S0-BKT-718

ERNEST HEMINGWAY: THE CRITICAL HERITAGE

THE CRITICAL HERITAGE SERIES

General Editor: B. C. Southam

The Critical Heritage series collects together a large body of criticism on major figures in literature. Each volume presents the contemporary responses to a particular writer, enabling the student to follow the formation of critical attitudes to the writer's work and its place within a literary tradition.

The carefully selected sources range from landmark essays in the history of criticism to fragments of contemporary opinion and little published documentary material, such as letters and diaries.

Significant pieces of criticism from later periods are also included in order to demonstrate fluctuations in reputation following the writer's death.

ERNEST HEMINGWAY

THE CRITICAL HERITAGE

Edited by

JEFFREY MEYERS

London and New York

First published in 1982
Reprinted in 1997 by Routledge

11 New Fetter Lane
London EC4P 4EE
&
29 West 35th Street
New York, NY 10001

Printed in Great Britain by
TJ Press, Padstow, Cornwall

Printed on acid-free paper

British Library Cataloguing in Publication Data

ISBN 0-415-15934-2

General Editor's Preface

The reception given to a writer by his contemporaries and near-contemporaries is evidence of considerable value to the student of literature. On one side we learn a great deal about the state of criticism at large and in particular about the development of critical attitudes towards a single writer; at the same time, through private comments in letters, journals or marginalia, we gain an insight upon the tastes and literary thought of individual readers of the period. Evidence of this kind helps us to understand the writer's historical situation, the nature of his immediate reading-public, and his response to these pressures.

The separate volumes in the *Critical Heritage Series* present a record of this early criticism. Clearly, for many of the highly productive and lengthily reviewed nineteenth- and twentieth-century writers, there exists an enormous body of material; and in these cases the volume editors have made a selection of the most important views, significant for their intrinsic critical worth or for their representative quality – perhaps even registering incomprehension!

For earlier writers, notably pre-eighteenth century, the materials are much scarcer and the historical period has been extended, sometimes far beyond the writer's lifetime, in order to show the inception and growth of critical views which were initially slow to appear.

In each volume the documents are headed by an Introduction, discussing the material assembled and relating the early stages of the author's reception to what we have come to identify as the critical tradition. The volumes will make available much material which would otherwise be difficult of access and it is hoped that the modern reader will be thereby helped towards an informed understanding of the ways in which literature has been read and judged.

B.C.S.

For Robert Bone

Contents

Acknowledgments

The editor and publishers would like to thank the following for permission to reproduce copyright material: William Abrahams for No. 122; John Aldridge for No. 115; 'The Atlantic Monthly' for Nos. 62 and 66 (Copyright © 1939 ® 1967 © 1940 ® 1968, by The Atlantic Monthly Company, Boston, Mass. Reprinted with permission); Carlos Baker for Nos. 74 and 111; Malcolm Bradbury for No. 109; Brandt & Brandt for Nos. 97 and 108 (Copyright © 1964 by Stanley Kauffmann. Copyright © 1967 by Stanley Kauffmann); Jonathan Cape Ltd. for Nos. 27 and 39, from 'Now and Then,' Winter 1929 and Spring 1934; Curtis Brown Ltd. for No. 92; Elizabeth H. Dos Passos for No. 25; Editions Gallimard and Jean Drieu La Rochelle for No. 31, Préface by Pierre Drieu La Rochelle to 'L'Adieu aux armes'(© Editions Gallimard 1932); Richard Ellmann for No. 98; Farrar, Straus and Giroux, Inc., for Nos. 1 and 119, Mr. Hemingway's Dry-Points from 'The Shores of Light' by Edmund Wilson (Copyright 1952 by Edmund Wilson), and An Effort at Self-Revelation by Edmund Wilson (Copyright © 1971 by Edmund Wilson. This selection appeared originally in 'The New Yorker'); Northrop Frye for No. 80; Harcourt Brace Jovanovich, Inc., for Nos. 58 and 68 (Copyright 1939 by Lionel Trilling. Copyright 1941 by Lionel Trilling. Reprinted by permission of the Estate of Lionel Trilling); 'Harper's' for No. 85 (Copyright © 1952 by Harper's Magazine. All rights reserved. Reprinted from the October 1952 issue by special permission); A. Norah Hartley for No. 26; Irving Howe for Nos. 93 and 118; 'The Hudson Review' for No. 90, pp. 146-8 of Eccentrics' Pilgrimage by R.W.B. Lewis (Reprinted by permission from 'The Hudson Review,' vol. 6, no. 1 (Spring 1953). Copyright © 1953 by The Hudson Review, Inc.); I.H.T. Corporation for Nos. 11 and 16, from 'New York Herald Tribune Books' (© I.H.T. Corporation. Reprinted by permission); 'Kansas City Star' for No. 2; Alfred Kazin for Nos. 47, 54, and 77; Frank Kermode for No. 101; the Executors and Trustees of the Estate of Mrs. G.A. Wyndham Lewis for No. 40, from Wyndham Lewis, 'Life and Letters' (Copyright, Mrs. G.A. Wyndham Lewis); London Express News and Feature Services for No. 24; Louisiana State University Press for No. 52, from 'Southern Review'; Dwight Macdonald for No. 67; T.S. Matthews for No. 22; W.H. Mellers for Nos. 57 and 73; Marvin Mudrick for No. 105; 'The Nation' (New York) for Nos. 4, 8, 13, 34, 38, 49, 56, 60, 76, and 100 (Copyright 1926, 1932, 1933, 1937, 1938, 1940, 1950, 1964 The Nation Associates); 'New Statesman' for Nos. 14, 18, 46, and 117; 'The New Yorker' for Nos. 33 and 59; 'The New York Times' for Nos. 88 and 91 (© 1952 and 1953 by The New York Times Company. Reprinted by permission); Harold Ober Associates Incorporated for No.5 (Copyright 1926 by George H. Doran Company. Copyright renewed 1953 by Frances Scott Fitzgerald Lanahan); 'The Observer' for No. 83; 'Partisan Review' for Nos. 51 and 87 (Copyright May, 1938, by Partisan Review; Copyright November-December, 1952, by Partisan Review); A.D. Peters & Co. Ltd. for No. 71; George Plimpton for No. 96; Laurence Pollinger Ltd. for No. 70; Laurence Pollinger Ltd., the Estate of the late Mrs. Frieda Lawrence Ravagli, and the publishers, William Heinemann Ltd. and Viking Penguin Inc., for No. 6, a review by D.H. Lawrence of Ernest Hemingway's 'In Our Time' from 'Phoenix: The Posthumous Papers of D.H. Lawrence' edited with an Introduction by Edward D. McDonald (Copyright 1936 by Frieda Lawrence. Copyright © renewed 1964 by the Estate of the late Frieda Lawrence Ravagli); Mario Praz for No. 21; Peter Quennell for No. 10; Random House, Inc., for No. 32, Ford Madox Ford, Introduction to 'A Farewell to Arms' (Copyright 1932 by Random House, Inc.); Christopher Ricks for No. 114; Alan Ross for No. 103; Louis Rubin for No. 121; 'Saturday Review' for Nos. 41, 45, 64, and 94 (© Saturday Review, 1935, 1937, 1940, 1961); Ruth Schorer for Nos. 69 and 84; Martin Secker & Warburg Ltd. and Farrar, Straus and Giroux, Inc., for No. 95, Nothing Amen from 'Man as an End' by Alberto Moravia, translated from the Italian by Bernard Wall (English translation Copyright © 1965 by Martin Secker & Warburg Ltd.); 'Sewanee Review' for Nos. 82 and 106; 'Shenandoah' for No. 86 (Copyright 1952 by Washington and Lee University, reprinted from 'Shenandoah': The Washington and Lee University Review, with the permission of the Editor); 'Spectator' for No. 99; Stephen Spender for No. 113; 'The Tablet' for No. 78; Tony Tanner for Nos. 102 and 110; Paul Theroux for No. 120; Vanderbilt University Press for No. 23, Perfect Behavior from 'The Spyglass,' ed. John

Tyree Fain; 'The Washington Post' for No. 116; A.P. Watt Ltd. and David Garnett for No. 9, Introduction to 'The Torrents of Spring'; Andrew D. Weinberger, Esq., for No. 17 (© 1927, 1955 The New Yorker Magazine, Inc., assigned to NAACP), and for No. 63; 'The Yale Literary Magazine' for No. 44 by Sinclair Lewis; Philip Young for Nos. 104, 107, and 112.

Note on the Selection and Text

Hemingway's work has inspired an abundance of excellent contemporary criticism, much of it written by fellow novelists. I have based this representative selection on the inherent interest of the work and on the authority of the critic; and have deliberately included a number of essays by English, French, Italian, Spanish, German and Russian as well as American critics. I have dispensed with trivial and uninteresting reviews; the opinions of the critics included in this volume are significant.

Scribner's refused permission to use Robert Penn Warren's essay; Christopher Isherwood and John Wain did not wish to reprint their critiques of 'For Whom the Bell Tolls' and 'Islands in the Stream.' I was forced to omit reviews by James Farrell and John O'Hara, by Malcolm Cowley, Horace Gregory and Carl Van Doren, and by Cyril Connolly when the 'New York Times,' the 'New York Herald Tribune' Corporation and the 'Sunday Times' of London demanded unrealistic fees. These notices are discussed in the Introduction; John Wain, Malcolm Cowley and Cyril Connolly are represented by other work. Apart from these few disappointments, I was able to reprint all the reviews that I wished to include - despite the limitations of my budget. I am grateful to authors, editors, publishers and agents for their generous cooperation.

The reviews and essays printed in this volume follow the original texts. Quotations from Hemingway's works have been retained, and typographical errors corrected.

Introduction

IMAGE

Ernest Hemingway, like Mark Twain and Stephen Crane, was a journalist and war correspondent before he became a writer, and this valuable experience enabled him to describe - with unusual authority - the bloody conflicts and exotic settings that appear in his work. In boyhood he had hunted and fished with Indians in the wilds of northern Michigan. While still in his teens he worked as a reporter for the 'Kansas City Star,' covered the police station and the hospital, and constantly saw violence and death. He served in a Red Cross ambulance unit on the Italian front during the Great War, witnessed the bitter fighting on the Piave, and was traumatically wounded in the legs by shrapnel and machine guns during the Austrian offensive at Fossalta in July 1918. As a correspondent for the 'Toronto Star Weekly' during 1920-23, he saw the atrocities of the Greco-Turkish War on the quay at Smyrna and during the retreat of the Greek army in Thrace. He reported the Genoa and Lausanne Conferences and the conflict in the Ruhr, interviewed Lloyd George and Mussolini, and witnessed the rise of Fascism in Italy. In a stimulating essay on Hemingway's style, Hugh Kenner suggests the vital connection between detachment and emotion, between the substance and the surface of his art: 'Hemingway learned one role early, that of Special Correspondent, professionally detached from the public horrors which he owed it to his readers to write down.... This role, in the inter-chapters of "In Our Time," established a center from which to write of private horrors as well.'(1)

In 1923 Hemingway abandoned journalism for fiction, lived an impoverished expatriate life in the attics and cafés of Paris, helped Ford Madox Ford to edit the 'transatlantic review,' and won respect and recognition with his first book, 'Three Stories and Ten Poems.' His friend Archibald MacLeish recalled his prodigious career in Years of the Dog:

Or the lad in the Rue de Notre Dame des Champs
At the carpenter's loft on the left-hand side going
  down -
The lad with the supple look like a sleepy panther -
And what became of him? Fame became of him.
Veteran out of the wars before he was twenty:
Famous at twenty-five: thirty a master -
Whittled a style for his time from a walnut stick
In a carpenter's loft in a street of that April city.(2)

Hemingway boxed in Paris, skied in Austria, fished in Spain and tested his courage against the bulls in Pamplona. He described this world of men without women in his books, and suggested that the same courage and skill were required for both killing and creating. Like the bull-fighter Pedro Romero, Hemingway wanted to hold 'his purity of line through the maximum of exposure.'(3)

His extraordinary good looks (Clark Gable with biceps) also influenced his image, for he was rugged, handsome and muscular when young; bearded, patriarchal and powerful when old. Man Ray's 1928 photograph of Hemingway standing in front of the Shakespeare & Co. bookshop with a bandaged head (after a skylight fell onto his skull), and the photos of his broken body and fractured fuselage after two African plane crashes and the 'grossly exaggerated' reports of his death in 1954 ('*Look*, we have come through!'), confirmed the legend of the hero who inscribed his experience on his body and seemed able to survive anything.(4) He had four attractive wives - one for each big book - fathered three sons, and became a model of how to live as well as how to write, of the art of life as well as the life of art. The timid Joyce, whose wife thought 'Jim could do with a spot of that lion-hunting,' admired the books that were authenticated by danger and pain: 'He's a good writer, Hemingway. He writes as he is. We like him. He's a big, powerful peasant, as strong as a buffalo. A sportsman. And ready to live the life he writes about. He would never have written it if his body had not allowed him to live it. But giants of his sort are truly modest; there is much more behind Hemingway's form than people know.'(5)

Hemingway retained the provincial notion that the artist was effeminate and he compensated for his profession by using his art as a weapon for competition and combat. His pugnacious stance and refusal to speak, act and write like an intellectual - even if he thought and felt like one - and his glorification of machismo, blood sports, physical violence and war, made him appear to be far less intelligent than he actually was. As Lionel Trilling observed: 'skilful physical effort is perhaps something intellectuals too quickly dismiss as a form of activity' (No. 58).

Hemingway's public image attracted a vast number of readers and his major novels - unlike those of Conrad, Ford, Lawrence and Joyce - achieved immense popular and financial success. He was introduced to Scribner's by Fitzgerald, was edited by the expert Max Perkins and soon became the firm's most important author. The first printing of 5,090 copies of 'The Sun Also Rises' (1926), which established Hemingway's literary reputation and public fame, sold out quickly. The novel was reprinted six times during the first year, reached its tenth printing in November 1929, and had sold more than a million copies by the time of Hemingway's death in 1961. 'A Farewell to Arms' (1929) sold more than 79,000 copies in the first four months, earned Hemingway $30,000 in book royalties and reached 1,400,000 copies by 1961. 'For Whom the Bell Tolls' (1940) sold half a million copies in the first six months; and 'The Old Man and the Sea' (1952) had even greater success. The entire novella appeared in 'Life' magazine - which then had a circulation of 5½ million - ten days before publication. The first Book-of-the-Month printing was 153,000, and the book still sells more copies than any other work by Hemingway.

All of Hemingway's major works became successful films: 'A Farewell to Arms' (1932), 'For Whom the Bell Tolls' - sold to Paramount for $100,000 plus royalties (1943), 'To Have and Have Not' (1944), 'The Killers' (1946), 'The Macomber Affair' (1947), 'The Snows of Kilimanjaro' (1952), 'The Sun Also Rises' (1957), 'The Old Man and the Sea' (1958), the second 'A Farewell to Arms' (1958) and 'Islands in the Stream' (1977). These movies helped to make him a millionaire; and his well-publicized friendships with Marlene Dietrich, and with Ingrid Bergman and Gary Cooper (who starred in these films and personified his heroic characters), enhanced his glamorous legend. The Hemingway image has continued with his granddaughters, who have recently achieved fame as models and movie stars.

In 1953 Saul Bellow, whose Augie March is an eagle-flying hero in the Hemingway tradition, praised him (in Emerson's words) for his ability to withstand the threatening test of violent experience and sudden fame, and said his dramatic characters were an expression of his inner strength: 'Hemingway thinks of himself as a representative man, one who has had the necessary qualifying experiences. He has not been disintegrated by the fighting, the drinking, the wounds, the turbulence, the glamor, he has not gotten lost in the capitals of the world, nor has he disappeared in the huge continents, nor has he been made anonymous within the oceanic human crowd. He keeps the outlines of his personality. This is why his characters are so dramatic; they offer the promise of a strong and victorious identity.'(6)

Though Hemingway was honored with the Pulitzer Prize in 1953 and the Nobel Prize for Literature the following year, he seemed by then to have lost what he called 'the most essential gift for a good writer - a built-in, shockproof, shit detector.'(7) In 'Green Hills of Africa' he reflected on the sad fate of Scott Fitzgerald and shrewdly listed the things that harm a writer: 'Politics, women, drink, money, ambition. And the lack of politics, women, drink, money and ambition.' He also explained: 'Our writers when they have made some money increase their standard of living and they are caught. They have to write to keep up their establishments, their wives, and so on, and they write slop.'(8) At the end of his life he succumbed to the dangers he had prophesied.

In his last decade, the years of his greatest fame and most radical deterioration, the Papa legend - which found its fullest and least attractive expression in A.E. Hotchner's book of 1966 - undermined the literary reputation and exposed the widening fissure between the two Hemingways: the private artist and public figure. The bitterness, boastfulness and self-indulgence that had flawed 'Death in the Afternoon' (1932) and 'Green Hills of Africa' (1935) were rigorously excised from 'The Old Man and the Sea' - a poor man's 'Moby Dick'. But his authorial intrusions seeped into and nearly swamped 'Across the River and into the Trees' (1950), The Dangerous Summer bullfighting articles that appeared in 'Life' in 1960, and the posthumously published 'Islands in the Stream' (1970).

The heroic image was inevitably modified after Hemingway's suicide in 1961. His public persona was then re-examined and his 'simple' manly style was seen as a sophisticated device for both hiding and revealing an obsession with courage that was rooted in anxiety. Another disciple, Norman Mailer - whose brawling character Sergius O'Shaughnessy and brilliant story 'The Time of Her Time' would be inconceivable without the example of Hemingway - saw him as a tragic figure wrestling, like the biblical Jacob, with destructive self-knowledge: 'It is not likely that Hemingway was a brave man who sought danger for the sake of the sensations it provided him. What is more likely the truth of his own odyssey is that he struggled with his cowardice and against a secret lust to suicide all his life, that his inner landscape was a nightmare, and he spent his nights wrestling with the gods. It may even be that the final judgment on his work may come to the notion that what he failed to do was tragic, but what he accomplished was heroic, for it is possible that he carried a weight of anxiety with him which would have suffocated any man smaller than himself.' (9)

REPUTATION

Hemingway's literary reputation, which was frequently confused with his public image, was established among his fellow writers even before he published his first book. In the early 1920s he received sympathetic encouragement and practical help from Sherwood Anderson, Gertrude Stein, Ford Madox Ford, Ezra Pound and Scott Fitzgerald. He was the rising star of American literature and seemed to have the surest future.

The stylistic influence of Ring Lardner, Anderson and Stein has been much discussed and vastly over-rated. One need only compare Hemingway's early style - in 'In Our Time' and 'The Sun Also Rises' - with that of his supposed teachers to see immediately that he is very different - and infinitely superior. Hemingway's ambition was 'to write what I've seen and known in the best and simplest way.' His classic style, stripped of adjectives, is bare, sharp and direct. He emphasizes dialogue rather than description, sensations rather than thought, and achieves an astonishing immediacy: an 'exaltation of the instant.' As Wallace Stevens remarked: 'Most people don't think of Hemingway as a poet, but obviously he is a poet and I should say, offhand, the most significant of living poets, so far as the subject of EXTRAORDINARY ACTUALITY is concerned.'(10) Hemingway's influence, his gift of evoking a sense of place, are matched in this century only by D.H. Lawrence.

Hemingway expresses his characteristic themes of violence, stoicism, war and death in perfectly controlled prose; and seems to excise all emotion from his work while allowing it to move powerfully beneath the surface. 'By presenting a succession of images,' writes Harry Levin, 'each of which has its brief moment when it commands the reader's undivided attention, he achieves his special vividness and fluidity.... He derives his strength from a power to visualize episodes through the eyes of those most directly involved.'(11) Tony Tanner adds: 'It is this elevation of intensity over continuity, the "now" over history, and the evidence of the senses over the constructs of the mind that determines the whole point of view and strategy of Hemingway's prose and explains his essential preoccupation with what we might call the "over-sensitized hero."'(12) Hemingway explained this technique of understatement, first adumbrated in a well-known passage in 'Death in the Afternoon,' in an interview with George Plimpton that portrayed him as a dedicated if unreflective artist: 'I always try to write on the principle of the iceberg. There is seven eighths of it under water for every part that shows. Anything you know you can eliminate and it only strengthens your iceberg. It is the part that doesn't show.'(13)

Criticism 'has played an unusually important part in Hemingway's career,' writes Lionel Trilling. 'Perhaps no American talent has so publicly developed as Hemingway's: more than any writer of our time he has been under glass, watched, checked up on, predicted, suspected, warned. One part of his audience took from him new styles of writing, of love-making, of very being' (No. 58). He immediately attracted serious attention and his early work received enthusiastic praise from Edmund Wilson, Allen Tate, D.H. Lawrence, Conrad Aiken and Edwin Muir as well as Stein, Ford and Fitzgerald. The original reactions and later judgments about the quality of his books are surprisingly similar. Critics noticed that his novels appeared in alternating phases and his finest fiction was inevitably succeeded by minor works. 'In Our Time' was followed by 'The Torrents of Spring,' 'The Sun Also Rises' by 'Men Without Women,' 'A Farewell to Arms' by 'To Have and Have Not,' 'For Whom the Bell Tolls' by 'Across the River and into the Trees,' 'The Old Man and the Sea' by 'Islands in the Stream.' Critics tend to agree that he did his best work between 'In Our Time' (1925) and 'For Whom the Bell Tolls' (1940), and that his books - apart from 'The Old Man and the Sea' - significantly declined during the last twenty years of his career.

Hemingway could not help attacking people who had tried to help him advance his career, and his discarded benefactors served a secondary purpose as satiric victims. His bitter public controversies with other writers aroused the hostility of the critics, hurt his reputation and cost him many valuable friendships. For a great many friends and former friends reviewed his books. Hemingway, who was unusually vindictive, parodied Anderson in 'The Torrents of Spring' (1926), condemned Stein and Ford in 'A Moveable

Feast' (1964), satirized Harold Loeb in 'The Sun Also Rises.' He condemned Scott Fitzgerald in the magazine version of The Snows of Kilimanjaro, quarreled with John Dos Passos about the politics of the Spanish Civil War and savaged Sinclair Lewis in 'Across the River and into the Trees.'

Hemingway's books were very favorably received in the 1920s; but when 'Death in the Afternoon' and 'Winner Take Nothing' (1933) drew adverse criticism, he was deeply wounded and began to express publicly his intense hostility to reviewers. In 'Green Hills of Africa' he called critics 'the lice who crawl on literature' and condemned these parasites for destroying serious writers: 'If they believe the critics when they say they are great then they must believe them when they say they are rotten and they lose confidence. At present we have two good writers who cannot write because they have lost confidence through reading critics.'(14)

Apart from the numerous reviews, a good many long and serious essays - including the two most influential works, by Wyndham Lewis and Edmund Wilson - have been included in this volume. But four other influential essays by Kazin, Cowley (both of whom have several reviews in this book), Warren and Leavis, published between 1942 and 1952, are worth noticing. Alfred Kazin's perceptive chapter, which appeared two years after 'For Whom the Bell Tolls' and before the decline became apparent, explained the connection between Hemingway's art and life, and defined his artistic greatness as well as his intellectual limitations:

> To Hemingway life became supremely the task of preserving oneself by preserving and refining one's art. Art was the ultimate, as it was perhaps the only, defense. In a society that served only to prey upon the individual, endurance was possible only by retaining one's identity and thus proclaiming one's valor. Writing was not a recreation, it was a way of life; it was born of desperation and enmity and took its insights from a militant suffering. Yet it could exist only as it purified itself; it had meaning only as it served to tell the truth. A writer succeeded by proving himself superior to circumstance; his significance as an artist lay in his honesty, his courage, and the will to endure....
>
> Hemingway is one of the great half-triumphs of literature; he proved himself the triumphal modern artist come to America, and within his range and means, one of the most interesting creators in the history of the American imagination.... [But] there is no real

> continuity in him, nothing of the essential greatness of spirit which his own artistic success has always called for.... [We] realize, with respect and sympathy, that it is a triumph in and of a narrow, local, and violent world - and never superior to it.(15)

In his Introduction to 'The Portable Hemingway' (1944), Malcolm Cowley rejected the notion that Hemingway was a primitive, emphasized his use of ritual and myth, and placed him in the imaginative tradition of the American symbolists, rather than of the naturalists: 'His kinship [is] with a wholly different group of novelists, let us say with Poe and Hawthorne and Melville: the haunted and nocturnal writers, the men who dealt in images that were symbols of an inner world.'(16) Robert Penn Warren, whose long essay appeared in 1947 and was later used as an Introduction to 'A Farewell to Arms,' also shifts the traditional emphasis and characterizes Hemingway as 'essentially a lyric rather than a dramatic writer, and for the lyric writer virtue depends upon the intensity with which the personal vision is rendered.' Warren also justifies Hemingway's violence and explains how his code opposes the nihilism of the modern world:

> The code and discipline are important because they can give meaning to life which otherwise seems to have no meaning or justification. In other words, in a world without supernatural sanctions, in the God-abandoned world of modernity, man can realize an ideal meaning only in so far as he can define and maintain the code. The effort to define and maintain the code, however limited and imperfect it may be, is the characteristically human effort and provides the tragic or pitiful human story....
>
> The violence, although in its first aspect it represents a sinking into nature, at the same time, in its second aspect, represents a conquest of nature, and of nada in man. It represents such a conquest, not because of the fact of violence, but because the violence appears in terms of discipline, a style and a code.(17)

And F.R. Leavis, who influenced the views of the young W.H. Mellers that were published in his influential journal 'Scrutiny,' took a rather patronising attitude toward Hemingway in 1952 and helped to explain why his reputation (battered by Wyndham Lewis in 1934) never achieved the same stature in England as it did on native ground: 'In Hemingway we have, it may be granted, something positively

American. But it is hard to see why, in this, he should be thought to promise well for an American literary future - in saying which one is registering the portentous distance between Hemingway and Mark Twain.... Compared with the idiom cultivated by Hemingway, Huck's language, as he speaks it, it is hardly excessive to say, is Shakespearean in its range and subtlety.'(18) The critical response to Hemingway has oscillated between two positions. Most critics have admired his technical virtuosity, emotional intensity and heroic code, while a minority have found him too imaginatively limited by his spare style, violent world and mindless characters.

Hemingway's reputation has had five distinct phases and has fluctuated wildly during each decade of his career. He received almost universal praise in the 1920s and reached the peak of his contemporary reputation with 'A Farewell to Arms' in 1929. His books of the 1930s - 'Death in The Afternoon,' 'Winner Take Nothing,' 'Green Hills of Africa,' 'To Have and Have Not' - were severely criticized by disenchanted reviewers; but he made a major recovery with 'For Whom the Bell Tolls' in 1940. He published no significant work in the 1940s, which culminated in the almost universally condemned novel, 'Across the River and into the Trees' (1950). But two years later he achieved an astonishing critical triumph with 'The Old Man and the Sea.' He brought out no books during the last nine years of his life, but regained his reputation with the posthumously published 'A Moveable Feast' in 1964. Though most critics found 'Islands in the Stream' disappointing, the retrospective view of his entire career has now placed him securely with the leading novelists of his time.

INFLUENCE

Despite the reservations of reviewers, the technique and style of Hemingway's books, which were translated into more than thirty-five languages, had a profound effect on modern European writers. For he offered a way of seeing and recording experience which matched his contemporaries' belief that art is a means of telling the truth. Sartre and Camus, as well as Elio Vittorini and Giuseppe Berto, Wolfgang Borchert and Heinrich Böll, were strongly influenced by his work.(19) Camus liked to emphasize his own place in the French tradition and said he would give a hundred Hemingways for a Stendhal or a Benjamin Constant, but Sartre defined his friend's debt to the American master: 'The comparison with Hemingway seems more fruitful [than with Kafka]. The relationship between the two styles is obvious. Both men write in the same short sentences. Each sentence refuses to exploit the momentum accumulated by preceding ones. Each is a new beginning. Each is like a snapshot of a gesture or object. For each new gesture and word there is a new and corresponding sentence.... Even in "Death in the Afternoon," which is not a novel, Hemingway retains that abrupt style of narration that shoots each separate sentence out of the void with a sort of respiratory spasm. His style is himself.... What our author [Camus] borrows from Hemingway is thus the discontinuity between the clipped phrases that imitate the discontinuity of time.'(20)

Hemingway, who was first published in Russia in 1934 and praised as an active anti-Fascist, soon became the favorite foreign author of both the intellectuals and the masses. More than a million copies of his works have appeared in the Soviet Union. He has received a poetic tribute from Yevgeny Yevtushenko and critical appreciation in several essays by Ivan Kashkeen, who presents the most appealing social and political aspects of Hemingway to Russian readers: 'The struggle of the common people for a decent existence, their simple and straightforward attitude towards life and death serve as a model for Hemingway's more complex and contradictory characters.' He also states the reasons why Hemingway is attractive to younger writers: 'The fact that he can look at life without blinking; that his manner is all his own; that he is ruthlessly exacting on himself, making no allowances, and straightforward in self-appraisal; that his hero keeps himself in check, and is ever ready to fight nature, danger, fear, even death, and is prepared to join other people at the most perilous moments in their struggle for a common cause.'(21)

Hemingway's life and work, which taught a generation of men to speak in stoical accents, have also had a profound influence on a school of hard-boiled American writers - Dashiell Hammett, James Farrell, John O'Hara, Nelson Algren, James Jones and Norman Mailer - who were affected not only by his style and technique, but also by his horrific content and his heroic code that seemed to represent the essence of American values.(22) Ralph Ellison has described the psychological and aesthetic effect of Hemingway's life and language, and explained why he was an even more important model for him than the black novelist Richard Wright: 'Because he appreciated the things of this earth which I love.... Because he wrote with such precision.... Because all that he wrote was involved with a spirit beyond the tragic.... Because Hemingway was a greater artist than Wright.... Because Hemingway loved the American language and the joy of writing.... Because he was in many ways the true father-as-artist of so many of us who came to writing during the late thirties.'(23)

CRITICAL REACTIONS TO HEMINGWAY

'Three Stories and Ten Poems' and 'in our time'

Hemingway's first, thin, 58-page book, 'Three Stories and Ten Poems,' expressed his characteristic mood, style and themes. It contained Up in Michigan, Out of Season and My Old Man, and six poems that had appeared in Harriet Monroe's 'Poetry' in January 1923. The volume was dedicated to his first wife, Hadley, and privately printed in July 1923, in a limited edition of 300 copies, by Robert McAlmon's Contact Publishing Company in Paris. Hemingway had met his fellow expatriate McAlmon, who was married to an English shipping heiress, in Rapallo, travelled with him in Spain and saw a good deal of him in Paris.

The first, 100-word review appeared in the Paris edition of the 'Chicago Tribune' on 27 November 1923 and was written by Gertrude Stein. Hemingway had met the older writer in Paris, through an introduction from Sherwood Anderson, and had published parts of her novel 'The Making of Americans' while editing Ford's 'transatlantic review.' Miss Stein graciously, if tautologically, acknowledged: 'Three stories and ten poems is very pleasantly said.... As he sticks to poetry and intelligence it is both poetry and intelligent.' But she advised Hemingway to 'stick to poetry and intelligence and eschew the hotter emotions and the more turgid vision.'(24) (The two friends later quarreled when each claimed to have taught the other how to write. In a nasty chapter of 'The Autobiography of Alice B. Toklas' (1933), Stein condemned Hemingway as a cowardly Rotarian; in 'Green Hills of Africa' he called her jealous and malicious, and had the last word after her death (and his own) in 'A Moveable Feast.')

'in our time,' whose lower-case title followed the fashion of the 'transatlantic review,' contained eighteen short, untitled chapters, including six that had been published in the spring 1923 issue of the 'Little Review.' The 38-page book was also privately published, in March 1924, in an even more limited edition of 170 copies, by William Bird's Three Mountains Press in Paris. It was sold at Sylvia Beach's Shakespeare & Co. The small book was one of six works, edited by Ezra Pound, that formed an

'Inquest into the state of contemporary English prose' and included Pound's 'Indiscretions,' Ford's 'Men and Women' and William Carlos Williams' 'The Great American Novel.'

When Hemingway heard that Edmund Wilson had read his six prose sketches in the Exiles number of the 'Little Review,' co-edited by Pound, he sent Wilson review copies of his first two books. Wilson was an early admirer and consistent reviewer of Hemingway's works, and wrote an Introduction to the second edition of 'In Our Time' (1930). But he later became an outspoken critic and published a damaging chapter on Hemingway in 'The Wound and the Bow' (1941) (No. 62). Wilson's 'Dial' review of 'Three Stories and Ten Poems' - which was a great breakthrough for Hemingway and helped to establish his serious literary reputation - immediately recognized the essence of Hemingway's talent. Wilson states 'his prose is of the first distinction,' links him with Anderson and Stein, and notes that their colloquial diction conveys 'profound emotions and complex states of mind.' He also perceives that in 'in our time' Hemingway 'is remarkably successful in suggesting moral values by a series of simple statements,' and that his 'harrowing record of barbarities' has the sharpness and elegance of lithographs by Goya (No. 1). When this review appeared Hemingway wrote to Wilson that 'he was "awfully glad" his early books had pleased so good a critic' and praised Wilson's review as 'cool, clear-minded, decent, impersonal and sympathetic. Such intelligence as Wilson had displayed was "a damn rare commodity."'(25)

The anonymous review in the 'Kansas City Star,' which notes that Hemingway had been a reporter on that newspaper, calls him 'one of the most promising young writers in the English language' and claims that his vivid, realistic, objective yet emotionally charged stories reveal 'distinguished talent, if not absolute genius' (No. 2). Max Perkins was equally enthusiastic and wrote to Fitzgerald, who had been promoting Hemingway at Scribner's: 'As for Hemingway: I finally got his "In our time" which accumulates a fearful effect through a series of brief episodes, presented with economy, strength and vitality. A remarkable, tight, complete expression of the *scene*, in our time, as it looks to Hemingway.'(26)

Only H.L. Mencken, the cantankerous panjandrum of American letters, seemed unimpressed by the avant-garde antics of the young writer. He calls the book 'The sort of brave, bold stuff that all atheistic young newspaper reporters write. Jesus Christ in lower case. A hanging, carnal love, and two disembowelings. Here it is set forth solemnly on Rives hand-made paper, in an edition of

170 copies, and with the imprimatur of Ezra Pound.' In retaliation, Hemingway sardonically dedicated 'The Torrents of Spring' to H.L. Mencken and S. Stanwood Menken, 'a wealthy vice-crusader who stood for everything H.L. Mencken hated.' (27)

'In Our Time'

'In Our Time,' Hemingway's first commercially published book, was brought out by Boni & Liveright in October 1925 in an edition of 1,335 copies. The volume was significantly different and much thicker than the earlier work with the same (but lower-case) title. 'In Our Time' used the sixteen short chapters of its predecessor as interchapters between sixteen short stories. Two of the stories came from 'Three Stories and Ten Poems,' two had previously been sketches in 'in our time,' seven (one of them now in two parts) had been published in the 'transatlantic review,' the 'Little Review' and 'This Quarter,' and four appeared for the first time.

The dust jacket contained generous appreciations of Hemingway's work by Ford, Anderson, Dos Passos, Waldo Frank, Gilbert Seldes and Donald Ogden Stewart. Ford boldly - yet accurately - claimed: 'The best writer in America at this moment (though for the moment he happens to be in Paris), the most conscientious, the most master of his craft, the most consummate, is Ernest Hemingway.' And Anderson's puff maintained: 'Mr Hemingway is young, strong, full of laughter, and he can write. His people flesh suddenly up into those odd cohesive moments of glowing reality, the clear putting down of which has always made good writing so good.'

The reviewers were equally responsive. Paul Rosenfeld repeats the comparison with painting that had been made by Wilson and the 'Kansas City Star,' defines Hemingway's style as 'iron with a lyricism,' and enunciates his themes: 'the War, the bull-ring and the police-world, the excitement of combat, the cold ferocity of the mob, the insensibility of soldiering, the relief of nerves in alcoholic stupor.' He also recognizes that the violent subject matter is transcended by the positive aspect of Hemingway's values (No. 3). In his brief review, Allen Tate concentrates on the original technique: 'Hemingway has developed his chief distinction in prose through a careful rejection of "ideas"; he does not conceive his subject matter; he presents it (No. 4). Later writers, following Wyndham Lewis, would criticize Hemingway for this anti-intellectual stance.

Though Fitzgerald was older and had already established his literary reputation, he idolized Hemingway. At the end of his life he planned a 'medieval' novel, 'Philippe, Count of Darkness,' with a hero based on Hemingway. Fitzgerald mentions that he was first introduced to Hemingway's work by his Princeton classmate, Edmund Wilson; miscounts the number of stories in the book; and offers an enthusiastic, if diffuse, appreciation that sees Nick Adams as the unifying focus of the book (No. 5).

Like Fitzgerald, D.H. Lawrence says Nick is the thematic center of the 'fragmentary novel': 'It is a short book: and it does not pretend to be about one man. But it is.... The sketches are short, sharp, vivid, and most of them excellent.... These few sketches are enough to create the man and all his history: we need know no more' (No. 6). In these brief, introductory reviews of Hemingway's early work, the critics concentrated on his unusual diction, style, technique and moral values, and saw him as an important new force in modern literature. By 1925 the young Hemingway had fulfilled his early promise and launched his career.

'The Torrents of Spring'

'The Torrents of Spring,' whose title is taken from a story of 1870 by Ivan Turgenev, is a devastating mockery of the naive repetition and superficial psychology in Anderson's novel, 'Dark Laughter' (1925). It is also the first of many instances when Hemingway repaid kindness with malice. Hemingway's ability to parody Anderson reveals how well he had learned and then rejected the lesson of the master; and the satire was probably intended as a break with Boni & Liveright as well as with Anderson, who was the firm's best-selling author.

When Horace Liveright recovered from the shock of reading the typescript, he told Hemingway: 'Far from selling 20,000 copies, they would be lucky to ged rid of seven or eight hundred. To publish it would be in rotten taste and horribly cruel to Anderson.' When Liveright rejected the work, his contract with Hemingway, which included an option on his next three books, lapsed. This left Hemingway free to sign with Scribner's, as Fitzgerald had been urging him to do.

Just before Scribner's published the book, Hemingway explained to Anderson the reasons for his attack. Though he admitted that Anderson might think it was a 'lousy, snotty letter' about a 'lousy, snotty book,' he attempted to justify his behavior on the grounds of sincerity and suggested that Anderson's thought and style would be significantly improved by reading the severe strictures of a younger colleague. Carlos Baker explains: 'The whole thing had started the previous November while he and Dos Passos were having lunch and discussing "Dark Laughter." After lunch, said Ernest, he went back to the flat, "started the 'Torrents of Spring' thing," and completed it in a week. It was a joke, not meant to be mean, but absolutely sincere. Writers should not have to pull their punches among themselves. When a man like Sherwood, who was capable of great things, wrote something "rotten," it was Ernest's obligation to "call" him on it.... Since the book was not intended as a personal attack, the tougher it was, the better.'(28)

Harry Hansen, who alludes to Hemingway's ingratitude to Anderson and his break with Boni & Liveright, judges the book a failure: 'Hemingway has caught, I think, a glint of Anderson's professional naivete. Beyond that, however, parody is a gift of the gods. Few are blessed with it. It missed Hemingway. He is better as a writer of short stories' (No. 7). By contrast, Allen Tate says Hemingway's 'selective naturalism achieves its effects through indirect irony.' He finds the parody a better book than 'Dark Laughter' and calls the work 'a small masterpiece of American fiction' (No. 8).

David Garnett's intelligent Introduction to the English edition of 1933 over-rates the humor of the book. But he discusses the now-forgotten 'Dark Laughter,' places it in its sentimental primitivistic tradition, and notes that Hemingway is not parodying the story, 'but the ideas behind it, and the falsity of the author's approach.... It is characteristic of Anderson to think that negroes must be nearer Nature than white men are.' Garnett also observes that there is an element of self-parody in the book, which marked the end of Anderson's stylistic influence on his disciple (No. 9). Peter Quennell repeats Garnett's idea that 'besides being a satire on Sherwood Anderson, good-humoured if mercilessly acute, it is also a satire on Anderson's method as Hemingway himself has seen fit to adapt it.' He commends Hemingway's 'vivid, trenchant, and abrupt' style, and calls him 'perhaps the finest story-teller now writing in English' (No. 10). The critics seemed to feel that the feeble fiction by Anderson, who then had a distinguished reputation, provoked and deserved Hemingway's witty and well-executed condemnation.

'The Sun Also Rises'

'The Sun Also Rises' is based on Hemingway's observation of the postwar Lost Generation in Paris - a very different crowd from Henry James' genteel expatriates - and his participation in the festival of San Fermín in Spain. His enthusiasm for blood sports provides an illuminating contrast to D.H. Lawrence's expression of revulsion in the opening chapter of his Mexican novel, 'The Plumed Serpent' (also 1926). Hemingway's novel put Pamplona and bullfighting on the tourist map and the town has never recovered.(29) The title of the book comes from Ecclesiastes, the epigraph from Gertrude Stein, and the characters from recognizable people: Ford Madox Ford, Lady Duff Twysden and Harold Loeb - who sent out word that he was searching for Hemingway with a gun. It was published in October 1926, five months after 'The Torrents of Spring,' and received a mixed critical reception. But Malcolm Cowley soon discovered that Hemingway's influence was spreading far beyond Paris. College girls 'were modelling themselves after Lady Brett.... Bright young men from the Middle West were trying to be Hemingway heroes, talking in tough understatements from the sides of their mouths.' Two minor dissenters from the public acclaim were Hemingway's mother, who called it 'one of the filthiest books of the year,'(30) and Zelda Fitzgerald, who said it was about 'Bullfighting, bullslinging and bullshitting.'(31)

Allen Tate, who had praised 'In Our Time' and 'The Torrents of Spring,' and had great expectations for Hemingway's first novel, was profoundly disappointed. Tate, perhaps the first to use the term 'hard-boiled' to describe Hemingway, feels the book is flawed by sentimentality and caricature, and that Hemingway 'produced a successful novel, but not without returning some violence upon the integrity achieved in his first book' (No. 13). Tate's criticism is not very convincing and may have been influenced by his own premature and now embarrassing enthusiasm for the early works. In any case, he lost interest in Hemingway and stopped reviewing his books. Edwin Muir agrees with Tate and maintains: 'The original merits of the book are striking; its fault, equally apparent after one's first pleasure, is a lack of artistic significance. We see the lives of a group of people laid bare, and we feel that it does not matter to us' (No. 14). Both Muir and Tate seem to feel that the pleasure the novel gave and the success it achieved were somehow inconsistent with high art.

Conrad Aiken begins by airing the rumor - soon to become part of the Hemingway legend - that he once fought bulls in Spain for his livelihood; and he compares the novel to the fine bullfight story, The Undefeated. Aiken praises the brilliant dialogue, the profound revelation of character, the 'extraordinary effect of honesty and reality,' the dignity and detachment in telling the somewhat sordid yet intensely tragic story, and calls Hemingway the most exciting contemporary American novelist (No. 11). Herbert Gorman aroused interest in the novel by stating that it portrays a 'great spiritual debacle, a generation that has lost its guiding purpose and has been driven by time, fate or nerves ... into the feverish atmosphere of strained passions' (No. 12).

André Maurois, in another positive essay of 1929, repeats Muir's comparison with Maupassant, verifies the accuracy of Hemingway's portrayal of Paris, and observes: 'While he appreciates the poetic value of sports, they appeal to him above all scientifically. His vocabulary is always accurate, riveted and solid like a specialist's. He has Kipling's art of suggesting passions and feelings without calling them by name' (No. 15). Hemingway shares Kipling's confident tone and stoic attitude as well as his exoticism and expertise.

The retrospective essay by James Farrell, whose 'Studs Lonigan' (1932-35) had been strongly influenced by Hemingway, was published during World War Two. Farrell places the novel in the perspective of the 1920s and writes from the social-realist perspective of the 1930s. He says that Hemingway's influence had a liberating and salutary effect: 'The nihilistic character of Hemingway's writing helped to free younger people from the false hopes' of the thirties. But Farrell, like Kazin writing in 1942, believes that 'Hemingway is a writer of limited vision, one who has no broad and fertile perspective on life'; that his characters 'live for the present, constantly searching for new and fresh sensations'; and that his attitude is simply: 'an action is good if it makes one feel good.'(32) Though Farrell calls 'The Sun Also Rises' Hemingway's best book and one of the best novels of the twenties, he thinks that 'Hemingway's attitudes were firmly fixed at that time. He said pretty much what he had to say with his first stories and his first two novels.'(33) Contemporary critics were divided on the merits of the novel. But it has had a far greater effect on later generations who identified with rather than rejected the sordid and nihilistic lives of the protagonists, and recognized it as Hemingway's greatest work.

'Men Without Women'

Hemingway's collection of fourteen short stories, ten of them previously published, appeared in October 1927, and sold 19,000 copies in the first six months. Virginia Woolf, who had condemned 'Ulysses' as 'merely the scratching of pimples on the body of the bootboy at Claridge's,' (34) was unlikely to be impressed by the heroics of Hemingway. She circles around him, tests his weak spots, takes a feminist jab at the title of the book and pushes in her barbs. Though she concedes his merits, her conclusion is rather negative: 'Mr. Hemingway, then, is courageous; he is candid; he is highly skilled; he plants words precisely where he wishes; he has moments of bare and nervous beauty; he is modern in manner but not in vision; he is self-consciously virile; his talent has contracted rather than expanded; compared with his novel his stories are a little dry and sterile' (No. 16). Hemingway was extremely irritated by Woolf's review and told Max Perkins: 'All that Bloomsbury Group had appointed themselves the saviors of the republic of letters, habitually imputing dishonest motives to young challengers on the way up.'(35) Cyril Connolly was also fairly cool. But he grudgingly acknowledged that Hemingway's immaturity, ferocious virility and silent sentimentality were 'redeemed by humour, power over dialogue and an obvious knowledge of the people he describes' (No. 18).

In a sympathetic and witty review, Dorothy Parker traces the fluctuations of Hemingway's reputation and (in contrast to Woolf) states that his 'truly magnificent' short stories are more effective and more moving than his novel (No. 17). H.L. Mencken, in a composite review of 'Men Without Women' and Thornton Wilder's 'The Bridge of San Luis Rey,' warms to Hemingway, praises his technical virtuosity and suggests that increasing maturity should enable him to achieve his high promise (No. 20).

Mario Praz was introduced to Hemingway's writing by T.S. Eliot (whom he had translated into Italian) and wrote the first essay on Hemingway to appear in Italy. Thinking, perhaps, of the first sentence of In Another Country - 'In the fall the war was always there, but we did not go to it any more' - Praz neatly defines Hemingway's technique as 'a maximum of evocation with a minimum display of means' (No. 21).

Edmund Wilson, who still championed Hemingway at this stage of his career, castigates the superficial reviews of his colleagues and provides some shrewd insights about the stories. He defends Hemingway's characters as 'highly civilized persons of rather complex temperament and extreme sensibility' and observes that 'his drama usually turns on some principle of courage, of honor, of pity' that reveals his serious moral values (No. 19).

'A Farewell to Arms'

'Scribner's Magazine' paid Hemingway $16,000 for the serial rights of 'A Farewell to Arms,' whose title came from a poem by George Peele that Hemingway found in the 'Oxford Book of English Verse.' The novel was published in September 1929, a month before the Wall Street crash, and appeared on the best-seller lists with Erich Remarque's 'All Quiet on the Western Front.' Both works were banned by the censors in Boston because of 'immoral episodes and objectionable language.' A review by the serious novelist Robert Herrick agreed that Hemingway's '"beautiful love" is mere dirt, if anything' and maintained that 'no great loss to anybody would result if "A Farewell to Arms" had been suppressed.'(36) This unsavory publicity merely intensified the public's interest in the book and increased the substantial sales.

Malcolm Cowley, one of Hemingway's greatest admirers, discusses the extra-literary reasons for Hemingway's sudden fame: his distance from the jealousies of the New York literary world, his personal legend, his artistic pride, his use of sensational material, his ability to express the viewpoint of his postwar contemporaries. And he sees a new tenderness and seriousness in Hemingway's second novel: 'The emotions as a whole are more colored by thought; perhaps they are weaker and certainly they are becoming more complicated. They seem to demand expression in a subtler and richer prose.'(37) Tom Matthews (who later married Hemingway's third wife) also believes this novel is an advance on 'The Sun Also Rises.' He ambivalently notes that in his description of Frederic and Catherine, Hemingway 'has now invented the kind of ideal against which no man's heart is proof. In the conclusion of "A Farewell to Arms," he has transferred his action to a stage very far from realism, and to a plane that may be criticized as the dramatics of a sentimental dream' (No. 22). In the 'Criterion' of 1933, T.S. Eliot refutes the criticism that Hemingway was both hard-boiled and sentimental, and defends him as a writer who expresses his truest feelings: 'The illusion which pervades the whole various-climated American continent is the illusion of the hard-boiled. Even Mr. Ernest Hemingway - the writer of tender sentiment, and true sentiment, as in "The Killers" and "A Farewell to Arms" ... has been taken as the representative of hard-boiled.... Mr. Hemingway is a writer for whom I have considerable respect; he seems to me to tell the truth about his own feelings at the moment when they exist.'(38)

In a perversely doctrinaire review - a classic example of a misguided theoretical approach to literature - Donald Davidson completely misunderstands Hemingway's intention. He baldly states that the 'behaviorist' novel is 'a bold and exceptionally brilliant attempt to apply scientific method to art' (No. 23). When Allen Tate objected to the review, Davidson admitted: 'I am afraid I sacrificed Hemingway (to some extent) in order to make a point against science.'(39) Arnold Bennett, whose literary column in the mass circulation 'Evening Standard' had a powerful influence on public taste, also misses the point of the novel. He says that Hemingway should have written either a love story or a war story instead of attempting to write both. But he compensates for his obtuseness by conceding that Hemingway 'combines deep sympathy with breadth and impartiality of vision' (No. 24).

John Dos Passos, in a self-consciously low-brow review for a theoretically proletarian audience in the Communist organ, 'New Masses,' includes the requisite colloquial language, references to revolution and propaganda, and a little lecture on the joys of craftsmanship. He tries to convince his readers that the novel is great because Hemingway enjoyed the work (No. 25).

L.P. Hartley agrees that Hemingway's second novel is better than his first and observes that he 'has a gift for portraying friendship as well as love' (No. 26). Another English novelist, J.B. Priestley, notices in his literary puff for Jonathan Cape's house magazine that the characteristically modern lovers 'seem to be curiously lonely, without backgrounds, unsustained by any beliefs' and that this somehow adds to the 'terrible poignancy and force' of the concluding scene (No. 27). H.L. Mencken, by contrast, remains rather critical of Hemingway's stylistic tricks and shadowy characters. He wryly notes that the lovers conduct their affair 'under vast technical difficulties' and that 'the virtue of the story lies in its brilliant evocation of the horrible squalor and confusion of war' (No. 29). Lewis Galantière was probably the first to offer a psychological interpretation of Hemingway, which was later developed by Philip Young. Galantière concludes by remarking: 'There are two Hemingways: the positive, creative talent ... and the negative, fearful writer with the psychological impediments of a child' (No. 28).

Klaus Mann's high-flying retrospective review begins with a series of emotional generalities. He then compares Kafka's and Hemingway's 'primal anxiety' and explains

Hemingway's enormous attraction for European writers: 'He is a typical American but with the inner experiences of a European. He sees this world with the freshness of his youthful race and at the same time with the slyness of our old one' (No. 30). Drieu La Rochelle also compares Hemingway with European authors and concludes: 'We trade, with the Americans, our form for their raw life.... Hemingway is well aware of this happy exchange. An anxious barbarian, subtle and delicate ... [he] knows how to keep his strength and leave Rome with his booty intact' (No. 31). It is quite possible that Drieu La Rochelle's Preface of 1932 first drew André Gide's attention to the novel. In the 1940s French newspapers gave great publicity to Hemingway's service in World War Two, which enormously increased his popularity. In the late forties Gide joined in this enthusiasm, included Hemingway with Faulkner and Dashiell Hammett as writers of masterful dialogue, and recalled that 'A Farewell to Arms' 'seemed so remarkable' when he first read it.(40)

If Ford Madox Ford recognized himself and Stella Bowen as Mr. and Mrs. Braddocks in 'The Sun Also Rises,' he did not seem to mind. In his windy ramble on expatriate life in Paris Ford good-naturedly confirmed what he had said on the dust jacket of 'In Our Time': 'Hemingway writes extremely delicate prose - perhaps the most delicate prose that is today being written.'(41) In his charming Introduction to the Modern Library edition of 'A Farewell to Arms,' Ford reminisces about the early days in Paris when Hemingway published his first, small press books. Ford handsomely ranks Hemingway with Joseph Conrad and W.H. Hudson as one of 'The three impeccable writers of English prose that I have come across in fifty years of reading,' and says he has the supreme gift of using 'words so that they shall seem new and alive because of their juxtaposition with other words' (No. 32).

Critics felt that Hemingway expressed a new maturity and depth in 'A Farewell to Arms.' The novel received even more praise than his earlier works and he reached the pinnacle of his reputation in 1929. There were two dissenting voices, however, which claimed that he was egotistic and deliberately unintellectual; these charges would be frequently elaborated and used against Hemingway as his faults became more apparent and his work began to decline. In a letter of January 1930 the worldly Scottish writer R.B. Cunninghame Graham writes that 'A Farewell to Arms' was 'a mass of sentimental egotism and arrogance of attitude ... not badly written it is true, & with good dialogue. But like Joshua, he seems to have thought he could order the sun to stand still, or at least focus it on himself.'(42)

The second serious charge was made in 'Music at Night' (1931) by Aldous Huxley, the supreme example of a detached, intellectual writer. Huxley sharply observes: 'In "A Farewell to Arms," Mr. Ernest Hemingway ventures, once, to name an Old Master. There is a phrase, quite admirably expressive (for Mr. Ernest Hemingway is a most subtle and sensitive writer), a single phrase, no more, about "the bitter nail-holes" of Mantegna's Christs; then quickly, quickly, appalled by his own temerity, the author passes on ... passes on, shamefacedly, to speak once more of lower things.... It is not at all uncommon now to find intelligent and cultured people doing their best to feign stupidity and to conceal the fact that they have received an education.'(43) Hemingway (who did not attend a university) was clearly disturbed by this comment, for he took the trouble to answer Huxley's attack. In his next book, 'Death in the Afternoon,' Hemingway avoided the essence of the criticism - that he was a deliberately low-brow writer - and stated that he used the allusion as an effective way to reveal character: 'If the people the writer is making talk of old masters; of music; of modern painting; of letters, or of science, then they should talk of those subjects in the novel. If they do not talk of those subjects and the writer makes them talk of them he is a faker.'(44)

'Death in the Afternoon'

Hemingway, who had been to seven festivals at Pamplona and seen 1,500 bulls killed, was attracted to bullfights - the last pagan spectacle in the modern world - because he 'was trying to learn to write, commencing with the simplest things, and [felt] one of the simplest things of all and the most fundamental is violent death.'(45) His book is the classic work on bullfighting and has influenced everything written on the subject since it appeared. Yet the work did not please the critics. They attacked Hemingway's swaggering public persona who measured men by their machismo and *cojones*; gibed at his fellow writers: Huxley, Cocteau, Faulkner and Eliot; and arrogantly pontificated to his dummy interlocutor, the Old Lady. As H.L. Mencken writes in a review called The Spanish Idea of a Good Time, the book is 'an extraordinarily fine piece of expository writing, but ... often descends to a gross and irritating cheapness' (No. 36). Because of the Depression and the strange subject matter, the book sold poorly.

Robert Coates admits that like most American readers he knows nothing and cares less about bullfighting, and is bored by the exhaustive treatise. He calls Hemingway a romanticist 'in his inability to accept the idea of death as the end and completement of life' (No. 33). This would seem to be confirmed by Hemingway's suicide - an escape from rather than a completion of life. Granville Hicks defines Hemingway's method as 'a process of isolation - a deliberate setting apart of those segments of human experience he understands and likes to write about.' He also notes that Hemingway seems to believe: 'If ... you are troubled by the world, resort to personal violence' (No. 34).

In a more balanced review, Malcolm Cowley calls the book 'a Baedeker of bulls' that concerns 'the art of living, of drinking, of dying, of loving the Spanish land,' for bullfighting symbolizes 'a whole nation and a culture extending for centuries into the past.' He believes that for Hemingway bullfighting is 'an emotional substitute for war' and that his work is an 'elegy to Spain and vanished youth' (No. 35).

The first truly damaging critique was Max Eastman's Bull in the Afternoon, published in the 'New Republic' seven months after Cowley's review. Eastman argues that Hemingway's 'bull' is 'juvenile romantic gushing and sentimentalizing of simple facts' (46) about the brutal, shocking and ignoble aspects of a bullfight. He defines this, in opposition to Hemingway, as 'men tormenting and killing a bull.' After exposing Hemingway's posturings, Eastman moves - more menacingly - from his literary to his personal faults and seems to question his sexual capacity: 'It is of course a commonplace that Hemingway lacks the serene confidence that he *is* a full-sized man.... [He has] a continual sense of the obligation to put forth evidences of red-blooded masculinity.... [He has developed] a literary style, you might say, of wearing false hair on the chest' (No. 37).

This review provoked the rage of Hemingway, who was extremely sensitive to criticism. He told Max Perkins that he was tempted to stop publishing because swine like Eastman were not worth writing for and that he found the whole reviewing racket as disgusting as vomit. Four years later, in August 1937, Hemingway accidentally discovered Eastman in his editor's office. Perkins described the comic dénouement in a letter to Fitzgerald:

> Ernest ripped open his shirt and exposed a chest which was certainly hairy enough for anybody. Max laughed, and then Ernest, quite good-naturedly, reached over and opened Max's shirt, revealing a chest which was as bare as a bald man's head.... Then suddenly Ernest became

> truculent and said, 'What do you mean accusing me of impotence?' Eastman denied that he had.... [Then Ernest] hit Eastman with an open book. Instantly, of course, Eastman rushed at him. I thought Ernest would begin fighting and would kill him, and ran round my desk to try to catch him from behind, with never any fear for anything that might happen to Ernest. At the same time, as they grappled, all the books and everything went off my desk to the floor, and by the time I got around, both men were on the ground.... Ernest was on his back, with a broad smile on his face. - Apparently he regained his temper instantly after striking Eastman, and offered no resistance whatever.(47)

'Winner Take Nothing'

'Winner Take Nothing,' Hemingway's seventh book since the appearance of 'In Our Time' in 1925, contained fourteen short stories, eight of them previously published and only two of them major works: The Gambler, the Nun and the Radio and A Clean, Well-Lighted Place. Though Joyce criticized Hemingway for his journalistic technique and violent, superficial characters, he singled out the latter story for particular praise:

> Take Hemingway. He seems on the way to the top because he is original. But his originality is a venal one, and what he writes about smells in life, and in time it will smell in literature too: stories about alcoholics and nymphomaniacs and people who live in a waste land of violence and who have no emotional depth. I admit to his merit, of course, that he is very much of our time. But in my opinion he is too much of our time, in fact his writing is now more the work of a journalist than that of a literary man.
>
> [But] he has reduced the veil between literature and life, which is what every writer strives to do. Have you read A Clean, Well-Lighted Place?... It is masterly. Indeed, it is one of the best short stories ever written; there is bite there.(48)

The first printing was 20,300 copies, and 11,000 were sold the first month. But many critics agreed with Joyce and felt this volume was the weakest of Hemingway's three collections.

Horace Gregory, who admires Wine of Wyoming because in that story Hemingway interprets experience instead of merely presenting it, says that all his fictions 'have a single protagonist, himself ... [a] sensitive, disciplined, entirely civilized person.'(49) William Troy, writing in the 'Nation,' is much more severe. He remarks that the critical tide is turning against Hemingway because of his intellectual limitations and the monotonous repetition of his themes, and concludes: 'Unless Mr. Hemingway realizes within the next few years that fiction based on action as catharsis is becoming less and less potent,' he will lose his reputation (no. 38). In the most balanced and perceptive review, William Plomer observes: 'Combined with the motives of protest and escape, and lurking also beneath the manner - the fastidious brutality of this laconic wanderer - there is a genuine nihilism ... but it is the nihilism that so often goes with vitality' (No. 39).

Wyndham Lewis on Hemingway

Lewis had a dramatic introduction to Hemingway in July 1922 in the Paris studio of Ezra Pound: 'He was tall, handsome, and serene, and was repelling with his boxing gloves - I thought without undue exertion - a hectic assault of Ezra's. After a final swing at the dazzling solar plexus (parried effortlessly by the trousered statue) Pound fell back upon his settee.'(50) Lewis also met Hemingway with Archibald MacLeish in December 1927. Hemingway, who had recently published 'The Sun Also Rises,' was not confident about the dialogue of the English Lady Brett, but Lewis assured him that he had a good ear for speech and there was no occasion for anxiety. MacLeish recalled: 'I took Lewis to lunch in Paris and got Hemingway to come along. Walking back to the West Bank E.H. said: "Did you notice? He kept his gloves on all through lunch".... Since I hadn't and since he hadn't the question became lurid and memorable. But even as early as that Hemingway had decided not to care for him.'(51) Like Lewis, Hemingway created his own legend and was aggressive, hypersensitive, eager for recognition and intolerant of criticism. The two colossal egos were bound to clash.

The immediate cause of hostility was Lewis' incisive chapter on Hemingway in 'Men Without Art' - a title probably derived from 'Men Without Women' (1927). The Dumb Ox, one of Lewis' best-known essays, was first published in 'Life and Letters' (April 1934), reprinted in the 'American Review' (June 1934), in Lewis' 'Men Without Art' (1934), 'A Soldier of Humour' (1966) and 'Enemy Salvoes' (1976), and translated into Polish (1968). The essay is the most damaging attack ever made on Hemingway. It is original, substantial, witty and intelligent, it is written from an essentially sympathetic point of view and it influenced all subsequent English criticism on his work. Lewis attacks the very things Hemingway prided himself on: his originality, sophistication and admirable fictional heroes. He also shoots barbs into Hemingway's most vulnerable spots: his embarrassing caricature and echo of his literary midwife, Gertrude Stein; his lack of political awareness (a frequent criticism in the thirties, before the appearance of 'For Whom the Bell Tolls'); and his passive characters who possess the soul of a dumb ox: 'This brilliant Jewish lady has made a *clown* of him by teaching Ernest Hemingway her baby-talk!... [She has] strangely hypnotized him with her repeating habits and her *faux-naif* prattle ... [though] he has never taken it over into a gibbering and baboonish stage as has Miss Stein.' Lewis continues his assault by implying that Hemingway's characters reveal his own lack of ideology and intelligence: 'It is difficult to imagine a writer whose mind is more entirely closed to politics than Hemingway's.... Hemingway invariably invokes a dull-witted, bovine, monosyllabic simpleton ... a lethargic and stuttering dummy ... a super-innocent, queerly-sensitive, village-idiot of a few words and fewer ideas.' His characters are '*those to whom things are done*, in contrast to those who have executive will and intelligence' (No. 40). Lewis' criticism enraged Hemingway. He read the essay in the Shakespeare & Co. bookshop and confirmed the charge that he was anti-intellectual by punching a vase of tulips on Sylvia Beach's table and sending the fragments flying across the room.

In his fury, Hemingway failed to notice that Lewis also admired certain aspects of his work. Lewis praised Hemingway in 'Time and Western Man' (where he demolished 'Trudy' Stein) and followed the attack on Anderson's sentimental primitivism in 'The Torrents of Spring' with his own condemnation in 'Paleface.' When Lewis praised the satire, he received an enthusiastic response from Hemingway: 'I am very glad you liked "The Torrents of Spring' and thought you destroyed the Red and Black enthusiasm very finely in "Paleface." That terrible —— about the nobility of any gent belonging to another race than our own (whatever it is) was worth checking. Lawrence you know was Anderson's God in the old days - and you can trace his effect all through A's stuff.... In fact "The Torrents of Spring" was, in fiction form, performing the same purgative function as "Paleface."'

In 'Rude Assignment' Lewis said: 'I have always had great respect for Hemingway.... He is the greatest writer in America and (odd coincidence) one of the most successful.'(52) While in Canada he taught and lectured on 'For Whom the Bell Tolls.' Hemingway generously gave Lewis an influential and desperately needed endorsement when he was trying to obtain portrait commissions in St. Louis in 1944. But his vindictive cruelty to Lewis in 'A Moveable Feast' (where only Pound escaped whipping) was a pathetic response to the first serious critical essay on his work to be published in England: 'Wyndham Lewis wore a wide black hat, like a character in the quarter, and was dressed like someone out of "La Bohème." He had a face that reminded me of a frog, not a bullfrog but just any frog, and Paris was too big a puddle for him.... Lewis did not show evil; he just looked nasty.' And he added that Lewis, who was a triumphant seducer, had the eyes 'of an unsuccessful rapist.' (53)

'Green Hills of Africa'

In his brief Foreword to 'Green Hills of Africa,' which was based on a hunting expedition to Tanganyika in 1934, Hemingway wrote, somewhat defensively: 'Unlike many novels, none of the characters or incidents in this book is imaginary. Any one not finding sufficient love interest is at liberty, while reading it, to insert whatever love interest he or she may have at the time. The writer has attempted to write an absolutely true book to see whether the shape of a country and the pattern of a month's action can, if truly presented, compete with a work of the imagination.' The book was serialized in 'Scribner's Magazine,' which paid Hemingway $5,000, and had a first printing of 10,550 copies. Left-wing reviewers, most notably Granville Hicks and Edmund Wilson, attacked Hemingway for his escapist theme and for avoiding the economic and political issues of the Depression. And most critics felt that his obsession with blood-sports and death, though technically accurate, could *not* compete with his fictional work.

Bernard De Voto notes that Hemingway's nasty asides about critics mean 'Either the reviewers have been getting under his skin or he is uneasy about this book.' He says that much of this unimportant work - a curious mixture of description, straight fictional technique, literary discussion and exhibitionism - is dull, and he regrets the new experience of being bored by Hemingway (No. 41). Carl Van Doren, who is tolerant of Hemingway's exhibitionism and likes the book more than De Voto, observes: 'He is the center of the action, the sensorium on which the action is recorded. His book about Africa is a book about Ernest

Hemingway in Africa.' He too notices that Hemingway's prose style seems richer and more complex, and writes that though Hemingway is at times superficial and tiresome, 'he is mature as an artist, expounding his own art and exhibiting it in prose that sings like poetry without ever ceasing to be prose, easy, intricate and magical.'(54)

Writing in the Communist journal, 'New Masses,' Granville Hicks (who had disliked 'Death in the Afternoon') states 'I have always felt that Hemingway was by all odds the clearest and strongest non-revolutionary writer of his generation.' But he is seriously disappointed that Hemingway now concerns himself with dull and unworthy subjects on the margins of life and refuses to 'let himself look squarely at the contemporary American scene.' He concludes that in the six years since 'A Farewell to Arms' 'Hemingway has not produced a book even remotely worthy of his talents' (No. 42).

In his Letter to the Russians about Hemingway, later translated and published in the Soviet journal, 'International Literature' (February 1936), Edmund Wilson expresses - more forcefully and cogently - the same criticism as Granville Hicks. He calls it 'certainly far and away his weakest book,' asserts that Hemingway 'has chosen to treat his material in the wrong way' and maintains that he is losing interest in his fellow men (he wants only to kill the animals) and 'has become progressively more sterile and less interesting in proportion as he has become more detached from the great social issues of the day.' Wilson also identifies another radical defect, which became increasingly prominent as his work declined: 'he seems to lose all his capacity for self-criticism and is likely to become fatuous or maudlin ... as soon as he begins to write in the first person' (No. 43). Wilson's important review marked the beginning of his disenchantment with Hemingway and led directly to his major critique of 1939.

Hemingway began the quarrel with Sinclair Lewis, who reviewed his African book in the centennial number of the 'Yale Literary Magazine,' with an unpleasant article in the 'Toronto Star' of 5 August 1922. Lewis responded by praising Hemingway in his Nobel Prize speech of 1930. Hemingway continued to taunt the older, well-established writer - whom he clearly saw as a threatening rival - in 'Green Hills of Africa,' where he flatly states 'Sinclair Lewis is nothing.'(55) Lewis' review was understandably testy. He suggests that Hemingway enjoyed cruelty and says the volume 'tells how extremely amusing it is to shoot lots and lots of wild animals, to hear their quite-human moaning, and see them lurch off with their guts dragging,' Hemingway's obscene language also inspired Lewis' little squib:

Speak up, man! Be bravely heard
Bawling the four-letter word!
And wear your mind décolleté
Like Mr. Ernest Hemingway. (No. 44)

The battle continued with Lewis' attack on 'To Have and Have Not,' 'this thin screaming little book' about 'boresome and cowardly degenerates,'(56) which provoked Hemingway's savage vengeance in 'Across the River and into the Trees.' In that novel he described Lewis' pock-marks and ferret-features as looking 'like Goebbels's face, if Herr Goebbels had ever been in a plane that burned and had not been able to bail out before the fire reached him'(57)

Though Hemingway felt 'he had made the mistake of daring the critics to attack and they had taken the dare, "ganging up" on his book and refusing to judge it on its merits,'(58) he heeded their advice. For the Spanish Civil War intensified his political conviction and led to greater social commitment in 'To Have and Have Not' (1937). In that novel, the individualistic hero is placed in a corrupt society and shares the fate of other men.

'To Have and Have Not'

Two of the three sections of 'To Have and Have Not' were previously published as short stories in 'Cosmopolitan' (April 1934) and 'Esquire' (February 1936), and critics were quick to note that the three separate parts were imperfectly welded in the novel. The book Hemingway intended as his comeback in fiction received mostly negative reviews, but the public (after waiting for eight years) was eager for his work. The novel - which appeared while Hemingway was reporting the Spanish Civil War - was on the best-seller list from October to December 1937, and sold 36,000 copies in the first five months. 'To Have and Have Not' was Hemingway's first novel with an American setting, though Key West is on the extreme edge of the continent, next to the Caribbean and facing Cuba. The hero was named after the seventeenth-century Welsh buccaneer Sir Henry Morgan who also sailed and fought in these waters.

The editorial of Bernard De Voto (who disliked 'Green Hills of Africa') dismisses Hemingway's new social awareness - which had been praised by critics on the Left - as negligible. He continues in the tradition of Wyndham Lewis' criticism and asserts that his violent, amoral characters 'are incapable of ideas.... When they kill, they kill without guilt, without remorse, without rationalization' (No. 45). In his more perceptive review, Cyril Connolly observes (as James Joyce did in conversation): 'The great factor in determining Hemingway's style has been his body. His body is the opposite of Proust's, his style is the opposite of Proust's.' Connolly finds the novel 'morally odious' and lists the reasons for the decline in Hemingway's reputation: 'His book on big-game hunting, his flashy he-man articles in "Esquire" and his attitude to criticism have alienated a great many people.' But he still admires Hemingway and correctly predicts 'he is obviously the person who can write the great book about the Spanish war' (No. 46).

Alfred Kazin is more enthusiastic and, unlike De Voto and Connolly, finds that there is moral significance in the unusual hero of the novel: 'The hero of the book is not, like most of Hemingway's heroes, an elaborately self-conscious man against society; he is rather a mass man.... Harry Morgan's vice is his excessive self-reliance, the pride in his own tough loneliness.... Harry is unique because he is capable of struggle and casual about annihilation.' Kazin ends positively by stating that Hemingway 'is rather less sure of himself than usual, but a good deal more intense.... [He] is a genuine artist who has worked his way out of a cult of tiresome defeatism' (No. 47).

Like Kazin, Malcolm Cowley is one of Hemingway's best critics. He begins with a discussion of Hemingway's influence, which extends to detective stories, little magazines, newspapers, movies, highbrow novels and editorials, and believes he has had an excellent effect: he has encouraged authors to abandon affectation and 'to write as simply as possible about the things they really feel.' Cowley is, however, disappointed by the novel, which is defective in both plot and characterization, and is 'the weakest of Hemingway's books - except perhaps "Green Hills of Africa"'(No. 48).

In the most negative review, Louis Kronenberger asserts: 'it is a book with neither poise nor integration, and with shocking lapses from professional skill.' He feels the social theme is imposed and unconvincing because the sudden change in the main character is inconsistent: 'as Harry Morgan, the man born to stand alone, was about to go down to defeat, he [suddenly] came to realize that in this world the victims of society cannot stand alone' (No. 49). Edwin Muir, who was not impressed by 'The Sun Also Rises,' also finds a disparity between Hemingway's technique and theme: 'He clearly believes in sensation, and still distrusts thought, but he is also concerned about the state of the world, and his technique, fashioned exclusively to deal with the world of sensation, does not quite know how to deal with the change' (No. 50).

Philip Rahv states that Hemingway's 'favorite theme of human endurance and valor in the face of physical annihilation [is now] enacted on the stage of world events.' Like Cowley, he thinks the novel may begin a new phase of Hemingway's work, for Morgan 'represents Hemingway's review of his own past.... Morgan's death may presage Hemingway's social birth.' But Rahv, like most other critics, feels that the novelist has still not reached political maturity: 'In transcending his political indifference, he has not, however, at the same time transcended his political ignorance' (No. 51).

The long retrospective review by the poet Delmore Schwartz is the most complex consideration of the novel and one of the best essays on Hemingway. He begins by defining the pattern in Hemingway's work: 'there is an extraordinary interest in sensation; there is an extraordinary interest in conduct and the attitudes toward conduct; and there is always the background of war.' But Schwartz finds no 'clear link between the interest in sensation and the interest in conduct.' The pattern is completed by an outline 'of a morality and way of life which transcends the whole [narrow, violent] situation.' In this novel the pattern fails to work and Schwartz, after suggesting Hemingway's strengths, makes a startling judgment: it 'is a stupid and foolish book, a disgrace to a good writer, a book which should never have been printed.' Its main defects, as earlier critics noticed, are weak structure and commonplace conception (No. 52).

Though none of the reviewers really liked the novel, which was distinctly inferior to 'A Farewell to Arms,' many of them felt or hoped that there was a promising new social awareness in this transitional work. The novel was immortalized in the first Bogart-Bacall film, with a screenplay by William Faulkner, in which Bacall spoke the famous line: 'If you want anything, just whistle!'

'The Spanish Earth'

Hemingway was in Spain for nine months between March 1937 and May 1938, and reported the Civil War for the North American Newspaper Alliance. He saw the shelling of Madrid (including the Hotel Florida, where he was sharing a room with Martha Gellhorn), the fall of Teruel and the bombing of Tortosa. 'The Spanish Earth,' a documentary-propaganda film written and narrated by Hemingway and directed by the Dutch Communist Joris Ivens, was made in Spain during the Civil War. It was shown to President and Mrs. Roosevelt at the White House in July 1937; and the film script was published as a book in 1938, in a limited edition of 1,000 copies. In a review in the left-wing 'New Republic,' the distinguished young film critic Otis Ferguson states that the 'two simple themes [are] the suffering and dogged purposefulness of war for the cause; and ... the earth and its rightful function.' He praises Hemingway's script and narration, despite the high voice and flat Midwestern accent: 'Much of the carrying power in understatement should be credited to Ernest Hemingway's commentary.... [With his] feeling for the people of Spain which comes from his heart, the combination of experience and intuition directing your attention quietly to the mortal truth you might well have missed in the frame, there could hardly be a better choice' (No. 53).

'The Fifth Column and The First Forty-Nine Stories'

This composite volume contained Hemingway's only play - set in Spain and written during the Civil War, with a heroine clearly based on Martha Gellhorn - all of 'In Our Time,' 'Men Without Women,' 'Winner Take Nothing' and four uncollected stories, including his two masterpieces in this genre: The Short Happy Life of Francis Macomber and The Snows of Kilimanjaro. The cruel allusion to Scott Fitzgerald in the latter, just after he had published The Crack-Up articles and was particularly vulnerable, was changed to the less personal 'Julian' when the book appeared.

Like most critics, Alfred Kazin liked the stories (which were then being included in school textbooks) much better than the play, which failed to do justice to the important theme of commitment and to the complex politics of the war (No. 54). Malcolm Cowley believes the heroine negates the tragic implications of the play, for she is unintentionally presented 'as a chattering, superficial fool, a perfect specimen of the Junior Leaguer pitching woo [starting a courtship] on the fringes of the radical movement.' He also notes that Hemingway's violence, which once appeared excessive, now 'seems a simple and accurate description of the world in which we live' (No. 55).

Edmund Wilson's severe review asserts that the play is almost as bad as 'To Have and Have Not' and does not do 'very much either for Hemingway or for the revolution': 'the action is rather lacking in suspense and the final sacrifice rather weak in moral value.' Wilson shrewdly observes that the power of Hemingway's early stories, in contrast to the play, is his ability to identify himself with both the injurer and the injured. At their best, Hemingway's short stories represent 'one of the most considerable achievements of the American writing of our time' (No. 56).

The young W.H. Mellers adopts the condescending tone, derived from Wyndham Lewis, which English critics use as an antidote to American enthusiasm about Hemingway. He concedes that 'A Farewell to Arms' is an 'accomplished book'; and notes that the Hemingway values - resignation, fatalism, fortitude - 'as applied to human behaviour, are [like the Ten Commandments] in the main negative - one does *not* whine, one does *not* give in, one does *not* betray one's trust: and that in so far as they are positive they depend almost entirely on sensation.' But he feels these values are limited in that 'they can only live in the midst of destruction, being the values of a disintegrating society' (No. 57).

Lionel Trilling's persuasive and salutary essay opposes the critical trend of the entire decade and argues that literary works do not have to provide solutions to contemporary political problems. Trilling begins with Edmund Wilson's distinction between Hemingway the 'man' and the 'artist,' and attributes his failures to the intrusion of the former into his literary work. He then analyzes the enormous critical pressure - and misinterpretation - placed on Hemingway, and suggests the proper, detached perspective for reading his work: 'We looked for an emotional leader. We did not conceive Hemingway to be saying, Come, let us look at the world together. We supposed him to be saying, Come, it is your moral duty to be as my characters are. We took the easiest and simplest way of using the artist and decided he was not the "man" for us.... In short, the criticism of Hemingway came down to a kind of moral-political lecture, based on the assumption that art is - or should be - the exact equivalent of life.' Trilling concludes that we must not expect a political effect from a work of art: 'in removing from art a burden of messianic responsibility ... we may leave it free to do whatever it can actually do' (No. 58).

'The Fifth Column' (stage play)

In the spring of 1940, after the defeat of the Spanish Loyalists and the beginning of World War Two, 'The Fifth Column' was adapted for the stage by Benjamin Glazer.

Produced in New York by the Theater Guild and directed by Lee Strasberg, it ran for eighty-seven performances. Joseph Wood Krutch, who disagrees with most critics, does not like the play. He thinks the theme of 'reconciling the aims of a holy war with the methods which it must inevitably use' is not well-developed: 'what had begun as a complex picture of life in a war-torn city ends stagily as the love story of a hard-boiled hero whose grandiose gestures' are familiar and unconvincing (No. 60). Stark Young, who observes that Glazer has given more space to the love story and has added a drunken rape scene, finds the style uneven and the ending unconvincing. But he calls the acting and direction excellent (No. 61). Wolcott Gibbs writes that though the character of Dorothy has been weakened and 'Mr. Glazer has unquestionably simplified and cheapened the play here and there, I think it is emphatically worth seeing.' He also praises the 'remarkably fine performances' of the strong cast, led by Franchot Tone and Lee J. Cobb (No. 59).

Edmund Wilson on Hemingway

Edmund Wilson, the most learned and distinguished critic in America, wrote the most important and influential study of Hemingway. It drew heavily on Wilson's previous reviews of 'In Our Time,' 'Men Without Women,' 'Green Hills of Africa' and 'The Fifth Column and The First Forty-Nine Stories'; and it appeared in 1939 after the revelations of Russia's destructive role in Spain and the horrors of the Moscow Purge Trials had led to Wilson's disillusionment with Communism. This change in political attitude made Wilson less tolerant of Hemingway's brief, superficial flirtation with the Communists during the Spanish Civil War. Wilson offers a penetrating, analytical account of Hemingway's strengths and weaknesses; and his conclusive judgment of the first two decades of Hemingway's career still prevails.

Wilson, a great admirer of the early Hemingway, had published one of his stories in the 'New Republic' in May 1927. He now contrasts the successful artist of the 1920s with the public personality that eclipsed the writer, after 'A Farewell to Arms' in 1929, and dominated his work of the 1930s. Hemingway's radical decline is manifest in the deterioration of his prose: 'The master of that precise and clean style now indulges in purple patches which go on spreading for pages on end.' Instead of concentrating on his art, Hemingway has been 'occupied with building up his public personality' and exploiting this personality for profit: 'but Hemingway has created a Hemingway who is not only incredible but obnoxious. He is certainly his own worst-invented character.'

Yet Hemingway's surprising ability to recover his artistic integrity - revealed in the brilliant African stories of 1936 which compensate for the disastrous 'Green Hills of Africa' - allows Wilson to conclude his damaging essay on a positive note: 'His whole work is a criticism of society: he has responded to every pressure of the moral atmosphere of the time, as it is felt at the roots of human relations, with a sensitiveness almost unrivalled' (No. 62).

When Wilson's essay was reprinted in 'The Wound and the Bow' (1941), he added another page on 'For Whom the Bell Tolls' which summarized his review of the novel. Though Wilson thought it was superior to Hemingway's work of the thirties, it was still not equal to his finest books: 'The weaknesses of the book are its diffuseness ... and a romanticizing of some of the material, an infusion of the operatic.'(59)

'For Whom the Bell Tolls'

'For Whom the Bell Tolls,' Hemingway's longest and most ambitious novel, was written in Cuba and published in October 1940. It was a Book-of-the-Month Club choice and sold half a million copies in the first five months. The critical equalled the commercial success. Most reviewers received the book enthusiastically; thought it fulfilled the promise in 'To Have and Have Not' of a new social and political awareness - of a Hemingway 'involved in Mankinde'; and felt it compensated for the disappointing works of the 1930s and triumphantly re-established his literary reputation. The work was frequently compared to Malraux's great novel of the Spanish Civil War, 'Man's Hope' (1937), and Hemingway's book outsold Malraux's in France.

Despite Hemingway's clear sympathy for the Loyalists, the novel was attacked by Communist critics for portraying the atrocities of the Left as well as of the Right. Alvah Bessie, a veteran of the Lincoln Brigade, claimed in an open letter to the 'Daily Worker' that Hemingway had maligned the popular leader La Pasionaria, slandered the political commissar André Marty, and misrepresented Russia's attitude toward Spain. As Bessie lamented in the 'New Masses': 'He is found in bad company; in the company of his enemies, and the people's enemies who will fawn upon him and use him, his great talents and his passion for the people's cause, to traduce and betray those talents and those people.'(60)

Though Edmund Wilson had serious reservations about the merits of the novel, his review was more favorable than his judgment in 'The Wound and the Bow': 'There is in "For Whom the Bell Tolls" an imagination for social and political phenomena such as he has hardly given evidence of before.... What Hemingway presents us with in this study of the Spanish war is not so much a social analysis as a criticism of moral qualities' (No. 65). Dorothy Parker, who had admired Hemingway's stories in 1927, was ecstatic about the novel: 'It is written with a wisdom that washes the mind and cools it. It is written with an understanding that rips the heart with compassion' (No. 63). Howard Mumford Jones, who begins with an interesting comparison with 'A Farewell to Arms,' also praises the characters, style, theme and (unlike the Communist critics) the honesty: 'He has not omitted the drunkenness, the disorder, the cruelty, the selfishness, the confusion. The hero dies because of stupidity and treachery on his own side' (No. 64). And the playwright Robert Sherwood agrees that Hemingway's degree of delicacy proves that he 'is capable of self-criticism and self-development' and has achieved a rare 'sense of permanence and nobility of spirit' (No. 66).

The later and longer reviews in the quarterlies were inevitably more critical. In the same issue of the 'Partisan Review,' Dwight Macdonald and Lionel Trilling examine the political and the literary significance of the novel. Macdonald's essay quarrels with Edmund Wilson's view and seems to demand the kind of political discussion that Hemingway deliberately omitted from the novel. He criticizes the 'mixture of sentimental love scenes, too much talk, rambling narrative sequences, and rather dull interior monologues,' and calls it a failure 'because of its rejection of political consciousness' (No. 67). Trilling is more positive about the novel and believes Hemingway 'is wholly aware of the moral and political tensions which existed in actual fact.' He says the book reveals 'a restored Hemingway writing to the top of his bent' and that the episodes of El Sordo and Andres 'are equal to Tolstoy in his best battle manner.' He then proceeds to delineate the weaknesses: the 'astonishing melodrama' in place of tragedy, the 'devastating meaninglessness' of the death of Robert Jordan, the 'rather dull convention in which the men are all dominance and knowledge, the women all essential innocence and responsive passion.' After unfavorably contrasting Hemingway's attitude toward death with that of John Donne,

Trilling concludes: 'he is wholly at the service of the cult of experience and the result is a novel which, undertaking to celebrate the community of men, actually glorifies the isolation of the individual ego' (No. 68).

Mark Schorer is primarily concerned with the change and development in Hemingway's subject and style: 'from violent experience itself to the expressed evaluation of violence.... If the early books pled for sporting conduct on violent occasions, this book pleads the moral necessity of political violence.' Schorer believes that the novel disproves the thesis of Edmund Wilson's long essay, which was written before the book appeared and argued that Hemingway had no political persuasion, for in this work the individual 'vanishes in the political whole, but vanishes precisely to defend his dignity, his freedom, his virtue' (No. 69). Schorer's belief that Hemingway presents a 'poetic realization of man's *collective* virtues' is diametrically opposed to Trilling's view that he 'glorifies the isolation of the individual ego.'

The English critics were, as usual, less keen than the Americans. In a rather fanciful yet suggestive critique, written for Klaus Mann's 'Decision: A Review of Free Culture,' Christopher Isherwood sees 'Hemingway's three European novels as an artistic whole, a kind of metaphysical trilogy.... Hemingway's philosophy, in these three novels, is about the "Lost Generation," how it got lost, where it wandered to and how it might find itself again. His mysticism is about Death, Union through sexual love, and the problem of Evil in Time.... Through Love, we can transcend our consciousness of Time. That is the theme of "For Whom the Bell Tolls."(61) Mr. Isherwood writes, in a recent letter, that this essay 'expresses an enthusiasm for the novel which I no longer feel, although I remain a great admirer of much that Hemingway has written.'(62)

In a lively review in the 'Spectator,' Graham Greene criticizes the love story, 'told with Mr. Hemingway's usual romantic carnality,' but acknowledges that 'he has brought out of the Spanish war a subtlety and sympathy which were not there before' (No. 70). V.S. Pritchett, author of 'The Spanish Temper' (1954), repeats Wyndham Lewis' idea that Hemingway has been an unreflective and unself-critical writer, feels that Malraux is 'immeasurably superior' to Hemingway, and agrees with Greene that the novel is marred by the love affair which is 'fatal to the austerity of the narrative.' But he praises the dignity and pathos of the characters, the 'astonishingly real Spanish conversation' and the 'studied and intense narrative.' He concludes that the Spanish war has 'restored to

Hemingway his seriousness as a writer' (No. 71).

W.H. Mellers, who was critical of 'The Fifth Column and The First Forty-Nine Stories,' gives cool recognition to the merits of Hemingway's novel. He disagrees with Pritchett and states that the stylized speech of the Spaniards is 'another version of the stylization of the Hemingway language.' But he praises the 'precision and authenticity which came from first-hand experience' and says this meticulous clarity of detail 'gradually creates a resilient intensity.' He also accurately predicts that the 'book should make a superb film' (No. 73). E.M. Forster, writing a short moralistic paragraph in the 'Listener,' sees a penitential theme in the novel: '"For Whom the Bell Tolls" is a long, very serious book about the Spanish War, where Hemingway fought on the Republican side, and it deals with the blowing up of a bridge in the mountains, with Madrid, and with the Spaniards and the Americans who are engaged on the work. It is full of courage and brutality and foul language. It is also full of tenderness and decent values, and the idea running through it is that, though there must be a war in which we must all take part, there will have to be some sort of penance after the war if the human race is to get straight again.'(63)

A more recent anonymous evaluation in a volume edited by Geoffrey Grigson, a severe, authoritative and perceptive judge, echoes Ford's praise of Hemingway's style and suggests that English critics have now accepted this novel as his most important work: 'Hemingway's masterpiece was his novel of the Spanish Civil War, "For Whom the Bell Tolls" (1940). On the grand scale, it shows his prose at its most mature: exact, logical, muscular. One particularly admires the construction of the long sentences (it is a popular fallacy to suppose he used short ones all the time), in which one can see the whole structure, the bone as well as the flesh; each word, each subordinate clause, carries its exact weight, contributing what is required to the whole. He uses syntax as a sculptor uses stone.'(64)

The most unusual and provocative response to the novel is also a discussion of Spanish culture and mores by the novelist Arturo Barea who knew Hemingway during the Civil War. Barea argues that Hemingway understands very little of Spain beyond the bull-ring, has failed to render the reality of the Spanish War and has produced an unreal and deeply untruthful picture of the people and the period. Barea's five main criticisms are that the peasants of Old Castile could never have accepted as their leaders 'the old gypsy whore from Andalusia with her lover, the horse-dealer'; that the community of a Castilian village would never have followed Pablo to the end of the revolting organized butchery of the Fascists; that in the rape scene, it would be 'impossible for a Spaniard to want the union of his body with that of a woman still warm and moist from another male'; that Maria could not ask 'a foreigner to let her come into his bed the very first night after they had met ... and keep the respectful adoration of the members of her guerilla group'; and that Hemingway 'invents an artificial and pompous English' to convey the original Spanish (No. 72).

Though Barea is a Spaniard, his generalizations about the Spanish people are no more convincing than Hemingway's. The villagers might have accepted Pilar and Pablo as their leaders, during the unusual conditions of war, if they were the most effective military commanders; and the violence and hatred of wartime might well have led to the kind of brutal massacre that would otherwise have been impossible. The emotions aroused during rape - or indeed in a whorehouse patronized by a long line of eager soldiers - would be sufficient to dispel fastidious feelings about moist females. It is certainly unlikely that Maria would make sexual overtures to Jordan; but she has been deranged, and Hemingway is clearly writing a highly romanticized rather than a strictly realistic love story. Finally, Hemingway does not attempt to translate the Spanish but to provide an English version that will sound archaic, poetic and noble. In this novel, as well as in 'The Sun Also Rises,' he often achieves his effects by providing stilted latinate equivalents instead of colloquial idiomatic translations.(65)

'Men at War'

'Men at War,' an anthology of eighty-two war stories, edited and introduced by Hemingway, includes sections from 'A Farewell to Arms' and 'For Whom the Bell Tolls' and his dispatch from wartime Madrid. The book, which had a first printing of 20,000 copies, appeared in October 1942 - ten months after America entered the war - and reached first place on the non-fiction best-seller list in December. Carlos Baker suggests that though Hemingway did not have complete control of the selections, the best works are 'accurately observed and recorded with the utmost fidelity.... They have in common the factual flavor of eyewitness accounts, but have been matured by the artistic process beyond the level of reporting' (No. 74).

'The Portable Hemingway'

The Viking 'Portable Hemingway' was edited and annotated by Malcolm Cowley, whose valuable introduction helped to solidify Hemingway's reputation after the great success of 'For Whom the Bell Tolls.' This volume, which kept the public aware of Hemingway while he was reporting the war instead of writing books, contains passages from his four novels, all of 'In Our Time,' nine stories and the last chapter of 'Death in the Afternoon.' Granville Hicks observes that though Hemingway 'appears to be dealing with the surface behavior of bored and not very representative individuals, [he] is actually touching upon a profound and almost universal phenomenon. Perhaps that is why so many critics have felt in his work power and significance that their analyses did not account for' (No. 75).

'Across the River and into the Trees'

'Across the River and into the Trees' was condemned by all serious critics when it first appeared in September 1950 and is still considered Hemingway's worst novel. A few writers, like John O'Hara, praised the book out of loyalty to Hemingway or his past reputation; but Connolly, Zabel, Kazin, Waugh, Rosenfeld, Frye and Beach all agreed with Maxwell Geismar's evaluation in the 'Saturday Review of Literature': 'This is an unfortunate novel and unpleasant to review for anyone who respects Hemingway's talent and achievement. It it not only Hemingway's worst novel; it is a synthesis of everything that is bad in his previous work and throws a doubtful light on the future. It is so dreadful, in fact, that it begins to have its own morbid fascination.... The ideological background of the novel is a mixture of "True Romances," Superman, and the Last Frontier.'(66)

It would be foolish to claim that 'Across the River' is as good as Hemingway's best fiction. But the novel has been misinterpreted and maligned for purely external reasons, quite distinct from the merits of the literary text; when we separate Hemingway's hero from his public persona and recognize the confessional mode, it becomes a much better book than critical judgment has hitherto allowed. The novel presents an interesting case history of how biographical factors have distorted the meaning and ruined the reputation of a work that has considerable merit and that would have been hailed as impressive if it had been written by anyone but Hemingway. There are three biographical reasons why the novel received an intensely hostile reception: its place in Hemingway's literary career, his alienation of the critics and the decline of his personal legend. These factors led to a simplistic identification of the hero with the author and a misinterpretation of the book.

In 1950, Hemingway had not published a novel for ten years. Scribner's advance publicity had led readers to believe that 'Across the River' was a major work and would present Hemingway's experience in World War Two in the same way that 'A Farewell to Arms' and 'For Whom the Bell Tolls' had done for the Great War and the war in Spain. The publication of the novel had followed Malcolm Cowley's apotheosis of the Papa legend in 'Life' magazine (January 1949) and John McCaffery's admiring collection of essays (1950), which had heightened interest in Hemingway and aroused great expectations about his forthcoming book. The undignified serialization in the low-brow but high-paying ladies' magazine 'Cosmopolitan' (February-June 1950) was the first disappointment.

The critics inevitably compared Hemingway's latest novel with his greatest works. But it was impossible for him (or anyone else writing in 1950) to consistently maintain the standard of 'The Sun Also Rises' and 'A Farewell to Arms.' Critics who had staked - and in some cases established - their reputations by praising the greatness of Hemingway's earlier novels were intensely disappointed and irritated when their star failed to perform. Many of them felt they had over-rated his earlier work, expressed dissatisfaction by sharpening their knives on his abrasive novel and protected themselves by attacking him. The two main criticisms of the novel, as expressed by Philip Rahv in a 'Commentary' review, were that Hemingway was 'indulging himself in blatant self-pity and equally blatant conceit' and that 'there is hardly any aesthetic distance between the author and Colonel Richard Cantwell.... They have so much in common, in their private history and war experience no less than in their opinions, tastes, attitudes and prejudices, that there is no telling them apart.' (67)

Their hostility was also a form of retaliation. For Hemingway had repaid their previous praise with gratuitous attacks on literary parasites in his Introduction to Elio Vittorini's 'In Sicily' (1949), where he squeezed the last drop from the image of the critical wasteland: 'New York literary reviews grow dry and sad, inexistent without the watering of their benefactors, feeding on the dried manure of schism and the dusty taste of disputed dialectics, their only flowering a dessicated criticism as alive as stuffed birds, and their steady mulch the dehydrated cuds of fellow critics.' The critics were even more irritated when their negative reviews seemed to stimulate Hemingway addicts to buy the successful novel, which sold 125,000 copies in the first month.

As early as 1927 Edmund Wilson wrote: 'The reputation of Ernest Hemingway has, in a very short time, reached such proportions that it has already become fashionable to disparage him' (No. 19). Lillian Ross' 'New Yorker' profile, which appeared in May 1950 as an antidote to Cowley's sympathetic portrait, struck a devastating blow to the Hemingway legend. Though it is safe to assume that Hemingway played the role of tame bear and that he was not quite as stupid and boorish as Ross' malicious profile suggests, she did demonstrate that he had followed a descending path - characteristic of successful American novelists - from the charming Paris flat above the sawmill in the early twenties to the luxury and snobbery of the grand hotels of Venice in the late forties.

The profile also provided a bridge that connected the tone of the novel to the exhibitionistic hunting and fishing articles that had appeared in 'Esquire' in the mid-thirties, and to those manuals of expertise - 'Death in the Afternoon' and 'Green Hills of Africa' - in which he attempted to refute Gertrude Stein's admonition: 'Hemingway, remarks are not literature.'(68) And Hemingway's vainglorious boast, quoted in Ross' portrait of a pugnacious philistine, drinking heavily and grunting in pidgin English, invited disastrous retaliation: '"I started out very quiet and beat Mr. Turgenev," exclaimed the American author of "The Torrents of Spring" and Fathers and Sons. "Then I trained hard and I beat Mr. de Maupassant. I've fought two draws with Mr. Stendhal, and I think I had an edge in the last one. But nobody's going to get me in any ring with Mr. Tolstoy unless I'm crazy or I keep getting better."'(69) In October 1950, a few months after Hemingway's self-parodic interview, the 'New Yorker' also published E.B. White's witty send-up, Across the Street and into the Grill. Most critics, who seemed convinced that Hemingway had become too simple-minded to write a good book, accepted his pugilistic challenge and compared his work unfavorably with that of the nineteenth century masters.

Certain superficial details reinforce the autobiographical interpretation of the novel. The book is dedicated to Hemingway's fourth wife, Mary; expresses his adoration of the model of Renata, Adriana Ivancich, who designed the dust jacket; and contains a tasteless and transparent attack on his third wife, Martha Gellhorn, the only woman who ever stood up to him. Cantwell, like

Hemingway at Fossalta, ritualistically 'relieved himself in the exact place where he had determined, by triangulation, that he had been badly wounded thirty years before.'

Since these details encouraged critics to abolish the distinction between hero and author and equate Cantwell with Ross' image of Hemingway, they felt emboldened to expose his personal and artistic weaknesses by exposing his hero. But Hemingway was well aware of his radically defective fictional character. Though Hemingway revealed more of himself than he perhaps intended, he deliberately created and controlled a negative but essentially sympathetic hero who repeatedly confesses his own failure. The novel presents a severe self-portrait and scathing analysis of his own character, rather than a pitiful expression of self-indulgent egoism. As Edmund Wilson wrote in his review of 'Islands in the Stream': 'here is Hemingway making an effort to deal candidly with the discords of his own personality - his fears, which he has tried to suppress, his mistakes, which he has tried to justify, the pangs of bad conscience, which he has brazened out' (No. 119).

Cantwell shares many characteristics of Hemingway's heroes. He moves on familiar terrain, and runs his life through his mind to purge his bitterness. Wounded and defensive, he tries to control every aspect of his existence and walks with a slightly exaggerated confidence. Like the much admired Santiago in 'The Old Man and the Sea,' he exudes expertise and conveys to a devoted novice inside knowledge about everything from opening wine to cutting clams. His pride in trivial expertise is a feeble compensation for his overwhelming sense of failure. He has a desperate and rather pathetic desire to be liked and admired, and to be constantly reassured that he is liked and admired. He admits that he criticizes the universally praised heroes of the war, Generals Patton, Montgomery and Leclerc, because 'I have failed and I speak badly of all who have succeeded.' Like all Hemingway heroes, he is doomed to defeat and death; and the ultimate test of his character is the way he faces death.

The relationship of Othello and Desdemona (specifically mentioned in the novel) is vital to an understanding of Cantwell and Renata:

> She loved me for the dangers I had pass'd,
> And I loved her that she did pity them.

The allusion to 'Othello' suggests that Cantwell was also meant to be seen and judged from the less critical, more sympathetic viewpoint of the innocent, hero-worshipping

Renata; and that his mode of speech in the novel is confes-fessional. The function of Renata, who allows and encourages Cantwell to explore himself, is more as an interlocutor and extension of her lover than as an independent and substantial being. Cantwell frequently admits that his conversation about military matters is boring - to himself as well as to others - but he cannot stop confessing to such a sensitive and compassionate listener: a contessa who serves as a priest. Cantwell's recital of his faults continues throughout the novel. He is a shit, a mean son of a bitch, a brusque and brutal bastard; he exhibits a wild-boar truculence and loves his enemies more than his friends.

The source of his ineradicable bitterness is his failure as a general and subsequent demotion to colonel. Though he was forced to follow the orders of his inept superiors, he acknowledges that he must bear the ultimate responsibility. Hemingway, who saw literary life as competition with rivals and combat with critics, drew parallels between the life of the novelist and that of the soldier. Cantwell's confession of failure, his revelation of a certain hollowness at the core, his demotion from the highest rank, was perhaps Hemingway's admission of disappointment with his own novel and of a sense of declining powers after an impressive career. In his art, as opposed to his life, he conceded defeat and could no longer take on Mr. Turgenev, Mr. de Maupassant and Mr. Stendhal.

John O'Hara, a disciple of Hemingway and one of the few contemporary admirers of the novel, wildly overstated his case, on the front page of the 'New York Times Book Review,' by describing Hemingway as 'The most important author living today, the outstanding author since the death of Shakespeare.' The tone of his surprisingly simple-minded review, which attacks 'the pedants, the college professors, the litterateurs,' combines adulation with wisecracks. He calls Renata 'practically all that a middle-aged man with a cardiac condition could ask for'; and concludes, in Hemingway's boxing metaphor: 'He may not be able to go the full distance, but he can still hurt you.... Real class.'(70)

Cyril Connolly observes: 'it is not uncommon for a famous writer to produce one thoroughly bad book,' and states that Hemingway's 'Far-Western treatment of Death in Venice' is lamentable. He wryly remarks that though Hemingway's 'adventurous life has been an inspiration to writers who don't want to be publishers or Government officials,' his novel suffers from two unreal and unsympathetic characters. The Colonel is a 'drink-sodden and maundering old bore.... His ladylove is a whimsical waxwork.' Connolly believes that Hemingway must, at the age of fifty, abandon his romantic adolescent attitude and cease to be a repressed intellectual. He concludes with a shrewd prediction that Hemingway can still produce a valuable 'bestiary or a truthful autobiography'(71) - which is almost exactly what he did in his next two books.

In a review entitled A Good Day for Mr. Tolstoy, Morton Dauwen Zabel asserts 'this new novel is the poorest thing its author has ever done' and reveals the impasse that 'a talent arrives at when an inflexibly formulated conception of experience or humanity is pushed to the limits of its utility' (No. 76). Deb Wylder, who suggests that Hemingway, like Henry James, could profitably 'be examined in the light of the effect of European culture on the American type,' agrees that the book is a failure. He also feels that Hemingway has regressed to triviality and self-indulgence, and that the '"code" no longer acts as a set of rules to aid the protagonist to live in the world - it has now become an excuse ... to separate himself from the world' (No. 81).

Northrop Frye focusses on the disparity between the potential and the actual novel. The hero meets his fate 'with a compelling dignity,' 'his approaching death gives a bitter intensity to the ordinary events of his life' and 'his story is intended to be a study in isolation.' But Hemingway fails, in an embarrassing way, because he has not achieved the necessary technical detachment from his hero (No. 80). Joseph Warren Beach reads the novel as largely autobiographical. He remarks that 'the hero of Hemingway's novels is always much the same person' and that 'Colonel Cantwell is the oldest of all these avatars of Nick Adams.' He contrasts this book with the three earlier novels, and thinks it reveals 'a considerable strain on his stylistic resources,' is too thin a subject for a long book and, because of sentimentality, does not do full justice to the theme of love (No. 82). Alfred Kazin, as severe as Connolly, Zabel, Wylder, Frye and Beach, calls the book a distressing vulgar travesty. But he partially excuses it by noting that in 1949 Hemingway thought he would die of an eye infection and 'turned aside from the more ambitious novel he had been working over for some years to do this little book in the short time he felt was left' (No. 77).

Evelyn Waugh's unusual review notes the unanimous disapproval of the critics and explains the complex reasons for their hostility to 'one of the most original and powerful of living writers.' Waugh mentions Hemingway's even-handed criticism of the Loyalists in 'For Whom the

Bell Tolls,' Lillian Ross' blitz in the 'New Yorker,' his deliberately cultivated philistine image, his 'delight in the technicalities of every trade but his own' and, most importantly, his unfashionable, 'quite unforgivable - Decent Feeling' (No. 78). The psychoanalytically oriented review-essay by Isaac Rosenfeld is full of original insights: 'So good are the credentials of this [sparse] style, we honor it with our whole experience.... The Hemingway heroine has always been pure bitch, pure pal, or like Brett Ashley, two in one.' He states that Hemingway's reputation must soon decline because his 'attitude toward life has already begun to look like a hoax.' But he also perceives that the power of the novel derives from the 'courage to confess, even if it be only through self-betrayal, the sickness and fear and sad wreck of life behind the myth' (No. 79).

'The Old Man and the Sea'

Hemingway had planned his phenomenally successful novella, which won the Pulitzer Prize that had been denied to 'A Farewell to Arms' and 'For Whom the Bell Tolls,' for more than fifteen years. He had outlined the essence of the story in a paragraph of On the Blue Water which appeared in 'Esquire' in April 1936. 'Life' paid $40,000 for the serial rights, and bookstores rushed advance copies to their customers before magazine publication. Hemingway also sold the film rights for a handsome sum and became technical adviser for the fishing scenes that were shot off the coast of Peru. The novella, whose stark simplicity eliminated the obvious faults of 'Across the River and into the Trees,' was a triumphant recovery from the critical disaster of the previous novel and rapidly restored his reputation.

Most critics - forced to make a volte-face after pronouncing the writer dead - fell over each other in praising the work. Most of them shared the enthusiasm of Bernard Berenson, who exclaimed, in a public pronouncement that the great are called upon to make: 'Hemingway's "The Old Man and the Sea" is an idyll of the sea as sea, as un-Byronic and un-Melvillian as Homer himself, and communicated in a prose as calm and compelling as Homer's verse. No real artist symbolizes or allegorizes - and Hemingway is a real artist - but every real work of art exhales symbols and allegories. So does this short but not small masterpiece.'(72)

In his brief, early review Edwin Muir states: 'as soon as the long battle with the great fish begins the toughness and the sentimentality are gone, and Mr. Hemingway is in the world of free poetic imagination where he is really at home' (No. 83). Cyril Connolly, who had savaged 'Across the River and into the Trees,' compares the novella to Flaubert's A Simple Heart, calls it 'the best story Hemingway has ever written' and writes: 'a long physical struggle is described with the dynamic right words even as the changing qualities of the static sea are portrayed in their true colours, and the soul of the old man - humble, fearless, aromatic - is described perfectly too.'(73) The English advance orders reached 20,000 copies and these fine reviews inspired continuing sales of 2,000 a week.

'Everywhere the book is being called a classic,' says the influential critic Mark Schorer, who had written an appreciative review of 'For Whom the Bell Tolls.' He admires the religious theme, calls the work 'not only a moral fable, but a parable' and believes that 'Hemingway's art, when it is art, is absolutely incomparable, and that he is unquestionably the greatest craftsman in the American novel in this century' (No. 84). Gilbert Highet, who also notes the Conradian theme, emphasizes the epic pattern rather than the religious significance: 'A hero undertakes a hard task. He is scarcely equal to it because of ill luck, wounds, treachery, hesitation, or age. With a tremendous effort, he succeeds. But in his success he loses the prize itself, or final victory' (No. 85). Joyce Cary, responding to a questionnaire in the 'New York Times Book Review,' chooses the novella as his favorite book of the year: 'Hemingway's old man is profoundly original. It deals with fundamentals, the origins. Its form, so elaborately contrived, is yet perfectly suited to the massive shape of a folk theme' (No. 88). And William Faulkner's curt, mock-humble puff agrees with Schorer, Highet and Cary, stresses Hemingway's new element of pity (as opposed to toughness) and affirms: 'His best. Time may show it to be the best single piece of any of us, I mean his and my contemporaries' (No. 86).

After the first rave reviews, a much cooler reaction was inevitable in some of the more considered essays in the major quarterlies. F.W. Dupee allies himself with the admirers, and concentrates on interpreting the old man's character and his relation with the marlin which 'becomes his alter-ego as well as his catch, his victim and victimizer both.' For Dupee, the story shows Hemingway 'in what are no doubt his original capacities: as an exacting artist, a visionary of nature and human nature, a man committed to self-reliance' (No. 89). But R.W.B. Lewis, writing in the 'Hudson Review,' doubts 'if the book can bear the amount of critical weight already piled up on it.... [It] is not absolutely persuasive.... Our assent has to be partially withheld.' He praises Hemingway, however, for perceiving 'the stimulating and fatal relation between integrity of character and the churning abundance of experience. His style catches this perception with a good deal of its old power' (No. 90).

Like Gilbert Highet, Delmore Schwartz, who had blasted 'To Have and Have Not,' notes that the novella has the same theme as The Undefeated. In the most penetrating review of the book he also clarifies the reasons for the enthusiastic critical response: 'there was a note of insistence in the praise and a note of relief, the relief because his previous book was extremely bad in an ominous way, and the insistence, I think, because this new work is not so much good in itself as a virtuoso performance which reminds one of Hemingway at his best' (No. 87). If 'Across the River and into the Trees' was misread and condemned for external reasons, 'The Old Man and the Sea' - with its pervasive sentimentality, simple stoicism and forced religious symbolism - was Hemingway's most overrated work. It was also the last of his books to be published during his lifetime.

'The Hemingway Reader'

'The Hemingway Reader' (similar to 'The Portable Hemingway') was published in September 1953, with a first printing of about 16,000 copies, to capitalize on the enormous success of 'The Old Man and the Sea.' This comprehensive anthology, edited by Charles Poore who had favorably reviewed many of Hemingway's books, contained the complete 'Torrents of Spring,' excerpts from all six novels, chapters from 'Green Hills of Africa' and 'Death in the Afternoon,' and eleven of the best short stories. Stanley Edgar Hyman finds that 'The Sun Also Rises' 'survives undiminished, a small-scale masterpiece,' that 'For Whom the Bell Tolls' is marred by 'free-floating Hispanophile sentimentality,' and that even as early as A Way You'll Never Be (1933), 'the self-indulgence and egocentricism so repellent' in the later works are clearly visible. After surveying three decades of Hemingway's work, Hyman graphs a neat parabola that shows him sinking into the familiar and fatal trap of self-parody (No. 91).

Obituaries

In November 1961, four months after Hemingway's death,

Archibald MacLeish's elegy appeared in the 'Atlantic' and (retrospectively) suggested that a violent death seemed inevitable from the very beginning of Hemingway's intense career:

'In some inexplicable way an accident.'
Mary Hemingway

Oh, not inexplicable. Death explains
that kind of death: rewinds remembrance
backward like a film track till the laughing man
among the lilacs, peeling the green stem,
waits for the gunshot where the play began;

rewinds those Africas and Idahos and Spains
to find the table at the Closerie des Lilas,
sticky with syrup where the flash of joy
flamed into blackness like that flash of steel.

The gun between the teeth explains
The shattered mouth foretells the singing boy.(74)

The occasion of Hemingway's suicide demanded praise rather than summary judgment - the revaluation would come later. The critics, shocked by the sudden loss that made headlines around the world, were eager to render homage to a titanic figure. Ilya Ehrenburg, who knew him in Spain, says Hemingway was his favorite author. He discusses his enormous popularity in Russia and mentions that his 'death has meant the loss not only of a writer whom I love, but also a man of whose friendship I was proud' (No. 94). John Wain notes that 'Except for Macaulay, no writer in the English-speaking world has been so widely imitated as Hemingway.' His 'heroes are wounded because his view of life is a tragic stoical pessimism'; his major (Conradian) theme is that 'a defeat, if it is faced with courage and endured without loss of one's self-respect, counts as a victory' (No. 92). In a fine appreciation of Hemingway's art, Irving Howe states: 'He was always a young writer, and always a writer for the young. He published his best novel "The Sun Also Rises" in his mid-twenties and completed most of his great stories by the age of forty.' His finest stories 'are concerned to improvise a momentary truce in the hopeless encounter with fear' and 'are actually incitements to personal resistance and renewal' (No. 93).

In the most severe critique prompted by Hemingway's death, the Italian novelist Alberto Moravia argues that he exemplified the characteristic weakness of United States authors, and gives a negative twist to Irving Howe's idea: 'As a consequence of his lack of faith in culture, the American writer for the most part confines himself to recounting the story of his youth.... After he has made his début with a couple of books, the American writer tends to restrict himself to re-writing them.' After an extended comparison with the artists of action, D'Annunzio and Malraux, Moravia finds most of Hemingway's work inferior and concludes that his best books are 'The Sun Also Rises,' 'A Farewell to Arms' and 'The First Forty-Nine Stories' (No. 95).

'A Moveable Feast'

Hemingway's nostalgic memoir of his life in Paris during 1921-26 - when he was poor, in love with his wife and writing his most original work - was partly inspired by the astonishing recovery in 1957 of a suitcase of old documents that he had left in the basement of the Hotel Ritz in Paris in 1928. The book was mainly written in Cuba and Idaho during 1957-60; and after completing the work Hemingway confirmed the topographical accuracy by retracing his footsteps in Paris. But Hemingway was not, like Pound, loyal to his friends and their work. Though most of his distinguished companions and rivals were either hors de combat or dead, nearly all of his portraits were venomous and brutal.

The title had first appeared in 'Across the River and into the Trees' when Cantwell tells Renata: 'Happiness, as you know, is a moveable feast.'(75) After Hemingway's death the book was edited and prepared for press by his fourth wife, Mary. Passages from eleven of the twenty sketches appeared in 'Life' magazine (April 1964) a month before the publication of the book, which had a first printing of 85,000 copies. The memoir was on the best-seller list from May to December 1964, and held first place for nineteen weeks from June to October.

The critics, who took this occasion for a retrospective evaluation of Hemingway's career, praised his indirect self-portrait - his imposing presence was there 'by reflection' - for its clarity of recall and vividness of scene. Nearly everyone disapproved of his bitchiness and agreed that the nasty, funny and moving sections on Fitzgerald were the most interesting part of the book. Some reviewers, grateful for this gift from beyond the grave, were adulatory. Nelson Algren, a Hemingway apostle, points out in his tough-guy review 'how many Americans tried to *be* Hemingway, because the image felt true' and because the awareness that life was precarious made you 'become more alive' (No. 100). George Plimpton states, on the front page of the 'New York Herald Tribune Book Week': 'The Paris sketches are absolutely controlled, far enough removed in time so that the scenes and characters are observed in tranquillity, and yet with astonishing immediacy - his remarkable gift - so that many of the sketches have the hard brilliance of his best fiction.' He calls the memoir (which was written during a period of acute depression) a therapeutic work which still retains 'a note of impending chaos and death'; and then considers, at some length, the culinary and athletic aspects of the book (No. 96).

Morley Callaghan, who was on the scene in the 1920s, calls Hemingway 'an attractive, interesting, fascinating companion, dark and brooding though he might be, with strange shrewd hunches about people that turned into grudges.' Like Stanley Kauffmann and Richard Ellmann, Callaghan thinks the power of the book comes from Hemingway's recognition - in the twenties - that this would be the happiest period of his life: 'when the time came to write this book, maybe he knew what he had lost. And maybe this knowledge explains the book's bitter tone ... the quick leap for the jugular vein' (No. 99). In a long backward glance at Hemingway's early friendships and literary career, Stanley Kauffmann observes that his tremendous impact came from 'His increasingly rigorous and effective reticence, his insistent lucidity, his rejection of the formalities and flourishes of pre-war literature with an accompanying implicit rejection of pre-war social falsities' (No. 97). Richard Ellmann, in a witty and elegant review, notes that 'A Moveable Feast' fulfills the intention of the dying hero of The Snows of Kilimanjaro to describe his early life in Paris. After a long comparison with Fitzgerald, who squandered his prodigious talents, Ellmann remarks that though Hemingway 'wanted to be known as swashbuckling, his strength came from self-containment' (No. 98).

The longer reviews by three English writers were rather more critical of the memoirs. In an acute, off-beat analysis, Julian Maclaren-Ross (who could have drunk Papa under the table) expresses great admiration for the writer whose life and work had a considerable influence on his own career. He is not entirely uncritical, however; he remarks that 'A lot of nostalgic nonsense is often written about poverty and hunger by successful authors who no longer have to experience them,' and that Hadley, the first Mrs. Hemingway, seems to be the model for all the 'far too admiring and acquiescent' women in his fiction (No. 103). Tony Tanner also thinks that 'Hemingway certainly reveals himself more nakedly than he can have intended.... The book is written with a good deal of arrogance: every episode is turned to leave Hemingway looking tougher, more talented, more honest, more dignified than anyone else.' He too sees the book as a doomed idyll whose 'dawn brightness is occasionally darkened by sombre intimations of twilight' (No. 102). Frank Kermode ironically notes that Hemingway's famous built-in shit-detector 'can purge not only your prose but your acquaintance.' But he states that this essentially fictional work is 'about the heroic apprenticeship' of writing, that it is, 'in some ways, Hemingway's best book since the 1920s' and that (like Proust) it conveys with 'authority and distinction ... the sense of time regained' (No. 101).

The extended essays in the leading American quarterlies - 'Kenyon Review,' 'Hudson Review' and 'Sewanee Review' - found much to praise in what seemed to be Hemingway's last work. Philip Young, in his lively review, says that Hemingway's witty and hard-hitting memoir recaptures 'the great years of Americans in Paris, an ideal expatriation that thousands of literary people, born too late, have dreamed of ever since.' (76) For Young, it represents his 'most remarkable comeback' (No. 104). In a typically tough-minded, authoritative essay, Marvin Mudrick utilizes Edmund Wilson's distinction between 'the early master and the old impostor.' He notes that 'The reputation had its lethal effect on criticism, which either attacked the public image as if it were all there was of Hemingway, or praised virtually all of Hemingway as if the public image were quite unrelated to the work.' He calls Hemingway's early style 'as original and personal an invention as anything in literature' - and concludes: 'That Hemingway could have resolved to risk such a candor of private regret and longing [about his first marriage] against the grain of his so carefully cultivated reputation, less than a year before his death, is the proof of the strength he could still muster' (No. 105).

The one serious and significant dissent from the hallelujah chorus comes in Andrew Lytle's old-fashioned and frankly moralistic piece, which deliberately resists the seductions of Hemingway's art and rejects his moral values. Lytle finds two deep-rooted faults: his lack of charity and his rootless hedonism. Lytle, who agrees with Morley Callaghan about the first flaw, writes more forcefully than the other critics: 'There is not an associate of his, who conceivably might be his rival, or to whom he owed anything, that receives anything but denigration of character or profession.... The professional competence of each is betrayed through the deficiencies and follies of a personal and private nature.' And Lytle (a Southern regionalist writer) says of the second, self-destructive weakness: 'By its nature this set thrown up after the first world war is in exile, with only its appetites to depend upon.... Finally, this [hedonism] must have seemed meaningless, for it did not prevent Hemingway's first marriage from breaking up' (No. 106).

'By-Line: Ernest Hemingway'

This anthology of seventy-five dispatches from four decades of Hemingway's reporting was published in May 1967, sold 45,000 copies in the first month and was on the non-fiction best-seller list for six weeks. Philip Young, who wrote the Foreword and Commentaries for the English edition, is appropriately enthusiastic about the book. He convincingly justifies the publication, despite Hemingway's clearly expressed wish to keep his journalism buried in ephemeral periodicals, and observes that his role as journalist was 'a way of getting in on the action'; that some of his early political reporting reveals 'the precocious shrewdness of a writer who is supposed to have no politics,' and that for Hemingway hunting and fishing were 'an essentially aesthetic experience' (No. 107). Like Young, Stanley Kauffmann notices the striking differences between the writing of the young Hemingway, struggling for success in the early twenties, and that of the far less attractive public figure. He agrees that this volume is valuable both for its historical interest and for the original material that was later transformed into fiction (No. 108).

This volume was also well-received in England by two of the leading critics of American literature. Malcolm Bradbury begins by noting that Hemingway established his literary authority by not being a man of letters. For Bradbury, the reporting fuses Hemingway's three roles as journalist, sportsman and soldier of fortune: 'What they have in common is skill, expertise and the sense of having been there when it was happening - the sense of salvation through control and utter knowingness' (No. 109). Tony Tanner concentrates on the 'continuity between the prose of the reporter and that of the writer. It controls the same fears; it formulates the same strategies for survival; it holds onto the world in the same way. And like the fiction, the journalism is really about two things - war, and peace' (No. 110).

'The Fifth Column and Four Stories of the Spanish Civil War'

Critics writing in 1969 disliked 'The Fifth Column' as much as Kazin, Cowley and Wilson did when it was first published with 'The First Forty-Nine Stories' in 1938. The two old Hemingway war-horses, Carlos Baker and Philip Young, make the best possible case for the four minor stories in this composite volume and dismiss the play, which Hemingway himself called 'probably the most unsatisfactory thing I ever wrote.' After mentioning the considerable work by Hemingway that was inspired by his experience in the Spanish Civil War, even Carlos Baker admits that 'the years have not been kind to "The Fifth Column."' He concentrates instead on the uncollected stories, but tends to over-rate them (No. 111). Young notes that 'the book is unified in time, place and action' and that 'all four stories are deft and absorbing' (No. 112).

Stephen Spender, who did propaganda work in Spain for the Loyalists, is much more critical and penetrating. He concludes that when 'Hemingway was justifying war and toughness, he could be maudlin with a hideous inverted sentimentality, but that when he was simply observing and experiencing, war did move him to truthful observation and deep imaginative insight' (No. 113).

'Islands in the Stream'

If 'A Moveable Feast' was sometimes read as fiction, 'Islands in the Stream' was seen as pure autobiography. The novel, which returns to the Caribbean milieu of 'To Have and Have Not,' is Hemingway's second unsuccessful attempt to write a book about World War Two that would equal 'A Farewell to Arms' and 'For Whom the Bell Tolls.' The three-part work, written during 1946-47, 1950-51, was never completed and was kept in a bank vault during the last decade of Hemingway's life. Long excerpts from Parts 1 and 2 had previously appeared in 'Esquire' and 'Cosmopolitan'; the published version was edited by his wife, Mary. The novel, which finally came out in October 1970, was a Book-of-the-Month Club selection, sold 100,000 copies in the first three months and remained on the best-seller list for half a year. After A.E. Hotchner's widely read revelations of Papa (1966) and Carlos Baker's biography (1969), the public was especially eager for Hemingway. Just as 'A Moveable Feast' portrayed the most promising period of Hemingway's life, so 'Islands in the

Stream' depicted the most depressing. The novel was inevitably read with the knowledge that the author had killed himself.

The critics were far less responsive than the public to Hemingway's long-awaited last book, which John Aldridge calls 'the most widely publicized literary mystery of the last two decades.' The novelist John Wain finds it an essentially repetitive book and ranks it, on literary merit, above 'Across the River and into the Trees', slightly below 'For Whom the Bell Tolls' and 'well below the very best' work. 'When Hemingway has really described something,' Wain writes, 'he has saturated our minds in it, and it is difficult to feel the same freshness on a second visit.'(77) Joseph Epstein remarks that Hemingway's reputation has sharply declined since his death and that this good-bad book will do little to revive it. Nevertheless, its theme is significant: 'This is a novel about human loss, one in which a man's armor against the world is stripped away leaving him alone and exposed' (No. 116).

Christopher Ricks, writing in the 'New York Review of Books,' condemns the structural incoherence, the lack of motivation in the characters, the intrusive self-pity and the obsessive concern with suicide - clearly foreshadowed a decade before the tragic event (No. 114). Paul Theroux, after discussing his competitive instinct and fluctuating reputation, writes: 'The novel has no literary importance, but its personal candour is essential' for an understanding of Hemingway. He suggests that the book is an autobiography rather than a fictional portrayal of an 'embittered, heartless, unquestioning and deluded man' (No. 120). John Aldridge begins his long review with a detailed account of Hemingway's late unpublished works. He finds the novel strangely uneven and explains the reasons for its weakness: 'No longer positively committed to the early Hemingway values, he yet retains the early skepticism which in him is fast souring into hopelessness.... As the distance narrowed between himself and his heroes, his writing lost a crucial dimension. He began to try to *live out* his fantasies instead of projecting them in his fiction' (No. 115).

John Updike calls the book 'a gallant wreck of a novel paraded as the real thing.' The book inspires Updike 'with a worried concern for the celebrity who wrote it ... [for] the need to prove himself drives Thomas Hudson implacably toward violence and death.' He concludes by formulating the central artistic weakness: 'Love and death: fused complements in Hemingway's universe. Yet he never formulated the laws that bind them, never achieved the step of irony away from himself' (No. 117). Irving Howe, in another perceptive review, decides: 'Almost everything wrong with the book follows from this emotional overlap between author and protagonist.... The book moves ... on two planes: the external action, often interesting for pages at a time, and the inner life of Hudson, mostly tiresome.' Howe, who wrote a fine obituary notice of Hemingway, believes the essential weakness is the lack of a 'firm and disciplined vision of life' that pervades 'The Sun Also Rises' (No. 118).

The magisterial Edmund Wilson, who wrote the first serious notice of Hemingway's work in the 'Dial' in 1924, has virtually the last word on his last novel in the 'New Yorker,' nearly fifty years later. Wilson - who believes the book in the long run will appear more important than it now seems to be - makes two important points about the public and private Hemingway. His triumph 'seemed to satisfy two typical American ambitions: that of becoming an accomplished outdoorsman and that of making a great deal of money.' And the central theme of his last four novels - from 'A Farewell to Arms' to 'Islands in the Stream' - is that of a 'crucial game played against invincible odds' (No. 119).

The critics of this imperfect and sometimes preposterous novel were essentially sympathetic, as if they regretted their inability to praise the last work of an acknowledged master. There was no concurrence about which part of the novel was best or worst, but they agreed that the main faults were the same ones that had plagued Hemingway since 1940: a self-indulgent rather than disciplined attitude to art that resulted in a weak structure (the islands remained separate rather than attached to the mainland of the novel), lack of aesthetic distance and inability to portray a reflective character.

'The Nick Adams Stories'

'The Nick Adams Stories' was edited by Philip Young and published in April 1972 with a first printing of 25,000 copies. The volume contains twenty-four chronologically ordered tales - eight of them distinctly inferior and previously unpublished. They are rather vaguely unified by a consistent central character who made his first appearance in 'In Our Time' and brought readers back to the very beginning of Hemingway's literary career. Louis Rubin believes that the volume 'constitutes a fascinating and valuable bit of creative editing' for three reasons: it provides insight into Hemingway's creative process, reveals his sensibility and provides some excellent new writing (No. 121). William Abrahams is much more critical of Young's editorial assumptions. He doubts whether this arrangement makes these 'classic achievements' more meaningful and memorable. And he is sceptical about Young's attempt to reveal, for example, the nameless anxiety that haunts The Big Two-Hearted River and 'gives it its extraordinary depth and poetry' (No. 122).

BOOKS ON HEMINGWAY

Hemingway has been exhaustively anatomized in the vast number of books that have appeared since 1952. There is a superb bibliography and supplement (1967, 1975) by Audre Hanneman; anecdotal accounts by his sporting cronies; domestic recollections by his brother Leicester (1962), his sisters Marcelline (1962) and Madeleine (1975), his son Gregory (1976) and fourth wife, Mary (1976); memoirs by writers Harold Loeb (1959), Morley Callaghan (1963) and Nelson Algren (1965); a profile by Lillian Ross (1961); and biographies by A.E. Hotchner (1966), Carlos Baker (1969) and Scott Donaldson (1977).

The pioneering critical studies by Carlos Baker (1952) and Philip Young (1952) are still the best books on Hemingway. They have been followed by a number of more specialized works: Charles Fenton's useful study of the journalistic apprenticeship (1954), Nicholas Joost on the publication in little magazines (1968), Constance Montgomery on the Michigan days (1966), Castillo-Puché on Hemingway in Spain (1974), Wayne Kvam on Hemingway in Germany (1973) and Robert Gajdusek's photographs of Hemingway's Paris (1978).

John Atkins (1952), Stewart Sanderson (1961), Earl Rovit (1963) and Leo Gurko (1968) have produced rather bland general studies. Jack Killinger has written on Hemingway and existentialism (1960), Joseph DeFalco (1963) and Deb Wylder (1969) on Hemingway's heroes, Robert Lewis on Hemingway and love (1965), Robert Stephens on the non-fiction (1968) and Emily Watts on Hemingway and the arts (1971). Jackson Benson has edited a collection of criticism on the short stories (1975) and Matthew Bruccoli has considered the friendship with Fitzgerald (1978).

The most original and valuable recent book, which uses unpublished letters and manuscripts, source reading, historical background and literary biography to illuminate 'A Farewell to Arms,' is Michael Reynolds' 'Hemingway's First War.' Reynolds proves that Hemingway used military histories and newspaper accounts for the factual basis of the Italo-Austrian campaigns, which took place when he was still in high school in Oak Park.

Perhaps the only book that has not been written is one on Hemingway and film, which would consider the cinematic techniques in his fiction, his film script of 'The Spanish Earth,' the screen adaptations of his novels and his personal involvement in several of these films. Apart from Reynolds' book, there has been no study of Hemingway's manuscripts and, because of his will, no edition of his letters (the correspondence with Adriana Ivancich at the University of Texas is disappointingly dull). Unless new discoveries are made among the unpublished material, the books that inevitably follow at the fag-end of literary criticism will vary existing ideas, repeat what has already been said or offer madcap theories. Except for archival research, the essential work on Hemingway has already been done.

Malcolm Cowley, writing in 1937 when Hemingway had already completed his finest work, gave an accurate estimate of his place in world literature: 'I don't think that he is as great as Tolstoy or Thomas Mann, but I do think that he is perhaps as good as Mark Twain, and that is saying a great deal. In our own generation, he is the best we have' (No. 48). Though Hemingway has not equalled the greatest writers - with whom he compared himself - his stature, based on the highly innovative style and technique in three major novels and a dozen first-rate short stories, is secure. His reputation has survived his decline, his death and his detractors, and the intense critical revaluation of the last two decades has recognized him as the most important and influential American novelist of the twentieth century.

NOTES

1 Hugh Kenner, Small Ritual Truths, 'A Homemade World' (New York, 1975), 144.
2 Archibald MacLeish, Years of the Dog, 'Act Five' (New York, 1948), 53.
3 Ernest Hemingway, 'The Sun Also Rises' (New York, 1954), 168.
4 See Hemingway's account of the crashes, The Christmas Gift, 'Look,' 18 (20 April and 4 May 1954), 29-37, 79-89.
5 Quoted in Richard Ellmann, 'James Joyce' (New York, 1959), 708.
6 Saul Bellow, Hemingway and the Image of Man, 'Partisan

Review,' 20 (1953), 341.

7 George Plimpton, Ernest Hemingway, 'Paris Review,' 5 (1958), 89.

8 Ernest Hemingway, 'Green Hills of Africa' (New York, 1935), 23, 28.

9 Norman Mailer, Punching Papa, 'New York Review of Books,' 1 (August 1963), 13.

10 Wallace Stevens, 'Letters,' ed. Holly Stevens (London, 1966), 411-12.

11 Harry Levin, Observations on the Style of Ernest Hemingway, 'Kenyon Review,' 13 (1951), 601, 604.

12 Tony Tanner, Ernest Hemingway's Unhurried Sensations, 'Reign of Wonder' (Cambridge, England, 1965), 234.

13 Plimpton, 'Paris Review,' 84.

14 'Green Hills of Africa,' 23, 109.

15 Alfred Kazin, 'On Native Grounds' (New York, 1942), 327-8, 340. Jackson Benson's 'Hemingway: The Writer's Art of Self-Defense' (Minneapolis, 1969) is a book-length elaboration of Kazin's second sentence.

16 Malcolm Cowley, Introduction to 'The Portable Hemingway' (New York, 1944), vii.

17 Robert Penn Warren, Hemingway, 'Kenyon Review,' 9 (1947), 3, 11, 28. Cleanth Brooks, in 'The Hidden God' (New Haven, 1963), which discusses both Hemingway and Warren in a theological context, repeats Warren's main idea. See especially p. 8.

18 F.R. Leavis, Introduction to Marius Bewley's 'The Complex Fate' (London, 1952), xi.

19 See Roger Asselineau, ed., 'The Literary Reputation of Hemingway in Europe' (New York, 1965), 62, 83, 112, 117.

20 Quoted in Herbert Lottmann, 'Albert Camus' (London, 1979), 244; and Jean-Paul Sartre, Camus' 'The Outsider' (1943), 'Literary and Philosophical Essays,' trans. Annette Michelson (New York, 1955), 35, 38.

21 See Deming Brown, Hemingway in Russia, 'American Quarterly,' 5 (1953), 143; Yevgeny Yevtushenko, Encounter, 'Selected Poems' (New York, 1962), 79-80; and Ivan Kashkeen, Alive in the Midst of Death: Ernest Hemingway, 'Soviet Literature,' 7 (1956), 160-72, reprinted in Carlos Baker, ed., 'Hemingway and His Critics' (New York, 1961), 165, 177.

22. 'A separate peace,' a poignant phrase from 'In Our Time' and 'A Farewell to Arms,' became the title of a novel by John Knowles in 1959. Anthony Powell, in 'Messengers of Day,' has also acknowledged Hemingway's influence on his early novels.

23 Ralph Ellison, The World and the Jug, 'Shadow and Act' (New York, 1964), 140-1.

24 Stein's review is reprinted in Hugh Ford, ed., 'The Left Bank Revisited' (University Park, Pa., 1972), 257.
25 Carlos Baker, 'Ernest Hemingway: A Life Story' (New York, 1969), 171.
26 John Kuehl and Jackson Bryer, eds, 'Dear Scott, Dear Max' (London, 1971), 95.
27 [H.L. Mencken], Quackery, 'American Mercury,' 5 (August 1925), xxxviii; and Carlos Baker, 'Hemingway: The Writer as Artist' (Princeton, 1952), 41n. See 'The Sun Also Rises,' 42: 'I wondered where Cohn got that incapacity to enjoy Paris. Possibly from Mencken. Mencken hates Paris, I believe. So many young men get their likes and dislikes from Mencken.'
28 Baker, 'Ernest Hemingway,' 204, 212.
29 Plimpton, in 'Paris Review,' 76, suggests an interesting interpretation of the novel, based on an analogy with the bullfight, that is no less convincing because Hemingway denied it: 'Just as the bull is attracted and pacified by the presence of a steer, Robert Cohn defers to Jake who is emasculated precisely as is a steer. Mike is the picador, baiting Cohn repeatedly.... [I] wondered if it was your conscious intention to inform the novel with the tragic structure of a bullfight ritual.'
30 Quoted in Baker, 'Ernest Hemingway,' 224.
31 Quoted in Matthew Bruccoli, 'Scott and Ernest' (New York, 1978), 50.
32 See Ernest Hemingway, 'Death in the Afternoon' (Harmondsworth, Middlesex, 1966), 8: 'I only know that what is moral is what makes you feel good after and what is immoral is what you feel bad after.'
33 James Farrell, Ernest Hemingway, Apostle of a 'Lost Generation,' 'New York Times Book Review,' 1 August 1943, 6, 14.
34 Virginia Woolf, 'The Question of Things Happening: Letters, 1912-1922,' ed. Nigel Nicolson and Joanne Trautmann (London, 1976), 551.
35 Quoted in Baker, 'Ernest Hemingway,' 231-2.
36 Robert Herrick, What is Dirt?, 'Bookman,' 70 (November 1929), 261-2.
37 Malcolm Cowley, 'New York Herald Tribune Books,' 6 October 1929, 1.
38 T.S. Eliot, Commentary, 'Criterion,' 12 (April 1933), 471.
39 Donald Davidson, 'The Spyglass' (Nashville, Tenn., 1963), 88n.
40 André Gide, 'Journals,' trans. Justin O'Brien (London, 1951), 4:191, 198.

41 Ford Madox Ford, Some American Expatriates, 'Vanity Fair,' 28 (1 April 1927), 64.
42 Quoted in Cedric Watts and Lawrence Davies, 'Cunninghame Graham: A Critical Biography' (Cambridge, England, 1979), 264. See Joshua 10: 12-13.
43 Aldous Huxley, Foreheads Villainous Low, 'Music at Night' (London, 1931), 201.
44 'Death in the Afternoon,' 181.
45 Ibid., 6.
46 A curious satirical comment on this point was made by E.E. Cummings, No Thanks, 'Poems, 1923-1954' (New York, 1954), 294:

what does little Ernest croon
in his death at afternoon
(kow dow r 2 bul retoinis
wus de woids uf lil Oinis

[cow thou art to bull returning were the words of little Ernie].
47 Kuehl and Bryer, 'Dear Scott, Dear Max,' 239-40. Eastman gave his version of the story to the newspapers, and the next day the tactful Perkins was besieged by reporters. See: Hemingway slaps Eastman in Face, Eastman Claims Title and Literary Slug Fests, 'New York Times,' 14, 15 and 16 August 1937, 15, 31, 21.
48 Quoted in Arthur Power, 'Conversations with James Joyce' (Dublin, 1974), 107.
49 Horace Gregory, 'New York Herald Tribune Books,' 29 October 1933, 5.
50 Wyndham Lewis, Ezra: The Portrait of a Personality, 'Quarterly Review of Literature,' 5 (December 1949), 140.
51 Letters from Archibald MacLeish to Jeffrey Meyers (October 1977) and to W.K. Rose (25 April 1960), Vassar College Library.
52 Quoted in Wyndham Lewis, 'Rude Assignment' (London, 1950), 203-4.
53 Ernest Hemingway, 'A Moveable Feast' (New York, 1967), 109. For a complete discussion of Hemingway and Lewis, see Jeffrey Meyers, 'The Enemy: A Biography of Wyndham Lewis' (London, Routledge & Kegan Paul, 1980).
54 Carl Van Doren, 'New York Herald Tribune Books,' 27 October 1935, 3.
55 'Green Hills of Africa,' 8.
56 Sinclair Lewis, 'Newsweek,' 18 October 1937, 34.
57 Ernest Hemingway, 'Across the River and into the Trees' (Harmondsworth, Middlesex, 1966), 69.
58 Baker, 'Ernest Hemingway,' 340.

59 Edmund Wilson, 'The Wound and the Bow' (London, 1961), 217.
60 Alvah Bessie, 'New Masses,' 37 (5 November 1940), 29.
61 Christopher Isherwood, Hemingway, Death and the Devil, 'Decision,' 1 (1941), 58-9.
62 Letter from Christopher Isherwood to Jeffrey Meyers, 12 July 1979.
63 E.M. Forster, 'Listener,' 26 (10 July 1941), 63.
64 Geoffrey Grigson, ed., Hemingway, 'Concise Encyclopedia of Modern World Literature' (London, 1963), 205.
65 For further discussion of this point, see Edward Fenimore, English and Spanish in 'For Whom the Bell Tolls,' 'English Literary History,' 10 (1943), 73-86, and Robert Graves and Alan Hodge, 'The Reader Over Your Shoulder' (New York, 1944), 304-6.
66 Maxwell Geismar, 'Saturday Review of Literature,' 33 (9 September 1950), 18.
67 Philip Rahv, 'Commentary,' 10 (October 1950), 400-1. Delmore Schwartz, in The Fiction of Ernest Hemingway (1955), 'Selected Essays,' ed. Donald Dike and David Zucker (Chicago, 1970), 267, agrees with Rahv and dismisses the novel as 'a total indulgence in romantic fantasy ... a complete failure of the novelist to be critical of the hero's attitudes and feelings.'
68 Gertrude Stein, 'The Autobiography of Alice B. Toklas' (London, 1933), 235.
69 Quoted in Lillian Ross, 'Portrait of Hemingway' (New York, 1961), 35.
70 John O'Hara, 'New York Times Book Review,' 10 September 1950, 1, 30-1.
71 Cyril Connolly, 'Sunday Times' (London), 3 September 1950, 3.
72 Quoted in Baker, 'Ernest Hemingway,' 596.
73 Cyril Connolly, 'Sunday Times' (London), 7 September 1952, 5.
74 Archibald MacLeish, Hemingway, 'Atlantic,' 208 (November 1961), 46.
75 'Across the River and into the Trees,' 56.
76 For an amusing parody of nostalgic memoirs, see Woody Allen, A Twenties Memory, 'Getting Even' (London, 1973), 89-93.
77 John Wain, 'Observer,' 11 October 1970, 33.

'Three Stories and Ten Poems' (1923) and 'in our time' (1924)

1. EDMUND WILSON, 'DIAL'

77 (October 1924), 340-1

Edmund Wilson (1895-1972) was an influential American critic and intellectual historian, and the author of 'Axel's Castle' (1931), 'To the Finland Station' (1940) and 'The Wound and the Bow' (1941). The 'Dial,' edited by Scofield Thayer, was a distinguished literary monthly that championed modern artistic movements.

Mr Hemingway's poems are not particularly important, but his prose is of the first distinction. He must be counted as the only American writer but one - Mr Sherwood Anderson - who has felt the genius of Gertrude Stein's 'Three Lives' and has been evidently influenced by it. Indeed, Miss Stein, Mr Anderson, and Mr Hemingway may now be said to form a school by themselves. The characteristic of this school is a naïveté of language often passing into the colloquialism of the character dealt with which serves actually to convey profound emotions and complex states of mind. It is a distinctively American development in prose - as opposed to more or less successful American achievements in the traditional style of English prose - which has artistically justified itself at its best as a limpid shaft into deep waters.

Not, however, that Mr Hemingway is imitative. On the contrary, he is rather strikingly original, and in the dry compressed little vignettes of 'In Our Time' has almost invented a form of his own:

> They shot the six cabinet ministers at half-past six in the morning against the wall of a hospital. There were pools of water in the courtyard. There were dead leaves on the paving of the courtyard. It rained hard. All the shutters of the hospital were nailed shut. One of the ministers was sick with typhoid. Two soldiers carried him downstairs and out into the rain. They tried to hold him up against the wall but he sat down in a puddle of water. The other five stood very quietly against the wall. Finally the officer told the soldiers it was no good trying to make him stand up. When they fired the first volley he was sitting down in the water with his head on his knees.

Mr Hemingway is remarkably successful in suggesting moral values by a series of simple statements of this sort. His more important book is called 'In Our Time,' and below its cool objective manner really constitutes a harrowing record of barbarities: you have not only political executions, but criminal hangings, bull-fights, assassinations by the police, and all the cruelties and enormities of the war. Mr Hemingway is wholly unperturbed as he tells about these things: he is not a propagandist even for humanity. His bull-fight sketches have the dry sharpness and elegance of the bull-fight lithographs of Goya. And, like Goya, he is concerned first of all with making a fine picture. He is showing you what life is, too proud an artist to simplify. And I am inclined to think that his little book has more artistic dignity than any other that has been written by an American about the period of the war.

Not perhaps the most vivid book, but the soundest. Mr Hemingway, who can make you feel the poignancy of the Italian soldier deciding in his death agony that he will 'make a separate peace,' has no anti-militaristic *parti pris* which will lead him to suppress from his record the exhilaration of the men who had 'jammed an absolutely perfect barricade across the bridge' and who were 'frightfully put out when we heard the flank had gone, and we had to fall back.' It is only in the paleness, the thinness of some of his effects that Mr Hemingway sometimes fails. I am thinking especially of the story called Up in Michigan, which should have been a masterpiece, but has the curious defect of dealing with rude and primitive people yet leaving them shadowy.

'In Our Time' has a pretty and very amusing cover designed from scrambled newspaper clippings. The only objection I have to its appearance is that the titles are throughout printed without capitals - thus: 'in our time by ernest hemingway - paris.' This device, which used to be rather effective when the modernists first used to use it to call attention to the fact that they had something new to offer, has now grown common and a bore. The American advertisers have taken it over as one of their stock tricks. And it is so unsightly in itself that it is rather a pity to see it become - as in the case of Mr Hemingway's book and Mr Hueffer's 'transatlantic review' - a sort of badge of everything that is freshest and most interesting in modern writing.

2. UNSIGNED NOTICE, 'KANSAS CITY STAR'

20 December 1924, 6

Several years ago Ernest Hemingway was a reporter on the 'Star.' Now, in Paris, as correspondent of the Toronto Star,'(1) he is recognized, not simply as a journalist, but as one of the most promising young writers in the English language. When Ford Madox Ford, the distinguished novelist and poet, went to America for a visit, he selected Hemingway as the ablest available man to edit the 'transatlantic review' during his absence. In view of Ford's rank as an author and editor and of the position of the 'transatlantic' as one of the principal literary publications of Europe, the recognition amounts to a great deal.

One does not need to take the word of others, however, for Hemingway's ability. Although his published work, outside of newspaper articles, is slight in quantity, it has the quality that is associated with distinguished talent, if not absolute genius.

A little, unpretentious appearing book, with the simple descriptive title, 'Three Stories and Ten Poems,' written in English, but published in Paris, contains some of the best writing that I have seen from the pen of contemporary American authors. I say this primarily of the stories. In the poems one feels some of the excellent quality that appears in the prose, but somehow the verse more or less obscures it. The stories, simple, direct, revealing, one of them set in the middle West, the other two in Europe, are the real stuff.

In them are vividness and the firm sure texture of reality. These, however, are not uncommon in the work of a great many good writers. What Mr. Hemingway has added is a certain superior objectivity. He has taken hold of the best quality that modern journalism has, and he has carried it forward to a new point. Journalistic objectivity is content with the sense impressions of things, excluding both the opinions of the writer and the emotions of the actors except so far as the latter may be inferred from action.

Exclusion of opinion is all to the good. In many cases, however, the emotions of the actors are needed to make a story complete or significant. The 'yellow' newspaper recognizes this and pays a reporter to fake a portrayal of the emotions of a man before execution, for example - a portrayal which the murderer is persuaded to sign as his own. The result is always transparent bunk, for the reason that it requires something approaching genius to present the actors' emotions accurately and keep the author and his opinions and emotions out. It is this that Hemingway achieves. It puts into his work a fine, unsentimental understanding.

Add to this achievement Hemingway's real power in description, in picking out the essentials of an object or a person or an action in much the same way that contemporary painters are endeavoring to do; add also the spare inevitableness of his characters, and you have fiction which arouses the definitely esthetic emotions as much as does good music or good painting. We are prone to talk about 'literature and art,' as if literature were not one of the arts. When literature gets good enough, however, any reader sees it as art. And Mr. Hemingway's work is good enough.

Note

1 Hemingway had left the 'Toronto Star' on 1 January 1924.

'In Our Time' (1925)

3. PAUL ROSENFELD, 'NEW REPUBLIC'

45 (25 November 1925), 22-3

Paul Rosenfeld (1890-1946) was an American music and art critic. He was Associate Editor of 'Seven Arts,' 1916-17, and music critic of the 'Dial,' 1920-27.

Hemingway's short stories belong with cubist painting, 'Le Sacre du Printemps', (1) and other recent work bringing a feeling of positive forces through primitive modern idiom. The use of the direct, crude, rudimentary forms of the simple and primitive classes and their situations, of the stuffs, textures and rhythms of the mechanical and industrial worlds, has enabled this new American story teller, as it enabled the group to which he comes a fresh recruit, to achieve peculiarly sharp, decided, grimly affirmative expressions; and with these acute depictions and half-impersonal beats to satisfy a spirit running through the age. Hemingway's spoken prose is characteristically iron with a lyricism, aliveness and energy tremendously held in check. With the trip-hammer thud of Le Sacre his rhythms go. Emphatic, short, declarative sentences follow staunchly one upon the other, never precipitously or congestedly or mechanically, and never relenting. The stubby verbal forms are speeded in instances up to the brute, rapid, joyous jab of blunt period upon period. Hemingway's vocabulary is largely monosyllabic, and mechanical and concrete. Mixed with the common words, raw and pithy terms picked from the vernaculars of boys, jockeys, hunters, policemen, soldiers, and obscurely related to primitive impulse and primitive sex, further increase the rigidity of effect. There is something of Sherwood Anderson, of his fine bare effects and values coined from simplest words, in Hemingway's clear medium. There is Gertrude Stein equally obvious: her massive volumes, slow power, steady reiterations, and her intuition of the life of headless bodies. The American literary generations are learning to build upon each other. This newcomer's prose departs from the kindred literary mediums as a youngling from forebears. Wanting some of the warmth of Anderson and some of the pathos of Gertrude Stein, Hemingway's style none the less in its very experimental stage shows the outline of a new, tough, severe and satisfying beauty related equally to the world of machinery and the austerity of the red man.

It comes on the general errand of the group, the realization of a picture of the elements of life caught in barest, intensest opposition. In the world of Hemingway's stories, characters and principles are boxers crouched and proposing fists. Stocky rudimentary passions wrestle for a throw. The sport of the two youths snowshoeing in high Alps is brusquely, casually interrupted by consciousness of pregnancy and the responsibility seeking out the man. A lad sees his sensitive father beset by the active brutality of men and the passive brutality of women. Inside the hotel room in the rain male and female face each other for a swift passage of their eternal warfare. The sheer unfeeling barbarity of life, and the elementary humor and tenderness lying close upon it, is a favorite theme. The amazing single pages previously assembled in a booklet by the Three Mountains Press in Paris, sandwiched between the longer stories in the Liveright volume and connecting these with the doings of an epoch, bring dangerously close in instantaneous pictures of the War, of the bull-ring and the police-world, the excitement of combat, the cold ferocity of the mob, the insensibility of soldiering, the relief of nerves in alcoholic stupor, the naked, the mean, the comic brute in the human frame. Against these principles, set invariably in crude, simple, passionate opposition, the author plays the more constructive elements. We feel the absorption and fine helpfulness of the handicapped doctor performing a Caesarean operation with a jack-knife and releasing a child; the tender, subtle feeling for woman's life found among certain of the ordinary people of Europe; the enjoyment of the body in the physical play of life; the seriousness in the young man making him accept responsibility and automatically limit his narcissistic impulse to freedom. And both these forces and the uglier ones are given sharp physiognomies by the dramatic counterpoint; and what certain of them owe Sherwood Anderson is made good by the personal intensification of the passionate opposition between them.

There is little analysis in this narrative art. We are given chiefly, at times with marvelous freshness and crispness, what the eye sees and the ear hears. The conflicting principles are boldly established without psychologizings. Yet Hemingway's acceptation of the aesthetic responsibility of getting his material into action in instances remains near gesturing. His units are not brought into actual opposition in all his pieces. Or, formally introduced, they remain at inadequate degrees of tension, while a youthfully insolent sense of the stereotype in life blinds the author. Soldier's Home is one of Hemingway's forms half left in the limbo of the stencil. The happy relief to this and other incompleted pieces is furnished by stories like Cat in the Rain, Indian Camp, and My Old Man. In these, plastic elements accurately felt are opposed point against point, and a whole brought into view. It is a whole this newcomer has to show. It is one from which the many beauties of his book are fetched. He shares his epoch's feeling of a harsh impersonal force in the universe, permanent, not to be changed, taking both destruction and construction up into itself and set in motion by their dialectic. With the blood and pain, he makes us know the toughness of the earth, able to meet desire, nourish life, and waken in man the power to meet the brutalities of existence. This bald feeling is the condition of an adjustment to life begun in men before the War, but demanded even more intensely of them by its ghastlier train, and natural at all times to the products of primitive America. Through it men are reconciled to perpetual struggle, and while holding themselves tight work in relation to something in the universe. This adjustment is not the sole possible one. It is not necessarily the one of next year or of the year to follow, for any. But it had and still has its reality; and the rhythms, and tempi which communicate it share in its permanence.

Note

1 'The Rite of Spring,' a Diaghilev ballet with music by Igor Stravinsky, caused a riot at its Paris première in May 1913.

4. ALLEN TATE, 'NATION'

122 (10 February 1926), 161-2

Allen Tate (1899-1979) was an American poet, novelist and critic, the author of 'Reactionary Essays' (1936), 'The Fathers' (1938) and 'The Winter Sea' (1945).

Ernest Hemingway has developed his chief distinction in prose through a careful rejection of 'ideas'; he does not conceive his subject matter; he presents it. You will not be able to separate, in his facile accumulation of *petites sensations*, the observer from the observation, the reporter from the item reported; he never comments in excess of the immediate value of the object as a thing seen, of the event as a focus of observed motions. If he lacks the concept of character, he has an infallible deftness at projecting personality by isolating into typical significance some trivial accident of conduct. He lacks the ostentation of a writer inadequately equipped yet ambitious with a 'theory of reality.' Most typical of Mr. Hemingway's precise economical method is the story Big Two-Hearted River, where the time is one evening to the next afternoon and the single character a trout fisherman who makes his camp-fire, sleeps all night, gets up and catches a few trout, then starts home; that is all. But the passionate accuracy of particular observation, the intense monosyllabic diction, the fidelity to the internal demands of the subject - these qualities fuse in the most completely realized naturalistic fiction of the age. This sentence has much of the method of Mr. Hemingway's prose: 'When we saw the creature killed, I had a great mind to have the skin of her, and made signs to the prince that he should send some of his men to take the skin off' - and it would convey more of its quality had it not been written in 1720 by Daniel Defoe.

5. F. SCOTT FITZGERALD, 'BOOKMAN'

63 (May 1926), 264-5

F. Scott Fitzgerald (1896-1940) was an American novelist, author of 'The Great Gatsby' (1925), 'Tender is the Night' (1934) and 'The Last Tycoon' (1941).

'In Our Time' consists of fourteen stories, short and long, with fifteen vivid miniatures interpolated between them. When I try to think of any contemporary American short stories as good as Big Two-Hearted River, the last one in the book, only Gertrude Stein's Melanctha, Anderson's The Egg, and Lardner's Golden Honeymoon come to mind. It is the account of a boy on a fishing trip - he hikes, pitches his tent, cooks dinner, sleeps, and next morning casts for trout. Nothing more - but I read it with the most breathless unwilling interest I have experienced since Conrad first bent my reluctant eyes upon the sea.

The hero, Nick, runs through nearly all the stories, until the book takes on almost an autobiographical tint - in fact My Old Man, one of the two in which this element seems entirely absent, is the least successful of all. Some of the stories show influences but they are invariably absorbed and transmuted, while in My Old Man there is an echo of Anderson's way of thinking in those sentimental 'horse stories', which inaugurated his respectability and also his decline four years ago.

But with The Doctor and the Doctor's Wife, The End of Something, The Three Day Blow, Mr and Mrs Elliot, and Soldier's Home you are immediately aware of something temperamentally new. In the first of these a man is backed down by a half-breed Indian after committing himself to a fight. The quality of humiliation in the story is so intense that it immediately calls up every such incident in the reader's past. Without the aid of a comment or a pointing finger one knows exactly the sharp emotions of young Nick who watches the scene.

The next two stories describe an experience at the last edge of adolescence. You are constantly aware of the continual snapping of ties that is going on around Nick. In the half stewed, immature conversation before the fire you watch the awakening of that vast unrest that descends upon the emotional type at about eighteen. Again there is not a single recourse to exposition. As in Big Two-Hearted River, a picture - sharp, nostalgic, tense - develops before your eyes. When the picture is complete a light seems to snap out, the story is over. There is no tail, no sudden change of pace at the end to throw into relief what has gone before.

Nick leaves home penniless; you have a glimpse of him lying wounded in the street of a battered Italian town, and later of a love affair with a nurse on a hospital roof in Milan. Then in one of the best of the stories he is home again. The last glimpse of him is when his mother asks him, with all the bitter world in his heart, to kneel down beside her in the dining room in Puritan prayer.

Anyone who first looks through the short interpolated sketches will hardly fail to read the stories themselves. The Garden at Mons and The Barricade are profound essays upon the English officer, written on a postage stamp. The King of Greece's Tea Party, The Shooting of the Cabinet Ministers, and The Cigar-store Robbery particularly fascinated me, as they did when Edmund Wilson first showed them to me in an earlier pamphlet, over two years ago.

Disregard the rather ill-considered blurbs upon the cover. It is sufficient that here is no raw food served up by the railroad restaurants of California and Wisconsin. In the best of these dishes there is not a bit to spare. And many of us who have grown weary of admonitions to 'watch this man or that' have felt a sort of renewal of excitement at these stories wherein Ernest Hemingway turns a corner into the street.

6. D.H. LAWRENCE, 'CALENDAR OF MODERN LETTERS'

4 (April 1927), 72-3

D.H. Lawrence (1885-1930), English novelist, was author of 'Sons and Lovers' (1913), 'The Rainbow' (1915) and 'Women in Love' (1920). The 'Calendar of Modern Letters,' edited by the poet Edgell Rickword, published critical and creative work by some of the best modern writers.

'In Our Time' is the last of the four American books, and Mr. Hemingway has accepted the goal. He keeps on making flights, but he has no illusion about landing anywhere. He knows it will be nowhere every time.

'In Our Time' calls itself a book of stories, but it isn't that. It is a series of successive sketches from a man's life, and makes a fragmentary novel. The first scenes, by one of the big lakes in America - probably Superior(1) - are the best; when Nick is a boy. Then come fragments of war - on the Italian front. Then a soldier back home, very late, in the little town way west in Oklahoma. Then a young American and wife in post-war Europe; a long sketch about an American jockey in Milan and Paris; then Nick is back again in the Lake Superior region, getting off the train at a burnt-out town, and tramping across the empty country to camp by a trout-stream. Trout is the one passion life has left him - and this won't last long.

It is a short book: and it does not pretend to be about one man. But it is. It is as much as we need know of the man's life. The sketches are short, sharp, vivid, and most of them excellent. (The 'mottoes' in front seem a little affected.) And these few sketches are enough to create the man and all his history: we need know no more.

Nick is a type one meets in the more wild and woolly regions of the United States. He is the remains of the lone trapper and cowboy. Nowadays he is educated, and through with everything. It is a state of *conscious*, accepted indifference to everything except freedom from work and the moment's interest. Mr. Hemingway does it extremely well. Nothing matters. Everything happens. One wants to keep oneself loose. Avoid one thing only: getting connected up. Don't get connected up. If you get held by anything, break it. Don't be held. Break it, and get away. Don't get away with the idea of getting somewhere else. Just get away, for the sake of getting away. Beat it! 'Well, boy, I guess I'll beat it.' Ah, the pleasure in saying that!

Mr. Hemingway's sketches, for this reason, are excellent: so short, like striking a match, lighting a brief sensational cigarette, and it's over. His young love-affair ends as one throws a cigarette-end away. 'It isn't fun any more.' - 'Everything's gone to hell inside me.'

It is really honest. And it explains a great deal of sentimentality. When a thing has gone to hell inside you, your sentimentalism tries to pretend it hasn't. But Mr. Hemingway is through with the sentimentalism. 'It isn't fun any more. I guess I'll beat it.'

And he beats it, to somewhere else. In the end he'll be a sort of tramp, endlessly moving on for the sake of moving away from where he is. This is a negative goal, and Mr. Hemingway is really good, because he's perfectly straight about it. He is like Krebs, in that devastating Oklahoma sketch: he doesn't love anybody, and it nauseates him to have to pretend he does. He doesn't even *want* to love anybody; he doesn't want to go anywhere, he doesn't want to do anything. He wants just to lounge around and maintain a healthy state of nothingness inside himself, and an attitude of negation to everything outside himself. And why shouldn't he, since that is exactly and sincerely what he feels? If he really *doesn't* care, then why should he care? Anyhow, he doesn't.

Note

1 It is actually Lake Michigan.

'The Torrents of Spring' (1926)

7. HARRY HANSEN, 'NEW YORK WORLD'

30 May 1926, 4M

Harry Hansen (1884-1977) was an American critic, editor and anthologist.

This seems to be the open season for authors. First comes Llewelyn Powys, Englishman, and in a brilliant travel record, 'The Verdict of Bridlegoose,' brings down a whole flock of New York celebrities. Next at the bench, with a steady eye on half a dozen targets, comes Ernest Hemingway, the most promising American author in Paris. Hemingway gained critical praise a year ago when he published 'In Our Time,' a series of short stories, based for the most part on pathological variation in human beings, told with much economy of language. Hemingway has now elaborated on his own idea of authors and their methods in 'The Torrents of Spring,' which he also calls a 'romantic novel in honor of the passing of a great race.' The book is, for the most part, a parody of Sherwood Anderson's style and subject matter; to some extent also that of D.H. Lawrence. It is published not by Mr. Liveright, who issued Hemingway's first book and also publishes Sherwood Anderson, but by Mr. Scribner. Ergo, Mr. Scribner is able to announce that he will publish Hemingway's first novel in the fall.

Something seems to remind me that when Hemingway published 'In Our Time' it was Sherwood Anderson who turned handsprings and welcomed this newcomer to the ranks of

America's great men. Anderson trumpeted loudly, and now Hemingway pays him back by making him the principal butt of his parody. We may say, therefore, that Hemingway does not approve of logrolling. At least he is not going to 'lay off' Anderson merely because the latter was a hospitable host. He evidently regards Anderson as long-winded and boring, and something of his attitude can be gathered from the frequent quotations from Fielding sprinkled through the pages of the new book, of which the following comes opposite the first chapter: 'The only source of the true ridiculous (as it appears to me) is affectation.'

Well and good. There is nothing like parody to add to the gayety of nations. Christopher Ward(1) has hit the bull's-eye several times, but for real writing give me Beerbohm.(2) He has never been surpassed. He catches not merely the outward mannerism of the man but his essential mode of thinking. Hemingway had in Sherwood Anderson a remarkable subject. Taken superficially, Anderson should be easy to parody. He is always repeating himself, both in his words and in his attitudes. He shows no change, no many-sidedness. He is always the dreamy, searching groper, watching the commonplace facts of life with a sort of boyish amazement on his face. His prose is slow and simple. His stories haunt the reader, as they haunt him. He professes over and over again a love for words, without being able to use them as the dictionary indicates. But he also gives you the impression that he sees a bit beyond this external covering which buries men. He tries to dig down underneath the veneer of conventions. He goes about it slowly. His thoughts mature as slowly on paper as they mature slowly in the mind of the average plodding man.

So when Hemingway starts his story in a pump factory in Michigan and has Yogi Johnson talking to Scripps O'Neil about the weather - Scripps, who has two wives and a daughter he calls Lousy because her name is Lucy - you begin to get a glimmering of what is meant by superficial parody. Short sentences. Repetitious thoughts. References to 'that poet fellow' and 'that critic fellow, Mencken.' Wonderment, by Scripps, as to what goes on inside a passing train; about what telegraphers actually do: 'What sort of men went in for telegraphy? Were they like composers? Were they like the advertising men who write the ads, in our national weeklies?' And so on. At the end of a chapter now and then the sound of a far-off Indian warwhoop. Or perhaps the laughter of the Negro.

Here are a few samples of Hemingway's method, and if they interest you, you will know where to find more of them:

She had a man now. A man of her own. For her own. Could she keep him? Could she hold him for her own. She wondered.

Every night at the restaurant now, Scripps and Mandy talked together. The girl was trying to take him away. Him, her Scripps. Trying to take him away. Take him away. Could she, Diana, hold him?

Diana learned editorials by John Farrar by heart.(3) Scripps brightened. A little of the old light shining in Scripps's eye now. Then it died. Some little mistake in the wording, some slip in her understanding of a phrase, some divergence in her attitude, made it all ring false. She would go on. She was not beaten. She looked away from the window and slit open the covering of the magazine that lay on her table. It was Harper's Magazine. Harper's Magazine in a new format. Harper's Magazine completely changed and revised. Perhaps that would do the trick. She wondered.

A few other mannerisms. It is patent that D.H. Lawrence is in the mind of the author when he pictures Scripps marrying the waitress.(4) 'He felt vaguely uneasy. Something was stirring within him.' Notes by the author to the reader recounting his adventures with literary fellows in Paris: John Dos Passos and F. Scott Fitzgerald. Comment on 'The Making and Marring of Americans,'(5) perhaps a take-off on Lawrence's studies in American classical literature. I say perhaps. I don't know for sure. Hemingway has caught, I think, a glint of Anderson's professional naivete. Beyond that, however, parody is a gift of the gods. Few are blessed with it. It missed Hemingway. He is better as a writer of short stories.

Ernest Hemingway is a native of the Chicago area and had an interesting youth with his father, a physician. He frequently accompanied his father on medical errands, and some of the stories in 'In Our Time' are said to be transcripts of adventures up North. He lives in France, and most recently has been interested in the writings of younger Americans abroad in 'This Quarter,' a periodical edited by Ernest Walsh and Ethel Moorhead. A recent number contained a story of a bullfight by Hemingway(6) as well as contributions by Ezra Pound, Carl Sandburg, William Carlos Williams and many others.

Notes

1 Author of 'The Triumph of the Nut and Other Parodies' (1923).

2 Max Beerbohm (1868-1943) brilliantly parodied James, Conrad and other writers in 'A Christmas Garland' (1895).
3 Middle-brow editor of the 'Bookman,' 1921-27.
4 Hemingway was not satirizing D.H. Lawrence.
5 The allusion is to Stein's little-known 'The Making of Americans' (1925).
6 The Undefeated.

8. ALLEN TATE, 'NATION'

123 (28 July 1926), 89-90

Ernest Hemingway says he wrote this novel in ten days, and there is no reason for believing that Mr. Hemingway, besides being the best contemporary writer of eighteenth-century prose, is also a liar. The novel is short. But it would have done him or anybody else much credit had its author labored with its perfect style (perfect within honorable limitations) for ten months. 'The Torrents of Spring' differs in important features from Mr. Hemingway's first American volume, published last autumn; its differences from 'In Our Time' spring from a basically different intention. 'In Our Time' is naturalistic fiction done for purely creative ends. 'The Torrents of Spring' grew out of a motive a little this side of that; its motive is satire and, if one may produce an undemonstrable but wholly convincing bit of internal evidence, its object is Sherwood Anderson's 'Dark Laughter.'

'Pamela' is still worth reading; 'Joseph Andrews' is better worth reading. 'Dark Laughter' is a good novel, but, like 'Pamela,' it contains emotion in excess of the facts, and 'The Torrents of Spring' is better worth reading. Lacking, as Fielding did in 'Joseph Andrews,' a motive originally creative, Mr. Hemingway has nevertheless written a novel which is on its own account, irrespective of momentary aim, a small masterpiece of American fiction.

Mr. Hemingway's consistently limited performance is not generally due to missed intention. He knows what he wishes to do; he usually does it. His intention is fundamentally opposed to any other naturalism of the age. He gets his effects not by complete documentation but by the avoidance of explanatory statement; he keeps his explicit knowledge of the characters exactly equal to the reader's knowledge. Neither do the characters ever rationalize or generalize their successive predicaments. His naturalism is a modified naturalism, and its principles have become more and more unfamiliar since the influence of Zola caught up with the more difficult method of 'Bouvard et Pécuchet'(1) and obscured it; while Zola has actually instructed the American novel since Frank Norris, Flaubert has been simply admired. Mr. Hemingway, apparently careless about the choice of material, exercises the greatest zeal in isolating its significant aspects; his selective naturalism achieves its effects through indirect irony, the the irony of suppressed comment. Few of his characters are fools; all of them are Bouvards and Pécuchets in that their conduct is so arranged as to rouse the reader's sense of value to the appropriate judgment of it, while they are themselves immersed in a 'pure present' and lack the power of generalizing it at all. 'In Our Time' proved Hemingway to be a master of this irony. It is an irony pre-eminently fitted for sustained satire of the sort conspicuous in Defoe and Swift, and Hemingway's success with it in 'The Torrents of Spring' is a triumph, but not a surprise.

The material of the story is slight and insignificant in outline; a summary would be impertinent here. But Scripps O'Neil, Mrs. Scripps, Yogi Johnson, the big Indian and the little Indian, 'Brown's Beanery the Best by Test,' the drinking club of the educated Indians whence Yogi hears the 'dark Negro laughter' of the ebony bartender after he is kicked out for being not an Indian but a Swede - these characters and places focus the best genial satire of the 'spirituality' of roughnecks, the most deftly tempered ribaldry, and the most economically realized humor of disproportion that this reviewer has read in American prose.

Note

1 Gustave Flaubert's last book, 'Bouvard and Pécuchet' (1881), is a satire on dullness, pedantry and human stupidity.

9. DAVID GARNETT, INTRODUCTION TO 'THE TORRENTS OF SPRING'

1933

From 'The Torrents of Spring' (London, Cape, 1933), 9-20.

David Garnett (1892-1981) was an English novelist, the author of 'Lady into Fox' (1923) and an autobiography 'The Golden Echo' (1953).

> Who, or why, or which, or what, is the Akond of
> SWAT?
> Is he tall or short, or dark or fair?
> Does he sit on a stool, or a sofa or chair, or
> SQUAT,
> The Akond of Swat?(1)

We can all enjoy these lines without preparing our minds by reading an introduction, and what is true of Lear's Nonsense Verses is equally true of Hemingway's 'The Torrents of Spring'. For this reason it would be better if this Introduction were printed at the end of the book. Lest this seem to be too modest I may add that it would be best of all if it were to be inserted in the middle where there would be most chance of it being read. In the middle it would indeed be most useful, welcome, and hygienic, resting the reader exhausted by too much laughter, when he is just in the right limp and receptive condition to be educated.

Just as there are some people who like to know that it was Lord Tennyson's famous lines:

> But who hath seen her wave her hand?
> Or at the casement seen her stand?
> Or is she known in all the land,
> The Lady of Shallott?

which inspired Lear to scribble his nonsense, and that Abdul Ghafur, an Akond of Swat (one of the semi-divine potentates who acknowledge the paramountcy of the King-Emperor) got himself into the English newspapers during the Umbeyla campaign of 1863,(2) so there may well be readers of this book who will be interested to hear about its sources.

For though one cannot help laughing, one may just as

well know what started the joke and understand all the allusions to the underlying ideas implicit in it. But don't think for a moment that I'm going to tell you that you must read 'Dark Laughter' and wade all through the Chicago school of American writers. You can enjoy 'The Torrents of Spring' without.

Hemingway's first book, a collection of fine stories called 'In Our Time', was published in 1925. He had an admiration for Sherwood Anderson when he wrote these stories and was a bit under his influence, and Anderson, who was already at the height of his fame, contributed to the blurb on the cover of Hemingway's book. Anderson's next book 'Dark Laughter' was however too much for Hemingway to swallow, and these sentences culled from the first chapter, which describes two workmen looking out of the window into the factory yard may indicate why.

'Time very soon to push the windows up. Spring would be be coming soon now.... Sponge chewed tobacco and had a wife who got drunk with him sometimes on pay-days.... When he spoke of the other child, playfully called Bugs Martin, Sponge got a little upset. She had been a rip-terror right from the start. No doing anything with her. You couldn't keep her away from the boys. Sponge tried and his wife tried, but what good did it do?

'Sponge's old woman was all right. When she and Sponge were out that way after catfish, and they had both taken five or six drinks of "moon" she was like a kid.... When the old woman was a little lit up and acted like a kid it made Sponge feel that way too.'

In spite of certain temptations to do that sort of thing himself, the affectation of this was altogether too much for Hemingway who sat down and wrote 'The Torrents of Spring' (this high-spirited, good-tempered and good-natured parody) in a few days. It was published as his second book in 1925.(3)

The closest part of the parody is naturally at the opening, and the reader will not be kept long before he recognizes Sponge Martin, his sporty old wife, and their playful daughter Bugs. It is not the story however which Hemingway is parodying, but the ideas behind it, and the falsity of the author's approach to the story.

'Dark Laughter' is the story of a newspaper reporter who leaves his high-brow wife, gets work painting wheels in a wheel-factory, and draws upon himself the attentions of his boss's wife whom he inspires with 'the same subtle desires' as she once felt for a man in Paris. She engages him as the gardener.

The motif of 'Spring was coming on fast in Southern Indiana' runs through 'Dark Laughter' and symbolizes, and marches side by side with, the slow coming together of Bruce the workman and his boss's wife, whose subtle desires are at length assuaged. Unfortunately a pace which appears rapid to the gardener watching the asparagus in its bed, seems agonizingly slow when we are watching the gardener himself, and the reader wearies of these vegetable loves 'which grow vaster than empires and more slow'.(4)

Meanwhile below stairs, the negro women servants in the house watched and waited. Often they looked at each other and giggled. 'The air on the hilltop was filled with laughter, dark laughter.' The slowness of the lady and the gardener seems to them highly ridiculous as it would certainly also have done to more sophisticated spectators.

But the negroes, who in Hemingway's book are replaced by Indians, are more than negroes, and their laughter is not merely hysterical irritation with their mistress. They are the children of Nature, their laughter is the voice of Nature. It is characteristic of Anderson to think that negroes must be nearer to Nature than white men are, and that black is a more natural colour for the skin than white.

In one of his most brilliant critical essays, Wyndham Lewis has analysed in great detail the ideas underlying Anderson's 'Dark Laughter' and has compared them with D.H. Lawrence's ideas in 'Mornings in Mexico'. Nothing could be better than Wyndham Lewis's exposure of the stupidity of these ideas, and after roaring over 'The Torrents of Spring', the reader would do well to look up 'Paleface'.(5) The only fault to be found with Wyndham Lewis is that he is such an alarmist. According to him a deadly danger is lurking round the corner. But I cannot myself see anything in Anderson's ideas, or in Mencken's, which is very original. The view of the superiority of the simple negro, or the Red Indian, or of the child of nature, dates back beyond Wordsworth, Rousseau and Bernardin de St. Pierre.(6) The same idea is to be found in Daphnis and Cloe.(7) It is really no more than the belief that one can find a last surviving corner of the golden age lurking on some island or in some primitive community. And after all, sometimes one can.

'Silly American painters! They chase a Gauguin shadow to the South Seas,' exclaims Anderson who finds his golden age among the American negroes.

This seems to me as healthy a form of relaxation and no more dangerous than 'The Blue Lagoon',(8) or a passion for such primitive sports as hunting and fishing.

Just as it is the happy fortune of the Present to be able to invest the Past with whatever glamour it sees fit, so it is the privilege of civilized town-dwellers to sentimentalize primitive peoples. Both instincts appear to be healthy and normal.

Though Anderson appears to have adopted them occasionally, D.H. Lawrence's ideas are rather different and are more personal. The Mexican Indian appealed to him for reasons which are clearly different from those which led Wordsworth to idealize the simple English peasant. It was not the ordinary golden age which Lawrence wanted; what he loved in the Indian and was always advocating and praising was the absence of ideas. Had he but been able to practise what he preached how much better his books would have been!

I mention Lawrence only because several American critics have seen a satire on Lawrence as well as on Anderson in this book.(9) It may be so, but unassisted I have not been able to see it.

The tales from Ford, such as the Beautiful Thing which happened in Paris and the story of the French general, will be a joy to all. Ford is as fertile with stories as Boccaccio (10) and these are as good and as characteristic as any which I can remember.

The chief interest to me of 'The Torrents of Spring' lies not in its being a parody of Anderson, and least of all a counterblast to his stupidly expressed ideas, but in its being a parody of Hemingway himself, and in the light which it throws on his other work.

The short abrupt sentence, weighted with inarticulate masculinity such as is employed in the advertisements of men's boots and manly brands of tobacco, is a style which has been used by Hemingway. He is a great artist and he has got some of his best effects by this method. 'The Torrents of Spring' shows that he is a conscious artist who knows just what he is doing. One finds him continually laughing at himself.

Here are some jumbled passages taken from 'Dark Laughter', from 'In Our Time', Hemingway's first book of stories, and from 'The Torrents of Spring':

'There was something on his mind. It was spring, there was no doubt of that now, and he did not want a woman.... He passed a group of girls on their way home from High School. He looked carefully at all of them. He did not want a single one. Decidedly something was wrong. Was he going to pieces? Was this the end? A tree was a tree. One did not question it. Could a woman be just a woman for a time? She had to be that to be a woman at all.'

'He liked the girls that were walking along the other

side of the street. He would like to have one of them. But it was not worth it. They were such a nice pattern. He liked the pattern. It was exciting. But he would not go through all the talking. He did not want one badly enough. He liked to look at them all though. It was not worth it. Not now when things were getting good again.'

'Bruce was going about the garden plucking out of the ground the weaker plants. Already he had learned that much of gardening. It did not take one long to learn.'

'Everywhere men trying to explain the actions of their wives, women trying to explain the actions of their husbands. People didn't have to break up homes to get into a position where explanations had to be made. If life were not so complex it would be more simple.'

In conclusion I should say that although this book is a parody and most delightfully funny, it is of course a real work of art itself. Some of the scenes - particularly the one in which the magnificent squaw breaks into the beanery, completely sweep one off one's feet with enthusiasm as well as leave one rolling on the floor with laughter.

Notes

1 Edward Lear, 'Laughable Lyrics' (1877).
2 Vincent Smith, 'The Oxford History of India,' 2nd ed, (Oxford, 1923), 737: 'The only noticeable event of [Lord Elgin's] brief term of office was the "Umbeyla campaign" on the north-western frontier, rendered necessary by an outburst of Mohammedan fanaticism to the west of the Indus.'
3 It was actually published in 1926.
4 Andrew Marvell, To His Coy Mistress (1681).
5 At the time of 'Porgie,' 'All God's Chillun,' 'The Emperor Jones,' 'Nigger Heaven' and the cult of jazz, 'Paleface' (1929) wittily opposed the spurious expropriation of African culture, and rejected the fashionable assumption that the sensual life of the black race was superior to the white.
6 Author of the desert-island idyll, 'Paul et Virginie' (1787).
7 A Greek pastoral legend that inspired music by Maurice Ravel for a ballet produced by Diaghilev in 1910.
8 A popular romance of 1908 by Henry de Vere Stacpoole.
9 These critics included Harry Hansen (No. 7) and

Margery Latimer, 'New York Herald Tribune Books,' 18 July 1926, 16.

10 Italian author of 'The Decameron' (c. 1350).

10. PETER QUENNELL, 'NEW STATESMAN AND NATION'

5 (18 February 1933), 196

Peter Quennell (b. 1905), the English biographer of Byron (1935), Ruskin (1949) and Pope (1968), is also author of an autobiography 'The Marble Foot' (1976).

The Noble Savage (1) may have ceased to exist in fact - anthropologists have helped to undeceive us - but here and there in contemporary fiction he still manages to raise a nostalgic head. Lawrence romanticised the prancing Hopi; (2) Sherwood Anderson, better known to most English readers as the object of Wyndham Lewis's scorn - 'Paleface' holds him divertingly up to ridicule - than as a novelist who deserves attention on his own merits, in 'Dark Laughter' performed the same service for the American negro. This story of an amorous lady and a recalcitrant gardener, an intellectual who has run away from his wife, pulsates with umbrageous cachinnation.(3)

It is the negro maidservants whose mockery pervades the narrative. 'The two negro women in the house watched and waited. Often they looked at each other and giggled. The air on the hill-top was filled with laughter - dark laughter....' Meanwhile, as we are informed with hypnotic persistence, 'Spring was coming on fast in Southern Indiana.' The point is that although Spring was coming on fast, Bruce's desires were laggard and autumnal, and the dusky explosions from kitchen and pantry were bad for everybody's nerves.

Certainly, they begin to affect the reader's. Mr. Hemingway who, till 'Dark Laughter' saw the light, had been to some extent under the spell of Anderson's method - Anderson had sponsored his first book - was apparently both enchanted and disabused. He sat down and threw off a short parody; 'The Torrents of Spring,' published in 1925, caricatures Anderson's naive romanticism and his various irritating, yet occasionally persuasive, verbal tricks. It reproduces his habit of repetition. The same Spring wind blows insidiously through his tale; his characters, just as meaty and inarticulate, Yogi Johnson and the alcoholic Scripps O'Neil, struggle with their own formless, but portentous, thoughts. Like flies, newly escaped from a bath of molasses, they drag their inchoate musing across the page:

> Yogi Johnson stood looking out of the window of a big pump-factory in Michigan. Spring would soon be here. Could it be that what this writing fellow Hutchinson had said, 'If winter comes can spring be far behind?' (4) would be true again this year? Yogi Johnson wondered. Near Yogi at the next window but one stood Scripps O'Neil, a tall, lean man with a tall, lean face....

Scripps O'Neil, it may be as well to explain, is the reflection of a character called Sponge Martin:

> Time very soon to push the windows up. Spring would be coming soon now.... Sponge chewed tobacco and had a wife who got drunk with him sometimes on paydays.... When he spoke of the other child, playfully called Bugs Martin, Sponge got a little upset. She had been a rip-terror from the start.... Sponge's old woman was all right. When she and Sponge were out that way after catfish, and they had both taken five or six drinks of 'moon,' she was like a kid.... When the old woman was a little lit up and acted like a kid it made Sponge feel like that way too.

Scripps had a domestic background of a similar pattern:

> Scripps O'Neil had two wives. As he looked out of the window, standing tall and lean and resilient with his own tenuous hardness, he thought of both of them. One lived in Mancelona and the other lived in Petoskey.... (5) With his wife in Mancelona Scripps often got drunk. When he was drunk he and his wife were happy. They would go down to the railway station and walk out along the tracks, and then sit together and drink and watch the trains go by. They would sit under a pine tree on a little hill that overlooked the railway and drink.... Scripps had a daughter whom he playfully called Lousy O'Neil. Her real name was Lucy O'Neil. One night, after Scripps and his old woman had been out drinking on the railroad line for three or four days, he lost his wife. He didn't know where she

> was. When he came to himself everything was dark. He walked along the railroad track towards town. The tires were stiff and hard under his feet. He tried walking on the rails. He couldn't do it. He had the dope on that all right.... Finally he came to where he could see the lights of the switch-yard.

It will be noticed that not only does Hemingway's parody almost lovingly preserve the tone of the original - one quotation is not more ludicrous than the other - but that, particularly in the last lines of the second passage, the parodist is poking fun at his own style. Indeed, this is half the charm of 'The Torrents of Spring'; besides being a satire on Sherwood Anderson, good-humoured if mercilessly acute, it is also a satire on Anderson's method as Hemingway himself has seen fit to adapt it. Thus, Yogi is much perturbed by his lack of virility:

> Yogi was worried. There was something on his mind. It was spring, there was no doubt of that now, and he did not want a woman. He had worried about it a lot lately.... He couldn't explain it to himself. He had gone to the Public Library and asked for a book the night before. He looked at the librarian. He did not want her.... At the restaurant where he had a meal ticket he looked hard at the waitress who brought him his meals. He did not want her, either. He passed a group of girls on their way home from High School. He looked carefully at all of them. He did not want a single one.

- cogitations which inevitably take one back to a story, entitled Soldier's Home, printed in Hemingway's first book of tales:

> He liked the girls that were walking along the the other side of the street.... But the world they were in was not the world he was in.... It was not worth it.... He would not go through all the talking. He did not want one badly enough.... It was not worth it. Not now when things were getting good again.

Yogi is a more romantic creature than Krebs. Hemingway, except in 'The Torrents of Spring,' where the wild distant war-whoops of mysterious Indians take the place of the dusky laughter of negro serving-maids, lays on the 'atmosphere' with greater delicacy; but his characters are inclined to express their deepest feelings in the characteristic Andersonian telegraphese.

Hemingway succeeds and Anderson fails. The same masculine intermittences of thought and emotion, by Alfred Jingle out of Leopold Bloom, (6) with a touch of the modern collar-advertisement, are to be found in the novels and stories of both writers. They suggest conjurors perpetually rolling up their sleeves; there is nothing 'literary' or faked about the show; they are just 'regular fellows' doing their stuff. In Anderson, this attitude is immensely tiresome; in Hemingway, it must be admitted, on the other hand, the effect obtained - vivid, trenchant, and abrupt - usually justifies the means employed to compass it. So brilliant is Hemingway's gift of narrative - he is perhaps the finest story-teller now writing in English - that we can disregard the underlying pose.

'Torrents of Spring,' of course, is no more than a trifle. Nevertheless, for those who have covered the ground, have read 'In Our Time' and 'Men Without Women,' and caught from 'Paleface' an echo of 'Dark Laughter,' it is a long-expected and highly entertaining book.

Mr. Garnett adds a sympathetic foreword. He points out, as I have indicated above, that Hemingway's laughter is double-edged. This *jeu d'esprit* is a good-tempered essay in criticism, but has an astringency much needed at the present time.

Notes

1 In Rousseau's 'Émile' (1762), the Noble Savage symbolizes the innate goodness of natural man, uncorrupted by society.

2 A tribe of New Mexico Indians celebrated in Lawrence's 'Mornings in Mexico' (1927).

3 I.e. dark laughter.

4 Shelley, Ode to the West Wind (1820).

5 Both towns are in northern Michigan.

6 Wyndham Lewis, in 'Time and Western Man' (London, 1927), 121-2, was the first to point out that the effect of Bloom's word-stream in Joyce's 'Ulysses' 'was not unlike the conversation of Mr. Jingle in [Dickens'] "Pickwick Papers."'

'The Sun Also Rises' (1926) (English title: 'Fiesta')

11. CONRAD AIKEN, 'NEW YORK HERALD TRIBUNE BOOKS'

31 October 1926, 4

Conrad Aiken (1889-1973), American poet and novelist, was the author of 'Turns and Movies' (1916) and 'Blue Voyage' (1927).

It is rumored, with what accuracy I do not know, that Mr. Hemingway has at one time and another fought bulls in Spain as a mode of making a livelihood. Whether or not that is true, he writes of bull-fighting with extraordinary insight; he is clearly an expert. He is also, as clearly, *aficionado* - which is the Spanish term for a 'fan.' *Aficionado*, however, is a profounder word than fan, and suggests emotional intensities and religious zeals, not to mention psychotic fixations, which the baseball enthusiast does not dream of. If one likes bull-fighting, it has much the effect on one that half a course of psycho-analysis might have. One is thrilled and horrified; but one is also fascinated, and one cannot have enough. Perhaps the bull-fight only operates in this way on one who is too timid to descend into the ring himself - in which case one must absolve Mr. Hemingway from the charge of psychosis. Nevertheless, it is an interesting fact that his best short story, thus far, is a bull-fight story, The Undefeated, which in tragic intensity and spareness of outline challenges comparison with the very finest of contemporary short stories. And it is further interesting that in his new novel, 'The Sun Also

Rises,' the narrative works up to, and in a sense is built around, a bull-fight. Moreover, the story takes on, at this point, a force and tension which is nowhere else quite so striking.

This is not to suggest, however, that Mr. Hemingway's novel is lacking in these qualities, or that without the magnetism which the bull-fight exerts upon him he would be helpless. It has been apparent for some time that Mr. Hemingway is a writer of very unusual gifts; it has been merely a question as to what direction he would take. In 'The Sun Also Rises' he takes a decided step forward and makes it possible for me to say of him, with entire conviction, that he is in many respects the most exciting of contemporary American writers of fiction. To say that his literary debts are obvious is not to mitigate this assertion in the slightest. He has learned something from Mr. Anderson, and something, perhaps, from Mr. Fitzgerald's 'Great Gatsby'; he may even have extracted a grain or two of ore from Miss Gertrude Stein - which is in itself no inconsiderable feat.

But in the accomplished fact his work is not in the least like the work of any of these writers. If one thing is striking about it, furthermore, it is its extraordinary individuality of style. His publishers say of him, with a discernment unusual in publishers, that he has contrived, in his novel, to present his people and his actions not as perceptible through a literary medium but as if immediate, and that is true. If once or twice in his story he slips into something of Mr. Anderson's cumbersome and roundabout explanatory method, with its 'what I mean to say' and its 'the thing is this,' these echoes are few and unimportant. His own method lies at the other extreme. He simply states; he even, as a general rule, can be said to understate. It almost appears that he goes out of his way, now and then, to avoid the descriptive or the expansive methods - one has the feeling that he is a little afraid of being caught with any sort of purple on his palette, whether it be of rhetoric or of poetry. The action, he seems to say, must speak wholly for for itself.

This results, as might be expected, in a quite extraordinary effect of honesty and reality. The half dozen characters, all of whom belong to the curious and sad little world of disillusioned and aimless expatriates who make what home they can in the cafés of Paris, are seen perfectly and unsentimentally by Mr. Hemingway and are put before us with a maximum of economy. In the case of the hero, through whose mind we meet the event, and again in the cases of Brett, the heroine, and Robert Cohn, the sub-hero, Mr. Hemingway accomplishes more than this - he achieves an understanding and revelation of character which approaches the profound. When one reflects on the unattractiveness, not to say the sordidness, of the scene, and the (on the whole) gracelessness of the people, one is all the more astonished at the fact that Mr. Hemingway should have made them so moving. These folk exist, that is all; and if their story is sordid, it is also, by virtue of the author's dignity and detachment in the telling, intensely tragic.

If one feature of 'The Sun Also Rises' demands separate discussion, it is Mr. Hemingway's use of dialogue. The dialogue is brilliant. If there is better dialogue being written today I do not know where to find it. More than any other talk I can call to mind, it is alive with the rhythms and idioms, the pauses and suspensions and innuendoes and shorthands, of living speech. It is in the dialogue, almost entirely, that Mr. Hemingway tells his story and makes the people live and act. This is the dramatist's gift, and it reminds one of those novels of Henry James which were first projected as plays and then written, with something like an excess of talk, as fiction. Will Mr. Hemingway try his hand at a play? He clearly has the ability to make his story move, and move with intensity, through this medium. It is possible that he overuses this ability. One occasionally longs for a slowing down and expansion of the medium, a pause for more leisurely luxuriation in the instant, such as Mr. Hemingway only vouchsafes us in the fishing episode and in the account of the *fiesta* and the bull-fight. James himself, despite his sins in this regard, somewhere remarked that dialogue, the most trenchant of the novelists' weapons, should be used as sparely as possible, to be kept in reserve, its force and edge unimpaired, for those scenes in which the action took a definite and decisive turn; it is above all in dialogue that climax should flower. In a sense, therefore, Mr. Hemingway gives us the feeling of finality and climax a little too often and thus deprives himself and his reader of that long curve of crescendo without which a novel lacks final perfection of form. His spareness and economy, his objective detachment, would be only the more effective for an occasional offset, and his canvas greatly richer.

12. HERBERT GORMAN, 'NEW YORK WORLD'

14 NOVEMBER 1926, 10M

Herbert Gorman (1893-1954) was an American novelist and critic, and the biographer of James Joyce (1940).

The sense of cool repression that permeated Ernest Hemingway's book of short stories, 'In Our Time,' is again the most dominant aspect of his first novel, 'The Sun Also Rises.' Here, at last, is a writer who can assume (or, at least, appear to assume) an entirely impartial attitude toward his characters, drawing them with a surprising clarity through which no shadow of the author falls. Not once does the author intervene, either by implied moral or innuendo, between the reader and the group of slightly fantastic and deplorably febrile personages who act out the plotless incidents of 'The Sun Also Rises.' Neither is there any fine writing as such, any escape to the pleasurable subterfuges of overlarded description or mental analyses. The sentences are cold and direct. They are always statements.

The characters themselves are evolved from their conversations mainly, and it is a tribute to the uncanny skill of Hemingway to note that these people live with an almost painful reality. For those who know the stamping ground of the American expatriates in Paris - that district clustered about the corner where the Boulevard Raspail crosses the Boulevard Montparnasse - it will become speedily patent that practically all of these characters are directly based on actual people. This may add in some measure to the reality of the book but not enough so to take from Hemingway the credit of having created a group of vividly-conceived people existing in a somewhat febrile atmosphere.

The structure of the book is easily outlined. It is concerned with the effect of Lady Ashley on four men: Jake Barnes, who tells the story; Robert Cohn, a young Jew; Michael Campbell, engaged to Lady Ashley, and Romero, a young bullfighter. Through this group and through a shift of scene from the Left Bank in Paris to Pamplona in Spain during fiesta-time, Hemingway manages to achieve a vitriolic albeit manifestly impartial portrait of what might be called the over-nerved and over-sophisticated colony of expatriates in Europe. It is with keen wisdom that he set down Gertrude Stein's remark, 'You are all a lost generation,' at the beginning of his story. 'The Sun Also Rises' is, therefore, the tale of a great spiritual debacle, of a generation that has lost its guiding purpose and has been driven by time, fate or nerves (whatever one desires to call it) into the feverish atmosphere of strained passions. Behind the clarified paragraphs of the novel looms the pathetic figure of a great failure. There is hardly a character in the book that is not thwarted. Yet, in spite of this, a cold twilight of beauty informs the action.

Brett, Lady Ashley, spun about by her passions, or Jake Barnes, unsexed by the war, or Cohn, who crumbles to pieces beneath the weight of his desire for Brett, are all abandoned people, abandoned by the reasonability of time and left to struggle as they may with the disastrous prospects of living. The book rises to its most colorful and dramatic aspects in the account of the bull-fights and fiesta at Pamplona, a portion that is heightened by some of the finest and most restrained writing that this generation has produced, and there the reader has borne in upon him that these people have no more chance against fate than the bulls against the banderillos (1) of the fighters.

Hemingway has been wise enough to adorn his novel with no moral either stated or implied. But it is there nevertheless, a natural outgrowth of the action, and the reader may take it or leave it. With this novel Hemingway solidly places himself in the first rank of that younger group from whom we may expect so much, a group that has turned its back on pretty writing as such and turned its mind upon the phenomena of post-war life.

Note

1 Short barbed darts placed in the neck muscles of the bull to prepare him for the kill.

13. ALLEN TATE, 'NATION'

123 (15 December 1926), 642, 644

The present novel by the author of 'In Our Time' supports the recent prophecy that he will be the 'big man in

American letters.' At the time the prophecy was delivered it was meaningless because it was equivocal. Many of the possible interpretations now being eliminated, we fear it has turned out to mean something which we shall all regret. Mr. Hemingway has written a book that will be talked about, praised, perhaps imitated; it has already been received in something of that cautiously critical spirit which the followers of Henry James so notoriously maintain toward the master. Mr. Hemingway has produced a successful novel, but not without returning some violence upon the integrity achieved in his first book. He decided for reasons of his own to write a popular novel, or he wrote the only novel which he could write.

To choose the latter conjecture is to clear his intentions, obviously at the cost of impugning his art. One infers moreover that although sentimentality appears explicitly for the first time in his prose, it must have always been there. Its history can be constructed. The method used in 'In Our Time' was *pointilliste*, (1) and the sentimentality was submerged. With great skill he reversed the usual and most general formula of prose fiction: instead of selecting the details of physical background and of human behavior for the intensification of a dramatic situation, he employed the minimum of drama for the greatest possible intensification of the observed object. The reference of emphasis for the observed object was therefore not the action; rather, the reference of the action was the object, and the action could be impure or incomplete without risk of detection. It could be mixed and incoherent; it could be brought in when it was advantageous to observation, or left out. The exception, important as such, in Mr. Hemingway's work is the story Mr. and Mrs. Elliott. Here the definite dramatic conflict inherent in a sexual relation emerged as fantasy, and significantly; presumably he could not handle it otherwise without giving himself away.

In 'The Sun Also Rises,' a full-length novel, Mr. Hemingway could not escape such leading situations, and he had besides to approach them with a kind of seriousness. He fails. It is not that Mr. Hemingway is, in the term which he uses in fine contempt for the big word, hard-boiled; it is that he is not hard-boiled enough, in the artistic sense. No one can dispute with a writer the significance he derives from his subject-matter; one can only point out that the significance is mixed or incomplete. Brett is a nymphomaniac; Robert Cohn, a most offensive cad; both are puppets. For the emphasis is false; Hemingway doesn't fill out his characters and let them stand for themselves; he isolates one or two chief traits which reduce them to caricature. His perception of the physical object is direct and accurate; his vision of character, singularly oblique. And he actually betrays the interior machinery of his hard-boiled attitude: 'It is awfully easy to be hard-boiled about everything in the day-time, but at night it is another thing,' says Jake, the sexually impotent, musing on the futile accessibility of Brett. The history of his sentimentality is thus complete.

There are certain devices exploited in the book which do not improve it; they extend its appeal. Robert Cohn is not only a bounder, he is a Jewish bounder. The other bounders, like Mike, Mr. Hemingway for some reason spares. He also spares Brett - another device - for while her pleasant folly need not be flogged, it equally need not be condoned; she becomes the attractive wayward lady of Sir Arthur Pinero (2) and Michael Arlen.(3) Petronius's (4) Circe, the archetype of all the Bretts, was neither appealing nor deformed.

Mr. Hemingway has for some time been in the habit of throwing pebbles at the great - which recalls Mr. Pope's couplet about his contemporary Mr. Dennis.(5) The habit was formed in 'The Torrents of Spring,' where it was amusing. It is disconcerting in the present novel; it strains the context; and one must suspect that Mr. Hemingway protests too much. The point he seems to be making is that he is morally superior, for instance, to Mr. Mencken, but it is not yet clear just why.

Notes

1 A literary technique, derived from the Impressionist paintings of Georges Seurat, of constructing reality by the accumulation of small details.
2 English playwright, author of 'The Second Mrs. Tanqueray' (1893).
3 Armenian-English author of the phenomenally popular novel, 'The Green Hat' (1925), a combination of sexual farce and melodrama.
4 Roman author of the satirical and licentious 'Satyricon.'
5 The English critic John Dennis (1657-1734), who rashly attacked Pope and Swift, was permanently condemned in 'The Dunciad' (1728):

> She saw slow Philips creep like Tate's poor page,
> And all the mighty Mad in Dennis' rage. (I.105-6)

14. EDWIN MUIR, 'NATION AND ATHENAEUM'

41 (2 July 1927), 450, 452

Edwin Muir (1887-1959) was an English poet, critic and translator of Kafka, and author of 'The Structure of the Novel' (1928).

Mr. Hemingway is a writer of quite unusual talent. His observation is so exact that it has the effect of imagination; it evokes scenes, conversations, characters. His dialogue is by turns extraordinarily natural and brilliant, and impossibly melodramatic; when he has to describe anything he has a sureness and economy which recall Maupassant; he neither turns away from unpleasant details, nor does he stress them. There is, however, a curious inequality among his characters. Brett, the heroine, might have stepped out of 'The Green Hat'; she is the sentimentally regarded dare-devil, and she never becomes real. But most of the other characters, the majority of them American Bohemians living in Paris, are graphically drawn. The original merits of the book are striking; its fault, equally apparent after one's first pleasure, is a lack of artistic significance. We see the lives of a group of people laid bare, and we feel that it does not matter to us. Mr. Hemingway tells us a great deal about those people, but he tells us nothing of importance about human life. He tells us nothing, indeed, which any of his characters might not tell us; he writes with honesty, but as a member of the group he describes; and, accordingly, his narrative lacks proportion, which is the same thing as significance. But he is still a young writer; his gifts are original; and this first novel raises hopes of remarkable achievement. The Spanish scenes, Cohn's fight with the matador, the dance in the streets, the bull fight - these bring us in contact with a strong and original visual world.

15. ANDRÉ MAUROIS, 'THIS QUARTER'

2 (October 1929), 212-15

Translated by Florence Llona.

André Maurois (1885-1967) was the French biographer of Shelley (1924), Byron (1930) and Chateaubriand (1938). Hemingway had published The Big Two-Hearted River in the Spring 1925 issue of 'This Quarter,' a little magazine edited in Paris by Ernest Walsh and Ethel Moorhead.

When I visited Princeton University two years ago, the faculty were discussing a novel which had just been published by Ernest Hemingway. I wanted to know what it was called. '"The Sun Also Rises."' - 'Is it good?' - 'It's very hard, cynical, and extraordinarily true to life. I don't know whether you would care for it.' I bought it. It was very good indeed.

Not on account of the plot, which was practically non-existent. Lady Brett Ashley moves in a set of Montparnasse Americans, drinks, sleeps with men and is bored. She is engaged to a ruined Englishman and is loved by the American newspaper man who tells the story. She goes to San Sebastian with a Jewish boxer and leaves him for a young matador.... But any plot will do when a novelist knows how to create live human beings and Hemingway's characters are alive. They do not talk about their souls, they do not unravel their feelings. No, they merely order drinks and dinners, swear, have a good time, and yet you know them as well as you do Odette Swann, or Charlus, or Legrandin.(1) Cohn, the athletic Jew, glum, well meaning and clumsy, the others' reaction to Cohn's disposition, the Englishman's jealousy masked by a permanent drunk, were sketched with marvellously accurate touches, although the author did not once come forward nor did a single analytical sentence disturb the monotone of such conversations: 'Did you sleep well, Bill?' - 'I slept like a log,' said Bill. - 'Where were you?' - 'In a café,' said Bill.... This young American's technique seemed both perfect and mysterious.

I read his two volumes of short stories next. 'In Our Time' and 'Men Without Women.' 'In Our Time' was oddly constructed. The briefest of italicized sketches, more like blunt, cruel epigrams, alternated with stories as long as tales by Maupassant. Unity is achieved by the sameness of the feeling which runs through these tableaux and which is that life is hard. Bull's horns ripping men's skin. German soldiers fired at point-blank. Italians hung in an American prison. Greek ministers shot down in the mud. 'Our time' is brutal. Beneath its frail crust of civilization flourish practices as violent as ever the Rome of Suetonius (2) knew. Hemingway is not afraid of grim sights. He has a liking for boxers, for toreadors, for soldiers. 'Men Without Women' contains Fifty Grand, a really fine story about a boxer, and The Undefeated, which describes with restrained, forcible pathos an aging matador's last fight.

His tone and his choice of subjects mirrored a definite image of the author - and an accurate one. Hemingway's life is the one surmised. He was born in Oak Park, Illinois. His father, a physician, was also born near there. His family has lived in America for two hundred years. He spent his childhood in upper Michigan, and later roamed the United States and Canada, plying various small trades. During the war he enlisted in the Italian army,(3) was wounded and spent nine months in a hospital. He is decorated with the *Medaglia d'argento al Valore Militare.*(4) Since the war he has lived in Europe as foreign correspondent for American newspapers. He is an accomplished boxer. He skis in the winter and goes to Spain in the summer to see bull-fights. He is thirty-two years old.(5)

Where did he learn to write? What has he read? What does he admire? We do not know. If names were indispensable to give an idea of his style, I should mention Kipling and Mérimée,(6) but the resemblances are slight and the dissimilarities profound. His impassible narration recalls Mérimée, but Mérimée was a man of the drawing-room and library. Even if he rather fancied the rougher aspects of life, he gazed at them from the outside and held aloof. His smugglers are artists and philosophers. Hemingway's jockeys and boxers are jockeys and boxers, as they should be. While he appreciates the poetic value of sports, they appeal to him above all scientifically. His vocabulary is always accurate, riveted and solid like a specialist's. He has Kipling's art of suggesting passions and feelings without calling them by name, with less moral grandeur perhaps than Kipling because until now the scope of his subject matter has been less ample, but in Hemingway's stories there is an almost physical strength that does not exist in Kipling's, and a still sheerer starkness. A story by Hemingway is stripped to the bone. The facts are nearly always intimated by means of dialogue, without any commentaries. His descriptions are condensed into the least possible volume. Whenever he can, Hemingway lets the mere name of a place suggest the setting.... Boulevard Raspail.... Hôtel Crillon.... If this means that he is a realist, he is certainly very different from the 1880 school of French realists. His philosophy too is long a way from theirs. His picture of life is less pessimistic than theirs although just as somber. The 'miseries' common to us all pervade his work, but he supplies that powerful antidote, humour. The final impression is one of vigour and courage.

Sherwood Anderson, his senior, says of him:

'Mr. Hemingway's tales are full of the smells, the taste, the feel of life. He likes the sky, horses, running water, women, and men coming home from the hunt and I like his tales.

'That is something for me to say, for older writers do not much like to see such good young prosemen coming on in their own day.'

Anderson, who is so familiar with the plains and forests of the Middle West, knows that Hemingway's plains and forests are real. We Frenchmen feel that his Paris is real. There is no faulty drawing to destroy the illusion. He writes of nothing that he does not know.

The virtue of his construction is its simplicity. His dialogue is remarkable, although in 'The Sun Also Rises,' somewhat monotonous, unavoidably however, since the vocabulary of the characters is a meagre one. His style is made up of clean-cut, metallic elements. One is reminded of modern buildings - steel beams and cement. He achieves distinction through a horror of distinction. There are no Corinthian capitals nor processions of stereotyped naked women on Hemingway's façades. In one of his books, he defines a toreador's style thus: 'Romero never made any contortions, always it was straight and pure and natural in line. The others twisted themselves like corkscrews, their elbows raised, and leaned against the flanks of the bull after its horns had passed, to give a faked look of danger.... Romero's bull fighting gave real emotion, because he kept the absolute purity of line in his movements and always quietly and calmly let the horns pass him close each time.' This passage defines Hemingway's own style. The closer he works to the horns, the purer and quieter it is.

Notes

1 Characters in Marcel Proust's 'Remembrance of Things Past' (1913-27).

2 Roman historian, author of 'Lives of the Caesars.'
3 Hemingway was actually in a Red Cross ambulance unit on the Italian front.
4 Silver Medal for Military Valor.
5 Hemingway was 30 in 1929.
6 Prosper Mérimée, French novelist, was the author of 'Colomba' (1841) and 'Carmen' (1847).

'Men Without Women' (1927)

16. VIRGINIA WOOLF, 'NEW YORK HERALD TRIBUNE BOOKS'

9 October 1927, 1, 8

Virginia Woolf (1882-1941), English novelist, was the author of 'Mrs. Dalloway' (1925), 'To the Lighthouse' (1927) and 'The Waves' (1931).

Human credulity is indeed wonderful. There may be good reasons for believing in a King or a Judge or a Lord Mayor. When we see them go sweeping by in their robes and their wigs, with their heralds and their outriders, our knees begin to shake and our looks to falter. But what reason there is for believing in critics it is impossible to say. They have neither wigs nor outriders. They differ in no way from other people if one sees them in the flesh. Yet these insignificant fellow creatures have only to shut themselves up in a room, dip a pen in the ink, and call themselves 'we', for the rest of us to believe that they are somehow exalted, inspired, infallible. Wigs grow on their heads. Robes cover their limbs. No greater miracle was ever performed by the power of human credulity. And, like most miracles, this one, too, has had a weakening effect upon the mind of the believer. He begins to think that critics, because they call themselves so, must be right. He begins to suppose that something actually happens to a book when it has been praised or denounced in print. He begins to doubt and conceal his own sensitive, hesitating apprehensions when they conflict with the critics' decrees.

And yet, barring the learned (and learning is chiefly useful in judging the work of the dead), the critic is rather more fallible than the rest of us. He has to give us his opinion of a book that has been published two days, perhaps, with the shell still sticking to its head. He has to get outside that cloud of fertile, but unrealized, sensation which hangs about a reader, to solidify it, to sum it up. The chances are that he does this before the time is ripe; he does it too rapidly and too definitely. He says that it is a great book or a bad book. Yet, as he knows, when he is content to read only, it is neither. He is driven by force of circumstances and some human vanity to hide those hesitations which beset him as he reads, to smooth out all traces of that crab-like and crooked path by which he has reached what he choses to call 'a conclusion'. So the crude trumpet blasts of critical opinion blow loud and shrill, and we, humble readers that we are, bow our submissive heads.

But let us see whether we can do away with these pretences for a season and pull down the imposing curtain which hides the critical process until it is complete. Let us give the mind a new book, as one drops a lump of fish into a cage of fringed and eager sea anemones, and watch it pausing, pondering, considering its attack. Let us see what prejudices affect it; what influences tell upon it. And if the conclusion becomes in the process a little less conclusive, it may, for that very reason, approach nearer to the truth. The first thing that the mind desires is some foothold of fact upon which it can lodge before it takes flight upon its speculative career. Vague rumours attach themselves to people's names. Of Mr. Hemingway, we know that he is an American living in France, an 'advanced' writer, we suspect, connected with what is called a movement, though which of the many we own that we do not know. It will be well to make a little more certain of these matters by reading first Mr. Hemingway's earlier book, 'The Sun Also Rises', and it soon becomes clear from this that, if Mr. Hemingway is 'advanced', it is not in the way that is to us most interesting. A prejudice of which the reader would do well to take account is here exposed; the critic is a modernist. Yes, the excuse would be because the moderns make us aware of what we feel subconsciously; they are truer to our own experience; they even anticipate it, and this gives us a particular excitement. But nothing new is revealed about any of the characters in 'The Sun Also Rises'. They come before us shaped, proportioned, weighed, exactly as the characters of Maupassant are shaped and proportioned. They are seen from the old angle; the old reticences, the old relations between author and character are observed.

But the critic has the grace to reflect that this demand for new aspects and new perspectives may well be overdone. It may become whimsical. It may become foolish. For why should not art be traditional as well as original? Are we not attaching too much importance to an excitement which, though agreeable, may not be valuable in itself, so that we are led to make the fatal mistake of overriding the writer's gift?

At any rate, Mr. Hemingway is not modern in the sense given; and it would appear from his first novel that this rumour of modernity must have sprung from his subject matter and from his treatment of it rather than from any fundamental novelty in his conception of the art of fiction. It is a bare, abrupt, outspoken book. Life as people live it in Paris in 1927 or even in 1928 is described as we of this age do describe life (it is here that we steal a march upon the Victorians) openly, frankly, without prudery, but also without surprise. The immoralities and moralities of Paris are described as we are apt to hear them spoken of in private life. Such candour is modern and it is admirable. Then, for qualities grow together in art as in life, we find attached to this admirable frankness an equal bareness of style. Nobody speaks for more than a line or two. Half a line is mostly sufficient. If a hill or a town is described (and there is always some reason for its description) there it is, exactly and literally built up of little facts, literal enough, but chosen, as the final sharpness of the outline proves, with the utmost care. Therefore, a few words like these: 'The grain was just beginning to ripen and the fields were full of poppies. The pasture land was green and there were fine trees, and sometimes big rivers and chateaux off in the trees' - have a curious force. Each word pulls its weight in the sentence. And the prevailing atmosphere is fine and sharp, like that of winter days when the boughs are bare against the sky. (But if we had to choose one sentence with which to describe what Mr. Hemingway attempts and sometimes achieves, we should quote a passage from a description of a bullfight: 'Romero never made any contortions, always it was straight and pure and natural in line. The others twisted themselves like corkscrews, their elbows raised and leaned against the flanks of the bull after his horns had passed, to give a faked look of danger. Afterwards, all that was faked turned bad and gave an unpleasant feeling. Romero's bullfighting gave real emotion, because he kept the absolute purity of line in his movements and always quietly and calmly let the horns pass him close each time.') Mr. Hemingway's writing, one might paraphrase, gives us now and then a real emotion, because he keeps absolute purity of line in his movements and lets the horns (which are truth, fact, reality) pass him close each time. But there is something faked, too, which turns bad and gives an unpleasant feeling - that also we must face in course of time.

And here, indeed, we may conveniently pause and sum up what point we have reached in our critical progress. Mr. Hemingway is not an advanced writer in the sense that he is looking at life from a new angle. What he sees is a tolerably familiar sight. Common objects like beer bottles and journalists figure largely in the foreground. But he is a skilled and conscientious writer. He has an aim and makes for it without fear or circumlocution. We have, therefore, to take his measure against somebody of substance, and not merely line him, for form's sake, beside the indistinct bulk of some ephemeral shape largely stuffed with straw. Reluctantly we reach this decision, for this process of measurement is one of the most difficult of a critic's tasks. He has to decide which are the most salient points of the book he has just read; to distinguish accurately to what kind they belong, and then, holding them against whatever model is chosen for comparison, to bring out their deficiency or their adequacy.

Recalling 'The Sun Also Rises', certain scenes rise in memory: the bullfight, the character of the Englishman, Harris; here a little landscape which seems to grow behind the people naturally; here a long, lean phrase which goes curling round a situation like the lash of a whip. Now and again this phrase evokes a character brilliantly, more often a scene. Of character, there is little that remains firmly and solidly elucidated. Something indeed seems wrong with the people. If we place them (the comparison is bad) against Tchekov's people, they are flat as cardboard. If we place them (the comparison is better) against Maupassant's people they are crude as a photograph. If we place them (the comparison may be illegitimate) against real people, the people we liken them to are of an unreal type. They are people one may have seen showing off at some café; talking a rapid, high-pitched slang, because slang is the speech of the herd, seemingly much at their ease, and yet if we look at them a little from the shadow not at their ease at all, and, indeed, terribly afraid of being themselves, or they would say things simply in their natural voices. So it would seem that the thing that is faked is character; Mr. Hemingway leans against the flanks of that particular bull after the horns have passed.

After this preliminary study of Mr. Hemingway's first

book, we come to the new book, 'Men Without Women', possessed of certain views or prejudices. His talent plainly may develop along different lines. It may broaden and fill out; it may take a little more time and go into things - human beings in particular - rather more deeply. And even if this meant the sacrifice of some energy and point, the exchange would be to our private liking. On the other hand, his is a talent which may contract and harden still further, it may come to depend more and more upon the emphatic moment; make more and more use of dialogue, and cast narrative and description overboard as an encumbrance.

The fact that 'Men Without Women' consists of short stories, makes it probable that Mr. Hemingway has taken the second line. But, before we explore the new book, a word should be said which is generally left unsaid, about the implications of the title. As the publisher puts it ... 'the softening feminine influence is absent - either through training, discipline, death, or situation'. Whether we are to understand by this that women are incapable of training, discipline, death, or situation, we do not know. But it is undoubtedly true, if we are going to persevere in our attempt to reveal the processes of the critic's mind, that any emphasis laid upon sex is dangerous. Tell a man that this is a woman's book, or a woman that this is a man's, and you have brought into play sympathies and antipathies which have nothing to do with art. The greatest writers lay no stress upon sex one way or the other. The critic is not reminded as he reads them that he belongs to the masculine or the feminine gender. But in our time, thanks to our sexual perturbations, sex consciousness is strong, and shows itself in literature by an exaggeration, a protest of sexual characteristics which in either case is disagreeable. Thus Mr. Lawrence, Mr. Douglas,(1) and Mr. Joyce partly spoil their books for women readers by their display of self-conscious virility; and Mr. Hemingway, but much less violently, follows suit. All we can do, whether we are men or women, is to admit the influence, look the fact in the face, and so hope to stare it out of countenance.

To proceed then - 'Men Without Women' consists of short stories in the French rather than in the Russian manner. The great French masters, Mérimée and Maupassant, made their stories as self-conscious and compact as possible. There is never a thread left hanging; indeed, so contracted are they that when the last sentence of the last page flares up, as it so often does, we see by its light the whole circumference and significance of the story revealed. The Tchekov method is, of course, the very opposite of this. Everything is cloudy and vague, loosely trailing rather than tightly furled. The stories move slowly out of sight like clouds in the summer air, leaving a wake of meaning in our minds which gradually fades away. Of the two methods, who shall say which is the better? At any rate, Mr. Hemingway, enlisting under the French masters, carries out their teaching up to a point with considerable success.

There are in 'Men Without Women' many stories which, if life were longer, one would wish to read again. Most of them indeed are so competent, so efficient, and so bare of superfluity that one wonders why they do not make a deeper dent in the mind than they do. Take the pathetic story of the Major whose wife died - In Another Country; or the sardonic story of a conversation in a railway carriage - A Canary for One; or stories like The Undefeated and Fifty Grand which are full of the sordidness and heroism of bull-fighting and boxing - all of these are good trenchant stories, quick, terse, and strong. If one had not summoned the ghosts of Tchekov, Mérimée, and Maupassant, no doubt one would be enthusiastic. As it is, one looks about for something, fails to find something, and so is brought again to the old familiar business of ringing impressions on the counter, and asking what is wrong?

For some reason the book of short stories does not seem to us to go as deep or to promise as much as the novel. Perhaps it is the excessive use of dialogue, for Mr. Hemingway's use of it is surely excessive. A writer will always be chary of dialogue because dialogue puts the most violent pressure upon the reader's attention. He has to hear, to see, to supply the right tone, and to fill in the background from what the characters say without any help from the author. Therefore, when fictitious people are allowed to speak it must be because they have something so important to say that it stimulates the reader to do rather more than his share of the work of creation. But, although Mr. Hemingway keeps us under the fire of dialogue constantly, his people, half the time, are saying what the author could say much more economically for them. At last we are inclined to cry out with the little girl in Hills Like White Elephants: 'Would you please please please please please please stop talking?'

And probably it is this superfluity of dialogue which leads to that other fault which is always lying in wait for the writer of short stories: the lack of proportion. A paragraph in excess will make these little craft lopsided and will bring about that blurred effect which, when one is out for clarity and point, so baffles the reader.

And both these faults, the tendency to flood the page with unnecessary dialogue and the lack of sharp, unmistakable points by which we can take hold of the story, come from the more fundamental fact that, though Mr. Hemingway is brilliantly and enormously skilful, he lets his dexterity, like the bullfighter's cloak, get between him and the fact. For in truth story-writing has much in common with bullfighting. One may twist one's self like a corkscrew and go through every sort of contortion so that the public thinks one is running every risk and displaying superb gallantry. But the true writer stands close up to the bull and lets the horns - call them life, truth, reality, whatever you like - pass him close each time.

Mr. Hemingway, then, is courageous; he is candid; he is highly skilled; he plants words precisely where he wishes; he has moments of bare and nervous beauty; he is modern in manner but not in vision; he is self-consciously virile; his talent has contracted rather than expanded; compared with his novel his stories are a little dry and sterile. So we sum him up. So we reveal some of the prejudices, the instincts and the fallacies out of which what it pleases us to call criticism is made.

Note

1 Norman Douglas, homosexual author of 'South Wind' (1917) and 'Together' (1923).

17. DOROTHY PARKER, 'NEW YORKER'

3 (29 October 1927), 92-4

Dorothy Parker (1893-1967) was an American satirist and humorist, author of 'Enough Rope' (1927) and 'Here Lies' (1939), and a profile of Hemingway in the 'New Yorker' (30 November 1929) which quotes the famous phrase 'grace under pressure.'

Ernest Hemingway wrote a novel called 'The Sun Also Rises.' Promptly upon its publication, Ernest Hemingway was discovered, the Stars and Stripes were reverentially raised over him, eight hundred and forty-seven book reviewers formed themselves into the word 'welcome,' and the band played 'Hail to the Chief' (1) in three concurrent keys. All of which, I should think, might have made Ernest Hemingway pretty reasonably sick.

For, a year or so before 'The Sun Also Rises,' he had published 'In Our Time,' a collection of short pieces. The book caused about as much stir in literary circles as an incompleted dogfight on upper Riverside Drive. True, there were a few that went about quick and stirred with admiration for this clean, exciting prose, but most of the reviewers dismissed the volume with a tolerant smile and the word 'stark.' It was Mr. Mencken who slapped it down with 'sketches in the bold, bad manner of the Café du Dôme,' and the smaller boys, in their manner, took similar pokes at it. Well, you see, Ernest Hemingway was a young American living on the left bank of the Seine in Paris, France; he had been seen at the Dôme and the Rotonde and the Select and the Closerie des Lilas. He knew Pound, Joyce and Gertrude Stein. There is something a little - well, a little *you*-know - in all of those things. You wouldn't catch Bruce Barton or Mary Roberts Rinehart (2) doing them. No, sir.

And besides, 'In Our Time' was a book of short stories. That's no way to start off. People don't like that; they feel cheated. Any bookseller will be glad to tell you, in his interesting *argot*, that 'short stories don't go.' People take up a book of short stories and say, 'Oh, what's this? Just a lot of those short things?' and put it right down again. Only yesterday afternoon, at four o'clock sharp, I saw and heard a woman do that to Ernest Hemingway's new book, 'Men Without Women.' She had been one of those most excited about his novel.

Literature, it appears, is here measured by a yard-stick. As soon as 'The Sun Also Rises' came out, Ernest Hemingway was the white-haired boy. He was praised, adored, analyzed, best-sold, argued about, and banned in Boston; (3) all the trimmings were accorded him. People got into feuds about whether or not his story was worth the telling. (You see this silver scar left by a bullet, right up here under my hair? I got that the night I said that any well-told story was worth the telling. An eighth of an inch nearer the temple, and I wouldn't be sitting here doing this sort of tripe.) They affirmed, and passionately, that the dissolute expatriates in this novel of 'a lost generation' were not worth bothering about; and then they devoted most of their time to discussing them. There was a time, and it went on for weeks, when you could go nowhere without hearing of 'The Sun Also Rises.' Some thought it without excuse; and some, they of the cool, tall foreheads, called it the greatest American novel, tossing 'Huckleberry Finn' and 'The Scarlet Letter' lightly out the window. They hated it or they revered it. I may say, with due respect to Mr. Hemingway, that I was never so sick of a book in my life.

Now 'The Sun Also Rises' was as 'starkly' written as Mr. Hemingway's short stories; it dealt with subjects as 'unpleasant.' Why it should have been taken to the slightly damp bosom of the public while the (as it seems to me) superb 'In Our Time' should have been disregarded will always be a puzzle to me. As I see it - I knew this conversation would get back to me sooner or later, preferably sooner - Mr. Hemingway's style, this prose stripped to its firm young bones, is far more effective, far more moving, in the short story than in the novel. He is, to me, the greatest living writer of short stories; he is, also to me, not the greatest living novelist.

After all the high screaming about 'The Sun Also Rises,' I feared for Mr. Hemingway's next book. You know how it is - as soon as they all start acclaiming a writer, that writer is just about to slip downward. The littler critics circle like literary buzzards above only the sick lions.

So it is a warm gratification to find the new Hemingway book, 'Men Without Women,' a truly magnificent work. It is composed of thirteen (4) short stories, most of which have been published before. They are sad and terrible stories; the author's enormous appetite for life seems to have been somehow appeased. You find here little of that peaceful ecstasy that marked the camping trip in 'The Sun Also Rises' and the lone fisherman's days in Big Two-Hearted River, in 'In Our Time.' The stories include The Killers, which seems to me one of the four great American short stories. (All you have to do is drop the nearest hat, and I'll tell you what I think the others are. They are Wilbur Daniel Steele's Blue Murder, (5) Sherwood Anderson's I'm a Fool, and Ring Lardner's Some Like Them Cold, that story which seems to me as shrewd a picture of every woman at some time as is Chekhov's The Darling. Now what do *you* like best?) The book also includes Fifty Grand, In Another Country, and the delicate and tragic Hills Like White Elephants. I do not know where a greater collection of stories can be found.

Ford Madox Ford has said of this author, 'Hemingway writes like an angel.' I take issue (there is nothing better for that morning headache than taking a little issue). Hemingway writes like a human being. I think it is impossible for him to write of any event at which he has not been present; his is, then, a reportorial talent, just as Sinclair Lewis's is. But, or so I think, Lewis remains a reporter, and Hemingway stands a genius because Hemingway has an unerring sense of selection. He discards details with a magnificent lavishness; he keeps his words to their short path. His is, as any reader knows, a dangerous influence. The simple thing he does looks so easy to do. But look at the boys who try to do it.

Notes

1 A musical tribute played to the President of the United States.
2 Popular middle-brow writers of religious and mystery novels.
3 Parker's joke was prophetic. 'The Sun Also Rises' was not banned in Boston, but 'A Farewell to Arms' was.
4 There are fourteen stories in the book.
5 A murder story set in Wyoming that appeared in 'Harper's,' 151 (October 1925), 559-70.

18. CYRIL CONNOLLY, 'NEW STATESMAN'

30 (26 November 1927), 208

Cyril Connolly (1903-74) was a critic, editor of 'Horizon,' and author of 'Enemies of Promise' (1938) and 'The Unquiet Grave' (1945).

With Mr. Hemingway, we at once enter the front line of modern literary warfare. We are face to face with the largest and wildest of the game that Mr. Wyndham Lewis chivvies through the warrens of the Rive Gauche (1) and with the only one of its fauna on whose tail he has tried to place a pinch of commendatory salt, apparently in vain.(2)

'Men Without Women' is a collection of grim little stories told in admirable colloquial dialogue with no point, no moral and no ornamentation. They are about bull-fighters, crooks, crook prize-fighters, crook peasants, dope fiends, and soldiers in hospital. The title is intended to strike the note of ferocious virility which characterises the book, which is, however, by no means free from the strong silent sentimentality latent in this attitude. They are, in fact, a blend of Gertrude Stein's manner, Celtic childishness, and the slice of life (the real thing!) redeemed by humour, power over dialogue and an obvious knowledge of the people he describes. Yet as far as realism goes, he can make little advance on Vernon Lee,(3) to whom the raw slice of life would be as unpleasant as the decomposing prose of Gertrude Stein. Here, for instance, is her account of the conversation of Italian peasants with an Englishman (about 1880):

> Was it true that it always rained in England? Was it true that one could pick up lumps of gold somewhere in England? Was there any town as large as M—— in that country? The priest thought these questions foolish, and enquired with much gravity after the health of Milord Vellingtone,(4) who, he understood, had been seriously unwell of late ... and asked me whether I had been to the neighbouring Bologna; informed me that the city was the mother of all art, and that the Carracci (5) especially were her most glorious sons. Meanwhile the rain continued coming down in a steady pour.

There is no artifice employed. Yet anyone who has sheltered from a storm in a Latin country must have undergone just that questioning, the earnest vanity of the peasants, the smug patronage of the priests. Here is Mr. Hemingway describing another fatuous dialogue, only with two Americans and a waitress in Spezia:

> 'It is my country,' she said; 'Spezia is my home, and Italy is my country.'
>
> 'She says that Italy is her country.'
>
> 'Tell her it looks like her country,' Guy said.
>
> 'What have you for dessert?' I asked.
>
> 'Fruit,' she said, 'we have bananas.'
>
> 'Bananas are all right,' Guy said. 'They've got skins on.'
>
> 'Oh, he takes bananas,' the lady said. She embraced Guy.
>
> 'What does she say?' he asked, keeping his face out of the way.
>
> 'She is pleased because you take bananas.'
>
> 'Tell her I don't take bananas.'
>
> 'The signor doesn't take bananas.'

'Ah,' said the lady, crestfallen, 'he doesn't take bananas.'

'Tell her I take a cold bath every morning.'

'The signor takes a cold bath every morning.'

'No understand,' the lady said.

Here the Mutt and Jeff (6) dialogue is elaborated by the soporific echoes of Miss Stein's tom tom. Yet beneath the dressing the humour is only Mark Twain's; the fertile situation of the Anglo-Saxon confronted with the foreigner. Mr. Hemingway really represents an acute phase of post-war dissatisfaction. Unfortunately the post-war period is nearly over; the violent and exciting confusion of those years has passed and with it the vogue for those talented authors who substituted impatience for ambition and struggled bravely on without the great driving power of tradition. The literature of the future will be in the hands of a bland and orderly generation about which absolutely nothing is known. Meanwhile Mr. Hemingway remains easily the ablest of the wild band of Americans in Europe and is obviously capable of a great deal of development before his work reaches maturity. At present this work is irritating, but very readable and full of a power and freshness that will interest anyone who prefers the terser examples of American realism to the laborious chronicles of dull families and dull crimes. Mr. Hemingway is considered, falsely, a second Joyce in America; at present he is more of a dark horse than a white hope, but his book makes a good test of one's own capacity to appreciate modernity. In descriptions of bull fights and of the normal life of unromantic Spain he is unexcelled.

Notes

1 Left Bank (of the Seine).
2 In 'Time and Western Man,' Wyndham Lewis launched devastating attacks on Pound, Joyce and Stein, but called Hemingway 'an admirable writer, almost universally admired' (p. 63).
3 Pseudonym of Violet Paget (1856-1935), who lived in Florence and wrote about the history, art and landscape of Italy.
4 Lord Wellington.
5 Ludovico and Annibale Carracci were sixteenth-century Italian painters.
6 American comic-strip characters.

19. EDMUND WILSON, 'NEW REPUBLIC'

53 (14 December 1927), 102-3

The reputation of Ernest Hemingway has, in a very short time, reached such proportions that it has already become fashionable to disparage him. Yet it seems to me that he has received in America very little intelligent criticism. I find Lee Wilson Dodd, for example, in the 'Saturday Review of Literature,' with his usual gentle trepidation in the presence of contemporary life, deciding with a sigh of relief that, after all, Ernest Hemingway (a young man who has published only three books) is not Shakespeare or Tolstoy; and describing Hemingway's subjects as follows: 'The people he observes with fascinated fixation and then makes live before us are ... all very much alike: bull-fighters, bruisers, touts, gunmen, professional soldiers, prostitutes, hard drinkers, dope fiends.... For what they may or may not be intellectually, esthetically or morally worth, he makes his facts ours.' In the 'Nation,' Joseph Wood Krutch, whose review is more sympathetic than Mr. Dodd's, describes Hemingway as follows: 'Spiritually the distinguishing mark of Mr. Hemingway's work is a weariness too great to be aware of anything but sensations.... Mr. Hemingway tells us, both by his choice of subject and by the method which he employs, that life is an affair of mean tragedies.... In his hands the subject matter of literature becomes sordid little catastrophes in the lives of very vulgar people.'(1) I do not know whether these reviewers of 'Men Without Women' have never read Hemingway's other two books, or whether they have simply forgotten them. Do the stories in 'In Our Time' and in 'The Sun Also Rises' actually answer to these descriptions? Does 'Men Without Women' answer to them? The hero of 'In Our Time' who appears in one or two stories in the new volume, and the hero of 'The Sun Also Rises,' are both highly civilized persons of rather complex temperament and extreme sensibility. In what way can they be said to be 'very vulgar people'? And can the adventures of even the old bull-fighter in The Undefeated be called a 'sordid little catastrophe'?

One of the stories in 'Men without Women' also appeared in 'The American Caravan,'(2) and was thus twice exposed to the reviewers; yet in all the reviews I have read of both volumes I cannot remember one which seemed to me to give an accurate account of it. It has almost invariably been mentioned, briefly, as a simple tale of horror or a tale of brutality, or something of the sort. Let us examine this story a moment. Two young men have been skiing in the Alps: it is spring and the sun is terrifically strong; but in the shade the sweat freezes in their underclothes. They have begun to find it oppressive and are glad to get down to an inn. On their way, they have passed a burial, and at the inn they hear the story of the woman who is dead. She was the wife of a peasant and died during the winter, but the husband was snow bound and could not bring her out till spring. The peasant put the body in the wood-shed, laying it on a pile of wood; but when he had to use the wood, he stood the corpse up in a corner, and got into the habit of hanging the lantern in its mouth. Why, we ask ourselves for a moment, have we been told about the skiing expedition? Then, immediately, we realize that Hemingway, with his masterly relevance in apparent indirection, has, in the oppression felt by the tourists, supplied us with the explanation of the brutalization of the peasant. This brutalization by itself is not, however, the theme of the story. We do not see the point till the end. The peasant will not drink at the inn, where he has come immediately after the burial, but goes on to a neighboring one. '"He didn't want to drink with me," said the sexton. "He didn't want to drink with *him*, after he knew about his wife," said the innkeeper.' Similarly, A Pursuit Race is, as Mr. Dodd would say, a story about a dope-fiend; but what is more interesting and important, it is also about a man who has just lost a desperately prolonged moral struggle, and it derives its whole significance from the last paragraph, in which the manager of the burlesque show, understanding what has happened and pitying his recreant advance man, refrains from waking him. So in A Simple Inquiry, in which we are shown that strange demoralization of army life which is scarcely distinguishable from stoicism, the value of the incident lies entirely in the fact that the major refrains from dismissing the boy.

It would appear, then, that Hemingway's world was not quite so devoid of interest as it has been represented by Mr. Krutch and Mr. Dodd. Even when he deals with rudimentary types - as he by no means always does - his drama usually turns on some principle of courage, of honor, of pity - in short, of sportsmanship in its largest human sense - which he discovers in them. I do not say that the world which Hemingway depicts is not a bad world; it is a bad world and a world where much is suffered. Hemingway's feelings about this world, his criticism of what goes on in it, are, for all his misleadingly simple and matter-of-fact style, rather subtle and complex; but he has, it seems to me, made it sufficiently plain what sort of emotions and ideas he intends to communicate. His first book was called 'In Our Time,' and it was made up of a series of brief and brutal sketches of barbarous happenings mostly connected with the War, alternated with a series of short stories about a sensitive and healthy boy in the American northwest.(3) We were, I take it, to contrast these two series. When Hemingway gave them this title, he meant to tell us that life was barbarous, even in our civilized age; and that the man who sees the cabinet ministers shot and who finds himself potting at the Germans from the 'perfectly priceless barricade' has had to come a long way from the boy who, with the fresh senses of youth, so much enjoyed the three days' fishing trip at Big Two-Hearted River. Yet has he really come so far? Is not the very principle of life essentially ruthless and cruel? What is the difference between the gusto of the soldier all on edge to hunt his fellow humans and the gusto of the young fisherman hooking grasshoppers to catch trout? Hemingway is primarily preoccupied with these problems of suffering and cruelty.

The barbarity of the world since the War is also the theme of Hemingway's next book, 'The Sun Also Rises.' By his title and by the quotations which he prefixes to this book, he makes it plain what moral judgment we are to pass on the events he describes: 'You are all a lost generation.' What gives the book its profound unity and its disquieting effectiveness is the intimate relation established between the Spanish fiesta with its processions, its revelry and its bull-fighting and the atrocious behavior of the group of Americans and English who have come down from Paris to enjoy it. In the heartlessness of these people in their treatment of one another, do we not find the same principle at work as in the pagan orgy of the festival? Is not the brutal persecution of the Jew as much a natural casualty of a barbarous world as the fate of the man who is accidentally gored by the bull on the way to the bull-ring? The whole interest of 'The Sun Also Rises' lies in the attempts of the hero and the heroine to disengage themselves from this world, or rather to arrive at some method of living in it honorably. The real story is the story of their attempts to do this - attempts by which, in such a world, they are always bound to lose in everything except honor. I do not agree, as has sometimes been said, that the behavior of the people in 'The Sun Also Rises' is typical of only a small and special class of American and English expatriates. I believe that it is more or less typical of certain phases of the whole western world today; and the title 'In Our Time' would have applied to it with as much appropriateness as to its predecessor.

Hemingway's attitude, however, toward the cruelties and treacheries he describes is quite different from anything else which one remembers in a similar connection. He has nothing of the generous indignation of the romantics: he does not, like Byron, bid the stones of the prisoner's cell 'appeal from tyranny to God'; nor, like Shelley, bid the winds to 'wail for the world's wrong.'(4) Nor has he even that grim and repressed, but still generous, still passionate feeling which we find in the pessimist-realists - in Hardy's 'Tess,' in Maupassant's Boule de Suif,(5) even in those infrequent scenes of Flaubert where we are made to boil at the spectacle of an old farm servant or of a young silk-weaver's daughter at the mercy of the bourgeoisie. In his treatment of the War, for example, Hemingway is as far as possible from Barbusse (6) or from John Dos Passos. His point of view, his state of mind, is a curious one, and one typical of the time - he seems so broken in to the agonies of humanity, and, though even against his will, so impassively resigned to them, that his only protest is, as it were, the grin and the oath of the sportsman who loses the game. Furthermore, we are not always quite sure on which side Hemingway is betting. We are sometimes afflicted by the suspicion that what we are witnessing is a set-up, with the manager backing the barbarian. Yet, to speak of Hemingway in these terms is really to misrepresent him. He is not a moralist staging a melodrama, but an artist presenting a situation of which the moral values are complex. Hemingway thoroughly enjoys bull-fighting as he enjoys skiing, racing and prize-fights; and he is unremittingly conscious of the fact that, from the point of view of life as a sport, all that seems to him most painful is somehow closely bound up with what seems to him most enjoyable. The peculiar conflicts of feeling which arise in a temperament of this kind, are the subject of his fiction. His most remarkable effects, effects unlike anything else one remembers, are those, as in the fishing trip in 'The Sun Also Rises,' where we are made to feel, behind the appetite for the physical world, the falsity or the tragedy of a moral situation. The inescapable consciousness of this discord does not arouse Hemingway to passionate violence; but it poisons him and makes him sick, and thus invests with a singular sinister quality - a quality perhaps new in fiction - the sunlight and the green summer landscapes of 'The Sun Also Rises.' Thus, if Hemingway is oppressive, as Mr. Dodd complains, it is because he himself is oppressed. And we may find in him -

in the clairvoyant's crystal of that incomparable art - an image of the common oppression.

Notes

1 Dodd, 'Saturday Review of Literature,' 4 (19 November 1927), 322-3, and Krutch, 'Nation,' 125 (16 November 1927), 548.
2 An Alpine Idyll, 'American Caravan,' ed. Van Wyck Brooks (New York, 1927).
3 The stories take place in the Midwest.
4 Byron, Sonnet on Chillon (1816), and Shelley, A Dirge (1824).
5 The Dumpling, a famous story of a prostitute (1880).
6 French novelist, author of 'Under Fire' (1916).

20. H.L. MENCKEN, 'AMERICAN MERCURY'

14 (May 1928), 127

H.L. Mencken (1880-1956) was an American critic and editor, and author of 'Prejudices' (1919-27) and 'The American Language' (1919).

Mr. Hemingway and Mr. Wilder have made huge successes of late, and received a great deal of uncritical homage. I believe that both are too sagacious to let it fool them. It is technical virtuosity that has won them attention; it is hard and fundamental thinking that must get them on, if they are to make good their high promise. I gather from both of them the feeling that they are yet somewhat uncertain about their characters - that after their most surprising bravura passages they remain in some doubt as to what it is all about. As a result, their work often seems fragmentary: it charms without leaving any very deep impression. But that is a defect that the years ought to cure. Meanwhile, Mr. Hemingway's Fifty Grand, first printed in the 'Atlantic,' and The Killers, first printed in 'Scribner's' and Mr. Wilder's The Marquesa de Montemayor and Uncle Pio are things to be sincerely thankful for. They may not be masterpieces, but masterpieces might surely be written in their manner.

21. MARIO PRAZ, 'LA STAMPA'

14 June 1929, 3

Mario Praz (b. 1896) is Emeritus Professor of English at the University of Rome and the author of 'The Romantic Agony' (1930) and 'Mnemosyne' (1970).

The article was reprinted as: Hemingway in Italy, in 'Hemingway and His Critics,' ed. Carlos Baker (New York, 1961), 116-18. It has been translated by Mario Praz. 'La Stampa' is a daily newspaper published in Turin.

Our present period seems to mark the triumph of narrative art. I do not only speak of France and England, where the traditions of the novel and the short story can be traced back to a distant date, but even Italy teems with skillful storytellers. Nowadays, nearly everybody in Italy seems to know how to write a plausible story. It is the gold reserve of narrative genius accumulated during the last century which allows so much paper currency in our time. Because, after all, we live on the crumbs of the banquet of the great French, Russian, and English novelists of the nineteenth century; and today's stories are well contrived, and convincing, because their authors have learned a lesson either from Chekhov, or from Henry James, or from Proust. It is not even strictly necessary that young authors should take the trouble of reading the classics of the novel: their lesson is in the air. The short story has reached its moment of perfection and saturation just as the sonnet had done in the sixteenth century, when sonnets, so to say, got written by themselves, so saturated was the air with Petrarchan (1) strains. And as in the sixteenth century even grammarians knew how to polish off a pretty sonnet, so nowadays even critics know how to write a plausible short story. One wonders what is going to survive out of so much fecundity. The case of the sixteenth-century sonneteers, all perfect and interchangeable - seldom if ever read by posterity - is a warning.

Now Ernest Hemingway has a new accent in this multitude of story-tellers; it would be next to impossible to find in him an echo of the current recipes. Maybe because he is an American, and America may be considered relatively virgin soil, so far as literary traditions are concerned. If you have to think of somebody else, you may think of Defoe, who in 'Moll Flanders' causes his heroine to talk in a sublimated version of the style of a maidservant's letter. Nothing, at first, seems simpler than Hemingway's technique: he confines himself to repeating speeches almost dryly, to describing the scene with the barest particulars. His style adheres to the outlines of things with an almost impersonal firmness. If one can talk of an objective style, it is his. There is nothing in him of that cerebral tendency which cannot do away with certain standards and categories, and no sooner contemplates an object than it deforms and judges it, so as to give an artificial, rhetorical, vision of the world.... It would be difficult to imagine a more elementary style than Hemingway's: the greatest possible economy of means, as in a natural process. He wraps things round by a repeated verbal contact; he seems to possess the spontaneous wisdom of the dowser, who divines the presence of underground water. Hemingway relates half a sentence, sketches the expression of a face, a twitching of the lips, a nothing; but this nothing throws light on a whole situation: a maximum of evocation with a minimum display of means. One may object that this can be said of the art of every great storyteller; but the novelty consists in this, that the austere fitness which in a European is, as a rule, the result of a laborious process of simplification, seems to exist naturally in this American. He cannot help adhering to the things he describes, so much so that a sophisticated reader may find his way of approach monotonous in the long run. Any subject is good for Hemingway: a fishing party, a conversation overheard in a military hospital or in a sleeping car or in a bar, a boxing match, a bullfight. He has a definite propensity for subjects of this latter description, since he seems sometimes to identify 'life' with the display of violence and brutality, so that blows and blood appear occasionally to be regarded as high human values. But Hemingway has not read Pirandello, so that his boxers are not suffering from metaphysical languors. And he knows next to nothing about the history of religions, so that his *matadores* in the act of stabbing the bull between its horns are not reminded, like Montherlant's, of Mithra's sacrifice.(2) One is indeed at a loss to imagine what his readings may have been. Hemingway's point of view has so little in common with the esthete's that occasionally it may even appear strictly utilitarian. He singles out details of a practical character with the humdrum precision of the man in the street.

Notes

1 Francesco Petrarca (1304-74), Italian poet.
2 Henri de Montherlant, French novelist, author of 'Les Bestiaires' (1925). The ancient Mithraic cult worshipped the bull.

'A Farewell to Arms' (1929)

22. T.S. MATTHEWS, 'NEW REPUBLIC'

60 (9 October 1929), 208-10

T.S. Matthews (b. 1901), American editor of 'Time' magazine, was the author of 'Great Tom' (1974) and 'Under the Influence' (1977).

The writings of Ernest Hemingway have very quickly put him in a prominent place among American writers, and his numerous admirers have looked forward with impatience and great expectations to his second novel. They should not be disappointed: 'A Farewell to Arms' is worthy of their hopes and of its author's promise.

The book is cast in the form which Hemingway has apparently delimited for himself in the novel - diary form. It is written in the first person, in that bare and unliterary style (unliterary except for echoes of Sherwood Anderson and Gertrude Stein), in that tone which suggests a roughly educated but sensitive poet who is prouder of his muscles than of his vocabulary, which we are now accustomed to associate with Hemingway's name. The conversation of the characters is as distinctly Hemingway conversation as the conversation in one of Shaw's plays is Shavian. But there are some marked differences between 'A Farewell to Arms' and Hemingway's previous work.

For one thing, the design is more apparent, the material more solidly arranged. Perhaps the strongest criticism that could be levelled against 'The Sun Also

Rises' was that its action was concerned with flotsam in the eddy of a backwater. It was apparently possible for some readers to appreciate the masculinity of Hemingway's 'anti-literary' style, to admit the authenticity of his characters, and still to say, 'What of it?' This criticism I do not consider valid - there has always been, it seems to me, in the implications of Hemingway's prose, and in his characters themselves, a kind of symbolic content that gives the least of his stories a wider range than it seems to cover - but such a criticism was certainly possible. It is not, however, a criticism that can possibly be directed against 'A Farewell to Arms.' Fishing, drinking, and watching bullfights might be considered too superficial to be the stuff of tragedy, but love and death are not parochial themes.

The story begins in the summer of one of the middle years of the War. The hero is an American, Frederic Henry, in the Italian army on the Isonzo, in charge of a section of ambulances. It is before America has declared war, and he is the only American in Gorizia. But an English hospital unit has been sent down: he meets one of the nurses, Catherine Barkley, and falls in love with her. In the Italian offensive, he is wounded, and taken back to the base hospital in Milan where she too manages to be transferred. He is ordered to the front again just in time to be caught in the Caporetto retreat. In the mad scramble across the plains he loses the main column, is almost cut off by the Germans, and then almost shot by the Italians for not being with his section. He escapes, makes up his mind to desert from the army, and gets to Milan, where he eventually finds Catherine again. He is in mufti, the police are suspicious, and with the connivance of a friendly barman they row across the border into Switzerland. Their passports are in order, so they escape being interned. Catherine is going to have a baby. They spend the winter in a little cottage in the mountains, and in the spring go down to Lausanne, where the baby is to be born. Everything goes well for a time; then the doctor advises a Caesarean operation; the baby is born dead, and Catherine has an unexpected hemorrhage and dies. Here the story ends. Or not quite here. Hemingway's characteristic last sentence is: 'After a while I went out and left the hospital and walked back to the hotel in the rain.'

The book has more in it than 'The Sun Also Rises'; it is more of a story; and it is more carefully written. Sometimes this care is too evident.

I had gone to no such place but to the smoke of cafés

> and nights when the room whirled and you needed to look at the wall to make it stop, nights in bed, drunk, when you knew that that was all there was, and the strange excitement of waking and not knowing who it was with you, and the world all unreal in the dark and so exciting that you must resume again unknowing and not caring in the night, sure that this was all and all and all and not caring. Suddenly to care very much and to sleep to wake with it sometimes morning and all that had been there gone and everything sharp and hard and clear and sometimes a dispute about the cost.

This is a good description, but it is Hemingway gone temporarily Gertrude Stein. There is one other striking example of this manner, not new to Hemingway, but new to his serious vein:

> 'I love your beard,' Catherine said. 'It's a great success. It looks so stiff and fierce and it's very soft and a great pleasure.'

This speech of Catherine's occurs toward the end of the book. When she is first introduced, she talks, plausibly enough, in a manner which, though distinctly Hemingway, might also pass as British. In the last half of the book, (except for the Gertrude Stein lapse quoted above), she is pure Hemingway. The change that comes over her, the change that comes over both the main characters, is not, I think, due to the author's carelessness. Whether he deliberately planned this metamorphosis or half-consciously allowed it to take place is of minor interest. The interesting and the significant thing is the nature of the change. A typical Hemingway hero and a not-quite-so-typical Hemingway heroine are transformed, long before the end, into the figures of two ideal lovers.

Hemingway has been generally regarded as one of the most representative spokesmen of a lost generation - a generation remarkable chiefly for its cynicism, its godlessness, and its complete lack of faith. He can still, I think, be regarded as a representative spokesman, but the strictures generally implied against his generation will soon, perhaps, have to be modified or further refined. As far as Hemingway himself is concerned, it can certainly no longer be said that his characters do not embody a very definite faith.

> 'They won't get us,' I said. 'Because you're too brave. Nothing ever happens to the brave.'

Rinaldi, the Italian surgeon who is the hero's room-mate in the first part of the book, has what almost amounts to a breakdown because he can discover nothing in life outside his three anodynes of women, wine and work. The note of hopelessness that dominated the whole of 'The Sun Also Rises' is not absent in 'A Farewell to Arms,' nor is it weaker, but it has been subtly modified, so that it is not the note of hopelessness we hear so much as the undertone of courage. Hemingway is now definitely on the side of the angels, fallen angels though they are. The principal instrument of this change is Catherine. Brett, the heroine of 'The Sun Also Rises,' was really in a constant fever of despair; the selfless faith which Catherine gives her lover may seem to come from a knowledge very like despair, but it is not a fever. When we look back on the two women, it is much easier to believe in Brett's actual existence than in Catherine's - Brett was so imperfect, so unsatisfactory. And, like an old soldier, it would have been wrong for Brett to die. The Lady in the Green Hat died, but Brett must live. But Catherine is Brett - an ennobled, a purified Brett, who can show us how to live, who must die before she forgets how to show us - deified into the brave and lovely creature whom men, if they have never found her, will always invent.

This apotheosis of bravery in the person of a woman is the more striking because Hemingway is still the same apparently blunt-minded writer of two-fisted words. He still has a horror of expressing delicate or noble sentiments, except obliquely.

> I did not say anything. I was always embarrassed by the words sacred, glorious, and sacrifice and the expression in vain. We had heard them ... and had read them, on proclamations that were slapped up by billposters over other proclamations, now for a long time, and I had seen nothing sacred, and the things that were glorious had no glory and the sacrifices were like the stockyards at Chicago if nothing was done with the meat except to bury it. There were many words that you could not stand to hear and finally only the names of places had dignity.

And his prophecy of individual fate is, if anything, more brutally pessimistic than ever:

> The world breaks every one and afterward many are strong at the broken places. But those that will not break it kills. It kills the very good and the very gentle and the very brave impartially. If you are

> none of these you can be sure it will kill you too but there will be no special hurry.

He will not even call Catherine brave, except through the lips of her lover. Here he is describing how she acted in the first stages of labor:

> The pains came quite regularly, then slackened off. Catherine was very excited. When the pains were bad she called them good ones. When they started to fall off she was disappointed and ashamed.

Hemingway is not a realist. The billboards of the world, even as he writes about them, fade into something else: in place of the world to which we are accustomed, we see a land and a people of strong outlines, of conventionalized shadow; the people speak in a clipped and tacit language as stylized as their appearance. But Hemingway's report of reality is quite as valid as a realist's. The description of the War, in the first part of 'A Farewell to Arms,' is perhaps as good a description of war just behind the front as has been written; and a fresh report from a point of view as original as Hemingway's is an addition to experience. But this book is not essentially a war-story: it is a love-story. If love-stories mean nothing to you, gentle or hard-boiled reader, this is not your book.

The transition, indeed, from the comparative realism of the war scenes to the ideal reality of the idyll is not as effective as it might be. The meeting of the lovers after Henry's desertion from the army, and their escape into Switzerland, have not that ring of authenticity about them which from Hemingway we demand. We are accustomed to his apparent irrelevancies, which he knows how to use with such a strong and ironic effect, but the scene, for instance, between the lovers and Ferguson in the hotel at Stresa seems altogether too irrelevant, and has no ironic or dramatic value, but is merely an unwanted complication of the story. From this point until the time when the lovers are safely established in Switzerland, we feel a kind of uncertainty about everything that happens; we cannot quite believe in it. Why is it, then, that when our belief is reawakened, it grows with every page, until once more we are convinced, and passionately convinced, that we are hearing the truth?

I think it is because Hemingway, like every writer who has discovered in himself the secret of literature, has now invented the kind of ideal against which no man's heart is proof. In the conclusion of 'A Farewell to Arms,' he has transferred his action to a stage very far from realism, and to a plane which may be criticized as the dramatics of a sentimental dream. And it is a dream. Catherine Barkley is one of the impossibly beautiful characters of modern tragedy - the Tesses, the Alyoshas, the Myshkins (1) - who could never have existed, who could not live even in our minds if it were not for our hearts. In that sentimentalism, that intimation of impossible immortality, poets and those who hear them are alike guilty.

Hemingway himself is doubtless a very different sort of man from the people pictured in his books: he may well have very different ideas about the real nature of life; but as long as books remain a communication between us, we must take them as we understand them and feel them to be. 'Nothing ever happens to the brave.' It is an ambiguous statement of belief, and its implications are sufficiently sinister, but its meaning is as clear and as simple as the faith it voices. It is a man's faith; and men have lived and died by much worse.

Note

1 The protagonists of Hardy's 'Tess of the D'Urbervilles' (1891), Dostoyevsky's 'The Brothers Karamazov' (1880) and 'The Idiot' (1868).

23. DONALD DAVIDSON, 'NASHVILLE TENNESSEAN'

3 November 1929, 7

Donald Davidson (1893-1968) was an American professor, poet and critic, and was associated with the Southern Fugitive group.

Ernest Hemingway's novel 'A Farewell to Arms' is like a direct and most remarkable answer to the recent wish of Dr. Watson,(1) prophet of behaviorism, that somebody would write a novel containing people who act in a lifelike and scientific manner. That is exactly what Mr. Hemingway does, with such astounding verity as to overwhelm, befuddle and profoundly impress all readers. Mr. Hemingway here is playing scientist, and he is watching people behave. It is a mistake to suppose that people behave morally or immorally, becomingly or unbecomingly. That is not the point at all: they merely behave. There is no good, no ill, no pretty, no ugly - only behavior. Behaviorism argues that there is stimulus and response, nothing else, and Mr. Hemingway's books contain (ostensibly, but not quite) nothing else. The novel is a bold and exceptionally brilliant attempt to apply scientific method to art, and I devoutly hope that all the scientists will read it and admire it intensely.

This comment on a book that is apparently taking the public by storm requires further demonstration, which I shall attempt to give.

Look first at the people of the book, who happen to be people, not cockroaches or mice, acting and reacting in wartime Italy rather than in a laboratory. But they are only people, not highly differentiated individuals. That is to say they are, in a manner of speaking, laboratory specimens. In the interest of the scientific 'experiment' or observation, they must be as normal and average as possible, and so they are. It is regrettable, perhaps, that they are nice healthy creatures, not without animal charm (even if without souls), but we must presume that their occasional sufferings are in the interest of some scientific investigation which will eventually declare the 'whole truth' about something, possibly war and love.

Thus we have first a Male with no characteristics other than might be noted in a description like this: Henry, Frederic; American; commissioned in Italian ambulance corps; speaks Italian (with accent); reactions, normally human. And then of course a Female: Barkley, Catherine; nurse; English; normally attractive and equipped with normal feminine reactions. The subordinate characters, too, are just as colorless: Rinaldi, Italian officer, inclined to be amorous; a priest, unnamed; other officers, soldiers, police, nurses, surgeons, bawdyhouse keepers and inmates, restaurant keepers, Swiss officials, family folk. All of these, notice, talk alike and all do nothing but behave, offering given responses to given stimuli.

Then we must have a situation. It is simply this. Put the Male and Female under the disorderly and rather uninviting conditions of war, including battle, wounds, hospitalization, return to the front, retreat and bring the Male and Female into propinquity now and then. What will happen?

I am tempted to describe what does happen - it is all, of course, 'natural' - in such a catechism as James Joyce uses in one part of 'Ulysses.'(2) It would run something like this:

Question: What do soldiers do in war?

Answer: They fight, drink, eat, sleep, talk, obey commands, march, go on leave, visit brothels, are tired or sick or dead or alive, wonder when the next battle will be, sometimes meet respectable women, sometimes fall in love hastily.

Question: Was the same true in the case of Henry, Frederic?

Answer: It was invariably true.

Question: What do nurses do in a war?

Answer: They eat, sleep, drink, talk, obey commands, tend the wounded, are tired or sick or dead or alive, wonder when the next battle will be, sometimes meet attractive officers, sometimes fall in love hastily.

Question: Was the same true in the case of Barkley, Catherine?

Answer: It was invariably true.

Question: What not very special circumstances modified the case of Henry, Frederic?

Answer: He was wounded in the leg, and was thus entitled to prosecute a love affair with Barkley, Catherine.

Question: What wholly natural thing did Henry, Frederic do during the Caporetto retreat?

Answer: He retreated, was arrested, saw police shooting fugitives, jumped in the river, escaped, joined Catherine, quit the war, went to Switzerland.

Question: What not unnatural consequences to Barkley, Catherine, attended her love affair with Henry, Frederic?

Answer: Ineffective labor in childbirth, Caesarean operation, death.

Question: And what were the results for Henry, Frederic?

Answer: Results unknown. He merely walked back in the rain.

The application of the scientific method may be further demonstrated by a scrutiny of other features of the novel. A scientific report of events requires that there be no comment, no intrusion of private sentiments, no depreciation or apology. The 'bare facts' must be given - or tabulated.

Therefore style (as style is generally known) is wiped out, or is reduced to its lowest, most natural, terms. It will take the form of simple, unelaborated predications, not unlike the sentences in a First Reader. For instance: The dog is black. The sky is blue. Catherine is pretty. I did not love Catherine at first but now I love Catherine. I drank the wine and it did not make me feel good. She was unconscious all the time and it did not take her very long to die.

And that, as I see it, is the gist of Mr. Hemingway's hypothetical case, which by the unthinking may be called an indictment of war or of civilization or an apology for free love or what you will. But its method does not justify any of these interpretations, however latently they may exist.

What of it, then? On the surface it is assuredly a most remarkable performance. To those who take pleasure in contemplating a world of mechanisms doing nothing but acting and reacting, it must be a nearly perfect book. Let us leave them with their admirations, which are no doubt justifiable under the circumstances.

But what of those who, without knowing exactly why, have an uneasy sense of dissatisfaction with Mr. Hemingway's book and ask for something more than a remarkably natural series of conversations, daydreams, and incidents? Mr. Hemingway's book will have plenty of defenders to fly up and condemn those who are dissatisfied. I want to supply a little ammunition to the dissatisfied, out of pure sympathy for the underdog if for no other reason.

First of all, don't complain about vulgarity or obscenity. There you lose the battle. For to a scientist, nothing is vulgar or obscene any more than it is genteel or pretty. And Mr. Hemingway apparently is trying to be a scientist. Attack him instead at the point where a fundamental contradiction exists. Can there be such a thing as a scientific work of art? The nature of the contradiction can be immediately seen. Mr. Hemingway could treat human affairs scientifically only in a scientific medium. That is, he would have to invent equations, symbols, vocabularies, hypotheses, laws, as scientists are in the habit of doing. By so doing he would achieve all the 'reality' that science is capable of achieving - which might perhaps be of practical use, but could not be vended as a novel, even by so respectable a house as Charles Scribner's Sons.

Obviously Mr. Hemingway did not, could not, go to such a logical limit. He was forced to compromise by using the vocabulary and the forms of art. The minute he made the compromise, he failed fundamentally and outrageously. His novel is a splendid imitation, but only an imitation, of science. It is a hybrid beast, ill-begotten and sterile. It is a stunt, a tour de force, and no matter how blindingly brilliant, no matter how subtle in artifice, it is in in effect a complete deception (possibly a self-deception) and can exist only as a kind of marvelous monstrosity.

Note that he falls short even of science. Committed to the form of the novel, he must be selective where science is inclusive. He cannot destroy his own personality and bias, for from his book we get the distinct impression that he wishes us to believe war is unheroic, life is all too frequently a dirty trick, and love may be a very deadly joke on the woman. Even in his effort to get away from style he creates a new style that is in effect a reaction against all decorative imagistic prose.

'A Farewell to Arms,' which is apparently intended to give us a perfect example of pure behavior, turns out after all to be only the behavior of Mr. Hemingway, stupendously overreaching himself in the effort to combine the role of artist and scientist and producing something exactly as marvelous and as convincing as a tragic sculpture done in butter.

Notes

1 John Watson was Professor of Psychology at Johns Hopkins University and author of 'Behaviorism' (1925). Behaviorism is a concept of psychology in which the organism is seen as responding to stimuli set by the outer environment and inner biological processes.
2 Joyce uses this method in the Ithaca section of the novel.

24. ARNOLD BENNETT, 'EVENING STANDARD'

14 November 1929, 5

Arnold Bennett (1867-1931) was an English novelist, the author of 'The Old Wives' Tale' (1908) and 'Clayhanger' (1910).

Ernest Hemingway is a youngish American, whose work, in short stories, to which I have referred once or twice in this column, began to impress me first about a couple of years ago.

'A Farewell to Arms' deals with the Italian front. Gorizia, Udine, Piave, Milan, are some of the place-names that occur prominently in it. Its detail is as marvellous as any yet given. The description of the wounding of the hero in a bombardment is as tremendously effective as anything current. In fact, I seriously question whether this description has been equalled. Its dialogue, possibly over-plenteous here and there, is masterly in reproductive realism. Short sentences, page after page, admirably marshalled and grouped. Its detachment is perfect. No flush and no fever in this novel; but the sane calmness of a spectator who combines deep sympathy with breadth and impartiality of vision.

The book is hard, almost metallic, glittering, blinding by the reflections of its bright surface, utterly free of any sentimentality. But imbued through and through with genuine sentiment. A strange and original book. Whatever it may not do to you, it will convince you of its honesty and veracity. You will never be able to say as you read: 'This isn't true. This is exaggerated. This is forced.'

The weakness of the novel, if it has one, springs from the author being in two minds about his purpose in writing it. He seems to be to be undecided whether he is writing a description of the war as his hero saw it, or the love-story of his hero. The heroine is a nurse, or a sort of nurse; a heroical character. The love-story is quite as fine as the war-story, but a divided aim is bound to have some deleterious influence. In 'A Farewell to Arms,' either the military background should have been less, or there should have been more of the sexual passion, or the two should have been more cunningly intermingled. (I could not suggest how.) Alternate layers of war and of love are scarcely satisfactory.

Withal, the book is a superb performance. I have specified a striking scene of battle. But the escape of hero and heroine into Switzerland is equally striking. And the birth of the baby in a Swiss hospital is even more striking. I have read nothing in that line so graphic, so beautiful, so harrowing. It need not fear comparison with the coming into the world of Anna Karenina's child.

The author, while often tactful in his omissions, permits himself a freedom of expression hitherto unexampled in Anglo-Saxon fiction printed for general sale. Some readers will object to it. I don't.

25. JOHN DOS PASSOS, 'NEW MASSES'

5 (1 December 1929), 16

John Dos Passos (1896-1970), American novelist, was author of 'Three Soldiers' (1922) and 'USA' (1930-36). He was Hemingway's friend in the 1920s.

Hemingway's 'A Farewell to Arms' is the best written book that has seen the light in America for many a long day. By well-written I don't mean the tasty college composition course sort of thing that our critics seem to consider good writing. I mean writing that is terse and economical, in which each sentence and each phrase bears the maximum load of meaning, sense impressions, emotions. The book is a firstrate piece of craftsmanship by a man who knows his job. It gives you the sort of pleasure line by line that you get from handling a piece of wellfinished carpenter's work. Read the first chapter, the talk at the officer's mess in Gorizia, the scene in the dressingstation when the narrator is wounded, the paragraph describing the ride to Milan in the hospital train, the talk with the British major about how everybody's cooked in the war, the whole description of the disaster at Caporetto to the end of the chapter where the battlepolice are shooting the officers as they cross the bridge, the caesarian operation in which the girl dies. The stuff will match up as narrative prose with anything that's been written since there was any English language.

It's a darn good document too. It describes with reserve and exactness the complex of events back of the Italian front in the winter of 1916 and the summer and fall of 1917 when people had more or less settled down to the thought of war as the natural form of human existence, when every individual in the armies was struggling for survival with bitter hopelessness. In the absolute degradation of the average soldier's life in the Italian army there were two hopes, that the revolution would end the war or that Meester Weelson would end the war on the terms of the Seventeen Points.(1) In Italy the revolution lost its nerve at the moment of its victory and Meester Weelson's points paved the way for D'Annunzio's bloody farce at Fiume (2) and the tyranny of Mussolini and the banks. If a man wanted to learn the history of that period in that sector of the European War I don't know where he'd find a better account than in the first half of 'A Farewell to Arms.'

This is a big time for the book business in America. The writing, publishing and marketing of books is getting to be a major industry along with the beauty shoppes and advertising. Ten years ago it was generally thought that all writers were either drunks or fairies. Now they have a halo of possible money around them and are respected on a par with brokers or realtors. The American people seem to be genuinely hungry for books. Even good books sell.

It's not surprising that 'A Farewell to Arms,' that accidentally combines the selling points of having a love-story and being about the war, should be going like hot-cakes. It would be difficult to dope out just why there should be such a tremendous vogue for books about the war just now. Maybe it's that the boys and girls who were too young to know anything about the last war are just reaching the book-buying age. Maybe it's the result of the intense military propaganda going on in schools and colleges. Any how if they read things like 'A Farewell to Arms' and 'All Quiet on the Western Front,' they are certainly getting the dope straight and it's hard to see how the militarist could profit much. Certainly a writer can't help but feel good about the success of such an honest and competent piece of work as 'A Farewell to Arms.'

After all craftsmanship is a damn fine thing, one of the few human functions a man can unstintedly admire. The drift of the Fordized world seems all against it. Rationalization and subdivision of labor in industry tend more and more to wipe it out. It's getting to be almost unthinkable that you should take pleasure in your work, that a man should enjoy doing a piece of work for the sake of doing it as well as he damn well can. What we still have is the mechanic's or motorman's pleasure in a smooth-running machine. As the operator gets more mechanized even that disappears; what you get is a division of life into drudgery and leisure instead of into work and play. As industrial society evolves and the workers get control of the machines a new type of craftsmanship may work out. For the present you only get opportunity for craftsmanship, which ought to be the privilege of any workman, in novelwriting and the painting of easelpictures and in a few of the machinebuilding trades that are hangovers from the period of individual manufacture that is just closing. Most of the attempts to salvage craftsmanship in industry have been faddy movements like East Aurora and Morris furniture (3) and have come to nothing. 'A Farewell to Arms' is no worse a novel because it was written with a typewriter. But it's a magnificent novel because the writer felt every minute the satisfaction of working ably with his material and his tools and continually pushing the work to the limits of his effort.

Notes

1 Woodrow Wilson's idealistic plan for the postwar world had Fourteen Points.
2 In 1919 the Italian poet Gabriele D'Annunzio defied the Allied powers, captured the Adriatic town of Fiume and personally ruled it for sixteen months.
3 East Aurora is a town in New York State where, in the early twentieth century, the Roycroft Workshops produced fine handicrafts. William Morris (1834-96) was a poet, artist and influential designer.

26. L.P. HARTLEY, 'SATURDAY REVIEW' (LONDON)

148 (7 December 1929), 684, 686

L.P. Hartley (1895-1973), the English novelist, was author of 'The Go-Between' (1953) and 'The Hireling' (1957).

Mr. Hemingway is a novelist of the expatriated. 'Fiesta' showed us a group of Americans and one Englishwoman being violently idle, first in Paris and then in Spain. They went to bull-fights, they made love, they drank. Above all, they drank. They were not congenial company even in a book, but they knew how to get the utmost out of their emotions, and though bored and desperate, they were seldom dull.

The same characters, or others like them, reappear in 'A Farewell to Arms.' There is an English woman serving as a nurse in the Italian Red Cross, there is an American who has joined the Italian army for no better reason than that he speaks the language. There is the Continental scene as envisaged by a thirsty Anglo-Saxon: cafés, vermouths, drinks - unlimited drinks. There is the same dialogue between the lovers, the American soon cuts out Catherine's Italian admirer - trivial, pregnant, witty, yet coming from the heart and charged with a plangent emotion.

'A Farewell to Arms' contains most of the ingredients of its predecessor, but it has others as well, and it is a much better book. The Italian officers, with whom the hero was on intimate terms (Mr. Hemingway has a gift for portraying friendship as well as love), are excellently drawn and the war passages are vivid and exciting. No doubt the war in Italy is easier to describe than the war on the Western Front: there was more movement, hope ran higher, disappointment was more acute; the emotions aroused were more comparable to those of everyday life. And, as chronicler of the war in Italy, Mr. Hemingway has the field almost to himself: the novelist writing of the Western theatre must first disentangle his impressions from those of scores of others before he can be certain that he is drawing on his own experience. Warfare in the Italian campaign was still warfare in the old style, stimulating not stultifying, to the imagination; at least so it seems, from the American 'tenente's' partial glimpses of it.

But he was glad to escape with his mistress to a neutral country: all for love and the war well lost. Mr. Hemingway comes as near as a novelist can to making unmixed, lyrical love his central theme. Other people's happiness is difficult to enjoy, in life or in fiction; we experience, even before Fate does, a kind of envy at the spectacle of so much bliss, and long to prove the unworthiness of its possessors. Certainly, this particular unmarried couple, rejoicing in their sin, present a broad target to the censorious; and even to a less jaundiced view, there is something wanton and wasteful in their happiness. But, if it is an offence to be happy, they certainly pay for it a thousandfold; the concluding scenes are unbearably painful, and would wring tears from a stone. The hypercritical may question whether Henry would have been granted such freedom of access to Catherine's accouchement; but he was headstrong and hard to cross and had no respect for circumstances:

> If people bring so much courage to this world the world has to kill them to break them, so of course it kills them. The world breaks everyone and afterward many are strong at the broken places. But those that will not break it kills. It kills the very good and the very gentle and the very brave impartially. If you are none of these you can be sure it will kill you too, but there will be no special hurry.

Closing the book, the reader will agree that the narrator had every reason for espousing this gloomy view.

27. J.B. PRIESTLEY, 'NOW AND THEN'

34 (Winter 1929), 11-12

J.B. Priestley (b. 1894), an English novelist, is the author of 'The Good Companions' (1929) and 'Angel Pavement' (1930). 'Now and Then' was a literary magazine published by Jonathan Cape Ltd to stimulate interest in their books. It reprinted Priestley's essay, which was originally written for an English book club.

Ernest Hemingway's 'A Farewell to Arms' is one of the very best novels that have passed through the hands of the Book Society Committee. Why, then, didn't we choose it? Well, I think anybody who reads our first choice, 'Whiteoaks,'(1) and then this novel will understand why. 'Whiteoaks,' an equally good piece of writing, is one of those novels that all sensible readers can enjoy. 'A Farewell to Arms,' far rougher and more outspoken, a brutally masculine performance, is not everybody's book. I am sorry about this, but, at the same time, I am not going to make the fashionable mistake of supposing that this limitation necessarily makes Mr. Hemingway more important than he already is. Literature is not a matter of pleasing Aunt Susan. But we must also remember that it is equally not a matter of simply shocking Aunt Susan.

For some time now, good critics have regarded Mr. Hemingway as one of the most important of the younger American writers of fiction. He is in his thirties, was born in the Middle West, but has lived in Europe, chiefly in Paris, for several years, and most of his work is not about America at all, but has a European background. (And I believe that work will be even better than it is now when he goes home again to interpret the life of his own people. This is the customary thing to tell these American artists who have exiled themselves, but then, like a good many customary things, it happens to be true.) Mr. Hemingway is really very American; though he may be writing about boulevards and bullfights, he could not possibly be mistaken for an English writer. He has a curious manner and idiom which are based on characteristic American speech. He tells his tales in a succession of short, direct sentences, piling up the facts, and avoiding all obvious 'literary' airs and graces. You feel as if he were riddling his subjects with a machine-gun. But through the medium of this bluff, masculine, 'hard-boiled,' apparently insensitive style, he contrives to give you a very vivid and sometimes poignant picture of the life he knows.

He has done this superbly in 'A Farewell to Arms,' which is the story of a young American who does ambulance work on the Italian Front during the War. This tough young man falls in love with an English girl who is nursing out there. He is wounded, returns to the Front only to participate in the famous and horrible retreat of 1917, finally escapes from Italy with his girl, only to see her die, after the birth of their child, in Switzerland. It may be objected that the figures of mortality after childbirth are already far too high in fiction, but I think even the objectors will admit the terrible poignancy and force of Mr. Hemingway's concluding scene.

Even better though, and quite new to us, are the Italian Front scenes, especially those during the retreat, which are horribly alive. And then, dominating the whole grim chronicle, is the queer, almost inarticulate love story of the two unfortunates, who, like so many chief characters is modern fiction, seem to be curiously lonely, without backgrounds, unsustained by any beliefs of any kind, hardly looking on further than the next cocktail, at heart puzzled and melancholy barbarians. Mr. Hemingway, setting every possible obstacle in his way, yet achieves a beautiful tenderness and pathos in this love story, heightened no doubt by the cunning suggestion throughout of inarticulacy. A Hemingway character, suddenly finding himself rapturously in love, cannot do neat rhetorical things with moons and stars and flames and flowers; he can only mutter: 'Aw, what the hell!'; but the emotion comes through all right, perhaps with all the more force because there is no suspicion of deft literary juggling in the scene.

I implore every member of this society who has a good head and a stout heart to acquire at least this one additional novel this month. I believe it will not be long before readers will be able to boast of the fact that they bought a first edition of 'A Farewell to Arms.'

Note

1 A family chronicle novel (1929) by the Canadian writer Mazo de la Roche.

28. LEWIS GALANTIÈRE, 'HOUND AND HORN'

3 (January 1930), 259-62

Lewis Galantière (1893-1977) was the American translator of Anouilh, the Goncourts, Jules Romains and Saint-Exupéry. He was a friend of Hemingway in Paris and helped to introduce his books when they first appeared in the early 1920s. 'Hound and Horn' was a little magazine, edited by the poet and critic R.P. Blackmur, which published the best avant-garde authors and established the reputations of many important modern writers.

Hemingway's strongest and most moving writing is still in 'Men Without Women.' In those short stories of gunmen, prizefighters, drug addicts, and bullfighters, he was entirely without self-consciousness, unevasively absorbed by the creation of figures in which he found something to admire and much to pity. He projected them confidently out of himself, and these creatures of his imagination stood like models while he drew them firmly, surely, carefully, divining and surprising their most secret changes of countenance and most characteristic movements. The present novel, although in matters relating to 'mere' writing and the organization of materials it marks an advance upon the author's earlier work, is fundamentally retrograde: it represents a return to his uneasy concern with himself. While the novel was being published serially in 'Scribner's,' there was repeated protest in the chit-chat department at the back of that magazine to the effect that this was emphatically not an autobiographical novel. This protest (accompanied - so vulgar is the practice of our publishers -- by references to Hemingway's Italian war cross and photographs of the author in skiing costume), this protest despite, the novel gives off an odour of autobiography.

Every fictional composition is of course a compound of experience. But the motive of experience and the motive of art are not the same: we endure experience for ourselves, whereas we re-create it for others, for an imagined and ideally comprehending reader. An experience, and the emotion which accompanies it, are unimportant except to him who is experiencing, for the reason that they are not being shared; and to be made art, there must be injected into the experience a different, indeed a superior sort of emotion, the emotion of the artist over and above that of the protagonist. It is the artist's emotion (not the protagonist's) that we are able to share, and it is likely that the measure of sincerity and seriousness in art, may very well be merely the depth and the genuineness of the artist's emotion. In certain episodes of 'A Farewell to Arms' the impression is irresistible that the author has endeavoured not to reveal or traduce emotions he has experienced, while yet retaining the episodic *cadre* (1) of experience, and in so doing he has been forced to substitute sensation for emotion. In a superficial formula, instead of detaching Frederic and Catherine from himself - the artist's creative gesture - he has detached himself from them, in the gesture of the observer. Born of a desire to evade the autobiographical, there was in him a curious *will to not-create*. The contrary will produced 'Men Without Women'; it gave us all the figures save that of Jake Barnes in 'The Sun Also Rises': the will manifest in 'A Farewell to Arms' is one which Hemingway cannot be urged too strongly to defeat.

If we examine this will in the light of the data afforded by 'A Farewell to Arms' we find at bottom, I believe, a phenomenon which is at once an ideal and a fear: the ideal is that of our boyhood friend the Redskin; the fear is the fear of displaying emotion. We have had the ideal before, in, for example, novels of the Wild West (I doubt that Homer's heroes refrained from crying out when they were in pain); but I do not know an age before our own in which it could be understood that such an ideal might be accompanied by such a fear. In Hemingway's novel, the Brave is not afraid of war, and the Squaw does not flinch at the thought of birth pangs. The story of their young love in the spring of the year is swiftly told, for most of us reminiscentially stirring, and for the young a simulacrum of Tristan and Iseut.(2) Frederic is a somewhat morose young man, and Catherine is a rather desperately happy young woman. He, the male, is served and adored and complacently spreads his peacock tail before her who serves and adores. Beyond this there is no discernible difference between them: they are wraiths, *deux formes qui ont tout à l'heure passé*.(3) Our knowledge of them is limited to their sensations. There is no need that we be shown conflict *between* them (though one has the impression that a woman would find it hard to live nine or ten months with the Frederic of this novel and not have been pretty well tortured by him); but of conflict *within* them, of their personality, their common humanity, we know nothing. Even in what is presented as their bravery they are the same person, avid of sensation, submissive to the flesh and the world (which is war), grimly gay in their unprotesting acceptance of circumstances, seeking and finding a haven in bed, with a bottle of *fine* (4) or Chianti to stand guard over their exaltation. This return to the primitive, accomplished by Hemingway as skilfully and naturally as Voltaire transported Candide about an impossible world, has as movement, as episode, the merit which Barrès (5) used to call credibility, but the protagonists remain insignificant, a pair of silhouettes. Now and then their dialogue possesses a warm charm, is swept by an all too brief wind of sympathetically heedless youth - and charm and breeze vanish before the reader is able to fix these people in his imagination and love them as young lovers should be loved.

The war story, which fills nearly two-thirds of the book, is very much more successful. Only one engagement is described, for Frederic was an ambulance officer, not an infantryman, and his experience of war was had just behind the lines. Yet that too was war, and the sound and smell of it in the streets in which this American volunteer and his men were billeted, over the hills and on the highways that led to the line of battle, are admirably rendered. Fine as they are, and of thrilling actuality as is the magnificent account of the retreat of the Italian horde from Caporetto, one retains a stronger sense of the characters who people the scene than of the war itself. It is these secondary characters of the novel who are the most vivid. The author knew about Catherine only that she was inexplicably in love with Frederic; she was Frederic's creature, not his, and what Frederic knew about her nobody will ever know. But the men at the front are Hemingway's creatures: he imagined them, knew them, gave them personality and life. It is not simply that Rinaldi is intended to be liked, the priest to be stupid and yet too helpless to draw one's rudeness, Passini and Manera to be socialists, Aymo and Piani and Bondello to be sterling comrades-in-arms. The intention in these and other minor figures is fulfilled; they are what they are purported to be; and moreover it is only when they are on the scene that the novel is lifted above the level of selective autobiography, that Hemingway's creative gift expands and enjoys free play, that his profound feeling for men of simple desires and his sardonic and occasionally subtle humour emerge, and that his work is of a quality commensurate with the unreserved enthusiasm of which he is for the time being the object.

As for the writing, it seems to me the best Hemingway has done. The book is welded together with great care and scrupulous attention to detail. There are surprises in the novel, but only because we do not read attentively enough: the tone of each situation is sounded in advance; the colour of each character is indicated somewhat before he moves completely into view. In the descriptive passages, Hemingway shows for the first time that he can write by ear as well as by eye, so to say. Even the haphazard punctuation is not an obstacle to enjoyment of the fluidity and the rhythmical beauty of many of his periods. He has remembered, besides, all the lessons of his arduous, self-taught apprenticeship. Echoes are here of those steely paragraphs which comprized the first Paris publication of 'In Our Time,' and of much that he has learned since. Now and then there is a line of gibberish, of unfortunate Joyce or bad Stein; his eye for objects and excessive concern with detail lead him into dull cataloguing; his meticulousness about *should* and *would* (which does not prevent his using *whom* in the nominative) lures him into affectation; he sprays the words 'nice' and 'fine' and 'lovely' a bit too monotonously through his pages.

There are two Hemingways: the positive, creative talent skilfully at work in a being who sees and understands the anguish and bravery of men struggling with forces whose purpose they cannot divine; and the negative, fearful writer with the psychological impediments of a child afraid of the dark and conjuring it away with a whistle as hopeless as it is off key. From the first of these we may look for work of great merit.

Notes

1 Frame.
2 A Celtic legend of doomed lovers, a frequently recurring theme in literature and music.
3 Two forms who have just passed.
4 Brandy.
5 Maurice Barrès (1862-1923), French novelist, essayist and politician.

29. H.L. MENCKEN, 'AMERICAN MERCURY'

19 (January 1930), 127

Mr. Hemingway's 'Farewell to Arms' is a study of the disintegration of two youngsters under the impact of war. The man, Frederic Henry, is a young American architect, turned into a lieutenant of the Italian Ambulance; the woman is Catherine Barkley, a Scotch nurse. They meet just after Catherine has lost her fiancé, blown to pieces on the Western front, and fall into each other's arms at once. For six months they dodge about between Milan and the Italian front, carrying on their affair under vast technical difficulties. Henry is badly wounded; the Italians, broken, retreat in a panic; earth and sky are full of blood and flames. Finally a baby is on its way, and the pair escape to Switzerland. There Catherine dies in childbirth, and Henry wanders into space. 'It was like saying good-bye to a statue. After a while I went out and left the hospital and walked back to the hotel in the rain.'

The virtue of the story lies in its brilliant evocation of the horrible squalor and confusion of war - specifically of war *à la Italienne*. The thing has all the blinding color of a Kiralfy spectacle.(1) And the people who move through it, seen flittingly in the glare, are often almost appallingly real. But Henry and Catherine, it seems to me, are always a shade less real than the rest. The more they are accounted for, the less accountable they become. In the end they fade into mere wraiths, and in the last scenes they scarcely seem human at all. Mr. Hemingway's dialogue, as always, is fresh and vivid. Otherwise, his tricks begin to wear thin. The mounting incoherence of a drunken scene is effective once, but not three or four times. And there is surely no need to write such vile English as this: 'The last mile or two of the new road, where it started to level out, *would be able* to be shelled steadily by the Austrians.'

Note

1 Imre Kiralfy (1845-1919), author and organizer of international exhibitions.

30. KLAUS MANN, 'NEUE SCHWEIZER RUNDSCHAU' [NEW SWISS REVIEW]

24 (April 1931), 272-7

Klaus Mann (1906-49) was the son of Thomas Mann, and author of a novel on Tchaikovsky (1935) and a study of Gide (1943). The 'Neue Schweizer Rundschau' was a literary magazine published in Zürich. This article was translated by William M. Calder III and Jeffrey Meyers.

I

The style of every great new writer is a fully incomprehensible, an inexplicable, a disconcerting phenomenon. It is nothing short of a miracle. The world is seen as it was never seen before. It stands in a new light. Thus the world itself becomes new. It is transformed under the creative gaze which perceives it and by perceiving it reforms it. Every great new writer reveals the world anew.

It is always like Columbus and the egg.(1) You say to yourself, after you have grown familiar with the new revelation: 'Of course, that is the way it is; you must tell the tale precisely that way. My God, why haven't we always done it that way?' With Hemingway we feel this particularly strongly. The reason is that his manner is as simple and understandable as it is original. Of course, you think, how else could you describe this mysterious life? This way you grasp its very kernel. This way you banish its sorrow and, with sorrow, its pleasure. Now it is simple, But this extraordinary American had to come to show us how.

He appears to grasp life in its externals. Yet in almost every line he penetrates its hidden center. He usually passes over feelings in silence in order to present the most trivial facts. It often seems to us like a retreat to naturalism, and is really a step further 'In Another Country' (2) where important secrets dwell. He describes how someone orders a whisky and soda, drinks it and pays; how someone requests his hotel bill at the front desk; chats with the bartender about the weather. With a reticence which I have never yet found in any other writer, with such consistency and persistence, he conceals the mystery that lies behind external symbols. The most factual statements lie like trapdoors over depths which plunge God knows where.

In order to put this epic technique, which has a thorough and therefore a sophisticated artlessness, more or less into its literary setting, you might say that it lies somewhere between the impressionism of Herman Bang,(3) saturated as that is with sadness, and the laconic mysticism of Franz Kafka. Only, in contrast to Bang's, Hemingway's melancholy is thoroughly *male*. It is so extreme that occasionally it can almost have the effect of toughness. It is concealed, while that of Bang, with all its purity, is overt. A detailed comparison with Kafka seems inappropriate. Nonetheless, I believe it is justified. Though the two differ fundamentally, they have something decisive in common: the reticent, mysterious veiling of the heart; reserve, economy, withdrawal, which scarcely impinges, where others would blatantly intrude. Of course, there remains decisive in Kafka the element of Jewish piety. It gives to his whole world the mystical dignity of an unapproachable secret kingdom, where everything stands joined in an hierarchic order of worship. An ambiguous, special sense dwells deep in everything.

Hemingway is an Anglo-Saxon, and hence is more relaxed, more worldly. He is no secret priest but remains an American boy, albeit one with knowing eyes. He is not without religion - no intellect of real quality could be so - rather he is primitive in religious matters without feeling for arcane mysteries of worship. In 'A Farewell to Arms' an experienced old nobleman says to the young officer who insists that he is without religion: 'But you love. Don't forget, that is a religious feeling.' Hemingway feels - he is American - the mystery of this world; he does not concern himself with the other. The *mysterium* is itself immanent in the phenomenon of life, and in its most trivial facts too. One has no need to export it to the other world. Because no one knows why, for what purpose, and how long he is here, there remains one fundamental feeling in all living creatures: *anxiety*. This fundamental feeling has daemonic power in Hemingway's books. *The creature fears*, for it does not know whether it will receive a curse or a blessing.

In the midst of a conversation, in the midst of a lovers' chat: anxiety. I recall the love scene in 'A Farewell to Arms'; it is raining, and suddenly the woman is afraid of this pouring rain: an atavistic reaction, primal anxiety. She could just as well fear time, which races by. This element of anxiety, of the most profound terror of life, is after all another bond between Hemingway and Kafka. Behind all the lives devised by Kafka stands inexplicable, deeply veiled, merciless, ice cold and pedantic, like a machine toiling with deadly accuracy - the curse, the law court, that determines every man's activity down to the tiniest detail.

In Hemingway, too, one is always conscious only of a curse a priori, never of being ensnared in guilt. To be alive is to be guilty. *Why* is the man in 'The Sun Also Rises' mutilated? *Why* does the beloved Catherine die? In many passages in 'Men Without Women' this terror before fate is condensed into a horror of the breathtaking sort that is also found only in Edgar Allan Poe. On the other hand, as I have already implied, we ought not to include Hemingway among those writers for whom the horror of life forms and determines everything. His cynicism is a very healthy protection. Life is frightening, but we know nothing more beautiful.

The great attraction which Hemingway exercises upon the most fastidious young Europeans probably lies in his mingling of fresh vitality and mystery. He preserves the powerful feeling of a young American, while his soul seems experienced and at home in other regions, the most remote ones. Mere complexity, abstract mysticism, discourage and exhaust us easily: likewise mere strength. His robust complexity, his vital melancholy fascinate.

That this puzzling, simple life deserves to be loved is a foregone conclusion. Somebody asks: 'Do you value life?' The other: 'Yes.' 'I too because it is all I have.' Whoever loves life in this way, so unconditionally, so uncritically, with such pious cynicism, loves death equally: simply because it, even more than life, is all, all, all that we have.

II

At the moment [1931] there are three books by Hemingway available in German: 'The Sun Also Rises,' 'Men Without Women' and 'A Farewell to Arms.'

'The Sun Also Rises' takes place partly in Paris, partly in Spain. In a small group of bohemian Americans there is a wonderful, eccentric lady, called Brett. There is continual drunkenness in the book, punctuated with expert descriptions of fishing and bullfighting. The whole book has a particular dry briskness; one might say a sportive liveliness. From where does the sorrow which fills the book come?

The man who narrates the story loves the woman called Brett. Because of a wound the man is impotent. Brett loves him; but she cannot be his. So her vitality is a little despairing; her sexual excesses seem forced.

Behind the bits of conversation casually tossed away, lies the grief of a hopeless love. This grief is the secret of the novel 'The Sun Also Rises.'

One could say a great deal about Hemingway's female characters. They have a very special magic. It is a fresh yet melancholy charm, of the sort that only Anglo-Saxon women of good breeding possess. Brett of 'The Sun Also Rises' and Catherine of 'A Farewell to Arms' are of the same family. They are both cheerful, energetic, and heroic, and have an aristocratic and courageous toughness. When everything goes dreadfully wrong, they insist: 'I feel perfectly wonderful, darling.' Brett is more extravagant than Catherine; this comes above all from the milieu in which she lives. Catherine, whom we meet as a nurse, and who wears her uniform while making love, would probably in Montparnasse be as easy-going and as fond of alcohol as Brett; and she would remain just as perfect a lady as Brett does in the most dangerous situations. In order not to do Brett an injustice one ought never to forget that Catherine loves successfully, while she, in the nature of things, has a hopeless love. Death ends Catherine's bliss. Brett must take as a surrogate for happiness the handsome young bullfighter. Naturally that cannot turn out well. Brett is unsatisfied and therefore a bit hysterical. Catherine is satisfied and a bit sentimental. Both have a wonderful neatness: extreme reserve and extreme devotion at the same time.

'Men Without Women' is Hemingway's most concentrated book. It is also his toughest. Women scarcely appear in it. In stories which are often no more than bits of conversations whole lives are captured: the tragedy of the morphine addict, the tragedy of the wounded man who cannot sleep, of the ageing boxer, of the bullfighter. The anecdotal technique often recalls de Maupassant, but everything is at once harder and more profound. One will also think of Bang's 'Exzentrische Novellen,' and not only in regard to the subject matter. Several of Bang's unforgettable circus stories could also be in 'Men Without Women,' if stripped of any sentimentality.

Take one of the shortest pieces, like An Alpine Idyll or A Simple Enquiry. They are masterpieces, so much life is compressed into them. They are distilled life, every word is loaded with fate. The essence tastes bitter but magnificently strong.

Hemingway will never surpass this volume of stories. Even in 'A Farewell to Arms' he did not surpass it. This book that bids farewell to arms is no ordinary war-novel. War is the background for a love-story, a background, of course, whose shadow darkens the idyll and pitilessly determines its progress and its end.

Henry's love for Catherine blooms slowly and expands to great magnificence. Catherine dies; she seems to die with the same meaninglessness with which the young American must flee from the country for which he has fought as a volunteer.

I am reluctant to speak of the scene which describes the death of the gallant and sweet Catherine as a literary matter. I have the immediate feeling that I have shared in it myself. We have lived a piece of life. The woman who stood in the center of this life must now die.

The young American has fled with the woman he loves to Switzerland. The young American lay wounded in Milan; she cared for him. He returned to the front; he deserted during the retreat; he was to be arrested and shot. He escapes; he finds his love again; she is expecting his child; she dies in childbirth. While she struggles against death, Henry stands outside and prays: 'But what if she should die? She can't die.' But God has no mercy.

No contemporary writer could portray the scene of Catherine's death as well as Hemingway. With its tense reserve about what happens within and with its uncanny exactitude about what happens outside, it is uniquely characteristic; and it is the most shattering passage that he has written. We sense at the end a really physical sympathy that chokes us up, when the woman, whom till then the ether has spared the most horrible pain, cries: 'It doesn't work any more. It doesn't work!' No one but Hemingway would have omitted the farewell to the dead woman with such grim toughness. No mention of tears. The narrator concludes factually: 'I walked back to the hotel in the rain.' This sentence is his lament for the dead. Behind this sentence sorrow opens like an abyss.

III

I could say more about Ernest Hemingway, who came to Europe from America; who tramped through France, Spain, Italy, who went trout fishing and was a taxi-driver in Paris. (4) He is the type to whom we can say 'Yes' as we can to very few writers. He has the best American qualities contained with our own virtues. One ought not to say that he is a Europeanized American. He has remained too profoundly and essentially American for that. He is a typical American but with the inner experiences of a European. He sees this world with the freshness of his youthful race and at the same time with the slyness of our old one. I should like him to be read more than anyone else. He is an outstanding poet of our time.

Notes

1 When Columbus was told that his discovery was not so difficult, he asked who could stand an egg on its end. When no one could, he cut off an end and stood it up.
2 'In einem andern Land' [In Another Country] was the German title of 'A Farewell to Arms.'
3 Danish novelist, author of 'Eccentric Stories' (1895).
4 Hemingway was never a taxi-driver.

31. PIERRE DRIEU LA ROCHELLE, PRÉFACE TO 'L'ADIEU AUX ARMES'

1932

From 'L'Adieu aux armes' (Paris, Gallimard, 1933), 9-12. This preface is translated by Valerie Meyers.

Pierre Drieu La Rochelle (1893-1945) was a French novelist and critic, Fascist collaborator and suicide. He wrote 'The Comedy of Charleroi' (1934) and 'Gilles' (1939).

A real writer is a man who knows things; he knows them too well to talk about them, so he writes. Hemingway is clearly that sort of man. He knows the things he's done, the places he's been to and the people he's been with. And he knows nothing else. With these things only he creates his world.

But he knows these places, these things, these people, very well; he grasps them with the surest and deepest human knowledge: a knowledge acquired first by using his senses, and later by exercising that capacity for feeling and reason created by the balance of all five senses. His world is therefore a solid world. It is a solid world one can reach out and touch. It lacks intellectual elaboration but it has the power that objects, and art-objects, have: the power of suggestion.

Hemingway knows American Indians, boxers, jockeys, Italians in the war, Americans in Paris, some women, some writers. It's not much, you say? Well, read it, read 'A Farewell to Arms.' And you will see if this isn't something more than a handful of Italians and a Scottish nurse, when Hemingway puts his hand to it.

I met Hemingway just once: we had dinner together with some mutual friends, in a yellow house on the banks of the Seine, where so many Americans have strolled. He is a very hefty fellow. I liked him very much. I had no desire to chat with him, I wished I had been his friend for ten years, and had no need to talk rubbish to make contact. He is the sort of man you ought to go hunting or fishing with.

Imagine a Maupassant who hadn't been shut up in a ministry or in Paris, and who, when young, had set off in his boat on the open sea; a Maupassant who had seen half-savage countries, who had known war, poverty and the common people.

Hemingway has the same gifts as Maupassant: the gifts of the senses, an inexhaustible power of receiving, or recording. He is a man who is at once a camera and a phonograph, but who is none the less a man. He is a man who is flesh and blood and for whom others are above all flesh and blood, with nerves, tears, laughter, desires, fears - and he sums this all up in their voices.

One can only admire the richness of the dialogue in Hemingway's novels and stories. He has little description or narrative; but you receive a clear impression of the atmosphere of a place or a person through a certain dialogue, redolent with suggestions of sight and taste as well as sound.

There is indeed something else in Hemingway's dialogue; above all there is Hemingway's spirit. This spirit is not of humor or irony but of health; what moves you about it is the very *tone* of his life, his health, his high spirits. He has the shoulders of a porter and the soul of a hunting-dog, desperately aware of every living scent, pursuing every quarry with a tender and implacable desire.

I have often doubted whether Americans are ever young; but I think they are when I read Hemingway (and some others). You immediately feel a force, in contact with the earth and nature, big enough to bear the heavy apparatus of society and industry; it crosses the old, stone Europe and iron America like a joyful rhinoceros who has taken its morning bath and rushes to its breakfast.

What attracts me to a Sherwood Anderson, to a Hemingway, to a Dos Passos, is that they know the great uninhibited spaces of their continent where the exposed towns are swamped by the wilderness, and they know how to return there. In doing so they continue a powerful tradition of the Nordic races, that of solitary commerce with nature - the tradition of Walt Whitman, Thoreau, Melville - Hardy, Kipling, Meredith, Keats and Shelley - the tradition of Hamsun - the tradition of Tolstoy and Turgenev.

This youth or health does not exclude pessimism. There is pessimism in Hemingway, a sacred pessimism. I remember an old American lady who said to me: 'Why are the European literatures so sad?' I replied, 'You have not looked at your own'. I thought of Whitman, Thoreau, Poe.

Pessimism is the prerogative of strength and youth. Re-read Nietzsche's 'Birth of Tragedy': the stronger man is, the more he enters into life; and when he enters into the heart of life, he has to find a tragic vision. These young writers have a tragic life. They are wanderers; they dash from America to Europe and to Asia, looking for something of value everywhere and finding it nowhere. They carry on their backs the obscure fate of their civilization, which scares and seduces them at the same time. They want to be and are Americans, and yet they still need Europe badly.

They come to work in Europe, then return to live in America. They get drunk, they swim, they get angry, they snatch women from the idiotic life in big American cities, they go to the devil, they come back, they write, they despair and in that very moment they create works which prove that America decidedly exists, that Americans have finished building their house. They are already settling down and beginning to sing.

The young writers have a public, they have success, their pockets are stuffed full of dollars (the novelists at least, not the poets, of course); but they are nevertheless misunderstood, and they have to fight their public, which is also healthy and exciting.

The art they are creating is robust, direct, anxious, full of new, yet confident rhythms. We need them. The European public eats up American translations. We devour the good and bad haphazardly; but the good never comes without the bad. And in any case, some really good things come to us from over there. Thus, up to a point, we are also in their debt.

We trade, with the Americans, our form for their raw life. We need the healthy excess they send us, to revive our form; but they still need our form to contain and direct their outpourings. Hemingway is well aware of this happy exchange. An anxious barbarian, subtle and delicate (like all barbarians), he is also a happy barbarian, who knows how to keep his strength and leave Rome with his booty intact.

32. FORD MADOX FORD, INTRODUCTION TO 'A FAREWELL TO ARMS'

1932

From 'A Farewell to Arms' (New York, Modern Library, 1932), ix-xx.

Ford Madox Ford (1873-1939), English novelist, was the author of 'The Good Soldier' (1915) and 'Parade's End' (1924-28).

I experienced a singular sensation on reading the first sentence of 'A Farewell to Arms.' There are sensations you cannot describe. You may know what causes them but you cannot tell what portions of your mind they affect nor yet, possibly, what parts of your physical entity. I can only say that it was as if I had found at last again something shining after a long delving amongst dust. I daresay prospectors after gold or diamonds feel something like that. But theirs can hardly be so coldly clear an emotion, or one so impersonal. The three impeccable writers of English prose that I have come across in fifty years or so of reading in search of English prose have been Joseph Conrad, W.H. Hudson (1) . . . . and Ernest Hemingway.... Impeccable each after his kind! I remember with equal clarity and equal indefinableness my sensation on first reading a sentence of each. With the Conrad it was like being overwhelmed by a great, unhastening wave. With the Hudson it was like lying on one's back and looking up into a clear, still sky. With the Hemingway it was just excitement. Like waiting at the side of a coppice, when foxhunting, for the hounds to break cover. One was going on a long chase in dry clear weather, one did not know in what direction or over what country.

The first sentence of Hemingway that I ever came across was not of course:

> In the late summer of that year we lived in a house in a village that looked across the river and the plain towards the mountains.

That is the opening of 'Farewell to Arms.' No, my first sentence of Hemingway was:

'Everybody was drunk.' *Tout court!* Like that!

Exactly how much my emotion gained from immediately afterwards reading the rest of the paragraph I can't say.

It runs for the next few sentences as follows:

> Everybody was drunk. The whole battery was drunk going along the road in the dark. We were going to the Champagne. The lieutenant kept riding his horse out into the fields and saying to him, 'I'm drunk, I tell you, mon vieux. Oh, I am so soused.' We went along the road in the dark and the adjutant kept riding up alongside my kitchen and saying, 'You must put it out. It is dangerous. It will be observed.'

I am reading from *'No 3 of 170 hand-made copies printed on* rives *hand-made paper'* which is inscribed: 'to robert mcalmon and william bird *publishers of the city of paris* and to captain edward dorman-smith m.c., of *his majesty's fifth fusiliers* this book is respectfully dedicated.' The title page, curiously enough bears the date 1924 but the copy is inscribed to me by Ernest Hemingway 'march 1923' (2) and must, as far as I can remember have been given to me then. There is a nice problem for bibliophiles.

This book is the first version of 'In Our Time' and is described as published at 'paris, *printed at* the three mountains press *and for sale at* shakespeare & company *in the rue de l'odéon; london:* william jackson, *took's court, cursitor street, chancery lane.'*

Those were the brave times in Paris when William Bird and I, and I daresay Hemingway too believed, I don't know why, that salvation could be found in leaving out capitals. We printed and published in a domed wine-vault, exceedingly old and cramped, on the Ile St. Louis with a grey view on the Seine below the Quais. It must have been salvation we aspired to for thoughts of fortune seldom came near us and Fortune herself, never. Publisher Bird printed his books beautifully at a great old seventeenth-century press and we all took hands at pulling its immense levers about. I 'edited' in a gallery like a bird-cage at the top of the vault. It was so low that I could never stand up. Ezra also 'edited' somewhere, I daresay, in the rue Notre Dame des Champs. At any rate the last page but one of 'In Our Time' - or perhaps it is the *feuille de garde*, (3) carries the announcement:

Here ends *The Inquest* into the state of
contemporary English prose, as
edited by EZRA POUND and printed at
the THREE MOUNTAINS PRESS. The six
works constituting the series are:
Indiscretions *of* Ezra Pound
Women and Men *by* Ford Madox Ford

Elimus *by* B. C. Windeler
with Designs *by* D. Shakespear
The Great American Novel
by William Carlos Williams
England *by* B. M. G. Adams
In Our Time *by* Ernest Hemingway
with portrait *by* Henry Strater.

Mr. Pound, you perceive did believe in CAPITALS and so obviously did one half of Hemingway for his other book of the same date - a blue-grey pamphlet - announces itself all in capitals of great baldness. (They are I believe of the style called *sans-sérif*): (4)

THREE STORIES
& TEN POEMS
ERNEST HEMINGWAY

it calls itself without even a '*by*' in italics. There is no date or publisher's or distributor's name or address on the title page but the back of the half-title bears the small notices

Copyright 1923 by the author
Published by
Contact Publishing Co.

and the last page but one has the announcement

PRINTED AT DIJON
BY
MAURICE DARANTIERE
M. CX. XXIII

This copy bears an inscription in the handwriting of Mr. Hemingway to the effect that it was given to me in Paris by himself in 924. That seems almost an exaggeration in antedating.

Anyhow, I read first 'In Our Time' and then My Old Man in 'Ten Stories' [sic] both in 1923.

Those were exciting times in Paris. The Young-American literature that today forms the most important phase of the literary world anywhere was getting itself born there. And those were birth-throes!

Young America from the limitless prairies leapt, released, on Paris. They stampeded with the madness of colts when you let down the slip-rails between dried pasture and green. The noise of their advancing drowned all sounds. Their innumerable forms hid the very trees on the boulevards. Their perpetual motion made you dizzy. The falling plane-leaves that are the distinguishing mark of grey, quiet Paris, were crushed under foot and vanished like flakes of snow in tormented seas.

I might have been described as - by comparison - a nice quiet gentleman for an elderly tea-party. And there I was between, as it were, the too quiet aestheticisms of William Bird, publisher supported by Ezra Pound, poet-editor, and, at the other extreme, Robert McAlmon damn-your-damn-highbrow-eyes author-publisher, backed by a whole Horde of Montparnasse from anywhere between North Dakota and Missouri.... You should have seen those Thursday tea-parties at the uncapitalled 'transatlantic review' offices! The French speak of 'la semaine a deux jeudis' ... the week with two Thursdays in it. (5) Mine seemed to contain sixty, judging by the noise, lung-power, crashing in, and denunciation. They sat on forms - school benches - cramped round Bird's great hand press. On the top of it was an iron eagle. A seventeenth-century eagle!

Where exactly between William Bird, hand-printer and publisher and Robert McAlmon, nine-hundred horse power linotype-publisher Hemingway came in I never quite found out. He was presented to me by Ezra and Bill Bird and had rather the aspect of an Eton-Oxford husky-ish young captain of a midland regiment of His Britannic Majesty. In that capacity he entered the phalanxes of the 'transatlantic review.' I forget what his official title was. He was perhaps joint-editor - or an advisory or consulting or vetoing editor. Of those there was a considerable company. I, I have omitted to say, was supposed to be Editor in Chief. They all shouted at me: I did not know how to write, or knew too much to be able to write, or did not know how to edit, or keep accounts, or sing 'Franky & Johnny,' or order a dinner. The ceiling was vaulted, the plane-leaves drifted down on the quays outside; the grey Seine flowed softly.

Into the animated din would drift Hemingway, balancing on the point of his toes, feinting at my head with hands as large as hams and relating sinister stories of Paris landlords. He told them with singularly choice words in a slow voice. He still struck me as disciplined. Even captains of his majesty's fifth fusiliers are sometimes amateur pugilists and now and then dance on their toe-points in private. I noticed less however of Eton and Oxford. He seemed more a creature of wild adventures amongst steers in infinitudes.

All the same, when I went to New York, I confided that review to him. I gave him strict injunctions as to whom not to print and above all whom not to cut.

The last mortal enemy he made for me died yesterday. Hemingway had cut *his* article and all those of my most cherished and awful contributors down to a line or two apiece. In return he had printed all *his* wildest friends *in extenso*. So that uncapitalised review died. I don't say that it died of Hemingway. I still knew he must somehow be disciplined.

But, a day or two after my return, we were all lunching in the little bistro that was next to the office. There were a great many people and each of them was accusing me of some different incapacity. At last Hemingway extended an enormous seeming ham under my nose. He shouted. What he shouted I could not hear but I realised I had a pencil. Under the shadow of that vast and menacing object I wrote verses on the table-cloth.

Heaven over-arches earth and sea
Earth sadness and sea-hurricanes.
Heaven over-arches you and me.
A little while and we shall be
Please God, where there is no more sea
  And no....

The reader may supply the rhyme.

That was the birth of a nation.

At any rate if America counts in the comity of civilised nations it is by her new writers that she has achieved that immense feat. So it seems to me. The reader trained in other schools of thought must bear with it. A nation exists by its laws, inventions, mass-products. It lives for other nations by its arts.

I do not propose here to mention other names than those of Ernest Hemingway. It is not my business to appraise. Appraisements imply censures and it is not one writer's business to censure others. A writer should expound other writers or let them alone.

When I thought that Hemingway had discipline I was not mistaken. He had then and still has the discipline that makes you avoid temptation in the selection of words and the discipline that lets you be remorselessly economical in the number that you employ. If, as writer you have those disciplined knowledges or instincts, you may prize fight or do what you like with the rest of your time.

The curse of English prose is that English words have double effects. They have their literal meanings and then associations they attain from other writers that have used them. These associations as often as not come from the Authorised Version or the Book of Common Prayer. You use a combination of words once used by Archbishop Cranmer or Archbishop Warham (6) or the Translators in the XVI & XVII centuries. You expect to get from them an overtone of awfulness, or erudition or romance or pomposity. So your prose dies.

Hemingway's words strike you, each one, as if they were pebbles fetched fresh from a brook. They live and shine, each in its place. So one of his pages has the effect of a brook-bottom into which you look down through the flowing water. The words form a tessellation, each in order beside the other.

It is a very great quality. It is indeed the supreme quality of the written art of the moment. It is a great part of what makes literature come into its own at such rare times as it achieves that feat. Books lose their hold on you as soon as the words in which they are written are demoded or too usual the one following the other. The aim - the achievement - of the great prose writer is to use words so that they shall seem new and alive because of their juxtaposition with other words. This gift Hemingway has supremely. Any sentence of his taken at random will hold your attention. And irresistibly. It does not matter where you take it.

> I was in under the canvas with guns. They smelled cleanly of oil and grease. I lay and listened to the rain on the canvas and the clicking of the car over the rails. There was a little light came through and I lay and looked at the guns.

You could not begin that first sentence and not finish the passage.

That is a great part of this author's gift. Yet it is not only 'gift.' You cannot throw yourself into a frame of mind and just write and get that effect. Your mind has to choose each word and your ear has to test it until by long disciplining of mind and ear you can no longer go wrong.

That disciplining through which you must put yourself is all the more difficult in that it must be gone through in solitude. You cannot watch the man next to you in the ranks smartly manipulating his side-arms nor do you hear any word of command by which to time yourself.

On the other hand a writer holds a reader by his temperament. That is his true 'gift' - what he receives from whoever sends him into the world. It arises from how you look at things. If you look at and render things so that they appear new to the reader you will hold his attention. If what you give him appears familiar or half familiar his attention will wander. Hemingway's use of the word 'cleanly' is an instance of what I have just been saying. The guns smelled cleanly of oil and grease. Oil and grease are not usually associated in the mind with a clean smell. Yet at the minutest reflection you realise that the oil and grease on the clean metal of big guns are not dirt. So the adverb is just. You have had a moment of surprise and then your knowledge is added to. The word 'author' means 'someone who adds to your consciousness.'

When, in those old days, Hemingway used to tell stories of his Paris landlords he used to be hesitant, to pause between words and then to speak gently but with great decision. His temperament was selecting the instances he should narrate, his mind selecting the words to employ. The impression was one of a person using restraint at the biddings of discipline. It was the right impression to have had.

He maintains his hold on himself up to the last word of every unit of his prose. The last words of My Old Man are:

> But I don't know. Seems like when they get started they don't leave a guy nothing.

The last words of 'In Our Time':

> It was very jolly. We talked for a long time. Like all Greeks he wanted to go to America.

'A Farewell to Arms' ends incomparably:

> But after I had got them out and shut the door and turned out the light it wasn't any good. It was like saying good-by to a statue. After a while I went out and left the hospital and walked back to the hotel in the rain.

Incomparably, because that muted passage after great emotion still holds the mind after the book is finished. The interest prolongs itself and the reader is left wishing to read more of that writer.

After the first triumphant success of a writer a certain tremulousness besets his supporters in the public. It is the second book that is going to have a rough crossing.... Or the third and the fourth. So after the great artistic triumph of William Bird's edition of 'In Our Time' Hemingway seemed to me to falter. He produced a couple of books that I did not much like. I was probably expected not much to like them. Let us say that they were essays towards a longer form than that of the episodic 'In Our Time.' Then with 'Men Without Women' he proved that he retained the essential gift. In that volume there is an episodic-narrative that moves you as you will - if you are to be moved at all - be moved by episodes of the Greek Anthology. (7) It has the same quality of serene flawlessness.

In the first paragraph I have explained the nature of my emotion when I read a year or so ago that first sentence of 'Farewell to Arms.' It was more than excitement. It was excitement plus re-assurance. The sentence was exactly the right opening for a long piece of work. To read it was like looking at an athlete setting out on a difficult and prolonged effort. You say, at the first movement of the limbs: 'It's all right. He's in form.... He'll do today what he has never quite done before.' And you settle luxuriantly into your seat.

So I read on after the first sentence:

> In the bed of the river there were pebbles and boulders dry and white in the sun, and the water was clear and swiftly moving and blue in the channels. Troops went by the house and down the road and the dust they raised powdered the leaves of the trees. The trunks of the trees were dusty and the leaves fell early that year and we saw the troops marching along the road and the dust rising and the leaves, stirred by the breeze falling and the soldiers marching and afterwards the road bare and white except for the leaves.

A wish I could quote more, it is such pleasure to see words like that come from one's pen. But you can read it for yourself.

'A Farewell to Arms' is a book important in the annals of the art of writing because it proves that Hemingway, the writer of short, perfect episodes, can keep up the pace through a volume. There have been other writers of impeccable - of matchless - prose but as a rule their sustained efforts have palled because precisely of the remarkableness of the prose itself. You can hardly read 'Marius the Epicurean.' You may applaud its author, Walter Pater. But 'A Farewell to Arms' is without purple patches or even verbal 'felicities.' While you are reading it you forget to applaud its author. You do not know that you are having to do with an author. You are living.

'A Farewell to Arms' is a book that unites the critic

to the simple. You could read it and be thrilled if you had never read a book - or if you had read and measured all the good books in the world. That is the real province of the art of writing.

Hemingway has other fields to conquer. That is no censure on 'A Farewell to Arms.' It is not blaming the United States to say that she has not yet annexed Nicaragua. But whatever he does can never take away from the fresh radiance of this work. It may close with tears but it is like a spring morning.

Notes

1 English naturalist and novelist, author of 'The Purple Land' (1885) and 'Green Mansions' (1904).
2 Hemingway meant to write March 1924.
3 Endpaper.
4 Form of type without cross-lines finishing off a stroke of a letter.
5 I.e. two half-holidays.
6 William Wareham (c. 1450-1532), Archbishop of Canterbury; and Thomas Cranmer (1489-1556), Archbishop of Canterbury, who was mainly responsible for the Book of Common Prayer (1552).
7 The first collection of Greek poems, including Sappho's, made by Meleager of Gadara.

'Death in the Afternoon' (1932)

33. ROBERT COATES, 'NEW YORKER'

8 (1 October 1932), 61-3)

Robert Coates (1897-1973) was an American novelist and critic.

I must say (though it disappoint you) that Ernest Hemingway's long-awaited new book, 'Death in the Afternoon,' just published by Scribner, is likely to be thoroughly enjoyed by only two very distinct types of people; those who have a consuming interest in the more technical details of bullfighting as a sport, and those who have an equally profound interest - apart from the mere amusement value of his separate books - in Mr. Hemingway himself as a writer, and in the point of view on which his work is based.

Now, to the first class I do not personally belong. The book is an exhaustive treatise on bullfighting in all its aspects, from the breeding of the bulls to the moment of their dispatch in the ring, with a critical analysis of the technique of the various matadors besides; and I confess that a little of this goes a long way with me. I have never seen a bullfight, and though I have no idea what my reactions to one might be, I am sure at least of this: that I'd a thousand times rather see one than be told about it, even by one so skilled in description as Mr. Hemingway undeniably is. Indeed, I found the illustrations - of which there must be almost a hundred, all excellent - far more enlightening about the actual conduct of the fights than anything he had to say.

But for those who, so to speak, can pay more attention to Mr. Hemingway than to the bull, I think the book should hold considerable interest. Certainly, none that I have recently read has been so revealing, both consciously and unconsciously, of its author's point of view.

You'll see, for instance, distorted as an object doubly reflected, what he thinks you think his writings are about. You think, for one thing, that all he's good at is dialogue, so he creates in your image a mythical Old Lady, who says 'I like it when you write about love,' and acts as his interlocutor while he expresses some pretty bitter opinions on readers, writers, and things in general. But then, I take it that no romantic writer (and I had occasion last week to state, without intent of derogation, my belief that Mr. Hemingway *is* a romantic, and not a classical realist at all) is ever satisfied by any interpretation of his work but his own. And though there are passages in which his bitterness descends in petulance (as in his gibes at William Faulkner, who has done him no harm save to come under his influence, and at T.S. Eliot, Aldous Huxley, Jean Cocteau, and others, living and dead), there are also passages of a bright, appealing honesty in which he reveals, almost involuntarily, the tremendous labor of simplification, the searching for the particularizing detail, that goes into his own work.

Another great characteristic of the romanticist - the one, perhaps, that separates him most definitely from the classicist - is his inability to accept the idea of death as the end and complement of life. Now, of Mr. Hemingway's six other books, all - except the unfortunate 'Torrents of Spring' - had to do with death or the threat of it, and in this book death seems to take on for him the intimacy, the nearness, of a personal enemy.

Death in wartime: it still preoccupies him, and he cannot find words strong enough in his determination to make you, too, feel the horror of it. Death in peacetime, too: in the arena it is, of course, the climactic touch, and this is avowedly the reason he went there to study it, but it is always around us. After telling of the beauty of Madrid he can find only this to say of it: 'It makes you feel very badly, all questions of immortality aside, to know that you will have to die and never see it again'; and when the Old Lady, after one of his anecdotal asides, remarks 'I find that a very sad story, sir,' he replies 'Madam, all stories, if continued far enough, end in death, and he is no true story-teller who would keep that from you.... If two people love each other there can be no happy end to it.' I take it that this is the clearest statement yet heard of Mr. Hemingway's artistic point of view. But it is because death so almost actually *hurts* him that he can write so movingly about it, and in this book, too, there are many moments when those flat, unaccented sentences of his suddenly take up their march, and you are made to feel again, with him, the bitterness, and the pity, and the injustice of it.

To sum up, then: a strange book, childish, here and there, in its small-boy wickedness of vocabulary; bitter, and even morbid in its endless preoccupation with fatality. As far as momentary popularity goes, it seems almost a suicidal book in its deliberate flouting of reader and critic alike, and I feel sure that because of it Mr. Hemingway has let himself in for some hard panning from those who have been most hysterical in praise of him. But, in spite of this, I think it contains some of the most honest and some of the best writing he has done since 'In Our Time.'

34. GRANVILLE HICKS, 'NATION'

135 (9 November 1932), 461

Granville Hicks (b. 1901) is the American author of 'The Great Tradition' (1934) and 'John Reed' (1936); he founded the Communist magazine 'New Masses' in 1926 and resigned from the Party in 1939.

Though no one can doubt the genuineness of Hemingway's interest in bullfighting, 'Death in the Afternoon' seems to have been written with one eye on the proverbial wolf. It may be just as well; a book that tried to maintain the level of The Undefeated or of the bullfight descriptions in 'The Sun Also Rises' would undoubtedly become painful and might become ridiculous. Certainly the uninitiated reader can learn all that he is likely to need or want to know about bulls, fights, and fighters, and he has some fine photographs, an elegant binding, and a certain amount of humor thrown in.

If anyone else had written the book, there would be

little more to say; but because Hemingway ranks so high among contemporary novelists, and because more people will read the book because they are interested in Hemingway than will read it because they are interested in bullfighting, one is justified in going on to talk about the author. Fortunately the author, fully aware of the interest in his personality, has made a vigorous effort to put as much of himself as possible into his book. As a rule these intimate revelations are placed, for the convenience of the author, who obviously prefers to do a craftsmanlike job, as well as for the convenience of the reader, at the end of each chapter. At first they take the form of dialogues between the author and an old lady, dialogues that suggest both Frank Harris and A.A. Milne (1) at their most objectionable. Later on - but none too soon, as Mr. Hemingway candidly observes - the old lady disappears, and the author speaks directly to his readers.

We have, then, a series of observations on life and letters that provide glimpses of the mind of Ernest Hemingway; and there are, of course, other less premeditated revelations. The net impression is not unlike that received from the novels and stories. There is, it is true, a suggestion, especially in his comments on his critics, that Hemingway is less sure of himself than might have been supposed. But in general the book confirms previous judgments. It is surely not surprising to learn that he went to his first bullfight because he 'was trying to learn to write, commencing with the simplest things, and one of the simplest things of all and the most fundamental is violent death.' It is not surprising to find him speaking of 'mountain skiing, sexual intercourse, wing shooting, or any other thing which it is impossible to make come true on paper, or at least impossible to attempt to make more than one version of at a time on paper, it being always an individual experience.' It is not surprising to read: 'If two people love each other there can be no happy end to it'; or to come across a brutal and quite quite irrelevant description of the horrors of death in war time. All these things fit the picture.

There is considerable humor in the book, but Hemingway always speaks respectfully of bullfighting and of writing. In his peroration, which is largely concerned with the latter activity, he says: 'Let those who want to save the world if you can get to see it clear and as a whole. Then any part you make will represent the whole if it's made truly.' This is obviously sound, and it would be hard to find any novelist who, as novelist, would disagree with it. The only questions it raises are concerned with Hemingway's own efforts to see the world clear and as a whole. Is his literary process one of selection - a selection based on and dictated by a knowledge of the whole? Or is it a process of isolation - a deliberate setting apart of those segments of human experience he understands and likes to write about? It would take a good deal of space to answer these questions, and a good many references to the stories and novels to support one's answers. But there is a kind of answer suggested in a passage in this book: 'After one comes, through contact with its administrators, no longer to cherish greatly the law as a remedy in abuses, then the bottle becomes a sovereign means of direct action. If you cannot throw it, at least you can always drink from it.' If, in other words, you are troubled by the world, resort to personal violence; and if personal violence proves, as it usually does, to be dangerous, ineffective, and undignified, console yourself with drink - or skiing, or sexual intercourse, or watching bullfights. Now though this is certainly a poor way to save the world, it no doubt is a fine way to 'get to see it clear and as a whole.' Yah, as Mr. Hemingway would say, like hell it is!

Note

1 Frank Harris was the egoistic author of 'My Life and Loves' (1923-27). A.A. Milne was the author of enormously successful children's books, including 'Winnie the Pooh' (1926).

35. MALCOLM COWLEY, 'NEW REPUBLIC'

73 (30 November 1932), 76-7

Malcolm Cowley (b. 1898), American critic and poet, is the author of 'Exile's Return' (1934) and 'The Literary Situation' (1954), and one of Hemingway's greatest admirers.

Just why did Ernest Hemingway write a book on bullfighting? It is, make no mistake, a good book on bullfighting, full of technical writing as accurate as anything printed in Spanish newspapers like 'El Sol' or

'A.B.C.' and general information presented more vividly and completely than ever before in Spanish or English. Hemingway writes for those who have seen their first bull-fight, or shortly intend to see it, or are wondering whether to do so if they ever visit Spain. He tells them what, where, when, how - the seats to buy, the buses or trains to take, the things to watch for and which of them to applaud, which to salute with a volley of oranges, empty bottles and dead fish. He tells how the bulls are bred and tested, how the matadors are trained, glorified and, in the end, killed off like bulls. He illustrates the text with dozens of good photographs. In appendices, he gives further information, the dates of the principal *corridas* (1) in Spain, Mexico and Peru, the reactions of typical Anglo-Saxons and the achievements of Sidney Franklin the one American matador. Everything is there, even a store of pathetic or hilarious stories to read during dull moments of the fight, if there be any. In a word, he has written a Baedeker (2) of bulls, an admirable volume, but -

Being a good artist, he does a good job, never faking, skimping or pretending. He often talks about himself, but meanwhile keeps his eye on the thing outside, the object to be portrayed; by force of prolonged attention, he makes the object larger than life, fills it with all his knowledge and feeling, with himself. His book about bull-fighting thus becomes something more, a book about sport in general and, since this particular sport is really an art, a book about artistic appreciation and literary criticism, yes, and the art of living, of drinking, of dying, of loving the Spanish land. But all this being said -

Like every good artist, Hemingway employs a double process of selection and diversification, of contraction and expansion. He says: 'Let those who want to save the world if you can get to see it clear and as a whole.' Writing in Anglo-Saxon words of one syllable he is sometimes more difficult than Whitehead or Paul Valéry, (3) but what he means in this case is made clear enough by the addition of two more monosyllables and a comma. Let those who want to do so save the world, if *you* can get to see it clear and as a whole. Then, he continues, 'any part you make will represent the whole if it's made truly.' This book, being truly made, represents in its own fashion the whole of life. But all this being said, one must add that the whole it represents is discolored and distorted by the point of view; that the book is full of self-conscious cruelty, bravado, pity and, especially when dying horses are concerned, a sort of uneasiness that ends by communicating itself to the reader. 'Death in the Afternoon' is a less important book than 'A Farewell to Arms'; its style is often labored and sometimes flowery (and isn't rendered any less so by Hemingway's apologies for fine writing; apologies never help); its best descriptions of bull-fights are less moving than the brief description in 'The Sun Also Rises.' For three years, in the midst of a world more tumultuous and exciting than any bull-fight, Hemingway has been writing and repolishing this book. Why did he choose this particular subject, this part to represent the whole?

The answer carries us back fifteen years. During the War, Hemingway served on the Italian front, first as an ambulance driver, later in the shock troops, the Arditi; he was seriously wounded and received two medals. The War, to judge from his books, has been the central experience in his career; he shows the effects of it more completely than any other American novelist. In an article recently printed in the 'New Republic,' I tried to describe these effects in their relation to the writers of Hemingway's generation, which is also mine, reader, and possibly your own. (4) I said that the War uprooted us, cut us off from our own class and country; that it taught us to assume what I called a spectatorial attitude toward life in general; that it encouraged us to write once more about old themes, simple themes like love and death; and, though I did not emphasize the point, that it gave us a sense of self-pity and self-esteem, a bitter aloofness in the midst of armies. The War, I said, 'infected us with the slow poison of irresponsibility and unconcern for the future - the poison of travel, too ... and the poison of danger, excitement, that made our old life intolerable. Then, as suddenly as it began for us, the War ended' - leaving behind it desires and habits which were difficult to satisfy in a world at peace.

Bull-fighting perhaps could serve as an emotional substitute for war. It provided everything, travel, excitement, crowds like armies watching the spectacle of danger. Hemingway says on the second page of his new book, 'The only place where you could see life and death, *i.e.*, violent death now that the wars were over, was in the bull ring and I wanted very much to go to Spain where I could study it.' His motives were not merely emotional; he was 'trying to learn to write, commencing with the simplest things,' and bull-fighting was an ideal subject; it dealt with fundamentals; apparently it was independent of morality, of social implications, of any connection with politics. 'So I went to Spain to see bull-fights and try to write about them for myself.... It might be good to have a book about bull-fighting in English and a serious book on such an unmoral subject may have some value.'

But the book when he came to write it ten years later disproved a good many of the ideas which he carried with him into Spain. There are contradictions between Hemingway's ideas and the ideas suggested to readers by his narrative. To give an obvious example, 'Death in the Afternoon' is not at all an unmoral book, nor does it treat bull-fighting as an unmoral subject. If Hemingway praises the performance of a great matador, almost all his adjectives are rich in moral connotations: they are words like true, emotional, not tricked, pure, brave, honest, noble, candid, honorable, sincere. Other matadors are not merely inartistic: they are low, false, vulgar, cowardly; they are even 'cynical.'

A second contradiction is more important. 'All art,' he says, 'is only done by the individual. The individual is all you ever have.' But almost from beginning to end, 'Death in the Afternoon' is a refutation of this idea. It is true that the art of the matador, the great individual, provides the 'moment of truth' which is the climax of a good bull-fight, but Hemingway makes it clear that the matador's performance would be impossible without the collaboration of nameless people, dozens of them, hundreds, thousands, in circles gradually widening till they include almost a whole nation and a culture extending for centuries into the past. The matador, to begin with, must depend on the work of his own team, his *cuadrilla*, which is charged with the function of conducting the bull through the first two stages of the fight, of regulating his speed and carriage, of preparing him for the 'moment of truth' when the sword goes in between the shoulder blades and bull and matador are for the moment one. But the bull, too, must play his part; he must be a brave, 'candid' bull of a type that can be raised only by breeders of knowledge and integrity, encouraged by audiences which howl at the sight of inferior animals. The audience, moreover, must appreciate the finer points of the art, must know when to throw small dead animals of all sorts, including fish; it must hold a certain attitude toward bravery and death; it must, in short, be the sort of audience that exists only in Castille, Navarre, Andalusia and perhaps in Mexico City. The government, finally, must grant at the very least an intelligent toleration if the art of bull-fighting is to survive. The government might easily abolish it, not by jailing the matadors, but simply by seizing the ranches where bulls are raised and sending the animals to the slaughterhouse. As for the bull-fighters themselves, they grow up unencouraged, 'having a natural talent as acrobats or jockeys or even writers have, and none of them are irreplaceable....' And so the author has described a complete circle. He began by saying that the individual, in art, is all you ever have; he ends by deciding that the individual, even the greatest matador, is replaceable and nonessential.

Hemingway is a master at not drawing implications. In this respect as in others, it is interesting to compare 'Death in the Afternoon' with 'Les Bestiaires,' a novel about bull-fighting written by a Frenchman of the same age. Henry de Montherlant sees implications everywhere. The modern *corrida de toros* implies the ancient sacrifice of a white bull to Mithra, which in turn leads him to consider the beauties of ritual, the mysteries of sacrifice, the glories of tradition, Royalism, Catholicism, patriotic ecstasy, till shortly the bulls, the author and his readers together are lost in a haze of emotion. Montherlant is inferior to Hemingway in hardness, honesty, freshness, keen perception, and yet in a sense I think he is justified. Bull-fighting really does imply a certain attitude toward life, a willingness to accept things as they are, bad as they are, and to recompense oneself by regarding them as picturesque tragedy. Bull-fighting does, I think, imply an aristocracy, an established Church, a proletariat resigned to suffering pain in return for the privilege of seeing pain inflicted on others, and a rabble of gladiators, bootlickers and whores; but I am just as glad that Hemingway does not consciously draw these implications.

I don't mean to say that the book is without political meanings or contradictions. Hemingway detested the dictator Primo de Rivera - for many reasons, probably, but he mentions only one: Primo insisted on protecting the horses with belly-pads and thereby spoiled one part of the *corrida*. (5) Hemingway hates policemen. Hemingway had many friends among the republican politicians when they were being hunted through the Pyrenees, but now they have come into power he is beginning to detest them also: he suspects them of wishing to abolish bull-fights 'so that they will have no intellectual embarrassments at being different from their European colleagues when they meet at the League of Nations.' Hemingway is disturbed by the peasant jacquerie (6) in Andalusia, which is threatening the bull-breeding ranches, but at the same time he feels an instinctive friendship toward the peasants. I think he realizes the possibility that the Spanish people themselves, and not their government, might put an end to the bull-fight, replacing it by sports and arts more appropriate to a revolutionary society. On this matter, however, he takes no stand. To do so would force him to think about the present and the future, and he has fallen into the habit of writing with his eyes turned backwards.

This habit, revealed engagingly in all his books, is now becoming a vice. During the War, he dreamed about his boyhood in Michigan, where trout lay thickly in the cool streams in July. 'One year they had cut the hemlock woods.... You could not go back' - but you could write about it nostalgically; and later, in Paris and Spain, you could write about the brave days of the War; and still later, in Key West, (7) you could write about Madrid and Pamplona and the bull-fights, always with an elegiac note, a tenderness for things past and never to be recaptured. All through the present book, but especially in the last chapter, one finds this note repeated, this regret for 'the one year everyone drank so much and no one was nasty. There really was such a year.' 'Make all that come true again,' he cries. But, 'Pamplona is changed.... Rafael says things are very changed and he won't go to Pamplona any more.... Pamplona is changed, of course, but not so much as we are older.' Always there is this grief for something that has died within us, for a state of security or felicity existing in youth or in the mind. 'We will never ride back from Toledo in the dark, washing the dust out with Fundador, (8) nor will there be that week of what happened in the night of that July in Madrid.' It is all very brave, hard-boiled and wistful, but there are other chords for Hemingway to strike.

In a sense, every book he has written has been an elegy. He has given us his farewell to Michigan, to Montparnasse, his 'Farewell to Arms'; his new book is a sort of elegy to Spain and vanished youth and the brave days of Belmonte and Maera. Hemingway's talent is great enough to justify us in making demands on it. Will he ever give us, I wonder, his farewell to farewells?

Notes

1 Bullfights.
2 Famous series of German guide books.
3 Alfred North Whitehead was an English philosopher and mathematician, and co-author with Bertrand Russell of 'Principia Mathematica' (1910-13). Paul Valéry was a French poet, author of 'La Jeune parque' (1917) and 'Le Cimetière marin' (1920).
4 Malcolm Cowley, The Homeless Generation, 'New Republic,' 72 (26 October 1932), 281-5.
5 Miguel Primo de Rivera, Premier of Spain 1925-30. The

belly pads prevented the horses from being disembowelled by the bulls.
6 Rising.
7 From 1928 Hemingway had spent part of the year in Key West, Florida.
8 A Spanish brandy.

36. H.L. MENCKEN, 'AMERICAN MERCURY'

27 (December 1932), 506-7

Mr. Hemingway has been before the public for ten years and in that time he has published seven books. He has been praised very lavishly, but has somehow failed to make his way into the first rank of living American authors. Nevertheless, he has made some progress in that direction, and his last novel, 'A Farewell to Arms', was unquestionably his best. In the present book, which is not fiction but fact, his characteristic merits and defects are clearly revealed. It is, on the one hand, an extraordinarily fine piece of expository writing, but on the other hand it often descends to a gross and irritating cheapness. So long as the author confines himself to his proper business, which is that of describing the art and science of bullfighting, he is unfailingly clear, colorful and interesting. Unfortunately, he apparently finds it hard to so confine himself. Only too often he turns aside from his theme to prove fatuously that he is a naughty fellow, and when he does so he almost invariably falls into banality and worse. The reader he seems to keep in his mind's eye is a sort of common denominator of all the Ladies' Aid Societies of his native Oak Park, Ill. The way to shock this innocent grandam, obviously, is to have at her with the ancient four-letter words. Mr. Hemingway does so with moral industry; he even drags her into the story as a character, to gloat over her horror. But she is quite as much an intruder in that story as King George V would be, or Dr. Irving Babbitt, (1) or the Holy Ghost, and the four-letter words are as idiotically incongruous as so many booster's slogans or college yells.

Mr. Hemingway's main purpose in 'Death in the Afternoon' is to describe bullfighting as he has observed it in Spain. He admits frankly that he enjoys it, and he conveys a good deal of that enjoyment to the reader. The sport is brutal, but there is no evidence that it is any more brutal than football. The common American idea, I suppose, is that the bull is a senile and sclerotic beast with no chance against the matador, but Mr. Hemingway shows that this is very far from the truth. The bull, in fact, is always a youngster, and he is selected for his stamina and warlike enterprise. If he shows no pugnacity the fight is a flop, and the fans indicate their discontent by bombarding the matador with empty bottles. Moreover, the matador is not permitted to kill his antagonist in the safest way possible, which would probably also be the easiest. On the contrary, he must expose himself deliberately to the maximum of risk, and his rank in his profession is determined very largely by his ingenuity in devising new hazards, and his courage in facing them. When the formal jousting prescribed by the canon is over, and he prepares to kill, he must approach the bull so closely and so openly that a miscalculation of half an inch may well cost him his life.

Mr. Hemingway has seen hundreds of fights, and no less than 3,000 (2) bulls have been dispatched before his eyes. He has cultivated bullfighters and studied the immense literature of their mystery, and at one time he even ventured into the ring himself. Thus he knows everything about bullfighting that anyone save an actual matador can hope to learn, and this large and particular knowledge is visible on every page of his book. No better treatise on the sport has ever been written in English, and there is not much probability that better ones are to be had in Spanish. The narrative is full of the vividness of something really seen, felt, experienced. It is done simply, in English that is often bald and graceless, but it is done nevertheless with great skill. Take out the interludes behind the barn, for the pained astonishment of the Oak Park *Damenverein*, (3) and it would be a really first-rate book. Even with the interludes it is well worth reading. Not many current books unearth so much unfamiliar stuff, or present it so effectively. I emerge cherishing a hope that bullfighting will be introduced at Harvard and Yale, or, if not at Harvard and Yale, then at least in the Lynching Belt of the South, where it would offer stiff and perhaps ruinous competition to the frying of poor blackamoors. Years ago I proposed that brass bands be set up down there for that purpose, but bullfights would be better. Imagine the moral stimulation in rural Georgia if an evangelist came to town offering to fight the local bulls by day and baptise the local damned by night!

Mr. Hemingway's main text fills about half of his book. There follows a series of excellent full-page photographs of bullfighters in action, including several which show the bull getting the better of it. There is also an elaborate and amusing glossary of bullfighting terms, running to nearly a hundred pages, and at the end is a calendar of the principal bullfights of Spain and Latin-America, for the convenience of tourists. A four-page note on Sidney Franklin, the Brooklyn matador, completes the book. Señor Franklin first came to fame in Mexico, but of late he has been enjoying great success in Spain. Mr. Hemingway says that 'he kills easily and well. He does not give the importance to killing that it merits, since it is easy for him and because he ignores the danger.' But ignoring it has not enabled him to avoid it, for he has been gored twice, once very badly. Mr. Hemingway describes his principal wounds in plain English. They will give the Oak Park W.C.T.U. (4) another conniption fit. The Hemingway boy is really a case.

Notes

1 Professor of French at Harvard, author of 'Rousseau and Romanticism' (1919).
2 According to Carlos Baker in 'Ernest Hemingway: A Life Story' (New York, 1969), 484, Hemingway had seen 1,500 bulls killed.
3 Ladies' club.
4 Women's Christian Temperance Union.

37. MAX EASTMAN, 'NEW REPUBLIC'

75 (7 June 1933), 94-7

Max Eastman (1883-1969) was an American poet and critic, and author of 'The Enjoyment of Poetry' (1913) and 'Leon Trotsky' (1925).

There are gorgeous pages in Ernest Hemingway's book about bullfights - big humor and reckless straight talk of what things are, genuinely heavy ferocity against prattle of what they are not. Hemingway is a full-sized man hewing his way with flying strokes of the poet's broad axe which I greatly admire. Nevertheless, there is an unconscionable quantity of bull - to put it as decorously as possible - poured and plastered all over what he writes about bullfights. By bull I mean juvenile romantic gushing and sentimentalizing of simple facts.

For example, it is well known and fairly obvious that bulls do not run and gallop about the pasture; they stand solid 'dominating the landscape with their confidence' as Hemingway brilliantly says. Therefore when they have dashed about the ring some minutes, tossed a few horses, repeatedly charged and attempted to gore a man and thrown their heads off because he turned out to be a rag, they soon get winded and their tongues hang out and they pant. Certain bulls, however, for reasons more or less accidental, go through the ordeal in a small area without much running and therefore get tired in the muscles before they get winded. These bulls do not hang their tongues out and pant. This plain fact, which would be obvious to anybody without smoke in his eyes, is romanticized by Hemingway to mean that some bulls are so 'brave' that they will never let their tongues out, but hold their mouths 'tight shut to keep the blood in' even after they are stabbed to death and until they drop. This is not juvenile romanticism, it is child's fairy-story writing. And yet Hemingway asks us to believe that what drew him to bullfights was the desire to learn to put down 'what really happened in action; what the actual things were which produced the emotion that you experienced.'

In pursuit of this rigorous aim he informs us that bullfights are 'so well ordered and so strongly disciplined by ritual that a person feeling the whole tragedy cannot separate the minor comic-tragedy of the horse so as to feel it emotionally.' And he generalizes: 'The *aficionado*, or lover of the bullfight, may be said, broadly, then, to be one who has this sense of the tragedy and ritual of the fight so that the minor aspects are not important except as they relate to the whole.' Which is just the kind of sentimental poppycock most regularly dished out by those Art nannies and pale-eyed professors of poetry whom Hemingway above all men despises. Hemingway himself makes plain all through his book that the performance itself is not an artistic tragedy as often as one time out of a hundred. When it is, there is about one man out of a thousand in the grandstand who would know what you were talking about if you started in on 'the whole tragedy' as opposed to the 'minor comic-tragedy of the horse.' The *aficionado*, or bullfight fan, is the Spanish equivalent of the American baseball fan. He reacts the same way to the same kind of things. If you could get the authorization to put on a bullfight in the Yankee Stadium, (1) you would see approximately the same crowd there that you do now, and they would behave, after a little instruction from our star reporters and radio announcers, just about the way the Spanish crowd behaves. And they would not be - 'broadly' - the kind of people, if there are such people, who can see an infuriated bull charge across a bull ring, ram his horns into the private end of a horse's belly and rip him clear up to the ribs, lifting and tossing his rider bodily in the air and over against the fence with the same motion, and keep their attention so occupied with the 'whole tragedy' that they cannot 'separate' this enough to 'feel it emotionally.' Bullfights are not wholly bad, but sentimentalizing over them in the name of art-form and ritual is.

Whatever art may be, a bullfight is not art in exactly that particular which exempts art from those rules of decent conduct which make life possible and civilization a hope - namely, that its representations are not real. A bullfight - foolishly so called by the English for it does not except for a moment resemble a fight - is real life. It is men tormenting and killing a bull; it is a bull being tormented and killed.

And if it is not 'art' in a sense to justify Hemingway's undiscriminating recourse to that notion, still less is it 'tragedy' in a sense to sustain the elevated emotions which he hopes to pump over it with this portentous term.

Suppose that you attend a bullfight with your eyes and emotional receptors recklessly wide open, as a poet should. What do you see to admire and what to despise? Men moving in the risk of wounds and death with skill, grace, suavity and courage. That is something to admire - and the wild free fighting force of the animal as he charges into the arena, a sight so thrilling that words fail utterly. They fail Hemingway. Until Christians thought up the sickly idea of worshipping a lamb, this noble creature symbolized the beauty of divine power in a good half of the great religions of the earth.

Here, then, are two things to admire and they command admiration; they command sympathy. And then you see these admirable brave men begin to take down this noble creature and reduce him to a state where they can successfully run in and knife him, by a means which would be described in any other situation under the sun as a series of dirty tricks, these tricks being made possible by his well known and all too obvious stupidity - the limitations of his vision and rigidity of his instincts - this stupidity being further assured by breeding, by keeping him in a dim light before the running and by never giving him a second chance in the ring. You see this beautiful creature, whom you admire because he is so gorgeously equipped with power for wild life and despise for his stupidity, trapped in a ring where his power is nothing, and you see him put forth his utmost in vain to escape death at the hands of these spryer and more flexible monkeys, whose courage you admire and whose mean use of their wit you despise. You see him baffled, bewildered, insane with fright, fury and physical agony, jabbed, stabbed, haunted, hounded, steadily brought dreadfully down from his beauty of power, until he stands horribly torpid, sinking leadlike into his tracks, lacking the mere strength of muscle to lift his vast head, panting, gasping, gurgling, his mouth too little and the tiny black tongue hanging out too far to give him breath, and faint falsetto cries of anguish, altogether lost-babylike now and not bull-like, coming out of him, and you see one of these triumphant monkeys strike a theatrical pose, and dash in swiftly and deftly - yes, while there is still danger, still a staggering thrust left in the too heavy horns - and they have invented statistics, moreover, and know exactly how much and how little danger there is - dash in swiftly and deftly and plunge a sword into the very point where they accurately know - for they have also invented anatomy, these wonderful monkeys - that they will end that powerful and noble thing forever.

That is what a bullfight is, and that is all it is. To drag in notions of honor and glory here, and take them seriously, is ungrown-up enough and rather sophomoric. But to pump words over it like tragedy and dramatic conflict is mere romantic nonsense and self-deception crying to heaven. It is not tragic to die in a trap because although beautiful you are stupid; it is not tragic to play mean tricks on a beautiful thing that is stupid, and stab it when its power is gone. It is the exact opposite of tragedy in every high meaning that has ever been given to that word. It is killing made meaner, death more ignoble, bloodshed more merely shocking than it has need to be.

Fortunately it is no great trick to close one's receptors in a certain direction, to deaden sympathies that are unfruitful. We all go through life with these emotional blinders on; we could not go through otherwise. I remember an anxious mother in fits of anxiety because her husband had taken their infant son into one of those sidewalk horror exhibitions - it was an illuminated view of a 'famous painting of Nero throwing Christians to the lions.'

'George, George, how could you subject Bobby's tender little growing soul to that shocking experience? What *did* he do? What *did* he say?'

'He said, "Oh, Papa, there's one poor lion hasn't got any Christian!"'

This being the nature of the human infant, it is obvious that if you grow up in a society which does not extend sympathy to bulls in the bull ring, barring some heightened consciousness or gift of reflection in you amounting to an eccentricity, you will not do so either. For this reason the idea that bullfights prove Spaniards to be cruel, or as Havelock Ellis (2) says, 'indifferent to pain both in themselves and others,' seems to me - with all respect to that eminent authority - the veriest nonsense. The appetites to which bullfighting appeals are a universal human inheritance, and if its survival in Spain must have some explanation other than cultural accident, I should associate it with the almost feminine gentleness of character to be felt in that country which seems to have need of this stoical overprotest of courage without mercy. At any rate, we expect an American poet who goes down there to see more and not less than a Spanish adolescent, whose one-sided obtundity in this matter is as inevitable as the misshapen callous on the bottom of any man's foot.

Why then does our iron advocate of straight talk about what things are, our full-sized man, our ferocious realist, go blind and wrap himself up in clouds of juvenile romanticism the moment he crosses the border on his way to a Spanish bullfight? It is of course a commonplace that Hemingway lacks the serene confidence that he *is* a full-sized man. Most of us too delicately organized babies who grow up to be artists suffer at times from that small inward doubt. But some circumstance seems to have laid upon Hemingway a continual sense of the obligation to put forth evidences of red-blooded masculinity. It must be made obvious not only in the swing of the big shoulders and the clothes he puts on, but in the stride of his prose style and the emotions he permits to come to the surface there. This trait of his character has been strong enough to form the nucleus of a new flavor in English literature, and it has moreover begotten a veritable school of fiction-writers - a literary style, you might say, of wearing false hair on the chest - but, nevertheless, I think it is inadequate to explain the ecstatic adulation with which Hemingway approaches everything connected with the killing of bulls in the bull ring.

He says that he went to see these spectacles because he was trying to learn how to write, and he wanted something 'simple' to write about; violent death, he thought, was one of the simplest things; he had seen a great deal of violent death in the War, but the War being over and he still learning to write, it seemed necessary to see some more. I do not think you can call it psychoanalysis to remark that the only simple thing here is Ernest Hemingway. A man writes about - and travels over the earth to see - what he likes to dwell on. Moreover, it is not death Hemingway writes about or travels to see, but killing. Nobody above fourteen years old will contend that he has got into his book that 'feeling of life and death' which he says he was working for. He has got into it an enthusiasm for killing - for courage and dominating and killing. Hemingway cannot feel - he cannot even see - the hero of his 'tragedy' staggering toward death in blood loss and bewilderment. He withdraws automatically from any participation in that central fact. He did once feel, he tells us, the surprise of pain which makes the animal toss awkwardly like a great inflexible box when the banderillos are jabbed into his withers, but this live feeling vanished instantly and by an extraordinary magic the moment he learned that the bull is more and not less dangerous after he has been 'slowed' in this way, and will now make better aimed, because more desperate, efforts to defend his life. After learning that, Hemingway felt 'no more sympathy' for the bull 'than for a canvas or the marble a sculptor cuts or the dry powder snow your skis cut through.' Which is a clear statement - is it not? - of indifference to 'the feeling of life and death,' and total preoccupation with the art of courageous killing.

A like numbness of imagination afflicts this poet when the life and death of the matador is in question. The climax of his enterprise of learning how to write, at least the last mention of it, occurs on page 20, where after seeing a matador gored by a bull, he wakes in the night and tries to remember 'what it was that seemed just out of my remembering and that was the thing that I had really seen and, finally, remembering all around it, I got it. When he stood up, his face white and dirty and the silk of his breeches opened from waist to knee, it was the dirtiness of his slit underwear and the clean, clean, unbearably clean whiteness of the thigh bone that I had seen, and it was that which was important.' Is the clean whiteness of a man's thigh bone the 'important' thing to a poet working for the feeling of life and death, or is it merely the most shocking thing, and therefore the most sought after by an ecstatic in the rapture of killing?

'Do you know the sin it would be,' he says, 'to ruffle the arrangement of the feathers on a hawk's neck if they could never be replaced as they were? Well, that would be the sin it would be to kill El Gallo.' And we turn the page with a shudder for El Gallo.

It seems, then, that our ferocious realist is so romantic about bullfights, and so blind to much of what they 'actually are,' because he is enraptured with courageous killing. He is athirst after this quality of act and emotion with that high-fevered thirst of the saint after the blood of the living God, so that little else can open its way into his eyes or down to his heartstrings. He is himself, moreover, courageous enough - and with a courage rarer than that of toreros - to state plainly that he loves killing, and try to state why. It is because killing makes him feel triumphant over death.

'Killing cleanly and in a way which gives you esthetic pride and pleasure,' he says, 'has always been one of the greatest enjoyments of a part of the human race.... One of its greatest pleasures ... is the feeling of rebellion against death which comes from its administering. Once you accept the rule of death thou shalt not kill is an easily and a naturally obeyed commandment. But when a man is still in rebellion against death he has pleasure in taking to himself one of the godlike attributes; that of giving it. This is one of the most profound feelings in those men who enjoy killing.'

Hemingway is quite right about the pleasure derived by a part of our race, and, in imagination, indeed, by all of it, from killing. One need only read the Old Testament to see how easy it was for our most pious ancestors in morality to cut a whole people out of the tiny circle of their tribal sympathy like the ring of light round a campfire, and enjoy with free hearts the delight of slaughtering them 'so that there was none left in that city, man, woman or child.' And one need only remark the popularity of murder stories - or of Hemingway's own book so gorgeously full of horse's blood and bull's blood, and matador's blood, and even the blood of 'six carefully selected Christs' crucified in his riotous imagination to make a holiday for his readers, in order to see that this little-satisfied thirst is wellnigh universal.

Had men not enjoyed killing, they would not be here, and the bulls would be doing it all. That is a significant fact. But nevertheless the important part of the killing has been done, and the present tendency is to suppress, to sublimate in representative art, even in some measure to breed out this dangerous taste. For this we have the authority of Gene Tunney, (3) a writer who stands at the opposite pole from Hemingway, having abundantly established his prowess in action, and in literature therefore being somewhat concerned, strangely enough, to establish his sensibility. Speaking in his biography of the 'killer-instinct boys,' he remarks that 'the higher in human development one goes, the more controlled one finds this reaction.' And if that is true in the prize ring, it is more certainly true among poets and artists and sensitive young men generally.

It is so true that the nervous horror of these young men, and their mental and moral sickness, after forcing themselves through the insensate butchery of the World War, may be said almost to have created an epoch in our literature. One by one they have recovered their tongues and stood up during these fifteen years, those stricken poets, and confessed that they were devastated and broken clear down and shattered by that forced discipline in the art of wholesale killing - those have who were not too shattered to speak. And their speech with the silence of the others is the true aftermath in poetry of the Great War - not the priggish trivialities of the Cult of Unintelligibility, not the cheap moral of decorum (that shallow cult so admirably exterminated root and branch by Ernest Hemingway in a paragraph of this book), not the new Bohemianism of the synthetic-gin period, (4) not the poetry of the new scientific hope in Russia, for it has had no poetry - but the confession in language of blood and tears of the horror unendurable to vividly living nerves of the combination of civilized life with barbaric slaughter.

Will it be too much like a clinic if I point out that Ernest Hemingway is one of the most sensitive and vivid-living of these poets, one of the most passionately intolerant, too, of priggery and parlor triviality and old maids' morals and empty skulls hiding in unintelligibility? I am not strong for literary psychoanalysis, but I must record a guess rising toward the middle of his book and growing to conviction in the end, that 'Death in the Afternoon' belongs also among those confessions of horror which are the true poetry and the only great poetry of this generation. It does not matter much whether Ernest Hemingway knows this fact or not. We may hope he will find out, for a man cannot grow to his height without self-knowledge. But the important thing is for us to know.

We took this young man with his sensitive genius for experience, for living all the qualities of life and finding a balance among them - and with that too obvious fear in him of proving inadequate - and we shoved him into our pit of slaughter, and told him to be courageous about killing. And we thought he would come out weeping and jittering. Well, he came out roaring for blood, shouting to the skies the joy of killing, the 'religious ecstasy' of killing - and most pathetic, most pitiable, killing as a protest against death.

Notes

1 A baseball park in New York City.
2 English psychologist, author of 'Studies in the Psychology of Sex' (1897-1910).
3 American heavyweight boxing champion, author of an autobiography 'A Man Must Fight' (1932).
4 Prohibition, 1920-33.

'Winner Take Nothing' (1933)

38. WILLIAM TROY, 'NATION'

137 (15 November 1933), 570

William Troy (1903-61), American critic, was the author of 'Selected Essays' (1967).

It is among Mr. Hemingway's admirers that the suspicion is being most strongly created that the champion is losing, if he has not already lost, his hold. In the current 'Contempo,' for example, Henry Hart administers a sharp castigation to those ungrateful people who were the first to applaud him when he was in his prime. (1) Briefly stated, Mr. Hart's thesis is that the generation into whose veins Hemingway poured such a badly needed flow of rich red blood should be the last to revile him now that his task is done. Despite his eloquent recapitulation of the champion's past glories, however, Mr. Hart only succeeds in delivering what is really a politely modulated funeral oration. Similarly, in a review of the newest Hemingway volume, Horace Gregory lauds the author of 'In Our Time' and 'The Sun Also Rises' for his services to his generation, of which he is still represented as the principal spokesman, without anywhere making clear whether those services ever did, or do now, include an intellectually satisfactory statement of its position. (2) The reason in both cases for this manifest attempt to let the champion down as easily as possible is not very hard to discover. Whatever have been Hemingway's limitations of mind and sensibility, he has stood out for his generation in

America as preeminently the type of pure artist, concentrated on experience and on its disciplined expression in literature. His very limitations have seemed at times to be his greatest virtues. At any rate they have saved him from saga-making, from vatic exuberances, and from the mechanical illustration of politico-economic ideologies. To turn against this writer, therefore, seems almost tantamount to turning against an art itself or against the artist's role in culture or society. It is to take sides with the Philistines - by whatever name they may now call themselves.

Now some such reservations must be understood when one reports that Mr. Hemingway's latest collection of stories includes what is actually the poorest and least interesting writing he has ever placed on public view. One cannot but regret, for instance, that a specimen like One Reader Writes should ever have been exposed to that view. As for most of the stories in the volume, their dulness may be traced either to a lack of growth or to growth along what is for Hemingway a new and unfortunate direction. There is, first of all, a recurrence of all the old nostalgias - the nostalgia for Europe (Wine of Wyoming), for the church (The Gambler, the Nun, and the Radio), for adolescence (Fathers and Sons), and for death (A Clean, Well-Lighted Place). There is also the monotonous repetition of the subjects attached to these themes - eating and drinking, travel, sport, coition. In one story the café waiter sums it all up in the now celebrated prayer: 'Our nada who art in nada, nada be thy name thy kingdom nada thy will be nada in nada as it is in nada....'

The new direction mentioned is an increasing fondness for subjects and characters which are usually distinguished by the label 'special.' Ignoring the preoccupation with death, which in the reprinted Natural History of the Dead almost amounts to an enthusiastic *delectatio morbosa*, (3) there are enough other indications that Hemingway is in danger of becoming as *fin de siècle* as his contemporary, William Faulkner. At its worst this tendency results in such delicacies as Mother of a Queen, which deals with a homosexual bullfighter who permits his mother's bones to be thrown on a dump heap, and God Rest You Merry, Gentlemen, which deals with a sex-crazed adolescent who commits self-mutilation. As it happens, the real objection to this kind of subject matter has quite recently been expressed once and for all by Mr. Hemingway's own literary godmother: 'She [Gertrude Stein] says she dislikes the abnormal, it is so obvious.'

The Gambler story is from every point of view the most successful in the book: Sister Cecilia and the Mexican

Cayetano are both admirably realized characterizations, the narrative is dense, and there is one remarkable passage of serious reflection. Examining the statement that religion is the opium of the people, (4) the convalescent Mr. Frazer decides that economics, patriotism, sexual intercourse, the radio, gambling, and ambition, each in its way, are also opiums of the people. The real, the actual opium of the people, he concludes, is bread. 'Revolution, Mr. Frazer thought, is no opium. Revolution is a catharsis; an ecstasy which can only be prolonged by tyranny. The opiums are for before and after. He was thinking well, a little too well.'

Too well? One wonders whether Mr. Hemingway can produce any more interesting volumes so long as he stops off as abruptly as this, turning to play the radio so loud that it can no longer be heard. Fiction is an opium as long as it contents itself with playing over the surface of things. Action, too, is an opium if it is thought of simply as a catharsis and not as an expression. Unless Mr. Hemingway realizes within the next few years that fiction based on action as catharsis is becoming less and less potent as an opium, he will not be able to hold the championship much longer.

Notes

1 Henry Hart, I Come Not to Bury Hemingway, 'Contempo,' 3 (25 October 1933), 1-2.
2 Horace Gregory, 'New York Herald Tribune Books,' 29 October 1933, 5.
3 Morbid delight.
4 Karl Marx, 'Critique of the Hegelian Philosophy of Right' (1844).

39. WILLIAM PLOMER, 'NOW AND THEN'

47 (Spring 1934), 22-3

William Plomer (1903-73) was a South African biographer, poet and novelist. He wrote 'Cecil Rhodes' (1933), an autobiography 'Double Lives' (1943) and 'Museum Pieces' (1952).

Mr. Hemingway's new book of short stories begins with

two men fighting. One of them produces a knife.

> He was choking me and hammering my head on the floor and I got the knife out and opened it up; and I cut the muscle right across his arm and he let go of me.

In another story a boy mutilates himself, at Christmas time, with a razor. In another a military doctor flings a saucerful of iodine in the eyes of a wounded officer. Attention is drawn to these episodes of violence, because episodes of violence are a particular choice of Mr. Hemingway, war veteran and connoisseur of bull-fighting, and may be taken as having a particular significance. 'Pourquoi alors', in the words of Edmond Jaloux, 'ne pas s'expliquer franchement sur le sadisme et ne pas vouloir accepter qu'il soit un des ferments les plus naturels de l'âme humaine?' (1)

Mr. Hemingway writes as an artist, in many ways representative of his race and time, and one might regard him as cutting right across the muscle of the arm of Convention; one might read into the incident of the boy who mutilates himself at Christmas time, in a belief that sexual excitement is 'a sin against our Lord and Saviour', an indictment of Christianity; and one could wish for no clearer exposures of modern warfare. His writings belong, quite as much as the writings of, say, D. H. Lawrence, to the literature of protest and escape. Although this book is destined to lie on tables of glass and steel in clean, empty, modern rooms, neither book nor table can be regarded as some pure, new, effortless fancy; the book, like that furniture and those rooms, is a protest against old conventions and an effort to escape from them, and at the same time an effort towards the establishment of a new convention. Sexual inversion, male and female; the War and its effects; the pleasant or unpleasant follies of various sorts of 'ordinary' people in this present century - these are some of Mr. Hemingway's preoccupations, some of the subjects he treats with that technical skill, that economy, and that peculiarly American kind of sophistication, which have helped to make his name. Irony plays over the surface, and is often intensified to a terrible directness, as in A Natural History of the Dead, whom 'one has seen in the hot weather with a half-pint of maggots working where their mouths have been.' That irony is often humorous, but here and there a phrase reveals that the legacy of puritanism is not yet spent: would it occur to any but a 'Western' man to write, even in fun, 'the position prescribed for procreation is indecorous, highly indecorous'? And sometimes Mr. Hemingway is content just to express disgust, taking up a touch-me-not attitude.

Combined with the motives of protest and escape, and lurking also beneath the manner - the fastidious brutality of this laconic wanderer - there is a genuine nihilism, like that of the waiter in A Clean, Well-Lighted Place who says to himself, 'Hail nothing full of nothing, nothing is with thee' and 'Our nada who art in nada, nada be thy name'. This is partly the nihilism of our time, the time of the War and of our permanent Crisis and of our spiritual dislocation, but it is also the nihilism that so often goes with vitality. Mr. Hemingway's vitality, which has led him into the waiting rooms of Swiss railway stations and the Spanish bullring, to Milan or Kansas City, observing various sorts of people, the French exiles in Wyoming, the bull-fighter who was a 'queen', the sick child in bed, or 'the biggest whore I ever saw in my life' - this vitality quickens his eye and shapes his style. To me he is the most interesting contemporary American short-story writer. Vivid, adroit, and an expert in brevity, he can put more point into an anecdote than many writers can into a novel.

Note

1 'Then why not discuss sadism frankly and recognize that it is one of the most natural actions of the human soul?' Edmond Jaloux (1878-1949), French critic.

Wyndham Lewis on Hemingway (1934)

40. WYNDHAM LEWIS, THE DUMB OX: A STUDY OF ERNEST HEMINGWAY, 'LIFE AND LETTERS'

10 (April 1934), 33-45

Wyndham Lewis (1882-1957) was an English painter and writer, author of 'Tarr' (1918), 'The Apes of God' (1930), 'The Revenge for Love' (1937) and 'Self Condemned' (1954). 'Life and Letters,' edited in London by Desmond McCarthy, published excellent critical evaluations of modern literature. The essay was reprinted in 'Men Without Art' (London, 1934), 17-41.

Ernest Hemingway is a very considerable artist in prose-fiction. Besides this, or with this, his work possesses a penetrating quality, like an animal speaking. Compared often with Hemingway, William Faulkner is an excellent, big-strong, novelist: but a conscious artist he cannot be said to be. Artists are made, not born: but he is considerably older, I believe, than Hemingway, so it is not that. But my motive for discussing these two novelists has not been to arrive at estimates of that sort.

A quality in the work of the author of 'Men Without Women' suggests that we are in the presence of a writer who is not merely a conspicuous chessman in the big-business book-game of the moment, but something much finer than that. Let me attempt to isolate that quality for you, in such a way as not to damage it too much: for having set out to demonstrate the political significance of this artist's work, I shall, in the course of that demonstration, resort to a dissection of it - not the best way, I am afraid, to bring out the beauties of the finished product. This dissection is, however, necessary for my purpose here. 'I have a weakness for Ernest Hemingway,' (1) as the egregious Miss Stein says: it is not agreeable to me to pry into his craft, but there is no help for it if I am to reach certain important conclusions.

But *political significance!* That is surely the last thing one would expect to find in such books as 'In Our Time,' 'The Sun also Rises,' 'Men Without Women,' or 'Farewell to Arms.' And indeed it is difficult to imagine a writer whose mind is more entirely closed to politics than is Hemingway's. I do not suppose he has ever heard of the Five-Year Plan, (2) though I dare say he knows that artists pay no income tax in Mexico, and is quite likely to be following closely the agitation of the Mexican matadors to get themselves recognized as 'artists' so that they may pay no income tax. I expect he has heard of Hitler, but thinks of him mainly, if he is acquainted with the story, as the Boche (3) who went down into a cellar with another Boche and captured thirty Frogs and came back with an Iron Cross. He probably knows that his friend Pound writes a good many letters every week to American papers on the subject of Social Credit, but I am sure Pound has never succeeded in making him read a line of 'Credit-Power and Democracy.'(4) He is interested in the sports of death, in the sad things that happen to those engaged in the sports of love - in sand-sharks and in Wilson-spoons (5) - in war, but *not* in the things that cause war, or the people who profit by it, or in the ultimate human destinies involved in it. He lives, or affects to live, *submerged*. He is in the multitudinous ranks of *those to whom things happen* - terrible things of course, and of course stoically borne. He has never heard, or affects never to have heard, that there is another and superior element, inhabited by a type of unnatural men which preys upon that of the submerged type. Or perhaps it is not quite a submerged mankind to which he belongs, or affects to belong, but to something of the sort described in one of Faulkner's war stories: 'But after twelve years,' Faulkner writes, 'I think of us as bugs in the surface of the water, isolant and aimless and unflagging. Not on the surface; in it, within that line of demarcation not air and not water, sometimes submerged, sometimes not.' (6) (What a stupid and unpleasant word 'isolant' is! Hemingway would be incapable of using such a word.) But - twelve, fifteen years afterwards - to be *submerged*, most of the time, is Hemingway's idea. It is a little bit of an *art pur* notion, but it is, I think, extremely effective, in his case. Faulkner is much less preoccupied with art for its own sake, and although he has obtained his best successes by submerging himself again (in an intoxicating and hysterical fluid) he does not like being submerged quite as well as Hemingway, and dives rather because he is compelled to dive by public opinion, I imagine, than because he feels at home in the stupid medium of the sub-world, the bêtise (7) of the herd. Hemingway has really taken up his quarters there, and has mastered the medium entirely, so that he is of it and yet not of it in a very satisfactory way.

Another manner of looking at it would be to say that Ernest Hemingway is the Noble Savage of Rousseau, but a white version, the simple American man. That is at all events the rôle that he has chosen, and he plays it with an imperturbable art and grace beyond praise.

It is not perhaps necessary to say that Hemingway's art is an art of the surface - and, as I look at it, none the worse for that. It is almost purely an art of action, and of very violent action, which is another qualification. Faulkner's is that too: but violence with Hemingway is deadly matter-of-fact (as if there were only violent action and nothing else in the world): whereas with Faulkner it is an excited crescendo of psychological working-up of a sluggish and not ungentle universe, where there *might* be something else than high-explosive - if it were given a Chinaman's chance, which it is not. The latter is a far less artistic purveyor of violence. He does it well: but as to the manner, he does it in a way that any fool could do it. Hemingway, on the other hand, serves it up like the master of this form of art that he is, immeasurably more effective than Faulkner - good as he is; or than say the Irish novelist O'Flaherty (8) - who is a *raffiné* (9) too, or rather a two-gun man; Hemingway really banishes melodrama (except for his absurd escapes, on a Hollywood pattern, in 'Farewellto Arms').

To find a parallel to 'In Our Time' or 'Farewell to Arms' you have to go to 'Colomba' or to 'Chronique du règne de Charles ix': (10) and in one sense Prosper Mérimée supplies the historical key to these two ex-soldiers - married, in their literary craft, to a theatre of action à *l'outrance*. (11) The scene at the siege of La Rochelle in the 'Chronique de Règne de Charles ix' for instance: in the burning of the mill when the ensign is roasted in the window, that is the Hemingway subjects-matter to perfection - a man melted in his armour like a shell-fish in its shell - melted lobster in its red armour.

> 'S'ils tentaient de sauter par les fenêtres, ils tombaient dans les flammes, ou bien étaient reçus sur la pointe des piques.... Un enseigne, revêtu d'une armure complète, essaya de sauter comme les autres par une fenêtre étroite. Sa cuirasse se terminait, suivant une mode alors assez commune, par une espèce de jupon en fer qui couvrait les cuisses et le ventre, et s'élargissait comme le haut d'un entonnoir, de manière à permettre de marcher facilement. La fenêtre n'était pas assez large pour laisser passer cette partie de son armure, et l'enseigne, dans son trouble, s'y était précipité avec tant de violence, qu'il se trouva avoir la plus grande partie du corps en dehors sans pouvoir remuer, et pris comme dans un étau. Cependant les flammes montaient jusqu'à lui, échauffaient son armure, et l'y brûlaient lentement comme dans une fournaise ou dans ce fameux taureau d'airain inventé par Phalaris. (12)

Compare this with the following:

> We were in a garden at Mons. Young Buckley came in with his patrol from across the river. The first German I saw climbed up over the garden wall. We waited till he got one leg over and then potted him. He had so much equipment on and looked awfully surprised and fell down into the garden. Then three more came over further down the wall. We shot them. They all came just like that. (13)

'In no century would Prosper Mérimée have been a theologian or metaphysician,' and if that is true of Mérimée, it is at least equally true of his American prototype. But their 'formulas' sound rather the same, 'indifferent in politics ... all the while he is feeding all his scholarly curiosity, his imagination, the very eye, with the, to him ever delightful, relieving, reassuring spectacle, of those straightforward forces in human nature, which are also matters of fact. There is the formula of Mérimée! the enthusiastic amateur of rude, crude, naked force in men and women wherever it could be found ... there are no half-lights.... Sylla, the false Demetrius, (14) Carmen, Colomba, that impassioned self within himself, have no atmosphere. Painfully distinct in outline, inevitable to sight, unrelieved, there they stand, like solitary mountain forms on some hard, perfectly transparent day. What Mérimée gets around his singularly sculpturesque creations is neither more nor less than empty space.' (15)

I have quoted the whole of this passage because it

gives you 'the formula,' equally for the author of 'Carmen' and of 'The Sun also Rises' - namely *the enthusiastic amateur of rude, crude, naked force in men and women:* but it also brings out very well, subsequently, the nature of the radical and extremely significant *difference* existing between these two men, of differing nations and epochs - sharing so singularly a taste for physical violence and for fine writing, but nothing else. Between them there is this deep gulf fixed: that gifted he of today is 'the man that things are done to' - even the 'I' in 'The Sun also Rises' allows his Jew puppet to knock him about and 'put him to sleep' with a crash on the jaw, and this first person singular conveys a very aimless, will-less person, to say the least of it: whereas that *he* of the world of 'Carmen' (so much admired by Nietzsche for its bright Latin violence and directness - *la gaya scienza*) (16) or of Corsican vendetta, he was in love with *will*, as much as with violence: he did not celebrate in his stories a spirit that suffered bodily injury and mental disaster with the stoicism of an athletic clown in a particularly brutal circus - or of oxen (however robust) beneath a crushing yoke: *he*, the inventor of Colomba, belonged to a race of men for whom action meant *their* acting, with all the weight and momentum of the whole of their being: *he* of post-Napoleonic France celebrated intense spiritual energy and purpose, using physical violence as a mere means to that only half-animal ideal. *Sylla, Demetrius, Colomba*, even *de Mergy*, summon to our mind a world bursting with purpose - even if always upon the personal and very animal plane, and with no more universal ends: while Hemingway's books, on the other hand, scarcely contain a figure who is not in some way futile, clown-like, passive, and above all *purposeless*. His world of men and women (*in violent action*, certainly) is completely empty of will. His puppets are leaves, *very violently* blown hither and thither; drugged or at least deeply intoxicated phantoms of a sort of matter-of-fact shell-shock.

In 'Farewell to Arms' the hero is a young American who has come over to Europe for the fun of the thing, as an alternative to baseball, to take part in the Sport of Kings. It has not occurred to him that it is no longer the sport of kings, but the turning-point in the history of the earth at which he is assisting, when men must either cease thinking like children and abandon such sports, or else lose their freedom for ever, much more effectively than any mere *king* could ever cause them to lose it. For him, it remains 'war' in the old-fashioned semi-sporting sense. Throughout this ghastly event, he proves himself a thorough-going sport, makes several hairbreadth, Fenimore Cooper-like (17), escapes, but never from first to last betrays a spark of intelligence. Indeed, his physical stoicism, admirable as it is, is as nothing to his really heroic imperviousness to thought. This 'war' - Gallipoli, Paschendaele, Caporetto (18) - is just another 'scrap.' The Anglo-Saxon American - the 'Doughboy' - and the Anglo-Saxon Tommy - join hands, in fact, outrival each other in a stolid determination absolutely to ignore, come what may, what all this is about. Whoever may be in the secrets of destiny - may indeed be destiny itself - *they* are not nor ever will be. They are an integral part of that world *to whom things happen:* they are not those who cause or connive at the happenings, and that is perfectly clear.

Pack up your troubles in your old kit bag,
Smile boys, that's the style

and *keep smiling*, what's more, from ear to ear, a *should-I-worry?* 'good sport' smile, as do the Hollywood Stars when they are being photographed, as did the poor Bairnsfather 'Tommy' - the 'muddied oaf at the goal' (19) - of all oafishness!

I hope this does not seem irrelevant to you: it is not, let me reassure you, but very much the contrary. The roots of all these books are in the War of 1914-1918, as much those of Faulkner as those of Hemingway: it would be ridiculous of course to say that either of these two highly intelligent ex-soldiers shared the 'oafish' mentality altogether: but the war-years were a democratic, a *levelling*, school, and both come from a pretty thoroughly 'levelled' nation, where personality is the thing least liked. The rigid organization of the communal life as revealed in 'Middletown' (20) for instance (or such a phenomenon as N.R.A.) (21) is akin to the military state. So *will*, as expressed in the expansion of the individual, is not a thing we should expect to find illustrated by a deliberately typical American writer.

Those foci of passionate personal energy which we find in Mérimée, we should look for in vain in the pages of Hemingway or Faulkner: in place of Don José (22) or of Colomba we get a pack of drugged or intoxicated marionettes. These differences are exceedingly important. But I shall be dealing with that more carefully in my next chapter.

So any attempt to identify 'the formula' for Prosper Mérimée with that of Ernest Hemingway would break down. You are led at once to a realization of the critical difference between these two universes of discourse, both employing nothing but physical terms; of how an appetite for the extremity of violence exists in both, but in the one case it is personal ambition, family pride, romantic love that are at stake, and their satisfaction is viollently sought and undertaken, whereas in the other case purposeless violence, for the sake of the 'kick,' is pursued and recorded, and the 'thinking subject' is to regard himself as nothing more significant than a ripple beneath the breeze upon a pond.

If we come down to the manner, specifically to the style, in which these sensational impressions are conveyed, again most interesting discoveries await us: for, especially with Mr. Hemingway, the story is told in the tone, and with the vocabulary, of the persons described. The rhythm is the anonymous folk-rhythm of the urban proletariat. Mr. Hemingway is, self-consciously, a folk-prose-poet in the way that Robert Burns was a folk-poet. But what is curious about this is that the modified *Beach-la-mar* (23) in which he writes, is, more or less, the speech that is proposed for everybody in the future - it is a volapuk (24) which probably will be ours tomorrow. For if the chief executive of the United States greets the Roman Catholic democratic leader (Al Smith) (25) with the exclamation 'Hallo old potato!' today, the English political leaders will be doing so the day after tomorrow. And the Anglo-Saxon *Beach-la-mar* of the future will not be quite the same thing as Chaucer or Dante, contrasted with the learned tongue. For the latter was the speech of a race rather than of a class, whereas our 'vulgar tongue' will really be *vulgar*.

But in the case of Hemingway the folk-business is very seriously complicated by a really surprising fact. He has suffered an overmastering influence, which cuts his work off from any other, except that of his mistress (for his master has been a *mistress*!). So much is this the case, that their destinies (his and that of the person who so strangely hypnotized him with her repeating habits and her *faux-naif* (26) prattle) are for ever interlocked. His receptivity was so abnormally pronounced (even as a craftsman, this capacity for being *the person that things are done to* rather than the person who naturally initiates what is to be done to others, was so marked) and the affinity thus disclosed was found so powerful! I don't like speaking about this, for it is such a first-class complication, and yet it is in a way so irrelevant to the spirit which informs his work and must have informed it had he never made this apparently overwhelming 'contact.' But there it is: if you ask yourself how you would be able to tell a page of Hemingway, if it were unexpectedly placed before you, you would be compelled to answer, *Because it would be like Miss Stein!* And if you were asked how you would know it was not by Miss Stein, you would say, *Because it would probably be about prize-fighting, war, or the bull-ring, and Miss Stein does not write about war, boxing or bull-fighting!*

It is very uncomfortable in real life when people become so captivated with somebody else's tricks that they become a sort of caricature or echo of the other: and it is no less embarrassing in books, at least when one entertains any respect for the victim of the fascination. But let us take a passage or two and get this over - it is very unpleasant. Let us take Krebs - the 'he' in this passage is Krebs, a returned soldier in a Hemingway story:

> When he was in town their appeal to him was not very strong. He did not like them when he saw them in the Greek's ice-cream parlor. He did not want them themselves really. They were too complicated. There was something else. Vaguely he wanted a girl but he did not want to have to work to get her. He would have liked to have a girl but he did not want to have to spend a long time getting her. He did not want to get into the intrigue and the politics. He did not want to have to do any courting. He did not want to tell any more lies. It wasn't worth it.
>
> He did not want any consequences. He did not want any consequences ever again. He wanted to live along without consequences. Besides he did not really need a girl. The army had taught him that. It was all right to pose as though you had to have a girl. Nearly everybody did that. But it wasn't true. You did not need a girl. That was the funny thing. First a fellow boasted how girls meant nothing to him, that he never thought of them, that they could not touch him. Then a fellow boasted that he could not get along without girls, that he had to have them all the time, that he could not go to sleep without them.
>
> That was all a lie. It was all a lie both ways. You did not need a girl unless you thought about them. He learned that in the army. Then sooner or later you always got one. When you were really ripe for a girl you always got one. You did not have to think about it. Sooner or later it would come. He had learned that in the army.
>
> Now he would have liked a girl if she had come to

> him and not wanted to talk. But here at home it was all too complicated. He knew he could never get through it all again. It was not worth the trouble. That was the thing about French girls and German girls. There was not all this talking. You couldn't talk much and you did not need to talk. It was simple and you were friends. He thought about France and then he began to think about Germany. On the whole he liked Germany better. He did not want to leave Germany. He did not want to come home. Still, he had come home. He sat on the front porch.
>
> He liked the girls that were walking along the other side of the street. He liked the look of them much better than the French girls or the German girls. But the world they were in was not the world he was in. He would like to have one of them. But it was not worth it. They were such a nice pattern. He liked the pattern. It was exciting. But he would not go through all the talking. He did not want one badly enough. He liked to look at them all, though. It was not worth it. (27)

So much for Krebs: now open Miss Stein and 'meet' Melanctha.

> Rose was lazy but not dirty, and Sam was careful but not fussy, and then there was Melanctha.... When Rose's baby was coming to be born, Rose came to stay in the house where Melanctha Herbert lived just then, ... Rose went there to stay, so that she might have the doctor from the hospital.... Melanctha Herbert had not made her life all simple like Rose Johnson. Melanctha had not found it easy with herself to make her wants and what she had, agree.
>
> Melanctha Herbert was always losing what she had in wanting all the things she saw. Melanctha was always being left when she was not leaving others.
>
> Melanctha Herbert always loved too hard and much too often. She was always full with mystery and subtle movements ... etc., etc., etc. (28)

Or here is a typical bit from 'Composition as Explanation':

> There is singularly nothing that makes a difference a difference in beginning and in the middle and in ending except that each generation has something different at which they are all looking. By this I mean so simply that anybody knows it that composition is the difference which makes each and all of them then

> different from other generations and this is what makes everything different otherwise they are all alike and everybody knows it because everybody says it. (29)

There is no possibility, I am afraid, of slurring over this. It is just a thing that you have to accept as an unfortunate handicap in an artist who is in some respects above praise. Sometimes it is less pronounced, there are occasions when it is *almost* absent - Krebs, for instance, is a full-blooded example of Hemingway steining away for all he is worth. But it is never quite absent.

How much does it matter? If we blot out Gertrude Stein, and suppose she does not exist, does this part of Hemingway's equipment help or not? We must answer *Yes* I think. It does seem to help a good deal: many of his best effects are obtained by means of it. It is so much a part of his craft, indeed, that it is difficult now to imagine Hemingway without this mannerism. He has never taken it over into a gibbering and baboonish stage as has Miss Stein. He has kept it as a valuable oddity, even if a flagrantly borrowed one - ever present it is true, but one to which we can easily get used and come to like even as a delightfully clumsy engine of innocence. I don't mind it very much.

To say that, near to communism as we all are, it cannot matter, and is indeed praiseworthy, for a celebrated artist to take over, lock, stock and barrel from another artist the very thing for which he is mainly known, seems to me to be going too far in the denial of the person, or the individual - especially as in a case of this sort, the trick is after all, in the first instance, a *personal* trick. Such a practice must result, if universally indulged in, in hybrid forms or monstrosities.

And my main criticism, indeed, of the *steining* of Hemingway is that it does impose upon him an ethos - *the Stein ethos*, as it might be called. With Stein's bag of tricks he also takes over a *Weltanschauung*, (30) which may not at all be his, and does in fact seem to contradict his major personal quality. This infantile, dull-witted dreamy stutter compels whoever uses it to conform to the infantile, dull-witted type. He passes over into the category of *those to whom things are done*, from that of those who execute - if the latter is indeed where he originally belonged. One might even go so far as to say that this brilliant Jewish lady had made a *clown* of him by teaching Ernest Hemingway her baby-talk! So it is a pity. And it is very difficult to know where Hemingway proper begins and Stein leaves off as an artist. It is an uncomfortable situation for the critic, especially for one who 'has a weakness' for the male member of this strange spiritual partnership, and very much prefers him to the female.

Hemingway's two principal books, 'The Sun also Rises' (for English publication called 'Fiesta') and 'Farewell to Arms,' are delivered in the first person singular. What that involves may not be at once apparent to those who have not given much attention to literary composition. But it is not at all difficult to explain. Suppose you, Raymond Robinson, sit down to write a romance; subject-matter, the War. You get your 'I' started off, say just before the outbreak of war, and then there is the outbreak, and then 'I flew to the nearest recruiting station and joined the army' you write. Then the 'I' goes off to the Western Front (or the Italian Front) and you will find yourself writing 'I seized the Boche by the throat with one hand and shot him in the stomach with the other,' or whatever it is you imagine your 'I' as doing. But this 'I,' the the reader will learn, does not bear the name on the title page, namely Raymond Robinson. He is called Geoffrey Jones. The reader will think, 'that is only a thin disguise. It is Robinson's personal experience all right!'

Now this difficulty (if it be a difficulty) is very much enhanced if (for some reason) Geoffrey Jones is *always* doing exactly the things that Raymond Robinson is known to have done. If Raymond Robinson fought gallantly at Caporetto, (31) for instance, then Geoffrey Jones - with the choice of a whole earth at war to choose from - is at Caporetto too. If Raymond Robinson takes to the sport of bull-fighting, sure enough Geoffrey Jones - the 'I' of the novel - is there in the bull-ring too, as the night follows day. This, in fine, has been the case with Hemingway and *his* First-person-singular.

Evidently, in this situation - possessing a First-person-singular that invariably copies you in this flattering way - something must be done about it. The *First-person-singular* has to be endowed so palpably with qualities that could by no stretch of the imagination belong to its author that no confusion is possible. Upon this principle the 'I' of 'The Sun also Rises' is described as sexually impotent, which is a complete alibi, of course, for Hemingway.

But there is more than this. The sort of First-person-singular that Hemingway invariably invokes is a dull-witted, bovine, monosyllabic simpleton. This lethargic and stuttering dummy he conducts, or pushes from behind, through all the scenes that interest him. This burlesque First-person-singular behaves in them like a moronesque version of his brilliant author. He *Steins* up and down the world, with the big lustreless ruminatory orbs of a Picasso doll-woman (of the semi-classic type Picasso patented, with enormous hands and feet). (32) It is, in short, the very dummy that is required for the literary mannerism of Miss Stein! It is the incarnation of the Stein-stutter - the male incarnation, it is understood.

But this constipated, baffled 'frustrated' - yes, deeply and Freudianly 'frustrated' - this wooden-headed, leaden-witted, heavy-footed, loutish and oafish marionette - peering dully out into the surrounding universe like a great big bloated five-year-old - pointing at this and pointing at that - uttering simply 'CAT!' - 'HAT!' - 'FOOD!' - 'SWEETIE!' - is, as a companion, infectious. His author has perhaps not been quite immune. Seen for ever through his nursery spectacles, the values of life accommodate themselves, even in the mind of his author, to the limitations and peculiar requirements of this highly idiosyncratic puppet.

So the political aspects of Hemingway's work (if, as I started by saying, one can employ such a word as *political* in connection with a thing that is so divorced from reality as a super-innocent, queerly-sensitive, village-idiot of a few words and fewer ideas) have to be sought, if anywhere, in the personality of this *First-person-singular*, imposed upon him largely by the Stein-manner.

We can return to the folk-prose problem now and face all the questions that the 'done gones' and 'sorta gonnas' present. Mr H.L. Mencken in his well-known, extremely competent and exhaustive treatise, 'The American Language' (a classic in this field of research, first published fifteen years ago) affirmed that the American dialect had not yet come to the stage where it could be said to have acquired charm for 'the purists.' If used (at that time) in narrative literature it still possessed only the status of a disagreeable and socially-inferior jargon, like the cockney occurring in a Dickens novel - or as it is still mostly used in William Faulkner's novels, never outside of inverted commas; the novelist, having invoked it to convey the manner of speech of his rustic or provincial puppets, steps smartly away and resumes the narrative in the language of Macaulay or Horace Walpole, (33) more or less.

'In so far as it is apprehended at all,' Mencken wrote in 1920, 'it is only in the sense that Irish-English was apprehended a generation ago - that is, as something uncouth and comic. But that is the way that new dialects always come in - through a drum-fire of cackles. Given the poet, there may suddenly come a day when our *theirns* and *would'a hads* will take on the barbaric stateliness of the peasant locution of old Maurya in "Riders to the Sea."'(34)

The reason that the dialect of the Aran Islands, (35) or that used by Robert Burns, were so different from cockney or from the English educated speech was because it was a mixture of English and another language, Gaelic or lowland Scotch, and with the intermixture of foreign words went a literal translation of foreign idioms and the distortions arrived at by a tongue accustomed to another language. It was 'broken-English,' in other words, not 'low-English,' or slum-English, as is cockney.

Americans are today un-English in blood - whatever names they may bear: and in view of this it is surprising how intact the English language remains in the United States. But the *Beach-la-mar*, as he calls it, to which Mencken is referring above, is as it were the cockney of America. It has this great advantage over cockney, that it is fed with a great variety of immigrant words. It is, however, fundamentally *a class-jargon*; not a jargon resulting from difference of race, and consequently of speech. It is the *patois* of the 'poor white,' the negro, or the uneducated immigrant. It is not the language spoken by Mrs. Alice Roosevelt Longworth, (36) for instance, or by Ernest Hemingway for that matter. But it is very *American*. And it is a *patois*, a fairly good rendering of which any American is competent to give. And you have read above the affectionate way Mencken refers to *our* 'theirns' and 'would'a hads.'

English as spoken in America is more vigorous and expressive than Oxford English, I think. It is easy to mistake a native from the wilds of Dorsetshire for an American, I have found: and were 'educated' English used upon a good strong reverberant Dorsetshire basis, for instance, it would be all to the good, it is my opinion. Raleigh, Drake, and the rest of them, must have talked rather like that.

But with cockney it is not at all the same thing. There you get a degradation of English - it is *proletariat*, city-slum English, like Dublin-slum English. That is in a different category altogether to the weighty, rapid and expressive torrent of the best Dorsetshire talk; and, as I have said, the *best* American is in the same category as the Dorsetshire - or as non-slum Irish - a good, sound accent, too. But the question to be answered is whether the *Beach-la-mar* Mr. Mencken has in mind is not too much the deteriorated pidgin tongue of the United States; and whether if that is *affectionné* too much by the *literati* (37)

- as being the most *American* thing available, like a jazz - it is not going to be a vulgar corruption, which will vulgarize, as well as enrich, the tongue. So far it exists generally in inverted commas, as in Mr. Faulkner's books. Is it to be let out or not? A question for Americans.

For fifty years dialect-American has tended, what with negro and immigrant pressure, to simplify itself grammatically, and I suppose is still doing so at this moment.

> His (the immigrant's) linguistic habits and limitations have to be reckoned with in dealing with him and the concessions thus made necessary have a very ponderable influence upon the general speech. Of much importance is the support given to the native tendency by the foreigner's incapacity for employing (or even comprehending) syntax of any complexity, or words not of the simplest. This is the tendency towards succinctness and clarity, at whatever sacrifice of grace. One English observer, Sidney Low, (38) puts the chief blame for the general explosiveness of American upon the immigrant, who must be communicated with in the plainest words available, and is not socially worthy of the suavity of circumlocution anyhow. In his turn the immigrant seizes upon these plainest words as upon a sort of convenient Lingua Franca - his quick adoption of *damn* as a universal adjective is traditional - and throws his influence upon the side of the underlying speech habit when he gets on in the vulgate. Many characteristic Americanisms of the sort to stagger lexicographers - for example, *near-silk* - have come from Jews, whose progress in business is a good deal faster than their progress in English. (39)

While England was a uniquely powerful empire-state, ruled by an aristocratic caste, its influence upon the speech as upon the psychology of the American ex-colonies was overwhelming. But today that ascendancy has almost entirely vanished. The aristocratic caste is nothing but a shadow of itself, the cinema has brought the American scene and the American dialect nightly into the heart of England, and the 'Americanizing' process is far advanced. 'Done gones,' 'good guys' and 'buddies' sprout upon the lips of cockney children as readily as upon those to the manner born, of New York or Chicago: and there is no politically-powerful literate class any longer now, in our British 'Banker's Olympus,' to confer prestige upon an exact and intelligent selective speech. Americanization - which is also for England, at least, proletarianization - is too far advanced to require underlining, even for people who fail usually to recognize anything until it has been in existence for a quarter of a century.

But if America has come to England, there has been no reciprocal movement of England into the United States: indeed, with the new American nationalism, England is deliberately kept out: and all the great influence that England exerted formally - merely by being there and speaking the same tongue and sharing the same fundamental political principles - that is today a thing of the past. So the situation is this, as far as our common language is concerned: the destiny of England and the United States of America is more than ever one. But it is now the American influence that is paramount. The tables have effectively been turned in that respect.

But there is a larger issue even than that local to the English-speaking nations. English is of all languages the simplest grammatically and the easiest to make into a *Beach-la-mar* or *pidgin* tongue. Whether this fact, combined with its 'extra-ordinary tendency to degenerate into slang of every kind,' is against it, is of some importance for the future - for it will have less and less grammar, obviously, and more and more cosmopolitan slang. - Mr. Mencken is of opinion that a language cannot be too simple - he is all for *Beach-la-mar*. The path towards analysis and the elimination of inflection, has been trod by English so thoroughly that, in its American form, it should today win the race for a universal volapuk. Indeed, as Mr. Mencken says, 'the foreigner essaying it, indeed, finds his chief difficulty, not in mastering its forms, but in grasping its lack of form. He doesn't have to learn a new and complex grammar; what he has to do is to forget grammar. Once he has done so, the rest is a mere matter of acquiring a vocabulary.'(40)

There is, it is true, the difficulty of the vowel sounds: but that is easily settled. Standard English possesses nineteen distinct vowel sounds: no other living European tongue except Portuguese, so Mr. Mencken says, possesses so many. Modern Greek, for instance, can only boast of five, we are told. 'The (American) immigrant, facing all these vowels, finds some of them quite impossible: the Russian Jew, for example, cannot manage *ur*. As a result, he tends to employ a neutralized vowel in the situations which present difficulties, and this neutralized vowel, supported by the slip-shod speech-habits of the native proletariat, makes steady progress.'(41)

That that 'neutralized vowel' has made great progress in America no one would deny who has been there; and, starting in the natural language-difficulties of the Central European immigrant, the above-mentioned 'neutralized vowel' will make its way over here in due course, who can doubt it? These vowels must be watched. *Watch your vowels* should be our next national slogan! The fatal grammatical easiness of English is responsible, however, for such problems as these, as much as the growing impressionability of the English nation, and the proletarianization, rather than the reverse, of the American.

As long ago as 1910 an English traveller, Mr. Alexander Thompson, in a book called 'Japan for a Week,' expresses himself as follows:

> It was only on reaching Italy that I began fully to realize this wonderful thing, that for nearly six weeks, on a German ship, in a journey of nearly ten thousand miles, we had heard little of any language but English!
>
> It is an amazing thing when one thinks of it.
>
> In Japan most of the tradespeople spoke English. At Shanghai, at Hong-Kong, at Singapore, at Penang, at Colombo, at Suez, at Port Said - all the way home to the Italian ports, the language of all the ship's traffic, the language of such discourse as the passengers held with natives, most of the language on board ship itself, was English.
>
> The German captain of our ship spoke English more often than German. All his officers spoke English.
>
> The Chinese man-o'-war's men who conveyed the Chinese prince on board at Shanghai, received commands and exchanged commands with our German sailors in English. The Chinese mandarins in their conversations with the ships' officers invariably spoke English. They use the same ideographs in writing as the Japanese, but to talk to our Japanese passengers they had to speak English. Nay, coming as they did from various provinces of the Empire, where the language greatly differs, they found it most convenient in conversation among themselves to speak English. (42)

If you place side by side the unfortunate impressionability of Hemingway, which caused him to adopt integrally the half-wit simplicity of repetitive biblical diction patented by Miss Stein, and that other fact that Mr. Hemingway, being an American nationalist by temperament, is inclined to gravitate stylistically towards the national underdog dialect, in the last resort to the kind of *Beach-la-mar* I have been discussing, you have the two principal factors in Hemingway as artist in prose-fiction, to make of what you can.

Take up any book of his, again, and open it at random: you will find a page of stuff that is, considered in isolation, valueless as writing. It is not written: it is lifted out of Nature and very artfully and adroitly tumbled out upon the page: it is the brute material of every-day proletarian speech and feeling. The *matière* (43) is cheap and coarse: but not because it is proletarian speech merely, but because it is *the prose of reality* – the prose of the street-car or the provincial newspaper or the five and ten cent store. I have just opened 'Farewell to Arms' entirely at random, for instance, and this is what I find:

> 'If you had any foreign bodies in your legs they would set up an inflammation and you'd have fever.'
> 'All right,' I said. 'We'll see what comes out.'
> She went out of the room and came back with the old nurse of the early morning. Together they made the bed with me in it. That was new to me and an admirable proceeding.
> 'Who is in charge here?'
> 'Miss Van Campen.'
> 'How many nurses are there?'
> 'Just us two.'
> 'Won't there be any more?'
> 'Some more are coming.'
> 'When will they get here?'
> 'I don't know. You ask a great many questions for a sick boy.'
> 'I'm not sick.' I said, 'I'm wounded.'
> They had finished making the bed and I lay with a clean smooth sheet under me and another sheet over me. Mrs. Walker went out and came back with a pyjama jacket. They put that on me and I felt very clean and dressed.
> 'You're awfully nice to me,' I said. The nurse called Miss Gage giggled. 'Could I have a drink of water?' I asked.
> 'Certainly. Then you can have breakfast.'
> 'I don't want breakfast. Can I have the shutters opened, please?'
> The light had been dim in the room and when the shutters were opened it was bright sunlight, and I looked out on a balcony and beyond were the tiled roofs of houses and chimneys and the sky very blue.
> 'Don't you know when the other nurses are coming?'
> 'Why? Don't we take good care of you?'
> 'You're very nice.'
> 'Would you like to use the bedpan?'
> 'I might try.'
> They helped me and held me up, but it was not any use. Afterward I lay and looked out the open doors on

to the balcony.
'When does the doctor come?' (44)

It is not writing, if you like. When I read 'Farewell to Arms' doubtless I read this page as I came to it, just as I should watch scenes unfolding on the screen in the cinema, without pictorial criticism; and it, page eighty-three, contributed its fraction to the general effect: and when I had finished the book I thought it a very good book. By that I meant that the cumulative effect was impressive, as *the events themselves* would be. Or it is like reading a newspaper, day by day, about some matter of absorbing interest - say the reports of a divorce, murder, or libel action. If you say *anyone could write it*, you are mistaken there, because, to obtain that smooth effect, of commonplace reality, there must be no sentimental or other heightening, the number of words expended must be proportionate to the importance and the length of the respective phases of the action, and any false move or overstatement would at once stand out and tell against it. If an inferior reporter to Hemingway took up the pen, that fact would at once be detected by a person sensitive to reality.

It is an art, then, from this standpoint, like the cinema, or like those 'modernist' still-life pictures in which, in place of *painting* a match box upon the canvas, a piece of actual match box is stuck on. A recent example of this (I choose it because a good many people will have seen it) is the cover design of the French periodical 'Minotaure,' in which Picasso has pasted and tacked various things together, sticking a line drawing of the Minotaur in the middle. Hemingway's is a poster-art, in this sense: or a *cinema in words*. *The steining* in the text of Hemingway is as it were the hand-made part - if we are considering it as 'super-realist' design: a manipulation of the photograph if we are regarding it as a film.

If you say that this is not the way that Dante wrote, that these are not artistically permanent creations - or not permanent in the sense of a verse of Bishop King,(45) or a page of Gulliver, I agree. But it is what we have got: there is actually *bad* and *good* of this kind; and I for my part enjoy what I regard as the good, without worrying any more about it than that.

That a particular phase in the life of humanity is implicit in this art is certain. It is one of the first fruits of the *proletarianization* which, as a result of the amazing revolutions in the technique of industry, we are all undergoing, whether we like it or not. But this purely political, or sociological side to the question can be brought out, I believe, with great vividness by a quotation. Here, for instance, is a fragment of a story of a mutiny at sea.

> I opened the door a little, about two inches, and saw there was a rope round the companion, which prevented the doors opening. Big Harry and Lips asked me what I wanted. I said I wanted to go down to the galley. Big Harry said: 'Plenty of time between this and eight o'clock; you stop down below.' I then went into the chief mate's room, which was the nearest to me. There was nobody there. I went to the second mate's room, he was not there. I went to the captain's pillow, it was standing up in his bed, and I found two revolvers loaded, one with six shots and one with four. I took possession of them and put them in my pockets. I then stood on the cabin table in the after cabin, and lifted the skylight up and tried to get out there. Renken was standing at the wheel, and he called out, 'Come aft, boys, the steward is coming out of the skylight.' I then closed the skylight and came down again. The after-skylight was close to the wheel, about 10 feet as near as I could guess. I could see him. The light used for the compass is in the skylight, and the wheel is in the back of it. The light is fastened to the skylight to light the compass, and the compass is just in front of the wheel. Before I could get the skylight closed I heard their steps coming aft, and I went down into the cabin and told the boy to light a fire. Shortly afterwards I heard five shots fired on deck ... about a second afterwards the same as if somebody was running on deck. I could not judge which way they were running; the noise on the deck, and the vessel being in ballast, you could hear as well aft as forward. That was about twenty minutes after hearing the captain call out. I put the revolvers away in my locker. I then took it into my head to take the revolvers into my possession and chance it; if the men came down to me to do anything wrong, to save myself. I put them in my pockets, one on each side. About 5.30 Green, the boatswain, came down first, and French Peter, Big Harry, and all the other lot followed. The deck was left without anybody, and the wheel too, they came into the cabin; Trousillot was there as well. They did not speak at first. The first thing they did was to rub me over. They could not feel anything. I had the two revolvers with me, but they did not feel them. French Peter and Big Harry felt me over. All the others were present. Green said, 'Well, steward, we

> have finished now.' I said, 'What the hell did you finish?' He said, 'We have finished captain, mate and second.' He said, 'We got our mind made up to go to Greece; if you like to save your own life you had better take charge of the ship and bring us to Greece. You bring us to Gibraltar, we will find Greece: you bring us there you will be all right, steward. We will take the boats when we get to Greece, and take the sails and everything into the boats, and sell them ashore and divide the money between ourselves. You will have your share, the same as anybody else; the charts and sextants, and all that belongs to the navigation, you can have. Me and my cousin, Johny Moore, have got a rich uncle; he will buy everything. We will scuttle the ship. My uncle is a large owner there of some ships. We will see you right, that you will be master of one of those vessels.' I said, 'Well, men, come on deck and get them braces ready, and I hope you will agree and also obey my orders!' The other men said, 'All right, steward, very good, very good, steward, you do right.' That was all I could hear from them, from everybody. The conversation between me and Green was in English, and everybody standing round. He spoke to the other men in Greek. What he said I don't know. I said, 'Where are the bodies? Where is the captain?' Green said, 'Oh they are all right, they are overboard,' and all the men said the same....(46)

That is not by Hemingway, though it quite well might be. I should not be able to tell it was not by Hemingway if it were shown me as a fragment. But this is by him:

> Across the bay they found the other boat beached. Uncle George was smoking a cigar in the dark. The young Indian pulled the boat way up the beach. Uncle George gave both the Indians cigars.
>
> They walked up from the beach through a meadow that was soaking wet with dew, following the young Indian who carried a lantern. Then they went into the woods and followed a trail that led to the logging road that ran back into the hills. It was much lighter on the logging road as the timber was cut away on both sides. The young Indian stopped and blew out his lantern and they all walked on along the road.
>
> The came around a bend and a dog came out barking. Ahead were the lights of the shanties where the Indian bark-peelers lived. More dogs rushed out at them. The two Indians sent them back to the shanties. In the shanty nearest the road there was a light in the window.

> An old woman stood in the doorway holding a lamp.
>
> Inside on a wooden bunk lay a young Indian woman. She had been trying to have her baby for two days. All the old women in the camp had been helping her. The men had moved off up the road to sit in the dark and smoke out of range of the noise she made. She screamed just as Nick and the two Indians followed his father and Uncle George into the shanty. She lay in the lower bunk, very big under a quilt. Her head was turned to one side. In the upper bunk was her husband. He had cut his foot very badly with an axe three days before. He was smoking a pipe. The room smelled very bad. Nick's father ordered some water to be put on the stove, while it was heating he spoke to Nick. 'This lady is going to have a baby, Nick,' he said. 'I know,' said Nick. 'You don' know.' said his father. 'Listen to me. What she is going through is called being in labour. The baby wants to be born and she wants it to be born. All her muscles are trying to get the baby born. That is what is happening when she screams.' 'I see,' Nick said. Just then the woman cried out.(47)

The first of these two passages is from a book entitled 'Forty Years in the Old Bailey.' It is the account of a mutiny and murder on the high seas, the trial occurring on May 3 and 4, 1876. It was evidence verbatim of one Constant von Hoydonck, a Belgian, twenty-years of age, who joined the vessel 'Lenni' at Antwerp, as chief steward, on October 22. This is a *Querschnitt*, (48) a slice, of 'real life': and how close Hemingway is to such material as this can be seen by comparing it with the second passage out of 'In Our Time.'

That, I think, should put you in possession of all that is essential for an understanding of the work of this very notable artist: an understanding I mean; I do not mean that, as a work of art, a book of his should be approached in this critical and anatomizing spirit. That is another matter. Where the 'politics' come in I suppose by this time you will have gathered. This is the voice of the 'folk,' of the masses, who are the cannon-fodder, the cattle outside the slaughter-house, serenely chewing the cud - *of those to whom things are done*, in contrast to those who have executive will and intelligence. It is itself innocent of politics - one might almost add alas! That does not affect its quality as art. The expression of the soul of the dumb ox would have a penetrating beauty of its own, if it were uttered with genius - with bovine genius (and in the case of Hemingway that is what has happened): just as much as would the folk-song of the baboon, or of the 'Praying Mantis.' But where the politics crop up is that if we take this to be the typical art of a civilization - and there is no serious writer who stands higher in Anglo-Saxony today than does Ernest Hemingway - then we are by the same token saying something very definite about that civilization.

Notes

1 Gertrude Stein, 'The Autobiography of Alice B. Toklas' (London, 1933), 231.
2 Soviet economic program.
3 Derogatory French word for 'German.'
4 A crankish economic book by C.H. Douglas (1921), whose theories had an unfortunate influence on Pound.
5 A kind of hooked, metal fishing bait.
6 Ad Astra (1930), 'Collected Stories of William Faulkner' (New York, 1948), 408.
7 Stupidity.
8 Liam O'Flaherty, Irish author of 'The Informer' (1926).
9 Subtle person.
10 'Chronicle of the Reign of Charles IX' (1829), an historical novel about the massacre of St. Bartholomew.
11 To the bitter end.
12 (Paris, 1957), 269: 'If they tried to leap out of the windows, they would fall into the flames, or be impaledon the pikes. Then we saw a dreadful sight. An ensign, dressed in full armor, tried to jump, like the others, out of a narrow window. In a fashion that was fairly common in those days, he wore below his breastplate a kind of iron skirt which covered his thighs and belly, and widened out like the opening of a tunnel, to make walking easier. The window was not wide enough to allow this part of his armor through, and the ensign, in his confusion, had thrown himself so violently that he found himself with most of his body outside, yet unable to move, stuck as if in a vice. But the flames rose right up to him, heated his armor and slowly burned him in it, as in a furnace or in that famous bronze bull invented by Phalaris.' Phalaris, tyrant of Sicily, was notorious for the brazen bull in which he burned alive the victims of his cruelty.
13 'In Our Time,' inter-chapter 3.
14 Sylla, hero of 'The Social War' (1841). 'The False Demetrius' concerns an episode from sixteenth-century Russian history.

15 Walter Pater, Prosper Mérimée, 'Miscellaneous Studies' (London, 1895), 3-5.
16 Nietzsche, 'The Joyful Wisdom' (1882).
17 Fenimore Cooper was an American author of frontier novels, 'The Last of the Mohicans' (1826) and 'The Deerslayer' (1841).
18 Major battles of the Great War in Turkey, Flanders and Italy.
19 Rudyard Kipling, The Islanders (1902).
20 An influential sociological study by Robert and Helen Lynd (1929).
21 National Recovery Administration, created by Franklin Roosevelt to provide work during the Depression.
22 Tragic hero of Mérimée's 'Carmen.'
23 Jargon English used in the Western Pacific.
24 Artificial international language invented about 1879 by J.M. Schleyer.
25 Alfred E. Smith (1873-1944), American politician, governor of New York State, was defeated by Herbert Hoover in the presidential election of 1928.
26 Falsely naive.
27 Soldiers Home, 'In Our Time' (New York, 1970), 71-2.
28 Gertrude Stein, 'Three Lives' (1908), (London, 1927), p. 89.
29 Gertrude Stein, 'Composition as Explanation' (London, 1926), 5.
30 World view.
31 The battle of Caporetto took place in October 1917, *before* Hemingway arrived in Italy.
32 See, for example, 'Seated Woman' (1923).
33 Thomas Babington Macaulay was an English historian and statesman, and author of 'The History of England' (1848-52). Horace Walpole (1717-89), was an English novelist, historian and letter-writer.
34 H.L. Mencken, 'The American Language' (New York, revised ed. 1922), 386. 'Riders to the Sea' is a play by John Millington Synge (1904).
35 Off the west coast of Ireland, in Galway Bay.
36 Aristocratic daughter of President Theodore Roosevelt.
37 Used affectedly by literary types.
38 Editor of 'The Dictionary of English History' (1884).
39 Mencken, 204-5.
40 Ibid., 377.
41 Ibid., 317
42 Alexander Thompson, 'Japan for a Week' (London, 1911), 225-6.
43 Subject.
44 'A Farewell to Arms' (Harmondsworth, Middlesex,1963), 69-70.

45 Henry King (1592-1669), English poet and Bishop of Gloucester.
46 Frederick Lamb, 'Forty Years in the Old Bailey' (London, 1913), 190-2. Lamb was a shorthand writer.
47 'In Our Time', 15-16.
48 Cross-section.

'Green Hills of Africa' (1935)

41. BERNARD DE VOTO, 'SATURDAY REVIEW OF LITERATURE'

12 (26 October 1935), 5

Bernard De Voto (1897-1955), American editor of the 'Saturday Review,' was the author of several books on Mark Twain.

'The writer has attempted to write an absolutely true book to see whether the shape of a country and the pattern of a month's action can, if truly presented, compete with a work of the imagination.' So Mr. Hemingway describes his intention, in a preface that is shorter than the average sentence that follows it. Later, in one of the 'bloody literary discussions,' he praises prose that is 'without tricks and without cheating' - a phrase which sums up an ambition that has been constant in all his work. Then he records his satisfaction 'when you write well and truly of something and know impersonally you have written in that way and those who are paid to read it and report on it do not like the subject so they say it is all a fake.' In another passage, 'the lice who crawl on literature will not praise' a work of art. Either the reviewers have been getting under his skin or he is uneasy about this book.

Mr. Hemingway should have his answer: 'Green Hills of Africa' cannot compete with his works of the imagination. It is not exactly a poor book, but it is certainly far from a good one. The trouble is that it has few fine and no extraordinary passages, and long parts of it are dull. And being bored by Ernest Hemingway is a new experience for readers and reviewers alike. The queer thing is that this novelty springs from the same intense literary self-consciousness that has been a large part of the effectiveness of his books up to now. He kills this one by being too assiduously an experimental artist in prose, out to register sensation and find the right words for the country-side and activity and emotion, and, by way of the bush and the campfires and the rhinoceros dung, carry his prose to the 'fourth and fifth dimension that can be gotten.' He has reverted to his café-table-talk days, he is being arty, and Africa isn't a good place for it.

Only about forty percent of the book is devoted to the shape of the country and the pattern of action. That part isn't too good. He is magnificent when he is rendering the emotions of the hunt and the kill, but those passages are less frequent than long, confusing, over-written descriptions, and these are lush and very tiresome. Besides, there are a lot of tricks and some cheating. Mr. Hemingway plunges into the rhetoric he has monotonously denounced, and he overlays a good many bits of plain brush-work with very eloquent and highly literary researches into past time.

The rest of it runs about twenty percent literary discussion, twenty percent exhibitionism, and twenty percent straight fiction technique gratefully brought into this unimaginative effort. The literary discussion, though it contains some precious plums, is mostly bad; the exhibitionism is unfailingly good. Mr. Hemingway is not qualified for analytical thought. His flat judgments and especially his papal rules and by-laws are superficial when they aren't plain cockeyed. He has written about writing, probably, more than any other writer of his time: he is much better at writing and we should all be richer if he would stick to it. But he is a first-rate humorist, and the clowning is excellent. When he gives us Hemingway in the sulks, Hemingway with the braggies, Hemingway amused or angered by the gun-bearers, Hemingway getting tight, Hemingway at the latrine, Hemingway being hard-boiled, or brutal, or swaggering, or ruthless, Hemingway kidding someone or getting sore at someone - the book comes to life. It comes to life, in fact, whenever he forgets about the shape of the country and the pattern of action, and brings some people on the stage.

Working with real people, Pop, P.O.M., (1) Karl, the casuals, he is quite as effective a novelist as he is with imaginary ones. He imparts the same life to the natives, some of whom do not even speak. Droopy, Garrick, and The Wanderobo are splendid creations; one sees and feels them, accepts them, experiences them. They live. And that is creation of a high order, a *tour de force* all the more remarkable since it is done without the dialogue that is Mr. Hemingway's most formidable weapon. When he is being a novelist, he achieves his purpose. His book has the life and validity he tells us he set out to give it; he gets the experience itself into prose. It successfully competes with the imagination - because it uses the tools and technique of an imaginative artist.

The big news for literature, however, is that, stylistically, there is a new period of Hemingway. He seems to be fighting a one-man revolution to carry prose back to 'The Anatomy of Melancholy' (2) or beyond. There have been omens of it before now, of course, and Mr. Hemingway, in his café-table days, pondered Gertrude Stein to his own gain. The repetitious Stein of 'Tender Buttons' (3) doesn't show up here, but the Stein who is out to get four or five dimensions into prose is pretty obvious. But he also appears to have been reading a prose translation of 'The Odyssey' too closely, and something that sounds like a German translation of Hemingway. With the result that whereas the typical Hemingway sentence used to run three to a line it now runs three to a page. And whereas he used to simplify vocabulary in order to be wholly clear, he now simplifies grammar till the result looks like a marriage between an e. e. cummings simultaneity and one of those ground-mists of Sherwood Anderson's that Mr. Hemingway was burlesquing ten years ago.

The prize sentence in the book runs forty-six lines, the one I should like to quote as typical ('Now, heavy socks ...' p. 95), though less than half that long is still too long, and a comparatively straightforward one must serve. 'Going downhill steeply made these Spanish shooting boots short in the toe and there was an old argument, about this length of boot and whether the boot-maker, whose part I had taken, unwittingly, first, only as interpreter, and finally embraced his theory patriotically as a whole and, I believed, by logic, had overcome it by adding onto the heel.'

This is simpler than most, but it shows the new phase. Usually the material is not so factual as this and we are supposed to get, besides the sense, some muscular effort or some effect of color or movement that is latent in pace and rhythm rather than in words. But, however earnest the intention, the result is a kind of etymological gas that is just bad writing. The five-word sentences of 'The Sun Also Rises' were better. You know where you stood with them, and what Mr. Hemingway was saying. He ought to leave the fourth dimension to Ouspensky (4) and give us prose.

An unimportant book. A pretty small book for a big man to write. One hopes that this is just a valley and that something the size of 'Death in the Afternoon' is on the other side.

Notes

1 Poor Old Mama, Hemingway's wife, Pauline. This coy device may have been taken from D.H. Lawrence, who refers to his wife Frieda as 'Q.B.' (Queen Bee) in 'Sea and Sardinia' (1921).
2 A treatise on the causes, symptoms and cures of melancholy, written in an elaborate prose style by Robert Burton (1621).
3 A book of verse, published in 1914, whose title alludes to nipples.
4 P.D. Ouspensky, a crackpot Russian mystic and disciple of Gurdjieff, first used the term 'fifth dimension' in 'A New Model of the Universe' (1931).

42. GRANVILLE HICKS, 'NEW MASSES'

17 (19 November 1935), 23

It ought to be said that I approached 'Green Hills of Africa' with a sincere desire to find something to praise in it. Hemingway's piece in the 'New Masses,' Who Murdered the Vets?, (1) put me in a frame of mind to forgive everything, even 'Death in the Afternoon.' I have always admired most of 'The Sun Also Rises,' some of 'A Farewell to Arms' and several of the short stories. I have always felt that Hemingway was by all odds the clearest and strongest non-revolutionary writer of his generation. The passion of Who Murdered the Vets? not only strengthened my conviction; it made me want to emphasize the good things that can be said about Hemingway, not the bad. This was not because I had any notion that Hemingway would become a revolutionary novelist if the 'New Masses' patted him on the back; it was because Who Murdered the Vets? had a quality that had been disastrously absent from his previous work. A reviewer has a right to interpret an author's work in terms of his direction. Who Murdered the Vets? suggested that Hemingway was going somewhere and I hoped to find further evidence in 'Green Hills of Africa.'

The autobiographical preface is advisable, for what I have to say about 'Green Hills of Africa' is that it is the dullest book I have read since 'Anthony Adverse.' (2) There are perhaps ten pages that are interesting, and of these I shall speak later on. The rest of the book is just plain dull. Hunting is probably exciting to do; it is not exciting to read about. Hemingway got up very early in the morning and went out and chased a lion or a rhinoceros or a kudu, and he either shot him or he didn't, and if he did, some one named Karl shot a bigger one. So that evening they all got a little tight. This went on for a month, and finally they found themselves beside the Sea of Galilee, drinking, and Karl made a good crack about not walking on the water because it had been done once, and Hemingway said he would write a book so that P.O.M. (Poor Old Mama, i.e. Mrs. Hemingway) could remember what Mr. J.P. (their guide) looked like. And so we have 'Green Hills of Africa.'

After a good deal of thinking about why the book is dull, the only reason I can see is its subject-matter. On pages 148-150, Hemingway has a very long sentence - which proves that he does not have to write short ones and that, I suspect, is what it is intended to prove. The sentence begins by talking about the feeling that comes 'when you write well and truly of something and know impersonally you have written in that way and those who are paid to read it and report on it do not like the subject so they say it is all a fake, yet you know its value absolutely.' Now I do not like the subject of 'Green Hills of Africa'; but it would never occur to me to say that it is in any respect a fake. It is a perfectly honest book, and that is why I think it is dull because the subject is dull. Another clause in the same sentence concerns the feeling that comes 'when you do something that people do not consider a serious occupation and yet you know, truly, that it is as important as all the things that are in fashion.' This applies, I suppose, to either bull-fighting or hunting, and the only possible comment is that though they may be important to Hemingway, they aren't to most people. The proof is in the response to 'Death in the Afternoon' and 'Green Hills of Africa.' Since they are, it seems to me, as good books as are likely to be written on bull-fighting and hunting, the trouble must be with the subjects.

A certain amount of nonsense is written about the subject-matter of literature. No critic in his right mind will try to prescribe an author's subjects; the author has to start with what he feels and knows. But that is not equivalent to saying that one subject is as good as another. 'To write a great novel,' Herman Melville said, 'you must have a great theme.'(3) The whole history of literature proves that he was right. When an author, starting out to write on some trivial theme, has produced a great book, it is because the trivial theme hitched on to a great one. (You might have a great novel about people who were hunting, but it wouldn't be about hunting.) (4) A great theme concerns the issues of life and death as they present themselves in the age in which the author lives.

It comes down to an argument over values, in which Mr. Hemingway's judgment is set against the judgment of history. The ten interesting pages in the book are all given over to discussions of the nature of literature and the function of the author. It is a subject on which Mr. Hemingway feels deeply and when he feels deeply he writes well. But he is always on the defensive, just as he was in the literary conversations in 'Death in the Afternoon.'

He is very bitter about the critics, and very bold in asserting his independence of them, so bitter and so bold that one detects a sign of a bad conscience. No one will deny that sports are pleasant and even important, but to be wholly wrapped up in them is not a sign of intellectual maturity. And the truth is, as he constantly reveals, that Hemingway is not wholly wrapped up in them. He has ideas about war, revolution, religion, art and other adult interests; ideas that the readers of the 'New Masses' wouldn't always like, but ideas. And still he goes on writing about bulls and kudus.

Would Hemingway write better books if he wrote on different themes? Who Murdered the Vets? suggests that he would, for in that piece all his talents were suddenly lifted onto a higher level. That is why a great theme is important; it calls out so much more of what is in an author. I should like to have Hemingway write a novel about a strike, to use an obvious example, not because a strike is the only thing worth writing about, but because it would do something to Hemingway. If he would just let himself look squarely at the contemporary American scene, he would be bound to grow. I am not talking about his becoming a Communist, though that would be good for the revolutionary movement and better for him, I am merely suggesting that his concern with the margins of life is a dangerous business. In six years Hemingway has not produced a book even remotely worthy of his talents. He knows that the time is short and that it is difficult in this age and country for a writer to survive. There is bigger game in the world than kudus, and he had better start going after it now if he ever wants to get it.

Notes

1 'New Masses,' 16 (17 September 1935), 9-10, on a Florida hurricane that destroyed a work-camp and killed 458 veterans.
2 A best-selling romance on the Napoleonic era, by Hervey Allen (1933).
3 'Moby Dick' (London, 1961), 394: 'To produce a mighty book, you must choose a mighty theme.'
4 See Faulkner's novella, 'The Bear' (1942).

43. EDMUND WILSON, 'NEW REPUBLIC'

85 (11 December 1935), 135-6

The new book of Ernest Hemingway has been to me a great disappointment. 'Green Hills of Africa' is certainly far and away his weakest book, in fact the only really weak book he has written (leaving out of consideration the burlesque 'Torrents of Spring').

'Green Hills of Africa' is an account of a hunting expedition, in which 'the writer has attempted,' as Hemingway says, 'to write an absolutely true book to see whether the shape of a country and the pattern of a month's action can, if truly presented, compete with a work of the imagination.' In my opinion, he has not succeeded. The sophisticated technique of the fiction-writer comes to look artificial when it is applied to a series of real happenings; and the necessity of sticking to what really happened prevents the writer from supplying the ideal characters and incidents which give point to a work of fiction. 'Green Hills of Africa' is thus an instructive experiment: it brings out very clearly the difference between actual experience and the imaginary experience of fiction, but it is a warning of reefs to steer clear of.

Aside from this - or perhaps for the very reason that he has chosen to treat his material in the wrong way - Hemingway's literary personality appears here in a slightly absurd light. He delivers a self-confident lecture on the high possibilities of prose writing, with the implication that he himself, Hemingway, has realized or hopes to realize these possibilities; and then writes what are certainly, from the point of view of prose, the very worst pages of his life. There is one passage which is hardly even intelligible - the most serious possible fault for a writer who is always insisting on the supreme importance of lucidity. He inveighs with much scorn against the literary life and against the professional literary man of the cities; and then manages to give the impression that he himself is a professional literary man of the most touchy and self-conscious kind. As one of the newspaper writers has said of Hemingway, he went all the way to Africa to hunt and then when he thought he had found a rhinoceros, it turned out to be Gertrude Stein (1) - an old friend and admiration of Hemingway's, who wrote of him disparagingly in her recent autobiography and upon whom Hemingway in 'Green Hills of Africa' has taken the opportunity to revenge himself. He affirms in accents of defiance his perfect satisfaction with the hunter's life and his passionate enthusiasm for Africa; and then writes what seems to me the only book I have ever read which makes Africa and its animals seem dull.

When the Soviet critic, I. Kashkeen, who has published in the English edition of 'International Literature' a very able essay on Hemingway - what is in fact perhaps the only serious and thoroughgoing study of him which has yet been written (2) - when Kashkeen comes to read 'Green Hills of Africa,' he will no doubt find much confirmation for his theory that the author of 'In Our Time' has become progressively more sterile and less interesting in proportion as he has become more detached from the great social issues of the day. And it is true that one of the things which strikes us most and which depresses us as we read 'Green Hills of Africa' is the apparent drying-up in Hemingway of his interest in his fellow beings. Animals can be made extremely interesting; but the animals in this book are not interesting. Almost the only thing we hear about them is that Hemingway wants to kill them. Nor do we learn much about the natives: there is one fine description of a tribe of marvelous runners but the principal impression we carry away is that the natives were simple people who enormously admired Hemingway. Nor do we learn much more about his hunting companion than that the latter has better luck than Hemingway and inspires Hemingway's envy; nor much more about Mrs. Hemingway than that she is fond of Hemingway. Nor does he seem even to take much real interest in himself: the picture of Hemingway we get seems mainly inspired by the idea which he imagines his public have of him when they read the rubbishy articles he writes for the men's-wear magazine, 'Esquire.' (3)

Yet I am not sure that it is true - as perhaps Kashkeen would conclude - that it is Hemingway's material which is here at fault. It is not the fact that 'Green Hills of Africa' deals with an African hunting expedition instead of with the American class struggle which is really at the bottom of its failure; but rather the technical and psychological approach of the writer to his subject. One can imagine the material of 'Green Hills of Africa' being handled quite successfully in short stories or as a background to one of Hemingway's novels. But for reasons which I cannot attempt to explain, something frightful seems to happen to Hemingway as soon as he begins to write in the first person. In his fiction, the conflicting elements of his personality, the emotional situations which obsess him, are externalized and objectified; and the result is an art which is severe, intense and deeply serious. But as soon as he talks in his own person, he seems to lose all his capacity for self-criticism and is likely to become fatuous or maudlin. His ideas about life, or rather his sense of what happens and the way in which it happens, is in his stories sunk deep below the surface and is conveyed not by argument or preaching but by directly transmitted emotion: it is turned into something as hard as a crystal and as disturbing as a great lyric. When he expounds this sense of life, however, in his own character of Ernest Hemingway, the Old Master of Key West, he has a way of sounding silly. Perhaps he is beginning to be imposed on by the American publicity legend which has been created about him and which, as Kashkeen has pointed out, has very little to do with what one actually finds in his stories. But, in any case, among his creations, he is certainly his own worst-drawn character, and he is his own worst commentator. His very prose style goes to pot - or rather, he writes a different prose style from the one which he has perfected in his fiction and which is, it seems to me, without question one of the finest that has been written in America and one of the finest that is being written anywhere.

This vein of Hemingway maudlin, this vein of unconscious burlesque, had already broken out in the personal interludes of 'Death in the Afternoon,' his book on bull-fighting, but in that book there was so much objective writing, so much solid information, that these interludes could not spoil it. 'Green Hills of Africa' is *all* such an interlude - and I doubt whether it is anything more than an interlude in Hemingway's work as a whole. His last volume of short stories certainly showed a further developing mastery, rather than any degeneration, of his art. One of them, a simple anecdote of a man who goes out to plunder a wreck and finds that he cannot even crack open the port-hole - this short story, (4) with its implications of the irreducible hazards and pains of life and of the code of honor which one must evolve to live among them, is more than worth the whole of 'The Green Hills of Africa.'

These moral implications of Hemingway, as one finds them in the story I have mentioned, Kashkeen seems to me to underestimate. To the Marxist, it is no doubt true that there should be no irreducible hazards and pains. But these will not be eliminated next year, nor even five years from now, nor even after five years more. And in the meantime? If Hemingway were to address himself to writing about the social conflict, there is no reason to believe that his stories would cease to illustrate the same tragic sense of the way in which things happen. We can get some idea of what we might expect from the introduction he wrote to the exhibition of the drawings of the Spanish revolutionary painter, Luis Quintanilla. (5) He has an acute sense of the cost and danger of doing anything worth doing, including revolution; and he knows that people do not always live to get what they pay for. 'The world breaks everyone and afterward many are strong in the broken places. But those that will not break it kills. It kills the very good and the very gentle and the very brave impartially. If you are none of those you can be sure that it will kill you too but there will be no special hurry' - says the hero of 'A Farewell to Arms.' (6) This is not in the least the same thing as saying that there is no use in being good or brave. The truth is that, though, as Kashkeen says, Hemingway is very much given to writing about the end of things, his effect is bracing rather than dispiriting. Is The Undefeated, which deals with the humiliation and death of an old bull-fighter, really a story of defeat? Of course not. The old man's courage is in itself a victory. It is true that Hemingway writes about decadence, but there is always something else which is opposed to the decadence. He writes about death, but to write tellingly about death you have to have the principle of life.

And is it not true on the highest plane of imaginative writing, the plane on which one must consider Hemingway, that what is written about an old bull-fighter is written, also, about other kinds of men? Is not real genius of moral insight a motor that will start any engine? The non-Marxist who reads a banal Marxist fable, written without real imagination or feeling, does not feel or imagine anything. The Marxist who reads the story of a conflict, though that conflict may have nothing to do with the class struggle, will, if the story is written with passion and skill, identify himself with the hero. Do we not translate what moves us in literature into terms of whatever we do in our lives?

But that, Kashkeen might reply, is an extremely dangerous doctrine. Suppose the hero of the story in question is frankly a counter-revolutionary. How can we be sure that the reader will translate the hero's counter-revolutionary courage into terms of revolutionary activity? How do we know that he will not simply be persuaded to admire the counter-revolution? We cannot know, of course. But we may be assured that wherever the main current of human hope and progress runs the readers will get out of literature of all kinds the kind of inspiration they need for their own particular activities, the kind of consolation they need for their own particular defeats. That the Soviets assume this to be true is indicated by the fact that they are at present translating wholesale the classics both of antiquity and of the modern world and republishing their own classics with pious care. I observed when I was recently in Russia (7) that even the creations of the counter-revolutionary Dostoevsky were still of interest to Soviet readers and that the government was bringing out his notebooks. And surely there is more in the increasing popularity of Shakespeare on the Soviet stage than a desire on the part of Russian audiences to study the failures of feudal princes. Individuals in Russia still suffer their failures, their griefs and their frustrations; and people still go to the theatre to have their souls purged through pity and terror. (8)

I feel that Soviet critics, and also Marxist critics elsewhere, sometimes underestimate the positive qualities of modern non-Marxist masters. A writer like Kashkeen might reply that today the only positive forces are those which are working for the destruction of the rotten old capitalist world and for the realization of human possibilities through socialism. I can only adduce, as an example of the law of moral interchangeability which I would invoke in behalf of Hemingway, that on my recent visit to Russia the passage from literature which came most often into my head, which seemed to me to express most eloquently the effect of the Revolution on all kinds and conditions of people in the Soviet Union, was from the writings of that arch-bourgeois, arch-snob, arch-esthete and arch-decadent, Marcel Proust. It is the conclusion of the section on the death of one of his characters, the novelist Bergotte, in which Proust speaks of the moral obligations which make themselves felt in spite of everything, and which seem to reach humanity from some source outside its own wretched self - obligations 'invisible only to fools - and are they really even to them?' (9) Proust was speaking here of the obligations of the artist - for him, in his world of dissolving values, art was the only thing which seemed to keep its validity and endure. But when I was traveling in the Soviet Union, the words would come back into my mind and I would find that the obligations involved in the ideal of the Leninist tradition, permeating even parts of society, motivating even individuals, by whom at first sight it seemed least to be felt, had substituted themselves for the obligations involved in Proust's ideal of art. 'Invisible only to fools - and are they really even to them?'

Notes

1 In John Chamberlain's extremely negative review, 'New York Times,' 25 October 1935, 19.
2 Ivan Kashkeen, Ernest Hemingway: A Tragedy of Craftsmanship, 'International Literature,' 5 (May 1935), 72-90. Wilson ignores the perceptive essay by the right-wing Wyndham Lewis.
3 Hemingway published nine articles about Spain, Africa and Cuba in 'Esquire' (January-September 1934).
4 After the Storm, 'Winner Take Nothing.'
5 'Luis Quintanilla: Catalogue' (New York, Pierre Matisse Gallery, 1934).
6 'A Farewell to Arms,' 193.
7 Wilson was in Russia during May-October 1935.
8 Aristotle's definition of tragedy in the 'Poetics.'
9 Marcel Proust, 'The Captive,' trans. C.K. Scott-Moncrieff (London, 1971), I, 251.

44. SINCLAIR LEWIS, 'YALE LITERARY MAGAZINE'

101 (February 1936), 46-7

Sinclair Lewis (1885-1951), an American novelist, wrote 'Main Street' (1920), 'Babbitt' (1922) and 'Arrowsmith' (1923).

This article begins with Lewis' Rambling Thoughts on

Literature as a Business and ends with this extract on Hemingway.

In 'Men without Women,' 'Farewell,' and 'Sun Also Rises' it was indicated that Tom Wolfe and he are far the best among the fictioneers now under forty, but in his new book, 'Green Hills of Africa,' a volume in which he tells how extremely amusing it is to shoot lots and lots of wild animals, to hear their quite-human moaning, and see them lurch off with their guts dragging, Mr. Hemingway notes:

'Emerson, Hawthorne, Whittier, and Company.... All these men were gentlemen, or wished to be. They were all very respectable. They did not use the words that people always have used in speech, the words that survive in language. Nor would you gather that they had bodies. They had minds, yes. Nice, dry, clean minds. This is all very dull.' (Check!)

I told you this essay would be rambling. As always, Mr. Hemingway has inspired me; this time to the following Lines to a College Professor:

Mister Ernest Heminway
Halts his slaughter of the kudu
To remind you that you may
Risk his sacerdotal hoodoo
If you go on, day by day
Talking priggishly as you do.
Speak up, man! Be bravely heard
Bawling the four-letter word!
And wear your mind décolleté
Like Mr. Ernest Hemingway.

No, if you take my advice and combine the delights of selling coffee and pickles and figs with the delights of writing about them, you will never be allowed to throw the bull with Mr. Hemingway. (1) But I wonder if you will care much.

Note

1 An allusion to Max Eastman's review.

'To Have and Have Not' (1937)

45. BERNARD DE VOTO, 'SATURDAY REVIEW OF LITERATURE'

16 (16 October 1937), 8

So far none of Ernest Hemingway's characters has had any more consciousness than a jaguar. They are physiological systems organized around abdomens, suprarenal glands, and genitals. They are sacs of basic instinct. Their cerebrums have highly developed motor areas but are elsewhere atrophied or vestigial. Their speech is rudimentary, they have no capacity for analytical or reflective thought, they have no beliefs, no moral concepts, no ideas. Living on an instinctual level, they have no complexities of personality, emotion, or experience.

Working exclusively with such people, Mr. Hemingway has created the most memorable prize-fighters, bull-fighters, literary hangers-on, fishermen, duck-shooters, and thugs that American literature has ever seen. With Frederic Henry, a man without consciousness caught up in a catastrophic mob-panic, and Catherine Barkley, a woman who lives in completely unconscious obedience to instinct, he has composed a novel that will last as long as any in its generation. No one else writing in America today can give a scene the reality that Mr. Hemingway gives it, or can equal his dialogue, which reaches the reader as living speech.

That is an achievement on which any writer who ever lived might well rest, but Mr. Hemingway seems uneasy about it. He has grown, as our reviewer (1) says, increasingly belligerent about personalities more complex than those he creates, about ideas, about every kind of experience that is not localized in or near the viscera.

But if his characters are incapable of ideas, Mr. Hemingway is not. Their mindlessness is itself the assertion of an idea. It is one of Mr. Hemingway's root ideas and has come to dominate his work. Every so often it should be taken out and scrutinized.

Since the thinking of the Hemingway characters has been confined to a form of omphalic irritation, they have not usually had any social awareness. The social significance of 'To Have and Have Not' is also negligible. The dice which Mr. Hemingway is rolling are so openly and flagrantly loaded that he cannot mean us to think of his sterile millionaires and his gonadotropic 'conchs' (2) in economic terms. The social assertions and findings are so naive, fragmentary, and casual that they cannot be offered as criticism of the established order: beside them, the simplest of the blue-jeans-and-solidarity Cinderella stories that the 'New Masses' was praising three or four years ago would seem profound. The significance of the title is not sociological: it is one with the significance of Jake's wound in 'The Sun Also Rises' and with the symbolism of the plaster cast in which the hero of 'A Farewell to Arms' had to make love. The millionaires and the literary lice are not the 'haves' - they are the 'have-nots.' The 'haves' are the conchs, and particularly Harry Morgan. Just what it is that Harry Morgan has and his oppressors lack we are told specifically and repeatedly. Mr. Hemingway has given us the supporting argument before.

It is curious where that argument takes you - where it has taken Mr. Hemingway. 'Since he was a boy,' one of his companions says of Harry Morgan, 'he never had no pity for nobody. But he never had no pity for himself either.' Quite clearly, for Mr. Hemingway the second half of that antithesis is a complete justification of the first half. If you do not pity yourself you need not pity anyone, and conversely you must not pity yourself lest you grow weak by pitying someone else. Yet one wonders whether a man is completely vindicated and sufficiently praised when it is said of him that he does not pity himself. One wonders if refusal to pity himself is enough to make Harry Morgan so admirable as Mr. Hemingway considers him. He breaks faith with and murders the Chinaman who employs him; after rum-running and miscellaneous violence, he becomes an accessory to bank robbery and more murder; and he finishes up with a quadruple murder. But floods of adrenalin are always surging into his blood stream, and, when he is wounded, both his central and his sympathetic nervous systems are polarized in support of his will to live. Mr. Hemingway is in the position of saying that nothing else matters.

'He never had no pity for nobody. But he never had no

pity for himself either.' It is not by chance that that analysis summons up an image of a trapped animal escaping by gnawing off its foot. 'She watched him go out of the house, tall, wide-shouldered, flat-backed, his hips narrow, moving, still, she thought, like some kind of animal, easy and swift and not old yet.' Also, 'Him, like he was, snotty and strong and quick, and like some kind of expensive animal.' We have reached the end of a path that Mr. Hemingway has been traveling for a long time. The highest praise he can give a man is to say that he is like an animal.

You see, it is only the animals who never deny life by forsaking the level of pure instinct. They are clean, honest, unpitying. They live in the reality of blood-consciousness, (3) immersed in primary and direct experience: hunger, thirst, desire, alertness, wariness, aggressiveness. When they couple they do not weave a dishonest poetry over the clean delight of physiological function. When they kill, they kill without guilt, without remorse, without rationalization. They do not pose; they do not talk nobly; they do not live in a fog of thought, in the diseased secretion of the mind that betrays and enfeebles man. They do not kid themselves with ideas; they do not delude themselves with reason or reverie; instead, they are clean, sure, and very strong. They pity neither themselves nor other animals. They live instinctively, they defend themselves to the death, and every mammal pleases but only man is vile. What gave the death of the bull its tragic beauty was the fact that it perished at the moment of total aggressiveness, charging at its mortal enemy with all the physiology of its animal nature concentrated in the instinctive, self-justifying act of destruction. And now, compared with the human world which gives the sterile dominion over the potent, how beautiful is the long curve of the shark diving for gouts of blood.

Every man to his preference. Mr. Hemingway is certainly entitled to fall in love with sharks if he wants to, and our literature is the richer for his admiration. There has been, of course, much anthropophobia in modern literature. If the admirers of D.H. Lawrence, for instance, have not consciously loved alligators, they are at least accustomed to praise the faculties of alligators that may be discerned in man. But it is hard to see just how man himself may profitably employ the idea and just what reference either the alligator or the bull has to the problems man is working with in the modern world. And it will be interesting to see how the literary left, which temporarily regards Mr. Hemingway as an ally, (4) will adapt his conclusions when adopting them. The cult of blood-consciousness and holy violence, as well as the clean beauty of the shark, has so far been the property of their political opponents.

It would be even more interesting to find out what Mr. Hemingway thinks of Mr. Robinson Jeffers. (5) Utilizing the diseased secretion of thought to the utmost, Mr. Jeffers has also reached the conclusion that the animals are superior to man, but he finds the waving grasses still more admirable. Unpitying alligator or undeluded chlorophyll - which shall we prefer, which shall be the measure of things?

Notes

1 George Stevens, in 'Saturday Review of Literature,' 16 (16 October 1937), 6-7, calls the book 'less than profound and short of impressive.'
2 Resident of the Florida keys.
3 D.H. Lawrence's phrase. See 'Letters,' ed. James Boulton (Cambridge, 1979), I, 503.
4 Because of his commitment to the Spanish Loyalists.
5 American poet, author of 'Tamar' (1924) and 'Roan Stallion' (1925), who renounced humanity in his works and relied on nature.

46. CYRIL CONNOLLY, 'NEW STATESMAN AND NATION'

14 (16 October 1937), 606

Let us start with Hemingway. 'To Have and Have Not,' while a much better book than 'Green Hills of Africa,' and very exciting and readable, represents no sort of advance on his other short stories, nor is there any sign of him having profited from Lewis' Dumb Ox article. His new hero is the dumbest ox of all. In this book Hemingway is the victim of his style. He does not parody himself, but he is unable to tackle anything that does not fit into it. His style was originally formed by two influences I should guess, 'Huckleberry Finn' and Gertrude Stein-Sherwood Anderson. It was a reaction to the verbose highbrow style of the literary mandarins, (1) Henry James, Conrad, the American men of letters, and aimed at complete simplicity and co-ordination between the written word and the violent emotions behind it. Long sentences, allusions, analogies, ideas, all that is thoughtful or educated is alien to it. It is an admirable medium, a technique like Seurat's for rendering the life of the body, its inarticulate pleasures and pains, heroism and lust, but is not capable of any enlargement. The novelist must always remain on the same level as his characters and must not stand aside from them. Like the king he must never say anything that might not have been said by the dullest of his subjects. Hence the Dumb Ox charge of Lewis, who does not see what admirable results are gained by the method, how essential the author's dumbness is to it. The great factor in determining Hemingway's style has been his body. His body is the opposite of Proust's, his style is the opposite of Proust's. Hemingway is a very large athletic man possessed of enormous physical vitality. Boxing, bull-fighting, big-game shooting, tarpon-fishing, soldiering are as necessary to him as a walk in the park to you or me or cork walls (2) and complete silence were to Proust. But this huge frame that knows no illness, except when it stops a bullet, has a healthy contempt for all constipated and meditative colleagues, and has passed on its schoolboy prejudices to the extremely alert and intelligent artist who inhabits it.

> I know about love. Love always hangs up behind the bath-room door. It smells like lysol. To hell with love. Love is you making me happy and then going off to sleep with your mouth open while I lie awake all night afraid to say my prayers even because I know I have no right to any more. Love is all the dirty little tricks you taught me that you probably got out of some books. All right. I'm through with you and I'm through with love. Your kind of picknose love. You writer.... If you were just a good writer I could stand for all the rest of it maybe. But I've seen you bitter, jealous, changing your politics to suit the fashion, sucking up to people's faces and talking about them behind their backs.

So speaks the Irish wife of a villain in 'To Have and Have Not,' as she casts her vile literary husband out of the house and home, and so speaks the whole physique of Hemingway, longing to get at another Max Eastman, and so speak most Germans, Italians, business men, he-men and schoolboys. Grrr! *You writer!*

'To Have and Have Not' consists of three long short stories which form three sections in the life of Harry Morgan, a Key West character who makes a living by rum-running, gun-running and man-running between Florida and

Cuba. This active passionate life on the verge of the tropics is perfect material for the Hemingway style, and the reader carries away from the book a sense of freshness and exhilaration; trade winds, southern cities, and warm seas all admirably described by the instrument of precision with which he writes. Against the background move Harry Morgan, the chivalrous buccaneer, the 'Rummies,' Revolutionaries, and decayed longshoremen, and the even more decayed winter visitors who bring the vices of the rich. What French papers call *Le Tragique Bilan* (3) is exceptionally high, even for a Hemingway. Jaws crack like 'a bag of marbles,' necks are broken ('Don't think you can't hear it crack either') and a great many people are shot. Morally I find the book odious. When a winter visitor doesn't pay Morgan for fishing lessons he makes up for it by breaking the man's neck. Because Richard Gordon is a writer everyone is justified in taking a poke at him. Morgan has 'cojones' (4) (polite translation, guts) and is therefore a hero. Gordon is a villain, he has not. At the end of the book Hemingway abandons his sentimental underdog attitude, and substitutes Left-wing propaganda by analysing, in the O'Hara (5) manner, the people on the yachts. This lands him in difficulties with his style again, and in some confusion over the dual scale of values, potency versus impotency, and capitalism versus communism. Alas, in real life the Right are often more potent than the Left.

It is the fashion to say that Hemingway is finished. His book on big-game hunting, his flashy he-man articles in 'Esquire' and his attitude to criticism have alienated a great many people. But I do not think he is. These three stories are not very new, but they show an admirable handling of his material, within its limitations. But Hemingway has been in Spain for some time now and he is obviously the person who can write the great book about the Spanish war. And in Spain he will not be able to write about people who feel without writing about people who think, since the Government troops are not dumb oxen, like the Moors, and consequently he can get rid of his anti-highbrow complexes. He will have to write about people like himself. 'Cojones' are not enough.

Meanwhile, in spite of all the warbooks, sport books, talkies, and crime-books, and the articles in the 'Daily Express' which imitate him, he is still a delight to read. 'You know how it is there early in the morning in Havana' his book begins, and if you get that far you had better put off all engagements till it is finished.

Notes

1 'Mandarin' is Connolly's well-known term for elaborate prose stylists.
2 Proust was a neurasthenic invalid who worked in a cork-lined room to keep out noise and dust.
3 The tragic balance.
4 Balls.
5 John O'Hara (1905-70), an American novelist in the Hemingway tradition, was author of 'Appointment in Samarra' (1934) and 'Butterfield 8' (1935).

47. ALFRED KAZIN, 'NEW YORK HERALD TRIBUNE BOOKS'

17 October 1937, 3

Alfred Kazin (b. 1915) is an American critic and autobiographer, and author of 'On Native Grounds' (1942) and 'New York Jew' (1978).

In the eight years since the publication of 'A Farewell to Arms,' the Hemingway legend has lost its luster with the gradual recession of a world that nourished that legend with emulation and empty flattery. He has written books, but they have been elaborate and sometimes threadbare excuses for one solid book; and as the years have gone by, we have grown accustomed to him standing like Tarzan against a backdrop labeled Nature, while little men with nothing of his stabbing talent and pride of craftsmanship have done the work. One wondered if the end of 12, Rue de Fleurus, (1) Gertrude Stein like some immense priestess of nonsense expounding her text in nonsense syllables, dear Ezra Pound and all the rest, was not his end, too. Had the lost generation gone down with a whimper? Would it never go beyond the pat theatrics of saying America, farewell?

The answer - troubled, sketchy, feverishly brilliant and flat by turns, and only a little heartening - is 'To Have and Have Not.' It happens to be the first full-length book Hemingway has ever written about his own country and his own people; and that explains a good deal. In the earlier books America was the last frontier of his

Michigan boyhood, a mountainous jumble of forests against which we saw him as the inquisitive but tight-lipped youth, the doctor's son, violently athletic, hard, curt, and already a little sad. And then America went out of the picture altogether, and there was the dry crackle of the boozed cosmopolitans eating their hearts out in unison, with a shift of scene to Malaga (2) or Paris or the African jungle, with the famous style getting more mechanical book by book, the sentences more involved, the head-shaking over a circumscribed eternity more obvious.

It is significant that the America of 'To Have and Have Not' is Key West. For like the Paris of 1925, Key West is at once an outpost of a culture and its symbol. It is a home for disabled and unemployed veterans, a night resort for writers who talk great books, a harbor for the sleek yachts of the newer millionaires. Being a tip of the continent, it is an open door to Cuba, a window on the Gulf Stream, the Florida of the boom all over again, albeit a little tarnished; and a bit of Latin America. It is by Key West that Hemingway went home, and it is Key West, apparently, that remains America in cross-section to him: the noisy, shabby, deeply moving rancor and tumult of all those human wrecks, the fishermen and the Cuban revolutionaries, the veterans and the alcoholics, the gilt-edged snobs and the hungry natives, the great white stretch of beach promising everything and leading nowhere.

For this is a Hemingway who can get angry and snarl with his heart open. It means a novel thrown together with a fury that leaps from one page to another, a succession of styles instead of a chopped, frozen manner; it means that as he wrote the book he was forced to see his way through in terms of his own position, so that chapters are broken nervously, speeches are begun but never finished, characters enter from all sides and at all times. Wyndham Lewis once wrote that the 'I' in all Hemingway's books is 'the man things are done to'; but here there are several narrators, for in place of Jake Barnes and Frederic Henry, who were always being hurt so badly that they leaned over backward to conceal their pain, there are the people to whom things are being done every day in Hemingway's America, and they talk right out.

The hero of the book is not, like most of Hemingway's heroes, an elaborately self-conscious man against society; he is rather a mass-man, a man like any other, whose life has a beginning, a middle, and a significant end. Harry Morgan's vice is his excessive self-reliance, the pride in his own tough loneliness; but he differs from Jake and Frederic as much as he differs from those sullen, tight-lipped men of action who play the role of natural man, the present version of the romantic savage, in Hemingway's works. Harry is unique because he is capable of struggle and casual about annihilation; and through his effort, though it consists largely of hard-fisted industry, chances taken at night, terrible suffering, he learns the folly of isolation.

The essential point about him is that he earns a living by primitive means in a world rotten with waste. Harry has been a bruiser, a policeman, a bootlegger, a smuggler; he has cheated men, for they have cheated him; killed them when he thought it necessary. His motorboat alone provides sustenance for himself and his family, and the fact that he is a good husband and father, that he is capable of romantic affection, gives him an unconscious virtue when he is set against the men who pay him for their their cheap pleasure. The world is a jungle and Harry finds an appropriate realism in being a rover. During prohibition he was a rum-runner; afterward he shipped any contraband people would give him - rifles for another Cuban revolution, fleeing Cubans, emigrant Orientals and what not. Revolutionaries and wealthy fishermen are all customers to him, and he finds bitter affirmation of his suspicions when he is betrayed, or when some captain of industry blithely loses his expensive rod and apparatus and runs out on him.

When an Oriental gentleman, wonderfully smooth-spoken and therefore suspect, pays him to dump dozens of Chinese across the water, Harry pockets the money, kills the Oriental gentleman, and leaves the Chinese in Cuba. Reduced to running booze again, he is shot by the police and loses an arm. He does business with crooked lawyers and insults them magnificently. Disappointed in his children, humbled and a little scared by the loss of his arm, he goes on fooling the police, getting caught and slipping out, losing his boat to officials, doing business with gunmen and getting hurt. But Harry is not conscious of any fundamental dishonesty, for the only alternative is the shamefaced starvation of living on relief. When he strays into the bars of Key West and listens to the visitors from New York giggling over their drunken animal play, he gains new courage to go his own way by the only means he knows.

As Harry's career draws to its shaped end, Hemingway, as if under the force of some new emotion, enlarges the novel steadily, putting it on two planes - one for life and death of Harry Morgan, battered American; one for the wastrels whom he hates with so much relish. In a marvelous scene, Harry and his boat are seized by some Cuban terrorists and he is forced to run it for them. By a pretext he steals his way to the hold, and there proceeds, in the grand style, to slaughter them methodically, but at the cost of a mortal wound. The boat, stocked with the dead, drifts crazily in the Gulf Stream. Farewell, Harry. And just at this point, with a withering fury that throws him out of breath, Hemingway turns his attention to the yachts sleeping in the harbor, and breaks them open, one by one, to make verbal mincemeat of their owners - the chronic drunks, the perverts, the young aesthetes (somewhat chastened since pater's stocks went down), the expensive blondes, the pot-bellied jugglers resting from their labors on 'change.

A new Hemingway? Not altogether. There are pages and pages in which the old icy brilliance comes through, with the slippery rhythm, the virtual assonance, the artful grace of phrases fused with such laborious cleverness that the click-clack of the beat is like a hiss. But where before there was one style for one chill elegy on the war and wasted youth, here there are many new twists and turns. even an unusual clumsiness, for this is a Hemingway who is rather less sure of himself than usual, but a good deal more intense. That clumsiness makes uncomfortable reading; it contributes to the impression one gets as a whole that the book is hardly up to snuff; but it tells us that here, in a country notorious for its one-book geniuses and despite an interminably autobiographical generation, is a genuine artist who has worked his way out of a cult of tiresome defeatism; and who may, on this path, yet write a book worthy of him. There's just a chance that Ernest Hemingway is a promising young novelist.

Notes

1 Gertrude Stein's address in Paris.
2 'The Sun Also Rises' takes place in Pamplona and Madrid.

48. MALCOLM COWLEY, 'NEW REPUBLIC'

92 (20 October 1937), 305-6

Chief among Hemingway's virtues as a writer is his scrupulous regard for fact, for reality, for 'what happened.' It is a rare virtue in the world of letters. Most writers want to please or shock, to be 'accomplished craftsmen' or to be 'original'; in both cases their work is determined by literary fashions, which they either follow or defy. From the very first, Hemingway did neither, since his aim was simply to reproduce the things he had seen and felt - 'simply,' I say, but anyone who has tried to set down his own impressions accurately must realize that the task is enormously difficult; there is always the temptation to change and falsify the story because it doesn't fit into a conventional pattern, or because the right words are lacking. Hemingway himself had to find a whole new vocabulary, one in which old or popular words like 'good,' 'nice' and 'rotten' are given fresh values. But it always makes me angry to hear people speaking of his 'lean, hard, athletic prose.' Sometimes his prose is beautiful, poetic in the best sense, in its exact evocations of landscapes and emotions. Sometimes it is terse and efficient. Sometimes, with its piling up of very short words, it gives the effect of a man stammering, getting his tongue twisted, talking too much but eventually making us understand just what he wants to say.

During the last ten years Hemingway has been imitated more widely than any other American or British writer, even T.S. Eliot. You find his influence everywhere from the pulp-paper true-detective-story weeklies to the very little magazines making no compromise with the public taste. You find it in newspapers and the movies, in English highbrow novels and even in this weekly journal of opinion. Partly it has been a bad influence. It has made people copy the hard-boiled manner of The Killers and Fifty Grand - this latter being the cheapest story that Hemingway ever signed. It has encouraged them to boast in print of their love affairs and drinking bouts - though God knows they needed little encouragement. Worst of all, it has caused many young writers to take over Hemingway's vocabulary and his manner of seeing the world - thereby making it impossible for them to be as honest as Hemingway. But in general I think that his influence has been excellent. It has freed many writers - not only novelists but poets and essayists and simple reporters - from a burden of erudition and affectation that they thought was part of the writer's equipment. It has encouraged them to write as simply as possible about the things they really feel, instead of the things they think that other people think they ought to feel. Critics in particular owe a debt to Hemingway; and many of them, including myself, have been slow to acknowledge it. So let me put the record straight. I don't think he is as great as Tolstoy or Thomas Mann, but I do think that he is perhaps as good as Mark Twain, and that is saying a great deal. In our generation, he is the best we have.

His new novel I found easy to read, impossible to lay down before it was finished, and very hard to review. It contains some of the best writing he has ever done. There are scenes that are superb technical achievements and other scenes that carry him into new registers of emotion. As a whole it lacks unity and sureness of effect.

Part of its weakness is a simple matter of plot structure, a department in which Hemingway was never strong. The book falls apart at the beginning and the end. It begins with two long stories about Harry Morgan - both of them, I think, were first published in the 'Cosmopolitan' - and it ends with a fine soliloquy by Harry Morgan's widow. In the intervening pages, Hemingway deals with his principal theme, which is really two themes in counterpoint - on the one side, the life of the Have-Nots, that is, the Key West fishermen and relief workers who surround Harry Morgan; on the other side, the life of the Haves, that is, the wealthy yachtsmen and the drunken writers who winter in the Key West bars. These two themes never quite come together.

But a more serious weakness lies in the characters themselves, or rather in the author's attitude toward his characters. Some of them - the writers for example - are the same sort of people, leading the same sort of lives, as he described in 'The Sun Also Rises.' In those days Hemingway was unhappy about the lives they were leading, yet he approached the people with real sympathy, going to great pains, for example, to explain to himself why Robert Cohn was really a villain in spite of all his admirable qualities. But this time Hemingway really hates the people; he pictures them not as human beings but as the mere embodiments of lust or folly, as wolves or goats or monkeys disguised with little mustaches and portable typewriters. 'All right,' Helen Gordon says to her husband. 'I'm through with you and I'm through with love. Your kind of picknose love. You writer.' It is the final insult. But since Hemingway is a writer himself, this aversion is also a self-aversion, and prophesies a change in his own career - not from literature to fishing, for example, but rather from one kind of writing to another kind. And that change, that transition, is already foreshadowed in his characters. Among the very few that he portrays sympathetically are two Catholics (1) and a Communist war veteran. Harry Morgan himself begins as a tough guy capable of killing people in cold blood, either to get money or to save his hide; but he dies as a sort of proletarian hero.

There is a story behind this novel perhaps more interesting than the story that Hemingway has told. Some day we may know the whole of it; at present I have to reconstruct it from word-of-mouth information and from internal evidence. Hemingway has been working on the book for several years - at the very least, since 1933. It was practically finished a year ago, before he left for Spain. At that time it was a longer novel than in its present version, and it ended in a mood of utter discouragement. When Hemingway returned, full of enthusiasm for the Spanish Loyalists, he must have felt dissatisfied with what he had written; at any rate he destroyed large parts of it. It may have been then that he wrote a death scene for Harry Morgan - the scene in which he stammers out with his last few breaths: 'One man alone ain't got. No man alone now.... No matter how, a man alone ain't got no bloody f——g chance.' This might be the message that Hemingway carried back from Spain, his own free translation of Marx and Engels: 'Workers of the world unite, you have nothing to lose....' (2) The whole scene is beautifully done, but it doesn't grow out of what has gone before.

There are other scenes that are even stronger, and better integrated with the story- for example, the phantasmagorical drinking and slugging bout of the veterans on relief, and the quarrel between Helen Gordon and her husband, and Mrs. Morgan's last soliloquy. Almost all the women in the novel are portrayed with subtlety and sureness. As a whole, 'To Have and Have Not' is the weakest of Hemingway's books - except perhaps 'Green Hills of Africa' - but it is by no means the least promising. For some years now the literary hyenas have been saying that Hemingway was done for, but their noses have betrayed them into finding the scent of decay where none existed. From the evidence of this book, I should say that he was just beginning a new career.

Notes

1 Hemingway became a temporary Catholic during his marriage to Pauline Pfeiffer (1927-40).

2 '... but your chains,' 'The Communist Manifesto' (1848).

49. LOUIS KRONENBERGER, 'NATION'

145 (23 October 1937), 439-40

Louis Kronenberger (b. 1904) is an American anthologist and critic.

Hemingway's new novel - his first since 'A Farewell to Arms' - will strike many people as confused and some people as transitional. For despite a living hero and a handful of superb scenes, it is a book with neither poise nor integration, and with shocking lapses from professional skill. It splits up in the middle, not simply as a narrative, but also as a conception for a narrative: Hemingway, having told the story of a man, suddenly reinterprets it, and finds it necessary to contrast his hero with other men. Having shown us a lone wolf beaten down by the forces of a protected society, he goes on to picture a whole gallery of creatures drawn from that society.

Structurally all this is awkward and incompetent. It is like writing a letter and then adding to it an appalling number of postscripts. But the structural defect proceeds out of something more serious - out of an intellectual naivete which goes so far as to imagine that an explicit contrast between Harry Morgan and society is required. Actually the relationship has been obvious, not only in all the incidents of the story, but also in the very theme. It was implicit so soon as Hemingway ever conceived of Harry Morgan as an incorrigible individualist. Harry Morgan is doomed by the nature of his own conflicts and experiences; is doomed as his type has been doomed since it first arose in fiction; is doomed as the heroes of Balzac and Stendhal, or Dreiser and Conrad, were doomed. To drive the point home, Harry Morgan and society have only to interact, indeed they must interact; whereas Hemingway has thought to solve the problem by presenting them separately. But an even greater blunder on Hemingway's part was to suppose that he was presenting a true contrast. In reality Harry Morgan and the kind of society pitted against him were not divided in aim; they were merely unequal in strength.

Between the lines, however, one can read an *intention* on Hemingway's part which appeared to make the second half of the book a valid contrast with the first half. For by the time he had created Harry Morgan he had changed his conception of Harry Morgan's place in the scheme of things: the lone wolf had turned into the poor slob, the rebel had turned into the victim. The victim, to be sure, was there from the beginning; but not for Hemingway. Hemingway began by exalting Harry Morgan as the good type of hard guy - the fellow who pitied no one, least of all himself; the husband whose wife adored him extravagantly for his guts and his *cojones*; the fighter who knew how to take it on the chin. Then slowly the buccaneer began to dwindle, and someone who was a social problem, who had a social significance, began to take his place. And as Harry Morgan, the man born to stand alone, was about to go down to defeat, he came to realize that in this world the victims of society cannot stand alone.

This shift in values, coming as it does well after the book is under way, results in artistic ambiguity and confusion. But offstage we have advanced from the Hemingway who went to Spain to watch the bullfighters to the Hemingway who went to Spain to join the Loyalists. Death in the Afternoon has taken on a sterner meaning, and in that sense 'To Have and Have Not' would seem to mark a transition to the kind of book that Hemingway will write in the future. In that sense it was no bad thing to convert a successful novelette about Harry Morgan into an unsuccessful novel about Harry Morgan and society. But I must go on to say at once that I still find more of the old than of the new Hemingway in this book, and that in many respects he has still to come to grips with important social and ethical problems. The old love of violence - or is it no more than an unconscious exertion towards violence? - is as marked here as ever; the interest in sport is still too ritualistic; the harping on masculinity and potency is still a proof of either not enough perspective or not enough self-confidence; the hysterical exultation of a woman in her potent male is still a form of sentimentality.

Meanwhile with Hemingway taking on new and more significant interests, one is left wondering how well he will be able to cope with them. He is a very talented writer, but it remains to be proved how intelligent a one. When Clifton Fadiman some years ago drew the parallel between Hemingway and Byron, (1) I am sure that he extended it to include Goethe's celebrated remark about Byron: 'When he thinks, he is a child.' Nothing could be more inept here, more lacking in true insight, than Hemingway's brand of satire against literary loafers and the complacent rich. It is not only crude and slapdash, misunderstanding its own ends, but some of it is hardly professional. When one encounters such a remark as 'A man tapped for Bones (2) is seldom tapped for bed,' one is back on the Yale campus hearing one undergraduate wisecrack with another. Similarly, once action in the story is over, and reaction sets in - as with Harry's wife after he is dead - the sentimental note is sounded no more convincingly than the satiric was. Hemingway is writing, not as the woman felt, but as he would like her to feel. For he does not understand the woman.

These may seem like artistic rather than intellectual matters, but their failure as art is based on a defect of intelligence. And upon Hemingway's intellectual growth, it seems to me, his social and ethical growth - and hence his place as a really serious novelist - must hinge. As a writer he can portray scenes with what is little less than genius. As a thinking being he has still a very great deal to learn. His intentions in the matter are fairly clear. His qualifications are more in doubt. His temperament, I think, is in most doubt of all.

Notes

1 Clifton Fadiman, Ernest Hemingway: An American Byron, 'Nation,' 136 (18 January 1933), 63-4.
2 An elite undergraduate club at Yale.

50. EDWIN MUIR, 'LISTENER'

18 (27 October 1937), 925

Mr. Hemingway is an extraordinary writer. I am not thinking of his talent, which is undeniable, but of his attitude to the people and events he describes. In his first few stories he maintained a post of neutrality between good and evil; if he showed any sympathy it was with men who dismissed moral questions with an invitation to have a drink. He admitted as real the senses and the actions they drive people to; but he had little use for emotion or thought. He occupied himself ascetically with what Mr. Yeats has called 'the root facts of life'. The senses have an extreme directness, if we completely disconnect them from emotion and thought; for then their sole aim is satisfaction. They may be prevented from satisfying themselves by external circumstances, but by nothing else; consequently their logical expression is violence, for that is the natural response of the senses to something which prevents them from doing what they want to do. This accounts for the great amount of killing in Mr. Hemingway's stories, and this also makes it so plausible. By the actor killing is simply felt to be necessary, since his conflict is never with himself but always with something outside himself. He may kill in anger or with regret; but in either case it is because something is standing between him and his desires, and there is no other problem. If he is killed first it is his tragedy. If he survives he finds his fulfilment in love, drink and sport. This is more or less, it seems to me, Mr. Hemingway's picture of human life. It has the interest both of natural history and of any blood sport, but it is too specialised to be called human. It moves us because of Mr. Hemingway's complete honesty and very considerable skill as a writer; but in his latest novel he himself seems to recognise it as inadequate, for he has introduced a slight complication, a contrast, essentially a moral contrast, between the lot of the rich and the poor, between the ordinary man and the intellectual, the first of whom he describes as in some way real and the second as in some way false. He clearly believes in sensation, and still distrusts thought, but he is also concerned about the state of the world, and his technique, fashioned exclusively to deal with the world of sensation, does not know quite how to deal with the change. The story is therefore somewhat unconvincing, though it contains scenes as good as any he has ever written.

The main contrast in 'To Have and Have Not' is between Harry Morgan, a fisherman of Key West in Florida, and a crowd of rootless intellectuals who sprawl about the place. A visitor hires Harry's boat for a month and leaves without paying him. Harry, on his beam ends, is forced to accept an offer to ship to Cuba some Chinamen who are wanted by the police. He kills the Chinaman who makes the offer, after taking the money off him, and then he does not carry out the job. Later he loses an arm while rum-running. Finally he offers to take four revolutionaries across to Cuba, kills the four of them on the way across, but when everything seems safe is shot in the abdomen and dies in lingering pain. All these crimes are described simply as necessary. Harry is a fine animal; his walk and his bearing are mentioned several times; and he can only act like a fine animal. He is a hundred per cent. natural man who has lost one arm, and in spite of all the people he kills more in sorrow than in anger he is 'sympathetic'. But he is also a flagrantly romantic figure, with his wide shoulders, his bashed nose, his one arm and his walk. He is the noble roughneck, a modern sophisticated version of the noble savage. His ruin is indirectly brought about by those who have - whether what they have is money, or power, or intelligence, or cunning - just as the ruin of the noble savage was brought about, according to eighteenth-century worshippers of nature, by civilisation. The 'civilised' figures in the story have not even the few virtues that Harry has; they are rubbishy through and through. Several of the violent scenes are described with Mr. Hemingway's usually brilliant economy. The account of Harry's return in his boat from Cuba with a broken arm is an especially fine piece of imagination. The dialogue occasionally produces an effect of caricature, but it is very good, nevertheless. The account of Harry's death is disfigured by a first-class piece of hard-boiled sentimentality, supplied by the widow. The contrast between the haves and the have nots is unconvincing. But the story of Harry himself is extraordinary simply as a story.

51. PHILIP RAHV, 'PARTISAN REVIEW'

4 (December 1937), 62-4

Philip Rahv (1908-73) was an American editor and critic, founder of the Left-wing 'Partisan Review,' and author of 'Image and Idea' (1949).

Since Ernest Hemingway's recent activities of a public nature have forewarned us of a shift in his creative interests, the news that in his latest novel he has succumbed to the social muse is at the present moment hardly overwhelming. Yet his surrender, after nearly a decade of being wooed and reviled in turn by the critics of the Left, is an important literary event. It seems to have been the Spanish War that finally released him for a trial-flight into new country; and in this he has been true to his own legend. While in its ideological guise the significance of the social struggle seemed to him a mere superstition of the perverse intellect - and many are the sardonic asides he has written concerning the saviors of the world and revolution as an opium of the people (1) - it is something else again to see one's favorite theme of human endurance and valor in the face of physical annihilation enacted on the stage of world events. Once these events acquire a personal meaning, one has gotten hold of the individual link, peculiar to oneself alone, connecting one's old values with the new. And if we are conscious of the Hemingway mode as a whole, the fact that he comes into contact with the revolution precisely through its violence should convince us of his sincerity, rather than make us doubt it.

Hemingway's imagination defines itself most intimately within the pieties of combat. Hence, regardless how bizarre or naive it may appear to most of us, it must be realized that to him the difference between slaying the great kudu who roams the green hills of Africa and slaying the ogre Franco is as yet far from organic. At both alike he looks through the sights of a rifle. And the failure of the novel can be explained, I think, by his failure to understand this difference. In it he tries to reconcile elements that cannot function together and that, in the end, cancel each other out. If the book lacks unity of tone and structure, it is largely due to the contradiction between the old Hemingway manner and his new social direction.

What are Hemingway's values? To be alone, to be inarticulate, to be solemnly male and sense the world through an alert, supple, self-sufficient body, to face death with simplicity and to believe in it. Now if we take the great kudu as a symbol of these values - for intrinsically the kudu and the man who hunts him are really one, just as the bull and the bull-fighter are in essence identical - then it becomes evident that no matter how noble and powerful this animal may be in his native African haunts, it is ridiculous to put a rope around his neck and lead him down an American street to join a radical demonstration. The great kudu can never rebel against society - he is not in it. But in this novel about the rich and poor of Key West, the protagonist, Harry Morgan, is 'snotty and strong and quick and like some kind of *expensive animal*' (italics mine), and it is he who is charged with carrying through the theme of conversion. Morgan concentrates within himself the typical qualities of the Hemingway hero to the point of frenzy. An outlaw, owning nothing but his motor-boat which he uses to smuggle rum, guns, and his fellow-outlaws, he belongs to the breed of killers that live their lives 'all the way up'; the most violent character one has ever encountered in Hemingway, his one method of coping with life is to kill everyone who blocks the fulfilment of his needs. The story revolves around the successive murders he commits, and to shed blood is his only real necessity and the only means by which he can convince us of his existence. He and his wife Marie constitute an extra-social unit, a jungle cell of savage innocence in the midst of civilization. He is incapable of accomplishing the social task assigned to him and when he dies, killed by the bullet of a Cuban conspirator, his Stein stutter (2) of faith in the collective idea strikes us as false and imposed. He cannot breathe in the social air, and once forcibly converted by the author, he must die to disprove him. A character like Morgan can only be converted at the cost of losing his reality; his death is actually the only means the author has of saving himself the embarrassment of watching him fall apart.

But Hemingway cannot do without Morgan, for he has another meaning, a subjective one, one that is inherent in the ambivalent psychology of conversion. He represents Hemingway's review of his own past and of the type of man and mode of expression he had created: through him he is saying farewell to that past as well as testing its usability in the light of new needs. In this sense, Morgan's death may presage Hemingway's social birth.

Hemingway is shy about his conversion. He is afraid of the sentimentality attached to his new role, and of its possible melodramatic effects. Now Richard Gordon, a character in the story, corresponds exactly to the image that Hemingway would like the reader not to have of himself. Gordon is an insincere, false convert: he has changed his politics to suit the fashion and is writing a novel about a 'firm-breasted little Jewish agitator' leading a strike. Furthermore, whereas Morgan, with whom the author is to some extent identified, is sexually idealized, Gordon is shown mutilating his relation to his wife and finally losing her. And, indeed, in thus cunningly exemplifying in Gordon the negation of what he considers himself to be, he has purged his novel of those unctuous attitudes that so frequently vitiate the literary products of conversion.

'To Have and Have Not' is among the least successful of Hemingway's work, although in some of the scenes, as in the description of the veterans running amuck, the writing is superb. Yet it is valuable as an instance of a new beginning, as a thrust into a salient of new experience. But it is at this point that his problems really begin. In transcending his political indifference, he has not, however, at the same time transcended his political ignorance; and in turning away from individualism, he will find that the method of inarticulate virility is no substitute for consciousness. Emancipation from the most elementary bourgeois illusions is in itself no great achievement, unless it is but the first step in a development that leads one to perceive the world of materialist relations, and men themselves.

Notes

1 Karl Marx, 'Critique of the Hegelian Philosophy of Right' (1844).
2 Wyndham Lewis, 'Time and Western Man,' 67.

52. DELMORE SCHWARTZ, 'SOUTHERN REVIEW'

3 (Spring 1938), 769-82

Delmore Schwartz (1913-66), an American short story writer, poet and critic, wrote 'In Dreams Begin Responsibilities' (1938) and 'The World is a Wedding' (1948).

I

'Mr. Hemingway is preëminently the wise guy.' Such was Ezra Pound's succinct and idiomatic remark, which is mentioned for the sake of naming this popular and superficial aspect of his writing and immediately moving past it. It is worth saying, so that one can be aware of how much more his writing contains than cleverness, and of how very often the cleverness is a way of getting important feelings and attitudes upon the page. And now that this new novel presents an attempt to deal with the class structure of society, a review of this new book will be aided greatly by trying to get a whole and round view of what his writing has actually been concerned with besides cleverness and bright sayings.

Other aspects must be eliminated also. One must forget about the public figure, the legend, the athlete and sportsman, the American Byron, the one for whom Gertrude Stein has a weakness, with whom Morley Callaghan boxes and Max Eastman wrestles, and the professional funny man for a magazine whose chief purpose is the advertisement of men's clothing. These are very interesting aspects, no doubt, and Charles Scribner's Sons and the circulating libraries will not fail to appraise them at their true value. But one must forget about them if one is interested in serious criticism of a serious writer. It is precisely these aspects which obscure the serious writer: one would not be be astonished if they obscured the writer from himself at times. The serious writer is the one who tells us that he was working for a certain feeling of life and death, and that it is important to be critical of mysticism because mysteries actually exist.

Once a good writer has written five or six books, there is always a pattern present. The pattern can be observed in its simplest terms merely by watching for recurrent themes, or in a more detailed fashion. The important thing obviously is the writing itself, as a specific thing. The pattern is to be discarded as soon as it has been used or is useless. It is there, but the only reason for abstracting it is to aid one's gaze and get near as possible to the actual thing to be read. With this apology, and knowing well that one will not fail to forget some important element, I would like to name the pattern in Hemingway's writing as briefly as this: there is an extraordinary interest in sensation; there is an extraordinary interest in conduct and the attitudes toward conduct; and there is always the background of war, either one which has recently been concluded or one which is going on. Sometimes the background takes the form of the imminence of death, but it is the same thing, actually, because it is there for the same reason, to draw forth certain kinds of conduct. It would be neat and very helpful, if there were a clear link between the interest in sensation and the interest in conduct, but I am afraid that I can find none. It is true that during a time of war and when one is writing about war there will be a great heightening of sense-awareness because of danger, but Hemingway's interest in sensation is directed to daily gratification of the sense-organs as well as the feelings of peril.

One need not dwell very long on the attention paid to sensations. It is responsible in Hemingway for much good writing, and especially for the clean and hard character of the descriptive passages, which are also affected, I think, by certain kinds of modern painting. One interesting point may, however, be made. Any psychologist will tell us that the term *sensation* is very abstract because the whole history of the organism responds to any stimulus and actively determines its nature, so that we are experiencing our own past as much as the stimulus. But if a naked sensation is possible, then Hemingway is often engaged in describing it, and this seems to be significant of the fact that his characters are separate and alone at the present moment, having little or no history. They usually have a nationality, but mostly for the sake of their conversational idiom, which, as I intend to try to show in a moment, is the most characteristic aspect of Hemingway's style. Good eating, good drinking, good sport, good sexual intercourse, good landscapes - all these subjects have to do with sensation rather than with a more complex human experience, and these subjects constitute the texture of the writing.

By contrast, the interest in conduct and the attitudes toward conduct is central. The conduct with which Hemingway is chiefly concerned must be distinguished sharply from behavior, and the meaning of the word in which it is equivalent to human action. For it seems, of course, that every storyteller is concerned with conduct. With very different kinds of conduct, however, with the ultimate ends of human existence, with the *mores* of a given time or race. In no exact sense is the fiction of Hemingway about the one, nor the other, nor is it about the habits of daily living (as in 'Ulysses'), nor ideas (as in 'The Magic Mountain'), nor the way of life of a whole class (as in 'Buddenbrooks'), nor human passion amid an environment (as in 'Wuthering Heights' or 'The Return of the Native'), nor existence in every aspect (as in Tolstoy), nor the existence of a given society (as in Balzac), nor sensibility and time (as in Proust and Virginia Woolf), nor in moral obsessions of a special kind (as in Dostoyevsky and Gide), nor with the bureaucratic structure in which all human effort is involved (as in Kafka), nor with the growth and trials of character (as in George Eliot). This is a prolix list of negative examples, but they will serve to indicate the limitations of Hemingway's art as well as the kind of conduct in which he is not interested. Hemingway does not resemble any of the writers just mentioned; he does not resemble Gertrude Stein or Sherwood Anderson, although he has of course learned a method of style from them; he certainly does not resemble his imitators, but if a comparison is necessary, one could say, without meaning to be pretentious or astounding, that among novelists he most resembles Jane Austen, who was also very much interested in a special kind of conduct. Although she was not likewise concerned with sensations, she also used conversation for the sake of a kind of rhetoric.

There is a definite code by which characters are judged and by which they judge each other and which often provides the basis of the conversation. It is important to recognize that the code is relevant, and only relevant, to a definite period of time and to a special region of society. Courage, honesty, and skill are important rules of the code, but it is these human attributes as determined by a specific historical context. To be admirable, from the standpoint of this morality, is to admit defeat, to be a good sportsman, to accept pain without an outcry, to adhere strictly to the rules of the game and to play the game with great skill. To be repugnant and contemptible is to violate any of these requirements. It is sportsman-like morality, or equally, the morality of sportsmanship. It extends its requirements into the region of manners and carriage, and one must speak in clipped tones, avoid pretentious phrases, condense emotion into a few expletives or deliberately suppress it - noble, to borrow a pun from William Carlos Williams, equals no bull. (1)

Examples are, in fact, too plentiful. Cohn, in 'The Sun Also Rises,' is a prime example of one character who violates the code again and again. He does not play the game, he discusses his emotions at great length, he does not admit defeat with the lady whom he loves, and when he is hurt, he lets everyone know about it. Thus he must be one of the damned. He comes up against the blessed, the secular saint of Hemingway's morality, when he meets the matador who has won the lady whom he loves, and, being a good boxer, knocks him down again and again, only to have the matador take unending punishment and get up from the floor each time with no word and without being knocked out, until Cohn is finally defeated by the fortitude, the moral ascendancy, of the matador, and can only begin to cry and to wish to shake hands. In turn, the lady in question obeys the code and gives up the matador because she too recognizes his sanctity of character, and because 'it isn't the sort of thing one does,' and because she does not want to be 'one of those bitches that ruins children.' As this instance suggests, the whole code can be found explicitly in the book about bullfighting as well as in the stories.

Whether a person is capable of living up to the code can be found out fairly well in sport. As C.K. Ogden (2) has observed, the notion that modern sports are amusements is absurd - genuine recreations are one thing and involve no contest, but most games are actually among the most searching forms of existence. The best way, however, in which one's character is tested is by one's conduct in the face of death. It is, I think, this concern with conduct which directs Hemingway's plots to violent situations so often. And here again, one can recognize Hemingway's just intuitions, for one can scarcely doubt that the peril of dying is the most essential trial of any human being. But one would like, in passing, to protest against the frequent statement that Hemingway is interested in death, a notion which he himself seems to like. An interest in death is very unusual in the writers of our time, and it is with regret that one feels compelled to deny it of Hemingway. But he explains, in 'Death in the Afternoon,' that he went to the bullfights because he wanted to see violent death 'now that the wars were over' - a significant phrase - and the bullring was the only place to see it. He wanted to see violent death, not 'the complications of death by disease, or the death of a friend, or someone you have loved or have hated': which means, clearly, that he was not at all concerned either with dying, nor with the dead - which would be a truly impressive concern for a modern writer.

The morality in question has its own Arcady. (3) The priest who is held up for admiration in 'A Farewell to Arms' speaks of his own country, Abruzzi, where 'the roads were frozen and hard as iron, where it was clear cold and dry and the snow was dry and powdery and hare-tracks in the snow and the peasants took off their hats and called you Lord and there was good hunting.' (4) And we are given another version of it in the short stories about Switzerland - where the point in each story is the clear-cut integrity of the Swiss - and also in the story called A Clean, Well-Lighted Place, a café 'which is clean and pleasant and well-lighted and the light is good and there are shadows of the leaves.'

But there is always the background of the war and the despair consequent upon it. It is this which distinguishes the code sharply from the ones which it might seem to resemble very much, the codes of the gentleman, of chivalry, and of sport, of the past. For there is no reason for obeying the code, no sense that somehow it sustains a society and a way of life. Obedience to the code is an act of desire with no other basis, and the matador is admired and Cohn is condemned with the implication that everything is relative, if one cares to think about it. The values by which we live have been ruthlessly laid bare by the bloodshed, at one extreme, and by the political speeches and propaganda, at the other extreme. There is a remarkable passage in 'A Farewell to Arms' (much quoted, unless memory deceives me, when the book first was published) in which the destruction of values is explicitly recognized (A soldier says to the hero: 'What has been done this summer cannot have been done in vain.'):

> I did not say anything. I was always embarrassed by the words sacred, glorious, and sacrifice and the expression in vain. We had heard them, sometimes standing in the rain almost in earshot, so that only the shouted words came through, and had read them, on proclamations that were slapped up on billposters over other proclamations, now for a long time, and I had seen nothing sacred, and the things that were glorious had no glory and the sacrifices were like the stockyards at Chicago if nothing was done with the meat except to bury it. There were many words that you could not stand to hear and finally only the names of places had dignity.... Abstract words like glory, honor, courage, or hallow were obscene beside the concrete names of villages. (5)

And yet, although the hero of this book deserts from the army, and although it is true that the abstract words have become obscene, it is nevertheless precisely glory, honor, and courage which constitute the ideals of conduct in all of Hemingway's writing. Given the historical situation, given the war and the post-war world, the characters grasp these values by a fiat of will, as if they existed in a vacuum without support or basis. It is impossible to resume the desires and ambitions and the whole way of life which made existence supportable before the war occurred. One must send dispatches to a newspaper or get one's living in some other fashion not related to one's essential life, and then one will be free, for a time of holiday, to seek the intensity of feeling which was the one positive gift of the war. There are too many homosexuals in the drinking-places (much homosexuality has developed as a result of the war) and the *nouveaux riches* (who have become rich during the war) are also too prominent; and perhaps one has been wounded in the war and rendered impotent, or perhaps one's girl has died during the war. The reader will recognize the circumstances of 'The Sun Also Rises'; but whatever the specific context, the situation is identical. In a story called A Way You'll Never Be, a shell-shocked soldier says: 'Let's not talk about how I am, it's a subject I know too much about to want to think about it anymore.' (6)

And there is, to complete the pattern, an outline at a distance of a morality and way of life which transcends the whole situation. There are figures in the background who are not in that state of privation in which values lack a firm ground. When these figures come forward, there is always the implication that they are naïve and do not know what has happened and that the world has moved on: but in their naïveté and ignorance, they are nevertheless whole and integrated, a way which we'll never be. Twice or three times, Catholicism provides the basis for these figures, and in recognition of the superiority involved, the hero sometimes prays, or is very courteous and friendly to a priest, and the priest himself, though he is baited, is set forth as a lovable figure. Yet when the priest in 'A Farewell to Arms' asks the hero to go to his own happy country, in the passage already referred to, the hero does not go, although he had wanted to go, but he went instead 'to no such place but to the smoke of cafés and nights when the room whirled and you needed to look at the wall to make it stop, nights in bed drunk, when you knew that that was all that there was,' and then, in the morning, 'a sharp dispute about the cost.' (7)

There is one intricate method of style which bears the weight of the whole complex of attitudes, conduct, morality, and the disintegration of values. The method of style is constructed in the medium of conversation (and it is in his modification and extension of the rhetorical possibilities of speech that Hemingway has, I think, made his most valuable contribution to writing), and the speech is, by no means, as Wyndham Lewis maintains (having, as usual, nine or ten axes to grind) 'the rhythms of proletarian speech ... the voice of the "folk," of the masses, who are the cannon-fodder.' The conversation is, on the contrary, a great heightening of the kinds of speech of our time, an exaggeration in which the whole pattern is embodied. *The foreigner* is necessary for this rhetoric. The foreigner carries over into English the idiom of his native tongue, and in that modified English he makes clear the fact that he is living by the values which constitute the code. If, at times, it happens that the honorable one is an American and the foreigner is without honor, this makes no difficulties or falsity, for the honorable Americans are given a style of speech all their own, and the foreigner is made to speak like an American. The method is a fine example of how a writer's style and his values are fused. In the story called The Gambler, the Nun, and the Radio, a significant story in other respects also, we get the whole conversational system in action. A Mexican gambler has been shot and is being questioned by an American detective who wishes him to reveal his assailant and who tells him that he is going to die:

> 'Listen,' the detective said, 'this isn't Chicago. You're not a gangster. You don't have to act like a moving picture. It's all right to tell who shot you. That's all right to do.'

Here we have, of course, the concern with conduct set forth in usual American speech. The Mexican gambler understands English very well, but nevertheless this statement must be translated into his own terms, into a stylized foreign version. The translation is performed by a writer who is sick in the hospital at the same time:

> 'Listen, amigo,' said Mr. Frazer (the writer). 'The policeman says that we are not in Chicago but in Hailey, Montana. You are not a bandit and this has nothing to do with the cinema.'
>
> 'I believe him,' said Cayetano softly (because he is badly wounded this is not the cinema). 'Ya lo creo.'
>
> 'One can with honor denounce one's assailant. Everyone does it here, he says.' (8)

For emphasis, one ought to note that *the moving picture* becomes *the cinema* and *that's all right* becomes *one can with honor*, and the background is taken care of very well by the statement that everyone does it here, everyone denounces one's assailant to the police here.

Many other examples could be given, and will come readily to the mind of every reader of Hemingway.

Before going on to consider the new novel, it ought to be noted that the morality which seems so much the substance of Hemingway's writing is a fairly limited one. It is, as has been said already, peculiarly qualified by and linked to a specific historical background and a few definite situations. The morality cannot be directed to other kinds of situation and other ways of life without a thoroughgoing translation. It is a morality, to repeat, for wartime, for sport, for drinking, and for expatriates; and there are, after all, a good many other levels of existence, and on those levels the activities in question fall into place and become rather minor. Consider, for example, how irrelevant the morality would be when the subject matter was family life. The style, as has just been shown, is likewise focused upon certain key situations and contexts, and relative to them, and inseparable from them. This defines Hemingway's limitations as a writer, and it indicates that a genuine transformation would be needed if the same writer were to attempt to deal with the class structure of society directly. But this is precisely what Hemingway has tried to do in this new novel.

II

'To Have and Have Not' is a stupid and foolish book, a disgrace to a good writer, a book which should never have been printed. It contains passages of good writing, and the parts of three good short stories - when one of these parts appeared in 'Esquire' as a short story, it was much better there, and not broken up by the interposition of a chapter. But elsewhere and for the most part, it is appalling as a literary product: the conversation is repeatedly false, or rather falsetto, and the descriptive passages sometimes read like improvisations.

The central character of the book is Harry Morgan, a fisherman who has been earning his living by chartering his boat for fishing trips. When a wealthy man who owes him almost a thousand dollars for two weeks of fishing departs without paying him, Harry Morgan is driven to crime. Driven is scarcely the exact word, since he is naturally a violent man and he has recently rejected an offer to smuggle Chinese into the United States for no scruple other than prudence: he says that he is afraid human cargo will talk. Once launched upon his criminal career, the responsibility for which rests upon the welshing rich man, Harry Morgan makes rapid progress. He is forced to kill one Chinaman in order not to kill twelve others, and soon, while smuggling rum, he is badly wounded by the Coast Guard, loses an arm, and has his boat taken from him by the police. Finally, still trying merely to earn a living for his family, he engages to take four Cuban revolutionists back to Cuba after they have robbed a bank, and they, launched upon a career of adventitious violence, kill his assistant for no good reason, and are killed by him, but not before one of them manages to get a bullet into him, leaving him slowly bleeding to death of a stomach wound. The action of this whole passage is written very well. Harry Morgan does not die, however, before he has announced his conversion to the belief that all those who are, like him, merely trying to make a living, can get nowhere without solidarity. Hemingway tries very hard to make actual Morgan's realization of this fact, in his speech about it, in the half-delirium before he dies, but the whole dialogue is completely false. Quoted apart from its context, the falsity may not be as obvious as in the book itself, but the effort to syncopate the sentences, to resort to expletives, and tough-guy diction must be transparent:

> 'A man,' Harry Morgan said, looking at them both. 'One man alone ain't got. No man alone now.' He

stopped. 'No matter how a man alone ain't got no bloody ... chance.'

He closed his eyes. It had taken him a long time to get it out and it had taken him all of his life to learn it.... Harry Morgan looked at them but he did not answer [they, captain and mate, have asked the dying Morgan if he wants anything]. He had told them but they had not heard.

Throughout the narrative the rôle of the rich is underscored very heavily and they are presented in an unrelieved nastiness which amounts to little else than the worst caricature. There is, for example, the yachtsman, a member of the Administration, we are told, who sails by Harry Morgan's boat when he lies in it wounded, and wishes to get him and turn him over to the police because he thinks catching a bootlegger is better than catching fish. There are also passages in which Harry Morgan discusses the social problem with another of the 'have nots,' and these conversations are ridiculous despite Hemingway's perfect ear for conversation, and they are made more ridiculous by the effort to make them convincing by using a hard-boiled diction. There is the effort to make Harry Morgan an admirable character by observing him from the standpoint of his wife who celebrates him at some length because of his sexual powers.

And the progress of the story is as poorly constructed as it possibly could be by a writer who said once that writing is architecture and not interior decoration. The book begins in the first person singular of Harry Morgan, shifts to straight narrative, shifts to the first person singular of another person, resumes the straight narrative, which later becomes indistinguishable from a form of essay or biography, changes again to the first person singular of Morgan's wife for two pages, and concludes with straight narrative.

Such shifts in the standpoint would be less intolerable if there were any effort to make them systematic, and were it not for the fact that when the book is more than half completed and Harry Morgan is bleeding to death on his boat, we begin what is virtually a new book devoted to the break-up of the marriage of a writer who, crudely enough, is also writing about the social problem, but not - of course - like Hemingway. He is brought forward partly as another example of the contemptible lives of the 'haves,' partly to be a type of the insincere writer who, following literary fashions, is writing a novel about a textile strike. The most crude instances of the vicious literary attitude of the writer are given, and he is also condemned because he does not make love properly. Soon, however, the marital relationship becomes very interesting for its own sake, the writer becomes pathetic and moving, and the social theme has been lost sight of again. It is regained by bringing the writer to a saloon where there are abused, exploited, and punch-drunk veterans engaged in beating each other up. Here again the writing is very good in parts. The writer manages to get into a conversation with several of the veterans, one of whom, conveniently enough, turns out to be not only a communist, but also a reader of the writer's novels and their severest critic. The only relationship which the story of the writer bears to the story of Harry Morgan is that of geographical propinquity, and also there is one moment, the worst in the book, when the writer passes Morgan's wife in the street and mistakenly supposes her to be unsatisfied sexually, rather than one who is very well pleased.

But this is by no means all. Still feeling, one would suppose, that the theme has not received adequate exemplification, there is a new break in the narrative, again on the basis of geographical location, and we are treated to a series of brief character studies of the rich who are about to go to bed in their yachts in the harbor of Key West on the night that Harry Morgan is dying. Some of these studies are in themselves very well written - one of them suggests, almost a Jamesian augmentation in Hemingway's style. One of them concerns the relationship of a homosexual millionaire and one of his friends who will, six months after the end of the book, we are told, commit suicide because he has too small an income. It is at this point that we get a neat little editorial to the effect that the income which will be too small is one hundred and seventy dollars a month more than those on relief are getting. Another character study is that of a grain broker who has no past to look back upon but one consisting of successive betrayals for the sake of wealth. And lastly, we get a fine little close-up of a movie star whose lover has just become too drunk to make love to her and fallen asleep. These people are not related to each other, and their only relation to Harry Morgan is the fact that he is poor and they are rich, and they are near each other, spatially speaking.

The weakness of the structure and the commonplace character of the conception is in itself enough to show how poor the book is. This judgment can also be reinforced by examining the specific conversations, which are often farcical in their effort at satire, or simply false. But I do not think it is necessary to engage in further quotation of particular passages.

What is more important is the way in which Hemingway has shifted his literary situation without changing or modifying his style and method at all. First of all, he is writing about a theme which he does not know anything about and as a result the conception of character is constantly false. The immediate cause of Morgan's resort to crime, the fact that he has not been paid for his boat by the rich man, is not convincing as an explanation for the simple reason that he has been displayed as a violent individual to begin with, and thus one to whom crime would in no way be a degeneracy of character. Another curious attribute of the situation is that Harry Morgan has been getting thirty-five dollars a day during the fishing season and thus would presumably be one with a petty bourgeois mentality with regard to the economic situation and ripe for fascism. Another difficulty is his ability to generalize the evil from which he suffers, his ability to see it as a matter of the class structure and requiring solidarity. It would seem that, given Harry Morgan's mentality as presented in the book, he would tend to think always in terms of individuals, to fix evil-doing on individuals, on the man who did not pay, for example; and at most, if he did generalize about the matter, to make it a question of race-prejudice, or a prejudice against the nationality of the individual who has wronged him. It is not exact to say that Harry Morgan is a criminal, but he is criminal enough in his whole manner of approaching things, and the criminal is the one, among all, who presupposes and requires property relationships, so that the conversion of Harry Morgan at the end of the book comes bluntly against the fact that criminals when dying do not seem and cannot seem to understand their defeat as an exposure of the futility of individualism, the need of solidarity, and the evil of property relationships.

To repeat: in order to shift from the literary situation which I have tried to elucidate as the basis of Hemingway's writing and in order to grasp the social theme directly what is required is a reorientation of style and method. If it is felt, that is to say, that the social theme must be handled directly, then the satirized writer in 'To Have and Have Not' has at least chosen a subject matter proportionate to his theme in deciding to write about a textile strike, and thus taking up the evils of finance-capitalism in precisely the situations which show the conflict between the workers' need of wages and the employers' need of surplus value. In order to write about this, one needs what has been called 'a Marxist imagination,' the best example of which is to be found in

Trotzky's 'History of the Russian Revolution.' (9) It is the kind of imagination which Hemingway does not have, and exactly because he has an imagination of another sort. Perhaps he might, by a miracle of development, manage to acquire one, but it is at least certain that the social theme as involving the class structure of society cannot be grasped merely by deciding to write about it; especially after one has created a complicated instrument for describing the lives of individuals who are engaged in leisure-class pursuits, and are trying to maintain a code of values in a warring or post-war world.

Is it necessary, however, to handle the social theme directly? It would seem evident, on the contrary, that the character of the society in which we live, the hell of finance-capitalism, is revealed most adequately in certain important aspects by 'The Sun Also Rises' and 'A Farewell to Arms.' We see clearly how the simplest and most unoffending values are mercilessly perverted, abused, and befouled by modern war. Or, to put it even more crudely, the contemptible lives of the rich as they have previously been depicted by Hemingway are sufficient examples and sufficient judgments of our time, given Hemingway's own values. No other examples are possible for him, given his style, his interests, and his perceptions (all three are actually one), and he deceives himself and betrays us when he abandons them for an abstract paradigm, which falls apart at every moment in his book.

And now, as it happens, it seems to be possible to round out the picture patly, for, without for a moment doubting the good will involved, we read that Hemingway is once more in the midst of a war, sending dispatches about the battles to a newspaper syndicate, knocking out another correspondent who has doubted his motives and insinuated his bravado, and writing a play (10) about the war in a Madrid hotel amid the intermittent bombardments. I think it is not too much to say that we can hope for the best, both for the literary cause and the other one, so far as Hemingway is involved in it, because it is by no means a metaphor nor fanciful to say that he has now gone home.

Notes

1 William Carlos Williams, A Poem for Norman MacLeod, 'Collected Earlier Poems' (New York, 1951), 114.
2 Originator of Basic English; co-author, with I.A. Richards, of 'The Meaning of Meaning' (1923).
3 Idyllic region in Greek mythology.
4 'A Farewell to Arms' (Harmondsworth, Middlesex, 1963), 14.

5 Ibid., 143-4.
6 'Winner Take Nothing' (London, 1934), 79.
7 'A Farewell to Arms,' 14.
8 'Winner Take Nothing,' 197-8.
9 Published in London in 1919.
10 'The Fifth Column' (1938).

'The Spanish Earth' (film 1937, book 1938)

53. OTIS FERGUSON, 'NEW REPUBLIC'

92 (1 September 1937), 103

Otis Ferguson (1907-43) was an American film critic.

Top place in importance for the week goes to the set of pictures Joris Ivens brought back from the Madrid area and has finally got edited, scored for music and ready to go. His camera was in the fields, the rocking streets of the city, behind redoubts and with the tanks, sometimes in the advancing front line. He got as much of it as he could under such difficulties, sizing up not only perspective, sufficiency of lighting, the best points of shelter and focus, sizing up as well how each thing would fit with his idea. Then he took what he had and worked out his idea through it.

There are two simple themes: the suffering and dogged purposefulness of war for the cause; and the bulk and onward motion of the cause itself - the earth and its rightful function and what the chance to use and irrigate it will bring forth for men to eat, and how they will not be denied now at last even if they have to die for it. The film opens on the husbandry of the countryside, the look and meaning of the land. A spoken comment rushes in here to assume the unestablished, its faulty cuing presently demonstrated by the ease with which the film brings about the contrast in its own terms. Over the loaves of bread from the ovens, the war posters look down, and over the ordered fields and fruit trees the sound of firing comes to end the first sequence, the explosions growing louder, still unseen.

Then the defense of Madrid, the ravages within the city, the fighting itself, rifle and machine-gun fire from the gaunt shells of buildings, field-pieces in the orchard, citizens lined up to drill and become soldiers, soldiers lined up for attack or for soup, scattered in sleep or sniping positions or over newspapers. In the trenches as in the city life goes on, precarious but familiar, a strange world of death and strenuous doing, yet somehow the same, people clinging to their songs and houses, and in the fields there is yeoman work on the ditches and rude aqueducts: much of the old machine is down or silent but the life processes go on and a new machinery must be set up. And over all this, the strangeness itself becomes a part of routine, the heightened tempo of trucks hammering up with soldiers, the big planes out of the cloud somewhere and the air full of plaster dust, stretchers and ambulances by the door.

Though the camera never seems to get near enough the business end of things to catch the fearful symbol of the enemy or tell-tale thinning of the line (one figure falls; for the rest we get a particular group, the scream of a shell on the sound track, and cut to a stock explosion), the picture is definitely on the side of the harsh truth, for there are plenty of close-ups of violent death after the fact, and the comment is beautifully explicit on the price men will pay - that advance in echelons of six, the six becoming five and the four three and this is the way they go into action, not with trumpets. Yet one of the most convincing things about it is its abstention from bombast and sloganism.

Much of the carrying power in understatement should be credited to Ernest Hemingway's commentary. His voice doesn't come over too well, and what with his suggestion of some overrehearsed WNEW (1) announcer in an embarrassment it isn't vintage Hemingway; but with his knowledge and quiet statement of the odds against survival, that feeling for the people of Spain which comes from his heart, the combination of experience and intuition directing your attention quietly to the mortal truth you might well have missed in the frame, there could hardly be a better choice.

But the rest of the credit goes to Ivens and his unquenchable feeling for the life of people, at war or at work. He might have found a way around the sort of scene where 'natural' people are not natural at all but stiff and uneasy, and he skimped a little. But what he has brought back is convincing as the real thing, sparing neither cause nor effect, talking straightly as a man should talk. There are beautiful shots of ruin against the sky, and of the rise of native hills under it. There is no razzmatazz of angles, trick dissolves, symbols as such. He has saved for the last the advance that took the bridge and the running comment of symbol-in-fact represented by the completion of the business that loosed the water over the parched waiting land - but the whole film had been built up toward these two things, not just around them as spectacle. And though it is not a great film, it has been made so that somehow the power and meaning of its subject matter is there to feed the imagination of those who have any.

It isn't so much in the outward drama of the attack, the rattling trucks and tanks, breastworks and machine-gun placements and range-finders. These things are here but subordinated to a purpose, which is recorded in this camera simply because it is there in Ivens' and Hemingway's people - the serene grim cast of feature or carriage of the body, the fine figure of a man who comes up to address his brigade or parliamentary body. Men for the most part whose clouds of doubt and petty worry have burned off before a confident power imposing its symmetry from within. Relaxed, haggard or plain dirty, one after another is seen on the screen going through his heavy job as though in very token of the fact that a million or ten thousand or even fifty such cannot be wrong. There is no need for vilification and babble of glory here; showing the Spanish land and the people related to it, the film does not have to raise its voice to be undeniable, its report a plain testimonial to the way men can be lifted clear beyond themselves by the conception of and full response to the epic demand of their time.

Note

1 New York radio station.

'The Fifth Column and The First Forty-Nine Stories' (1938)

54. ALFRED KAZIN, 'NEW YORK HERALD TRIBUNE BOOKS'

16 October 1938, 5

Madrid in the old days was always a good place for Ernest Hemingway to work in. He wrote The Killers there, and part of 'The Sun Also Rises,' but in the fall and early winter of 1937 he was writing 'The Fifth Column' in the Hotel Florida, and Madrid was emphatically not a good place to work in. The hotel was some fifteen hundred yards from the front at times, and Francisco Franco's bi-lingual Castilians shelled it rather often. Witty people will say that the play reads as if it has been written under bombardment, and perhaps it does; but it is important to remember that the moral atmosphere in Madrid these last two years has been a little healthier than that of the sickened English-speaking world. (1)

No, 'The Fifth Column' is hardly a great play; it is an interesting Hemingway period piece - I almost said Hemingway short story, so nimbly do his stage people talk the clipped Hemingway speech - for it tells us more about him than it does about Spain. The heroism and the hunger of Spain flow a little into it, and a little of the treachery and the slow panic of Realpolitik, (2) but above and against the spectacle of martyrdom there is the old Hemingway hero, witty and sick, and the old Hemingway heroine, with her heart behind a Maginot (3) line, though this girl comes from Vassar, and Vassar ought to be mad at Mr. Hemingway for keeps. Ah, you will say, the old Hemingway hero, but surely with a new conscience? Well, yes. Do you remember Jake Barnes of Paris, 1925, and Lieutenant Frederic Henry at Caporetto? There is a difference, a very little one. Philip talking: 'We're in for fifty years of undeclared wars and I've signed up for the duration. I don't exactly remember when it was, but I've signed up all right.'

The scene, of course, is perfect; the very Hotel Florida in which Hemingway wrote the play; an American being casual and efficient in the service of the Loyalist Intelligence Service; the Vassar girl, Dorothy, living in a city at war (with so little hot water!) so she can write articles for magazines back home; German emigres fighting for the greater republic they never had; the swell of a battered world's undeclared hopes, and filtering through talk and love, the catastrophic twang of bombardment, like a great banjo deafeningly plucked; then the swish of shells, the screams, the hunger, and the shadow men of Franco's Fifth Column, the spies for the Unholy Alliance in Madrid, plotting nimbly while the city is rocked by fire.

Almost any one would have grown larger on this material, painted larger scenes, angrier ones, after seeing women and children murdered in line while waiting for food, but not Mr. Hemingway. When some years ago Clifton Fadiman so shrewdly noted Hemingway's resemblance to Byron, he could not have known that our Byron would find his own Greek war of independence, and that, as for his handsome prototype, war would mean the adventures of the eternally disillusioned among dead masterpieces. They sing Bandera Rossa (4) downstairs in the Hotel Florida, and Philip says: 'The best people I ever knew died for that song.' But he's not one of the best people; he may die with the mantle of a new world before his eyes, but sullenly, it's the thing to do, drinking's no longer any fun. He's Mr. Hemingway's Philip, sick in peace and sick in war, sick in the hearts of too many country-women. (5) It's a good war, yes, but war is what the Hemingway soul has moved through for fourteen years, the war against sobriety and against twentieth-century fate, the long, embattled journey by which Hemingway has gone around the world to find a little heroism in Madrid.

What it comes to is that this play - witty, noisy, full of crackle and home-driven insight - fails to master, because Hemingway has not yet mastered, that contemporary drama of which the Spanish war is but the most violent episode. There is a play of attitudes, Philip in love and Philip out of love, and which is more important, the Spanish Republic or the Vassar girl? She wants to get away. 'Don't you want all this to end? I mean you know, war and revolution?' Write a book on politics, live in Saint Tropez, she tells him: 'we'll just live somewhere

where it's lovely and you'll write.' And he must tell her that there's nothing for him to write but everything to do, and so in the end they fail. She just doesn't understand him.

Apparently, then, there will always be the same people against shifting backgrounds, Malaga, Paris, Key West, Toledo; apparently the eternal Lady Brett (Dorothy is a weaker sister), the eternal Jake (Philip is a waspish brother) will grow a little in new surroundings, drink less where the drink is scarce, turn on valves for heat in cold rooms, go mumbling their sick wisdom at each other through cities plagued by death. But when does the old charnel house come down? When will Hemingway in his vigorous, hopeful middle age reach up to the times that have in all their complexity made him the writer he is, given him his stage, displayed his forte, distinguished him from the others?

So much and so little for 'The Fifth Column.' With it are all of Hemingway's short stories, of which the first four - The Short Happy Life of Francis Macomber, The Capital of the World, The Snows of Kilimanjaro, and Old Man at the Bridge (dated Barcelona, 1938) - are new, and of which at least a half-dozen, as no one needs to be told, are simply terrific. They're printing Hemingway short stories in schoolbooks these days, and their author, it seems, is a little embarrassed. Ah, for the days when even the Treaty of Versailles (6) was young!

Notes

1 Kazin alludes to the refusal of America, England and France to intervene on the side of the Loyalists when Germany and Italy were actively helping the Fascists to win the war.
2 Realistic, i.e. brutal, politics.
3 Massive French fortifications which disastrously failed to prevent a German invasion.
4 The Red Flag, a Communist song, often sung in Spain.
5 An allusion to Henry Lee's eulogy of George Washington in 1799: 'First in war, first in peace, first in the hearts of his countrymen.'
6 1919.

55. MALCOLM COWLEY, 'NEW REPUBLIC'

96 (2 November 1938), 367-8

Hemingway says in his preface, 'This is only a play about counter espionage in Madrid. It has the defects of having been written in wartime, and if it has a moral it is that people who work for certain organizations have very little time for home life. There is a girl in it named Dorothy but her name might also have been Nostalgia.' I should judge that 'The Fifth Column' would need a little play-doctoring before production. There is too much commotion offstage, there are scenes that wouldn't be effective for lack of the proper timing, and no great skill is shown in the playwright's business of getting people in and out of doors. But the play reads like one of Hemingway's short stories, which is to say that it reads very well. The plot jumps ahead, the dialogue is sometimes tough, sometimes ourageously funny, and the minor characters are real creations - especially Max, the secret agent with a very tender heart and a face horribly deformed by torture.

The hero, Philip Rawlings, is the latest in a long line of Hemingway heroes, all of them brutal and reckless by day but wistful as little boys when alone at night with the women they love. As compared with Harry Morgan, of 'To Have and Have Not,' he shows an interesting development. Morgan, the lonely freebooter, had died in discovering the fellowship of the dispossessed: 'No matter how, a man alone ain't got no bloody f——g chance.' Philip is putting that discovery into action. He has the reputation of being a fancy war correspondent who spends his working hours wherever he can find women or whiskey. He likes to drink, that much is true. But in reality he is a hard-working agent in the counter-espionage service, acting under Communist Party orders. If he haunts the cafés along the Gran Via - 'and the embassies and the Ministerio and Vernon Rodgers' flat and that horrible Anita' - it is because he is looking for spies.

He longs for the carefree life he used to lead in the 1920's. You can hear the bitterness in his voice when he tells a very young and virtuous American volunteer, 'We of the older generation have certain leprous spots of vice which can hardly be eradicated at this late date. But you are an example to us.' Again he says, 'After this is over, I'll get a course of discipline to rid me of any anarchistic habits I may have acquired. I'll probably be sent back to working with pioneers.' It is as if he were talking over the heads of the audience, to the editors of the 'New Masses.' But in the midst of these sallies and asides, Hemingway is discussing an important theme, that of the individual serving an organization in which he believes, but not without moments of skepticism. Philip questions the means that must be employed - notably when there are prisoners to be given a third degree or fascist spies to be shot - and sometimes he questions the ends for which he is fighting. He wants to forget the war and take his girl to Kitzbühel (1) for the skiing. Then suddenly a boy is killed from ambush, or a dog is wounded by shell-fire and howls in the street, and Philip submits himself once more to party discipline. At the end, he decides to leave Dorothy because he loves her so much that she is interfering with his work. 'I do not ask that,' says poor tortured Max, his comrade. 'No. But you would sooner or later. There's no sense babying me along. We're in for fifty years of undeclared wars and I've signed up for the duration.'

The trouble is that although long-legged, bright-haired Dorothy is a symbol of the hero's nostalgia, and might be a symbol of ours if we saw her in the flesh, she is nothing of the sort when we read 'The Fifth Column.' She is presented there as a chattering, superficial fool, a perfect specimen of the Junior League pitching woo (2) on the fringes of the radical movement, with the result that she keeps the play from being a tragedy or even a valid conflict between love and duty. If Philip hadn't left her for the Spanish people, he might have traded her for a flask of Chanel No. 5 and still have had the best of the bargain.

This same big book contains Hemingway's forty-nine short stories, the entire contents of 'In Our Time,' 'Men Without Women' and 'Winner Take Nothing,' in addition to four new ones collected for the first time. Among them is The Snows of Kilimanjaro, the only story in which he has allowed himself to be conventionally poetic; it describes the death of a writer, with disquieting touches of self-loathing and self-pity. Another story is his very latest, Old Man at the Bridge, which was cabled from Barcelona in 1938. Six pages beyond it comes one of his oldest, On the Quai at Smyrna, written, I think, in 1921. Essentially they are the same story, that of people caught in the aftermath of a great military defeat.

During the seventeen years of his literary career, Hemingway's short stories have changed very little. He has broadened the range of his technical effects, and his geographical background, and to some extent his human sympathies. The new stories are not published like a few of the earlier ones, in the effort to be lurid or shocking. Yet those first stories defined his talent as a writer, and and some of them I still prefer to his more recent work. When he wrote them he seemed to be closer to his material and more directly moved by it. Has he ever shown more compassion than in The Battler and Indian Camp and My Old Man, all included in his first volume?

Reading the stories over again, you are impressed by how well they stand up in the face of a thousand products advertised to be just as good. You are also impressed by the number of them that deal with lust or violent death. In the first story - taking the order in which they are printed, not the order of writing - a rich woman shoots her husband in the back of the head with a hunting rifle. In the second, a Spanish boy plays at bull-fighting and is killed by an accidental thrust from a butcher knife. In the third, a writer dies of gangrene (3) after reliving his violent past. In the fourth, a old man waits for death in the midst of a general retreat. Some of the others deal with suicide, abortion, self-mutilation, war-time insanity, lesbianism, death on the racetrack, death in the bull ring; one story is called A Natural History of the Dead. People used to say that this choice of subjects was due to some unhealthy quirk, but I think there is another explanation. Every great writer - as Robert Cantwell said in his fine essay on Henry James (4) - is a prophet in spite of himself. He tries to express the underlying spirit of his age, and that spirit will sometime be carried into action. Hemingway's violence seemed excessive during the relatively quiet decade that followed the War. But now, after the fighting in Spain and China and the great surrender at Munich, it seems a simple and accurate description of the world in which we live.

Notes

1 A resort in the Austrian Tyrol.
2 The Junior League was an organization of American debutantes. Pitching woo is making love.
3 It is possible that Harry's thorn scratch, which leads to gangrene and death, was influenced by Rilke's scratch from a rose thorn, which precipitated his leukemia and led to his death in 1926. Hemingway discusses Rilke in 'Green Hills of Africa' (New York, 1935), 8.
4 Robert Cantwell, A Warning to Pre-War Novelists, 'New Republic,' 91 (23 June 1937), 179.

56. EDMUND WILSON, 'NATION'

147 (10 December 1938), 628, 630

Little did the critics of Hemingway know what they had in store for them when they were urging him a few years ago to interest himself in the large forces of society. Mr. Hemingway had a period of scathing indignation, during which he defied the 'world-savers' in the interests of his art and hobbies, and gibed fiercely at the insincerities of phony radicals; then he became aroused by the struggle of the Loyalists in Spain, the Stalinists took him in tow, and the first results are before us.

The earliest signs of Hemingway's new social consciousness had shown themselves in his book before this, 'To Have and Have Not,' in which he added nothing to the effect of several short stories by attempting to solder them together as a long story. This story was to have a moral of a kind that was new for Hemingway: the hero, a Florida smuggler, was finally to realize the hopelessness of fighting a bad world alone. Hemingway himself did not particularly labor this point; but in the meantime he had been helping to raise money for Spain and had appeared at a congress of the League of American Writers, and the Stalinists labored it for him. The literary fellow-travelers wrote as if 'To Have and Have Not' were the most creditable thing Hemingway had written, though from the literary point of view it was certainly by far the worst book he had written.

'The Fifth Column,' a play, is almost as bad. It opens very amusingly and rather dramatically, and it is good reading for the way the characters talk. But one can't see that it does very much either for Hemingway or for the revolution. The hero, though of Anglo-American origins, is a member of the Communist secret police, engaged in catching Fascist spies in Spain. His principal exploit in the course of the play is cleaning out, with the aid of only one other Communist, an artillery post containing seven Fascists - a scene which has as much plausibility and interest as the same kind of pushover and getaway in the cruder Hollywood Westerns. But the exploit that the play is really about is his affair with a girl magazine writer in a Madrid hotel under bombardment. What Hemingway's hero does for world communism is throw out this unfortunate woman, who has belonged to the Junior League and been to Vassar, after sleeping with her with enjoyment for several days, in favor of a Moorish whore who enables him to affirm by his reversion to her his solidarity with the people of Madrid. As he has treated the girl from Vassar with a good deal of frank contempt from the beginning, the action is rather lacking in suspense and the final sacrifice rather weak in moral value.

This heroic Anglo-American secret police agent is the same old Hemingway protagonist of 'The Sun Also Rises' and 'A Farewell to Arms,' though now rather more besotted and maudlin; but we never doubt that he will do his duty. Indeed, the more besotted and maudlin this familiar old character gets, the more completely he behaves like the hero of a book of adventure for boys. It does not make things any better for Hemingway to tell us in his preface that during the time when he was writing this play the hotel in which he himself was living was struck by 'more than thirty high-explosive shells.' In fact, it makes it worse.

The recent political activity of Hemingway has thus unquestionably its unfortunate aspect in that the spy hunt of the Loyalists in Spain has given him a pretext for turning loose without check in his writing the impulse to contemplate cruelty which has always played such a large part in his work. This impulse has been balanced in the past by the complementary impulse to show suffering; and he has made himself the master of a peculiar moral malaise, the source of much of the beauty of his stories, which derives from his identifying himself at once with the injurer and the injured. But here he is simply free to let the sadistic impulse have its way. Neither his hero's breaking-off with the girl nor the butchery by the Communists of the Fascists - which would have worried him at an early stage, when he used to write about wars very differently - seems to give rise to the slightest moral uneasiness. The Comintern agents in Spain have *carte blanche* to go as far as they like, because they are up against a lot of dirty bastards. Hemingway ignores the fact that the GPU (1) in Spain has been executing its opponents of the left as well as Fascist spies (though he does make his hero repudiate the idea of extorting a confession from one of his suspects). There is some attempt at compensation here, too, but it does not count for very much. Who can believe that our beloved bum, the greatest truant fisherman of all time, will ever be sent to mortify himself, as it is intimated at one point he may be, in a training camp for Young Pioneers? Who can believe it costs him any serious pain to throw over the Vassar girl? And in the meantime he has fun killing Fascists.

Now the bad news is told. Let us get on to the good. This book contains four new short stories which are among the best that Hemingway has written. The Short Happy Life of Francis Macomber seems to me to be one of his masterpieces. A story of big-game hunters in Africa, it is as good as 'Green Hills of Africa' was bad. The difference between Hemingway's work when he is writing on the one hand, objectively and when he is writing, on the other hand, directly about himself with a consciousness of what his public expects of him or about some character with whom it is easy for him to identify this public personality, is one of the odd phenomena of literature. The Short Happy Life of Francis Macomber deals with a theme that was implicit in 'Green Hills of Africa,' but it disengages and fully develops this theme.

So the story, in three pages, of the war in Spain - which might have been written about any war - is as telling as 'The Fifth Column' is silly. Hemingway's hand is as firm, his taste as sure, in his handling of this little anecdote, where he is concentrating artistically on something outside him, as they are inept in his dispatches from Spain, now collected and published in England in the series of left monographs called 'Fact,' where he is always diverting attention to his own narrow escapes from danger (though these, too, contain a couple of excellent anecdotes). So the story called The Capital of the World, another of Hemingway's very best, projects and judges in a poetic symbol those very adolescent obsessions which tend to spoil his other work. A young boy who has come up from the country and waits on table in a pension in Madrid gets accidentally stabbed with a meat knife while playing at bull-fighting with the dishwasher. This is the anecdote, but Hemingway has built in behind it all the life of the pension and the city: the priesthood, the working-class movement, the grown-up bull-fighters who have broken down or missed out. 'The boy Paco,' Hemingway concludes, 'had never known about any of this nor about what all these people would be doing on the next day and on other days to come. He had no idea how they really lived nor how they ended. He did not realize they ended. He died, as the Spanish phrase has it, full of illusions. He had not had time in his life to lose any of them, or even at the end, to complete an act of contrition.'

The Hemingway who wrote this fine story has looked at the fantasies of childhood with detachment and has registered the pathos of their discrepancy with the realities of the grown-up world. As an artist, he has bidden them goodbye. Yet he thinks that this boy from the village was lucky because he died while he still had them. The author of 'The Fifth Column' is still hanging on to these fantasies and they do not become him well.

The fourth story, The Snows of Kilimanjaro, another tragedy of African hunting, has some elements of the trashy moral attitudes which did such damage in 'The Fifth Column' and 'To Have and Have Not.' Here the central male, formerly a seriously intentioned writer, has allowed himself to marry a rich woman and now is dying in futility in Africa. He goes back poignantly to his early days in Paris, when he was happy, earnest, and poor, and he blames bitterly the rich bitch who has debased him. Yet this story, too, is one of the good ones. This new group of stories in general has more body than the last batch published in book form. There is a wonderful piece of writing at the end of The Snows of Kilimanjaro, in which the reader is made gradually to realize that what seems to be an escape by plane with the sick man looking down on Africa is only the dream of a dying man. (2)

When Loyalist Madrid is as far behind Hemingway as his former adventures in Africa, he will no doubt get something out of them as much better than the melodrama of 'The Fifth Column' as The Life of Francis Macomber is than 'Green Hills of Africa.' And in the meantime this omnibus volume, which contains all of Hemingway's short stories, represents one of the most considerable achievements of the American writing of our time, and ought, as they say, to be in every home.

Notes

1 Soviet secret police.
2 The frozen carcass of the leopard on the summit of Kilimanjaro, which Hemingway mentions in the epigraph and uses as an important symbol, may seem unrealistic. But the naturalist George Schaller writes in 'The Year of the Gorilla' (Harmondsworth, Middlesex, 1967), 40: 'Recently I came upon a fascinating account of a pack of wild dogs seen on the glaciers of Mt. Kilimanjaro at nearly twenty thousand feet.'

57. W.H. MELLERS, 'SCRUTINY'

8 (December 1939), 335-44

W.H. Mellers (b. 1914), English composer and critic,

Professor of Music at the University of York, is the author of 'François Couperin' (1950) and 'Man and His Music' (1957). 'Scrutiny,' edited in Cambridge, England, by F.R. Leavis, utilized the New Criticism and had a rather moralistic tone.

The ox, (1) as a literary hero, is no longer *à la mode*, and Mr. Hemingway himself has grown a little dusty. He has never again dazzled the literary skyline with another such rocket as 'A Farewell to Arms,' and it would indeed be difficult to imagine a pyrotechnic display more cunningly engineered to elicit the goggle-eyed oohs and ahs of a wider diversity of ill-assorted spectators. The highbrows ahed knowingly because the book had, or seemed to have, an Original Technique; the low-brows oohed excitedly because it was outspoken, a rattling war-cum-sex yarn, yet tragic too. And now the rocket has collapsed in ashes, nor has a re-issue in the Penguin Library done more than feebly re-animate the relics with a tawdry glow. Yet if it was overpraised as a work of art, and if Mr. Hemingway's growing reputation as Professional Clown and Tough Guy to the Great American Public has rather obscured his qualities as a writer, it does not follow that he has none, or that they are uninteresting. 'A Farewell to Arms' still seems to me an accomplished book, for whether it is valuable and whether it is false are two distinct questions which are often treated as though they were one.

In saying that it is accomplished I mean that it is competent with the slickness of the tougher type of Hollywood film. It is often said that Hollywood emotion is essentially synthetic but this, though true, is not the whole truth. It is wrong to assume that glycerine tears, because they are often inadequately motivated and always unsubtle, because they lack sensibility and hence any of the real passion that cannot exist apart from sensibility, have therefore no motivation at all; it is wrong to put all the blame on Hollywood for tapping the glycerine vats in people's hearts and none on people for possessing those vats waiting to be tapped at; and we must remember too that though there is much that is deliberately vicious in glycerine tears yet a form of art or entertainment so popular and universal cannot exist without incarnating, even if fortuitously, some of the values which the people who patronize it honestly live by.

Of course, to the intelligent and sensitive - to the Cultured Minority - toughness seems merely the most complacent form of stupidity, the reverse of being 'grown up,' rather an emotional immaturity, an inability to handle situations and experiences except by denying their validity. Yet it is only the complexity and difficulty of emotional experience that toughness denies, not emotion itself, for at heart toughness battens on virtues extravagantly soft, extravagantly sad and rather foolish. One believes in the simplest kind of sexual love and in intoxication; one takes an exhibitionist delight in manifestations of mechanic skill, whether in driving a car or slaughtering an animal; one holds steadfastly by courage (in the face of bulls, lions, guns, gangsters, women scorned and people who do not play the game), by sacrifice, and by a primitive kind of honour. It is true that one must not mention honour or courage or sacrifice by their names:

> I was always embarrassed by the words sacred, glorious and sacrifice, and the expression in vain. We had heard them sometimes standing in the rain almost out of earshot, so that only the shouted words came through, and had read them, on proclamations that were slapped up by billposters over other proclamations, now for a long time and I had seen nothing sacred and the things that were glorious had no glory and the sacrifices were like the stockyards at Chicago if nothing was done with the meat except to bury it.... There were many words that you could not stand to hear and finally only the names of places had dignity: (2)

but to admit fear of them is to admit belief in their existence, and it is the essence of the code that one must not whine, must accept what life offers fatalistically ('So this is what it's going to be like. Well, this is what it's going to be like, then' ... 'No pleasure in anything if you mouth it up too much.'). How simple and how extravagantly emotional the values of toughness really are is revealed not only in the love story of 'A Farewell to Arms' but also in such quasi-satirical stories about the warping of natural desire as Mr. and Mrs. Elliot, A Canary for One and A Very Short Story; while it is stated explicitly in a passage from the first chapter of the book about bull-fighting:

> So far about morals, I know only one, that what is moral is what you feel good after and what is immoral is what you feel bad after and judged by these moral standards, which I do not defend, the bull-fight is very moral to me because I feel very fine while it is going on and have a feeling of life and death and mortality

> and immortality, and after it is over I feel very sad but very fine.

Now you can consider this as amoral as you like, yet it is idiotic to say that for millions of people - though I do not mean specifically about bulls - it is, any more than the glycerine values of the cinema, false. Rather is it terrifyingly true, as true as the banal simplicity of Mr. Hemingway's prose. The infantile repetitions of dialogue in the story Hills like White Elephants, with its pathetic-bathetic 'I feel fine' conclusion, indicates how it is precisely the banality of the greater part of human experience, especially when it seems most intense, that Mr. Hemingway renders with such sinister acumen. And in this passage from 'A Farewell to Arms':

> If people bring so much courage to this world, the world has to kill them to break them, so of course it kills them. The world breaks everyone and afterward many are strong in the broken places. But those that will not break it kills. It kills the very good and the very gentle and the very brave impartially. If you are none of these you can be sure that it will kill you too but there will be no special hurry - (3)

even the sly, the dexterous tug at the heart-strings in the rhythm of the penultimate clause is honest in the sense that it is true, for we are none of us quite honest in our emotions, quite free from a self-pity that warps, staging them with a theatrical and appealing gesture. Hollywood and Mr. Hemingway's stories both genuinely represent an epoch in the history of human feeling - the situation in the last scene of Mr. Hemingway's play 'The Fifth Column' is itself one of Hollywood's ripest chestnuts except that of course Mr. Hemingway does not tack on the usually quite fortuitous happy ending; but there is this great difference between Hollywood and Mr. Hemingway, namely that whereas these values exist in the cinema only among much that is flabby, amorphous, infantile and adulterated, Mr. Hemingway presents them with the neatness, the concentration of a true if limited artist. This is really all people mean when they talk about Mr. Hemingway's gift for understatement. Every true artist has a 'gift for understatement' and if Mr. Hemingway's statement seems peculiarly under, that is merely because he has such a very simple statement to start from. It is at least a sort of tribute if we can say of Mr. Hemingway that, for the social historian, he makes Hollywood unnecessary.

I have already indicated that the Hemingway values, as applied to human behaviour, are in the main negative - one does *not* whine, one does *not* give in, one does *not* betray one's trust: and that in so far as they are positive they depend almost entirely on sensation - on delight in food and drink and women, in high speed and mechanic skill, in clean leaves and cool sheets, in tactile impressions and the sharp precision of landscape, particularly landscapes that are sunlit and frosty and sharply defined. (Mr. Hemingway's 'reporter's eye' as an aspect of descriptive technique, of which I shall have more to say later, is here relevant.) The reason for this is that the Hemingway values are not the sort of values on which human relationships could be based or by which a community could live for long. In this respect it is significant that the background to Mr. Hemingway's stories is almost always one of war and sudden death, not because he has any delight in, let alone understanding of, the simple violent realities of life and death in themselves - the amiably grim journalistic irony of A Natural History of the Dead shows no concern for the problem of death or the passion and suffering entailed in it - but merely because his values are such that they can live only in the midst of destruction, being the values of a disintegrating society: in other words they are a means of avoiding the complexity of human relations, of avoiding the necessity of living. I think there is probably - behind the grosser superficies, the more obvious symptoms of disintegration - a similar significance in the extreme simplicity of the values of the cinema; I am quite certain that it is the essence of the characteristic Hemingway situation.

This situation is stated patently in many of the stories about soldiers - for instance Soldiers' Home:

> Vaguely he wanted a girl but he did not want to have to work to get her. He did not want to get into the intrigue and politics ... he did not want any consequences ever again. He wanted to live along without consequences ... he would not go through all the talking ... he had tried so to keep his life from being complicated.

Other values may perhaps be hinted at, values more satisfying and even superior, as in the stories about the Swiss or references to the Catholic tradition in the portrait of the priest in 'A Farewell to Arms,' but it is always suggested that however sympathetic they are naïve, unreal, helpless in a disintegrating world. Should Mr. Hemingway ever indicate any conception of a better or happier life it is merely an intensification of the 'good' things in the present one, the things that make you Feel Fine: it is conceived, that is, like the account of bull-fighting which I have quoted earlier, entirely, entirely in terms of sensation. One of Mr. Hemingway's most perfect and most touching stories, A Clean, Well-lighted Place, emphasizes this point. The 'very old man walking unsteadily but with dignity,' the outcast cosmopolitan ('last week he tried to commit suicide. Why? He was in despair. What about? Nothing. How do you know it was nothing? He has plenty of money'); the waiter who would return to his wife; the other waiter who has only his insomnia to return to; these are all the stock Hemingway counters.

> 'We are two of different kinds,' the old waiter said.... 'It is not only a question of youth and confidence, although these things are very beautiful. Each night I am reluctant to close up because there may be someone who needs the café.'
>
> 'Hombre, there are bodegas (4) open all night long.'
>
> 'You do not understand. This is a clean and pleasant café.'
>
> 'It is well lighted. The light is very good, and also, now, there are the shadows of the leaves.... It is the light of course but it is necessary that the place be clean and pleasant. You do not want music. Certainly you do not want music. Nor can you stand before a bar with dignity although that is all that is provided for these hours. What did he fear? It was not fear or dread. It was a nothing that he knew too well. It was all a nothing and a man was a nothing too. It was only that and light was all it needed and a certain cleanness and order.'

You see it is no accident that so many of Mr. Hemingway's stories, if they do not take place in wars, have their setting in hotels, bars, or the waiting rooms of railway stations. The inhabitants of the Hemingway world are all homeless, and though they have neither confidence nor youth of spirit they believe, sentimentally but with melancholy honesty, that these qualities are 'very beautiful.' They wish above all to accept their homelessness and disillusion 'with dignity' and a stiff upper lip, and to be able to do so they ask little more than an average allowance of sensory and material comfort and cleanness and order. Nearly all the best stories in this volume deal with resignation in face of the biffs life gives one or - and perhaps the two are hardly separable - in face of the failure of an excessively simple scale of values. The quiet conclusion of A Clean, Well-lighted Place ('"After all," he said to himself, "it is probably only insomnia. Many must have it'") is typical, as is the behaviour of the major (of the story In Another Country) whose young wife has suddenly died:

> He stood there, biting his lower lip. 'It is very difficult,' he said, 'I cannot resign myself.'
>
> He looked straight past me and out through the window. Then he began to cry. 'I am utterly unable to resign myself,' he said, and choked. And then crying, his head up looking at nothing, carrying himself straight and soldierly, with tears on both his cheeks and biting his lips, he walked past the machines and out the door.
>
> The major did not come back to the hospital for three days. When he came back, there were large framed photographs around the wall, of all sorts of wounds before and after they had been cured by the machines. In front of the machine the major used were three photographs of hands like his that were completely restored. I do not know where the doctor got them. I always understood we were the first to use the machines. The photographs did not make much difference to the major because he only looked out of the window.

These things are typical and so is the peculiarly drab prose in which this resignation is incarnated. This is Mr. Hemingway's contribution to literature and if too topical and local to be permanent I think it is none the less a real one.

In trying to understand the means whereby Mr. Hemingway effects this incarnation we have first to consider his 'reporter's eye.' 'I was trying to write then,' he says in 'Death in the Afternoon,' 'and I found the greatest difficulty aside from knowing truly what you really felt, rather than what you were supposed to feel, and had been taught to feel, was to put down what really happened in action: what the actual things were that produced the emotion you experienced. In writing for a newspaper you told what happened and, with one trick and another you communicated the emotion aided by the element of timeliness which gives a certain emotion to any account of something that has happened on that day: but the real thing, the sequence of motion and fact which made the emotion and which would be as valid in a year or in ten years or, with luck and if you stated it purely enough, always, was beyond me, and I was working very hard to get it.' (5)

Here I think we can see the fundamentals of Mr. Hemingway's method, and also we can see how different they are from those of William Faulkner, a writer with whom he is often considered comparable. Faulkner tries to give a scrupulously realistic account of commonplace or even subnormal experience, but throughout so artificially intensifies the experience that it becomes a dishonest perversion. It is not merely that life is *not* like that, that the casual circumstance is not pregnant with such violent electrical cross-currents, but the dishonesty takes the form of an attempt to pump tragic significance into a conception of life that is quite as banal as Hemingway's and much more confused. Thus not only is its experimental technique (mainly a matter of interspersing straightforward statements with unnecessary clauses) factitious, but also its imaginative conception is chaotic - it is written from all points of view and none. Mr. Hemingway has his own brisk answer to this kind of Literature:

> No matter how good a phrase or a simile a writer may have if he puts it in where it is not absolutely necessary and irreplaceable he is spoiling his work for egotism. Prose is architecture, not interior decoration, and the Baroque is over....
>
> This too to remember. If a man writes clearly enough anyone can see if he fakes. If he mystifies to avoid a straight statement, which is very different from breaking so-called rules of syntax or grammar to make an effect which can be obtained in no other way, the writer takes a longer time to be known as a fake and other writers who are afflicted by the same necessity will praise him in their own defence. True mysticism should not be confused with incompetence in writing which seeks to mystify where there is no mystery but is really only the necessity to fake to cover lack of knowledge or the inability to state clearly. Mysticism implies a mystery and there are many mysteries; but incompetence is not one of them; nor is overwritten journalism made literature by the injection of a false epic quality. Remember this too: all bad writers are in love with the epic. (6)

I think it is a good answer if a simple one, and in its bluff way it really is consistent with Mr. Hemingway's practice. For though his reporter's eye may not see very much it sees what it does see very clearly - clearly enough to make his 'realism' not realistic but merely an acceptable literary convention. It is easy to see in such a passage as this:

> We were in the garden at Mons. Young Buckley came in

> with his patrol from across the river. The first German I saw climbed up over the garden wall. We waited till he got one leg over and then we potted him. He had so much equipment on and looked awfully surprised and fell down into the garden. Then three more came over farther down the wall. We shot them. They all came just like that,

or in such tiny tales as On the Quai at Smyrna and The Revolutionist how Mr. Hemingway uses the description of facts and incidents in the simplest language and most banal rhythms as a personal convention reconcilable with the characteristic Hemingway virtues of resignation, fatalism, and fortitude in the face of physical and occasionally mental suffering; while in Old Man at the Bridge we see the process carried a step further - a piece of reporting transformed, by *selection* of detail and control of rhythm, into a Hemingway situation, into a kind of minor art. I think it is clear from this story that Hemingway's prose, however colloquial, is no more realistic than, and as conventional as, that of (say) Meredith. (7) This, for instance, may be based on the movement of speech:

> There was nothing to do about him. It was Easter Sunday and the Fascists were advancing towards the Ebro. It was a grey overcast day with a low ceiling so that their planes were not up. That and the fact that cats know how to look after themselves was the only good luck that old man would ever have:

but essentially it is speech stylized for a specific end. So too, and much more obviously, is the private language, always consistent with the Hemingway virtues, which is spoken by Mr. Hemingway's heroines, where the extreme limitation of the stylization is the condition of the intention being clearly realized. ('You'll kill him marvellously,' she said, 'I know you will. I'm awfully anxious to see it.') Even when Mr. Hemingway dabbles in the Steinian trick as he does occasionally in order to express states of drunkenness, coition or hysteria, he does so strictly within the limits of his own convention, and not in a flatulent gallimaufry of everyone else's conventions that is supposed, as in Faulkner, to be realistic. You may think it awfully boring to be all the time making love and awfully brave and maybe awfully drunk, yet it's an awfully big thing and it's no use shutting your eyes to it.

> I was trying to learn to write, commencing with the simplest things, and one of the simplest things of all and the most fundamental is violent death.... I had read many books in which, when the author tried to convey it, he only produced a blur, and I decided that this was because either the author had never seen it clearly or, at the moment of it, he had physically or mentally shut his eyes, as one might do if he saw a child he could not possibly reach or aid about to be struck by a train. (8)

It is Mr. Hemingway's achievement that, in a fashion rather different from his intention, he really has presented us with the picture of a kind of death, and that he has done so without 'blur.' The death which is the Hemingway mentality is closer to us to-day than it has ever been, and it is stated in his art with the greatest possible neatness and condensation. We can take it or leave it; but we run the risk of being blurred ourselves if we try to be grateful to him and sad about him at one and the same time.

Notes

1 An allusion to Wyndham Lewis' essay.
2 'A Farewell to Arms' (Harmondsworth, Middlesex, 1963), 143-4.
3 Ibid., 193.
4 Wine-cellar.
5 'Death in the Afternoon' (Harmondsworth, Middlesex, 1966), 6.
6 Ibid., 181-2, 53-4.
7 George Meredith, English novelist, author of 'The Egoist,' (1879) and 'Diana of the Crossways' (1885).
8 'Death in the Afternoon,' 6.

58. LIONEL TRILLING, 'PARTISAN REVIEW'

6 (Winter 1939), 52-60

Lionel Trilling (1905-75) was an influential American critic, Professor of English at Columbia University, and author of 'Matthew Arnold' (1939), 'E.M. Forster' (1944) and the fine novel 'The Middle of the Journey' (1948).

Between 'The Fifth Column,' the play which makes the occasion for this large volume, and 'The First Forty-Nine Stories,' which make its bulk and its virtue, there is a difference of essence. For the play is the work of Hemingway the 'man' and the stories are by Hemingway the 'artist'. This is a distinction which seldom enough means anything in criticism, but now and then an author gives us, as Hemingway gives us, writing of two such different kinds that there is a certain amount of validity and at any rate a convenience in making it. Once made, the distinction can better be elaborated than defined or defended. Hemingway the 'artist' is conscious, Hemingway the 'man' is self-conscious; the 'artist' has a kind of innocence, the 'man' a kind of naivety; the 'artist' is disinterested, the 'man' has a dull personal axe to grind; the 'artist' has a perfect medium and tells the truth even if it be only *his* truth, but the 'man' fumbles at communication and falsifies. As Edmund Wilson said in his Letter to the Russians about Hemingway, which is the best estimate of our author that I know, '...something frightful seems to happen to Hemingway as soon as he begins to write in the first person. In his fiction, the conflicting elements of his personality, the emotional situations which obsess him, are externalized and objectified; and the result is an art which is severe, intense and deeply serious. But as soon as he talks in his own person, he seems to lose all his capacity for self-criticism and is likely to become fatuous or maudlin.' (1)

Mr. Wilson had in mind such specifically autobiographical and polemical works as 'Green Hills of Africa' (and obviously he was not referring to the technical use of the first person in fictional narrative) but since the writing of the Letter in 1935, we may observe of Hemingway that the 'man' has encroached upon the 'artist' in his fiction. In 'To Have and Have Not' and now in 'The Fifth Column' the 'first person' dominates and is the source of the failure of both works.

Of course it might be perfectly just to set down these failures simply to a lapse of Hemingway's talent. But there is, I think, something else to be said. For as one compares the high virtues of Hemingway's stories with the weakness of his latest novel and his first play, although one is perfectly aware of all that must be charged against the author himself, what forces itself into consideration is the cultural atmosphere which has helped to bring about the recent falling off. Insofar as we can ever blame a critical tradition for a writer's failures, we must, I believe, blame American criticism for the illegitimate emergence of Hemingway the 'man' and the resultant inferiority of his two recent major works.

It is certainly true that criticism of one kind or another has played an unusually important part in Hemingway's career. Perhaps no American talent has so publicly developed as Hemingway's: more than any writer of our time he has been under glass, watched, checked up on, predicted, suspected, warned. One part of his audience took from him new styles of writing, of love-making, of very being; this was the simpler part, but its infatuate imitation was of course a kind of criticism. But another section of his audience responded negatively, pointing out that the texture of Hemingway's work was made up of cruelty, religion, anti-intellectualism, even of basic fascism, and looked upon him as the active proponent of evil. Neither part of such an audience could fail to make its impression upon a writer. The knowledge that he had set a fashion and become a legend may have been gratifying but surely also burdensome and depressing, and it must have offered no small temptation. Yet perhaps more difficult for Hemingway to support with equanimity, and, from our point of view, much more important, was the constant accusation that he had attacked good human values. For upon Hemingway were turned all the fine social feelings of the now passing decade, all the noble sentiments, all the desperate optimism, all the extreme rationalism, all the contempt of irony and indirection - all the attitudes which, in the full tide of the liberal-radical movement, became dominant in our thought about literature. There was demanded of him earnestness and pity, social consciousness, as it was called, something 'positive' and 'constructive' and literal. For is not life a simple thing and is not the writer a villain or a counter-revolutionary who does not see it so?

As if under the pressure of this critical tradition, which persisted in mistaking the 'artist' for the 'man', Hemingway seems to have undertaken to vindicate the 'man' by showing that he, too, could muster the required 'social' feelings in the required social way. At any rate, he now brought the 'man' with all his contradictions and conflicts into his fiction. But 'his ideas about life,' - I quote Edmund Wilson again ' 'or rather his sense of what happens and the way it happens, is in his stories sunk deep below the surface and is not conveyed by argument or preaching but by directly transmitted emotion: it is turned into something as hard as crystal and as disturbing as a great lyric. When he expounds this sense of life, however, in his own character of Ernest Hemingway, the Old Master of Key West, he has a way of sounding silly.' If, however, the failures of Hemingway 'in his own character' were apparent to the practitioners of this critical tradition, they did not want Hemingway's virtues - the something 'hard' and 'disturbing.' Indeed, they were in a critical tradition that did not want artists at all; it wanted 'men,' recruits, and its apologists were delighted to enlist Hemingway in his own character, with all his confusions and naivety, simply because Hemingway had now declared himself on the right side.

And so when 'To Have And Have Not' appeared, one critic of the Left, grappling with the patent fact that the 'artist' had failed, yet determined to defend the 'man' who was his new ally, had no recourse save to explain that in this case failure was triumph because artistic fumbling was the mark of Hemingway's attempt to come to grips with the problems of modern life which were as yet too great for his art to encompass. Similarly, another critic of the Left, faced with the aesthetic inferiority of Hemingway's first play, takes refuge in praising the personal vindication which the 'man' has made by 'taking sides against fascism.' (2) In other words, the 'man' has been a sad case and long in need of regeneration; the looseness of thought and emotion, the easy and uninteresting idealism of the social feelings to which Hemingway now gives such sudden and literal expression are seen as the grateful signs of a personal reformation.

But the disinterested reader does not have to look very deep to see that Hemingway's social feelings, whatever they may yet become, are now the occasion for indulgence in the 'man'. His two recent failures are failures not only in form but in feeling; one looks at 'To Have And Have Not' and 'The Fifth Column,' one looks at their brag, and their disconcerting forcing of the emotions, at their downright priggishness, and then one looks at the criticism which, as I conceive it, made these failures possible by demanding them and which now accepts them so gladly, and one is tempted to reverse the whole liberal-radical assumption about literature. One almost wishes to say to an author like Hemingway, 'You have no duty, no responsibility. Literature, in a political sense, is not in the least important. Wherever the sword is drawn it is mightier than the pen. (3) Whatever you can do as a man, you can win no wars as an artist.'

Very obviously this would not be the whole truth, yet saying it might counteract the crude and literal theory of art to which, in varying measure, we have all been training ourselves for a decade. We have conceived the artist to be a man perpetually on the spot, who must always report to us in his precise moral and political latitude and longitude. Not that for a moment we would consider shaping our own political ideas by his; but we who of course turn for political guidance to newspapers, theorists, or historians, create the fiction that thousands - not, to be sure, ourselves - are waiting on the influence of the creative artist, and we stand by to see if he is leading us as he properly should. We consider then that we have exalted the importance of art, and perhaps we have. But in doing so we have quite forgotten how complex and subtle art is and, if it is to be 'used', how very difficult it is to use it.

One feels that Hemingway would never have thrown himself into his new and inferior work if the necessity had not been put upon him to justify himself before this magisterial conception of literature. Devoted to literalness, the critical tradition of the Left took Hemingway's symbols for his intention, saw in his stories only cruelty or violence or a calculated indifference, and turned upon him a barrage of high-mindedness - that liberal-radical highmindedness that is increasingly taking the place of thought among the 'progressive professional and middle class forces' and that now, under the name of 'good will' shuts out half the world. Had it seen what was actually in Hemingway's work, it would not have forced him out of his idiom of the artist and into the idiom of the man which he speaks with difficulty and without truth.

For what should have been always obvious is that Hemingway is a writer who, when he writes as an 'artist', is passionately and aggressively concerned with truth and even with social truth. And with this in mind, one might begin the consideration of his virtues with a glance at Woodrow Wilson. Hemingway has said that all genuine American writing comes from the prose of Huckleberry Finn's voyage down the Mississippi and certainly his own starts there. (4) But Huck's prose is a sort of moral symbol. It is the antithesis to the Widow Douglas - to the pious, the respectable, the morally plausible. It is the prose of the free man seeing the world as it really is. And Woodrow Wilson was, we might say, Hemingway's Widow Douglas. To the sensitive men who went to war it was not, perhaps, death and destruction that made the disorganizing shock. It was perhaps rather that death and destruction went on at the instance and to the accompaniment of the fine grave words, of which Woodrow Wilson's speeches were the finest and gravest. Here was the issue of liberal theory; here in the bloated or piecemeal corpse was the outcome of the words of humanitarianism and ideals; this was the work of presumably careful men of good will, learned men, polite men. The world was a newspaper world, a state-paper world, a memorial speech world. Words were trundled smoothly o'er the tongue - Coleridge had said it long ago -

> Like mere abstractions, empty sounds to which
> We join no feeling and attach no form
> As if the soldier died without a wound ...
> Passed off to Heaven, translated and not killed. (5)

Everyone in that time had feelings, as they called them; just as everyone has 'feelings' now. And it seems to me that what Hemingway wanted first to do was to get rid of the 'feelings,' the comfortable liberal humanitarian feelings: and to replace them with the truth.

Not cynicism, I think, not despair, as so often is said, but this admirable desire shaped his famous style and his notorious set of admirations and contempts. The trick of understatement or tangential statement sprang from this desire. Men had made so many utterances in such fine language that it had become time to shut up. Hemingway's people, as everyone knows, are afraid of words and ashamed of them and the line from his stories which has become famous is the one that begins 'Won't you please,' goes on through its innumerable 'pleases' and ends 'stop talking.' (6) Not only slain men but slain words made up the mortality of the war.

Another manifestation of the same desire in Hemingway was his devotion to the ideal of technique as an end in itself. A great deal can go down in the tumble but one of the things that stands best is a cleanly done job. As John Peale Bishop says in his admirable essay on Hemingway (which yet, I feel, contributes to the general misapprehension by asserting the evanescence of Hemingway's 'compassion'), professional pride is one of the last things to go. (7) Hemingway became a devotee of his own skill and he exploited the ideal of skill in his characters. His admired men always do a good job; and the proper handling of a rod, a gun, an espada (8) or a pen is a thing, so Hemingway seems always to be saying, which can be understood when speech cannot.

This does not mean that Hemingway attacks mind itself, a charge which has often been brought against him. It is perhaps safe to say that whenever he seems to be making such an attack, it is not so much *reason* as it is *rationalization* that he resists; 'mind' appears simply as the complex of false feelings. And against 'mind' in this sense he sets up what he believes to be the primal emotions, among others pain and death, met not with the mind but with techniques and courage. 'Mind' he sees as a kind of castrating knife, cutting off people's courage and proper self-love, making them 'reasonable,' which is to say dull and false. There is no need to point out how erroneous his view would have been were it really mind that was in question, but in the long romantic tradition of the attitude it never really *is* mind that is in question but rather a dull overlay of mechanical negative proper feeling, or a falseness of feeling which people believe to be reasonableness, and reasonable virtue. And when we think how quickly 'mind' capitulates in a crisis, how quickly, for example, it accommodated itself to the war and served it and glorified it, revulsion from it and a turning to the life of action - reduced, to be sure, to athleticism: but skilful physical effort is perhaps something intellectuals too quickly dismiss as a form of activity - can be the better understood. We can understand too the insistence on courage, even on courage deliberately observed in its purity: that is, when it is at the service of the most sordid desires, as in Fifty Grand.

This, then, was Hemingway's vision of the world. Was it a complete vision? Of course it was not. Was it a useful vision? That depended. If it was true, it was useful - if we knew how to use it. But the use of literature is not easy. In our hearts most of us are Platonists in the matter of art and we feel that we become directly infected by what we read; or at any rate we want to be Platonists, and we carry on a certain conviction from our Tom Swift (9) days that literature provides chiefly a means of identification and emulation. The Platonist view is not wholly to be dismissed; we *do* in a degree become directly infected by art; but the position is too simple. And we are further Platonistic in our feeling that literature must be religious: we want our attitudes formulated by the tribal bard. This, of course, gives to literature a very important function. But it forgets that literature has never 'solved,' though it may perhaps provide part of the data for eventual solutions.

With this attitude we asked, Can Hemingway's people speak only with difficulty? and we answered, Then it surely means that he thinks people should not speak. Does he find in courage the first of virtues? Then it surely means that we should be nothing but courageous. Is he concerned with the idea of death and of violence? Then it must mean that to him these are good things.

In short, we looked for an emotional leader. We did not conceive Hemingway to be saying, Come, let us look at the world together. We supposed him to be saying, Come, it is your moral duty to be as my characters are. We took the easiest and simplest way of using the artist and decided that he was not the 'man' for us. That he was a man and a Prophet we were certain; and equally certain that he was not the 'man' we would want to be or the Prophet who could lead us. That, as artist, he was not concerned with being a 'man' did not occur to us. We had, in other words, quite overlooked the whole process of art, overlooked style and tone, symbol and implication, overlooked the obliqueness and complication with which the artist may criticize life, and assumed that what Hemingway saw or what he put into his stories he wanted to have exist in the actual world.

In short, the criticism of Hemingway came down to a kind of moral-political lecture, based on the assumption that art is - or should be - the exact equivalent of life. The writer would have to be strong indeed who could remain unmoved by the moral pressure that was exerted upon Hemingway. He put away the significant reticences of the artist, opened his heart like 'a man,' and the flat literalness, the fine, fruity social idealism of the latest novel and the play are the result.

'The Fifth Column' is difficult to speak of. Summary is always likely to be a critical treachery, but after consulting the summaries of those who admire the work and regard it as a notable event, it seems fair to say that it is the story of a tender-tough American hero with the horrors, who does counter-espionage in Madrid, though everybody thinks he is just a playboy, who fears that he will no longer do his work well if he continues his liaison with an American girl chiefly remarkable for her legs and her obtuseness; and so sacrifices love and bourgeois pleasure for the sake of duty. Hemingway as a playwright gives up his tools of suggestion and tone and tells a literal story - an adventure story of the Spanish war, at best the story of the regeneration of an American Pimpernel (10) of not very good intelligence.

It is this work which has been received with the greatest satisfaction by a large and important cultural group as the fulfilment and vindication of Hemingway's career, as a fine document of the Spanish struggle, and as a political event of significance, 'a sign of the times,' as one reviewer called it. (11) To me it seems none of these things. It does not vindicate Hemingway's career because that career in its essential parts needs no vindication; and it does not fulfill Hemingway's career because that career has been in the service of exact if limited emotional truth and this play is in the service of fine feelings. Nor can I believe that the Spanish war is represented in any good sense by a play whose symbols are so sentimentally personal and whose dramatic tension is so weak; and it seems to me that there is something even vulgar in making Spain serve as a kind of mental hospital for disorganized foreigners who, out of a kind of self-contempt, turn to the 'ideal of the Spanish people.' Nor, finally, can I think that Hemingway's statement of an anti-fascist position is of great political importance or of more than neutral virtue. It is hard to believe that the declaration of anti-fascism is nowadays any more a mark of sufficient grace in a writer than a declaration against disease would be in a physician or a declaration against accidents would be in a locomotive engineer. The admirable intention in itself is not enough and criticism begins and does not end when the intention is declared.

But I believe that judgments so simple as these will be accepted with more and more difficulty. The 'progressive professional and middle class forces' are framing a new culture, based on the old liberal-radical culture but designed now to hide the new anomaly by which they live their intellectual and emotional lives. For they must believe, it seems, that imperialist arms advance proletarian revolution, that oppression by the right people brings liberty. Like Hemingway's latest hero, they show one front to the world and another to themselves, know that within they are true proletarian men while they wrap themselves in Early American togas; they are enthralled by their own good will; they are people of fine feelings and they dare not think lest the therapeutic charm vanish. This is not a political essay and I am not here concerned with the political consequences of these things, bad though they be and worse though they will be, but only with the cultural consequences. For to prevent the anomaly from appearing in its genuine difficulty, emotion - of a very limited kind - has been apotheosized and thought has been made almost a kind of treachery; the reviewer of 'The Fifth Column' to whom I have already referred cites as a virtue Hemingway's 'unintellectual' partisanship of the Spanish cause. The piety of 'good will' has become enough and Fascism is conceived not as a force which complicates the world but as a force which simplifies the world - and so it does for any number of people of good will (of a good will not to be doubted, I should say) for whom the existence of an absolute theological evil makes non-existent any other evil.

It is this group that has made Hemingway its cultural hero and for reasons that need not be canvassed very far. Now that Hemingway has become what this group would call 'affirmative' he has become insufficient; but insufficiency is the very thing this group desires. When Hemingway was in 'negation' his themes of courage, loyalty, tenderness and silence, tangentially used, suggested much; but now that they are used literally and directly they say far less than the situation demands. His stories showed a great effort of comprehension and they demand a considerable effort from their readers, that effort in which lies whatever teaching power there is in art; but now he is not making an effort to understand but to accept, which may indeed be the effort of the honest political man but not of the honest artist.

An attempt has been made to settle the problem of the artist's relation to politics by loudly making the requirement that he give up his base individuality and rescue humanity and his own soul by becoming the mouthpiece of a party, a movement or a philosophy. That requirement has demonstrably failed as a solution of the problem; the problem, however, still remains. It may be, of course, that politics itself will settle the problem for us; it may be that in our tragic time art worthy the name cannot be produced and that we must live with the banalities of 'The Fifth Column' or even with less. However, if the problem will be allowed to exist at all, it will not be solved in theory and on paper but in practice. And we have, after all, the practice of the past to guide us at least with a few tentative notions. We can learn to stop pressing the writer with the demand for contemporaneity when we remember the simple fact that writers have always written directly to and about the troubles of their own time and for and about their contemporaries, some in ways to us more obvious than others but all responding inevitably to what was happening around them. We can learn too that the relation of an artist to his culture, whether that culture be national or the culture of a relatively small recusant group, is a complex and even a contradictory relation: the artist must accept his culture and be accepted by it, but also - so it seems - he must be its critic, correcting and even rejecting it according to his personal insight; his strength seems to come from the tension of this ambivalent situation and we must learn to welcome the ambivalence. Finally, and simplest of all, we learn not to expect a political, certainly not an immediately political, effect from a work of art; and in removing from art a burden of messianic responsibility which it never has discharged and cannot discharge we may leave it free to do whatever it actually can do.

Notes

1 See No. 43
2 Edwin Berry Burgum, Hemingway's Development, 'New Masses,' 29 (22 November 1938), 21-4.
3 See Edward Bulwer Lytton, 'Richelieu,' II.i (1839): 'The pen is mightier than the sword.'
4 'Green Hills of Africa,' p. 22.
5 Fears in Solitude (1798).
6 Hills Like White Elephants in 'Men Without Women.'
7 John Peale Bishop, Homage to Hemingway, 'After the Genteel Tradition,' ed. Malcolm Cowley (New York, 1937), 186-201.
8 Sword.
9 Hero of books for boys by Edward Stratemeyer.
10 Hero of Baroness Orczy's romantic-adventure novel, 'The Scarlet Pimpernel' (1905).
11 Burgum, 'New Masses,' 21.

'The Fifth Column' (play produced 1940)

59. WOLCOTT GIBBS, 'NEW YORKER'

16 (16 March 1940), 44

Wolcott Gibbs (1902-58) was an American editor and humorist, and author of 'Season in the Sun' (1946).

In his preface to the published version of 'The Fifth Column,' Ernest Hemingway wrote, 'There is a girl in it named Dorothy but her name might also have been Nostalgia.' This Dorothy, this cheerful memory of the past, was quite a girl. The hero said that she was 'lazy and spoiled and rather stupid and enormously on the make,' but she was also very beautiful and not too much handicapped by chaste scruples. At the opening of the play in the book, if you remember, she was living with an English war correspondent who was always going on about his wife and children. 'These wife-and-children men at war,' said Dorothy indignantly. 'They just use them as a sort of entering wedge to get into bed with someone and then immediately afterwards they club you with them. I mean positively club you.' After she left her Englishman for the American counter-espionage agent, Philip Rawlings, what she wanted mostly was to get him away to some place where there was good skiing and champagne cocktails and a few people in nice clothes. That was Dorothy, beautiful and expensive, a little bit out of Anita Loos, (1) a little bit out of 'Vogue' and 'Harper's Bazaar' - Mr. Hemingway's half-contemptuous, half-rueful symbol of what has to be given up by men who have dedicated the rest of their lives to an idea.

I don't know whether Benjamin Glazer, who adapted 'The Fifth Column' for the Theatre Guild, ever read Mr. Hemingway's preface, but there is certainly not much left of the original Dorothy in the play at the Alvin. Mr. Glazer's Dorothy is rather vague politically, but that is about all that can be said against her, and, although the courtship opens with a seduction, most of the other niceties are preserved. The final impression left by this Dorothy is that if she succeeded in getting Philip out of Madrid it wouldn't have been to go batting around Europe, drinking champagne cocktails, but rather to get him settled in some neat little house in Scarsdale, (2) where he could join the Chamber of Commerce. In the great renunciation scene she says, 'It's better for him to risk dying for a chance of happiness than for a cause that is not his.' She talks like a kind of female Sidney Carton, (3) and I can't believe she is an improvement over what Mr. Hemingway had in mind in the first place.

Except, however, for this peculiar exchange of values - the idea of duty opposed to old pleasures exchanged for the idea of duty opposed to pure love - I think 'The Fifth Column' is astonishingly good. In 'A Farewell to Arms,' another of Mr. Hemingway's sparsely punctuated heroes said, 'I was always embarrassed by the words sacred, glorious and sacrifice and the expression in vain.' It may be that Mr. Glazer hasn't taken this remark quite seriously enough, because a great many words and expressions like these seem to have crept into his script - far more than there were when Hemingway first wrote it while the Fascist artillery was hammering the Hotel Florida down around him in Madrid. Like the spot-cleaning of Dorothy, this seemed to me unfortunate, but actually I don't believe it has done a great deal of harm to the play. Some of the speeches sound much nobler than they did in Mr. Hemingway's single-handed version, but the quality of the original dialogue, the sickness and disgust over what has to be done, is still there, even if it has been slicked up to some extent for the Broadway trade. On the whole, while Mr. Glazer has unquestionably simplified and cheapened the play here and there, I think it is emphatically worth seeing. I would recommend it especially to Miss Dorothy Thompson, (4) who recently placed on the stage her own impression of the behavior of people who can know no life worth living as long as there is Fascism in the world.

It is hard to say how much of the force and conviction of 'The Fifth Column' ought to be credited to Franchot Tone, but it is a lot. Mr. Tone, hitherto associated in my mind with a kind of boyish charm, even while imitating gangsters, plays the ex-journalist and counter-espionage agent with maturity and a disregard for romantic attitudes that would never have got him anywhere in Hollywood. It is a remarkably fine performance, and so are those given by Lee J. Cobb, as a soldier against Fascism all over the world; Emile Boreo, as the proprietor of the Hotel Florida and a master of strange syntax, and Arnold Moss, as a Loyalist leader not above any brutality necessary to the cause. Miss Katherine Locke, who had two strikes on her when the curtain went up, never seemed to me exactly the kind of girl you'd expect to find knocking around with newspaper-men in a war zone, but I doubt if anyone could have done much better. Miss Lenore Ulric played a Moorish tart, exhibiting an almost careless mastery of the rôle. It was a great pleasure to see her again.

Notes

1 American author of 'Gentlemen Prefer Blondes' (1925).
2 Wealthy northern suburb of New York City.
3 Revolutionary hero of Dickens' 'A Tale of Two Cities' (1859).
4 Dorothy Thompson, American foreign correspondent and political columnist, sometime wife of Sinclair Lewis, was co-author with Fritz Kortner of the play 'Another Sun,' performed in March 1940.

60. JOSEPH WOOD KRUTCH, 'NATION'

150 (16 March 1940), 371-2

Joseph Wood Krutch (1893-1970) was an American drama and literary critic, and author of 'Five Masters' (1930) and 'Samuel Johnson' (1944).

'The Fifth Column' was written and published in play form by Ernest Hemingway. It was 'adapted' by Benjamin Glazer and has now been performed by the Guild at the Alvin Theater. If a consensus of reviewers' opinions is sufficient evidence, it is a fine play and ought to be a great success. In my judgment, however, it is not quite the first nor very likely to become quite the second.

Mr. Hemingway's report on the war in Spain begins well. In fact, the first of the two acts is, in its entirety, tense and absorbing. But the expectations created by that first act are never fulfilled, and despite sincere, perhaps even brilliant acting and staging the very subject matter itself seems to elude the authors, and what had begun as a complex picture of life in a war-torn city ends stagily as the love story of a hard-boiled hero whose grandiose gestures may be authentic but are too familiar and expected to carry very deep conviction. The fault does not seem to lie where one would have been most inclined to expect a fault, for the writing in the first act at least is not only vivid and terse but little marred by that tendency toward exhibitionism which is its author's besetting sin. He does not wear his lack of heart on his sleeve; he is not, to revive the familiar taunt, too overwhelmingly aware of the hair on his chest. But he does abandon a complex and difficult subject for one that is relatively easy and already stereotyped, with the result that the spectator finds his interest declining step by step after the mid-point of the play has been reached and as the themes which had been brilliantly suggested in the first half of the piece recede farther and farther into the background.

These themes are all concerned in one way or another with the difficulty of reconciling the aims of a holy war with the methods which it must inevitably use, and with the contrast inevitably apparent between the cause for which one is fighting and the individuals in whose name the cause is fought for. It is not merely that the hero, a young American correspondent who has been drawn by his sympathy for the Loyalist government into the dangerous business of counter-espionage, cannot fail to realize that the drunken electrician of the hotel in which he lives is no very inspiring specimen of that proletariat for which he is endangering his life; it is also that his superior, the officer in charge of espionage, has been completely dehumanized by the process of fighting for humanity, and that the ruthlessness which he himself believes to be necessary remains nevertheless debasing when it is translated into a concrete instance - when, for instance, he has to bully a frightened boy wrongly suspected of treachery or shoot a fat German general in the back when the latter, a captive, will not walk fast enough. But these themes, brilliantly suggested, are never fully treated, and they are, I think, left undeveloped, not because they are not what the author is really interested in, but because it is plainly so much easier to develop instead the easily managed story of the hero's love affair with an American girl and his final decision not to follow her out of Spain to safety. Probably both original author and adapter are familiar with the fact that puzzled critics of the drama often fall back upon the statement that a play under discussion 'doesn't come to a focus.' The trouble with 'The Fifth Column' is that it does - at the wrong place. In the opening scenes several themes are in solution, and it is the least interesting of all that crystallizes.

In the past, when Mr. Hemingway has been beset with doubts he has sometimes seemed to imply that the sensible thing for any modern man faced with a difficult problem to do is just to forget all about it and go out and kill someone, or failing that, some animal - even if it is only a lion in Africa or a skilfully tortured bull in an arena. In the present instance there is little suggestion of that attitude, and he ends instead with a careful debate in which the girl who argues that Americans should leave dying Europe to wallow in its own blood is answered by a German refugee who explains that fascism cannot be fought with any chance of success except upon its own frontier. But the difficulty with this last conclusion is simply that by the time one has got around to it in the last few minutes of the performance the whole play has become so artificial that the argument has ceased to seem very real and has become merely the inevitable end of a play.

Franchot Tone plays the hero with great sincerity; Lee Cobb, the German equally well. Katherine Locke is also excellent in the faintly drawn role of the girl, and Lenore Ulric does what is required as the inevitable child of nature turned prostitute.

61. STARK YOUNG, 'NEW REPUBLIC'

102 (25 March 1940), 408

Stark Young (1881-1963) was an American theater critic and translator of French and Russian drama.

Mr. Hemingway's play, for several seasons about to be

produced or not to be produced, and in 1938 published, is now at last presented by the Theatre Guild, though in what is described as an adaptation. The adaptation is by Mr. Benjamin Glazer; and the two points of interest about the occasion are the test of Mr. Hemingway's writing as to its theatrical possibilities - a good deal thrown off by the fact that what we have is partly written by someone else - and Mr. Tone's presence on Broadway - a complete, undisputed and single triumph.

Nearly everyone at times reading some book of Mr. Hemingway's must have noted its dramatic quality and felt that it would make good theatre. There is not space to go into the discussion, but only to note that a thing's being highly dramatic does not necessarily mean that it is to that degree theatric. It may in fact be dramatic without being even possible for the stage at all. As for the Hemingway writing, I have of course read many pages where the stage possibilities seemed immense. At the same time, however, it was plain what a rare method would be needed to create the stage elements that must be added, and especially to do the necessary projection. In such a style of writing the matter of projection is a special problem, quite beyond the method and concentration of most of our directors and players.

The play tells the story of a newspaper man who has gone to Spain to join the fight against fascism. He serves as a sort of 'second-hand cop,' has a Spanish prostitute on the side, finds an American girl in the same hotel with him, rapes her - he is drunk at the moment - and falls in love with her. She too finally confesses her love for him; the war ends with fascism victorious under Franco; the two lovers plan to marry, they are to meet in France; she learns that the brother she came to find is dead; her lover arranges her departure. The German fighter, with the scarred face, has a final say about devoting his life all through to the cause of liberty, and the American decides not to join the girl as promised.

Such a dénouement gets nowhere. The character may behave as he likes, but the author is expected to see and judge his matter in scale as it were, and with reference to some point of view. And with all this coming overseas to Spain to die for liberty, for its sake giving up marriage, etc., etc., we should get some further definition of what this liberty is. Otherwise what remains has a very good chance of being largely gush, or cant, or impotent thinking, or some rehash of adolescent idealism and public vitality.

At its best this writing has at times the sense of some thrilling combination in reactions: at times it achieves a blaze of single motif, a complete isolation, that is unforgettable; and sometimes a handling of life, blood, sex, raw force that at its fullest pitch achieves a certain orgiastic clarity that is superb. At its less good, or its worst, this writing can give the sense of mere canceling and tricky simplification; at times it gives a far too tricky impression of the glamor of the libido. The appeal then is obviously that of a certain effeminate virility.

As compared with the published text, Mr. Glazer has re-written the play with more space given to the love story, and has added rape. These love scenes often lack the character and excitement and so on of Mr. Hemingway's style; but the point of view, or attitude toward love between men and women, the approach to the subject, seem to me quite in accord with that found in the novels.

Many of the play's admirable qualities are so closely bound up with the directing and acting that it is practically impossible to distinguish which is which and where the credit most lies. Certainly this is the case with Mr. Tone, who achieves the finest effects of tenderness - sudden insight into the quick heart, and conveys to us perfectly that sort of lyrical shock method that the writing employs, and that nostalgia for life - sweet wings that pass, that pass away.

And yet on the whole this play, whatever its limitations, is about something; about something even if now and again it is too much about something that is left out. Sometimes the writing itself is magical and thrilling, the interspaces of its mood filled with a breathless miracle. And this despite the fact that, as Mr. John Mason Brown of the 'New York Post' says in his review, 'its virtues are mainly deceptive because of the lack of distinction and genuine relevance in its writing' (1) - a keen and brilliant observation.

Mr. Lee Strasberg's direction of 'The Fifth Column' is a very fine asset, and the playing of his company in general is good. Miss Katherine Locke gives a sincere and often excellent performance of a role that as written is half silly and half poignant. Miss Lenore Ulric, as the Spanish prostitute, plays with her usual talent. If the result is like other such roles that she has played, that is not much against her, though this present role could be carried further if there were more of a harder, childlike, metallic quality. Mr Lee Cobb brings an admirable performance to the part of the German soldier. All of it is deeply felt and consistent, though in my opinion at times too slow and too much impeded by the foreign accent. There could be less of an accent after the first moments of his performance, or else the lines could change to words where no accent would be needed.

It is interesting to consider what effect might have derived for Mr. Tone's role if the heroine has been left as she is in the original. There she is the predatory young woman journalist, looking for her own where she may find it - in this case near the battle lines in tortured Spain. She is, after a fashion, then, another horror; and the sex motive would thus have become an added complication harrowing the situation for him. His resolving not to join her in France would then be quite another thing. The dénouement would make for much better sense and unity of tone. At the same time the leading male role would become to a greater extent the central interest in the play, the medium through which war's character is portrayed; and for the actor playing it the source of a greater singleness and concentration. The Glazer version, however, provides another sort of variety. Mr. Franchot Tone brings to his performance in general a precision, inner and outer, a fluidity, and a power to give and to evoke that draws out the players' fullest powers during their moments opposite him. In study and accomplishment, growth, maturity of approach, his performance is a reproach to the majority of actors and a lesson to the theatre.

Note

1 John Mason Brown, 'New York Post,' 7 March 1940, 10.

Edmund Wilson on Hemingway (1939)

62. EDMUND WILSON, ERNEST HEMINGWAY: GAUGE OF MORALE, 'ATLANTIC'

164 (July 1939), 36-46

Reprinted in 'The Wound and the Bow' (1941).

I

Hemingway's 'In Our Time' was an odd and original book. It had the appearance of a miscellany of stories and fragments; but actually the parts hung together and produced a definite effect. There were two distinct series of pieces which alternated with one another: one a set of brief and brutal sketches of police shootings, bull-fight crises, hangings of criminals, and incidents of the war; and the other a set of short stories dealing in its principal sequence with the growing-up of an American boy against a landscape of idyllic Michigan, but also with the return home of American soldiers. But it seems to have been Hemingway's intention - 'In Our Time' - that the war should set the key for the whole. The cold-bloodedness of the battles and executions strikes a discord with the sensitiveness and candor of the boy at home in the States; and presently the boy turns up in Europe in one of the intermediate vignettes as a soldier in the Italian army, hit in the spine by machine-gun fire and trying to talk to a dying Italian: '*Senta*, Rinaldi. *Senta*,' (1) he says, 'you and me, we've made a separate peace.'

But there is a more fundamental relationship between

the pieces of the two series. The shooting of Nick in the war does not really connect two different worlds: has he not found in the butchery abroad the same world that he knew back in Michigan? Was not life in the Michigan woods equally destructive and cruel? He went once with his father, the doctor, when he performed a Caesarean operation on an Indian squaw with a jackknife and no anaesthetic and sewed her up with fishing leaders, while the Indian wasn't able to bear it and cut his throat in his bunk. Another time, when the doctor saved the life of a squaw, her Indian picked a quarrel with him rather than pay him in work. And Nick himself sent his girl about her business when he found out how terrible her mother was. Even fishing in Big Two-Hearted River - away and free in the woods - he was conscious in a curious way of the cruelty inflicted on the fish, even of the silent agonies endured by the live bait, the grasshoppers kicking on the hook.

Not that life isn't enjoyable. Talking and drinking with one's friends is great fun; fishing in Big Two-Hearted River is a tranquil exhilaration. But the brutality of life is always there, and it is somehow bound up with the enjoyment. Bullfights are especially enjoyable. It is even exhilarating to build a simply priceless barricade and pot the enemy as they are trying to get over it. The condition of life is pain; and the joys of the most innocent surface are somehow tied to its stifled pangs.

The resolution of this discord in art made the beauty of Hemingway's stories. He had in the process tuned a marvelous prose. Out of the colloquial American speech, with its simple declarative sentences and its strings of Nordic monosyllables, he got effects of the utmost subtlety. F.M. Ford has found the perfect simile for the impression produced by this writing: 'Hemingway's words strike you, each one, as if they were pebbles fetched fresh from a brook. They live and shine, each in its place. So one of his pages has the effect of a brook-bottom into which you look down through the flowing water. The words form a tessellation, each in order beside the other.' (2)

Looking back, we can see how this style was already being refined and developed at a time - fifty years before - when it was regarded in most literary quarters as hopelessly non-literary and vulgar. There had been the nineteenth chapter of 'Huckleberry Finn': 'Two or three nights went by; I reckon I might say they swum by; they slid along so quick and smooth and lovely. Here is the way we put in the time. It was a monstrous big river down there - sometimes a mile and a half wide,' and so forth. These pages, when we happen to meet them in Carl Van Doren's anthology of world literature, stand up in a striking way beside a passage of description from Turgenev; and the pages which Hemingway was later to write about American wood and water are equivalents to the transcriptions by Turgenev - the 'Sportsman's Notebook' is much admired by Hemingway (3) - of Russian forests and fields. Each has brought to an immense and wild country the freshness of a new speech and a sensibility not yet conventionalized by literary associations. Yet it *is* the European sensibility which has come to Big Two-Hearted River, where the Indians are now obsolescent; in those solitudes it feels for the first time the cold current, the hot morning sun, sees the pine stumps, smells the sweet fern. And along with the mottled trout, with its 'clear water-over-gravel color,' the boy from the American Middle West brings up a fat little masterpiece.

In the meantime there had been also Ring Lardner, Sherwood Anderson, Gertrude Stein, using this American language for irony, lyric poetry, psychological insight. Hemingway seems to have learned from them all. But he is now able to charge this naïve accent with a new complexity of emotion, a malaise. The wholesale shattering of human beings in which he has taken part has given the boy a touch of panic.

II

The next fishing trip is strikingly different. Perhaps the first was an idealization. Is it possible to attain such sensuous bliss simply through being alone in the woods, smoking, fishing, and eating, with no thought about anyone else or about anything one has ever done or will ever be obliged to do? At any rate, today, in 'The Sun Also Rises,' all the things that are wrong with human life are there on the holiday, too - though one tries to keep them back out of the foreground and occupy one's mind only with the trout, caught now in a stream of the Pyrenees, with the kidding of the good friend from the States. The feeling of insecurity has deepened. The young American now appears in a seriously damaged condition: he has somehow been incapacitated sexually through wounds received in the war. He is in love with one of those international sirens who flourished in the cafés of the post-war period and whose ruthless and uncontrollable infidelities, in such a circle as that depicted by Hemingway, have made any sort of security impossible for the relations between women and men. The lovers of such a woman turn upon and rend one another because they are powerless to make themselves felt by *her*.

The casualties of the bullfight at Pamplona, to which these young people have gone for the *fiesta*, only reflect the bitings, bashings, betrayals, of demoralized human beings out of hand. What is the tiresome lover with whom the lady has just been off on a casual escapade, and who is unable to understand he has been discarded, but the man who, on his way to the bull ring, has been accidentally gored by the bull? The young American who tells the story is the only character who keeps up standards of conduct, and he is prevented by his disability from dominating and directing the woman, who otherwise, it is intimated, might love him. Here the membrane of the style has been stretched taut to convey the vibrations of these qualms. The dry sunlight and the green summer landscapes have been invested with a sinister quality which must be new in literature. One enjoys the sun and the green as one enjoys suckling pigs and Spanish wine, but the apprehension and uneasiness are undruggable.

Yet one can catch hold of a code in all the drunkenness and social chaos. 'Perhaps as you went along you did learn something,' Jake, the hero, reflects at one point. 'I did not care what it was all about. All I wanted to know was how to live in it. Maybe if you found out how to live in it you learned from that what it was all about.' '"Everybody behaves badly. Give them the proper chance,"' he says to Lady Brett. '"You wouldn't behave badly." Brett looked at me.' In the end, she sends for Jake, who finds her alone in a hotel. She has left her regular lover for a young bullfighter, and this boy has for the first time inspired her with a respect which has restrained her from 'ruining' him: 'You know it makes one feel rather good deciding not to be a bitch.' We suffer and we make suffer, and everybody loses out in the long run; but in the meantime we can lose with honor.

This code still markedly figures, still supplies a dependable moral backbone, in Hemingway's next book of short stories, 'Men Without Women,' Here Hemingway has mastered his method of economy in apparent casualness and relevance in apparent indirection, and has turned his sense of what happens and the way in which it happens into something as hard and clear as a crystal but as disturbing as a great lyric. Yet it is usually some principle of courage, of honor, of pity - that is, some principle of sportsmanship in its largest human sense - upon which the drama hinges. The old bullfighter in The Undefeated is defeated in everything except the spirit which will not accept defeat. You get the bull or he gets you: if you die, you can die game; there are certain things you cannot do. The burlesque show manager in A Pursuit Race refrains from waking his advance publicity agent when he overtakes him and realizes that the man has just lost a long struggle against whatever it is which has driven him to drink and dope. 'They got a cure for that,' the manager had said to him before he went to sleep; '"No," William Campbell said, "they haven't got a cure for anything."'

The burned major in A Simple Enquiry - that strange picture of the bedrock stoicism compatible with the abasement of war - has the decency not to dismiss the orderly who has rejected his proposition. The brutalized Alpine peasant who has been in the habit of hanging a lantern in the jaws of the stiffened corpse of his wife, stood in the corner of the woodshed till the spring makes it possible to bury her, is ashamed to drink with the sexton after the latter has found out what he has done.

This Hemingway of the middle twenties - 'The Sun Also Rises' came out in 1926 - expressed the romantic disillusion and set the favorite pose for the period. It was the moment of gallantry in heartbreak, grim and nonchalant banter, and heroic dissipation. The great watchword was 'Have a drink'; and in the bars of New York and Paris the young people were getting to talk like Hemingway.

III

The novel, 'A Farewell to Arms,' which followed 'Men Without Women,' is in a sense not so serious an affair. Beautifully written and very moving of course it is. Probably no other book has caught so well the strangeness of life in the army for an American in Europe during the war. The new places to which one was sent of which one had never heard, and the things that turned out to be in them; the ordinary people of foreign countries as one saw them when one was quartered among them or obliged to perform some common work with them; the pleasures of which one managed to cheat the war, intensified by the uncertainty and horror - and the uncertainty yet almost became a constant, the horror almost taken for granted; the love affairs, always subject to being poignantly broken up and yet carried on while they lasted in a spirit of irresponsible freedom which derived from having forfeited control of all one's other actions - this Hemingway got into his book, written long enough after the events for them to present themselves under an aspect fully idyllic.

But 'A Farewell to Arms' is a tragedy, and the lovers are shown as innocent victims with no relation to the forces that torment them. They themselves are not tormented within by that dissonance between personal satisfaction and the suffering one shares with others which it has been Hemingway's triumph to handle. 'A Farewell to Arms,' as the author has said, is a 'Romeo and Juliet.' And when Catherine and her lover emerge from the stream of action - the account of the Caporetto retreat is Hemingway's best sustained piece of narrative - when they escape from the alien necessities of which their romance has been merely an accident, which have been writing their story for for them, then we see that they are not in themselves convincing as human personalities. And we are confronted with the paradox that Hemingway, who possesses so remarkable a mimetic gift in getting the sense of social and national types and in making his people talk appropriately, has not shown any very solid sense of character, or, indeed, any real interest in it. The people in his short stories are satisfactory because he has only to hit them off: the point of the story does not lie in personalities, but in the emotion to which a situation gives rise. This is true even in 'The Sun Also Rises,' where the characters are hit off with wonderful cleverness. But in 'A Farewell to Arms,' as soon as we are brought into real intimacy with the lovers, as soon as the author is obliged to see them through a searching personal experience, we find merely an idealized relationship, the abstractions of a lyric emotion.

With 'Death in the Afternoon,' three years later, a new development for Hemingway commences. He writes a book not merely in the first person, but in the first person in his own character as Hemingway, and the results are unexpected and disconcerting. 'Death in the Afternoon' has its value as an exposition of bullfighting; and Hemingway is able to use the subject as a text for an explicit statement of his conception of man eternally pitting himself - he thinks the bullfight a ritual of this - against animal force and the odds of death. But the book is partly infected by a queer kind of maudlin emotion, which sounds at once neurotic and drunken. He overdoes his glorification of the bravery and martyrdom of the bullfighter. No doubt the professional expert at risking his life single-handed is impressive in contrast to the flatness, the timidity, and the unreality of much of the business of the modern world; but this admirable miniaturist in prose has already made the point perhaps more tellingly in the little prose poem called Banal Story. Now he offsets the virility of the bullfighters by anecdotes of the male homosexuals that frequent the Paris cafés, at the same time that he puts his chief justification of the voluptuous excitement of the spectacle into the mouth of an imaginary old lady. The whole thing becomes a little hysterical.

The master of that precise and clean style now indulges in purple patches which go on spreading for pages on end. I am not one who much admires the last chapter of 'Death in the Afternoon,' with its rich, all too rich, unrollings of memories of fine times in Spain, and with its what seem to me irrelevant reminiscences of the soliloquy of Mrs. Bloom in 'Ulysses.' Also, there are interludes of kidding of a kind which Hemingway handles with skill when he assigns them to characters in his stories, but in connection with which he seems to become incapable of exercising good sense or taste as soon as he undertakes them in his own person (the burlesque 'Torrents of Spring' was an early omen of this). In short, we are compelled to recognize that, as soon as Hemingway drops the burning glass of the disciplined and objective art with which he has learned to concentrate in a story the light of the emotions that flood in on him, he straightway becomes befuddled, slops over.

This befuddlement is later to go further, but in the meantime he publishes another volume of stories - 'Winner Take Nothing' - which is almost up to its predecessor. In this collection he deals much more effectively than in 'Death in the Afternoon' with that theme of contemporary decadence which is implied in his panegyric of the bullfighter. The first of the stories, After the Storm, is another of his variations - and one of the finest - on the theme of keeping up a code of decency among the hazards and pains of life. A fisherman goes out to plunder a wreck: he dives down to break in through a porthole, but inside he sees a woman with rings on her hands and her hair floating loose in the water, and he thinks about the passengers and crew being suddenly plunged to their deaths (he was almost killed himself in a drunken fight the night before), he sees the cloud of sea birds screaming around, and he finds that he is unable to crack the glass with his wrench and that he loses an anchor grapple with which he next tries to attack it; so he goes away and leaves the job to the Greeks, who blow the boat open and clean her out.

But in general the emotions of insecurity here obtrude themselves and dominate the book. Two of the stories deal with the hysteria of soldiers falling off the brink of their nerves under the strain of the experiences of the war, which here no longer presents an idyllic aspect;

another deals with a group of patients in a hospital, at the same time crippled and hopeless, still another (a five-page masterpiece) with an old man who has tried to commit suicide although he is known to have plenty of money and who now creeps into a café in search of 'a clean well-lighted place': 'After all, he said to himself, it is probably only insomnia. Many must have it.' Another story, like 'The Sun Also Rises,' centres around a castration; and four of the fourteen are concerned more or less with male or female homosexuality. In the last story, Fathers and Sons, (4) Hemingway reverts to the Michigan woods, as if to take the curse off the rest: young Nick had once made love to a nice Indian girl with plump legs and hard little breasts on the needles of the hemlock woods.

These stories and the interludes in 'Death in the Afternoon' must have been written during the years which followed the stock-market crash. They are full of the apprehension of losing control of oneself which is aroused by the getting out of control of a social-economic system, as well as of the fear of impotence which seems to accompany the loss of social mastery. And there is in such a story as A Clean Well-Lighted Place the feeling of having got to the end of everything, of having given up heroic attitudes, of wanting only the illusion of peace.

IV

And now, in proportion as the characters in his stories run out of fortitude and bravado, he passes into a phase where he is occupied with building up his public personality. He has already now become a legend, as Mencken was in the twenties; he is the Hemingway of the handsome photographs with the open neck and the outdoor grin, with the ominous resemblance to Clark Gable, who poses with giant marlin which he has just hauled in off Key West. And unluckily - but for an American inevitably - the opportunity soon presents itself to exploit this personality for profit: he is soon turning out regular articles for well-paying and trashy magazines.

This department of Hemingway's writing there is no point in discussing in detail. The most favorable thing one can say about it is that he made an extremely bad job of it, where a less authentic artist would probably had done somewhat better. The ordinary writer, when he projects himself, usually produces something which, though unlikely, is sympathetic; but Hemingway has created a Hemingway who is not only incredible but obnoxious. He is certainly his own worst-invented character.

But this journalism does seem to have contributed to the writing of some unsatisfactory books. 'Green Hills of Africa' (1935) owes its failure to falling between the two genres of personal exhibitionism and fiction. 'The writer has attempted,' says Hemingway, 'to write an absolutely true book to see whether the shape of a country and the pattern of a month's action can, if truly presented, compete with a work of the imagination.' He does try to present his own rôle objectively, and there is a genuine Hemingway theme - the connection between success at big-game hunting and sexual self-respect - involved in his adventures as he presents them. But the sophisticated technique of the fiction writer comes to look artificial when it is applied to a series of real happenings; and the necessity of sticking to what really happened makes impossible the typical characters and incidents which give point to a work of fiction. The monologues of the false - the publicity - Hemingway are almost as bad as his magazine articles. He inveighs with much scorn against the literary life and against the professional literary man of the cities; and then manages to give the impression that he himself is a professional literary man of the touchiest and most self-conscious kind. He delivers a self-confident lecture on the high possibilities of prose writing; and then produces such a sentence as the following: 'Going down-hill steeply made these Spanish shooting boots too short in the toe and there was an old argument, about this length of boot and whether the bootmaker, whose part I had taken, unwittingly first, only as interpreter, and finally embraced his theory patriotically as a whole and, I believed, by logic, had overcome it by adding onto the heel.' As soon as Hemingway begins speaking in the first person, he seems to lose his bearings, not merely as a critic of life, but even as a craftsman.

In another and significant way, 'Green Hills of Africa' is disappointing. 'Death in the Afternoon' did provide a lot of data on bullfighting and build up for us the bullfighting world; but its successor tells us little about Africa. Hemingway keeps affirming - as if in accents of defiance against those who would engage his attention for social problems - his passionate enthusiasm for the African country and his perfect satisfaction with the hunter's life; but he has produced what must be one of the only books ever written which make Africa and its animals seem dull. Almost the only thing we learn about the animals is that Hemingway wants to kill them. And as for the native, though there is one fine description of a tribe of marvelously trained runners, the principal impression we get of them is that they were simple and inferior people who enormously admired Hemingway.

It is not only that, as his critics of the Left had been complaining, he shows no interest in political issues, but that his interest in his fellow beings seems actually to be drying up. It is as if he were throwing himself on African hunting as something to live for and believe in, as something through which to realize himself; and as if, expecting of it too much, he had got out of it abnormally little, less than he is willing to admit. The disquiet of the Hemingway of the twenties had been, as I have said, undruggable - that is, in his books themselves, he had tried to express it, not drug it, had given it an appeasement in art; but now there sets in, in the Hemingway of the thirties, what seems to be a deliberate self-drugging. The situation is indicated objectively in The Gambler, the Nun, and the Radio, among the short stories of 1933, in which everything from daily bread to 'a belief in any new form of government' is characterized as 'the opium of the people' by an empty-hearted cripple in a hospital.

But at last there does rush into this vacuum the blast of the social issue, which has been roaring in the wind like a forest fire.

Out of a series of short stories he had written about a Florida waterside character he decided to make a little epic. The result was 'To Have and Have Not,' which seems to me the poorest of all his stories. Certainly some deep agitation is working upon Hemingway the artist. Craftsmanship and style, taste and sense, have all alike gone by the board. The negative attitude toward human beings has here become definitely malignant: the hero is like a wooden-headed Punch, always knocking people on the head (inferiors - Chinamen or Cubans); or, rather, he combines the characteristics of Punch with those of Popeye the Sailor in the animated cartoon in the movies. As the climax to a series of prodigies, this stupendous pirate-smuggler named Harry Morgan succeeds, alone, unarmed, and with only a hook for one hand, - though at the cost of a mortal wound, - in outwitting and destroying with their own weapons four men with revolvers and a machine gun, by whom he has been shanghaied in a launch.

The impotence of a decadent society has here been exploited deliberately, but less successfully than in the earlier short stories. Against a background of homosexuality, impotence, and masturbation among the wealthy holiday-makers in Florida, Popeye-Morgan is shown gratifying his wife with the same indefatigable dexterity which he has displayed in his other feats; and there is a choral refrain of praise of his virility - which wells up in the last pages of the book when the abandoned Mrs. Popeye regurgitates Mrs. Bloom's soliloquy.

To be a man in such a world of maggots is noble, but it is not enough. Besides the maggots, there are double-crossing rats, who will get you if they are given the smallest chance. What is most valid in 'To Have and Have Not' is the idea - conveyed better, perhaps, in the first of the series of episodes than in the final scenes of massacre and agony - that in an atmosphere (here revolutionary Cuba) in which man has been set against man, in which it is always a question whether your companion is not preparing to cut your throat, the most sturdy and straightforward American will turn suspicious and cruel. Harry Morgan is made to realize as he dies that to fight this bad world alone is hopeless. Again Hemingway, with his barometric accuracy, has seized the real moral feeling of the moment - a moment when social relations were subjected to severe tension, seemed already disintegrating. But the heroic Hemingway legend has at this point invaded his fiction and, inflaming and inflating his symbols, has produced an uncomfortable hybrid, half Hemingway-character, half nature myth.

Hemingway had not himself particularly labored this moral of individualism *versus* solidarity, but the critics of the Left labored it for him and received his least creditable piece of fiction as the statement of a new revelation. The progress of the Communist faith among the American writers since the beginning of the economic crisis has followed a peculiar course. That the aims and beliefs of Marx and Lenin should have come through to the minds of intellectuals who had been educated in the bourgeois tradition as great awakeners of conscience, a great light, was quite natural and entirely desirable. But the conception of the dynamic Marxist will, the exaltation of the Marxian religion, seized the members of the professional classes like a capricious contagion or hurricane, which shakes one and leaves his neighbor standing, then returns to lay hold on the second after the first has become calm again. In the moment of seizure, each one saw a scroll unrolled from the heavens, on which Marx and Lenin and Stalin, the Bolsheviks of 1917, the Soviets of the Five-Year Plan, and the GPU of the Moscow trials, were all a part of the same great purpose. Later the convert, if he were capable of it, would get over his first phase of snow blindness and learn to see real people and conditions, would study the development of Marxism in terms of peoples, periods, personalities, instead of logical deductions from abstract propositions or - as in the case of the more naïve or dishonest - of simple incantatory slogans. But for many there was at least a moment when the key to all the mysteries of human history seemed suddenly to have been placed in their hands, when the infallible guide to thought and behavior seemed to have been given them in a few easy formulas.

Hemingway was hit pretty late. He was still in 'Death in the Afternoon' telling the 'world-savers,' sensibly enough, that they should 'get to see' the world 'clear and as a whole. Then any part you make will represent the whole, if it's made truly. The thing to do is to work and learn to make it.' Later he jibed at the literary radicals, who talked but couldn't take it. Then, the challenge of the fight itself, - Hemingway never could resist a physical challenge, - the natural impulse to dedicate oneself to something bigger than big-game hunting and bull-fighting, and the fact that the class war had broken out in a country to which he was romantically attached, seem to have combined to make him align himself with the Communists as well as the Spanish Loyalists at a time when the Marxist philosophy had been pretty completely shelved by the Kremlin, now reactionary as well as corrupt, when the Russians were lending the Loyalists only help enough to preserve, as they imagined would be possible, the balance of power against Fascism while they acted at the same time as a police force to avert the real social revolution. (5)

Hemingway raised money for the Loyalists, reported the battle fronts. He even went so far as to make a speech at a congress of the League of American Writers, an organization rigged by the supporters of the Stalinist régime in Russia and full of precisely the type of literary revolutionists that he had formerly been ridiculing. Soon the Stalinists had taken him in tow, and he was feverishly denouncing as Fascists other writers who criticized the Kremlin. It has been one of the expedients of the Stalin administration in keeping its power and covering up its crimes to condemn on trumped-up charges of Fascist conspiracy, and even to kidnap and murder, its political opponents of the Left; and, along with the food and munitions, the Russians had brought to the war in Spain what the Austrian journalist Willi Schlamm called that diversion of doubtful value for the working class: 'Herr Vyshinsky's Grand Guignol.' (6)

The result of this was a play, 'The Fifth Column,' which, though it is good reading for the way the characters talk, is an exceedingly silly production. The hero, though an Anglo-American, is an agent of the Communist secret police, engaged in catching Fascist spies in Spain; and his principal exploit in the course of the play is clearing out, with the aid of a single Communist, an artillery post manned by seven Fascists. The scene is like a pushover and getaway from one of the cruder Hollywood Westerns.

The tendency on Hemingway's part to indulge such puerile fantasies appears perhaps first at the end of 'A Farewell to Arms,' where the hero, after many adventures of fighting, escaping, lovemaking, and drinking, rows his lady thirty-five kilometres against the wind on a cold November night; and we have seen what it could do for Harry Morgan. Now, as if with the conviction that the cause and the efficiency of the GPU have added several cubits to his stature, he has let this tendency loose; and he has also found in the GPU's grim duty a pretext to give rein to the appetite for killing which has always played such a large part in his work. He has progressed from grasshoppers and trout through bulls and lions and kudus to Chinamen and Cubans, and now to Fascists. Hitherto the act of destruction has given rise for him to complex emotions: he has identified himself not merely with the injurer but also with the injured; there has been a masochistic complement to the sadism. But now this paradox which splits our natures, and which has instigated some of Hemingway's best stories, need no longer present perplexities to his mind. The Fascists are dirty dogs, and to kill them is a holy act. He who had made a separate peace, who had said farewell to arms, has found a reason for taking them up again in a spirit of rabietic fury unpleasantly reminiscent of the spy mania and the sacred anti-German rage which took possession of so many civilians and staff officers under the stimulus of the last war.

Not that the compensatory trauma of the typical Hemingway protagonist is totally absent even here. The main episode is the hero's brief love affair and voluntary breaking off with a beautiful and adoring girl with whom he takes up in Madrid and who, having belonged to the Junior League and been to Vassar, represents for him the leisure-class play-world from which he is trying to get away. But as he has treated her from the very first scenes with considerable frank contempt, the action is rather lacking in suspense as the sacrifice is rather feeble in moral value. One takes no stock at all in the intimation that Mr. Philip may later be sent to mortify himself in a camp for training Young Pioneers. And in the meantime he has fun killing Fascists.

In 'The Fifth Column,' the drugging process has been

carried further still: the hero, who has become finally indistinguishable from the false or publicity Hemingway, has here dosed himself with whiskey; a seductive and desirous woman, for whom he has the most admirable reasons for not taking any responsibility; sacred rage; the excitement of bombardment; and indulgence in that headiest of sports, for which he has now the same excellent reasons - the bagging of human beings.

V

You may be afraid, after reading 'The Fifth Column,' that Hemingway will never sober up; but as you go in the new volume in which it appears, which includes also his most recent short stories, you find that your apprehensions were unfounded. Three of these stories have a great deal more body - they are longer and more complex - than the comparatively meagre anecdotes collected in 'Winner Take Nothing.' And here are his real artistic successes with the material of his experiences in Africa, which make up for the miscarried 'Green Hills': The Short Happy Life of Francis Macomber and The Snows of Kilimanjaro, which disengage, by dramatizing them objectively, the themes which in the earlier book never really got themselves presented. And here is at least a beginning of a real artistic utilization of Hemingway's experience in Spain: a little incident in two pages which outweighs the whole of 'The Fifth Column' and all his Spanish dispatches, about an old man, 'without politics,' who has occupied his life in taking care of eight pigeons, two goats, and a cat, and who has been dislodged and separated from his pets by the advance of the Fascist armies - a story which takes its place in the category of the war series of Callot (7) and Goya, whose union of elegance with sharpness Hemingway has already recalled in his earlier battle plates, a story which might have been written about almost any war.

And here - what is very remarkable - is a story, The Capital of the World, which finds an objective symbol for, precisely, what is wrong with 'The Fifth Column.' A young boy who has come up from the country and waits on table in a pension in Madrid gets accidentally stabbed with a meat knife while playing at bullfighting with the dishwasher. This is the simple anecdote, but Hemingway has built in behind it all the life of the pension and the city: the priesthood, the working-class movement, the grown-up bullfighters who have broken down or missed out. 'The boy Paco,' Hemingway concludes, 'had never known about any of this nor about what all these people would be doing on the next day and on other days to come. He had no idea how they really lived nor how they ended. He did not realize they ended. He died, as the Spanish phrase has it, full of illusions. He had not had time in his life to lose any of them, or even, at the end, to complete an act of contrition.' So he registers in this very fine story the discrepancy between the fantasies of boyhood and the realities of the grown-up world. The artist in Hemingway, who feels things truly and cannot help recording what he feels, has actually said good-bye to these fantasies at a time when the war correspondent is making himself ridiculous by attempting still to hang on to them.

The emotion which principally comes through in Francis Macomber and The Snows of Kilimanjaro - as it figures also in 'The Fifth Column' - is a growing antagonism to women. Looking back, one can see at this point that the tendency has been there all along. In The Doctor and the Doctor's Wife, the boy Nick goes out squirrel hunting with his father instead of obeying the summons of his mother; in Cross Country Snow, he regretfully says farewell to male companionship on a skiing expedition in Switzerland, when he is obliged to go back to the States so that his wife can have her baby. The young man in Hills Like White Elephants compels his girl to have an abortion against her will; another story, A Canary for One, bites almost unbearably but exquisitely on the loneliness to be endured by a wife after she and her husband shall have separated; the peasant of An Alpine Idyll abuses the corpse of his wife (these last three under the general title 'Men Without Women'). Brett in 'The Sun Also Rises' is an exclusive destructive force: she might be a better woman, it is intimated, in the company of Jake, the American; but actually he is protected against her and is in a sense revenging his own sex through being unable to do anything for her sexually. Even the hero of 'A Farewell to Arms' kills Catherine - after enjoying her abject devotion - by giving her a baby, itself born dead. The only women with whom Nick Adams's relations are perfectly satisfactory are the little Indian girls of his boyhood who are in a position of hopeless social disadvantage and have no power over the behavior of the white males - so that he can get rid of them the moment he has done with them. Thus in 'The Fifth Column' Mr. Philip brutally breaks off with Dorothy - he has been rescued from her demoralizing influence by his dedication to Communism, just as the hero of 'The Sun Also Rises' was saved by his physical disability - to revert to a little Moorish whore. Even Harry Morgan, who is represented as satisfying his wife on the scale of a Paul Bunyan, (8) deserts her in the end by dying and leaves her racked by the cruelest desire.

And now this instinct to get the women down presents itself frankly as a fear that the women will get the men down. The men in both these African stories are married to American harpies of the most soul-destroying sort. The hero of The Snows of Kilimanjaro loses his soul and dies of futility on a hunting expedition in Africa, out of which he is not getting what he had hoped. The story is not quite stripped clean of the trashy moral attitudes which have been coming to disfigure the author's work: the hero, a seriously-intentioned and apparently promising writer, goes on a little sloppily over the dear early days in Paris when he was earnest, happy, and poor, and blames a little hysterically the rich woman whom he has married and who has debased him. Yet it is one of Hemingway's remarkable stories. There is a wonderful piece of writing at the end when the reader is made to realize that what has seemed to be an escape by plane with the sick man looking down on Africa is only the dream of a dying man. The other story, Francis Macomber, perfectly realizes its purpose. Here the male saves his soul at the last minute, and then is actually shot down by his woman, who does not want him to have a soul. Here Hemingway has at last got what Thurber (9) calls the war between the sexes right out into the open and has written a terrific fable of the impossible civilized woman who despises the civilized man for his failure in initiative and nerve and then jealously tries to break him down as soon as he begins to exhibit any.

Going back over Hemingway's books today, we can see clearly what an error of the politicos it was to accuse him of an indifference to society. His whole work is a criticism of society: he has responded to every pressure of the moral atmosphere of the time, as it is felt at the roots of human relations, with a sensitiveness almost unrivaled. Even his preoccupation with licking the gang in the next block and being known as the best basketball player in high school has its meaning in the present epoch. After all, whatever is done in the world, political as well as athletic, depends on personal courage and strength. With Hemingway, courage and strength are always thought of in physical terms, so that he tends to give the impression that the bullfighter who can take it and dish it out is more of a man than any other kind of man, and that the sole duty of the revolutionary socialist is to get the counterrevolutionary gang before they get him.

But ideas, however correct, will never prevail by

themselves: there must be people who are prepared to stand or fall with them, and the ability to act on principle is still subject to the same competitive laws which work in sporting contests and sexual relations. Hemingway has expressed with genius the terrors of the modern man at the danger of losing control of his world, and he has also, within his scope, provided his own kind of antidote. This antidote, paradoxically, is almost entirely moral. Despite his preoccupation with physical contests, his heroes are almost always defeated physically, nervously, practically: their victories are moral ones. He himself, when he trained himself stubbornly in his unconventional, unmarketable art in a Paris which had other fashions, gave the prime example of such a victory; and if he has sometimes, under the menace of the general panic, seemed on the point of going to pieces as an artist, he has always pulled himself together the next moment. The principle of the Bourdon gauge, which is used to measure the pressure of liquids, is that a tube which has been curved into a coil will tend to straighten out in proportion as the liquid inside it is subjected to an increasing pressure.

Notes

1 Listen.
2 See No. 32
3 Published in 1852. Hemingway praises Turgenev in 'The Sun Also Rises' (New York 1954), 147, and 'Green Hills of Africa' (New York, 1935), 108.
4 The title comes from Turgenev's novel, 'Fathers and Sons' (1862).
5 George Orwell's brilliant reportage, 'Homage to Catalonia' (1938), was the first to reveal that the Communists had attacked their allies on the Left in order to prevent revolution in Spain.
6 Andre Vyshinsky (1883-1954) was Soviet prosecutor at the Moscow Purge Trials, 1936-38, later Foreign Minister. A Grand Guignol was a short nineteenth-century cabaret play, emphasizing violence and horrors.
7 Jacques Callot (1592-1635) was a French engraver of grotesque subjects.
8 Paul Bunyan was a mythical American giant lumberjack and folk hero.
9 James Thurber, American humorist and cartoonist, was author of 'The Secret Life of Walter Mitty' (1939).

'For Whom the Bell Tolls' (1940)

63. DOROTHY PARKER, 'PM'

20 October 1940, 42

'PM' was a lively New York newspaper.

Once I knew a woman who, by a set of circumstances which has been denied my understanding, got herself among people who chanced to be discussing 'War and Peace.' 'Now, let me see,' she said. '"War and Peace," now, did I read that, or didn't I? I sort of think I did, but I'm not really sure.'

I shall meet that woman again, for I have little luck in such matters. It will be with those who are talking about Ernest Hemingway's latest book. 'Now, let me see,' she will say. '"For Whom the Bell Tolls." Oh, yes, of course I read that. It's one of those books about the Spanish War, isn't it?'

I let her go, on the 'War and Peace' affair. But this time she shall die like a dog.

Ernest Hemingway's new book, that took two years in the writing, spans three days of the war in Spain. The war, they all know now, that should have been won against Fascism, so that this war could never be. Many did not know it then, and that is not terrible of them. For they were not told, and they read lies and heard them. But some who were high in power did know, and for their own brief advantage they lied and said it was not like that and everybody should do nothing about it. And theirs is the deed that cannot be forgotten.

This is a book, not of three days, but of all time. This is a book of all of us alive, of you and me and ours and those we hate. That is told by its title, taken from one of John Donne's sermons: 'No man is an *Iland*, intire of its selfe; every man is a peece of the *Continent*, a part of the maine; if a *Clod* bee washed away by the *Sea*, *Europe* is the lesse, as well as if a *Promontorie* were, as well as if a *Mannor* of thy friends or of *thine owne* were: any mans death diminishes me, because I am involved in *Mankinde*. And therefore never send to know for whom the *bell* tolls. It tolls for *thee*.'

This is a book about love and courage and innocence and strength and decency and glory. It is about stubbornness and stupidity and selfishness and treachery and death. It is a book about all those things that go on in the world night and day and always; those things that are only heightened and deepened by war. It is written with justice that is blood brother to brutality. It is written with a wisdom that washes the mind and cools it. It is written with an understanding that rips the heart with compassion for those who live, who do the best they can, just so that they may go on living.

It is a great thing to see a fine writer grow finer before your eyes. 'For Whom the Bell Tolls' is, and beyond all comparison, Ernest Hemingway's finest book. It is not necessary politely to introduce that statement by the words 'I think.' It is so, and that is all there is to it. It is not written in his staccato manner. The pack of little Hemingways who ran along after his old style cannot hope to copy the swell and flow of his new one. I cannot imagine what will become of those of them who are too old for the draft.

There are many authors who have written about love, all along the gamut from embarrassment to enchantment. There are many who have written about sex and have got rich and fat and pale at the job. But nobody can write as Ernest Hemingway can of a man and a woman together, their completion and their fulfillment. And nobody can make melodrama as Ernest Hemingway can, nobody else can get such excitement upon a printed page. I do not feel that the creation of excitement is a minor achievement.

'For Whom the Bell Tolls' is nothing to warrant a display of adjectives. Adjectives are dug from soil too long worked, and they make sickly praise and stumbling reading. I think that what you do about this book of Ernest Hemingway's is point to it and say, 'Here is a book.' As you would stand below Everest and say, 'Here is a mountain.'

64. HOWARD MUMFORD JONES, 'SATURDAY REVIEW OF LITERATURE'

23 (26 October 1940), 5, 19

Howard Mumford Jones (b. 1892), American educator and critic, is author of 'O Strange New World' (1964) and 'Revolution and Romanticism' (1974).

I think 'For Whom the Bell Tolls' is as great an advance over 'A Farewell to Arms' as 'A Farewell to Arms' was better than 'The Sun Also Rises.' 'The Sun Also Rises' was a striking book, but it was also something of a stunt. 'A Farewell to Arms' was a moving book, but it was also sentimental. 'For Whom the Bell Tolls' is not a stunt and is not merely sentimental. It is on the contrary, the finest and richest novel which Mr. Hemingway has written, it is one of the finest and richest novels of the year, and it is probably one of the finest and richest novels of the last decade. Gone now are the brittle surface, the clever concision of the early books. Gone is the self-conscious 'little Hemingway' of 'Death in the Afternoon.' Gone is the Hemingway manner. Manner has been replaced by style, and the mere author has died out in the artist. Hemingway disappears, and in his place is the sorrowful majesty of a cause in which he believed and which did not triumph, at least superficially. But it is only superficially that this lost cause is to be identified with the Spanish Republic. More deeply, the cause is *not* lost, because (and I am not trying to be magniloquent), it is the cause of Humanity itself - that vague and splendid cause in which the nineteenth century liberal believed with a faith that we have almost lost, and which inspired some of the best pages of Victor Hugo and Charles Dickens and Dostoievski and Tolstoy. 'For Whom the Bell Tolls' may seem to certain readers a tragic story because the war on the Republican side is so badly conducted that the hero is killed in futilely blowing up a bridge. But both the paradox and the force of the novel lie in the profounder truth that the death of the hero is, however pathetic, merely pathetic, and that the tragic issue, the cosmic issue, is not the death of Robert Jordan but the future of Humanity.

The plot will be compared with that of 'Farewell to Arms.' Again caught up in another military blunder, another hero meets a woman who swiftly and gladly gives herself to him and who has to suffer the physical discomforts of sex. Again there is a background of confusion and cruelty, a wrecked nation, stupid military power loose in the land like a blinded bull, and the wastage of human life in a black current of nihilism. Unlike the earlier couple, to be sure, in 'For Whom the Bell Tolls' the hero dies and the woman survives. Mr. Hemingway has been chary of inventing a new general framework for his tale.

But the comparison is merely mechanical. Hemingway looked at the retreat from Caporetto from the outside as a pitying spectator; he participates in the wreck of Spain as one of the combatants. Italian life and scenery furnished an interesting and picturesque backdrop for a pathetic love story in 'Farewell to Arms.' A pathetic love story in 'For Whom the Bell Tolls,' on the contrary, furnishes opportunity for an imaginative transcript of Spanish life so moving, so full and rich, so just and sympathetic, and yet so objective, that I can think of nothing quite comparable in the whole range of English fiction.

To be sure, this life is limited to Spain in war and to a particular sector of that struggle. Robert Jordan, an American teacher of Spanish, having joined the Republican forces, is sent as a dynamiter to blow up a bridge behind the fascist lines. He is instructed to make contact for that purpose with a small guerilla band in the mountains. The whole book is bounded in the little lapse of time between Roberto's arrival and his death three or four days later. He has been in Madrid, and in his reminiscences we learn something about municipal life in Spain. Hemingway occasionally interpolates the story of somebody else on the Republican side - usually I wish he wouldn't. But in general it is the lives and experiences of this small group of guerilla fighters, men and women, caught in these few days between the upper and the nether millstones, which serve as the vehicle for his imaginative triumph. Through them I think Hemingway has done for the Spanish Civil War the sort of thing that Tolstoy did for the Napoleonic campaigns in 'War and Peace.' At the end of 'For Whom the Bell Tolls,' the reader has not lived in Spain, he has lived Spain.

It is sometimes the mark of an imaginative and moving novel that the hero should vanish into the book. David Copperfield, for example, to all intents and purposes thus disappears. In 'Vanity Fair' the death of that half-hero, George Sedley, is merely trivial and incidental, though he dies at Waterloo; and yet 'Vanity Fair' is *par excellence* the English novel of Waterloo. In such cases the book is so vital it swallows up the character. Something of that sort happens in 'For Whom the Bell Tolls.'

Roberto Jordan is neither a David Copperfield nor a George Sedley, but he is in the main merely another Hemingway young man. Though we follow his adventures and the play of his mind with interest, though it is a matter of breathless consequence that he shall destroy his bridge, he is mainly the vehicle which calls into being the life of Spain.

The heroine just escapes being merely another Hemingway heroine. She is named Maria. Dreadful things have happened to her, and they are movingly told; she is tenderly presented - a new Haidee for a relatively chaste and very republican Don Juan; (1) and the love-making is beautiful and frank. But even Maria is little more than pathetic. Perhaps if she were not the technical heroine, she would escape into a fuller life. For, just as Amelia is dwarfed by Becky Sharp, (2) so Maria is dwarfed by another woman. In the rich and Falstaffian figure of La Pilar, wife of Pablo, disillusioned chieftain of the guerillas, Hemingway has created a character like a mountain. Whether Pilar is cooking, studying human nature, instructing Maria in the facts of life, cursing with the fulness of a Shakespearian shrew, inspiriting her husband, aiding Roberto, or philosophizing, she moves like a Titaness. Grouped around her, the other members of the gang are presented with a minute and sympathetic fidelity, a simplicity and sympathy, an intuitive insight into the mental processes of 'uncultivated' people that make them almost incredibly vivid. They dwarf the titular leads. The death of the old man at the bridge is, for example, much more pathetic than the love tale.

I have spoken of the style. In the descriptive and narrative portions Hemingway achieves a wider variety of effects than, I think, in any other story. But it is particularly in dialogue that the novel scores. The conversation is carried over almost literally from the Spanish, and it would appear that colloquial Spanish permits a combination of dignity, rhetorical precision, and wild poetry unattainable in a Germanic tongue. It is also rich in curses. Hemingway has solved the important problem of rendering the profanity and obscenity of the common people by using a device so simple and yet effective that I must leave it for the reader to discover. An immense part of the vitality of 'For Whom the Bell Tolls' lies in the imaginative force of its dialogue.

Everybody knows what an occasional poem is, and everybody knows that very few occasional poems survive the event which called them into being. I wish we had in criticism the phrase, 'occasional novel.' I refer to those books which, produced by such an event as the

Spanish Civil War, are impassioned and journalistic, and no more. Like occasional poetry, occasional fiction may often be impassioned, but the passion is not often shaped into enduring bronze. But somehow, sometime, somebody comes along and lifts the occasional novel out of contentiousness into the world of Humanity. Such a book is 'Uncle Tom's Cabin.' There is a small library of fiction on Negro slavery - who reads it today? But who doesn't know the story of Little Eva and Uncle Tom? There were a hundred novels about Waterloo - and only 'Vanity Fair' remains. Who doesn't know about Becky Sharp? I think it at least possible that 'For Whom the Bell Tolls' may be the 'Vanity Fair,' the 'Uncle Tom's Cabin' of the Spanish War. If the guess should prove accurate, the book will last, in my judgment, because it rises out of partisanship into imaginative comprehensiveness.

For, although Hemingway like Roberto is enlisted on the side of the Republic, neither he nor his hero blink the truth that a good deal of the material on that side is pretty sorry stuff. He has not omitted the drunkenness, the disorder, the cruelty, the selfishness, the confusion. The hero dies because of stupidity and treachery on his own side. Interpolated into the main action, there is a long and dreadful narrative about the murder by Pablo and others of twenty fascists in a Spanish village which is among the scenes of fiction I would rather forget. And yet, at the end, Pilar and her companions join the immortals. Their ride up the mountain is like riding into Valhalla (3) - a Valhalla inhabited by Jean Valjean (4) and Uncle Tom and the hero of 'Redemption' (5) and the legend that is Abraham Lincoln. Mere reporting, mere realism, mere enlistment on the right side - we have had dozens of books that could show these excellences only. 'For Whom the Bell Tolls' seems to me at least to spring from this great subterranean source of artistic energy.

Notes

1 In Byron's poem, Don Juan (1818-23).
2 In Thackeray's 'Vanity Fair' (1848).
3 In Norse mythology, the palace where the souls of slain heroes feasted.
4 Hero of Victor Hugo's 'Les Misérables' (1862).
5 Late, unfinished play by Tolstoy, produced in 1911.

65. EDMUND WILSON, 'NEW REPUBLIC'

103 (28 October 1940), 591-2

This new novel of Hemingway will come as a relief to those who didn't like 'Green Hills of Africa,' 'To Have and Have Not,' and 'The Fifth Column.' The big game hunter, the waterside superman, the Hotel Florida Stalinist, with their constrained and fevered attitudes, have evaporated like the fantasies of alcohol. Hemingway the artist is with us again; and it is like having an old friend back.

This book is also a new departure. It is Hemingway's first attempt to compose a full-length novel, with real characters and a built-up story. On the eve of a Loyalist attack in the Spanish civil war, a young American who has enlisted on the Loyalist side goes out into country held by the Fascists, under orders to blow up a bridge. He directs with considerable difficulty a band of peasant guerillas, spends three nights in a cave in their company, blows up the bridge on schedule, and is finally shot by the Fascists. The method is the reverse of the ordinary method in novels of contemporary history, Franz Hoellering's (1) or André Malraux's which undertake a general survey of a revolutionary crisis, shuttling back and forth among various groups of characters. There is a little of this shuttling in 'For Whom the Bell Tolls,' but it is all directly related to the main action: the blowing-up of the bridge. Through this episode the writer has aimed to reflect the whole course of the Spanish War, to show the tangle of elements that were engaged in it, and to exhibit the events in a larger perspective than that of the emergency of the moment.

In this he has been successful to a degree which will be surprising even to those who have believed in him most. There is in 'For Whom the Bell Tolls' an imagination for social and political phenomena such as he has hardly given evidence of before. The vision of this kind of insight is not so highly developed as it is with a writer like Malraux, but it is here combined with other things that these political novels often lack. What Hemingway presents us with in this study of the Spanish war is not so much a social analysis as a criticism of moral qualities. The *kind* of people people are rather than their social-economic relations is what Hemingway is particularly aware of.

Thus there is here a conception of the Spanish character, very firm and based on close observation, underlying the various social types; and in approaching the role of the Communists in Spain, Hemingway's judgments are not made to fit into the categories of a political line - since he has dropped off the Stalinist melodrama of the days of 1937, a way of thinking certainly alien to his artistic nature - but seem to represent definite personal impressions. The whole picture of the Russians and their followers in Spain - which will put 'The New Masses' to the trouble of immediately denouncing a former favorite at a time when they are already working overtime with so many other denunciations on their hands - looks absolutely authentic. You have the contrast between the exaltation of the converts and recruits of the headquarters of the International Brigade, and the luxury, the insolence and the cynicism of the headquarters of the emissaries of the Kremlin. You have the revolutionary stuffed shirt, André Marty, hero of the 1918 mutiny of the French fleet in the Black Sea, who has been magnified and corrupted in Moscow till he is no longer anything but a mischievous bureaucrat, obsessed with the idea of shooting heretics; and you have the Moscow insider Karkov, cold of head and serious of purpose while he repeats for the sake of conformity the venomous gibberings of Pravda. (2)

You have in the center of the stage the sincere fellow traveler from the States, teacher of Spanish in a Western college; and you have, traced with realism and delicacy, the whole chronicle of his reactions to the Communists, of his relations with the Spaniards he has to work with, and of the operation upon him in Spain of the American influences he brings with him. In the end, realizing fully the military futility of his mission and balked in his effort to save the situation, by the confusion of forces at cross-purposes that are throttling the Loyalist campaign, he is to stick by his gun sustained by nothing but the memory of his grandfather's record as a soldier in the American Civil War. In view of the dramatic declamations on the note of 'Look here, upon this picture, and on this!' (3) that the Stalinists were making a year or two ago over the contrast between Dos Passos' attitude and Hemingway's in connection with the Spanish war, it is striking that the hero of 'For Whom the Bell Tolls' should end up by cutting a figure not fundamentally so very much different from that of the hero of 'The Adventures of a Young Man.' (4)

Thus we get down out of the empyrean of Marxist political analysis, where the leaders are pulling the strings for the masses, and see the ordinary people as they come. And we see the actual layout - mile by mile and hill by hill - of the country in which they have to struggle. One of the most highly developed of Hemingway's senses is his geographical and strategical vision - what may be called his sense of terrain. It is no doubt from the Western frontier that he has inherited his vivid perception of every tree, every bush, every path, every contour and every stream that go to make up the lay of the land. He derives and he can communicate an excitement from the mere exploration and mastery of country that goes back to Fenimore Cooper; and he has succeeded in getting it into this new novel as he got it into his early stories. We are shown the Spanish conflict in its essential and primitive aspect of groups of imperfectly equipped and more or less groping human beings maneuvering over the surface of the earth.

The novel has certain weaknesses. A master of the concentrated short story, Hemingway is less sure in his grasp of the form of the elaborated novel. The shape of 'For Whom the Bell Tolls' is sometimes slack and sometimes bulging. It is certainly quite a little too long. You need space to make an epic of three days; but the story seems to slow up toward the end where the reader feels it ought to move faster; and the author has not found out how to mold or to cut the interior soliloquies of his hero. Nor are the excursions outside the consciousness of the hero, whose point of view comprehends most of the book, conducted with consistent attention to the symmetry and point of the whole.

There is, furthermore, in 'For Whom the Bell Tolls' something missing that we still look for in Hemingway. Where the semi-religious exaltation of communism has failed a writer who had once gained from it a new impetus, a vacuum is created which was not there before and which for the moment has to be filled. In Hemingway's case, there has poured in a certain amount of conventional romance. There is in 'For Whom the Bell Tolls' a love story that is headed straight for Hollywood. The hero falls in with an appealing little girl who has been captured and raped by the Fascists, who has never loved before and who wants him to teach her love. She adores him, lives only to serve him, longs for nothing but to learn his desires so that she can do for him what he wants, talks of her identity as completely merged in his. She is as docile as the Indian wives in the early stories of Kipling; (5) and since the dialogue of the characters speaking Spanish is rendered literally with its *thees* and *thous* and all the formalities of a Latin language, the scenes between Robert and Maria have a strange atmosphere of literary medievalism reminiscent of the era of Maurice Hewlett. (6) Robert keeps insisting to himself on his good fortune and on the unusualness of his experience in acquiring a girl like Maria; and, for all the reviewer knows, there may be a few such cases in Spain. But the whole thing has the too-perfect felicity of a youthful erotic dream. It lacks the true desperate emotion of the love affairs in some of Hemingway's other stories. And in general, though the situation is breathless and the suspense kept up all through, the book lacks the tensity, the moral malaise, that made the early work of Hemingway troubling.

But then this early work was, as it were, lyric; and 'For Whom the Bell Tolls' is an effort toward something else, which requires a steady hand. The hero of this new novel is no romantic Hemingway cartoon: his attitude toward his duty and the danger it involves are studied with more coolness and sobriety than in the case of perhaps any other of the author's leading juveniles. The young man is a credible young man who is shown in his relation to other people, and these other people are for the most part given credible identities, too. The author has began to externalize the elements of a complex personality in human figures that have a more complete existence than those of his previous stories.

That he should thus go back to his art, after a period of artistic demoralization, and give it a larger scope, that, in an era of general perplexity and panic, he should dramatize the events of the immediate past in terms, not of partisan journalism, but of the common human instincts that make men both fraternal and combative, is a reassuring evidence of the soundness of our intellectual life.

Notes

1 'The Defenders,' trans. Ludwig Lewisohn (1940).
2 Official Soviet newspaper, whose title means 'Truth.'
3 'Hamlet,' III.ii.
4 Published in 1939. Dos Passos' hero is an idealistic Communist, betrayed by the Party when he does not follow its program.
5 For example, Ameera in 'Without Benefit of Clergy' (1891).
6 Maurice Hewlett was author of popular historical romances, 'Richard Yea-and-Nay' (1900) and 'The Queen's Quair' (1904).

66. ROBERT SHERWOOD, 'ATLANTIC'

166 (November 1940), front section

Robert Sherwood (1896-1955), American playwright, was author of 'The Petrified Forest' (1935) and 'Abe Lincoln in Illinois' (1938).

One must be hesitant to apply the word 'artist' to a virile American writer. He is apt to feel that he has been insulted, that he has been ticketed as an escapist, or a literary embroiderer. However - here goes: Ernest Hemingway is an artist, and his new novel, 'For Whom the Bell Tolls,' is a rare and beautiful piece of work. It contains all the strength and brutality, the 'blood and guts' of all the previous Hemingway books (and more skillfully rendered profanity and obscenity than any of them); and it is written with a degree of delicacy which proves that this fine writer, unlike some other fine American writers, is capable of self-criticism and self-development. Hemingway has not been content merely to go on expending the huge natural force that is his, but has worked, and worked hard and intelligently, to give it form as well as substance.

He has succeeded magnificently and hearteningly and at the right moment.

There is in 'For Whom the Bell Tolls' not only the immediate stimulus of which Hemingway has always been an open-handed provider; there is in it a curious sense of permanence and nobility of spirit. Its characters are not represented as exceptional, as strange refugees from space and time. They are the eternal fighters of all wars, and the eternal victims. Theirs is the lost cause that can never be lost, the sacrifice that can never be futile. Thus the novel justifies the John Donne quotation from which came the title: 'No man is an *Iland*, intire of it selfe ... any mans *death* diminishes *me*, because I am involved in *Mankinde*; And therefore never send to know for whom the *bell* tolls; it tolls for *thee*.'

'For Whom the Bell Tolls' is another story of the Spanish Civil War, and its extraordinary merits seem all the more extraordinary because of that. Hemingway was there, in that war, in that prologue to war, and he felt it with a degree of intensity which was felt, God knows, by too few others. He now writes of it with detachment and objectivity, and with hardly a trace of rancor. I know that too much detachment and objectivity and too little rancor can be fatal to creation. But in this book he has achieved the true union of passion and reason, and that is why it is so preeminently a work of art.

He has painted on a small canvas. He has not attempted to sweep over a vast panorama, as in the retreat from Caporetto in 'A Farewell to Arms.' He tells of an exceedingly minor operation in the war; his central characters are few in number, and we see them during only seventy-two hours of their lives. But it seems to me that he tells the whole story of what was behind the Spanish tragedy, and what was to come of it for Spain and Europe and the rest of us. In one tremendous chapter (the tenth) he gives the story of how the movement started in one small town. Again, he tells of how an important message is delivered through the lines; and the difficulties involved in that delivery form the story of the centrifugal leadership of the Loyalist cause, which dissipated the hopes of the innocents of Spain. In these passages, Hemingway provides a masterpiece in the brief characterization of Comrade Marty, the political commissar, who was more eager to verify his own suspicions of his own associates than to gain victory over Fascism.

Hemingway's hero is named Robert Jordan. He bears a superficial resemblance to other Hemingway heroes, the clever ones and the dumb ones alike, in that he is resolutely resistant to illusion. But I should say that he is a better man than any of them. He is more grown-up. His consciousness is clearer. The love scenes between Robert Jordan and the girl Maria, to whom the Fascists had done 'bad things,' are complete love scenes. Complete love scenes are rare in modern literature. Any writer with knowledge of his craft can write skillfully about sex, but it takes an artist to write thus beautifully and truly about love.

When I said that Hemingway has written without rancor, I meant that he wrote with aching sympathy for all the victims of Fascism, including the Fascists themselves. He took no time out for denunciatory editorials. He did not feel the need to insult the reader's intelligence by telling him that Fascism is that which kills the spirit of man, which forbids man to be an artist. He has done his finest work, and, what is perhaps more important, he has dispelled any fears concerning his own limitations.

67. DWIGHT MACDONALD, 'PARTISAN REVIEW'

8 (January 1941), 24-8

Dwight Macdonald (b. 1906) was the American editor of 'Partisan Review' (1938-43) and 'Politics' (1944-49), and author of 'Memoirs of a Revolutionist' (1957) and 'Against the American Grain' (1962).

Hemingway's publishers advertise his new book as 'the novel that has something for everybody.' This seems to be an accurate statement. It is the biggest publishing success since 'Gone With the Wind': almost half a million copies have been sold and it is selling at the rate of 50,000 a week; Paramount has bought the movie rights at the highest price yet paid by Hollywood for a novel, and Gary Cooper, at Hemingway's insistence, is to play the hero; the initials FWTBT promise to become as familiar journalistic shorthand as GWTW. At the same time, the book has been extravagantly praised by the critics, from Mr. Mumford Jones of the 'Saturday Review of Literature' (who describes Pilar as a 'Falstaffian' character and thinks it is 'at least possible that "For Whom the Bell Tolls" may become the "Uncle Tom's Cabin" of the Spanish Civil War') to Mr. Edmund Wilson of the 'New Republic.' It is seldom that a novelist gathers both riches and reputation from the same book.

In the face of all this enthusiasm, I have to note that my own experience with 'For Whom the Bell Tolls' was disappointing. The opening chapters promised a good deal: they were moving, exciting, wonderfully keen in sensory description. They set the stage for major tragedy. But the stage was never really filled, the promise wasn't kept. The longer I read, the more of a let-down I felt, the more I had a sense that the author was floundering around, uncertain of his values and intentions, unable to come up to the pretensions of this theme. One trouble with the book is that it isn't a novel at all but rather a series of short stories, some of them excellent - Pilar's narratives of the killing of the fascists and of her life with the consumptive bullfighter; the description of Gaylord's Hotel; Andres' journey through the Loyalist lines; and the final blowing up of the bridge - imbedded in a mixture of sentimental love scenes, too much talk, rambling narrative sequences, and rather dull interior monologues by Jordan. So, too, with the characters; they are excellent when they are sketched in just enough for the purposes of a short story, as with El Sordo, the dignified Fernando, and the old man Anselmo. But when Hemingway tries to do more, he fails, as with the character of Pilar, which starts off well enough but becomes gaseous when it is expanded.

The worst failure is the central character, Robert Jordan. Like previous Hemingway heroes, Jordan is not an objectively rendered character but simply a mouthpiece for the author. The earlier heroes had at least a certain dramatic consistency, but Jordan is a monster, uniting - or trying to - the nihilism and cynicism of the usual Hemingway hero with a rather simpleminded political idealism - a sort of Hemingwayesque scoutmaster leading his little troop of peasants. For the Hemingway who speaks through Jordan is a Hemingway with a hangover, a repentant Hemingway who has been in contact with a revolution and has accepted it enough to be ashamed of his old faith and yet who cannot feel or understand deeply the new values. The result is that Jordan as a character is vague and fuzzy, destroyed by the continual friction of these irreconcilable viewpoints.

Jordan's confusion is shared and not understood by his creator, and this confusion is the root of the failure of the novel. Although Hemingway himself denies it frequently in the course of the book, and although most of the critics take his denial at face value, 'For Whom The Bell Tolls' is a political novel, both in that it deals with a great political event, the Spanish civil war, and that its author takes a definite (though largely unconscious) political attitude towards this event. And it is a failure because Hemingway lacks the moral and intellectual equipment to handle such a theme. Instinctively, he tries to cut the subject down to something he can handle by restricting his view of the war to the activities of a small band of peasant guerillas behind Franco's lines (and hence safely insulated from Loyalist politics) and by making his protagonist - in Karkov's words - 'a young American of slight political development but ... a fine partisan record.'

But such limitations negate the pretensions of the book. Hemingway's peasants have been so depoliticalized that it seems little more than chance that they are Loyalists rather than Rebels, and so the long novel is reduced to the scale of an adventure story. As for Jordan, on page 17 he admonishes himself: 'Turn off the thinking now, old timer, old comrade. You're a bridge-blower now. Not a thinker.' But what can be more fruitless than to follow through some five hundred pages the thoughts of a hero who has renounced thought?

I think the novel is a failure for precisely the reason that many critics seem to like it most: because of its rejection of political consciousness. 'The *kind* of people people are rather than their social-economic relations is what Hemingway is particularly aware of,' writes Edmund Wilson in the 'New Republic,' and it is clear from the rest of his review that he conceives of 'social-economic relations' as somehow conflicting with 'the kind of people people are.' This false antithesis, between politics and 'art,' or even between politics and 'life,' attractive enough always to the empirically-slanted American consciousness, is doubly seductive today when political creeds have been so discredited by the events of recent years. Mr. Wilson ends his review: 'That he should thus go back to his art, after a period of artistic demoralization, and give it a large scope, that in an era of general perplexity and panic, he should dramatize the events of the the immediate past in terms, not of partisan journalism, but of the common human instincts that make men both fraternal and combative - is reassuring evidence of the soundness of our intellectual life.'

Of course, posing the alternative in these terms, one must agree that 'For Whom the Bell Tolls' is vastly preferable to the 'partisan journalism' of 'The Fifth Column.' But there is another alternative, namely the treatment of revolutionary struggle as Malraux and Silone (1) have treated it in their novels, on the level of political consciousness. Mr. Wilson describes Hemingway's political understanding as 'not so highly developed as it is with a writer like Malraux,' adding 'but it is here combined with other things that these political novelists often lack.' Just what are these 'other things'? I find at least as profound an understanding of 'the kind of people people are' in Silone and Malraux as in Hemingway. Far from there being an antithesis between these two kinds of understanding, the human and the political, in these European novelists the one illuminates the other and is integrated with it. Politics is simply one category of human behavior - to the novelist who is writing about a revolution, the most important one.

To Mr. Wilson, however, 'politics' seems to mean the threadbare, vulgarized formulae, the treacheries and lies of Stalinism. Thus he actually describes the Hemingway of 'The Fifth Column' as infused with 'the semi-religious exaltation of communism,' whereas in fact Hemingway in that period expressed the most tepid sort of Popular Frontism. And Mr. Wilson can write of the new novel:

'Thus we get down out of the empyrean of Marxist political analysis, where the leaders are pulling the strings for the masses and see the ordinary people as they come.' It has never occurred to me that the defects of 'The Fifth Column' could be attributed to a too close study of the Marxist classics. And as for the leaders pulling the strings for the masses - Mr. Wilson should read again the passages in 'For Whom the Bell Tolls' dealing with the necessity for 'discipline,' and with the 'crazies,' the Anarchists.

This misconception of the nature of politics leads Mr. Wilson - and many others - to conclude that since Hemingway in 'For Whom the Bell Tolls' explicitly rejects the political catchwords of Stalinism, he has therefore liberated himself from 'politics' in general and from Stalinism in particular. Hemingway himself, whose conception of politics is essentially that of Mr. Wilson, may well suffer from the same delusion. But those who see no further into a political program than its catchwords are likely to imagine, when they lose faith in the catchwords, that to reject them is also to free themselves from the program. It may be, however, that they merely become *unconscious* of their political values.

Thus it is precisely that lack of political consciousness which Mr. Wilson finds so admirable that prevents Hemingway from really breaking with Stalinism. Jordan 'turns off the thinking' only to act the more freely in accordance with the very political formulae he has come to distrust so deeply as not to want to think about.

'Here in Spain the Communists offered the best discipline and the soundest and sanest for the prosecution of the war. He accepted their discipline because, in the conduct of the war, they were the only party whose program and discipline he could respect. What were his politics, then? He had none now, he told himself. But do not tell any one else, he thought....' Hemingway tries to write a non-political political novel and Jordan tries to participate in a revolutionary war and yet reject politics. But these are merely *other forms* of political thought and action.

'He would not think himself into any defeatism. The first thing was to win the war. If we did not win the war, everything was lost.' Here we see a false antithesis, between thinking and successful action (thought leads to defeatism) similar to that already noted between politics and human reality. This corresponds in turn to the false antithesis made by the Stalinists in Spain between the task of winning the war (a 'practical' matter which must be settled first) and that of creating a new society (a 'theoretical' matter, to be left to the distant future, a sort of dessert to be enjoyed after the war). But there was no real antithesis between the two tasks: the war could have been won only by carrying through the social revolution.

I will be told that Hemingway directly attacks the Stalinists in his portrait of Marty and in his rendering of the cynical atmosphere of Gaylord's. It is true that these represent a shift away from Stalinism - but of a superficial nature, like his rejection of the Party catch-words. Hemingway is at pains to indicate that Jordan's first reaction to Gaylord's was naive, that war is an ugly business, and that cynicism may be permitted those who are really facing the realities and 'doing the job.' And Marty is presented as literally half-crazy, his lunacy consisting in a passion for shooting Trotskyists and Anarchists - thus attributing the settled and rational (from its viewpoint) policy of the C.P. in Spain as the vagary of an eccentric individual!

It is notable that in his attempts to define to himself why he finds it increasingly harder to believe in the the Loyalist cause, Jordan often blames the Spanish national character (which he feels is treacherous, provincial, cruel, etc.) and sometimes even certain disturbing moral characteristics of individual Stalinists. But he never gives a thought to the really disillusioning development: the slow strangling, by the Stalino-bourgeois coalition, of the revolutionary upsurge of the Spanish masses. The most politically revealing thing in the book is Hemingway's vindictive picture of the Anarchists - 'the crackpots and romantic revolutionists,' 'the wild men,' or, most often, simply 'the crazies.' One character thinks of them as 'dangerous children; dirty, foul, undisciplined, kind, loving, silly and ignorant but armed.' (This character is not Karkov or Jordan but the simple peasant lad, Andres, who might have disliked the Anarchists but would certainly not have disliked them in these drillmaster's terms - a curious example of how Hemingway sometimes violates realism to voice his own prejudices.) What worries Hemingway about the Anarchists is that they were undisciplined and armed, which is a good short description of the masses in process of making a revolution. His counter-prescription is expressed in Jordan's evaluation of the Stalinist generals:

'They were Communists and they were disciplinarians. The discipline that they would enforce would make good troops. Lister was murderous in discipline.... But he knew how to forge a division into a fighting unit.'

I find it significant that the Communist Party seems to be undecided as to just what line to take towards 'For Whom the Bell Tolls.' While the book has been roundly denounced in classic C.P. style in the 'Daily Worker,' it is being sold in the Party bookshops. And Alvah C. Bessie in the 'New Masses' writes more in sorrow than in anger, taking the line that Hemingway, while still sincerely enlisted in the fight against 'our common enemy' (reaction), has been misled so that 'at the moment he is found in bad company. The Party has evidently not given up hope of welcoming back the straying sheep into the fold at some future (and happier) date. I should say this is a shrewd political judgment.

Note

1 Silone was an Italian political novelist, author of 'Fontamara' (1930) and 'Bread and Wine' (1937).

68. LIONEL TRILLING, 'PARTISAN REVIEW'

8 (January 1941), 63-7

To anyone who has been at all interested in its author's career - and who has not? - 'For Whom the Bell Tolls' will first give a literary emotion, for here, we feel at once, is a restored Hemingway writing to the top of his bent. He does not, as in the period of 'To Have and Have Not' and 'The Fifth Column,' warp or impede his notable talent with the belief that art is to be used like the automatic rifle. He does not substitute political will for literary insight nor arrogantly pass off his personal rage as social responsibility. Not that his present political attitude is coherent or illuminating; indeed, it is so little of either that it acts as the anarchic element in a work whose total effect is less impressive than many of its parts. Yet at least it is flexible enough, or ambiguous enough, to allow Hemingway a more varied notion of life than he has ever before achieved.

With the themes that bring out his skills most happily Hemingway has never been so good - no one else can make so memorable the events of sensory experience, how things look and move and are related to each other. From the beginning of the novel to the end one has the happy sense of the author's unremitting and successful poetic effort. So great is this effort, indeed, that one is inclined to feel that it is at times even too great, that it becomes conscious of itself almost to priggishness and quite to virtuosity. About some of the very good things - they are by now famous - one has the uneasy sense that they are rather too obviously 'performances': I mean things so admirable as the account of the massacre of the fascists by the republicans as well as things so much less good because so frankly gaudy as the description of the 'smell of death.' The really superlative passages are more modestly handled and the episodes of El Sordo on his hill and Andres making his way through the republican lines are equal to Tolstoy in his best battle-manner. But the sense of the writer doing his duty up to and beyond the point of supererogation is forced on us again in the frequent occurrence of that kind of writing of which Hemingway has always allowed himself a small and forgivable amount to deal with emotions which he considers especially difficult, delicate or noble. Obtrusively 'literary' and oddly 'feminine,' it is usually used for the emotions of love and it is always in as false and fancy taste as this:

> Now as they lay all that before had been shielded was unshielded. Where there had been roughness of fabric all was smooth with a smoothness and firm founded pressing and a long warm coolness, cool outside and warm within, long and light and closely holding, closely held, lonely, hollow-making with contours, happy-making, young and loving and now all warmly smooth with a hollowing, chest-aching, tight-held loneliness that was such that Robert Jordan felt he could not stand it....

Yet the virtuosity and the lapses of taste are but excesses of an effort which is, as a whole, remarkably successful. And if we cannot help thinking a little wryly about how much tragic defeat, how much limitation of political hope was necessary before Hemingway could be weaned from the novel of arrogant political will, neither can we help being impressed by what he has accomplished in the change.

I speak first and at some length of the style of 'For Whom the Bell Tolls' because it seems to me that the power and charm of the book arise almost entirely from the success of the style - from the success of many incidents handled to the full of their possible esthetic interest. The power and charm do not arise from the plan of the book as a whole; when the reading is behind us what we remember is a series of brilliant scenes and a sense of having been almost constantly excited, but we do not remember a general significance. Yet Hemingway, we may be sure, intended that the star-crossed love and heroic death of Robert Jordan should be a real tragedy, a moral and political tragedy which should suggest and embody the tragedy of the Spanish war. In this intention he quite fails; he gives us astonishing melodrama, which is something, but he does not give us tragedy. The clue to the failure is the essential, inner dulness of the hero, for Jordan is dull because he does not have within himself the tensions which, in historical fact, the events he lives through actually did have. Because Jordan does not reproduce in himself the moral and political tensions which existed in the historical situation, his story is at best cinematic; and since his story must provide whatever architectonic the novel is to have, the novel itself fails, not absolutely but relatively to its possibility and implied intention.

This failure illustrates as well as anything could the point of Philip Rahv's essay, The Cult of Experience in American Writing ('Partisan Review,' November-December 1940). For here again we have the imbalance which Mr. Rahv speaks of as characteristic of the American novel, on the one hand the remarkable perception of sensory and emotional fact, on the other hand an inadequacy of intellectual vitality. Consider as an illuminating detail the relation which Hemingway establishes between Robert Jordan and the leaders he admires, Golz the general and Karkov the journalist. Both are cynical and exceptionally competent men, wholly capable of understanding all the meanings of the revolutionary scene. But they are Europeans and Robert Jordan is not; like the hero of Henry James's novel, 'The American,' he knows that there are machinations going on around him, very wrong but very wonderful, which he will never be able to understand. Nor does he really want to understand as his friends do; he wants, as he says, to keep his mind in suspension until the war is won. He wants only to feel emotions and ideals, or, as a technician and a brave man, to *do* what he is told; the thinking is for others. Yet, like a Henry James character again, he must penetrate the complex secret; but he has no wish to use it, only to 'experience' it, for he likes, as he says, the feeling of being an 'insider,' which is what one becomes by losing one's American 'chastity of mind' telling political lies with the Russians in Gaylord's Hotel.

Hemingway himself, then, is wholly aware of the moral and political tensions which existed in actual fact.

Again and again, and always pungently, he brings to our notice the contradictions of a revolutionary civil war - describes the cynicism and intrigue and shabby vice of the Russian politicos, pointedly questions the political virtue of La Pasionaria, paints André Marty, in a brilliant and terrifying scene, as a homicidal psychopath under the protection of the Comintern, speaks out about the sins of Loyalist leaders and has only a small and uncertain inclination to extenuate the special sins of the Communists. Indeed, there is scarcely a charge that anti-Stalinists might have made during the war whose truth Hemingway does not in one way or another avow. Yet by some failure of mind or of seriousness, he cannot permit these political facts to become integral with the book by entering importantly into the mind of the hero. Robert Jordan, to be sure, thinks a good deal about all these things but almost always as if they were not much more than - to use the phrase of another anti-fascist - a matter of taste. He can, in Mr. Rahv's use of the word, 'experience' all the badness, but he cannot deal with it, dare not judge it.

In the end it kills him. And Hemingway knows, of course, that it kills him, for it is certainly true that of all the things that prevent Robert Jordan's despatch from arriving in time to halt the ill-fated attack and preserve his own life, it is the atmosphere of Gaylord's Hotel that is ultimately culpable; it is Marty's protected madness that makes it finally impossible to cancel the attack and that seals Jordan's fate. Were this kept in focus we should have had a personal tragedy which would have truly represented the whole tragedy of the Spanish war - the tragedy, that is, which was not merely a defeat by superior force but also a moral and political failure; for tragedy is not a matter of fact, it is a matter of value. To Robert Jordan his own death is bitter enough, but it is only the last incident of his experience; of its inherent tragic meaning, of its significance in relation to its cause, he has no awareness. Nor is his lack of awareness an intentional irony of which the reader is to be conscious; Hemingway lets the significance fade and the event becomes very nearly a matter of accident. It is, I find, rather terrifying to see where writing from naked experience can take an author; Hemingway knows that his hero must die in *some* moral circumstance and he lamely and belatedly contrives for Robert Jordan a problem of - courage. And so we get what we all like in the movies, a good fighting death, but in the face of all the potential significance of the event it is devastatingly meaningless. Courage, we are told as a last word, is all: and every nerve responds to the farewell, the flying hooves, the pain and the pathos, but we have been shuffled quite away from tragedy, which is not of fact and the nerves but of judgment and the mind.

What is the major movement of the novel is, then, a failure and a failure the more to be regretted because it has so many of the elements of great success. But there is another movement of the novel which does not fail - I mean all that part which deals with the guerilla bands of the mountains. One has to understand the genre of this to understand its success; one has to see that this part of the story is a social romance. I should like to draw on Mr. Rahv again: he remarks in another of his essays (Paleface and Redskin, 'Kenyon Review,' Summer 1939) that Hemingway may well be understood as a descendant of Natty Bumppo; (1) certainly in each of Hemingway's heroes there is a great deal of the Leatherstocking blood, though 'crossed' (as Leatherstocking himself would say) with the gentler, more sensitive blood of Uncas. And as Leatherstocking-Uncas, the perfect scout, Robert Jordan is all decision, action and good perception, far more interesting and attractive than in his character of looker-on at the political feasts of the Russians where he is a kind of Parsifal, (2) the culpable innocent who will not ask the right question. But more than the character of its hero takes its rise from Cooper - more, too, than Hemingway's 'sense of terrain' which Edmund Wilson speaks of as being like Cooper's; (3) for when we think of how clear a line there is between Uncas, Chingachgook and Tamenund, the noble Indians, and El Sordo and Anselmo and the rest of the guerilla band we see how very like Cooper's is Hemingway's romantic sense of the social and personal virtues. With Cooper, however, the social idealization is more formal and more frankly 'mythical' and perhaps it is Hemingway's greater realism which makes his social romance suspect, if not as fact then as feeling. For in a love affair with a nation, a people or a class, such as between Kipling and the sahibs or - to speak of a minor but socially interesting writer of today - between Angela Thirkell (4) and the English upper middle class, there is pretty sure to appear, sooner or later, a hatred of the outlander. Even when, like Hemingway, the lover is not himself a member of the beloved group, one cannot help sensing the implied rejection of the rest of humanity.

There is something suspect, too, I feel, in the love-story of this novel, which has so stirred and charmed the reviewers. By now the relation between men and women in Hemingway's novels has fixed itself into a rather dull convention in which the men are all dominance and knowledge, the women all essential innocence and responsive passion; these relationships reach their full development almost at the moment of first meeting and are somehow completed as soon as begun. Most significant, one feels of love in the Hemingway novels that it exists at all only because circumstances so surely doom it. We do not have to venture very deep into unexpressed meanings to find a connection between Hemingway's social myth and the pattern of his love-stories; in both there is a desperation which makes a quick grab for simple perfection, a desperation which, at the same time, makes understandable the compulsive turning to courage as the saving and solving virtue. The whole complex of attitudes is, we might guess, a way of responding to the idea of death.

About Hemingway's concern with death I do not find myself in agreement with the many critics who have found it irritating that anyone should deal with death except as a simple physical fact. I am not sure that our liberal, positive, progressive attitudes have taught us to be emotionally more competent before the idea of death, but only more silent; I cannot assume that anyone who breaks our habit of silence is, by that, doing wrong. But in Hemingway's treatment of death there is something indirect and thwarted, as though he cannot entirely break through our cultural reticences to speculate and poetize creatively upon the theme, as could, say a death-haunted man like John Donne, from whom Hemingway takes the epigraph and title of his novel. For Donne, death is the appalling negation and therefore the teacher of the ego, whereas for Hemingway it is the ego's final expression and the perfect protector of the personality. The great power of mind in Donne saved him from this sentimental error, just as it taught him how little the ego can exist by itself, how 'no man is an *Iland* intire of itselfe.' The nature and power of Hemingway's mind are such that he cannot exemplify in art the idea of the community of men, however moving and important it seems to him; he is wholly at the service of the cult of experience and the result is a novel which, undertaking to celebrate the community of men, actually glorifies the isolation of the individual ego.

Notes

1 Natty Bumppo is the woodsman-hero of Fenimore Cooper's 'Leatherstocking Tales' (1823-41).
2 Parsifal is the hero of Wagner's opera (1882), who seeks the Holy Grail.
3 See No. 65.

4 Angela Thirkell was a popular English novelist, author of 'The Brandons' (1939) and 'Love Among the Ruins' (1948).

69. MARK SCHORER, 'KENYON REVIEW'

3 (Winter 1941), 101-5

Mark Schorer (1908-77), an American novelist, critic and biographer, was the author of 'The Wars of Love' (1953), 'William Blake' (1946) and 'Sinclair Lewis' (1961). 'Kenyon Review,' edited by John Crowe Ransom in Gambier, Ohio, was a distinguished literary quarterly.

What was for long the sign of Ernest Hemingway's work - the curious tension between subject matter and style, between the themes of violence and the perfectly controlled prose - has gone. Hemingway was extraordinary among modern prose writers for exactly this reason, that he pressed his style into the service of his subject matter in a rather special way: the style was the immediate representation of the moral attitude of the author toward his material, it objectified the author's values and thus in itself was comment in writing otherwise unhampered by comment. When, however, the subject matter began to change - from violent experience itself to the expressed evaluation of violence - the manner began to change. The separation seems to take place in the story, The Snows of Kilimanjaro, but it is in the novel 'To Have and Have Not,' that the fumbling transition is clearest. The first third of this book is superb narrative in the old manner; but as Hemingway lets himself into the theme proper thereafter, the book begins to break down, and the end is a debacle, the noisy collapse of a style and technique simply unable to support their matter. Before, the style in itself was moral comment; with a change in moral attitude, that style was necessarily disrupted. In 'For Whom the Bell Tolls' we may witness a new style, less brilliant but more flexible, as it integrates itself. That is a very exciting literary spectacle.

'The Sun Also Rises' was a representation of the life that Hemingway lived and enjoyed and out of which his values came. The characters in this novel - without belief, without relation to a cultural or national past, without ideological relation to the future - submerge themselves in extravagant sensation and view life as a losing game, a sport like bullfighting which, while it is more nearly tragedy than sport because death is inevitable, is interesting only if it observes strict rules. Hemingway epitomized this not very difficult matter when, in an author's note in 'Scribner's Magazine,' he once said, 'I've known some very wonderful people who even though they were going directly to the grave ... managed to put up a very fine performance en route.' (1) This 'fine performance' is the sporting attitude, and it is dramatized in the gesture of Lady Ashley when she gives up her lover: 'You know I feel rather damned good, Jake ... it makes one feel rather good deciding not to be a bitch .... It's sort of what we have instead of God.' (2) Jake has himself observed that morality is what makes you feel good afterwards. Brett feels 'rather damned good' because she has behaved according to the tenets of that negative morality, that emphasis on the 'performance en route,' the *manner* of living, which the group has substituted for belief.

The preoccupation with bullfighting is not accidental; bullfighting is at once the most violent and the most stylized of sports. Its entire excitement depends on the degree to which the matador exposes himself to death *within the rules*. It disregards consequences, regards performance. Both are important. Courage, or unconcern for disaster, is a moral virtue: the best bullfighter works closest to the horns; the best man disregards present and impending catastrophe. Syphilis, the occupational disease of bullfighters, 'of all people who lead lives in which a disregard of consequences dominate,' is nearly commended. A blundering display of courage, however, is absurd: the matador should 'increase the amount of the danger of death'

> *within the rules provided for his protection* ... it is to his credit if he does something that he knows how to do in a highly dangerous but still geometrically possible manner. It is to his discredit if he runs danger through ignorance, through disregard of the fundamental rules....

Courage stylized, *style*, then, matters finally, and the experienced spectator looks for this; 'what they seek is honesty and true, not tricked, emotion and always classicism and the purity of execution of all the suertes, (3) and ... they want no sweetening.' Since the performance is a matter of the fighter's honor, bullfighting is a *moral* art, and style a *moral* matter.

> So far, about morals, [writes Hemingway] I know only that what is moral is what you feel good after and what is immoral is what you feel bad after and judged by these moral standards ... the bullfight is very moral to me.... (4)

In 'The Sun Also Rises,' Romero, who 'fakes' nothing in the fight, who has 'the old thing, the holding of his purity of line through the maximum of exposure,' is the one character who makes the others feel fine: he is the representation of artistic, hence of moral excellence.

All this carried directly over into Hemingway's concept of prose and into his own prose. The definition of morality and Brett's dramatization of it; the important counterpoint between danger and performance; the concept of art as moral insofar as its style is 'honest' or 'true' or 'pure' - this complex is translated as follows:

> It is much more difficult than poetry.... It can be written, *without tricks* and *without cheating*. *With nothing that will go bad afterwards*.... First, there must be talent.... Then there must be discipline.... Then there must be ... an *absolute conscience* as unchanging as the standard meter in Paris, to prevent *faking*. (5)

The style which made Hemingway famous - with its ascetic suppression of ornament and figure, its insistence on the objective and the unreflective (for good fighters do not talk), its habit of understatement (or sportsmen boast), the directness and the brevity of its syntactical constructions, its muscularity, the sharpness of its staccato and repetitive effects, 'the purity of its line under the maximum of exposure,' that is, its continued poise under the weight of event or feeling - this style is an exact transfiguration of Hemingway's moral attitude toward a peculiarly violent and chaotic experience. His style, in effect, is what he had instead of God.

Until God came.

Now that the evidence is in, the position taken by Edmund Wilson some time ago in The 'Atlantic Monthly' is indefensible. (6) Mr. Wilson argued that Hemingway's political persuasion was no persuasion at all, but a simple transfer from object to object of the desire to kill: kudu to fascist. No one would seriously contend, I think, that the very motive of 'For Whom the Bell Tolls' is not a tremendous sense of man's dignity and worth, an urgent awareness of the necessity of man's freedom, a nearly poetic realization of man's *collective* virtues. Indeed, the individual vanishes in the political whole, but vanishes precisely to defend his dignity, his freedom, his virtue. In spite of the ominous premium which the title seems to place on individuality, the real theme of this book is the relative unimportance of individuality and the superb importance of the political whole. (For fascists are men, too, and even when the bell tolls for them, it tolls for me, I believe; but the fascists in this book have scarcely any meaning as personalities, merely represent The Enemy.) Hemingway's title portends nothing more than that which we have all known: that the doom of Republican Spain was our doom. This novel is no 'War and Peace,' no 'Dynasts';(7) it is realistic, political, and deeply partisan. The defects of characterization are the conventional defects of partisan novels, in which personalities always threaten to vanish in abstractions, as, half the time, the woman Pilar becomes a Spanish Gaea, (8) Robert Jordan any vaguely attractive American, and Maria that perfect sexual creature of the private Hemingway mythology. As in so many partisan novels it is the minor characters, who bear no burden but their own, who are excellent: Sordo, the good old man Anselmo, the insane Marty, the politically exhausted Pablo, this last a magnificent portrait, and a dozen more. About their cause, which is his, Hemingway writes with a zealot's passion. And the old mould is as useless to him - as meaningless - as the old insistence on the individual's isolation, on the private pursuit of his pleasures, and on the exercise of his wholly private virtues. If the early books pled for sporting conduct on violent occasions, this book pleads the moral necessity of political violence. A different thing; indeed, a different writer.

Here is none of the grace of 'The Sun Also Rises,' none of the precise perfection of stories such as A Clean, Well-Lighted Place. This is by no means a perfect technical performance. The severe compression of the old work gives way to nearly complete relaxation. The first effect of this relaxation is evident in the pace of the narrative itself, which is leisurely. The second effect is in the fulness of detail, which Hemingway's sentences can suddenly accommodate. And the third effect is in the sentences themselves, which employ a wide variety of cadences, almost entirely new, and which are short and long, truncated and sinuous, bare or copious as they are needed. To my taste, this syntactical loosening up is almost excessive, for it quickly ramifies in many directions. Understatement is gone and overstatement too often replaces it; we are reminded of Hemingway's own remark that 'the dignity of movement of an iceberg is due to only one-eighth of it being above water.' (9) The older objectivity of style held the narrative in check in a way that this narrative is not held in check; and to this fact we may attribute many long passages of reflection not particularly well-written and not particularly necessary to the story, long reveries with which the older Hemingway would have had nothing to do. This easy method of exposition is a technical device which the older style made a luxury; here it is everywhere, and largely wasted.

Thus we gain and we lose. Because it is another story, this story could not have been told at all in the older style, and so, in the future, the flexibility of this new style, with its broader subject matter, gives us a bigger writer. How much do we care if, in relaxing, this style also sprawls sometimes, sometimes even snores a little in the sun? It is possible that moral greatness and the best manners are incompatible.

Notes

1 'Scribner's Magazine,' 81 (March 1927), 4 (excerpt of letter from Hemingway to Perkins, 7 December 1926).
2 'The Sun Also Rises' (New York, 1954), 245.
3 Predetermined maneuvers in a bullfight.
4 'Death in the Afternoon' (Harmondsworth, Middlesex, 1966), 23-4, 15, 8.
5 'Green Hills of Africa' (New York, 1935), 27.
6 See No. 62.
7 Epic poem by Thomas Hardy on the Napoleonic era (1904-8).
8 In Greek mythology, the Earth, mother of Titans.
9 'Death in the Afternoon,' 182.

70. GRAHAM GREENE, 'SPECTATOR'

166 (7 March 1941), 258

Graham Greene (b. 1904), English novelist, is the author

of 'The Power and the Glory' (1940), 'The Heart of the Matter' (1948) and 'The Human Factor' (1978).

It seems a long time now since Mr. Aldous Huxley picked a literary phrase out of one of Mr. Hemingway's books as evidence that his simple tough heroes were not quite so simple or tough as they looked. One of them, if I remember aright, had referred to Mantegna's 'bitter nails.' In return Mr. Hemingway in 'Death in the Afternoon' took Mr. Huxley and worried him as a terrier worries a rat, so that one had a vision of an odd elongated intellectual corpse tossed over Mr. Hemingway's massive shoulder. All the same, this one swallow did indicate summer. Now the title of his longest and perhaps his best novel is taken from one of Donne's sermons ('any new death diminishes me, because I am involved in Mankinde; and therefore never send to know for whom the bell tolls; it tolls for thee'), and the dialogue of his characters is heavy with the poetry of Spanish speech.

The hero, Robert Jordan, is a dynamiter in the International Brigade - 'involved in Mankinde.' He is sent behind the Fascist lines to make contact with a guerilla band, and with their help to blow up a certain bridge at the right time - so that a line of communication may be closed to reinforcements at the same moment as the Government troops under the German Golz launch a surprise attack. Everything goes wrong except the actual mission: the bridge is blown up, but the surprise fails, the attack fails, and Jordan is left stranded at the end with a broken leg, waiting to hold up for a few minutes the cavalry who are pursuing his guerilla comrades. This plain story of action is dubiously enriched by a romantic affair of love at first sight, a love which in the three days covered by the story progresses all the way from young lust to married tenderness and allows Mr. Hemingway to repeat the pathetic effects of untimely death and everlasting goodbye he worked so satisfactorily in 'Farewell to Arms' - only this time it is the man who dies. This love story - told with Mr. Hemingway's usual romantic carnality - is a pity; plot, as it were, pushes out subject, and Robert Jordan as the lover of Maria loses the kind of anonymous significance that would otherwise have attached to Jordan, the bridge-blower - he is more involved with a woman than mankind. As for Maria, she is a lay figure, chiefly remarkable for the fact that she has been violated by Fascists - this makes her to Mr. Hemingway a rather romantic character.

All the same, the bell does toll a fine and sombre note: Pilar, the ugly maternal gypsy woman, with her bull-fighting memories; Pablo, the cruel unreliable rebel who cannot even stick to treachery; Anselmo, the old hunter who hates the killing of men and misses God - these figures all stand around Jordan with the permanency of statues, and the long perspective of the hurried past and the uncertain future is filled with faces as vivid and simple as cartoons - Marty, the dangerous crazy Communist commissar who suspects treachery everywhere; Golz, the general, who knows that no attack will ever come off as it was intended; and nameless faces like that of the Spanish lieutenant-colonel, the professional soldier with his gentle manner and his care for his subordinates, and all the disappointing inhabitants of Gaylord's in Madrid - the peasant leaders who can talk Russian, La Pasionaria and the rest. And there are episodes here as fine as anything Mr. Hemingway has ever done: the appalling story of the massacre of some village Fascists, with the villagers dressed in their Sunday clothes and the drunkards spoiling the dignity of everything; the death of the guerilla leader Sordo and his band, bombed to death on a hilltop by 'planes; the scene where Pablo's followers, who are convinced of his treachery, try in vain to provoke him to some action or word that will give them the power to kill.

All these scenes were, perhaps, previously within Mr. Hemingway's range; but he has brought out of the Spanish war a subtlety and sympathy which were not there before and an expression which no longer fights shy of anything that literature can lend him (perhaps it is an advantage that his hero is a lecturer at an American university and is allowed thoughts, feelings, ideas that the old Hemingway would severely have pruned). Nobody need be afraid that this will be propaganda first and literature only second. It stands with Malraux's magnificent novel of the Republican air force as a record more truthful than history, because it deals with the emotions of men, with the ugliness of their idealism, and the cynicism and jealousy that are mixed up in the best causes - as we know now. Jordan's attitude stands, one cannot help feeling, for the author's, and is worth remembering by all writers today.

> The first thing was to win the war. If we did not win the war everything was lost. But he noticed, and listened to, and remembered everything. He was serving in a war and he gave absolute loyalty and as complete performance as he could give while he was serving. But nobody owned his mind, nor his faculties for seeing and hearing, and if he were going to form judgements he

would form them afterwards. And there would be plenty of material to draw them from.

71. V.S. PRITCHETT, 'NEW STATESMAN AND NATION'

21 (15 March 1941), 275-6

V.S. Pritchett (b. 1900), English critic, director of the 'New Statesman,' is the author of 'The Living Novel' (1946) and the autobiography 'A Cab at the Door' (1968).

After his last two books, the one about gun-running in the Caribbean and the other about big-game hunting in Tanganyika, one gave in to the hostile critics of Ernest Hemingway. Once more an American writer who had excited us by the precocity and originality of his gifts, had shown an incapacity to mature. For years Hemingway had carefully presented to us people with no thoughts in their heads; now we saw the end of the process, the empty head bashing itself against a brick wall in a frenzy of misery. Still tough on the surface, his people had become hysterical, sloppy and affected underneath, and the prose had become a manner. And then the Spanish war came. It was fortunate that the war was a Spanish war, for Hemingway, though at his best in war, had also been at his best about Spain; and instead of another visit to that country being a return to the dregs of earlier experience, the war gave him something new, gave him a new kind of intimacy with a people who were peculiarly suited to mature and deepen his type of mind. 'For Whom the Bell Tolls' is the product. It is a novel and though marred, I think, by its central love affair, it is the most adult and humane piece of writing he has done.

But before writing about this book, I should say something about the special place Hemingway occupies in the life of the last twenty years. For it is a special place. No other prose writer since Lawrence has had his influence. It lies partly in his manner of writing, which is a sort of stylisation of vernacular speech, but chiefly in his view of life and character. More than any other writer he has defined for us the personality of our own time. Such new definitions arise in every generation, for in every generation, if there has been sufficient chemical disturbance in society, a new kind of man is created and imposes himself on literature, until literature makes his outline clear for all to see - and imitate. I rather think that we have to go as far back as Byron and Byronism before we can find a type which has been stamped as vividly as Hemingway's upon a decade. Less extravagant, yet with a similar and disorientated, inverted or ambiguous romanticism, the Hemingway man, has, at any rate, captivated English-speaking society if it has not spread to the rest of Europe. It comes out above all in the poker-face reporters of the last ten years, their heads full of drink and cynicism, their hearts as sentimental as the hearts of schoolboys. More seriously, the Hemingway man is the tough technician, the average man on his own, a kind of Robinson Crusoe without spiritual life, about whose adventures there is always an aftermath of treachery, disgust, a bruised taste of suicide and death.

What has this to do especially with the last twenty years? Well, it is American, something from the dominant popular culture of the new world which has done more to set free the ordinary man than the last war or its revolutions. But that is only the background. Mr. Wyndham Lewis, in a brilliant essay, defined the Hemingway man, the typical character of his books, as 'the dumb ox,' or the helpless man in machine society who commands nothing, but 'to whom things are done.' This is a generalisation which must be applied very lightly. Compared with a character in Proust, for example, the Hemingway man seems, on the contrary, to be, above all, a 'doer.' He does not ruminate about the past; he lives in the present. He is essentially unreflective, non-sedentary, without judgment. Spiritually in chains, he has great physical freedom. He is a man on his own, who can only act. He cannot think or reflect or understand his position. His emotional responses are limited to what is 'fine' or what is 'like hell.' He is the killer who can only kill and gape at the vacuum afterwards; the 'bum' who merely 'goes places' and still finds himself; the boxer, the bullfighter, the hunter who faces the blankness of success and takes to women or the bottle to get away from it. The one satisfying thing in the lives of all the Hemingway characters is their technical efficiency. It is the only point on which they are self-critical. Their one fear - making a false judgment of the bull, pulling the trigger too soon, misreading the spoor, choosing the wrong moment to make love, not knowing how to take their drink, lacking 'one of the answers.' Failure in these respects makes them 'feel bad'; otherwise they just 'feel good.' Undisciplined in everything else they are intensely disciplined by their craft.

To a reflective man who knows how to live in the imagination, who has the leisure to cultivate his sensibility, who abhors violence, who does not wish to talk unless he has something to say, who mistrusts intuition, who is constantly concerned with putting an order on his experience and who, enjoying the freedoms of the mind, dislikes to be a dog wagged by the tail of his instincts, the tough Hemingway man is as boring as Robinson Crusoe would have been to Addison. (1) But the Addisons are at a disadvantage in our kind of world. Urbane, they are fixed and unadaptable. Sedate on the throne of civilisation they can only deplore that every few minutes a piece more of it is washed away. No; what has attracted us to the Hemingway man is his adaptability, the lightness of his luggage, his mobility, the way he has, so to speak, averaged down his demands. To anyone under 45 the natural climate of our lives has been war and a process of de-civilisation which disheartens our elders who have known better, but in which we have got to live out our lives. The Hemingway man has become an expert in de-civilisation. We admire him because he has made terms with his time.

It was Aldous Huxley who first pointed out the element of fake in Hemingway's attitude. An educated man, he was posing as non-educated and joining the general attack on culture. The criticism was well made, and the manner in which Hemingway's work went to pieces fully justifies it. In the end Hemingway had simply become sex, guns, booze and sons of bitches. A writer like Malraux, for example, is immeasurably superior to Hemingway in stating the intelligent and sensitive man's reactions to de-civilisation and war. He is also a far better writer on war and violence. But turning now to 'For Whom the Bell Tolls,' one can see that Huxley's criticism has been taken. It is not simply that the central character, the American dynamiter, Robert Jordan, is an educated man, which puts the book in the right key, though that is a big change. The point is that Hemingway has found a background of ideas he can respect. In the Spaniards he has discovered a non-thinking, instinctive people outside of our culture, refractory to Western ideas, whose values are fabulous and, ultimately, mystical, and who accept, as European humanism does not, the imminence of death. People who know the passions of action with a greater intensity than any other, the Spaniards know too the reactions from it, the aftermath, and upon what would otherwise be emptiness they have imposed the great ritual of their gravity and their remorse.

The scene of 'For Whom the Bell Tolls' is laid in the heights of the Guadarrama mountains in the second year of the civil war. This is an inaccessible no-man's-land neglected by either army, and hidden in a cave among the pines are a small guerilla band who from time to time have gone down to blow up the Fascist trains and loot them. The band, led by Pablo, are the relics of a party who had perpetrated a theatrical and awful massacre in their village. Jordan makes contact with them because he has to get their help in the blowing up of a bridge in one of the gorges, an act which is vital to the new Republican offensive. It is an essential part of the Hemingway philosophy that this act shall be futile, for the offensive is already betrayed to the Fascists. One sees a tragedy within a tragedy; that will be a futile doom in any case. The story itself moves elaborately and slowly through the two or three days with which it deals, and it reaches moments of intense drama. First of all Pablo has cold feet. The guerrillero is haunted by an incapacity to repeat the glory of his atrocities in the village. He is drinking hard and vacillating. He will either murder Jordan or betray everyone. Anyway, he realises, his game is up, his power gone. Alternatively Jordan or his band will murder Pablo in self-protection. Then there is a tremendous fight when the Fascists stumble upon a neighbouring guerilla leader; and, lastly, there is the long-drawn-out excitement of the mining of the bridge and the get-away. These, the main episodes, are linked by Jordan's love affair with the girl Maria, a lyrical piece of writing, charming in its rendering of the talk of the lovers, but fatal to the austerity of the narrative. The real tragedy is, after all, not Jordan's, but the maiming of this band of peasants, who are not so much scoundrels as medieval people torn up by the roots and no longer responsible outside the protective pattern of their normal lives. Pablo is a disgusting man, a killer, a sadist, a fat pig-eyed debauchee; yet he has an extraordinary dignity and pathos, the coward's tragic foresight. Pilar, his woman, once the mistress of bull-fighters, is a primitive force; the old man who humbly has devoted his life to the Republic and scrupulously maintains his new atheism against the ever-rising tide of his religious memories, is a most subtle and sympathetic portrait of a good man praying, not to avoid evil, but to be delivered from it; and the gypsy, irresponsible, witty, without conscience, childish, is a brilliant portrait. When the band is voting on the question of killing Pablo, all monotonously and calmly say, 'Kill him.' Until it comes to the gypsy who says with the childish simplicity of generations of hagglers, 'Sell him.'

The great quality, as we should expect, is in the talk. We know by now Hemingway's power with the words and accent of dialogue; but here, in his astonishingly real Spanish conversation, he has surpassed anything I have ever seen. Keeping close to the literal Castillian phrase with its Elizabethan nobility, he gets the laconic power of its simple statements and also the terrific rhetoric of its obscenity. The Spanish peasant divides his conversation between the two modes, reaching heights of classical formality, and depths of obscene rage, which have the air of incantation. Mr. Hemingway understands the hierarchy of Spanish blasphemy, the proper place of each rococo phrase. The scene in which Agustin attempts to provoke Pablo is both a fine piece of measured drama and excellent observation of the proper progress from one insult to the next.

The narrative in 'For Whom the Bell Tolls' is studied and intense. This is partly due to the breaking down of the prose into monosyllables and to the repetitions in people's thoughts and speech. Tedious as this sometimes is, it is an effective way of catching the murmur of life, the sort of sing-song which runs through human affairs. This kind of monologue is very impressive in such passages as when the old peasant is meditating on his dislike of the necessity of killing and his belief that a great act of penitence - 'something very strong' - will be needed afterwards, which reads like one of the Psalms. But the outstanding things in the book are not the episodes of the main story at all, in which we are indeed sometimes too conscious of each individual brick that has gone to make it; but the two stories, short stories they really are, told by Pilar, Pablo's woman. This woman in real life would be a born storyteller, one impelled to relate events as if she were the voice of all human suffering, ambition and fatality. She is, in her way, as formidable as La Celestina, a mixture of Lady Macbeth and the Wife of Bath. (2) She has two stories. One is her account of how the revolution started in the town where she and Pablo were living and how Pablo began his revolutionary career. She describes how one by one the Fascists were taken out of the Town Hall, beaten with flails, and then pitched over a cliff. Horrifying and sickening, the story has nevertheless that theatrical variety of incident, that primitive realism and capacity to catch every emotion that was felt by the people as a whole. It is like a crowd scene from Zola, but without any dubious symbolism written in. Her power as a storyteller is in making the horror human. The second story, from which I will quote a passage, is an account of her life with an earlier lover, a bull fighter, and of the banquet which was held in his honour. This is a wonderful story and Mr. Hemingway has set it in the midst of one of those pedantic Spanish disputes about the man's merits as a torero. She is describing the meal. The head of his last bull is on the wall covered by a cloth and will eventually be unveiled in his honour:

> I was at the table and others were there, Pastora, who is uglier than I am, and the Niña de los Peines, and other gypsies and whores of great category. It was a banquet, small but of great intensity and almost of a violence due to a dispute between Pastora and one of the most significant whores over a question of propriety. I myself was feeling more than happy and I was sitting by Finito and I noticed he would not look up at the bull's head, which was shrouded in a purple cloth as the images of the saints are covered in church during the week of the passion of our former Lord.

And Finito, the bull fighter sits there, smiling at everyone but staring now and then in a horror of fear at the shrouded head of the long horned bull on the wall and murmuring to himself, 'No, No, No,' and spitting blood into his napkin. He is dying of tuberculosis. Someone tells a story against a former manager, a story unfavorable to gypsies and the gypsy woman Pastora 'intervenes':

> I intervened to quiet Pastora and another *Gitana* (3) intervened to quiet me and the din was such that no one could distinguish any words which passed except the one great word whore which roared out above all other words.

But quiet was obtained at last, the speech made, the bull's head unveiled.

> Everyone shouted and applauded, and Finito sank further back in the chair and then everyone was quiet and looking at him and he said, 'No, No,' and looked at the bull and pulled further back and then he said, 'No' very loudly and a big blob of blood came out and he didn't even put up a napkin and it slid down his chin.... He looked around at the table and said 'No' once more and then he put the napkin up to his mouth and then he just sat there like that and said nothing and the banquet which had started so well and promised to mark an epoch in hilarity and good fellowship was not a success.

I have said little about the brief strictly political part of the book. Jordan is mainly struck by the religious fervour of the Communist rank and file and bewildered, though suspending judgment, by the 'realism' he found among the leaders. The thing was, he thought, to win the war. Afterwards he would see. The political portraits are short but they are packed with life, sceptical observation and shrewdness. His Marty is savage. His anarchists are very funny, his Russians very complicated. There is no doubt that, if you cut out Jordan's romance, the Spanish war has restored to Hemingway his seriousness as a writer.

Notes

1 Joseph Addison (1672-1719), the poet, essayist and statesman, was founder, with Richard Steele, of the 'Spectator.'
2 A bawd in 'La Celestina' (1499) by Fernando de Rojas, who serves as go-between for young lovers. The Wife of Bath is one of the principal pilgrims in Chaucer's 'Canterbury Tales' (1386-1400).
3 Gypsy.

72. ARTURO BAREA, 'HORIZON'

3 (May 1941), 350-61

Arturo Barea (1897-1957), a Spanish novelist and critic, was the author of 'The Forge' (1946), 'Lorca' (1944) and 'Unamuno' (1952), 'Horizon' was an excellent literary journal, edited in London by Cyril Connolly.

Ernest Hemingway's new novel, 'For Whom the Bell Tolls', was cast for the success it is now reaping along the whole front line from Left Wing reviewers to Hollywood producers.

It is a tale of violence, war and love, blood and thunder on the Spanish soil; it combines the romanticism and glamour of bullfighting with the ugly realism of a civil war; it is heroic, sensational, sensual, lyrical, and honestly anti-fascist without going in for politics; it contains one set of characters - Castilian peasants - which deserve the cliché praise 'sober in outline like an old woodcut', and another set of intellectually intriguing and exotic characters - Russian journalists and generals. It shows the inner problems of the author through his hero, the American scholar and Communist who is serving behind the Fascist lines, a true man of action, yet wrestling with his very uncommunistic, honest-to-god humanist soul. It describes the violence and horror of the Spanish War so that the reader who had been in love with a strange Spain of his own nostalgia sees all his vague imaginings assuming shape and life, and feels himself to be penetrating into the innermost recesses of the Spanish soul. It is written with an excellent technique of realism, and yet spares delicate feelings by putting the foulest oaths and obscenities in Spanish and italics (English readers may or may not look up the words in a dictionary; in any case they would not find half of them), thus noticeably reducing the amount of muckings, sons of bitches and hells.

I myself was fascinated by the book and felt it to be honest in so far as it renders Hemingway's real vision. And yet I find myself awkwardly alone in the conviction that, as a novel about Spaniards and their war, it is unreal and, in the last analysis, deeply untruthful, though practically all the critics claim the contrary, whatever their objections to other aspects of the book:

> 'You come to understand much of Spain which is not always, or even often, to be found in the histories.'
>
> 'Hemingway knows his Spain profoundly.... In miniature, Hemingway has written the war the Spanish were fighting.'
>
> '...here, in his astonishingly real Spanish conversation, he has surpassed anything I have ever seen.... Mr. Hemingway understands the hierarchy of Spanish blasphemy, the proper place of each rococo phrase.... Horrifying and sickening, the story has nevertheless that theatrical variety of incidents, that primitive realism and capacity to catch every emotion that was felt by the people as a whole....'
>
> 'The Spanish peasants who help him in his dangerous errand are superbly described ... all are alive and astonishingly themselves; Mr. Hemingway has never done anything better.'

As a Spaniard, and one who has lived through the period of our war which provides Hemingway with his stage setting, I came point by point to the following somewhat different conclusions:

Reading 'For Whom the Bell Tolls', you will indeed come to understand some aspects of Spanish character and life, but you will misunderstand more, and more important ones at that.

Ernest Hemingway does know 'his Spain'. But it is precisely his intimate knowledge of this narrow section of Spain which has blinded him to a wider and deeper understanding, and made it difficult for him to 'write the war we have been fighting'.

Some of his Spanish conversations are perfect, but others, often of great significance for the structure of the book, are totally un-Spanish. He has not mastered the intricate 'hierarchy of Spanish blasphemy' (anyhow the most difficult thing for a foreigner in any language, since it is based on ancient taboos and half-conscious superstitions). He commits a series of grave linguistic-psychological mistakes in this book - such, indeed, as I have heard him commit when he joked with the orderlies in my Madrid office. Then, we grinned at his solecisms because we liked him.

Hemingway has understood the emotions which our 'people as a whole' felt in the bull-ring, but not those which it felt in the collective action of war and revolution.

Some of the Castilian peasants Hemingway has created are real and alive, but others are artificial or out of place. Although all are magnificently described, in none of them has he touched the roots.

Ernest Hemingway himself and his book are of such importance that I think it necessary to specify, and if I can, to prove and explain my objections. After all, they cover not only the literary picture of Spaniards and their war, but also the quality of Hemingway's creative work in this instance, and the problem of his realism as a whole. The strength of his artistry makes fiction sound like distilled reality. The reader may well follow the lead of the critics; he may accept the book because it is a powerful work of art and implicitly believe in the inner truthfulness of Hemingway's Spain. For purely Spanish reasons I want to fight against this danger of a spurious understanding of my people.

The book relates an episode in the Republican guerilla warfare of May 1937. It takes place in the Sierra of the province of Segovia, and the *guerrilleros* concerned come from a small town, or rather village, in the province of Avila. (It is more correct to call these *pueblos* villages than towns, as does Hemingway.) Both the provinces are a part of Old Castile.

The men from those Castilian mountain villages are dour and hard, poor and distrustful. They have grown up on a soil which the snow covers half of the year and the sun scorches the other half. They are walled up in their own narrow lives, each working hard on his meagre bit of land and hunting the wild animals in the mountains. Their fierce self-defence against the hardships of their existence and of the very climate makes them shut the door of their community against any stranger, beyond a momentary and generous hospitality. They do not allow the gipsies to stay overnight in their villages, but often chase them away with stones. They have come to hate their *señores* (1) - all those who exploit them through money, position or power - and when they feel deceived by the highest power, their God, they turn against him with the same ferocious resentment. They do not talk much, nor do they talk easily; their turns of speech are heavy, simple and direct, with the dignity of simplicity and of pride in their manly strength.

I think Hemingway has seen all that and striven to express it. Some of his *guerrilleros*, above all Old Anselmo and El Sordo, belong to this soil. Yet he does not know the foundations of their lives and minds. Indeed, how could he? This is a Spain he has seen but never lived. And thus he commits the fatal error of putting the men of a Sierra village under the leadership of two people from the Spain he knows thoroughly, from the world of the *toreros* and their hangers-on: Pilar, the old gipsy tart, and Pablo, the horse-dealer of the bull-ring.

Such a situation is utterly impossible. The men from a township in the Sierra of Avila - from a place as primitive as Hemingway himself paints it - could never have admitted and accepted a Pilar and a Pablo as their leaders. The gipsy and the gipsified horse-dealer might have lived, and even become local leaders, in one of those villages in the Sierra de Guadarrama which Hemingway knows and which lives on tourists and week-enders from Madrid; but then again, these villages could never have produced Hemingway's peasant *guerrilleros*. That is to say, the old gipsy whore from Andalusia with her lover, the horse-dealer, grouped together with peasants from Old Castile constitute a glaring incongruity.

This lack of realism is, however, necessary for the pattern of Hemingway's book. It permits him to introduce, through Pilar, admirable descriptions of the people of the bull-ring a quarter of a century ago. It also permits him to construct scenes of savage brutality built round Pablo, whose whole mind is drenched with the smell of the Plaza de Toros and who is capable of studied, deliberate cruelty.

The scenes of the book which seem to have impressed themselves deeply on the minds of every non-Spanish reader as being barbarously realistic and true are thus the result of a purely artificial choice of dramatis personæ.

When Hemingway decided not to describe a group of purely Castilian guerilla fighters led by the most brutal and brave male among them, but to introduce the colourful gipsy woman and the bull-ring assassin, he blocked his own way to the reality of the Spanish War and Spanish violence.

Pilar relates in a painfully vivid narration what happened in the small Sierra township after the outbreak of the Rebellion. First she describes the assault on the barracks of the Guardia Civil, and this part of the tale is perfect in its realism. Just so it happened in many places throughout Spain. Then she tells how Pablo (who, as I must again emphasize, could never have become a leader in such a village in real life) organizes a monstrous and elaborate lynching of the local 'fascists', with the underlying intention of involving the whole population in the same blood guilt. He organizes this lynching like one of the old village bull-baitings or *capeas*. The men are in the square, most of them in their festive clothes, all with their wine-skins and armed with flails, sticks and knives. The doors of the Town Hall open to let out the prisoners one by one; they have to pass through the narrow space between a double line of men until they reach the edge of a cliff. The men in the lines, drunk with wine and cruelty, beat and knife their enemies to death, jeering at them the while. The bodies are thrown over the precipice. The women look on from the balconies, and in the end are shamefully drunk with blood and bestiality, just like the men.

Now, it happened in countless small towns and villages that underfed peasants and labourers killed the local *señores* who had starved them for years and sneered at them: 'Let the Republic feed you!' At first, there was almost everywhere some man or other, more savage than the rest, who wanted to lynch the 'fascists' and shouted: 'Let's tear their guts out!' - guts being a euphemism for which Hemingway uses the crude Spanish word in italics. Then two or three of the most hated men would be killed in the streets, brutally, in an outbreak of blind fury; but there was no deliberate torture. The others were shot at night on the threshing floors in the open fields where the women could not see it, nor even hear the shots. They were killed and then they were buried. Often those who had killed in revenge were naïve enough to give their victims a burial in the cemetery so that they should rest 'in hallowed ground'.

Hemingway must have sensed this. He had to invent his Pablo, the crafty, potential murderer, accustomed to seeing horses slit open in the bull-ring, in order to stage-manage this collective blood-orgy. Yet even if a Pablo could possibly have organized such a lynching, it is unthinkable that the community of a Castilian village would have followed him to the end of the revolting butchery, and not sooner have lynched Pablo himself. It is even more unthinkable that the butcher could have remained the leader of honest men who became guerilla fighters because of their own convictions.

The brutal violence of Spaniards, which exists together with a dark acceptance of life and death, is always individual. It draws strength and pride from a very simple awareness of their own masculinity. In the explosion of that stored-up violence people would agree to kill their enemies, to kill them quickly with a straight bullet or a straight knife, without investigation or trial. Nobody except of course the few with diseased brains who must have existed, thought, or could have thought, of organizing slaughter like a *fiesta* and of putting on festive clothes to get drunk on blood. In those village bull-baitings which Hemingway describes through the day-dreaming of his young guerrillero Andrés, the people would finish up intoxicated with mass cruelty; yet there is still a profound difference. Even if those *capeas* were nothing other than collective killings, the killing was not that of a tame cow but of a wild bull. Brutal, yes; but demanding personal bravery and the risk to life and limb from every individual. Thousands of young men have died in *capeas*. But if a milch cow had been put in the middle of the village square, nobody would have touched her, because a thing like that *no tiene gracia*, it would have held no attraction. The *gracia* does not consist in killing the bull, but in knowing that he can kill you. Everything else would destroy your claim to manliness.

Hemingway has forgotten this when he describes the collective killing of defenceless enemies in a bull-ring atmosphere. And yet, this is the kind of violence which the common reader would be apt to expect from Spaniards; the supreme skill of the narration makes it seem stark reality. To me, this is the worst aspect of Hemingway's fundamental mistake: he falsifies most plausibly the causes and the actual form of the tragic violence of my people - not knowing that he falsifies it, because much of what he describes does exist in the Spain of the bull-ring, the Spain he understands and seeks to find in every Spaniard.

The chain of errors prolongs itself, always springing from the same main source. Hemingway balances this story of a Republican atrocity by equally realistic-sounding and equally false stories of fascist atrocities. Again, the most important incident is one of collective violence. The heroine, Maria, has been violated by a group of fascists and she tells her lover about it.

At the beginning of the Civil War, Franco's Moorish soldiers committed rape. I myself knew of concrete cases. Afterwards, the Spanish fascist officers did their best to put an end to these outrages, although they themselves went on committing other forms of brutality inherent in civil war and fascist mentality. I have never heard of a collective violation by Falangists, and I do not believe it ever happened. Such a thing is contrary to Spanish psychology. I want to make it quite clear that I do not deny the potential and actual bestiality of Spaniards, but I do deny the psychological possibility of a collective sexual act. The consciousness of his own virility would make it impossible for a Spaniard to want the union of his body with that of a woman still warm and moist from another male. He would loathe it physically. Again, Hemingway describes most vividly what is intrinsically wrong; again, he is wrong because he fails to understand the individual quality of Spanish violence. Since these are the crucial parts of his psychological pattern, his whole picture of the Spaniards at war is distorted and unreal.

There is, however, another group scene which is magnificent in psychology and detail. The *guerrilleros* feel that Pablo is about to turn traitor, and try to provoke him to a step which would justify killing him. Although they believe his death to be necessary for their common good, they do not attack him together and finish him off, which would be easy; they stage a discussion which proceeds from insult to insult, true to life in its ceremonial violence, and try to incite Pablo to challenge one of them. That one would then be ready to kill him face to face. He would be ready to stab the bull - if the bull accepts the fight.

There are other Spanish scenes and characters which are excellently observed. The old Anselmo, with his grave problems of life and death, is completely genuine. The fascist officers are real, although their actions are artificially constructed. Everything connected with the world of the bull-fight is vivid and essentially truthful. El Sordo, the peasant leader of another guerilla band operating near Pablo's, is as much in the right place as Pablo is in the wrong. As far as he is described in his brief appearances, he is typical of his kind: primitive, harsh, straight, and ingenuous, continuing to live and fight though he knows that the future holds no hope. In the end he dies with a simple, brutal and unsentimental dignity: he dies, killing.

But even the genuine characters are curiously detached from their background. One never quite knows why they fight for the Republic, one only feels their stoic loyalty. There is no growth and no future in them. And yet it had been precisely their hope and belief in a constructive future which had set the Spanish labourers and peasants in motion.

Less relevant for Hemingway's treatment of the Spanish War, but interesting in view of his conception of the Spanish character, is the fact that the love story between the young American, Robert Jordan, and Maria is pure romancing, at least in so far as the Spanish girl is concerned. I cannot judge - for I cannot feel and associate in English - whether the love scenes are convincing. They may be good writing, though they do not seem so to me. They are certainly unrealistic in their psychology of the female partner.

A Spanish girl of the rural middle class is steeped in a tradition in which influences from the Moorish harem and the Catholic convent mix. She could not ask a stranger, a foreigner, to let her come into his bed the very first night after they had met. This, however, is what Maria does. She could not do it and keep the respectful adoration of the members of her guerilla group who know the history of her violation. They would call her a bitch on heat, not because she sleeps with a foreigner, but because she offers herself to him at once without even having been asked by him. Maria's ignorance of kissing and love is another impossible fiction. Such mental innocence may be found in other layers of Spanish society, among girls who had no other contact with life but their Father Confessor and the Holy Sisters of their convent school. In this, the most unreal character of the book, there is also a particularly marked discrepancy between social background and excessively lyrical language. This belongs, however, to the general question of the language used by the Spaniards throughout the book.

It is here that the artificiality of Hemingway's Spain and the gaps in his actual knowledge of the Spanish mind show themselves most clearly. The Castilian peasants speak forcefully and simply. Their language can be austere, it can express a sombre kind of hilarity. They often cover their resistance to expressing their own more complicated emotions by fierce blasphemy. All this has been said often, and Hemingway knows it. But when it comes to rendering the dignity and sobriety of their speech, he invents an artificial and pompous English which contains many un-English words and constructions, most of which cannot even be admitted as literal translations of the original Spanish. To prove this would require much space and would sound merely pedantic, but I want to give an example:

Agustin says: 'Also I have a boredom in these mountains.' (Hemingway-Jordan had commented on the fact that Spanish peasants use the abstract word *aburrimiento*, boredom; in reality, they hardly ever use it.) In such a case, the Castilian peasant would quite simply say: '*Además me aburro en estas montañas*,' or '*Estas montañas me aburren*,' of which the English equivalents are: 'Also, I'm bored in these mountains,' or 'These mountains bore me.'

The curious translation, which is no real translation, wants to impress on the reader the abstract quality of the peasant's speech. Yet it is precisely characteristic of the Castilian of the people that it shuns abstract nouns and rather expresses the abstract idea as personified concrete action such as 'the mountains bore me.' Hemingway continually sins against this spirit of the language in both the choice of words and the structure of the phrases in his dialogues between Spaniards. It seems to me that poise and simplicity of language should be rendered by equally poised, simple and natural language. The quality of dignity must flow out of directness, not out of hollow and artificial solemnity. I resent Spaniards in a serious book speaking like Don Adriano de Armado, the 'Fantastical Spaniard' of 'Love's Labour's Lost'. As a writer, I would be unhappy if Spanish dialogue I had written were to be translated into something as affected and artificial as: 'I encounter it to be perfectly normal,' when all I have said in Spanish was: *Lo encuentro perfectamente normal* - 'I find it perfectly normal'; or into: 'You have terminated already?', when I have said: *Habeis terminado ya?* - 'Have you finished already?'

Now, this matter of the treatment of idiomatic speech in a translation is most difficult, in any language. Yet Hemingway's solution, which sounds like utter realism, is in point of fact the very contrary. It makes the understanding of shades almost impossible to any reader who does not know Spanish, and it removes the Castilian figures to a plane of unreality where strange phrases and strange psychology run riot. The fact that geniune Spanish swear-words and idioms are copiously scattered all over the pages only adds to this unreality.

The erroneous use of blasphemy and obscene language reveals very neatly how Hemingway has failed to grasp certain subtleties of Spanish language and psychology. Instead of a long list I will give two instances, among the most striking in the book:

Robert Jordan continuously addresses Maria as 'Rabbit', in both English and Spanish, in intimacy and in public. Now, the Spanish word happens to be one of the more frequent and vulgar euphemisms for the female sexual organ. Jordan is described as knowing all the intricacies of Spanish double meanings. Had he really addressed his girl like this in public, it would have provoked a truly Rabelaisian outburst.

The other instance derives from a deeper misunderstanding.

One of the *guerrilleros* asks Robert about Maria: 'How is she in bed?' Another, who himself loves Maria and explains to Robert that she is no whore because she slept with him, says: 'And thy care is to *joder* with her all night?'

It is strictly impossible for a Spaniard to ask another man how his wife or lover is 'in bed'. It would break a taboo which is only lifted in the case of prostitutes. No Spaniard would use the word *joder*: the ugliest verb for the sexual act, and one which expresses not the joy but the nausea of sexual union, about a woman he respects and whom the other man loves. It would inevitably provoke a fight. But Hemingway-Jordan discusses the matter serenely, Jordan unaware that he has lost face by accepting an insult, Hemingway unaware that the use of the word by Agustin and its acceptance by Jordan gives away the fact that his own real knowledge of Spaniards is still confined to the world of 'Death in the Afternoon'.

When Hemingway came to Madrid in early Spring 1937, he came with the apprehensions of a man who had been hurt and twisted by the Great War, and who was now voluntarily exposing himself to bombs and shells, afraid of being afraid once more and eager to share the experience of a people's struggle. He came with the apprehensions of a man who, many years before, had found an escape from his inner helplessness in the animal brutality of the world of the Spanish bull-ring, after having been scarred by the disciplined and dull violence of modern war, and who now was afraid of having lost the Spain he knew and loved.

I remember him vividly now, as I knew him in those months: big and lumbering, with the look of a worried boy on his round face, diffident and yet consciously using his diffidence as an attraction, a good fellow to drink with, fond of dirty jokes 'pour épater l'Espagnol',(2) questioning, sceptical and intelligent in his curiosity, skilfully stressing his political ignorance, easy and friendly, yet remote and somewhat sad.

I think he had once taken Spain, the Spain of toreros, wealthy young *señoritos*, (3) gipsies, tarts, tipsters and so on, rather as one takes drugs. This colourful and purposeless game with life and death which followed rigid and ancient rules must have responded to some inner need of his. He wrote what to my knowledge is the best book on the bull-ring, 'Death in the Afternoon'. When he came back to Spain into our war, tired of describing and observing the flabby violence of American gangsterdom, he found few traces of the world he knew. The great toreros with whom he had been friends were on the side of the fascists. The gipsies had lost their market and had disappeared, many of them to the trenches.

Hemingway mixed with the soldiers in the bars more than with the pretentious Left-Wing intellectuals. He made many friends, as one makes friends drinking and joking together. Yet he lived the somewhat unreal life of a war correspondent in the shell-pitted Hotel Florida, among foreign journalists, officers of the International Brigades on leave, and a motley crowd of tourists and tarts. He could speak well with Spaniards, but he never shared their lives, neither in Madrid, nor in the trenches. The commander of the International Brigades, a man who appeared to us Spaniards the epitome of ugly prussianism, explained to him the strategic and tactical details of the battle of Madrid and the battle of Guadalajara.(4) Kolzoff, the correspondent of 'Pravda', gave him his cynical but shrewd explanations of life behind the scenes. Hemingway had access to the strictly guarded world of the Hotel Gaylord and he came to know its inmates, the Russians and the International Communist functionaries. And he admired them, secretly sceptical, and yet with a naïve longing to share their facility of decision. He must have had a bad conscience because he could not become part of the Spanish fight, nor part of that other political fight which seemed so clear-cut to those Russians and Communists.

In 'For Whom the Bell Tolls', there is the sublimation of all these experiences. The world of the Hotel Gaylord is evoked with an astonishing accuracy of detail; the non-Spanish figures of the book are all life-like portraits, some under their real names, such as the disastrous André Marty; others, like Kolzoff, slightly idealized and thinly disguised. What Hemingway did not do, but would have liked to be capable of doing, and what he actually felt is mirrored in his hero, Robert Jordan, who is left dying at the end of the book, not so much because the inner necessity of the tale demands it, as because Ernest Hemingway could not really believe in his future.

And then there is Spain. Hemingway could describe with truthfulness and art what he had seen from without, but he wanted to describe more. He wished for a share in the Spanish struggle. Not sharing the beliefs, the life and the suffering of the Spaniards, he could only shape them in his imagination after the image of the Spain he knew. His old obsession with violence pushed him into a track which only led him still further away from a share in that new and still chaotic Spanish life.

Thus the inner failure of Hemingway's novel - its failure to render the reality of the Spanish War in imaginative writing - seems to me to be due to the fact that he was always a spectator who wanted to be an actor, and who wanted to write as if he had been an actor. Yet it is not enough to look on: to write truthfully you must live, and you must feel what you are living.

Notes

1 Masters.
2 'To amaze the Spaniard,' a variant of 'pour épater le bourgeois.'
3 Fashionable men.
4 General Emilio Kléber commanded the XI International Brigade during the siege of Madrid.

73. W.H. MELLERS, 'SCRUTINY'

10 (June 1941), 93-9

'To Have and Have Not' was such a wickedly bad book that one began to despair of Mr. Hemingway's reputation. It was chaotic and it was insincere; and chaos and insincerity are not faults typical of his work. It is his neatness, his condensation, his honesty in accepting the stringent limitations of the extravagantly simple values he starts from, that have given his writing that restricted power and coherence which it may be said, at its best, to possess. For Mr. Hemingway can manage his own little estate with commendable efficiency, fearless of bulls and aggressive intruders; only outside the well-fenced paddock lurk dangers against which his brand of courage is helpless. We can see from 'To Have and Have Not' how, seeking to manage wider issues, he ceases to manage anything, least of all himself.

We might have thought Mr. Hemingway's day was over, yet now comes 'For Whom the Bell Tolls,' selling umpteen thousand copies and being transformed into a film on the one hand, and on the other being acclaimed by the high-brow critics as his most adult work to date, a major contribution and one of the great novels of the twentieth century. Now it is true that the book contains an amount of admirably clean and efficient writing, and that it is by a very hefty piece Mr. Hemingway's most extensive work of fiction; but it is not necessarily condemnatory if one adds that in no other respect should the book be referred to as 'great.'

The Spanish war presented Mr. Hemingway with what used to be known as a golden opportunity, because it enabled him to elaborate his stock counters and typical situations with a detailed precision and authenticity which came from first-hand experience - to turn reporting, as he has so often done, into a small kind of art. I have written previously in 'Scrutiny' (December, 1939) of what I take to be the essence of the Hemingway situation and the Hemingway world and there is no need to restate it. But it is important to stress that the new book deals in precisely similar counters - that in my opinion any talk of more complex and delicate values cannot be substantiated from the text. The hero, it is true, is a university professor who has moved in more exalted circles than (say) the hero of 'A Farewell to Arms'. But his background of 'old evenings in cafés, chestnut trees that would be in bloom now in this month ... book-shops, kiosks, galleries, the Parc Montsouris, the Stade Buffalo, the Butte Chaumont' and so forth, is not so far from the 'light and cleanness and order' which have always been Mr. Hemingway's positives, and is very close indeed to the cosmopolitan world of the curious creatures that made up the personnel of books like 'Fiesta.' Obviously, being 'formally educated and well-bred' or well-read won't turn a starling into a popinjay; and that Robert Jordan lives fundamentally by the values of the Hemingway code is stated explicitly in a conversation which he has with Pilar:

> You are a very cold boy.
> No, he said, I do not think so.
> No. In the head you are very cold.

It is that I am very preoccupied with my work.
But you do not like the things of life?
Yes. Very much. But not to interfere with my work.
You like to drink, I know. I have seen.
Yes. Very much. But not to interfere with my work.
And women?
I like them very much, but I have not given them much importance.

Jordan is too, then, the Hollywooden Hero: in a moment I will discuss his relations to the particular situation described in this novel.

The story tells how a young American fighting for the Republican cause is engaged upon the dynamiting of a bridge in a desolate mountain pass. He is living with, and is helped by, a band of peasants who have been waging guerilla warfare under the leadership of a somewhat dissipated desperado called Pablo. During the few days that comprise the action he has a brief love-affair with a girl, Maria, whom the peasants have rescued from the Fascists, there is anxiety over the weather and suspected treachery on the part of Pablo; but the bridge is finally blown and the band seeks to make its escape. During the migration Jordan is shot in the leg, the girl and the band are persuaded to continue their journey, and Jordan is left with a sub-machine gun to await the arrival of the Fascists and his death. It is not, you see, a cheerful story, especially since the utility of the bridge-blowing operation, on which the whole action hinges, is invalidated by the fact that the intended Government attack has been betrayed to the Fascists in advance. But the tragedy is as much that of the Spanish people as it is Jordan's. They are all people deprived of home and creed and the traditions of civilized life: the Spanish war is interpreted - it is one possible interpretation - as the most fundamental Hemingway situation.

Much has been written of Mr. Hemingway's understanding of the mentality of the Spanish people, probably justly enough. But that is not, I think, the point. Hemingway uses his Spaniards in a kind of choric fashion, their stylized speech being another version of the stylization of the Hemingway language. On the whole this chorus, particularly Anselmo, seems to indicate the attitude to a disintegrating society which Mr. Hemingway himself regards as most praiseworthy or (as he would say) 'honourable.' Anselmo, torn from his Catholic God and finding no other salvation, is in a sense the central figure, whose significance is summarized in any of his reflections on the moral implications of the war:

> Clearly I miss Him, having been brought up in religion. But now a man must be responsible to himself.... I think that after the war there will have to be some great penance done for the killing. If we no longer have religion after the war then I think there must be some form of civic penance organised that all may be cleansed from the killing or else we will never have a true and human basis for living.

Pilar also speaks of man's inevitable reliance on humanity ('Everyone needs to talk to someone. Before we had religion and other nonsense. Now for everyone there should be someone to whom one can speak frankly, for all the valour that one could have one becomes very alone'), while among the minor characters Andres reflects:

> I think that we are born into a time of great difficulty. I think any other time was probably easier. One suffers little because all of us have been formed to resist suffering.... But I would like to have it so that I could tie a handkerchief to that bush back there and come in the daylight and take the eggs and put them under a hen and be able to see the chicks of the partridge in my own courtyard. I would like such small and regular things.... But you have no house and no courtyard to your no-house, he thought. You have no family but a brother who goes to battle to-morrow and you own nothing but the wind and the sun and an empty belly.

This kind of attitude is summarized by Fernando when he says 'we must teach them. We must take away their planes, their automatic weapons, their tanks, their artillery, and teach them dignity,' and it is clear from all these passages that the key-words - valour, honour, dignity - do not apply specifically to the Spanish peasant but are ones which we have long been familiar with in Hemingway's writings, even though, with reference to an ancient and primitive civilization, they acquire, perhaps, a more gloomy poignancy. In any case Fernando is left 'standing there alone with his dignity' and it seems that for the good and brave of heart there is but little consolation. Anselmo himself is blown up with the futile destruction of the bridge, and Pilar achieves no spiritual victory. ('Neither bull force nor bull courage lasted, she knew now, and what did last? I last, she thought. Yes, I have lasted. But for what?'). The 'simple' nobility of Anselmo's attitude is if anything more tired and limp in its prose rhythm than anything comparable with it in

Hemingway's American or cosmopolitan world. For the believers in civilized society, however extravagantly simple-hearted, there is not, in a chaotic world, much hope.

If Anselmo and Pilar have nothing to turn to in the last resort but friendship and a human solidarity which will enable them to endure, Jordan himself attempts to live relatively successfully in a directionless universe by the process of ignoring anything which will be prejudicial to efficiency in the execution of a material duty. 'I am not of those who suffer' he says, and it is noteworthy that whenever he indulges in relatively noble reflections he immediately pricks the bubble with a pin of cynicism. ('You learned the dry-mouthed, fear-purged, purging ecstasy of battle and you fought that summer for all the poor in the world, against all tyranny.... It was in those days that you had a deep and sound and selfless pride - that would have made you a bloody bore at Gaylord's, he thought suddenly.') Because he is more sophisticated than Anselmo, he is also less serious: intellectually conscious of the hopes he fights for, of the futility of fighting, and of the imminence of death, whereas Anselmo emotionally accepts death and failure without rancour or bitterness, he must forget his friends and even his love in the pursuance of his duty, must pursue the maximum of sensation that is offered by a life that is taut on the brink of extinction. Such a conception has, no doubt, its compensations. If Anselmo - and Pilar too for all her resolution - is calm, fatalistically resigned and very tired, the fine-drawn wire of Jordan's existence tingles with a precarious joy. Partly of course it is joy in the 'Now and ever now,' in sensation, whether the sensation of desire that is 'smooth and young and lovely' or of the smell of smoked leather or of ground in spring after rain. 'If you love this girl as much as you say you do you had better love her very hard and make up in intensity what the relation will lack in duration and continuity,' he says in a passage which gives intimation of another of the Hemingway key-words, for being 'gay' is a sign of something too, 'like having immortality while you were still alive.' Yet this alone does not indicate the quality of the joy I have in mind and perhaps this short sentence conveys more accurately the blindingly clear nervous frenzy in which the closing section of the book takes place: 'He lay there holding her very lightly, feeling her breathe and feeling her heart beat, and keeping track of the time on his wrist watch.' It is like a white heady wine and death brings merely the release from tension. ('He felt empty and drained and exhausted from all of it and from them going and his mouth tasted of bile. Now finally and at last there was no problem.... I wish they would come, he thought. I do not want to get in any mixed up state before they come'). It is revealing to compare this typical Hemingway exit with the death of Sordo. Waiting to die, Jordan thinks actively of what he had done and not done and of the necessity of *not* thinking at all: Sordo does not need to tell himself not to think, it is sufficient to feel conscious of the life which death negates. ('Dying was nothing and he had no picture of it nor fear of it in his mind. But living was a field of grain blowing in the wind on the side of a hill. Living was a hawk in the sky. Living was an earthen jar of water in the dust of the threshing with the grain flailed out and and the chaff blowing....').

The clear cold frenzy which is the final impression left by this story of the inevitable abnegation of human ties and beliefs, this evocation of the still, painful ticking of the clock, is revealed through the curiously stealthy tread of Mr. Hemingway's prose, which we can examine in a simple passage of description:

> Earlier in the evening he had taken the axe and gone outside of the cave and walked through the new snow to the edge of the clearing and cut down a small spruce tree. In the dark he had dragged it, butt first, to the lee of the rock wall. There close to the rock, he had held the tree upright, holding the trunk firm with one hand, and, holding the axe-shaft close to the head had lopped off all the boughs until he had a pile of them. Then, leaving the pile of boughs, he had laid the bare pole of the trunk down in the snow and gone into the cave to get a slab of wood he had seen against the wall. With this slab he scraped the ground clear of the snow along the rock wall and then picked up his boughs and shaking them clean of snow laid them in rows, like overlapping plumes, until he had a bed. He put the pole across the foot of the bough bed to hold the branches in place and pegged it firm with two pointed pieces of wood he split from the edge of the slab. Then he carried the slab and the axe back into the cave, ducking under the blanket as he came in and leaned them both against the wall.

It is difficult to explain why this passage seems to me effective when most of the then-he-took-two-paces-forward-and-then-he-took-three-paces-back school of writing seems so utterly spurious, except that through the organization of the rhythm of the paragraph allied with the meticulous clarity of the detail an emotional aura is generated to what appears to be pure statement. However this may be, stretched to a wider canvas - embracing the ultimate degree of physical violence and the simpler type of psychological clash - this delicate step, this cat-like precision, this photogenic clarity, gradually creates a resilient sity, an impression of the painful isolation of even those who do their best to evade the difficulties with which life to-day might beset them. The process is so gradual that the stylized prose and the stylized dialect, continuing for hundreds of pages without the slightest variation of tempo or mood, are extraordinarily boring to read at long stretches - and the stretches must necessarily be much longer than in the short stories. Yet the boringness is maybe the condition of a certain kind of success, the slow unfolding of action paralleling the slow exfoliation of the prose; at least one can't imagine the end being as effective as it is except as the consummation of that laborious growth. Although I think Mr. Hemingway should restrict himself to short stories where the accuracy of his reporter's eye and his limitation of emotional range help rather than hinder him, I think one must also admit that if he is going to write a long novel the boringness of this one is implicit in the nature of his premises. Actually this book itself contains a number of excellent shorts - for instance some of the political portraits and, finest of all, the terrifying objective account of the massacre of Sordo and his band.

One thing is certain: treated with the honesty which is appropriate to it, this book should make a superb film. It has plenty of violent action, it is built around a single theme and an extravagantly simple but coherent scale of values, it conveys most of its point through a narrow formalized dialogue, and, most of all, it is extraordinarily photogenic even in the texture of its prose which produces - if I am not giving too subjective an account - an effect of transparent white light with sharply defined shadows. Mr. Hemingway himself can be trusted to insist on the piebald and to stamp vigorously on any suggestion of gorgeous technicolour; Mr. Gary Cooper can play the ox to perfection; and (given the opportunity as he may be) Mr. Aaron Copland, who wrote such intelligent and distinguished scores to 'Of Mice and Men' and 'Our Town,' could compose for it some transparently stringent and cinematic music.

'Men at War' (1942)

74. CARLOS BAKER, 'SEWANEE REVIEW'

51 (January 1943), 161-3

Carlos Baker (b. 1909) is Professor of English at Princeton University, and author of 'Hemingway: The Writer as Artist' (1952) and 'Ernest Hemingway: A Life Story' (1969).

Mr. Hemingway long ago decided that he belonged properly if not continually with Mars, and this anthology of men at war is evidently a compromise between what Mr. Hemingway wanted to include, and what the times made it expedient to exclude; between what Mr. Hemingway thought was sentimental trash, and what his publishers or nameless co-editors were set on putting in. It is a thematic anthology, and its theme is war. Insofar as it is a group effort, it falls short of the hopes of Mr. Hemingway, insofar as it falls short of his hopes, it corroborates his standards, - those (I mean) that underlie the best of his own writing.

The latest restatement of these standards is what renders valuable Hemingway's introduction to the anthology. 'A writer's job,' he says, 'is to tell the truth. His standard of fidelity to the truth should be so high that his invention, out of his experience, should produce a truer account than anything factual can be. For facts can be observed badly; but when a good writer is creating something, he has time and scope to make it an absolute truth.' Hemingway does not, of course, mean a transcendental absolute. He does mean something like unremitting conformity to the probable actual, that truth which is greater than the sum of its observed parts, the 'news that stays news' because it is true both to itself and to its constituents, which feed but do not compel it. I wish that there were time and space to examine the ramifications of this point of view in relation to Hemingway's development, but the principle involved does make a good starting-point for the evaluation of 'Men at War.'

Although relatively few of the selections conform to Hemingway's standards, the surprise is that so many should come so close. Among the two dozen which do conform, I should unhesitatingly include Crane's 'Red Badge of Courage' (here given complete), Hemingway's account of El Sordo's last fight from 'For Whom the Bell Tolls'; the extract from 'Her Privates We'; (1) the two episodes from Lawrence's 'Seven Pillars of Wisdom'; one or two by Colonel Thomason; (2) Stendhal's 'Personal View of Waterloo,' Bierce's Owl Creek Bridge; (3) Hillary's 'Falling Through Space,' (4) and perhaps a dozen others including one by Tolstoy. These twenty-odd are based on fact, accurately observed and recorded with the utmost fidelity, but illumined from within by a quality which goes beyond reporting as a good statue goes beyond stone. They contain the general in the particular; experience is rather a referant than a comptroller. They have in common the factual flavor of eyewitness accounts, but have been matured by the artistic process beyond the level of reporting. They have shaped forms which are recognizable as actuality from rough blocks of carefully ascertained fact. Their matter, to put it one more way, is informed with spirit.

Many, if not most of the remaining stories are history, approaching the others at various levels and to various degrees of nearness, yet always remaining history, tied to particularized fact. The rewards they offer are various: information about the great battles; demonstration of the part played by chance, ignorance, stupidity, or forethought (or these in combination) in the outcome of world-shaking issues. It is odd how flat some of them seem beside the genuine works of art. But the art of writing, like the art of war, has come a long way since David slew Goliath.

Notes

1 A novel of the Great War by Frederic Manning (1930).
2 Col. John Thomason, 'Lone Star Preacher' (1941), stories of World War Two.
3 An Occurrence at Owl Creek Bridge (1898), a short story about a wartime hanging, by Ambrose Bierce.
4 Richard Hillary, 'Falling Through Space' (1942), about the air force in World War Two.

'The Portable Hemingway' (1944)

75. GRANVILLE HICKS, 'NEW REPUBLIC'

111 (23 October 1944), 524, 526

Mr. Cowley's 'Portable Hemingway' contains the whole of 'The Sun Also Rises,' the description of the retreat from Caporetto from 'A Farewell to Arms,' the account of Harry Morgan's slaughter of the Cubans from 'To Have and Have Not' and the story of El Sordo's battle from 'For Whom the Bell Tolls.' It also contains the whole of 'In Our Time,' nine other short stories, and a brief passage from 'Death in the Afternoon.' I do not know for whom such a book is published, and I do not suppose it matters. People buy it and read it, and then perhaps they go and read the novels from which the extracts are taken and the other short stories, and that is all to the good, or else they read only what is in the book, and that is a good deal better than reading nothing. The selection is in some ways a strange one, but presumably it was dictated in part by practical considerations of publishing. The important thing is that there is nothing here that is not worth reading or rereading, and nothing has been omitted that is conspicuously better than what is here.

For people who have been reading Hemingway these twenty years, the book's great value - aside from the pleasant temptation to reread what one has always been promising oneself one would reread - lies in Malcolm Cowley's introduction and notes. The introductory essay, much of which appeared in the 'New Republic' last summer, (1) is the best critical discussion of Hemingway I have read. Curiously and even shockingly, it is one of the first discussions to examine Hemingway on his own grounds.

Hemingway, Cowley maintains, is not a naturalist, as the textbooks have said, but one of 'the haunted and nocturnal writers' in the tradition of Poe, Hawthorne and Melville. Like everyone else, I have always known that Hemingway did not describe fishing and skiing, boxing and bull-fighting, drinking and sexual intercourse for their own sake. I have thought and said that violent physical activity was for Hemingway the only possible escape from a world grown too complicated and difficult and disheartening. This is partly true, but the point Cowley makes is that the acts Hemingway so often describes have for him the quality of rites. Rites are a form of escape, too, I suppose, but when one reaches this level - the level, I mean, on which all primitive and most civilized men have lived - 'escape' cannot be used as a term of abuse. Hemingway, that is to say, though he appears to be dealing with the surface behavior of bored and not very representative individuals, is actually touching upon a profound and almost universal phenomenon. Perhaps that is why so many critics have felt in his work power and significance that their analyses did not account for.

Even writing, Cowley suggests, is a form of incantation or exorcism for Hemingway, and he quotes some of the many passages in which autobiographical characters speak of the catharsis writing can give. This, too, explains a good deal. Back in 1937, when John Peale Bishop was saying that Hemingway had gone bad as a writer, (2) two wonderful stories - The Short Happy Life of Francis Macomber and The Snows of Kilimanjaro - proved that his fears were exaggerated. Four years later 'For Whom the Bell Tolls' made it clear that Hemingway was the most disciplined craftsman of his generation. Because Hemingway has represented himself as a hard-boiled anti-intellectual, it has always seemed incongruous that he should care so much about the craft of writing, but now we can see the roots of his devotion. 'If he wrote it,' Nick thinks in Fathers and Sons, 'he could get rid of it. He had gotten rid of many things by writing them.' Craftsmanship has always been for Hemingway a means of getting at the truth, and one understands why: if he didn't get it right, it did no good.

All of Hemingway's compulsions stem from his feeling about death, with which he has been concerned in a way that few authors have since John Donne posed for a sculptor wrapped in his winding-sheet. Some evidence - Fathers and Sons, for example - suggests that this preoccupation took shape before his experiences in the First World War. At any rate it is to be felt in everything he has written. Bishop speaks of the apprehensiveness Hemingway displayed in the early twenties in Paris, and apprehensiveness is the mood of the majority of his characters. For some of them the fear of death becomes so acute that the only cure is defiance of death. This is what Wilson, the guide, knows and Macomber briefly learns, and it is what the bull-fighters know, the only people who ever live their lives all the way up. If the men who stalk death in the arena and the jungle do not live long, they live well: there is a law of compensation. Robert Jordan in 'For Whom the Bell Tolls' is resolved not to be one of those much possessed by death, but the certainty of death is there from the moment Pilar reads his hand, indeed from the moment Golz gives his orders; and the ultimate moral of the book for Hemingway is that the fullness of life in the three days before the dynamiting of the bridge negates the tragedy of Jordan's death. There is more to the novel than that, certainly, but nothing in it that is more important.

In discussing ritual and symbol, Cowley makes an interesting point about the influence of Hemingway's early contacts with Indians. He neglects, however, a greater influence, Hemingway's Catholicism. I do not know whether Hemingway has ever been a 'good' Catholic, but surely the fact of his being a 'bad' Catholic - like Jake Barnes and Frederic Henry - has to be reckoned with. As the lovely dialogue between Frederic Henry and Count Greffi in 'A Farewell to Arms' indicates, his fears and doubts are sharpened by an awareness of a conceivable faith in the order and purpose of the universe. This awareness is always present, but the response to it broadens from the anguish of Frederic Henry, who is *croyant* (3) at night, to the stoical affirmation of Anselmo in 'For Whom the Bell Tolls.' 'Let *them* have God,' Anselmo says. 'Clearly I miss Him, having been brought up in religion. But now a man is responsible to himself.'

Cowley is right in emphasizing the strain of primitivism in Hemingway, but it will not do to make too much of that particular theme. Next in importance to his concern with death, and closely related to it, is his concern with human loneliness. In the early work it is only in a rare kind of sexual relationship and in brief moments of male companionship that a man escapes loneliness, and both experiences are transient. Harry Morgan's discovery in 'To Have and Have Not' that a man cannot stand alone is not wholly convincing in terms of the novel, but its meaning for Hemingway became apparent in 'For Whom the Bell Tolls.' Here for the first time a Hemingway hero has a rich sense of the support that a beloved woman, a group of comrades and a cause can give - in death as well as life.

Now it is this sense of living in the group and

surviving in the group that is the primitive sense, whereas the feeling of isolation is sophisticated. Individualism in the philosophical sense is rare in most primitive societies and apparently nonexistent in many. Primitive man confronts all the experiences of life, including death, as part of a group, and his rituals - never private affairs like Hemingway's - grow out of and intensify the feeling of group solidarity. Civilizaton breaks down the small, integrated groups, and man comes to feel that he is alone. For us, the sense of belonging is something to be achieved, not a heritage, and, as is clear in 'For Whom the Bell Tolls,' it is always precarious.

It is strange that Hemingway, who has always hated pretentiousness, has found pretentious titles for all of his novels. If the titles are to be accepted at face value, he has written about a generation, about a war, about the struggle between rich and poor and about human solidarity. As a matter of fact, only the fourth of the novels lives up to the wider implications of its name, and even 'For Whom the Bell Tolls' is not wholly or with perfect success what it purports to be. It is perhaps unfortunate that his novels should have seemed to attempt so much. If one admits at the beginning that his men and women are in many respects not widely representative, one is more likely to see them for what they are, and to discover, as Cowley has discovered, that it is not their outward behavior that makes them important but their fears and their adjustments to their fears. If, that is, Jake Barnes is not representative of the postwar generation - and outwardly I don't see how he can be - he may, looked at closely, stand for an even larger segment of humanity.

To call Hemingway a great writer is not, it should be needless to say, to express agreement with all or any of his views. But Cowley has put this as well as it can be put:

> By now he has earned the right to be taken for what he is, with his great faults and greater virtues, with his narrowness, his power, his always open eyes, his stubborn, chip-on-the-shoulder honesty, his nightmares, his rituals for escaping them, and his sense of an inner and outer world that for twenty years were moving together toward the same disaster.

In the recent Collier's article (4) one sees pictures of Hemingway, the bearded, self-confident veteran surrounded by apprehensive kids in uniform, and one can smile, thinking of what he has said about war, thinking about his love of poses; but here, too, his demon is driving him, and some day we may be glad that he has again gone where his demon bade.

Notes

1 Malcolm Cowley, Hemingway at Midnight, 'New Republic,' 111 (14 August 1944), 109-5.
2 John Peale Bishop, The Missing All, 'Virginia Quarterly Review,' 13 (Winter 1937), 106-21.
3 A believer.
4 Hemingway wrote five war dispatches for 'Collier's' between 4 March and 7 October 1944.

'Across the River and into the Trees' (1950)

76. MORTON DAUWEN ZABEL, 'NATION'

171 (9 September 1950), 230

Morton Dauwen Zabel (1901-64) was an American professor and critic, and editor of 'Literary Opinion in America' (1937), 'The Portable Conrad' (1947) and 'The Portable James' (1951).

The story opens two hours before daylight on the lagoons north of Venice. 'The Colonel' - Richard Cantwell, ex-Brigadier General, aged fifty, and already under sentence of death - is going out to the duck-shooting. It is another of Hemingway's mornings - we've known them before, in Michigan, in Paris, in Wyoming, Africa, Spain, and Cuba - and for a moment an old spell is evoked: the cold half-light breaking over the islands, the ice-sheeted waters, the angry boatman flinging decoys from the boat, the first birds in the sky. Presently we cast back a day or two. The Colonel drives from his postwar station at Trieste to Venice. The Adriatic country he has known and loved since he fought in it as a boy in the other war unfolds its panorama of history and memories. He arrives at the Gritti Palace Hotel and goes to Harry's bar to meet the nineteen-year-old girl Renata whom he loves. From then on the tale recounts their last meetings, pledges of devotion, and defiance of despair until the Colonel, driving back to Trieste with his orderly, is killed by his heart and dies. His farewell to arms comes thirty years after Frederic Henry's and a dozen after Robert

Jordan's, but he is essentially the same man, this time 'half a hundred years' old.

This is the novel - Hemingway's fifth in thirty years of writing - we've awaited for ten years, certainly with every hope that it would augur the renewal of a talent that has given us several of the memorable books of the century. Briefly, it doesn't. What might, in, say, thirty pages, have been an effective *conte* on the order of Francis Macomber or The Snows of Kilimanjaro, has been stretched, beaten out, and enervated to the length of three hundred. The drama is almost static. The talk, retaining only a few of its old living accents, develops unbelievable prodigies of flatness, mawkishness, repetition, and dead wastes of words. The Colonel, advertised as 'perhaps the most complex character that Hemingway has ever presented,' proves to be a stereotype of earlier heroes: another existential man at his rope's end, faithful only to the ritual of soldiering and love; and the girl Renata repeats the submissive child-lover of 'For Whom the Bell Tolls,' serving also as counterfoil to another familiar type, the bitch ex-wife - an ambitious woman journalist in this case - who has sealed Cantwell's scepticism of all but the most rudimentary forms of human or sexual traffic.

The reader inevitably arrives at this book with a complex conditioning. It is, first of all, offered as a by-product of the larger novel Hemingway has been writing since 1940. We remember how the earlier novels and tales stamped the modern imagination with some of its most memorable fables and images. But we are also perforce reminded of how many other assaults the force and stubborn integrity of these have met in the last twenty years - confused performances like 'Death in the Afternoon' and 'To Have and Have Not'; fiascos of ineptitude like 'Green Hills of Africa; and 'The Fifth Column'; the muddled power of 'For Whom the Bell Tolls'; not to mention the dismal exhibitionism of the 'Esquire' articles in the thirties or the self-exploiting public character of the interviews and photographs (in this latter department rivalled by nothing in recent literary history so much as by the visions we've had of Truman Capote). The resentment induced by all this has hardly been improved on hearing Hemingway deliver himself of statements like the following: 'I started out very quiet and I beat Mr. Turgenev. Then I trained hard and I beat Mr. de Maupassant. I've fought two draws with Mr. Stendhal.... But nobody's going to get me in any ring with Mr. Tolstoy unless I'm crazy or I keep getting better.' The modesty *vis-à-vis* Tolstoy is appreciated, but one wonders if a little less certainty about having worsted the Messrs. Turgenev, Maupassant, and Stendhal might not, to put it mildly, have been tactful, or done Mr. Hemingway a little good. Of course there was also that 'New Yorker' profile last spring. With every allowance for calculated malice, one was left wondering what could possibly survive for the serious business of art and writing. The only answer provided by 'Across the River' is: very little.

The obvious truth is that this new novel is the poorest thing its author has ever done - poor with a feebleness of invention, a dulness of language, and a self-parodying of style and theme even beyond 'The Fifth Column' and 'To Have and Have Not.' It gives no sign of the latent rigor that has permitted Hemingway, in tales like The Undefeated, Old Man at the Bridge, Macomber, and Kilimanjaro, to pull himself together after he had given every evidence of having gone to pieces, and to declare his old powers. For a few small favors one must be grateful: this book at least lacks the supremely silly '(obscenity)' device that disfigured the pages of 'For Whom the Bell Tolls.' What one is left with (the analogy of Kipling once suggested by Edmund Wilson is again pertinent) is the impasse of routine mechanism and contrivance a talent arrives at when an inflexibly formulated conception of experience or humanity is pushed to the limits of its utility, excluding any genuine exploration of human complexity or any but the most brutally patented responses to character and conduct.

We are left to conclude that this talent, while nothing can efface what it achieved in at least two novels and a score of brilliant tales, will be subjected to some severely revised judgments in the coming years, and that when it is measured against some of its closer rivals - Fitzgerald, for instance, or Faulkner - it will meet rougher tests than the unlikely cases of Turgenev and Stendhal provide. 'Across the River and into the Trees' (the title badly mars the fine rhythm of Stonewall Jackson's last words) is an occasion for little but exasperated depression. But we are promised another novel soon. We must wait for it. And see.

77. ALFRED KAZIN, 'NEW YORKER'

26 (9 September 1950), 101-3

It is said that the new Hemingway novel, 'Across the River and Into the Trees,' was written because Hemingway thought at one period in 1949 that he would die of an eye infection caused by a hunting accident near Venice, and that he turned aside from the more ambitious novel he has been working over for some years to do this little book in the short time he felt was left. (1) The book was obviously written under great tension, is about an American in Venice waiting to die (an Army officer exactly Hemingway's age, which in 1949 was a furiously inconsolable fifty-one), one), and can only distress anyone who admires Hemingway. Considering the state of crisis in which it is supposed to have been written, it is hard to say what one feels most in reading this book - pity, embarrassment that so fine and honest a writer can make such a travesty of himself, or amazement that a man can render so marvellously the beauty of the natural world and yet be so vulgar.

The book reads as if it had been written as a premature summary of Hemingway's own life and work. It has the familiar Hemingway love affair, an abstractly ideal and doomed romance quite irrelevant to the real force and descriptive eloquence in the story; the familiar motifs of the satisfactions of hunting, eating, drinking, and comradeship in war; the usual refrain of slightly beery stoicism; the usual carefully loving descriptions of light, of water, of birds in flight, of the stoniness in the North Italian landscape. All of Hemingway is here - to the point of unconsciously quoting famous lines from the other works ('The finest people that you know'), the horrors remembered from shooting down Austrians on the Italian front in the First World War, the protracted, showy, and naively condescending negotiations with lovable bartenders and headwaiters in the better European restaurants, and the irritable reiteration that Valpolicella is better poured from flasks than from bottles; it gets too dreggy in bottles. The tough and battered hero, Colonel Richard Cantwell, of the American occupation forces in Trieste, is literally a composite of all the Hemingway heroes - is from the West, has fought with the Italian Army in the First World War, has been shot in the head and hit on the head, has a broken nose, has observed the Spanish Civil War, and is a terrific boxer, hunter, eater, and drinker. The girl, a Venetian countess of nineteen, is, simply, 'the most beautiful girl' in the world, the most loving, the most natural, and apparently of the best Venetian family. (Several of the doges were her ancestors.) Here is the way Hemingway introduces her: 'Then she came into the room, shining in her youth and tall striding beauty, and the carelessness the wind had made of her hair. She had pale, almost olive colored skin, a profile that could break your, or any one else's, heart, and her dark hair, of an alive texture, hung down over her shoulders.' When they kiss, they kiss 'hard and true'; when they make love, they use a stage talk that is mock Italian, either very tough or very maudlin, and remarkably false.

Hemingway's prose has been getting very gamy, and in this book the compulsion to use dirty words and show off is reminiscent more of the bullying American tank commanders he despises than of his old satiric gaiety. But never has the Hemingway hero's body been described with such meticulous and anxious self-love as now - 'half a hundred years old' and a 'beat-up old bastard.' At one point, the Colonel - his name is rarely mentioned in the book, as if he had been designed to remind us of a body in uniform rather than of a human being - is compared to the 'gladiator' with the broken nose 'in the oldest statues'; at another, he has the 'truculence' of a 'wild boar.' He expects any hour to die of heart disease, but, looking at himself in the mirror, he is glad that 'the gut is flat' and that 'the chest is all right except where it contains the defective muscle.' As a physical type, it must be said, the Hemingway hero has never been more distinct than he is here, just before dying. You see him very clearly, suffused in the light of Hemingway's love 'only for those who have fought or been mutilated' - he has the 'crooked' infantryman's walk, one leg 'hurts him always,' his eyes are like 'old used steel,' his battle-scarred face is lined with 'the different welts and ridges that had come before they had plastic surgery,' one hand is twisted, and he has heart disease; he keeps himself going with mannitol-hexanitrate (2) tablets.

The Colonel is all the Hemingway prizefighters, hunters, drinkers, and soldiers in one. Yet this book is different, for it is held together by blind anger rather than the lyric emotion that gives Hemingway's best work its unforgettable poignance. The thing most deeply felt in the book is the Colonel's rage at having to die - a rage that is deflected into one of the most confused and vituperatively revealing self-portrayals by an American I have ever seen. The Colonel understandably finds it very grim that he may die at fifty-one, especially now that he has the most beautiful girl in the world. But what apparently disturbs him most is not the fact that he must soon lose her (his love for her is often as vague to him as it is to us) but that his body has suddenly let him down. His pride is hurt. Moreover, he has been put back to his old rank of colonel - he was a brigadier general during the war, but made some trifling, if fatal, mistake in the Ardennes campaign - and he cannot forgive the Army top brass for this. Almost everything American now annoys him 'except me.' He snubs his Army chauffeur for entertaining opinions about Italian painters; he is scornful of the Army's 'comic-book readers,' of almost all its generals except Collins, Quesada, and (grudgingly) Bradley (3) ('a schoolmaster'), of American women, especially if they are correspondents (his ex-wife was a correspondent), of 'unsuccessful haberdashers' in the White House and their soprano daughters. (4) 'Now we are governed in some way by the dregs. We are governed by what you find in the bottom of dead beer glasses that whores have dunked their cigarettes in. The place has not even been swept out yet and they have an amateur pianist beating on the box.'

The Colonel spends his last two days duck-shooting, walking about Venice, eating hugely, drinking Valpolicella, making love to the Countess in a gondola, and denouncing the American scene as he lies with her in his hotel bed overlooking the Grand Canal. The Colonel seems to incarnate all of Hemingway's pride as an American who knows European comforts intimately, plus a savage contempt for Europe's ability to make war. He uses the word 'jerk' quite freely; at one point it is applied to his chauffeur, at another to D'Annunzio, at still another to Pacciardi, the present Italian Minister of Defense - what a joke that Italians should even think of defending themselves when they lack the atomic bomb! The Colonel is anti-Franco; Franco's physical appearance disgusts him, but apparently he is not entirely against totalitarianism, for he thinks of himself as a professional soldier and international sportsman quite above politics, and has no prejudice against his 'potential enemy,' the Russians, or his late enemy, the Germans. His idea of heaven would be to ski and talk shop endlessly with the Nazi Generals Rommel and Udet.

The Colonel likes nothing and nobody in this world but the Countess; the city of Venice, whose people are 'tough' and admire only 'tough' writers (there are dark remarks all through the book against Dante that I can attribute only to the fact that he came from Florence); certain sadly charming Italian hotelkeepers and noblemen and hunting dogs; and, of course, good wine, good food, good beds. The Colonel, like most Hemingway heroes, never spares you any of Hemingway's likes and dislikes in women, food, hotels, cities, and *le vin du pays*. The physiological and gastronomical detail in the book is generally so extraneous that it is impossible to believe Hemingway means anything by it; he is just sounding off. As you listen to the Colonel go on and on, it slowly and reluctantly comes home to you that his real quality is not, as you would expect from Hemingway's early work, one man's lonely fight against despair and bureaucratization and death but the oracular and naive self-importance of an American big shot who has been in all the countries and seen all the twentieth-century wars and has charmed a whole generation into believing that toughness is the same as valor.

In fact, what the Colonel represents is the flesh - the flesh in its most automatic impulses, with the sensory machine dying down, the heart threatening to burst at any moment, and the brain throbbing weakly on old obscenities. It is not a satiric portrait; the Colonel is too full of Hemingway's pettiest, most irrelevant opinions. There is, however, a great sense of guilt behind it; one of the most curious sides of the Colonel is his constant effort, 'remembering to be kind,' to hold himself in check, to be less brutal. As he says, he has usually lost women because of his brutality. So he tries very hard to be good, or at least to speak more nicely. But the effort never comes off. He has always lived by sensations; death is the last sensation, and so he waits for it - the flesh seeking to the end the satisfaction of each appetite, and indignant that it must die. It is wonderful to know that Hemingway has recovered, and that his book is not his last word.

Notes

1 This long abortive novel was begun in 1946. According to Baker: 'It was an experimental compound of past and present, filled with astonishing ineptitudes and based in part upon memories of his marriages to Hadley and Pauline' (p. 538).
2 A white crystalline powder used to reduce high blood pressure.
3 Gen. J. Lawton Collins (b. 1896), captured Cherbourg, led drives through Belgium and the Ruhr; Gen. Edward Quesada (b. 1904) was commanding general of IX Tactical Air Command in Europe; Gen. Omar Bradley (1893-1981) commanded the 12th Army in the final battles in Germany.
4 Harry and Margaret Truman.

78. EVELYN WAUGH, 'TABLET'

196 (30 September 1950), 290, 292

Evelyn Waugh (1903-66), English novelist, was the author of 'Decline and Fall' (1928), 'Brideshead Revisited' (1945) and 'The Loved One' (1948). The 'Tablet' is a Catholic weekly.

Mr. Ernest Hemingway's long-expected novel has been out for some weeks, and has already been conspicuously reviewed by all the leading critics. It is now impossible to approach it without some prejudice either against the book itself or against its critics, for their disapproval has been unanimous. They have been smug, condescending, derisive, some with unconcealed glee, some with an affectation of pity; all are agreed that there is a great failure to celebrate. It is the culmination of a whispering campaign of some years' duration, that 'Hemingway is finished.'

I read the reviews before I read the book, and I was in the mood to make the best of it. Mr. Hemingway is one of the most original and powerful of living writers. Even if he had written a completely fatuous book, this was not the way to treat it. What, in fact, he has done is to write a story entirely characteristic of himself, not his best book, perhaps his worst, but still something very much better than most of the work to which the same critics give their tepid applause.

It is the story of the death of an old soldier. He knows he is mortally ill, and he chooses to spend his last days in and near Venice, shooting and making love. The book is largely a monologue. The veteran ruminates bitterly over old battles. He exults in his young mistress. And all is written in that pungent vernacular which Mr. Hemingway should have patented.

It may be conceded at once that the hero is not an attractive character. He is a boor and a bore, jocular, humourless, self-centred, arrogant; he rose to command a brigade, but he is consumed by the under-dog's resentment of his superiors both in the army and elsewhere; the last man, in fact, to choose as one's companion in Venice. But these reviewers have been telling us for years that we must not judge novels by the amiability of their characters, any more than we must judge pictures by the beauty of their subjects. Mr. Hemingway makes a full, strong portrait of his obnoxious hero.

The heroine, a very young Venetian, is strangely unchaperoned. If social conventions have indeed relaxed so much since I was last in that city, this young lady's behaviour provides ample evidence that the traditional, rigid code was highly desirable. But are our reviewers the right people to complain of her goings-on? I think it is the troubadour in Mr. Hemingway which impels him to ennoble his heroines. He did the same thing in his first, startlingly brilliant 'Fiesta.' There is a strong affinity between that book and this. How it delighted and impressed us a quarter of a century ago! How flatly we accept the same gifts today!

Of course, between then and now there have been the shoals of imitators. It was so easy. You have to be an accomplished writer to imitate Henry James. Any journalist can produce a not quite passable imitation of Mr. Hemingway. But it was not only the inventions in technique that impressed us in 'Fiesta.' It was the mood. English literature is peculiarly rich in first-class Philistine novelists - Surtees (1) and Mr. P.G. Wodehouse, for example. But their characters were always happy. Mr. Hemingway has melancholy, a sense of doom. His men and women are as sad as those huge, soulless apes that huddle in their cages at the Zoo. And that mood is still with us.

'Across the River and into the Trees' is the nemesis of the philistine. The hero is fifty-one years of age, when the civilized man is just beginning the most fruitful period of his life. But the philistine is done for, a 'beat-up old bastard,' as he expresses it. He has lived for sport and drink and love-making and professional success, and now there is nothing left for him. He has to be decorated with a physical, mortal illness as with a medal. In accentuation of the pathos of his position, he regards himself as rather cultured and sophisticated. He has been places. He is one with that baffled, bibulous crew of 'Fiesta' who thought they were plunging deep into the heart of Europe by getting on friendly terms with barmen; who thought their café pickups the flower of decadent European aristocracy. He believes he is the sort of guy for whom the Old Masters painted, and to hell with the art experts.

All the faults of this latest book were abundantly present in the first; and most of the merits of the first are here again. Why has there been this concerted attack on Mr. Hemingway?

It began a few months ago with a softening-up blitz in the 'New Yorker.' That widely-read paper attached a female reporter to Mr. Hemingway to study him while he was on a holiday in New York. She ate and drank, went shopping and visited art galleries with him, and took careful note of every silly or vulgar thing he said or did during his spree. One might suppose that only a megalomaniac or a simpleton would expose himself to such an ordeal. She made a complete ass of him, of course; not altogether a lovable ass, either. I have never met Mr. Hemingway, but I think it probable that his own boisterous manners have contributed to his present unpopularity.

He has really done almost everything to render himself a 'beat-up old bastard.' His reputation was unassailable in 1936. Then, with much trumpeting, he went to Madrid and Barcelona. Here was something greater than bullfights and *bistros*. The greatest modern writer was devoting his art to the greatest modern theme. Picasso had painted Guernica; Messrs. Auden and Spender had written something or other; now the great warrior-artist of the New World was going to write the Modern Epic. But it did not turn out like that. 'For Whom the Bell Tolls' was not at all what the Socialists wanted. They had been busy denying atrocities; Mr. Hemingway described them in detail with relish. They had denied the presence of Russians; Mr. Hemingway led us straight into the front-door of the Gaylord Hotel. He made Marty and la Pasionaria as comic as any 'New Yorker' correspondent could have done. From then on he was on the wrong side of the barricades for the Socialists, while his pounding revolutionary heart still drove him from civilization.

His sense of superiority to Americans combined with his sense of inferiority to Europeans to give him the sort of patriotism which pleased no one. He could not abide the urban commercial development of his own country; he supposed, rather rightly, that the English were snooty about him, and the French wanted only his dollars. He had a Kiplingesque delight in the technicalities of every trade but his own. He remained, of course, an admirable technician, but, while he could talk for nights to fishermen about their tackle, he was nauseated by the jargon of other writers. Indeed, in this book he uses an American novelist as the typic contrast to his hero; a seedy, industrious fellow in the same hotel, sober, with no young mistress and no scars of battle, and no rollicking jokes with the servants.

When the second war came Mr. Hemingway could not be a soldier, and he despised war-correspondents; he became a war-correspondent. There is plenty to account for the bitterness and frustration of his present work. But our critics thrive on bitterness and frustration. They have forgotten that they once raised clenched fists to the red flag in Barcelona. Not more than a handful have been physically assaulted by the man. Why do they all hate him so?

I believe the truth is that they have detected in him something they find quite unforgivable - Decent Feeling. Behind all the bluster and cursing and fisticuffs he has an elementary sense of chivalry - respect for women, pity for the weak, love of honour - which keeps breaking in. There is a form of high, supercilious caddishness which is all the rage nowadays in literary circles. That is what the critics seek in vain in this book, and that is why their complaints are so loud and confident.

Note

1 Robert Surtees (1803-64) was the creator of John Jorrocks, the humorous sporting grocer.

79. ISAAC ROSENFELD, 'KENYON REVIEW'

13 (Winter 1951), 147-55

Isaac Rosenfeld (1919-56), an American critic and novelist, was the author of 'A Passage from Home' (1947) and 'An Age of Enormity' (1962).

It is not enough to say that 'Across the River and into the Trees' is a bad novel, which nearly everyone has said (the fact is, a good deal of it is trash), or to ascribe its failure to Hemingway's playing Hemingway. Such judgments fail to go deep; they make an artificial separation between the man and the artist, and attribute to the former, as though these were superficial mistakes, shortcomings which are the very essence of Hemingway's art. It seems to me that no writer of comparable stature has ever expressed in his work so false an attitude toward life. Now this is more than a matter of temperament, though the pompous boasting, the sounding off on life, love and literature in baseball, prize-ring and military metaphors (the purpose of which is to demonstrate that Hemingway is so great a literary figure that he is primarily an athlete, a hunter, a soldier, a lover of fine wines and women - anything but a writer; this is what I consider trash) that run all through this book, do help to create the impression that Hemingway has gone on a bender and deserted his art. But these monkeyshines are defenses, and to ignore the serious principle while criticizing Hemingway's legend of himself is to succumb to the strategy: at the expense of the man, to flatter the art.

It is easy to understand how Hemingway took hold of our imagination. The characters he created of the lost generation gave us an image of ourselves which we were glad to accept; it was a true image, and in the long run, ennobling. With considerable courage, he continued the work of realism in judging an old social order whose wars were not of our making, and for the wreck of whose values we were not responsible. Jake and his friends did not run out on life, they were pushed out; the separate peace which Frederic Henry concluded was the only sensible thing to do, and only the reactionary and the philistine would blame him for it. These characters, in their main outlines, were seen as the result of external force; the action of the world on them was recorded in the form of a wound. They were helpless. The drinking and the promiscuity were not to their liking. They were Puritan (which is to say, American) enough to hate themselves for it, and too Puritan to burn out the self-hatred. It was only on holiday - from the war, from their life in Paris after the war - that they had the chance to take their real pleasures, the few that weren't spoiled for them. These were simple pleasures after all - in 'A Farewell to Arms,' a love affair, and in 'The Sun Also Rises,' fishing, a trip to Spain. It is especially in the Spanish passages, celebrating Basque landscape and character, that Hemingway restores to his heroes a sense of value and participation in life, and he does so even with warmth which, considering his fear of sentiment, makes this evocation of the might-have-been a generous thing for him. The rituals of the bullfight have only private meaning; nevertheless, Hemingway derived from them the good news he had to give his generation, the virtue of grace under pressure. The only plea he made for his characters - the argument is implicit in the action - is that they have or at least once had the capacity to give themselves; if they no longer do so, it is because they have been wounded.

It was only natural that a whole generation should seize on the wound in justification of itself. The success myth, as the not yet successful Hemingway had the insight to observe, was overthrown, and nothing besides the wound had offered itself. He had no false comfort to give and he told, as far as it went, the truth. It was not the time to examine this argument closely; to do so would have seemed like compromising with society. It passed unnoticed that Hemingway himself was offering a compromise; not the kind the world desired or which it even recognized. All the same, in the character structure which he gave his heroes - an entity by itself, which we now call 'the Hemingway character' - the old values were never seriously questioned, and such clichés as manliness, courage and self-reliance remained unchanged. There is no objection to these values as such; the objection is to the meaning society has given them. Hemingway never examined their social meaning; he merely cut the traditional world of application out from under these values and put something unexpected in its place. He did not tell the lost generation to go out and in the name of these values sell, conquer, succeed, or otherwise overwhelm the world. He did tell it, in so many words, in his books and in the concomitant legend of himself, to attack and refashion itself in character, to be, precisely, self-reliant, courageous and manly - in a word, hard. It is here that he has been a misleading influence on a whole generation of American writers and their audience; and while he is not to be blamed for the army of imitators that has followed him or made (not without his example) an alliance, through the hard-boiled tradition, with bad taste, he is to be judged for what he himself has done. He has created his own subsection of the Myth of the American Male, supporting everything in this myth which is lifeless, vicious and false - the contempt for women and for every tender feeling, as for something effeminate and corrupt, the apotheosis of the purely forceful, tense and thrusting component of maleness as a phallic bludgeon to beat the female principle into submission, the perpetual adolescence of the emotions with its compensatory heroics to cover a fear, and consequent hatred, of sexual love; and this, not as a lapse from his art, but in its best practice.

In Hemingway's work there has always been a great lag between characterization and expression; the lives and characters of his heroes are set down to mean one thing, but they express something entirely different, frequently the opposite. Hemingway's men are hard, they contain their emotions; so runs their title to manliness. They contain their emotions because of a natural dignity and restraint, and this restraint becomes all the more appropriate as the strength of the emotion increases; it is only the trivial feeling that one can afford to let out freely. This creates an expectation for the reader, of a piece with the strong silent types of popular fiction - 'still waters run deep,' and similar over-evaluations of standard Anglo-Saxon behavior. The repetitious monosyllables of the dialogue, the closed self-sufficient gestures, are transformed by this dialectic into symbols of a heavy pressing force, barely held back from explosion. A great passion, such as Frederic Henry presumably feels for Catherine, is indicated as follows (my italics):

> I could remember Catherine *but I would get crazy if I thought about her when I was not sure yet I would see her, so I would not think about her, only about her a little,* only about her with the car going slowly and clickingly, and some light through the canvas and my lying with Catherine on the floor of the car. (1)

Instead of the actual feeling for Catherine, this presents us with a blank; a blank which the reader obligingly fills in. So good are the credentials of this style, we honor it with our whole experience. But when it is read for itself, without the usual expectations, what this passage expresses (as does the tone in which Hemingway always writes of love) is not a man's longing for a woman - where a man really would 'get crazy' and not 'only ... a little' - but his conscious suppression of that longing, which cannot have been very strong. Moreover, this suppression is made within a context of unconscious repressions, which show a fear of women, and defenses against sexuality and love.

The unconscious repression is expressed very clearly in an earlier passage of 'A Farewell to Arms.' Frederic is about to risk an operation on his knee, which will either shorten his recuperation or leave him a cripple. Catherine spends the night with him in his hospital room.

> That night a bat flew into the room through the open door that led onto the balcony and through which we watched the night over the roofs of the town. It was dark in our room except for the small light of the night over the town and the bat was not frightened but hunted in the room as though he had been outside. We lay and watched him and I do not think he saw us because we lay so still. After he went out we saw a searchlight come on and watched the beam move across the sky and then go off and it was dark again. A breeze came in the night and we heard the men of the

> anti-aircraft gun on the next roof talking.... Once in the night we went to sleep and when I woke she was not there but I heard her coming along the hall and the door opened and she came back to the bed and said it was all right she had been downstairs and they were all asleep.... She brought crackers and we ate them and drank some vermouth.... (2)

The expectation is that there will be a desperate tenderness in their love making, that they will try to give each other what reassurance they can in face of the present anxiety; this expectation may color even a second reading of the passage. But all affects are eliminated. The scene expresses infantile fear of the dark, with the bat symbolizing the castration anxiety. (The superstition is that bats get in the hair and can be removed only by cutting off the hair. This maintains the castration anxiety centered in the wounded leg.) The conversation and the light from outside are expressive again at the infantile level, representing the comfort the child takes, in his lonely room, to feel the presence of grown-ups about the house. The whole passage expresses loneliness, though the lovers are with each other. Catherine's presence is not felt, and it is not her part as mistress in the lovemaking that provides reassurance, but rather her re-entrance in the guise of mother, bringing food in the night, when the child wakes alone.

If this reading seems at all far fetched, it is no more so than the presence in the room, at a time like this, of the bat itself. How else did the bat get into the room? Moreover, this reading is borne out by the conversation between Catherine and Frederic on the following morning (it is the same conversation whenever 'Hemingway characters' try to express their tenderest feelings); they tinkle at each other, 'Didn't we have a lovely time, darling? Didn't we have a lovely night?' There is never real contact between Hemingway's lovers; there is chatter, eating, drinking and a lonely lying together. Nothing is deeply felt.

The style covers up this starvation with the honorific leanness. Dividing its skill between the suppression of feeling and the presentation of the clear, clean impression for which Hemingway is famous, it becomes a paraphrase of his philosophy, which considers emotion a disgraceful epiphenomenon, and holds a man to be most human when he is most like wood. This always happens. What was meant to be a full engagement with life, turns out to be a fear of life. All the softer emotions having been eliminated from the character structure of his heroes, the capacity for love and surrender vanish for good, leaving no counterpart in the outer world. Reality is to be read only in terms of violent action, the only kind of which his characters are capable; the world is that which answers to a man's capacity for dealing a blow. The only possible contact in such a world is that of devouring, the only yielding, death. Behaviorism is the only psychology, sickness, the only norm. There is nothing in this scheme to allow for growth, development, education of the feelings, since these do not exist. Hemingway is therefore one of the most static of novelists. His characters either learn nothing or, like Harry Morgan and Robert Jordan with their great discovery that there is some connection between man and man, reach, at the very end, the usual starting-point of the novel. Without this education, which is one of the basic patterns of life, there can be neither a great form nor a great subject in the novel. But in behaviorism there is nothing more to learn; once the reflex is conditioned, it is fixed.

If this were no more than a false philosophy and psychology, it would still be possible for Hemingway's art to succeed, in virtue of its own insight, unacknowledged in the doctrine. But this philosophy - as with all such anti-intellectualisms - is irrefutable. It has no theory, which one can correct by drawing the example from the practice; this is the practice. The philosophy is but another way of expressing the limitation and the falsehood of the art. It is only when Hemingway's style is freed of its defensive obligations that it reaches its best level, as when he writes of landscape and machines; there are no emotions to fend off with the latter, and with the former, the emotions are not suspect, since they have only symbolic reference to the feminine.

There is a critical problem in the disparity between Hemingway's direct treatment and his unintentional expression of character. What credit is he to receive for the compulsive masculinity, the guard raised against sentiment and all deep emotion, with the inevitable admission of sentimentality, which his characters show? I find this hard to answer. Even if we argue that these traits are not actually present in the characterization, but merely inferred from the behavior, the writer must still be given credit for presenting the material from which the inference is made. But when the author denies the inference, when he considers it vilification? It is a perfect irony to see Hemingway fight off the meanings which his critical audience attributes to him, the very meanings which give one reason to take his work seriously. He is as blind as

Oedipus, but his blindness must also be taken seriously. This leaves criticism in a hopelessly ambiguous position. It is no better when we offer to divide the credit between the writer and audience. This is a bad precedent. It makes the writer so incomplete that his work must be supplemented from without, over his dead knowledge. The artist no longer leads the response; he is determined by it. He presents a blank, which his more sophisticated audience returns to him, filled with insight. But we cannot afford to have artists so heavily in debt to their audience. It destroys literature, reducing it to anagrams and doctors' theses. But isn't this substantially the case with Hemingway? This is only one respect in which Hemingway, in his own work and through his imitators, has been a pernicious influence. For all these reasons, it seems to me that his reputation must soon decline, and while the excellent aspects of his style, at least in the earlier novels and some of the stories, the clear, clean writing that he does at his best, will retain their value, the deep moral significance that some critics (e.g. Cowley) have found or pretended to find in his attitude toward life has already begun to look like a hoax.

The curious thing about 'Across the River' is that while it is his worst novel, in one respect - but only in this respect - it is an improvement over all the earlier work. For once the severed halves of the characterization are joined, and the conscious and unconscious images of the hero closely resemble each other.

Richard Cantwell, Col., Infantry, U.S.A., who has come to Venice for several days to see his mistress and shoot ducks, is a man of fifty with a weak heart. He has the same structure as the earlier characters, with the same ascription of the inner anxiety to external causes, and the same discharge of that anxiety through substitutive behavior. He exists for the most part in conversation. Hemingway's clipped dialogue, which had always served the purpose of direct characterization (and of reflecting the unintentional characterization by keeping affect to a minimum), has now been loosened somewhat; it has a more complicated function - that of reducing the character to an even further simplicity. The gap between consciousness and behavior is now completely closed; at least, there is no language left to express it, as the displacement of tension through physical behavior (in Cantwell's case, battle) has been read back into the character, where it becomes the basic language: '... his ruined hand searched for the island in the great river with the high steep banks.... "Just hold me tight and hold the high ground, too (this is the girl speaking).... Please attack gently and with the same attack as before."' But now, though the hero is still meant to exemplify Hemingway's attitude toward life, he is presented as a sick man; he swallows pills all through the action, he must avoid excitement and strain, and he dies of a heart attack. (His mistress, the nineteen-year-old Italian countess Renata, a beautiful, wealthy and adoring pot of duck soup, has also been carried a step further in an even more disastrous simplification. The Hemingway heroine has always been pure bitch, pure pal, or like Brett Ashley, two in one. With Renata, the bitch has been dropped, and the great effort of the pal to please her man, all for him, is now no effort at all; it comes naturally, as it would to a doll. The result is something like one of the waxworks in Villiers de l'Isle-Adam.) (3) Cantwell has also a touch of the Shriner. (4) He plays a game with the head waiter of his hotel, complete with Secret Order, passwords, etc., and gladly interrupts his conversations with Renata, in which he treats her to encyclopedic pontifications, for a mystical pass or two with the *Gran Maestro*.

This may be a serious disintegration in the conception of character, a boring and pathetic attempt in and out of character to play the great man, but it is not a total loss. For once the hero, a man of the same cut and cloth as all the rest, is identified for what he is. The claims to universality are abandoned: Cantwell is not a figure of the lost generation, he is not the representative of something going on in our time, he is not learning through fatal experience what everyone with natural feeling knows to begin with, that no man is an island. He is a man on his own, lonely, grown old, demoted from the rank of General to nobody, in love or persuaded he is in love (there can never have been much difference for him) with a girl who may or may not exist (again no difference), prattling of war, of the good life and the true love with an unfeeling, monotonous, heartsick narcissism, not yet having learned what he is doing, having learned nothing from life, nothing beyond the one thing he knows now - that he is about to die. The defenses are down, the myth is overthrown. This is a poor sick bum, giving himself airs; as sick as all his brothers have been, and like them empty, compulsive and deluded, incapable of love. But for once Hemingway knows his man and for once it is possible to believe in his hero for what he is. He has come home, ruined, to something like humanity, the humanity, at least, of self-betrayal. What he acts out and what he expresses in his action, for once, are one.

This is the most touching thing Hemingway has done. For all the trash and foolishness of this book, perhaps even because of it, because he let himself be lulled and dulled by the fable of himself, he gave away some of his usual caution and let a little grief, more than ordinarily and not all of it stuck in the throat, come through his careful style. A little of the real terror of life in himself, with no defenses handy, not even a propitiatory bull to offer in sacrifice, nothing to kill but the hero. And a little real courage, more than it takes to shoot lions in Africa, the courage to confess, even if it be only through self-betrayal, the sickness and fear and sad wreck of life behind the myth. Wish him luck.

Notes

1 'A Farewell to Arms' (Harmondsworth, Middlesex, 1963), 180.
2 Ibid., 80-1.
3 Villiers de l'Isle-Adam was the French author of the stories 'Cruel Tales' (1883) and the play 'Axel' (1886).
4 American secret fraternal society.

80. NORTHROP FRYE, 'HUDSON REVIEW'

3 (Winter 1951), 611-12

Northrop Frye (b. 1912), a Canadian critic, is Professor of English at the University of Toronto, and author of 'Fearful Symmetry' (1947) and 'The Anatomy of Criticism' (1957).

The theme of 'Across the River and into the Trees' is death in Venice, with Colonel Cantwell, a reduced brigadier and a 'beat-up old bastard', as a military counterpart to Mann's beat-up old novelist. The colonel is a lonely man. Around him is an impersonal hatred directed, like a salute, at his uniform; behind him is the wreck of a marriage and of the career of a good professional soldier; in front of him is his next and last heart attack. He meets all this with a compelling dignity, and there is pathos in his struggles to control his temper, to be 'kind', and to avoid boring other people with his bitterness. It is not that he wants to be liked, but that he senses the rejection of humanity which is involved in every real breakdown of human contact. He has reached the rank in the army at which his superior officers give their orders in terms of a hideous 'big picture' in which strategy is based on politics and publicity stunts instead of on fighting. He cannot cope with this because he cannot relate it to his job of leading men into battle; and when the war is over, he feels his kinship with those who have been maimed and victimized by war, as he knows that no one has profited from it except profiteers. But he has gone far past the stage at which the word failure means anything to him. His approaching death gives a bitter intensity to the ordinary events of his life: to the food and drink of his last meals, to his last look at the violated beauty of Italy, and, above all, to his love for a nineteen-year-old Contessa who comes to him, a dream girl out of a dream city, to offer him an unconditional devotion. Everything that remains for him in life he accepts, simply and without question. The girl loves him, we are told, because he is never 'sad': there is no self-pity which rejects life by clinging to the ego. On the contrary, he has some tenderness for braggarts and charlatans who respond to the exuberance in life, and if there is a desire that still holds him, it is for children to continue his own life, which may be one reason why he calls the Contessa 'daughter'. It is a great theme, and in the hands of someone competent to deal with it - say Ernest Hemingway - it might have been a long short story of overwhelming power.

It is pleasant to dwell on the idea and postpone the fact. In the opening scene and in the curt description of the colonel's death, there is something of the old Hemingway grip. In between, however, the story lies around in bits and pieces, with no serious effort to articulate it. The colonel is entitled to rancorous prejudice - the reader doesn't expect him to be a Buddhist sage, and in his political and military reflections one wouldn't mind the clichés of a commonplace grouch if they built up to something bigger, but they don't. We expect to find the love scenes stripped of eloquence, but not to encounter a cloying singsong of 'I love you truly' and a repetitiousness that looks like padding. The role of the Contessa is that of a more attractive version of a deferential yes-man. The colonel wanders in an empty limbo between a dead and an unborn world, at no point related to other human beings in a way that would give his story any representative importance. As far as anyone can be, he is an island entire of itself.

This last, of course, is part of Hemingway's point. His story is intended to be a study in isolation, of how the standards of a decent soldier are betrayed by modern war. The colonel is not a writer, and the things that are happening to him he assumes to be incommunicable, because he has found them so. And he dominates the book so much that something of his distrust of communication seems to have leaked into the author and paralyzed his will to write. In this kind of story the hero's loneliness must be compensated for by the author's desire to tell the story and, to adopt one of his own cadences, tell it truly. But this involves the total detachment of author from character which comes when sympathy and insight are informed by professional skill. This detachment has not been reached, and the book remains technically on the amateurish level in which the most articulate character sounds like a mouthpiece for the author. Hence all the self-pity and egotism which have been thrown out the door reappear in the windows between the lines. The reader is practically compelled to read the story the wrong way, and the result is a continuous sense of embarrassment.

81. DEB WYLDER, 'WESTERN REVIEW'

15 (Spring 1951), 237-40

Deb Wylder (b. 1923), American professor and critic, is the author of 'Hemingway's Heroes' (1969).

> Finally I heard her [Gertrude Stein] say, Hemingway, after all you are ninety percent Rotarian. Can't you, he said, make it eighty percent? No, she said regretfully, I can't.
>
> from 'The Autobiography of Alice B. Toklas'(1)

It was not until the re-examination of the early Hemingway by the newer critics that we have been able to discover the complexity and truer significance of the works of Ernest Hemingway. It was for Robert Penn Warren, as an example, to point out that, after all, 'A Farewell to Arms' was a religious book. And Malcolm Cowley has stated that 'The Sun Also Rises' is 'a less despairing book than critics like to think.' (2) Those critics who had read Hemingway's first large-selling novel as the nihilistic treatment of a completely sterile society have obviously overlooked many important scenes of that novel, and have completely misinterpreted much of the work. Until recently, critics have failed to point out that Hemingway's selection of ritualistic material serves a moral or social, if not philosophical, purpose; that is, Jake and Frederic have perceived the inadequacies of organized society and have fallen back on a primitivistic series of rituals in order to protect themselves and their own integrity. Neither of these characters is as irresponsible as some critics would have us believe; their codes of living become almost a free man's religion in contrast with the highly institutionalized and ineffectual religion each man has rejected.

The world, 'Cosmopolitan' asserts, has waited ten long years for Hemingway's new novel. 'How do you like it now, gentlemen?' Mr. Hemingway constantly asks in a recent article by Lillian Ross in the 'New Yorker.' Probably the most frequent answer to this question will be, 'We don't.' And the tone of the answer will vary with the reader. For a generation that went to war feeling that what Hemingway had said about the first World War and its aftermath was as valid for the own generation as for his, the answer will be in the shocked voice of the betrayed. The voice of the critic and scholar, whom Hemingway has used every opportunity to badger these past few years, will be the voice of one who has long awaited a chance for reprisal. But even this voice may sound a bit startled at the change in Hemingway. For Hemingway has finally joined the 'lost generation' that has recently become totally lost.

If the generation of the 'twenties' could be classified as 'lost,' we must at least admit that they were searching. They were searching for an answer to the problems that an earlier generation had, without preparing them created and thrown in their faces. To use a Hemingway metaphor, they had been thrown in the game and had been given the rules - and then the world tried to catch them off base. And there was a distinct implication that they had even been handed a set of worthless, outmoded rules. Hemingway, himself, seemed to be looking for a new set of personal rules by which to live. And he found them in primitive rituals, and chose the traditional form of the bullfight to suggest the values inherent in a personal code, a code similar to the one of which Montaigne speaks in his essay Of Repentance. (3) The code of the bullfighter and the hunter could exemplify how to face life -

as well as death. With 'Across the River and into the Trees,' Ernest Hemingway has concluded his search, but from what Hemingway has found, one might say that he has finally become lost - irrevocably lost - at least in the world of values. He has, in effect, joined the ranks with Sinclair Lewis and John Dos Passos in an acceptance of those same institutionalized values which he had rejected in his youth.

Not that Hemingway accepts the 'American way of life' in a blind faith like Don Passos. Not that Colonel Richard Cantwell, the new Hemingway hero, does not have his personal code which embodies honesty, integrity, and action; for he does. We find that Colonel Richard Cantwell conducts his actions as carefully and unemotionally in his relationship with Renata as he does in the matter of the duck hunt, except in those moments when he is completely sentimental. The choice of whether or not to have lobster for dinner needs as much, if not more, calculation and concentration as whether or not the colonel should beat up on a pair of sailors. Moreover, we find that in such matters, as well as in his army career, the Colonel is a straight 'shooter' (Hemingway's own term for the duck hunter). But, underlying all this over statement of Colonel Cantwell's integrity, we find an acceptance of both the military and aristocratic hierarchies which becomes almost fascistic. True, the Colonel rejects the workings of the military hierarchy because it has become inefficient due to, primarily, its complexity. However, we are even more aware of the Colonel's personal dislike of the higher-ups who have refused to grant him a general's command in the regular army. The reason for this confusion lies, perhaps, in Hemingway's having forgotten some of the lessons taught him by Gertrude Stein. Before Hemingway had turned against Miss Stein, in 'Green Hills of Africa' where he tells how he taught her to write dialogue, he made this statement concerning his apprenticeship under Miss Stein and Ezra Pound: 'Ezra was right half the time, and when he was wrong he was so wrong you were never in any doubt about it. Gertrude was always right.' (4) And when Hemingway intended to publish his stories with his own meditations as additional material, Gertrude told him, 'Hemingway, remarks are not literature.' She was right, then; she is still right. Unfortunately, Hemingway seems to have forgotten this advice, for his new novel is filled with his own remarks thrust into the mouth of Colonel Cantwell. For example, Eisenhower is described as 'strictly Epworth League' (5) and a good politician. The other war leaders are classed as Rotarians, in general, and now and then Cantwell pauses to make specific charges against them as individuals. Which really, I suppose, doesn't seem such a terrible indictment when we learn a little more about Cantwell; he is not only an aristocratic Rotarian, but a legionnaire as well. In the vein reminiscent of the drunken legionnaire or the old army master sergeant, Cantwell tells us how 'rough' it was in the last war, that these boys (he refuses to dignify them by the name GI's) are not soldiers, they are comic-book reading technicians. Oddly enough, these boys seem to have won the war. Or as Cantwell would have us believe, under his direction the war was won in spite of the other officers and the soldiers themselves.

Cantwell is as Rotarian as the rest, and a little more dangerous about it. He tells Renata,

> In this club [Rotary Club] they have enameled buttons with their names and you are fined if you call them by their proper names. (page 125).

Cantwell has his own little club at the Gritti (the best hotel where he eats only the best food and drinks only the best wine) and the members call each other by titles of respect rather than proper names, such as 'My Colonel' and '*Gran Maestro*.' Here we have an aristocratic Rotary Club, and one presumes that Colonel Cantwell will, if not fine, at least reprimand those who forget to call him 'My Colonel' as he reprimands Jackson, the chauffeur, for not calling him 'Sir.' Cantwell's attitude might be typified in one sentence, on page 177, 'The hell with anything American except me.'

It has been pointed out that although the setting of most of Hemingway's novels has been in Europe, these novels remain curiously American. Like the earlier expatriate, Henry James, Hemingway may some day (and rightly so) be examined in the light of the effect of European culture on the American type - the examination of American cultural patterns (what James considered the lack of tradition) and the influence European tradition has upon the visiting American. And certainly there will be found some comparisons in ideas. But what James did, Hemingway cannot do - or, at least, has not done. James' style, as he examined the intricacies, the complexities, and the subtleties of European tradition, became more complex, more intricate, more subtle. His style, in a sense, grew out of the material he handled.

Ray B. West, Jr. has stated that 'ideology is not imposed upon the material, it grows out of it, and any attempt to impose it results in artistic failure.' (6)

But in 'Across the River and into the Trees,' the ideology has not only been forced upon the material, the ideology has been superficially attached to the protagonist. In other words, what is usually called the Hemingway 'code' no longer acts as a set of rules to aid the protagonist to live in the world - it has now become an excuse for an embittered old man (excluding his sexual virility and adolescent outlook) to separate himself from the world.

Hemingway has tried, in this novel, to present a more complicated and more subtle development through repetition and concentration on unimportant detail rather than through a corresponding complexity of style. In one scene, when Renata and the Colonel are ordering dinner from the *Gran Maestro*, this little Rotarian gathering spends so much time discussing the lobster that one does not care if that lobster's hard shell and fleshy interior correspond to the character of Colonel Cantwell - a reiteration of rose held in the brawny hand motif. Comparing these scenes with the one from 'The Sun Also Rises' in which you are suddenly reminded that Robert Cohn is a 'pickled herring' is an adequate reminder of the change in Hemingway's literary ability. And it is enough to say that the dialogue of 'Across the River and into the Trees' sounds like an imitation of Hemingway's worst imitators. The dialogue, moreover, is often used as a device to allow the unbelievable Colonel Cantwell to make Hemingway-inspired remarks about war and literature. The tone is closer to 'Green Hills of Africa' and 'Death in the Afternoon' than any of his novels. The result is a failure, for the imposition of such authoritative (and Hemingway *is* authority in this novel) material disrupts the novel form.

Hemingway has recently used every means in his power to strike at the critic. His introduction to Vittorini's 'In Sicily' was as much of a personal attack against critics as what it was intended to be - an introduction to a novel. His new novel bears a strong resemblance to this introduction. Forgetting Miss Stein's advice, he has misused the form of the novel as a vehicle for his own remarks.

Notes

1 Stein, 'Autobiography' (London, 1933), 236.
2 Malcolm Cowley, Introduction to 'The Portable Hemingway' (New York, 1944), xxi.
3 Michel de Montaigne, Of Repentance (c. 1585), 'Essays and Selected Writings,' trans. and ed. Donald Frame (New York, 1963), 317: 'No man ever treated a subject

he knew and understood better than I do the subject I have undertaken.... No man ever penetrated more deeply into his material, or plucked its limbs and consequences cleaner, or reached more accurately and fully the goal he set for his work. To accomplish it, I need only bring it to fidelity; and that is in it, as sincere and pure as can be found.'

4 Quoted in John Peale Bishop, Homage to Hemingway, 'After the Genteel Tradition,' ed. Malcolm Cowley (New York, 1937), 193.

5 American Methodist youth organization.

6 Ray West, Ernest Hemingway: The Failure of Sensibility, 'Sewanee Review,' 53, (1945), 135.

82. JOSEPH WARREN BEACH, 'SEWANEE REVIEW'

59 (Spring 1951), 311-16

Joseph Warren Beach (1880-1957) was an American professor and critic, and author of books on Henry James (1918) and Thomas Hardy (1922). This review is the first third of a long retrospective essay on Hemingway.

I

With his latest novel, Ernest Hemingway has caused a good deal of embarrassment to the many eminent critics and the large body of readers who have whole-heartedly admired him and defended him against all who challenged his perfection as an artist. Indeed, he has rather put his admirers on the spot. He is making it necessary for them to pass his earlier work in review in the light of his latest performance and satisfy themselves whether the faintly disagreeable odor that emanates from 'Across the River and into the Trees' is an evidence of decay already present in the work they have admired so much, or simply an accidental feature of a story turned out in a moment of weakness.

The champion of Hemingway suffers under a double handicap if he has examined the self-portrait of the author exhibited by Lillian Ross in a May number of the 'New Yorker.' It is painful to find that a serious artist, in the fullness of maturity and fame, can be such a boyish -

and bearish - show-off, that a distinguished manipulator of words should depend so much on mere profanity for emphasis and characterization, that an experienced man of the world should be willing to expose to the world so many intimate personal secrets, or that a man who has seen so much and thought so much about life should be so shamelessly self-confident and self-absorbed. But then one reflects that the famous man may be genuinely embarrassed by what he considers the necessity for making a public appearance, that sensitiveness to criticism may have made him self-conscious, and that the crudity of his conversational style may be a defense against those who mistake veneer for culture, or culture for 'life.' Besides, it is a democratic tradition for the public man, when in the public eye, to be a bit easygoing in his manner of speech. And since we are all infinitely curious about the ways and thoughts of genius, what is expected of the noted writer is that he should talk about himself.

If there is one thing that interests Mr. Hemingway more than writing it is manly sports, and nearly everything he has to say to Miss Ross is in terms of boxing, baseball, flying, or hunting. He is interested in the techniques of all these games; he is very much interested in excellent performance; and he is equally interested in the competitive aspects of a sport. In writing, he does not pretend to compete with Tolstoi, who is *hors concours*. But he does consider that he has beat Turgenev and Maupassant at their game; he has fought two draws with 'Mr. Stendhal,' and he thinks he has an edge in the last one. In the United States he is much concerned with 'defending the title' against all comers; though he has stated elsewhere that he does not consider himself in a class with Faulkner.

There is plenty of evidence that Hemingway is a scrupulous artist, bent on turning out the best writing he is capable of. In the days before he had proved a good seller - living in a Paris attic, and serving an apprenticeship to Ezra Pound and Gertrude Stein - he turned down magazine offers that would have supported him handsomely for years. He is certainly devoted to this game for its own sake, and he does himself an injustice spreading his tail feathers even in this half-joking way. Defending the title is a proper and manly thing to do; but it is perhaps just here that the reader has a clue to what often makes him uneasy in Hemingway. In his talk, and sometimes in his writing, one is a trifle bored by the heavy emphasis laid on *virility*. we know, of course, that *virtue* is derived from the same word - signifying adult manhood. We know that virility is a very important factor in human life, and the root of many admirable qualities. The

Romans and Greeks knew this, and so did the people of the Renaissance. American writers have long since made up for the neglect of this truth on the part of the Victorians. And Mr. Hemingway has borne his part in disseminating this important knowledge. It is almost time we returned to the attitudes of Chaucer and Shakespeare and Donne, who took this thing for granted and did not think it necessary to be forever shouting it from the housetops.

And this brings us to the subject of Hemingway's latest novel.

II

'Across the River and into the Trees' is the pathetic 'Liebestod' (1) of a certain Colonel Cantwell, who died of heart failure in an automobile while returning from a duck hunt in the marshes near Venice. Hemingway says 'the book is about the command level in the Second World War.' And that is true too; for the tactical errors and all-round stupidity of the generals in that war make the chief subject of conversation between Colonel Cantwell and his girl-friend while they do their eating and drinking at the Gritti Palace Hotel, and it is this conversation that occupies most of the pages of the book. The Colonel had had the rank of general, and had been demoted as a result of the stupid orders from above which resulted in the decimation of his regiment.

Colonel Cantwell is a genuine fighting man, whose most admirable trait is the purity of his devotion to the honorable and dirty 'trade' of war. But he is a down-to-earth realist, as keen in the exposure of every sort of buncombe as Captain Bluntschli in 'Arms and the Man'. (2) And the loss of rank has not made him any more indulgent toward those who direct war or talk about it without any firsthand knowledge of fighting. He speaks the rough language of the soldier, which alternatively shocks and fascinates his girl-friend. She is drawn to him by his honest character, his manliness, his interesting and uneven temper, by the intensity of his love for her, and perhaps even by the fact that he is more than twice her age and that his heart condition presages a short term of life. She is nineteen, very beautiful, and a contessa. He gives a dubious air of innocence to their relation by calling her 'daughter.' Circumstances seem to make marriage out of the question, and the Colonel prays God he may do her no harm. But the girl's love is too strong and prevails over his good intentions.

A dozen details, big and little, make it clear to one

acquainted with Hemingway's career that a large part of this story is autobiographical. The duck-shooting is a transcript of many passages in his sporting life, as when, in these same Venetian marshes, he 'shot two high doubles, rights and lefts in a row,' and the Italian gardener 'cried with emotion.' There is even the ambitious journalist wife of the Colonel, and his taking of Paris in '44. (See Malcolm Cowley's Portrait of Mr. Papa in 'Life' for January 10, 1949.) Many of the sayings of the Colonel are borrowed from other works of Hemingway ('Better to die on our feet than to live on our knees,' (3) from 'For Whom the Bell Tolls'; 'If you ever fight, then you must win it. That's all that counts,' from Hemingway's introduction to 'Men at War'). (4) A strong head for Martinis and champagne is a phenomenon of wide occurrence. More intimate touches are the Colonel's age, his serious illness, his lameness, the early rising of the old campaigner and the pillbox with the champagne. We are at liberty to assume that the Contessa and the adventure in the gondola are fictive; but they would fit in well with our imaginary life of Hemingway, either as actuality or as wish fulfillment. In one point there is a startling difference between the sentiments of Hemingway and Colonel Cantwell. In 1942 Hemingway was ready to sterilize all members of Nazi party organizations in order to secure the future peace of the world. In 1950 Colonel Cantwell is very fond of both Russians and Germans: 'Do we have to hate the Krauts because we kill them?' But that might be simply the difference between 1942 and 1950.

It has often been noted that the hero of Hemingway's novels is always much the same person - that Jake Barnes and Frederic Henry and Robert Jordan are grown-up versions of the boy Nick Adams of 'In Our Time,' who is so obviously a rendering of the boy Ernest Hemingway. Well, Colonel Cantwell is the oldest of all these avatars of Nick Adams; but one is not sure that he is actually the most adult in his attitude toward himself. And the sense of psychological regression here is one thing that makes us hesitate to rate this book among the best of his work.

Apart from incidental talk about fighting and brass hats, the action of the story consists of three things: the love-making of Renata and the Colonel, the duck-hunt on the following day, and the death of the Colonel on his way back to Venice. It is a slight ground of substance for so long a piece. This is not the serious book about the war on which Hemingway has been at work for many years. It is something thrown off in passing. Hemingway began the present work as a short story. 'Then I couldn't stop,' he says. 'It went on into a novel.' (5) The question is whether he would not have been wiser to stop it. The situation of the man of fifty, with a bad heart, falling in love with a beautiful young girl, and realizing that here, too late, is the true love of which he has always dreamed, is entirely plausible and deeply moving. The question is whether, as it stands, this subject is big enough, strong enough, for the weight he puts upon it.

For one thing, it has proved a considerable strain on his stylistic resources, which have generally been adequate to all his needs. He has seldom allowed himself so many soft, blank-check adjectives for characterizing towns or persons or feelings. The distant view of Venice was 'wonderful' and 'beautiful' to the Colonel as it was when he was eighteen. It was 'like going to New York the first time ... in the old days when it was shining, white and beautiful.' The author is conscious that this is a trifle cliché (and not exactly 'precise'), and he tries again: 'We are coming into my town, he thought. *Christ, what a lovely town.*' He probably feels that the soldier's blasphemy takes the curse off the esthete's la-di-da. And he tries it again with the fishing boats. Picturesque? '*To hell with the picturesque. They are just damned beautiful.*' And so, as Miss Ross would say, 'that settled that.'

When it comes to the sentiment of love, the old Hemingway is still harder to find. Renata 'turned her head ... and the Colonel *felt his heart turn over inside* him, as though some sleeping animal had turned over in its burrow,' etc. (Cf. May Sarton, 'Shadow of a Man,' p. 221: 'His heart turned over inside him.') Hemingway seems to be vaguely aware that his figure of the heart turning over, though violent enough, may have lost its force through frequent use, and he tries to take off the curse of the cliché with the added vividness of the sleeping animal in its burrow. This really distracts the reader's attention altogether from the heart and supplants the mood of the lover with that of the natural historian. But Hemingway is in love with this figure and the trick to save it. At another point: 'and he looked at Renata and *his heart rolled over as a porpoise* does in the sea.' And then, for the instruction of those who cannot realize the mystical importance of what he is saying, he adds: 'It was a beautiful movement and only a few people in the world can feel it and accomplish it.' It remains somewhat dubious whether the rare and beautiful movement in question is that of the loving heart or the porpoise in the sea.

And then there is the oft-repeated assurance of the

Colonel to Renata that she is his 'last and true and only love,' which is not quite in the Hemingway manner. Well, you may say that in his tenderness the Colonel is whimsically adapting the words of some old ballad. (For the girl is incidentally perfecting her English.) You may say that there is a spice of conscious wit in this paradox of a *last* and *only* love. You may say, if you like, that these lovers are performing a ritual, and that repetition is of the essence of all rituals. Well, yes, but the rituals of love are for lovers, and require some cutting down in transcription.

You may say that the belated discovery of true love is a tragic circumstance, not unknown in human experience, and one that may well draw our tears. Draw our tears yes. But whether it is correct to use the word tragic in this connection depends on one's conception of tragedy. According to Aristotle tragedy is associated with an important action and one in which the character of the participants is a main determinant in the catastrophe.(6) Hemingway does not succeed in giving this abortive love the sort of importance that Aristotle calls for and Shakespeare exemplifies. And it is not the character of Renata or the Colonel that provokes the tragedy here, but the accidental circumstance that they have met thirty years too late. It is more exact to say that this story is *pathetic*, and that the pathos is rather too much drawn out for the happiest effect.

There is one other thing that may well be disturbing to many readers whom it would be rash to dismiss as simply prudish. In the gondola ride, in his effort to persuade us of the 'truth' of this love, Hemingway feels called on to emphasize the continued virility of the aged and ailing soldier. This is a ticklish undertaking, in which he runs the risk of appealing to the ribald more than to the compassionate reader. All the more so as the display of virility on the part of the Colonel is followed so closely by his death, after the related (and perhaps symbolic) display of the same quality in the duck-shooting. There is much danger here that the frivolous reader may put the love-making and the death together and, in view of the man's condition, may be as much inclined to laugh at the old fool as to pity the true lover.

Notes

1 Literally 'love-death'; the aria sung by the doomed lovers in Wagner's 'Tristan und Isolde' (1865).

2 Captain Bluntschli is the cynical soldier in Bernard Shaw's play of 1894.
3 Ernest Hemingway, 'For Whom the Bell Tolls' (New York, 1968), 309.
4 Ernest Hemingway, Introduction to 'Men at War' (New York, 1971), 5.
5 Lillian Ross, 'Portrait of Hemingway' (New York, 1961), 35.
6 Aristotle, 'Poetics.'

'The Old Man and the Sea' (1952)

83. EDWIN MUIR, 'OBSERVER'

7 September 1952, 7

Muir reviews Hemingway's novel with Evelyn Waugh's 'Men at Arms.'

These books, both by experienced novelists, are somewhat unlike what we have come to expect. We are surprised by a slight lack of professional assurance and accomplishment. The authors seem to be reaching after something more significant; and imperfection has slipped in. How the novelist is to deal with imperfection now that the novel has become recognised as a technical feat, is hard to say. It was not a question which worried novelists in earlier times. But now the novelist must offer a triumph and avoid any sign of a struggle with his subject. And since the novelist offers it, the reader has come to require it, for a triumph is a reassuring thing.

Yet we apply other standards to the great novelists of the past; we accept Scott's insipid heroes and heroines (and how many of them there are) for the sake of the scores of living characters, knowing that these could never have breathed in the conditioned atmosphere of a neat contemporary novel. Melville's Moby Dick and Captain Ahab tear wide gaps in his imaginative structure. We accept the faults for the sake of the greatness. It is true that the greatness, both in Scott and Melville, is something that breaks in: there are enough chinks to admit it. But the contemporary novel has become so neat and tight that only a double miracle would allow the miracle to happen.

Neither of these novels may be great; but there is one character in 'Men at Arms' of a quite different size from any other that Mr. Waugh has produced, and a really heroic piece of narrative in 'The Old Man and the Sea,' told with a simplicity which shows that Mr. Hemingway has forgotten that he is a tough writer. He does, at the start, expose his sentimentality more openly than he has done before; but that is a thing which we have to accept for the sake of the superb writing which follows, just as we accept the tears of Dickens. The first few pages are almost strangely sentimental, with relapses into the 'ands' of children's storybooks:

> Everything about him was old except his eyes and they were the same colour as the sea and were cheerful and undefeated.

But this gush of sentimentality is a mere discharge of inhibitions, a sort of ceremonial purification; and as soon as the long battle with the great fish begins the toughness and the sentimentality are gone, and Mr. Hemingway is in the world of free poetic imagination where he is really at home. If the reader can survive the first few pages which introduce him to the old man, the boy, and the fish, he will be rewarded. For Mr. Hemingway is essentially an imaginative writer, and his imagination has never displayed itself more powerfully than in this simple and tragic story.

84. MARK SCHORER, 'NEW REPUBLIC'

127 (6 October 1952), 19-20

The only guts that are mentioned in this story are the veritable entrails of fish, but we are nevertheless reminded on every page that Hemingway once defined this favorite word, in its metaphorical use, as 'grace under pressure.' Grace, in the fullest sense, is the possession of this old man, just as grace was precisely what Colonel Cantwell, in 'Across the River and into the Trees,' was totally without. But here it is, complete and absolute, the very breath of this old man, so thoroughly his in his essence as in his *ambiente*, that it can only be there under pressure as at all other times, and indeed, even under the greatest pressure, he hardly alters. Grace, by which one means now not the old stiff upper lip (this old man's upper lip is not so very stiff) which came to some of the older heroes a little easily sometimes, a quality more nearly a manner of speaking than of being; not that now, but benignity, nothing less, and beautifully, masterfully presented, so that the satisfaction one has in this creation is plain happiness, and then, I suppose, gratitude.

The old man has a Franciscan quality that so pervades his habit of thought as to support and give the body of dramatic plausibility, even inevitability to the suggestion of Christian martyrdom which comes at the end. Early in the story, when the old man is being helped by the boy, he thanks him for the food he gives him. 'He was too simple to wonder when he had attained humility. But he knew he had attained it and he knew it was not disgraceful and it carried no loss of true pride.' Humility - the assumption without self-consciousness and therefore without sentimentality - is the old man's strength.

He was very fond of flying fish as they were his principal friends on the ocean. He was sorry for the birds, especially the small delicate dark terns that were always flying and looking and almost never finding, and he thought, 'The birds have a harder life than we do except for the robber birds and the heavy strong ones. Why did they make birds so delicate and fine as those sea swallows when the ocean can be so cruel? She is kind and very beautiful. But she can be so cruel and it comes so suddenly and such birds that fly, dipping and hunting, with their small sad voices are made too delicately for the sea.'

And again, now of porpoises, and then of the marlin itself:

> 'They are good,' he said. 'They play and make jokes and love one another. They are our brothers like the flying fish.'
>
> Then he began to pity the great fish that he had hooked. He is wonderful and strange and who knows how old he is, he thought. Never have I had such a strong fish nor one who acted so strangely. Perhaps he is too wise to jump. He could ruin me by jumping or by a wild rush. But perhaps he has been hooked many times before and he knows that this is how he should make his fight.

> He cannot know that it is only one man against him, nor that it is an old man. But what a great fish he is.... I wonder if he has any plans or if he is just as desperate as I am?

And thus, with a kind of Biblical abstraction that always assumes the independence of all things in their own character from his character, which is likewise independent and separate (in this recognition lie the true sources of brotherhood as of pity), he speaks to a bird, to his fish, and to the parts of his own body, his hands and his head. With a few wavering exceptions, Hemingway sustains the perilous poise of all this with great beauty over pits of possible bathos.

Everywhere the book is being called a classic. In at least one sense, the word cannot be applied, for here and there, where the writing wavers, its pure lucidity is muddied by all that hulking personality which, at his worst, Hemingway has made all too familiar. I do not have in mind the talk about baseball, which has bothered at least one reviewer. 'The baseball' is a near obsession with most Caribbean natives, but we do not have to know this to accept the old man's interest as his own rather than as Hemingway's. (After all, DiMaggio's (1) father *was* a fisherman, as the old man tells us, and the sword of the marlin is 'as long as a baseball bat.') But a murky paragraph that has to do with 'mysticism about turtles' is a case in point. Or a sentence such as this: 'He did not truly feel good because the pain from the cord across his back had almost passed pain and gone into a dullness that he mistrusted' - is it a quibble to suggest that the word 'truly' and its location spoil this sentence, jar us out of the mind of the old man whom we are coming to know into the reflection that we've read Hemingway before? Or a brief passage such as this:

> After he judged that his right hand had been in the water long enough he took it out and looked at it.
>
> 'It is not bad,' he said. 'And pain does not matter to a man....
>
> 'You did not do so badly for something worthless,' he said to his left hand. 'But there was a moment when I could not find you.'
>
> Why was I not born with two good hands? he thought. Perhaps it was my fault in not training that one properly. But God knows he has had enough chances to learn. He did not do so badly in the night, though, and he has only cramped once. If he cramps again let the line cut him off. (2)

The last sentence tells us with dramatic concreteness what the generalization, 'pain does not matter to a man,' which is really Hemingway's, does not tell us at all. It should not have been written, precisely because what *is* written must make *us* speak that conclusion, it should be our generalization from his evidence.

But the old man seldom lapses into dramatic falseness. In his age, alone at sea, he has taken to speaking aloud, and instead of dialogue between characters by which most fiction moves, this story moves by little dialogues in the old man himself, the exchange of what is spoken and what is not spoken. This is almost a running drama between that which is only possible and that which is real:

> 'Fish,' he said, 'I love you and respect you very much. But I will kill you dead before this day ends.'
>
> Let us hope so, he thought.

The threat of over-generalization is almost always in the spoken words, which, then, are immediately rooted in actuality by the reservations of the unspoken. And of course, Hemingway's incredible gift for writing of the natural life serves the same function. Whether he is describing plankton, jelly fish, the sucking fish that swim in the shadow of the marlin, the gutting of a dolphin that contains two flying fish, or turtles, they are all always there before us, actualities, and the old man is an actuality among them.

The novel is nearly a fable. The best fiction, at its heart, always is, of course, but with his particular diction and syntax, Hemingway's stories approach fable more directly than most, and never so directly as here. It is the quality of his fiction at its very best, the marvelous simplicity of line. ('"Be calm and strong, old man", he said.') There has been another strain in his fiction, to be sure - his personal ambition to become a character in a tall tale, folklore as opposed to fable. That is the weaker man pushing aside the great novelist. The strain glimmers once in this story when we are told of the old man's feat of strength in his youth: 'They had gone one day and one night with their elbows on a chalk line on the table and their forearms straight up and their hands gripped tight.' Take it away.

The true quality of fable is first of all in the style, in the degree of abstraction, which is not only in some ways Biblical but is always tending toward the proverbial rhythm. ('The setting of the sun is a difficult time for fish.') Next, it is in the simplicity of the narrative, and in the beautiful proportion (about three-fourths to one-fourth) of its rise and fall. Finally, of course, it is in the moral significance of the narrative, this fine story of an ancient who goes too far out, 'beyond the boundaries of permitted aspiration,' (3) as Conrad put it ('You violated your luck when you went too far outside,' the old man thinks), and encounters his destiny:

> His choice had been to stay in the deep dark water far out beyond all snares and traps and treacheries. My choice was to go there to find him beyond all people. Beyond all people in the world. Now we are joined together and have been since noon. And no one to help either one of us.

In this isolation, he wins a Conradian victory, which means destruction and triumph. We permit his martyrdom because he has earned it. His sigh is 'just a noise such as a man might make, involuntarily, feeling the nail go through his hands and into the wood.' He stumbles under the weight of his mast when he carries it across his shoulder, up a hill. He sleeps, finally, 'with his arms out straight and the palms of his hands up.' There is more than this, and for those who, like this reviewer, believe that Hemingway's art, when it is art, is absolutely incomparable, and that he is unquestionably the greatest craftsman in the American novel in this century, something that is perhaps even more interesting. For this appears to be not only a moral fable, but a parable, and all the controlled passion in the story, all the taut excitement in the prose come, I believe, from the parable. It is an old man catching a fish, yes; but it is also a great artist in the act of mastering his subject, and, more than that, of actually writing about that struggle. Nothing is more important than his craft, and it is beloved; but because it must be struggled with and mastered, it is also a foe, enemy to all self-indulgence, to all looseness of feeling, all laxness of style, all soft pomposities.

> 'I am a strange old man.'
> 'But are you strong enough now for a truly big fish?'
> 'I think so. And there are many tricks.'

Hemingway, who has always known the tricks, is strong enough now to have mastered his greatest subject. 'I could not fail myself and die on a fish like this,' the old man reflects. They win together, the great character, the big writer.

Notes

1 Joe DiMaggio, star center fielder of the New York Yankees, later married Marilyn Monroe.
2 See Matthew 5: 29: 'if thy right eye offend thee, pluck it out.'
3 Joseph Conrad, Heart of Darkness, 'Three Short Novels' (New York, 1960), 80: 'this alone had beguiled his unlawful soul beyond the bounds of permitted aspirations.'

85. GILBERT HIGHET, 'HARPER'S'

205 (October 1952), 102, 104

Gilbert Highet (1906-78) was a Scottish-born critic, Professor of Latin at Columbia University, and the author of 'The Classical Tradition' (1949), 'The Art of Teaching' (1951) and 'Juvenal' (1954).

Ernest Hemingway's 'The Old Man and the Sea' is a good story. It is about courage. It tells of a fisherman who fights old age and the loss of his strength, poverty and the loss of his luck, loneliness and the gigantic sea in which he hunts, almost completely solitary except for the birds, the flying-fish, and the friendly dolphins. It tells how he caught a huge fish; how the fish fought him, pulling him many miles out to sea; how he killed it; how the sharks attacked his magnificent prize before he could get it home; and how bravely and hopelessly he fought them - even the sharks are brave, in their way.

This always was a good story. It was good when Mr. Hemingway first told it, in an essay called On the Blue Water, on page 184 of 'Esquire' for April 1936. It was good when variations of it were told by other American writers. Walter Van Tilburg Clark did it proud in 'The Track of the Cat.' (1) Mr. Hemingway's closest predecessor, Jack London, made fun of it in a mammoth-hunt called

'A Relic of the Pliocene.' (2) There was also a long novel about a sea captain and a whale.

Mr. Hemingway's feelings do not change much, so it is natural that this should be a plot familiar to his readers. It is an epic pattern. A hero undertakes a hard task. He is scarcely equal to it because of ill luck, wounds, treachery, hesitation, or age. With a tremendous effort, he succeeds. But in his success he loses the prize itself, or final victory, or his life. Still, his gallantry remains. Mr. Hemingway has used this pattern in Francis Macomber, 'For Whom the Bell Tolls,' and several other tales. What is new here is his thinking about age and about death: not the energetic death of the fighter or hunter, nor the silly chance death of the pedestrian, but the inevitable death of which old age is a degrading part. A number of his early stories had aging athletes in them: My Old Man, about racing: The Undefeated, about bullfighting: 'To Have and Have Not,' about smuggling. His last book, about the garrulous colonel, approached this problem again, from the point of view of the sufferer, not of the spectator. But the colonel was elderly, boozy, and a bore. The lonely fisherman here is old, ascetic, and noble.

Notes

1 A symbolic novel about hunting a panther (1949).
2 A story in 'The Faith of Men' (1904).

86. WILIAM FAULKNER, 'SHENANDOAH'

3 (Autumn 1952), 55

William Faulkner (1897-1962) was an American novelist, the author of 'The Sound and the Fury' (1929), 'Light in August' (1932) and 'Absalom, Absalom!' (1936). 'Shenandoah' is a literary journal published in Lexington, Virginia.

His best. Time may show it to be the best single piece of any of us, I mean his and my contemporaries. This time, he discovered God, a Creator. Until now, his men and women had made themselves, shaped themselves out of their own clay; their victories and defeats were at the hands of each other, just to prove to themselves or one another how tough they could be. But this time, he wrote about pity: about something somewhere that made them all: the old man who had to catch the fish and then lose it, the fish that had to be caught and then lost, the sharks which had to rob the old man of his fish; made them all and loved them all and pitied them all. It's all right. Praise God that whatever made and loves and pities Hemingway and me kept him from touching it any further.

87. DELMORE SCHWARTZ, 'PARTISAN REVIEW'

19 (November 1952), 702-3

The ovation which greeted Hemingway's new novel was mostly very nice. For it was mostly a desire to continue to admire a great writer. Yet there was a note of insistence in the praise and a note of relief, the relief because his previous book was extremely bad in an ominous way, and the insistence, I think, because this new work is not so much good in itself as a virtuoso performance which reminds one of Hemingway at his best. The experience of literature is always comparative, and we have only to remember a story like The Undefeated, which has almost the same theme as 'The Old Man and the Sea,' or the account of the Caporetto retreat in 'A Farewell to Arms,' to see exactly how the new book falls short. Whenever, in this new book, the narrative is concerned wholly with fishing, there is a pure vividness of presentation. But when the old man's emotions are explicitly dealt with, there is a margin of self-consciousness and a mannerism of assertion which is perhaps inevitable whenever a great writer cannot get free of his knowledge that he is a great writer. Perhaps this is why the old fisherman is too generalized, too much without a personal history; the reader cannot help but think at times that Hemingway, the publicized author and personality bewitched by his own publicity and an imitator of his own style, is speaking to him directly.

Nevertheless this book does not exist in isolation from the author's work as a whole, which gives it a greater significance and to which it gives a new definition and clarity. We see more clearly how for Hemingway the kingdom of heaven, which is within us, is moral stamina; experience, stripped of illusion, is inexhaustible threat. Which should make the reader recognize how purely American a writer Hemingway is. For what is this sense of existence but the essential condition of the pioneer? It is the terror and the isolation of the pioneer in the forest that Hemingway seeks out in his prizefighters, gunmen, matadors, soldiers and expatriate sportsmen. The hunting and fishing which were necessities of life for the pioneer may be merely sports and games now, but they are pursued with an energy and passion absent in other areas of existence because only within the conditions of sport can a man be truly himself, truly an individual, truly able to pit an isolated will and consciousness against the whole of experience. In 'To Have and Have not,' Hemingway tried to repudiate this sense of existence; in 'For Whom the Bell Tolls' he tried to go beyond it, but he wrote with all of his power under control only when the hero was contained within guerilla warfare, which is obviously Daniel Boone again; in 'Across the River and into the Trees' there is an hysterical fury against modern warfare, for in modern warfare the isolated individual can have no role purely as an isolated individual. Now, after the bluster, bravado and truculence of that book, his fresh possession of his own sensibility suggests the possibility of a new masterpiece.

88. JOYCE CARY, 'NEW YORK TIMES BOOK REVIEW'

7 December 1952, 4

Joyce Cary (1888-1957), Irish novelist, was the author of 'Mister Johnson' (1939) and 'The Horse's Mouth' (1944).

Of the books I have read this year, Hemingway's 'The Old Man and the Sea' struck me as the most complete job. Hemingway at his best is unique. He tells a folk tale, but it is a sophisticated folk tale. It has been said that this great artist belongs essentially to the world of the strip cartoon and there is something in judgment for those who understand the difference between 'Lear' and 'Silver King.' (1) Both are melodramas for barnstormers but one is tailored by genius and the other is a reach-me-down from the slop-shop. They are different in effect because they are different in cause. Lear's tragedy was written by a man who loved melodrama for its richness of theme. Silver King began and ended as a tear-jerker. It is stale now because it was a dead thing then. It has no root in experience or reflection. Hemingway's old man is profoundly original. It deals with fundamentals, the origins. Its form, so elaborately contrived, is yet perfectly suited to the massive shape of a folk theme.

Note

1 A popular melodrama by Henry Arthur Jones and Henry Herman, produced in 1882.

89. F.W. DUPEE, 'KENYON REVIEW'

15 (Winter 1953), 150-5

F.W. Dupee (1904-79), an American professor and critic, was the author of books on Henry James.

Hemingway's next to last book, 'Across the River and into the Trees,' may some day be admired more liberally than it seems to have been on its first appearance. That novel was at least a powerful expression of Hemingway's legend. His new novel, 'The Old Man and the Sea,' has nothing to do with the legend, except as it registers a determination to shake the legend off. In this story the author is revealed rather than exposed. He is shown in what are no doubt his original capacities: as an exacting artist, a visionary of nature and human nature, a man committed to self-reliance *jusqu'au feu* (1) and beyond.

One of his best stories, 'The Old Man and the Sea' is also a first-rate example of that literature of the big hunt to which so many American writers have contributed, affirming through this image the frontier virtues and the natural basis of our life. Certain of Hemingway's early tales renewed the hunting subject for the present age; he comes back to it now with a difference. His protagonist is no longer an enchanted boy in the woods but an aging man enacting a general tragedy. This sounds ambitious; and it must be added that 'The Old Man and the Sea' is no such elaborate performance as 'Moby Dick' or Faulkner's The Bear, two eminent narratives of the big hunt. But Hemingway's short novel or long story has its own way of being ambitious: it is a quintessential if not a complex revelation, as this author's best work usually is. Its simplicity is of an urgent kind, like that of a cry of alarm at night or a command shouted across water.

There are only two characters of any consequence and one of them is a fish. The other, the principal character, is a Cuban fisherman who is getting on in years and is also down on his luck. Between his bad luck and his time of life there is an unavowed but strongly felt connection. The one seems to confirm the other, in his own mind as in that of his fellow fishermen. Even the boy whom he has lovingly instructed in their trade is advised by his parents to leave the old man alone. 'The setting of the sun is a difficult time for all fish,' as the old man observes; and old age is a difficult time for active men. But this still active man is determined to repair his luck and redeem his years. 'My big fish must be somewhere,' he insists, putting out by himself in his small skiff. What happens next shows him to have been only too right. He hooks a sixteen-foot marlin,(2) a fish so huge and so game as to challenge any two men to handle it; and the old man, besides being alone, is poorly equipped for such an encounter. As it is, he accomplishes what few could hope to accomplish. He plays the big fish through the days and nights in defiance of hunger and fatigue, he kills it at last with a harpoon, and he makes for port with his carcass in tow. But meanwhile the fish has dragged him in his skiff far out to sea, and before he can get the carcass ashore and to market it is eaten to the bone by sharks.

'I am sorry that I went too far out. I ruined us both,' he confesses to the fish's remains, which he tows ashore as a sorry witness to his bad-good luck. But nothing can console him for a fate which has been confirmed on such a grand scale. It is true that in his skill and resolution he has been exemplary. His exercise of those qualities shows what such a man may still be despite his years. But the 'going too far out' and the resulting loss of the substance of his catch make up the unredeemable part of his situation, the sheer bad luck of being old. It is different for the tourists looking on from the portside cafés. They are impressed by the mere bigness of the fish's skeleton, which they take for that of an outsized shark. To the fisherman and his kind, the value of the meat and the right name of the fish are matters of absolute importance. After all, fish are their livelihood; and a man's excellent performance does not compensate his failures. The natives shrug, the boy weeps, and the old man returns to the newspaper-lined bed in his draughty shack.

But neither do a man's failures compromise his performance. Hemingway is committed to a careful accounting of the profit and loss of life; and in general the two must occupy to infinity their separate columns in the ledger. Only at moments of intense experience are they felt to compose a sum, and then but magically, as in a dream or in art. Many of Hemingway's stories are about just such moments, however, and 'The Old Man and the Sea' is one of those stories. If the old man has not succeeded in getting the fish to market, he has nevertheless exerted himself to his limits and in doing so has fully shown what he is.

He is a preeminently natural man who is at the same time and by the same token entirely human, his human-ness manifesting itself partly in the various items that make him an individual: the brown blotch on his face, his peculiar idiom, his taste for big-league baseball, his dreams of lions on a yellow African beach. If he is a superior individual that is probably because the natural, the human and the unique are all markedly present in him. And he *is* superior: like all first-rate heroes he suffers abysmally but is equal to his sufferings; and because he has freely elected to endure them in what to him is a good cause, they even seem just and beautiful. His story is perhaps the saddest in Hemingway's work but it is among the least painful. It is also one of the least theatrical, although the glare of theatre that plays on much of Hemingway's work is a prime attraction of it. The usual theatricality arises from the fact that the solitude and suffering of his heroes regularly exceed their given circumstances. They pine and suffer, not only personally but, so to speak, historically. They agonize in the name of all the superior individuals 'in our time': the men and women whose skills come to nothing, the doomed artists of sport and battle and love. 'The Old Man and the Sea,' which shows the tourists in the cafés and the glow of Havana in the night sky, keeps to the historical pattern; and thanks to that fact it remains firmly within Hemingway's usual line of vision. Yet the story's sadness is uncommonly intelligible on the story's own terms, and thus is less of the footlights. As the old man suffers for a good reason, so he is lonely in the quite predictable sense that he requires the companionship and help of others.

Besides, his assets are perfectly tangible, his resources are there for all to see. He has his sustaining sense of community with created things. This includes the big fish, which, in the heightened consciousness brought on by the old man's ordeal, becomes his alter-ego as well as his catch, his victim and victimizer both. It includes the sharks of various kinds that attack and devour the fish when it is dead and which the old man frankly hates, saying, 'I'll fight them until I die.' It includes the stray land bird that perches momentarily on his taut lines, as exhausted as he is. It includes everything above and beneath 'the blue water that the old man saw now with his lines going down into the water that was a mile deep.' And this sympathy for the created, this passion for the particular, extends to his own person and being: to his words, which he speaks carefully as if counting out change; to his hands - the bad left one that is subject to cramps and the more dependable right one; to his very sins, which he remembers although professing himself incompetent to deal with them ('There are people who are paid to do it,' he thinks). For himself he has a detached awareness and respect, as if he were part of the whole world of forces. Indeed his physical side is inseparable from any other side of him. His conscience is at one with his powers of endurance. If he has a soul, its seat is in his two hands.

But he and the marlin are not at one. His community with nature is perfect enough so that he feels no need to confound himself with its purer products. If the fish is a character, as I said, it is on the condition of his remaining a fish; the old man talks to him but he does not talk to the old man. The old man's entire mental life is predicated on a recognition of differences. He is different in that he practices the arts and exhibits the morale of his human trade, feeling the responsibility that goes with his mastery. This responsibility he acknowledges when he says, 'I am sorry I went so far out, I ruined us both.' An old unlucky man may still be a man. 'It is better to be lucky. But I would rather be exact,' he says.

Such is the old fisherman's portrait as it emerges from the swiftly presented minutiae of his conduct in the process of the action. The portrait brings to a high pitch of consciousness that humane naturalism which Hemingway professes, in common with Faulkner and other American writers of their generation. Hemingway's hatred of merely acquisitive and destructive men is as the old man's hatred of the sharks; and his naturalism serves him as a counter-irritant, a cry of battle. It is therefore frequently distorted into forms of violence, lust and muscular snobbishness; but in the distortion resides the art. If his feeling for nature receives in this story an uncommonly ideal expression, that does not necessarily mean that the anger is any less. It may mean that the anger has now reached the stage of the ineffable. The story is not a demonstration but a dream. It is like the dream of the lions on the yellow beach that recurs to the old fisherman in the extremity of his age and misfortune.

Notes

1 To the limit.
2 The marlin is actually eighteen feet.

90. R.W.B. LEWIS, 'HUDSON REVIEW'

6 (Spring 1953), 146-8

R.W.B. Lewis (b. 1917), American critic, Professor of English at Yale University, is the author of 'The American Adam' (1955) and 'Edith Wharton' (1975).

Hemingway's brief parable of the old fisherman, the giant marlin and the sharks has an authentic beauty, but I doubt if the book can bear the amount of critical weight already piled upon it. I have read a comic-strip parody of it which is less funny than it might be, because the original itself has an elusive strain of parody - a very faint breath of mockery of the representative Hemingway style and hero and adventure and athletic ritual. The work is not, somehow, altogether and finally *serio* (1) (the Italian word distinguishes, better than its English translation, between the good quality and its corruptions into the stuffy and pretentious); and our assent has to be partially withheld. Yet it has its rare and gentle humanities.

The story (I assume it need not be rehearsed) is an autumnal song celebrating anew and in his old age the staunch, solitary and self-communing figure who has attained to the qualities Hemingway thinks necessary for survival in a wolfish world. In his own right, so to speak, the old man is a moving and even a noble individual; love has gone into him, and goes out of him; he is really, and without insistence, at home with the weather. It is only when his inventor tampers with him, makes him dream of lions on the beach, and the like, that he verges on the antic. His crisis is the classic contest between *virtu* and *fortuna*: between the old man's skill and tenacity ('I know many tricks and have resolution') and the unpredictable swerve of things which Hemingway calls 'luck' ('Luck is a thing that comes in many forms and who can recognise her?'). Hemingway has remarked rather often that such is also the crisis of every creative enterprise; and we may be supposed to take the story as an allegory of its own history. If so, however, it is an allegory too banal to warrant much analysis. It is the ultimate sizing up of experience that interests us. And where, at the end of 'To Have and Have Not' (1937), the dying Harry Morgan concluded that, 'A man alone doesn't have a bloody chance,' here the old man, awesomely alone, reflects in all humility that 'Man is not made for defeat.... A man can be destroyed but not defeated.' This is the sign of *virtu* prepared to survive any calamity; even the appalling *fortuna* represented by the sharks, who devour the greatest catch - an eighteen-foot marlin - the old man has ever dreamed of.

Although 'The Old Man and the Sea' is not absolutely persuasive, Hemingway regains in it much of the poise so vexatiously missing in the unlucky 'Across the River.' The distinction of Hemingway's best work has rested upon the insight by which he managed to avoid the tempting alternatives I have mentioned. 'Let those who want to save the world,' he once wrote, 'if you can get to see it clear and as a whole.'(2) In 'Across the River,' Hemingway seemed intent on the world's salvation, though for what hodge-podge of purposes, one scarcely dares to guess. Now, with this curiously peaceful account of the old man's splendid failure, Hemingway returns to the role of the perceiver; and what he perceives is once again the stimulating and fatal relation between integrity of character and the churning abundance of experience. His style catches this perception with a good deal of its old power: in the relation (mentioned by Harry Levin) (3) between an abundance of nouns, the signs of things in experience, and the simplicity and paucity of adjectives - signs of the ways we clutch at experience, seek to punch it into shape and hang on to it. The old man's old man is realised in prose that honors them both.

Notes

1 Sincere, honest.
2 'Death in the Afternoon' (Harmondsworth, Middlesex, 1962), 263.
3 Harry Levin, Observations on the Style of Ernest Hemingway, 'Kenyon Review,' 13 (1951), 581-609.

'The Hemingway Reader' (1953)

91. STANLEY EDGAR HYMAN, 'NEW YORK TIMES BOOK REVIEW'

13 September 1953, 28

Stanley Edgar Hyman (1919-70) was an American professor and critic, and the author of 'The Armed Vision' (1952) and 'The Tangled Bank' (1962).

Ernest Hemingway has been publishing for almost thirty years, and it was inevitable that sooner or later the Viking 'Portable Hemingway' would be succeeded by a more comprehensive selection from Scribner's. Charles Poore has edited this with intelligence and discrimination, including the whole of 'The Torrents of Spring' and 'The Sun Also Rises,' well-chosen chapters from the other five novels, 'Green Hills of Africa,' and 'Death in the Afternoon,' and eleven short stories. His prefaces, despite a tone of somewhat indiscriminate approval, are brief and relevant, often pointing up details of technique that might otherwise be missed.

One can suspect that 'The Torrents of Spring,' which now seems a crashing bore, was included to have a novel otherwise unavailable, and The Fable of the Good Lion, a dreadful piece of whimsey that appeared in 'Holiday' in 1951, to have a story not previously in book form. One can quibble with the choice of stories (if much-reprinted ones like The Short Happy Life of Francis Macomber and The Snows of Kilimanjaro, why not The Killers and The Undefeated; why not My Old Man instead of the melodramatic Fifty Grand?) or note that Mr. Poore's bias is for the details of physical action, and that scenes of this sort tend to represent the novels rather than more complicated and elusive rituals. In the last analysis no anthology of Hemingway's work, including the reviewer's ideal selection, could be free of such surmises, quibbles, and reservations.

The larger issue the book raises is that of Hemingway's own development. A compilation covering three decades of work is a merciless test, with a writer competing at every moment against his own absolute best. Except for a few pages of puerile private joking and an inadequate ending, 'The Sun Also Rises' survives undiminished, a small-scale masterpiece, as do the parts Mr. Poore has printed of 'A Farewell to Arms' and 'To Have and Have Not,' as well as a high percentage of the stories, particularly The Light of the World. But even as early as A Way You'll Never Be the self-indulgence and egocentrism so repellent in the later war correspondence are clearly visible; 'Death in the Afternoon' has all the free-floating Hispanophile sentimentality that was to mar 'For Whom the Bell Tolls' a decade later, and irrelevant dogmatic opinions were just as obtrusive in 'Green Hills of Africa' as they are in 'Across the River and Into the Trees.'

After the tough economy of After the Storm it is embarrassing to read the same thing done less well in 'The Old Man and the Sea,' and if The Undefeated, which resembles 'The Old Man' in theme and structure and has none of its faults, had been included, the note of self-parody in Hemingway's recent work would have been painfully evident. Colonel Cantwell is monstrous after we have just known love and war with Lieutenant Henry.

It is true that we cannot always expect a writer to write at his best, and it is true that the worst things Hemingway ever wrote are better than much of today's prose, but these thoughts are no comfort when a chronological selection graphs a neat parabola. Sinking into a self-parody in later years is a fate that has befallen many fine writers before Hemingway and no doubt awaits many after him.

Obituaries (1961)

92. JOHN WAIN, 'OBSERVER'

9 July 1961, 21

John Wain (b. 1925) is an English novelist and critic, the author of 'Hurry On Down' (1953), 'The Living World of Shakespeare' (1964) and the autobiography 'Sprightly Running' (1962).

If the word 'classical' still has any meaning except just as the opposite of 'romantic,' then we can say that Ernest Hemingway was a classical writer. He was terse, lucid, economical; he pared life down to what he took to be the essentials, and then worked with great care and concentration to embody these essentials in imaginative form. He had neither the romantic interest in the untypical nor the adventure-story writer's interest in action for its own sake.

His characteristic form is the heroic fable. If Homer (assuming one single person of that name to have existed) could return to earth and read modern literature, he would find very little in it that was congenial to him - until he got to Hemingway. There, in 'A Farewell to Arms,' in Fifty Grand, in The Undefeated, in 'The Old Man and the Sea,' he would find himself back in his own world, of heroic simplicities that are not simple, of unreflective action that is yet more action of the mind than of the body.

Except for Macaulay, no writer in the English-speaking world has been so widely imitated as Hemingway. Even

Byron was not copied by so many, nor for so long. At any given time since the late twenties there has been a huge tribe of would-be Hemingways who have taken from the master the little they could use and left the much they could not. They have imagined that all one had to do to be a Hemingway was to write about violence and use short sentences. Yet, to a thoughtful reader, it is clear that hunting and fighting are important to him only secondarily. His vision of life embodied itself in fables concerning physical activity and the outdoor world, but there is never any doubt that for Hemingway, as for all sensitive men, the real battleground is inward.

Hemingway's soldiers, hunters, boxers and bullfighters are all men who have to face their personal testing-time in isolation, drawing strength, if they are fortunate enough to have strength, from the resources of their innermost being. So does every man; the same laws that apply to these picturesque men of action apply equally to curate or bank clerk; and this, so far from banishing Hemingway to the triviality of the adventure-story writer, is precisely what gives him his universality and greatness. It is nowhere suggested in his work that men who do not kill wild animals, or risk their lives in the bullring, are less real and significant than men who do. It is simply that his imaginative vision was able to refract itself through these tales of courage, fear, hunger, sweat, loneliness and death.

Hemingway is a very physical writer; the 'objective correlative,' (1) in Eliot's famous phrase, is always to him a matter of the concrete, the seen and touched and experienced. Happiness is the kick of a salmon on one's line, or a glass of cold beer in the hot spring sunshine, or making love to a girl in a sleeping-bag. Tragedy is death, bereavement or mutilation. We all know that every Hemingway story has a Wounded Hero - a roll-call of his principal characters would hardly produce a whole man - but I think there is a danger of making too much of this. Serious fiction has always dealt with the Wounded Hero; its chief characters are all people who have to struggle against some blemish or deficiency in themselves. Hemingway, following his bent, expressed this in directly external terms, by lopping off an arm, or making his hero impotent or afflicting him with heart disease. But this does not mean that he exalted the external matter over the inward essence.

Hemingway's heroes are wounded because his view of life is a tragic stoical pessimism. It is the losing fight, or the fight carried on under some cruel disadvantage, that interests him. He sees life as essentially a losing battle, but instead of reasoning from this that nothing matters much he takes the attitude that is, in fact, normal among lofty tragic writers: that a defeat, if it is faced with courage and endured without loss of one's self-respect, counts as a victory. If a man can dig down to his own deepest springs, and find something good there, he can go ahead and die, because the most important business of his life is completed.

Another feature of Hemingway's work which his imitators failed to take over is his deep compassion. He has a large-hearted sympathy for those who carry impossible burdens or whose luck has failed them. One sees this at its simplest level in his writing about poverty. Much of his life was spent in countries where the poor were very poor, as indeed they were for most of his lifetime in the United States. His books abound in sketches of simple, dignified people who face without complaint a life of unending hardship; in these sketches, his respect for men who earn their living with their bodies was able to merge with his sense of tragic stoicism.

There is no blinking of the facts, no sentimentalisation of poverty as something ennobling. Being poor does bring out some godlike attributes in people, and also some savage animal ones. The first chapter of 'To Have and Have Not' shows how Harry Morgan, bilked by the rich summer visitor who ruined some expensive fishing equipment and then left without paying, is thrown back on the necessity to use his fishing-boat in an illegal emigration voyage which involves him in murder and cruelty; what makes the story so magnificent is that Hemingway has sympathy for Morgan, for the murdered go-between, and for the desperate emigrants who fail to make their getaway, in about the same proportion; this, he is saying, is what life has done to these people; the only moral outcast is the swindling vacationer.

It is this all-embracing tragic and compassionate vision that sets Hemingway so firmly apart from the action writers who aped his style. But there is an equally evident separation on the plane of art. Hemingway was one of those writers to whom language matters. He had a passionate fastidiousness about words and rhythms, a contempt for imprecision, and the wholeheartedness of a Flaubert. Though there were many imitators there was never truly a 'school of Hemingway,' because the standard he set was too severe.

On this side, Hemingway belongs with the poets. And it was from the poets that he learnt to write. His training started in a newspaper office, but it was completed in the Paris days when he was associated with the group of experimental, expatriate writers presided over by Ezra Pound.

'Nothing can please many, or please long, but just representations of general nature.' (2) Dr. Johnson's remark gives the classicist's position in one sentence. Most modern literature is 'romantic' in that it explores the possibilities of the extreme; it eagerly pursues madness, eccentricity, the solitary and the perverse. Where it is not romantic, it becomes gregarious, concerning itself with the social questions which men face all together. Ionesco and Genet on the one side, Arthur Miller and C.P. Snow on the other.

Hemingway's attitude was exceptional because classical art, nowadays, is exceptional. He took men singly, not forgetting the collective world they belonged to, but seeing them as individuals, amid the individual's ultimate loneliness, within that world. He placed them in positions of extreme stress. And he showed them behaving under that stress as men behave: not as civil servants behave, or factory workers, or Americans, or lepers, or bohemian intellectuals. His aim was to get below the skin and present the universal, underlying truth to experience that Johnson had in mind when he spoke of 'just representations of general nature.' In my submission, he succeeded. And for that reason his books please many, and will surely please long.

Notes

1 T.S. Eliot, Hamlet and His Problems (1919), 'Selected Prose,' ed. Frank Kermode (London, 1975), 48: 'the only way of expressing emotion, in the form of art, is by finding an "objective correlative"; in other words, a set of objects, a situation, a chain of events, which shall be the formula for that poetic emotion.'

2 Johnson makes the same point in chapter 10 of 'Rasselas' (1759) when Imlac says: 'The business of the poet is to examine, not the individual, but the species; to remark general properties and large appearances.'

93. IRVING HOWE, 'NEW REPUBLIC'

145 (24 July 1961), 19-20

Irving Howe (b. 1920) is Professor of English at City University of New York, and the author of 'Sherwood Anderson' (1951), 'William Faulkner' (1952) and 'Politics and the Novel' (1957).

Now that he is dead and nothing remains but a few books and the problem of his dying, perhaps we should ask the simplest, most radical of questions: what was there in Hemingway's writing that enabled him to command the loyalty of a generation? Even those of us who disliked some of his work and most of his posture, why did we too feel compelled to acknowledge the strength and resonance of his voice?

Answering such questions can never be easy, and with Hemingway, master that he is of false leads and distracting personnae, it demands a touch of ruthlessness. The usual business of literary criticism will yield only limited returns, for if you were to spend the next decade studying the narrative techniques of his stories you would still be far from the sources of his power. Most of his late work was bad, Papa gone soft, desperately in search of the image of self he had made in his youth. 'The Old Man and the Sea' - a confection of synthetic wisdom, an exercise in pidgin-classicism, a parody of composure and lilt. 'Across the River and into the Trees' - the swagger of a failing conqueror, all garrulous and fantasy, but as a personal revelation unbearably sad, the pose crumbling, the terror of getting old finally breaking past his guard.

For the past twenty years the public Hemingway, who cannot after all be so readily separated from Hemingway, was a tiresome man. The old African hunter, the connoisseur of bulls, women and wars, the experience-dropper, was a show-off who had stopped watching the audience to see if it remained interested. Nothing more cruel has happened to an American writer than the Lillian Ross interview in a 1950 'New Yorker': a smear of vanity and petulance that only a journalistic Delilah would have put into print. Miss Ross, a few days ago, wrote in anger to say that Hemingway had approved her article, (1) and one believes her implicitly. That is just the trouble. Years earlier

Hemingway had written, 'Something happens to our good writers at a certain age....' (2) Yes; they devote the first half of their lives to imitating human experience and the second to parodying their imitation.

But there was another Hemingway. He was always a young writer, and always a writer for the young. He published his best novel 'The Sun Also Rises' in his mid-twenties and completed most of his great stories by the age of forty. He started a campaign of terror against the fixed vocabulary of literature, a purge of style and pomp, and in the name of naturalness he modelled a new artifice for tension. He was a short-breathed writer, whether in the novel or story. He struck past the barriers of culture and seemed to disregard the reticence of civilized relationships. He wrote for the nerves.

In his very first stories Hemingway struck straight to the heart of our nihilism, writing with that marvellous courage he then had, which allowed him to brush past received ideas and show Nick Adams alone, bewildered, afraid and bored, Nick Adams finding his bit of peace through fishing with an exact salvaging ritual in the big two-hearted river. Hemingway struck straight to the heart of our nihilism through stories about people who have come to the end of the line, who no longer know what to do or where to turn: nihilism not as an idea or a sentiment, but as an encompassing condition of moral disarray in which one has lost those tacit impulsions which permit life to continue and suddenly begins to ask questions that would better be left unasked. There is a truth which makes our faith in human existence seem absurd, and no one need contemplate it for very long: Hemingway, in his early writing did. Nick Adams, Jake Barnes, Lady Brett, Frederic Henry, and then the prizefighters, matadors, rich Americans and failed writers: all are at the edge, almost ready to surrender and be done with it, yet holding on to whatever fragment of morale, whatever scrap of honor, they can. Theirs is the heroism of people who have long ago given up the idea of being heroic and wish only to get by without being too messy.

It has been said that Hemingway, obsessed with the problem of fear, sought in his fiction for strategies to overcome it; (3) and that is true, but only partly so. Hemingway was not so foolish as to suppose that fear can finally be overcome: all his best stories, from Fifty Grand to The Short Happy Life of Francis Macomber are concerned to improvise a momentary truce in the hopeless encounter with fear. Hemingway touched upon something deeper, something that broke forth in his fiction as the most personal and lonely kind of experience but was formed by the pressure of 20th Century history. His great subject, I think, was panic, the panic that follows, so to speak, upon the dissolution of nihilism into the bloodstream of consciousness, the panic that finds unbearable the thought of the next minute and its succession by the minute after that. And we all know this experience, even if, unlike Jake Barnes, we can sleep at night: we know it because it is part of modern life, perhaps of any life, but also because Hemingway drove it fearlessly into our awareness.

But there was more. Hemingway's early fiction made his readers turn in upon themselves with the pain of measurement and consider the question of their sufficiency as men. He touched the quick of our anxieties, and for the moment of his excellence he stood ready to face whatever he saw. The compulsive stylization of his prose was a way of letting the language tense and retense, group and regroup, while beneath it the panic that had taken hold of the characters and then of the reader kept spreading inexorably. The prose served both as barrier and principle of contrast to that shapelessness which is panic by definition, and through its very tautness allowed the reader finally to establish some distance and then perhaps compassion.

This Hemingway forced us to ask whether as men we had retained any thrust and will, any unbreakable pride. He asked this question in the most fundamental sexual way, moving from the desperateness of 'The Sun Also Rises' to the comforts but also final return to bleakness in 'Farewell to Arms,' from the sleeping-bag fantasia - with Maria as a sort of Fayaway (4) with politics - of 'For Whom the Bell Tolls' to the boozy ruminations of 'Across the River and into the Trees.' But he also asked the question in other ways.

The poet John Berryman once said that we live in a culture where a man can go through his entire life without having once to discover whether he is a coward. (5) Hemingway forced his readers to consider such possibilities, and through the clenched shape of his stories he kept insisting that no one can escape, moments of truth come to all of us. Fatalistic as they often seem, immersed in images of violence and death, his stories are actually incitements to personal resistance and renewal. Reading them, one felt stirred to a stronger sense - if not of one's possible freedom - then at least of one's possible endurance and companionship in stoicism.

Hemingway's vision was narrow. It was, as an Italian critic has remarked, 'a brilliant half-vision of life,'(6) in which a whole range of behavior, not least of all the behavior of man thinking, was left out. But there were moments when he wrote with a sudden enlarged sensibility, so that one forgot the limits of his stance and style, feeling that here, for these few pages, one was in the presence of a great writer. There is a little story called A Clean Well-Lighted Place and a passage in that story where the older waiter explains to the younger one that he must be patient with the homeless men sitting in the café, because everyone needs a clean well-lighted place in which to stare at his aloneness. I cannot imagine that this story will ever be forgotten.

Notes

1 In the 'New York Times,' 5 July 1961, 32.
2 'Green Hills of Africa' (New York, 1935), 19.
3 Philip Young's thesis in 'Ernest Hemingway' (1952).
4 Fayaway is the heroine of Melville's 'Typee' (1846), the lovely, undemanding girl the narrator finds in the South Seas.
5 Berryman's remark was made to Howe in conversation in the late 1940s. Berryman committed suicide in 1972.
6 Emilio Cecchi, quoted in Pier Francesco Paolini, The Hemingway of the Major Works, 'Hemingway and His Critics,' ed. Carlos Baker (New York, 1961), 133.

94. ILYA EHRENBURG, 'SATURDAY REVIEW'

44 (29 July 1961), 20

Ilya Ehrenburg (1891-1967) was a Soviet novelist and journalist who reported the Spanish Civil War with Hemingway.

Some thirty years ago in Spain Ernst Toller (1) gave me a novel, 'The Sun Also Rises,' by Ernest Hemingway, a writer then unknown to me. 'This may interest you,' said Toller. 'There seems to be something about Spain in it....' At the same time I also bought a copy of 'A Farewell to Arms.' Both these books greatly moved me, and

Hemingway has been my favorite writer ever since.

As a reader I found Hemingway's novels very human: in them were life, love, death, brief joy, long wars. After James Joyce's 'Ulysses' and 'The Counterfeiters,' by Gide, these novels seemed to rehabilitate life. As a writer I was astonished by Hemingway's skill. I feel content whenever I understand how a book is composed, but I have never understood, to this day, how Hemingway achieved his powerful dialogue. More than once I have had occasion to listen to men's conversation after it was taped: all of us tend to talk at much greater length and in a far more 'literary' and pallid way than what Hemingway offered, which was not dialogue overheard, but a concentrate of it, often made up of superficially insignificant elements - mere fragments of everyday phrases, which always managed to convey what was most important. When other writers try to imitate Hemingway's dialogue, the result is a poor parody: his discovery was not a key to a new method, but something deeply individual and inimitable.

It is, perhaps, thanks to his command of dialogue that Hemingway became such a master of the short story. After Chekhov no one else, it seems, has been able to say so much about man in that genre. I recall a conversation I once had with Isaac Babel, the foremost writer of the Soviet short story. Babel was extremely enthusiastic about that story of Hemingway's in which the action takes place at a small Swiss resort. (2) 'I read a very stupid article,' Babel told me, 'where it is argued that Hemingway is very observant and, above all, knows how to listen to people talking. The fool who wrote that fails to understand that one cannot "overhear" such conversation or, if one can, one can do so only within one's self....' Neither Babel nor I was alone in our enthusiasm for Hemingway.

In the middle 1930s 'International Literature,' (3) a monthly journal then published in Moscow, sent out a questionnaire asking Soviet writers to state which contemporary authors in the West they considered to be most significant. In almost all the answers Hemingway came first.

Towards the end of July 1941 we had air alerts in Moscow - nearly every night. Boris Lapin, my son-in-law, who was a young writer, had just arrived from the front on his way to the army of the South. He and I decided to spend the night at a vacant *dacha* (4) belonging to some friends, where we hoped to get a good night's rest. But we had just been given the manuscript of a recently completed translation of 'For Whom the Bell Tolls.' (5) We never got to bed: we read all night, taking our turn over each page. I, too, was due to leave for the front, but wanted to read the novel to the end. When we had both finished, we glanced at each other and smiled. We did not even hear the rumble of the anti-aircraft guns or the explosions of the bombs.

I recall Boris Lapin saying, 'Very bitter and very virile....' Two weeks later Lapin was killed in the fighting around Kiev. Hemingway's novel was the last book he read.

Hemingway is loved not only by our writers, but also by our readers. Some five years ago it was announced that a new two-volume edition of his works would be sold by advance subscription. The subscribers had to register personally in a bookshop situated in the apartment house where I was living. It was a cold winter evening. As I drove up to the house, I saw a long queue, the tail of which was made up predominantly of young people. It turned out that they had come there the night before the subscription opened so as not to be outnumbered the next morning and thus miss their chance to subscribe. Not all of our books get sold out; there are books that lie on the shelves of bookshops and in the warehouses, but Hemingway's works are unobtainable unless one makes a strenuous effort.

Hemingway's death has meant the loss not only of a writer whom I love, but also a man of whose friendship I was proud. I first became acquainted with him in Madrid at the home of the Soviet correspondent for 'Pravda,' Michael Koltzov. Rarely have I been as excited as I was that evening early in 1937; for at last I met the writer for whom I had a regard like that of an apprentice for his master. I said many flattering things to Hemingway, but he only frowned suspiciously. Then an odd discord developed. Hemingway talked to me in Spanish, and I answered in French. He told me that he had been sent to Spain by an American newspaper agency. (6) I asked him whether his assignment was to cable only feature stories or also news - '*nouvelles.*' This last word precipitated a stormy scene: Hemingway misinterpreted '*nouvelles*' to mean 'novellas,' that is, novels. He shouted, 'I spotted at once that you were being sarcastic!...' When the misunderstanding was cleared up, he explained with a laugh that his detractors used to reproach him for his 'telegraphic style.' I answered that the same thing had been written about me. We then became friends.

I remember the artillery-shattered hotel on the Gran Via where he was staying, the kerosene stove, the coffee, the whiskey, a page of manuscript: he was writing a play at the time. (7) I was with him at the front during the battle of Guadalajara. It was the only Republican victory, and Hemingway had a smile on his face.

I still have in my possession a small photograph taken near Ibarra Castle: (8) it shows Hemingway, Joris Ivens, the film man, Gustav Regler, the German writer, and me. I often met Hemingway at the headquarters of the Twelfth International Brigade, which was then commanded by General Lukacz, as the Hungarian writer Mate Zalku was known in Spain. One day Hemingway and Lukacz got to reminiscing about the First World War, when, it seems, they had sat opposite each other in the trenches of two hostile armies. As a writer Hemingway was fascinated by war but, at the same time, he passionately hated it.

In 1946, when I visited the United States, I received a long, friendly letter from him. Hemingway recalled our days in Spain, and invited me to stay with him in Cuba. At the time I was unable to accept, and so I have never seen him with a beard except in his photographs. In my memory he lives on as a tall sturdy man with a sad expression and a vague smile.

I was asked to say a few words on television about the loss that millions of my countrymen were now suffering. When I arrived at the studio I was surrounded by the technicians, who questioned me about the circumstances under which Ernest Hemingway died. It was his readers who were asking me about him. The loss of this major writer hurts.

It hurts, too, that a man should have died who, through the love felt for him, has brought together people and nations otherwise remote from each other.

Notes

1 Ernst Toller was a German Expressionist playwright and political activist, and author of 'Men and the Masses' (1920).
2 Probably An Alpine Idyll in 'Men Without Women' (1927).
3 The response to the questionnaire was published in 1937.
4 Country house.
5 'A Farewell to Arms' was translated by E. Kalashnikova and published in Moscow in 1936.
6 North American Newspaper Alliance.
7 Hemingway was writing 'The Fifth Column' in the Hotel Florida.
8 Outside Brihuega, northeast of Guadalajara.

95. ALBERTO MORAVIA, 'L'ESPRESSO'

20 August 1961, 8

Alberto Moravia (b. 1907), an Italian novelist, is the author of 'The Indifferent Ones' (1932) and 'The Woman of Rome' (1949).

This article was reprinted in Alberto Moravia, Nothing Amen, 'Man as an End' (New York, 1966), 231-6. It was translated by Bernard Wall. 'L'Espresso' is a daily newspaper published in Rome.

A significant feature of modern American literature is the inability of many of the writers to get beyond the world of their adolescence and youth, so as to add to it and develop it. The American writer often starts off splendidly, with courage, candour, curiosity, a sense of adventure, and a thirst for experience. But unfortunately a maximum charge of vitality is matched by a minimum of cultural equipment. In other words, faith in life is accompanied by a lack of faith in the resources of culture, which the American writer sees as cramping and weighing down the immediacy and authenticity of direct experience. Naturally this attitude is also a fact of culture, though of a minor, degraded and anti-humanistic culture.

As a consequence of his lack of faith in culture, the American writer for the most part confines himself to recounting the story of his youth. For him it is an inspirational capital that must be spent without delay and without thinking about profitable investments to assure him a tranquil old age. Metaphor apart, in the United States literary careers such as those of Thomas Mann or André Gide - who went on developing a train of writing begun fifty years earlier up to the last days of their life - are rare. After he has made his début with a couple of books, the American writer tends to restrict himself to re-writing them, and so increasingly falls into imitating himself and his own particular mannerisms. That is, he seems incapable of developing his themes by gradually dropping the worn-out and decaying parts and bringing the vigorous and lasting ones to leaf and flower. If we wanted to trace the writer back to the civilisation to which he belongs, we could almost say that despite himself the American writer imitates the standardised industrial production that is the dominant characteristic of his country's economy. He sets out from a prototype designed when he was young, and spends the rest of his life turning out a standardised production based on the blueprint of his original prototype. What is the explanation of this unfortunate development? Let us point out at the outset that writers in the past, such as Emily Dickinson and Herman Melville, went on writing in an original and fresh way right up to their death without declining into mannerism and self-imitation. So we get the impression that the modern American writer has failed to extract himself from the general alienation of society in the United States. After the deceptive freshness of youth he mirrors increasingly, in the mechanisation of his own work, the general mechanisation of the society for which he is writing.

In these observations we are aware that we have involuntarily drawn almost a portrait of Ernest Hemingway. Hemingway was our contemporary, and he met his death when he was still young, yet, precisely because of the infantile and precocious state of arrested development we have just described, his work as regards our time is as discounted and anachronistic as any, and for this same reason ranks with all that is most classical and beyond discussion.

Where did Hemingway come from? By his origins he was a 'frontiersman', that is he inherited the view of life peculiar to those American social groups that moved westwards towards the great spaces open to conquest and colonisation. Strange to say, this by and large healthy, youthful, brave and frank view of life was to reveal itself through Hemingway as related to all the most refined, tired and corrupt lucubrations of old Europe during the same period. I mean the spirit of decadence at its most superficial and exasperated level, the sort of decadence which, finding literature insufficient, was later to spread to *mores* and politics by way of D'Annunzianism and Nazism. This amounts to saying that the sporting, boisterous young man from Chicago was related, in the great family of writers, to two such different figures as D'Annunzio and Malraux. (1) We could easily trace him back to Theodore Roosevelt who was also a great huntsman, explorer and man of action and even to Byron who swam the Hellespont, was a *carbonaro* (2) in Italy and a patriot in Greece. Whereas with his real contemporary, Proust, Hemingway had nothing in common. We have mentioned Proust so as to situate Hemingway. The French novelist, in fact, was saved from decadentism by his faith in culture; his work is far removed from the superficial and brand new temptations to decadence of his time owing to his character as humanist and moralist. Memory is reason reclaimed, life reordered, rationality never betrayed. Proust is the last of the great European realists whereas Hemingway belongs to the irrationalist wave of men like Lawrence and Malraux.

Surely nothing could throw light on Hemingway better than a comparison with D'Annunzio and Malraux. What has Hemingway in common with these two writers? With D'Annunzio he shares the ambition of creating a myth about himself, that is to say, building himself a pedestal in his own mythological monument not only by means of literature but also, and chiefly, by a tendentious choice of modes of action - bull-fighting, big game hunting, civil war, world war, revolution. This myth of self outlives literary creativeness; the writer is already dead and embalmed, whether at Gardone (3) or Cuba, but the man of action goes on firing off cannon or lion hunting, taking part in politics, or war. Of course the myth makes heavy demands: D'Annunzio had to live it to the bitter end, that is, until he became ridiculous and senile; Hemingway, who was more modern and less rhetorical, lived it up to a splendid suicide with a bullet from a big game rifle in the temple. Despite the undoubted sincerity of both Hemingway and D'Annunzio, what remains of such myths? Nothing, even less than nothing. They are fabricated for the masses, and and the masses forget them as soon as other more up-to-date and beguiling myths arise.

The comparison with Malraux, on the other hand, involves an examination of Hemingway's themes. Malraux, in his life, is not an actor like D'Annunzio, but a terribly serious European intellectual, a sort of Parisian Raskolnikoff. (4) So with Malraux Hemingway has in common the ambition to interpret, and live, the great modern revolutionary movements in an individualistic, super-mystical and Nietzschean key. Malraux starts off with the adventure of a theft of valuable statues in the depths of the forests of Indo-China, (5) then passes through Stalinist Communism and ends up as one of de Gaulle's ministers. With him the parabola from decadentism to Fascist-type nationalism is complete. Hemingway, who is less coherent and rational, more artistic and voluble, stops halfway; he attempts to insert his cowboy individualism, in love with courage and death, into the Spanish revolution, fails, and withdraws in time into private life. How are we to explain the failure of both Hemingway and Malraux? It was because their idea that revolution was an adventure like any other was fundamentally mistaken. Revolution was not an adventure, though there were many adventures involved in it and it was often adventurous; it was a struggle for a ruthless order and one without imagination, as was made perfectly clear with the development of Stalinism. It was therefore not unexpected that Hemingway's Marxism, picked up by flipping through a popular handbook, evaporated as soon as could be after the unfortunate effort of 'To Have and Have Not.' Yet Hemingway wrote 'For Whom the Bell Tolls,' his most ambitious and careful work, whose cruel episodes and conventional characters betrayed his decadence and lack of ideas, and then re-crossed the Atlantic. Africa - 'Green Hills of Africa' - was a mere intermezzo; the return to Italy after the second world war - 'Across the River and into the Trees' - a fiasco. Finally, with 'The Old Man and the Sea,' a bad book if an enormous success, Hemingway seemed to reach out once more to the original motifs of American literature and his own. With 'The Old Man and the Sea' he tried to write his 'Moby Dick.' All he really did was to imitate himself in a painstaking, clumsy and mannered way.

His best books are far removed from our time and are really fine. They are the only ones we like and are ready to re-read. Unfalsified reality shines through them, and they have preserved intact the fascination of his infantile, one-dimensional and boisterous prose, apparently simple and ordered, in reality full of poetic ambiguity (there is no shadow of rationality in Hemingway's prose). Anyone who has tried to translate it has experienced how it falls to pieces, and one has to start again from the beginning, luminous, and always a trifle conventional; these books, written between 1920 and 1930, will live as examples of the literary idea of a whole epoch. All told they amount to two novels, 'The Sun Also Rises' ('Fiesta') and 'A Farewell to Arms,' and a volume of short stories, 'The First Forty-Nine Stories.' Hemingway's simplicity, or rather his lack of ideas, makes him better as a short story writer than a novelist. He was the creator of that lyrical and autobiographical way of telling stories which in Italy, after various modifications, came to be known as neo-realism.

In 'A Farewell to Arms' Hemingway's inclination to create a myth of himself is blended in a natural way with his rejection of the traditional novel endowed with plot, characters, psychology and conflicts. In this novel, which relates his war experience in Italy, as in 'The Sun Also Rises,' which describes the sojourn of a group of Americans in Spain, and as also in 'Men Without Women,' a collection of stories about sport and sporting champions, Hemingway blueprinted an ethics and a type of hero of his own that he repeated in all his subsequent books: the ethics of physical courage, or the capacity or incapacity to face one's adversary without fear, the adversary being in turn a boxer, a lion, a bull, an enemy soldier, death; and a hero of American intellectual nomadism, a war correspondent, a hunter, a journalist, a traveller. Physical courage is no more than an infantile and puritan sublimation of sexual energy and it is possibly for this reason that the portraits of women in Hemingway's books are all conventional, rather like those of Kipling, another writer of physical courage with whom he has some affinities. As for the hero, at first glance he seems an energetic and adventurous Stendhalian character but in reality he is a weak-nerved man always hunting for new sensations and distractions, who acts as he drinks and drinks as he acts to conceal the nothingness inside him and around him. Hemingway's famous dialogues, even before they are literary invention, are the direct expression of this desolation of action divorced from any meaning and any justification. Their elegance is not, as many imitators have believed, a question of style but of ethics. So if it be true, as would appear, that Hemingway killed himself, it may well be worthwhile recalling his story, A Clean, Well-lighted Place, in which two waiters are talking on the very subject, precisely, of an old regular who had tried to kill himself a few days earlier:

> 'Last week he tried to commit suicide,' one waiter said.
> 'Why?'
> 'He was in despair.'
> 'What about?'
> 'Nothing.'
> 'How do you know it was nothing.'
> 'He has plenty of money.'

Later the old man goes away, one of the waiters goes to bed, and the other one, now alone, repeats to himself his night prayer:

> 'Our nada who art in nada, nada be thy name thy kingdom nada thy will be nada in nada as it is in nada...' amen.

Hemingway wrote the story when he was young and confident. But - once again following the tradition of modern American literature - he was incapable of developing or adding anything of value to his early, naïve nihilism. So it truly can be said of him that he died as he had lived.

Notes

1 In 'Across the River and into the Trees' (Harmondsworth,

Middlesex, 1966), 42, Hemingway calls D'Annunzio: 'Writer, poet, national hero, phraser of the dialectic of Fascism, macabre egotist, aviator, commander, or rider, in the first of the fast torpedo attack boats, Lieutenant-Colonel of Infantry without knowing how to command a company, nor a platoon properly, the great, lovely writer of "Notturno" whom we respect, and jerk.'

2 Member of Italian revolutionary secret society.

3 Village on Lake Garda where D'Annunzio retired in splendor after Fiume.

4 Murderer-hero in Dostoyevsky's 'Crime and Punishment' (1866).

5 Malraux fictionalized these adventures in 'The Royal Way' (1930).

'A Moveable Feast' (1964)

96. GEORGE PLIMPTON, 'NEW YORK HERALD TRIBUNE BOOK WEEK'

3 May 1964, 1, 12-13

George Plimpton (b. 1927) is an American novelist and sportswriter, the author of 'Paper Lion' (1966) and editor of 'Writers at Work' (1957, 1963).

Thinking back on it, there were two subjects Hemingway detested talking about. He felt any discussion of his craft was a waste of time, possibly injurious, and he was particularly sensitive to questions put to him on the subject. I can remember, in the course of doing an interview with him in Cuba on the art of fiction some years ago, (1) venturing a question to him, an especially callow one:

'You have used a bird,' I said, '... a white bird ... occasionally ... in the love-making scenes in the short-stories, and it flies ... well, out of the gondola in "Across the River"....'

I had to stop before making a question of it. He was absolutely furious. We were standing above the little bay at Cohima - the wind was coming strong off the Gulf Stream, whipping his whiskers as he turned to me, his face bristling. He was hunched forward with rage. 'You think of some better way!' he said. I thought he was going to throw me in the bay.

I said: 'Well ... ah....' There was not much one could say. One learned quickly not to pick at the fabric of his method.

And similarly, his apprenticeship as a writer, his years in newspaper work, the Paris of the Twenties, his tutelage with Gertrude Stein, his friendships with Ezra Pound, Archibald MacLeish, the literary life there - such questions, though not met with as violent a reaction, were answered, if at all, with reluctance. 'The literary gossip of 30-odd years ago is disgusting and boring,' he said.

His attitude seemed less inflexible after the African plane-crashes. (2) His injuries were serious, and his friends remarked that their effect seemed to make him turn inward, particularly to the past - never in any maudlin sense, or as a refuge, but that the stories and reminiscences seemed to come more easily from him. The early Paris years had been a very good time for him. Some of the stories were essentially comic, but almost all are extremely personal, and one can see why he would want to harbor them. He finally decided to let them go, to record them - finishing them in Idaho in 1960 - and they are now available in 'A Moveable Feast,' a series of 20 personal narratives, the shortest only four pages, the longest a 30-page account of a hilarious trip to Lyon with Scott Fitzgerald to pick up an abandoned car. The period they cover is 1921-26 - when Hemingway was in his early twenties and married to Hadley Richardson. They have one child, Bumby, and a cat, Mr. F. Puss.

Edmund Wilson, who did the first critical appraisals of Hemingway in the 'Dial' in 1927, later wrote harshly of Hemingway's personal narratives: '...something frightful seems to happen to Hemingway as soon as he begins to write in the first person.' (3) Certainly, this indictment would hold for the almost frenzied self-consciousness of the articles entitled The Dangerous Summer, the account of the rivalry between the matadors Antonio Ordoñez and Luis Miguel Dominguin (4) which Hemingway put aside 'A Moveable Feast' to write. It is difficult to believe both works were done essentially at the same time. The Paris sketches are absolutely controlled, far enough removed in time so that the scenes and characters are observed in tranquillity, and yet with astonishing immediacy - his remarkable gift - so that many of the sketches have the hard brilliance of his best fiction. Indeed, in a short prefatory note Hemingway says the book may be regarded as fiction - by which he means not that the incidents described are imaginary, but that the techniques utilized are those of the fiction writer. He informs not as a sociologist might look at the period, or a literary historian - which will disappoint those expecting to find portraits-in-depth of Joyce or Stein or the others. He makes no pretense of exploring their complexities.

Instead, the portraits, vivid and sharp, are used as a short story writer might use them - as characters in a set piece, so that their names could be substituted without diminishing the value of the whole. It is better, of course, to have them as they are, if only to watch Hemingway settle old scores with his detractors. Wyndham Lewis comes in for a terrible pasting, and so does the Eliot cult, in a gentle way, and Alice Toklas, and Ford Madox Ford, and a few others.

But mainly, the tone of 'A Moveable Feast' is reflective and comfortable as Hemingway returns to one of the basic themes of his early work - the release that comes with the relish of sensation, the gratification of appetite. In many ways, the book is close to the concept of the famous short story, The Big Two-Hearted River, in which Nick Adams returns in near shock from the wars to find release, perhaps sanity, in the carefully relished sensations of trout fishing in the timber country, a refurbishing through a lucid and aesthetic appreciation of the physical world.

Hemingway's return to Paris in 'A Moveable Feast' suggests the same sort of therapeutic visit - his health crippled in the plane-crashes, his consciousness sensing decline, a robust middle age behind him - returning in print to the ties of Paris to touch down at specific landmarks, certain streets, cafés, even remembered bottles of wine and long past meals, as if these physical entities could bring serenity and order. It is a therapeutic measure Hemingway has often put his characters to: one remembers the night walk in 'The Sun Also Rises' through a directory of streets, and the fishing near Pamplona, so carefully detailed that Nathan Asch, the novelist, who Hemingway said had a strong accent, was prompted to say of the first draft, 'Hem, vaht you mean saying you wrote a novel? A novel, huh. Hem, you are riding a trahvel buch.'

Boris Pasternak's wife once complained that this aspect of Hemingway - the acute consciousness of sensation - bored her finally, particularly the directories of streets, the endless meals and drinks with little else happening to the heroes. Pasternak disagreed. 'The greatness of a writer,' he said, 'has nothing to do with subject matter itself, only with how much the subject matter touches the author. It is the density of style which counts. Through Hemingway's style you feel matter, iron, wood.' (5)

Madame Pasternak would have her troubles with 'A Moveable Feast,' aptly named, since literally dozens of meals, with attendant wines, are chronicled, with such 'density of style' that one's stomach moans: a dozen *portugaises* oysters appear on page six to lead off the gastronomic parade, which includes *crabe mexicaine, truite au bleu,* jugged hare, venison with chestnut sauce, *poularde de bresse*, truffled roast chicken, American ham and eggs (a breakfast he has in Lyon with Scott Fitzgerald), cherry tarts (a number of these - apparently Hemingway's favorite dessert), mutton, *foie de veau*, *cervelas* (which is a big sausage split in two), *marennes*, *tournedos* (6) with sauce Bernaise, and *goujon* which is the little silvery fish caught in the Seine with the long-jointed poles and which Hemingway ate by the plateful.

As for the liquid refreshment, that is considerable - beginning on the third page of the first sketch with a rum St. James, then on to *kirsch*, *quetsche*, *mirabelle*, *framboise*, *muscadet*, (7) Sancerre, Sion, Chambery Cassis, Cahors wine, Corsican wine, Chateauneuf du Pape, cherry brandy (which a bicycle rider sucks up through a straw from a hotwater bottle under his shirt), St. Emilion, Macon, whisky sours, Fleury, champagnes, lemonade and whisky (which is prepared for Scott Fitzgerald on that Lyon trip - he imagines he is ailing), Capri and fruit cup, Montagny, and Enzian *schnappes*, along with a number of *fines*, *distingués*, and *demis*. (8) The only liquid described which Hemingway did not take to was goat's milk - bought early every morning from the goatherd by the woman on the floor above him.

The meals are never intrusive, though they are triumphs, as Pasternak would say, in the art of suggesting pleasant sensations: there is one chapter, Hunger Was Good Discipline, describing Hemingway's first meal on the proceeds of a check from 'Der Querschnitt' he has picked up from Sylvia Beach's bookshop, which will induce an appetite in any one who has not just stepped away from his fill of *goujons*.

But for all the cataloguing of meals, of wines, of Paris streets (over 30 are identified), and even pervading the fine humor of the sketches (both Faulkner, in certain sections of 'The Reivers,' and Hemingway seem to have done their best humorous writing in their last years) there is a note of impending chaos and death. The therapy does not work. Hemingway sees ruin in the faces of his Paris friends - Ernest Walsh, Ford, Pascin, (9) and the smell of it seems to be with many others.

Of the writers, Ezra Pound is the only life force in the book, Scott Fitzgerald's face seems suddenly a death's head to Hemingway, watching him in a café. It is indicative that Hemingway moves the last chapter of 'A Moveable

Feast' to Schruns in the Vorarlberg in Austria, the only sketch removed from France. The Hemingways had a couple of good years (Hemingway finished 'The Sun Also Rises' there) until the place was ruined by the influx of the rich, the time consumers, and even their marriage began to drift apart. They had gone there to ski. Skiing itself had a particular identification for Hemingway - revitalizing him as Antaeus (10) is by contact with the earth, of all the physical sensations perhaps the most identified with life: '...the great glacier run, smooth and straight, forever straight if our legs could hold it, our ankles locked, we running so low, leaning into the speed, dropping forever and forever in the silent hiss of the crisp powder. It was better than any flying or anything else, and we built the ability to do it and to have the long climbs carrying the heavy rucksack.' One remembers from the short story, Cross Country Snow, (11) that one of the skiers says to Nick Adams, 'Maybe we'll never go skiing again, Nick.' Nick replies: 'We've got to. It isn't worth while if you can't.'

Notes

1 George Plimpton, Ernest Hemingway, 'Paris Review,' 5 (1958), 60-89.
2 In January 1954.
3 See No. 43. Wilson's 'Dial' essay appeared in 1924.
4 'Life,' 5, 12 and 19 September 1960.
5 Boris Pasternak, 'Writers at Work: The "Paris Review" Interviews,' ed. George Plimpton, Second Series, London, 1963, 114.
6 In the Portuguese style: crab in the Mexican style; poached trout; capon from the region of Bresse; calves' liver; whitefish; filet steak.
7 Cherry brandy; plum brandy; plum liqueur; raspberry liqueur; white wine.
8 Spirits; brandy; large glass of beer; half-pint of beer.
9 Ernest Walsh, poet and editor of 'This Quarter,' died of consumption in 1926. Jules Pascin, Bulgarian-born French painter, hanged himself in 1936.
10 Antaeus was a giant wrestler in Greek mythology who was invincible as long as he touched his mother, the Earth.
11 Cross-Country Snow, 'In Our Time' (1925).

97. STANLEY KAUFFMANN, 'NEW REPUBLIC'

150 (9 May 1964), 17-18, 20-1, 23-4

Stanley Kauffmann (b. 1916), an American editor, critic and novelist, is the author of 'The Philanderer' (1952).

The very first entry in Camus' 'Notebooks' might serve as epigraph to Hemingway's posthumous memoirs: 'What I mean is this: that one can, with no romanticism, feel nostalgic for lost poverty.' It is the city of Paris, in memory and effect, that is the moveable feast; to it, Hemingway sat again in these recollections, written between 1958 and 1960, of his Paris life in the early 20's. This book, highly affecting and biographically invaluable, is an anomalous performance in literature. An author, who slipped in critical esteem during the second half of his writing life, reminds us after his death of his earlier claims to greatness.

'What a book,' Gertrude Stein and Sherwood Anderson once agreed, 'would be the real story of Hemingway, not those he writes but the confessions of the real Ernest Hemingway. It would be for another audience than the audience Hemingway has now but it would be very wonderful.' (1) By and large he now has a different audience from the one he had when that comment was made. This book is probably not the confession that Miss Stein and Anderson envisioned - it is only a collection of sketches - but their intuition was sound. The Hemingway who went back to himself found much of himself and made this book about his youth the best work of his later years.

There are 20 sections, most of them self-contained but each one a glimpse that adds to a prospect. One cannot learn from this book all of Hemingway's life in the period; it is not a chronicle. But these sketches give us, for the first time, an intimate view of him as he evolved his art, of his first marriage, of others around him. He provides (deliberately posthumously, one can assume) insight and information that, for all the publicity and public *persona*, he never afforded during his life.

To get the worst out of the way at once, the conversations between him and his wife - quoted after 35 years - will simply strengthen the hands of the satirists. If he and she really talked like that, then one wonders what the struggle was - noted elsewhere in the book - to work out his style. He needed only to set down his domestic chat, which was the Hemingway style already over-ripened.

> 'Let's walk down the rue de Seine [she says] and look in all the galleries, and in the windows of the shops.'
> 'Sure. We can walk anywhere and we can stop at some new café where we don't know anyone and nobody knows us and have a drink.'
> 'We can have two drinks.'
> 'Then we can eat somewhere.'
> 'No. Don't forget we have to pay the library.'
> 'We'll come home and eat here and we'll have a lovely meal and drink Beaune from the co-operative you can see right out of the window there with the price of the Beaune on the window. And afterwards we'll read and then go to bed and make love.'

If it were a novel, it would cry for a touch or two of E.B. White. (2) In autobiography, it paralyzes even parody.

All the dialogue between the pair is in that vein. Eventually we get a clue as to why he has been sentimentalizing his marriage into the worst kind of 'brave and true' Hemingwayesque idyll. At the end of the book his marriage is breaking up and he is already sorry, but seems powerless to prevent it. ('When I saw my wife standing by the tracks as the train came in by the piled logs at the station, I wished I had died before I ever loved anyone but her.') His sugary treatment may be an attempt to ease his conscience and pay a deferred debt.

Little of the rest of the book is less than best Hemingway. There is some of his usual reverse-provincialism: all Frenchmen, particularly those wounded in the war, are wonderful. There is the wine and food and private café and quaint-character snobbism that later wrecked so many imitators. (Hemingway spent little of his adult life in America. Our Man in the Picturesque Old World became his principal role.) There is also his private caste system, with him and his wife at the top. He attempts to laugh at it, saying that in their poverty they looked down on the rich; but the dominant tone here, as in his whole life, is a belief in an aristocracy of the chivalrous, aswirl in a sea of cowards and cheapjacks.

But after these lesser streaks in the book, we are left with a small diamond mine. The most easily describable treasures are the portraits of friends, acquaintances, enemies. Some are passé figures, interesting now only because they interested him then: Ernest Walsh, the poet who was 'marked for death' and made quite a good thing out of it; Evan Shipman, an American bohemian whom Hemingway liked and who said, 'We need more true mystery in our lives, Hem. The completely unambitious writer and the really good unpublished poem are the things we lack most at this time. There is, of course, the problem of sustenance.'

Better-known figures are sketched: Ford Madox Ford 'breathing heavily through a heavy,stained mustache and holding himself as upright as an ambulatory, well clothed, up-ended hogshead'; Wyndham Lewis ('Some people show evil as a great race horse shows breeding.... Lewis did not show evil; he just looked nasty'). Pre-eminently, of course, there is the great trinity of this period in his life: Stein, Pound, Fitzgerald.

The story of Gertrude Stein's influence on Hemingway is familiar, but here it is seen with a special gratitude, appraisal, and egotism. Hemingway knows what she did for him, but he also wants to make clear that he performed several services for her, particularly in helping to prepare and publish 'The Making of Americans.'

He never refers to Alice Toklas by name, only as 'her companion' - possibly as retaliation for the comments in the 'Autobiography.' Throughout the book there are anecdotes that seem almost accidentally permissive, like cracks in the façade of literary history. One of these is his account of why he ceased to be a good friend of Miss Stein's. He inadvertently overheard a conversation between her and, presumably, Miss Toklas. He and Miss Stein had evidently felt no qualms about discussing homosexuality; he quotes her comparison of the male and female sorts. But he overheard her pleading with her friend in such an abject and painful way that he could never look at her again without remembering it, and it changed the entire color of his relationship with her. Obviously he never told her about it.

'Ezra Pound was always a good friend and he was always doing things for people.' Hemingway does not here explore the poet's subsequent behavior and fate, but he is unafraid to assert what is no secret: that, in addition to his own achievements, Pound was an extraordinary friend of writers he admired. The extent of Pound's editorial advice on 'The Waste Land,' for instance, is generally known; less known is the fact that he started a fund in Paris to free Eliot of his duties in a London bank, an effort happily made superfluous by an award and a subsidy that soon came Eliot's way. (3) Hemingway published Homage to Ezra in 'This Quarter' in 1925. His own political feelings were subsequently well manifested, but his loyalty to Pound - on the Forsterian plane (4) above politics and patriotism - remained constant.

Among these portraits and reminiscences, certainly the most fascinating are those of Fitzgerald, the golden unfortunate, the prince of pathos, who seemed in his very lifetime to be consciously discharging his role as a man with an unfulfilled life. Because his name and Hemingway's have so long been linked in comparison and contrast, it is now forgotten that, when they first met, Fitzgerald was successful, Hemingway quite poor and (as fiction writer) known only to a few readers of small magazines. In 1924, the year before their meeting, Fitzgerald had already written to Maxwell Perkins drawing attention to Hemingway's stories. When Fitzgerald looked him up in Paris, there were polarities of resistance-attraction on Hemingway's part to this 'older and successful' writer. (Thus Hemingway in 1960. Fitzgerald was all of three years older.)

Because of these polarities, Hemingway saw Fitzgerald steadily and saw him less than whole. But it is notable that the only chapter in this book with an epigraph is the first one on Fitzgerald, in which Hemingway makes a comparison with a butterfly, a statement whose sentimentality diminishes on re-reading. (Curiously, Andrew Turnbull, in a biography of Fitzgerald published after Hemingway's death, uses the same figure in a different way, saying that a comparison between the two men at that time 'would be like comparing a butterfly and a bull.')(5) His physical descriptions of Fitzgerald are the most vivid I have ever read.

He knew none of Fitzgerald's serious work when they met, but was aware of the 'older' man's success and was perhaps flattered by his attention. He accepted Fitzgerald's invitation to go by train with him to Lyon to pick up a car the Fitzgeralds had left there, then drive back to Paris. The story of the trip (among other things, there was no top on the car because Zelda hated tops, so the two men had to stop every time it rained) is possibly the funniest story about two famous writers since Tolstoy fell asleep while Turgenev read 'Fathers and Sons' to him. What with Fitzgerald's sudden, stark drunkenness, his hypochondria and dramatics, Hemingway was well weary of him by the time they reached Paris. Then Fitzgerald gave him a copy of 'The Great Gatsby,' which had just been published.

> When I had finished the book I knew that no matter what Scott did, nor how he behaved, I must know it was like a sickness and be of any help I could to him and try to be a good friend.... If he could write a book as fine as 'The Great Gatsby' I was sure he could write an even

> better one. I did not know Zelda yet, and so I did not know the terrible odds that were against him.

He soon got to know Zelda, and soon thought her insane. His view of her is the key to his view of Fitzgerald. His portrait of Fitzgerald emphasizes three elements: the drinking, the relation with Zelda, the sexual beliefs and status. As for the first, he makes clear that Fitzgerald was not, in the usual sense, a really heavy drinker but did not need to be. A relatively small amount not only made him drunk and irresponsible, it acted like a terrible poison on him, transforming his face into a death mask, making him sweat, grow rigid and strange. Eight years later Fitzgerald wrote to Perkins that he had gone on the wagon, 'but don't tell Ernest because he has long convinced himself that I am an incurable alcoholic, due to the fact that we almost always meet on parties. I am *his* alcoholic just like Ring [Lardner] is mine and do not want to disillusion him....' (6) The illusion of course was Fitzgerald's, because the parallel with Lardner was unfortunately apt. Still, there seemed at times to be some conviviality in Lardner's drinking; Fitzgerald's usually seemed like the sickness of a little boy who has been dared to overeat, is miserable, but will take the dare again tomorrow.

The dare came from Zelda, in Hemingway's opinion; she was jealous of her husband's writing and did what she could to interfere. When he seemed to be settling down to work, she either started a flirtation with another man to distract him or else taunted him into partying with her. Saner women than Zelda have loved their husbands at the same time that they wanted to compete with them, or were furious at being unable to compete and used the husband's love against him.

And Zelda was also responsible, says Hemingway, for a fear of physical incompetence on Fitzgerald's part. In sexual matters he was obviously a Victorian - in naïveté and prudishness - transported into the Jazz Age. The first question he asked Hemingway after he knew him well enough to call him Ernest was whether he had slept with his wife before marriage. It was a patent effort to compare notes: which failed. One day Fitzgerald confided to him at lunch that Zelda had told him he was too small. Hemingway was direct enough; he asked Fitzgerald to accompany him to *le water*. (7) (The vision of these two Olympians engaged in measurement in the men's room must have given the Muses a bit of a turn.) When they returned to their table Hemingway tried to assure him that everything was all right, that Zelda wanted to destroy him, and he added some technical advice. (8) 'But,' says Hemingway, 'he was still doubtful.'

The story is irresistibly amusing and in fact has a distinct serious value towards illuminating a certain mistiness, substitution, evasion about sexual matters in Fitzgerald's writing. The first really sexual scene in his work is in his last, unfinished novel. Yet Hemingway's retailing of this story has an inescapable tinge of smoking-room masculine superiority. Despite his declaration quoted above, he had and always retained an edge of dislike for Fitzgerald. In later Paris years he did not even want the other man to know his address (says Morley Callaghan) (9) for fear he would come barging in at any hour; but it was probably more than a wish for privacy. One may conjecture that this dislike was compounded of reaction to Fitzgerald's somewhat pretty good looks, Fitzgerald's liking for the tinselly life that he himself despised, Fitzgerald's willingness to compromise his writing for money which Hemingway, once he was on his own, never did. His own latter-day works were inferior, not compromised. There may also have been some residual resentment because the 'older' man had been successful first, had helped him to Scribner's - a favor hard to forget and therefore hard to forgive. In any event, in 1936, when Fitzgerald was small threat to him, he took the notorious crack at him in The Snows of Kilimanjaro. (10)

There was unquestionably a mean streak in Hemingway. He admits to a very bad, quick temper 'in those days'; it persisted. His mockery of Gertrude Stein in 'Green Hills of Africa' and 'For Whom the Bell Tolls' (11) can conceivably be justified as revenge for the remarks about him in the 'Autobiography of Alice B. Toklas,' particularly the use of the one word that could never be forgivable to him: yellow. But, similar to his rough treatment of his benefactor Sherwood Anderson in the short-novel parody 'The Torrents of Spring,' his blow at the drunken, sick, bankrupt, discouraged Fitzgerald can only be explained as deeply impelled abscission from those to whom he was indebted - like Thomas Wolfe's (more gentle) abandonment of Maxwell Perkins.

Above all the engrossing biographical details, items of portraiture and revealing anecdotes in the book, there tower two elements. The first of these, despite the marital chat quoted earlier, is the sad, lovely, moving warmth with which it is written. The second is his account (in some measure) of how he acquired the abilities with which to write it.

'When spring came, even the false spring, there were no problems except where to be happiest.' Youth, strength, joy of love, pride of poverty, delight in the city where he lived with his wife and child - all these fused into happiness, sheer happiness: rare in any good 20th Century author; rarer still in Hemingway. Memory may have gilded matters, but the facts as they were have less relevance than the memory.

But it is not gauzy Arcadian happiness; it is related closely to his work: to the sense that he was free of newspaper work and was settling firmly to his true vocation, that he had made the rock-deep right decision and was growing. To appreciate this fully, we must understand that he had been no mere cub reporter. (12) He had been a responsible correspondent entrusted by a large newspaper and a syndicate with important assignments. For example, he covered the Genoa Economic Conference in April, 1922, the Greco-Turkish war later that year; he interviewed Clemenceau and Mussolini. (His comments on the latter, which he wrote when he was 23, were, as Charles Fenton points out, remarkably prescient.) (13) He had given up a potentially big career, he had the responsibility of a wife and infant, and he had now cut himself loose even from occasional journalism. Influenced most immediately by Lardner and Anderson and Stein, and positively enjoined by the last to quit reporting, he had set out to find himself, and he knew, in his blood and bones, that he was succeeding.

In this book then we are in some degree present at one of the epochal moments in 20th Century literature: Hemingway's forging of his prose. What makes the joy in the book specially poignant is not only that we know now it was the high period of his life; the author himself, looking back after 35 years to the time when he was happiest, seems to know that he knew *then* that he would never be happier, stronger in his work, more imperial.

Speaking of why he did not include the old man's suicide, which is implied, in his story Out of Season:

> This was omitted on my new theory that you could omit anything if you knew what you omitted and the omitted part would strengthen the story and make people feel something more than they understood.

The evolution of understatement in his style - in his *concept* or art - connects with, among other matters, what he was learning from painters. (All his life painting was of prime importance to him.) 'I was learning something from the painting of Cézanne that made writing simple true sentences far from enough to make the stories have the dimensions that I was trying to put in them.'

His increasingly rigorous and effective reticence, his insistent lucidity, his rejection of the formalities and flourishes of pre-war literature with an accompanying implicit rejection of pre-war social falsities and pomposities - these touched quick nerves in his contemporaries around the world. Before he was thirty he was an immense literary power, one of the two or three most influential living writers of English. Faulkner took longer to become an influence. Joyce's influence, though more profound, was not so wide. For instance, Hemingway was the obvious stylistic father of Dashiell Hammett, as Hammett was of Chandler and of much lesser writers in the *genre*. Hemingway also had a strong influence outside of literature. It is impossible to conceive of Humphrey Bogart's film image without benefit of Hammett and Chandler and also without the direct influence of Hemingway abroad. As recent a film as 'The Hustler' (14) is virtually unimaginable - not only in story but in cinematic method - without the prior existence of Hemingway. I do not cite these examples as major art but only as evidence of his staggeringly large pervasive influence.

To younger readers, those who came to Hemingway after World War II, he could not possibly look the same as to previous generations because the later group saw him in a different context. (The different audience that Gertrude Stein said he needed?) Those who began to read him in the mid-20's, or soon after, experienced a small epiphany, saw a powerful and incredibly timely writer appear, almost as a savior bringing curt truth to a windy and shaken society. Change ensued. The first newly published book of Hemingway's that I read was 'Death in the Afternoon' (1932), and I can remember the quiet shock it caused among my friends, a shock allayed by 'Winner Take Nothing,' then amplified by 'Green Hills of Africa.' By the time we all reached 'For Whom the Bell Tolls,' Hemingway was just another writer, in the sense that he now wrote good books and bad books, or books with good and bad components in them. Even when he was better than good, he was not a god any more. The savior was gone, replaced by Papa who, it seemed, could not function - as a novelist, at least - without a war to stimulate him. Of his two novels unconnected with war, 'To Have and Have Not' prepared us long ago for the vacuities of 'The Old Man and the Sea.' 'Across the River and into the Trees' is almost an allegory of the author longing for past wars. His short stories, which contain his finest work, are much less dependent on war; but they dwindled away in the late 30's, and he published no story of consequence after 1940.

Younger readers missed this transition of attitude

towards Hemingway. For them he was, from the start, a mixed blessing. To them especially, then, this latest book may be a happy surprise. It is like getting a clear view back through the thick forest of his own self-imitation and the imitations of others, of the big-game gamesmanship and the worship of the bull. And he achieved it thirty-five years later, even at the same time (according to a prefatory note) that he was writing the stale, tired Dangerous Summer for 'Life.' It is rumored that there will be more posthumous books, probably fiction. Whatever their quality, it is unlikely that they will strike more touchingly this strong note of rejuvenation.

Rejuvenation from what? The quintessence of Hemingway is that he wrote realistically, even naturalistically, about romantic situations and characters. Jake Barnes, the mutilated hero of 'The Sun Also Rises,' is in effect Cyrano de Bergerac (15) in the 20th Century. His physical affliction is one of removal instead of enlargement, but it serves the same purpose as Cyrano's nose: to make him a lover who cannot love, attendant all his life (we feel) on his lady's wishes. Lieutenant Henry and his nurse enact a delicate little love poem - with the pathetic, not tragic, end of death in childbirth - its delicacy heightened by being set in the midst of a war that is unsparingly perceived and is under-described with magnificent ruthlessness.

This basic romanticism was not a flaw in the young writer, as these two still-potent novels prove. The flaw was in concentrating on this essentially youthful outlook as he grew older, his insistence that true and interesting life meant risk of death, large physical gesture, gallantry, and the rest of the doctrine of action as saving grace in a world grown morally as well as literally sedentary. This view clogged his development; and as, in the last twenty years, he struggled to write or did not write, he seemed to acquire an almost savage aloofness, combined with a capitalization of that aloofness, that aggravated this lack of growth. Edmund Wilson reminds us that 'it is a mistake to accuse [Hemingway] of an indifference to society. His whole work is a criticism of society.'(16) But it is significant that of the many gifted Americans who went to Paris in the twenties because they felt that only there could they become writers, Hemingway along never really returned to America (notwithstanding his Key West residence for some of the thirties). To provide himself with a life that was more than that of a conventional expatriate, a floating observer, he plunged even more heavily into the synthetic life of strenuous sports - which also served him as little wars. After Paris, excepting the two real wars, he lived in abstraction: in the formal rules of deep-sea fishing, rhino hunting, bullfighting, anywhere except where life as men were actually living it could touch and possibly enlarge him. Certainly he had little part in contemporary American life.

His style, which he had simplified to deal simply with genuinely great events, became pseudo-simple and self-conscious when, in later years, he dealt with lesser events on which he tried to enforce great stature. After 'For Whom the Bell Tolls' his writing continued to have a quality about it of translation, as from Spanish, possibly in the hope that formality would lend quality. The old fisherman had to be Cuban, of course, to talk about the Tigers of Detroit (17) and to call the fish 'thou'; an old American fisherman would have destroyed the pentateuchal grandiosity. Hemingway was always trying to make everything return to the time when he was young and strong as a writer, when his experience was fitted to his style.

In this book he accomplishes the return. Dealing with the high days (for him) when it was created, the simple style, for the most part, seems at home again: is relatively free of sludge, runs clean and clear and refreshing.

His career, at its height, was very short - less than 15 years. By taking us back to its birth, this book helps to explain its sudden and enormous impact, and raises again, after a considerable silence on the matter, the queston of his greatness. A novelist once said to me: 'We all know what it takes to be a great writer, even if you have the talent. You have to give your life.' Hemingway gave his life; then, by circumscribing his growth, he took it back again. This book suggests that he came to realize it and that, at the last, he wanted to say so.

Notes

1 Stein, 'Autobiography,' (London, 1933), 232.

2 E.B. White (b. 1899), is an American humorist. In October 1950 he published a parody of 'Across the River River' in the 'New Yorker.'

3 Eliot left Lloyd's bank in 1925, when he joined the publishing firm of Faber & Gwyer.

4 E.M. Forster, What I Believe, 'Two Cheers for Democracy' (1951) (Harmondsworth, Middlesex, 1965), 76: 'if I had to choose between betraying my country and betraying my friend, I hope I should have the guts to betray my country.'

5 Andrew Turnbull, 'Scott Fitzgerald' (New York, 1962) 188.

6 'The Letters of F. Scott Fitzgerald,' ed. Andrew Turnbull (London, 1963), 230.
7 The water-closet.
8 Fitzgerald's convincing statement in The Crack-Up that he slept with prostitutes as an undergraduate in 1917 casts doubt on Hemingway's version of the incident.
9 In his memoir, 'That Summer in Paris' (1963).
10 Hemingway wrote: 'He remembered poor Scott Fitzgerald and his romantic awe of [the rich].... He thought they were a special glamorous race and when he found out they weren't it wrecked him just as much as any other thing wrecked him.'
11 'For Whom the Bell Tolls' (New York, 1968), 289: 'A rose is a rose is an onion ... a stone is a stein is a rock is a boulder is a pebble.'
12 See 'Ernest Hemingway, Cub Reporter: The Kansas City Star Stories,' ed. Matthew Bruccoli (1970).
13 Charles Fenton, 'The Apprenticeship of Ernest Hemingway' (1954).
14 Robert Rossen's film (1961) about pool players, with Paul Newman and Jackie Gleason.
15 Hero of a popular play (1897) by the French author Edmond Rostand.
16 See No. 62.
17 A baseball team.

98. RICHARD ELLMANN, 'NEW STATESMAN'

67 (22 May 1964), 809-10

Richard Ellmann (b. 1918), Professor of English at Oxford, is the author of 'The Identity of Yeats' (1954) and 'James Joyce' (1959), and editor of Joyce's 'Letters' (1966, 1975).

Four paragraphs on Fitzgerald's 'Letters,' which Ellmann also reviewed, have been omitted.

In the last decade of his 61 years Hemingway fell into writing about veterans who knew the ropes only too well. In Italy and then in Cuba, the centre of attention was an unvanquishable old man, dressed up in martial or littoral costume, condensing into new saws for the benefit of some devoted novice (the younger the better) a lifetime's knowhow. Hemingway was so eager to depict characters tired, opposed, yet indomitable, that he seemed to be displaying his own toughness to the critics - by this time numerous - who thought he was no longer out in front. The sense of being himself under test led him to those dreams of senile glory in which decrepit heroes triumphantly outfaced old age and death - harshest critics of all. His books took on the air of ripostes, conceived in defiance, executed in mawkish gestures monosyllabically enforced, that Hemingway as well as his imitators had stereotyped.

The new book comes as a relief because the defensive tactics of the old man are left out, and we are back among the up-and-coming. In 1956 (1) Hemingway unearthed some old notebooks of his first years in Paris, kept (but of course) in the cellar of the Paris Ritz. These prompted him to reconstruct the time of his first espousal to a woman, to literature, and to Paris between 1921 and 1926, with some later information superimposed upon the early incidents. In these years, with the 'Byronic intensity' that Scott Fitzgerald envied him, Hemingway was making a style, missing lunch, sorting a subject-matter, throwing off the burden of journalism, nurturing his infant talent like his baby son, Mr. Bumby. In Paris his best subjects came from the life he had experienced years before in Michigan, and now he wrote, from Ketchum, Idaho and San Francisco de Paula in Cuba, more fully than ever before about Paris. The hero of The Snows of Kilimanjaro regretted on his deathbed that he would never be able to describe how he lived near the Place Contrescarpe, or how he wintered in Schruns, but Hemingway carries out posthumously Harry's unfulfilled intentions.

The book is made up of a series of short stories or near-stories, the form in which Hemingway always did his best. While autobiographical, they offer no direct self-portraiture, but look at the old comrades generally with a beady eye. No attempt is made at a consecutive chronicle, and in spite of unspecified rearranging and cutting by Mary Hemingway some episodes fit more loosely than others into the scheme, which is the association between Paris and himself, the rise and decline of his first marriage to Hadley Richardson, and, in the end - inadequately prepared but still powerfully expressed - the sudden yielding of a tensely organised young man to the lax temptations, hitherto resisted, of the rich. The book echoes somewhat the situation in 'The Sun Also Rises', with the writer instead of the bullfighter as the vulnerable material, and several of the characters from that earlier book flit through this one, mysteriously unnamed.

In writing about the early Twenties, Hemingway returned to what reads more like the account of a battle than a feast. The participants, savagely articulate to a man, have nearly all written books about the time, and more often than not they converge on Hemingway as a favourite target, partly because he was so much more successful than they. Gertrude Stein, Robert McAlmon, Wyndham Lewis and Harold Loeb (better known as Robert Cohn in 'The Sun Also Rises') struck at Hemingway in turn, and during his lifetime he offered no direct reply. (2) Among these assailants, Gertrude Stein, (as Hemingway's brother Leicester confirms) (3) particularly annoyed by depicting him as an ungrateful pupil, a coward, and (to cap it all) a bad boxer. Hemingway saved his retort for more than 25 years, and now offers a counter-image of Gertrude Stein as a woman formidable in talk but lazy and corrupt, piqued at his not remaining subordinate and unknown, quick to instruct (though his style had already been formed) but suspicious of her pupils after their graduation. Among other things, she explained to Hemingway that female homosexuality was beautiful and the male correlative ugly. Hemingway politely conceded the distinction until one day he overheard some masochistic byplay in Miss Stein's own flat. If anyone belonged to the lost generation, he suggests with unwonted primness, it was Gertrude Stein.

The most amusing part of the book describes Hemingway's meeting with Scott Fitzgerald, especially a drive they took by car from Lyons to Paris. Hemingway represents his companion, comically and adroitly, as a hypochondriac, a morning drinker, a victim of Zelda Fitzgerald's hawk-like cruelty and envy, and in sum as 'poor Fitzgerald' - the label which, when afterwards conferred in print, so irritated its recipient. The letters of Fitzgerald, on the other hand, indicate that he enjoyed the Lyons trip immensely and found Hemingway 'a peach of a fellow'. The one who spoiled the trip bore the other no ill will.

It was like Fitzgerald to abase himself further before someone who already had contempt for him, and so to Hemingway, of all people, he confessed that Zelda found him sexually insufficient. Hemingway was prepared, over a good lunch, to reassure him, to give him tips, to detect Zelda's villainy, and after lunch to present circumstantial evidence at the Louvre. With the revelation of Fitzgerald's problem Hemingway opens a new biographical vista, and sexual measurement may well occupy during the next half-century the place held by phlebotomy 100 years ago.

From external colouring to inner substance, the two men were opposites. Hemingway's posture was impregnability, while Fitzgerald's was the admission of more weaknesses than he had. He made no scruple about assessing himself as 'very second-rate'; he printed stationery identifying himself as 'Hack Writer and Plagiarist'. He recognised later that his own tendency was toward self-disparagement (he called it 'melancholy') as surely as Hemingway's was towards megalomania. Their early association must have been a continual pummelling of Fitzgerald, who would confess changing his stories' endings to suit the market, only to have Hemingway claim total indifference to such considerations. Fitzgerald called himself an 'old whore', while Hemingway, on higher and higher wages, still claimed virginity. By Hemingway's standards, Fitzgerald should not have been able to write at all, but he acknowledged with surprise that his friend could sometimes write well.

While Fitzgerald was expending his subject-matter prodigally in his early years, Hemingway was always gathering, absorbing, hoarding, withholding. He prided himself, 'The Moveable Feast' makes clear, on his secrets, such as a method of giving his stories added power by not mentioning a large part of their subject. The Big Two-Hearted River dates from this period, and keeps back the information that the hero's immersion in nature is so rapturous because he is just back from the war. 'You'll lose it if you talk about it,' says Jake in 'The Sun Also Rises', and here Hadley Hemingway volunteers a similar remark.

For Hemingway writing was a kind of suppression with only partial release, and this book inadvertently reveals many examples of this habit of mind. He would go without food in order to save the money, then indulge later in some gush of expense, and at the same time keep a secret money heap in reserve. The propensity goes beyond good housekeeping. His capacity for retention of his notebooks for so many years, for storing manuscripts in bank vaults for future exploitation, seems connected with this mode of writing and living. Even his method of composing a paragraph in circles around key words suggests a kind of peristaltic movement. Though he wanted to be known as swashbuckling, his strength came from self-containment.

As an ant he could not bear grasshoppers (4) - mistimedly drunk, ungainly, ill-smelling, bad-spelling people. The quality for which he has been so dispraised, by Morley Callaghan and others - his competitiveness and reluctance to recognise value in his rivals' work (a quality he noted in Stein but not in himself) - seems to have been more than anything an attempt to protect his winter stores. The book does not show him liking many people except his wife, an unknown poet, Sylvia Beach, two waiters and Ezra Pound, the last in spite of Pound's startling ignorance of Russian novels....

Each writer finds the other pathetic, though Fitzgerald arrives at the conclusion more slowly. What gradually became apparent to him in the Thirties was that Hemingway's method of saving, of holding himself back, of reserving subjects for future use, of restraining plots almost out of existence, was capable of becoming quite as formula-ridden as his own spending and self-squandering. If Hemingway thought of him as drunk, he considered Hemingway 'punch-drunk'; when 'For Whom the Bell Tolls' was published he estimated it accurately, and took his turn to patronise it as a book that would 'please the average type of reader, the mind who used to enjoy Sinclair Lewis.'

> It is full of a lot of rounded adventures on the *Huckleberry Finn* order and of course it is highly intelligent and literate like everything he does. I suppose life takes a good deal out of you and you never can quite repeat. (5)

By another, deliberate irony, Hemingway, so proudly disciplined, ends 'The Moveable Feast' with an admission of his fall. In imagery reminiscent of 'The Old Man and the Sea', he speaks of a pilot-fish, a kind of primitive bane in human form, who flatters and softens him up in Schruns for the advent of the rich. The pilot-fish, unnamed but doubtless an actual person, (6) prepares him like Fitzgerald's Zelda for destruction. When the rich arrive they lionise him and persuade him to read aloud some of 'The Sun Also Rises' before it is finished, a premature release which remains one of his bitterest memories. The result of this and other concessions is that his marriage to Hadley is broken, as if it were bound up with the constrained, secret marriage to his art. The knit and private joys of art, love and the city begin to fall apart into public postures.

Evidently good literature can be written by ants and grasshoppers alike. In Hemingway there is more to stir respect, in Fitzgerald more to evoke sympathy. At his best, in the edged dialogues of this book, Hemingway exhibits the intensity Fitzgerald admired in him. The language, seemingly simple, has poetic undertones, as when he writes of Paris, 'in those days, though, the spring always came finally,' or describes Fitzgerald in a fancied illness.

> Scott was lying with his eyes closed, breathing slowly

and carefully and with his waxy colour and his perfect features, he looked like a little dead crusader.

Occasionally, it's true, Hemingway lapses into the flaw of his manner, the rather precious winding about with words such as 'wonderful' or 'true' or 'warm'. But as a rule the style is eccentric, narrow, powerful, and all his own. Fitzgerald's manner, less concentrated, somewhat diffuse, a little careless, but slipping in and out of distinction, is now attracting the imitators who grew tired of the old battered idol.

Notes

1 Actually, 1957.
2 Hemingway had, in fact, attacked Stein in 'Death in the Afternoon,' 'Green Hills of Africa' and 'For Whom the Bell Tolls.' Lewis' work was literary criticism, not a memoir. Hemingway had, of course, provoked the quarrel with Harold Loeb.
3 Leicester Hemingway, 'My Brother, Ernest Hemingway' (1962).
4 An allusion to the fable of the Ondt and the Gracehoper in chapter 13 of James Joyce's 'Finnegans Wake' (1939).
5 'Letters of Fitzgerald,' ed. Turnbull, 128.
6 The pilot-fish was his wealthy second wife, Pauline Pfeiffer.

99. MORLEY CALLAGHAN, 'SPECTATOR'

212 (22 May 1964), 696

Morley Callaghan (b. 1903) is a Canadian novelist and short story writer, and author of the memoir 'That Summer in Paris' (1963) which describes Hemingway's circle of friends.

The book opens with the young Hemingway sitting at a café on the Place St. Michel, and straightway the old familiar and terribly determined elegiac note is sounded. It is very disquieting. Is he going to try to recapture the rhythms of 'A Farewell to Arms,' one wonders unhappily? But soon, and mainly because he is able to recapture some of the feeling he had had for his first wife, Hadley, and their small son in those Paris days between 1921 and 1926, the style gets straightened out; the sad, disturbing and often funny book gets going in its own right. Once again after all these years we seem to see him sitting alone at the café, writing and hoping. It is very moving. We see him, too, as he watches the fishermen on the banks of the Seine, or goes into the Musée du Luxembourg to study the paintings of Cézanne, and wonders if he could get the same landscape effects in prose.

It was the time when he was writing those little stories that were something new in the language. Working in poverty, and in love with his wife, he was strangely happy. Having given up newspaper work, he was committed to writing and was turning out a kind of story that was so suggestive, so stripped, so objective, so effective in capturing pure sensation that it became a unique kind of poetry. Never again was he to be as original or as objective as he had been in those days. When the time came to write this book, maybe he knew what he had lost. And maybe this knowledge explains the book's bitter tone.

But in those days he wasn't as self-absorbed or as isolated as he makes out. In fact, long before he wrote 'The Sun Also Rises,' he had had a peculiar underground fame. And the wonderful thing about him at the time was that he had a generous interest in the work of other unknown writers, was in touch with them, and would go out of his way to try and get them published in the little Paris magazines. Did he forget about the young writers who adored him? Why is it that the main thing he wanted to remember, or get down on paper, was that he had found perfect happiness in isolation, work and love - till other people came into the picture? And the only wisdom he has to offer now, looking back on it, is that other people, any people, are always the enemies of two who are in love and the enemies of the artist also. They smell out happiness, they move in to destroy it. It is always people, never himself, who are to blame.

And so he manages to give the impression that two star-crossed lovers, himself and Hadley, the 'Farewell to Arms' theme again, had their happiness destroyed by the great enemy - people. A man's fate is in the people who are interested in him, and if you are ski-ing in the Alps with your girl and people find you there you can't prevail against them. This is, surely, a pretty childish view of life.

Some of the people to be looked down on are done in the book as set pieces, and not at all in the flow of memories. This faulty structure is the great weakness of the book. And what frightening sketches of people who at one time knew and liked him! There is Ford Madox Ford, who, as editor of the 'Transatlantic Review,' had printed some of Hemingway's early work, and who, even before the triumphant appearance of 'The Sun Also Rises,' had written a front-page article in the 'Herald Tribune Books,' (1) New York, calling him the best young writer in America; Ernest Walsh, the Irish poet, an editor of 'This Quarter,' who had first printed Big Two-Hearted River and The Undefeated; Gertrude Stein, once his motherly friend, who had belittled him in print; Wyndham Lewis, who over the years had deplored Hemingway's love of violence; Pascin, the painter, and Scott Fitzgerald, who as he says had been a loyal friend for years - until they fell out.

The touch he uses in these portraits is controlled, expert, humorous and apparently exact; he is like a proud pool player, who lines up the balls with his cue, says, 'That one in the corner pocket,' and sinks it cleanly. But underneath the surface humour - it's really a gallows humour - there is a long-nourished savagery, or downright venom, and in his portraits there is the quick leap for the jugular vein.

What a relief it is to find him expressing tenderness and respect and loyalty to Ezra Pound - or affection for Sylvia Beach. And a relief, too, to discover there was a young poet named Evan Shipman whom he liked. Otherwise one could gather he had no capacity for friendship at all. In a prefatory note he says there were many good friends. There were indeed. It is unfortunate that he didn't get some of his old simple friendliness into the book. How much fairer he would have been to himself in revealing what he was really like in those days. He was actually an attractive, interesting, fascinating companion, dark and brooding though he might be, with strange shrewd hunches about people that turned into grudges. He was likeable and simple in manner, too. Savagery that was in him only broke out when he went berserk. What a pity that he withheld so much of himself that was so boyish and engaging. It was all here for him to tell. He isn't berserk in this book. He is a mockingly amusing, cold killer with a weapon he often controls so beautifully - his own prose.

In those days he would tell you he disliked Ford. He would openly scoff at him. But his brother, in his hero-worshipping book, tells how Ford had been sent to visit the Hemingway family home in Chicago. Yet in the sketch

Hemingway does of Ford, the two of them sitting at a café, a very expert, very funny sketch, he pictures Ford as a liar and a clown who gave off a body odour that fouled up the air. Was this all there was to Ford? Of course not, and he knew it.

It is true, too, that Wyndham Lewis was a difficult man to meet. He was so self-conscious, so worried that his importance would not be recognised, that he was always ill at ease and without any grace of manner. Hemingway and Lewis met in Pound's studio when Hemingway was teaching Pound to box. Looking back on the meeting, he believed he hated Lewis on sight. He can hardly express his loathing for 'the meanest-looking man I ever met.' And here again Hemingway overdoes it. And why? Only God knows! He had no more interest in trying to understand Lewis than he had in understanding Ford. And yet these highly prejudiced, personal reactions are interesting. In them may be found the keynote to the brilliance of much of his work. With him everything was personal, his work became the projection of his personality. He was not concerned with fairness or charity, or moral judgments, just with his own sensations.

But I, for one, don't care whether or not he was fair to Gertrude Stein. The domineering woman had talked her way into a reputation, and had taken her cracks at him. Now he goes to work on her. It's the literary life, I suppose.

The best and happiest writing in the book, and in some ways the fairest picture he gives of anyone, is of Scott Fitzgerald. The writing turns free and easy. He forgets the Biblical rhythms. He is at home and happy with his subject. The description of a trip to Lyon with Fitzgerald is simply hilarious; it is more than that; he gives a wonderfully vivid glimpse of Fitzgerald in all his changing moods, drunk and sober, and recognises his talent. Yet on end, aside from recognition of the talent, Fitzgerald is so cut down as a person - well, as Hemingway tells it, even the bartender at the Ritz, where Fitzgerald spent so much time, can't even remember him, but promised to try to do so, if old Hem will write about him and make him memorable.

The terrible disorder in Fitzgerald's life Hemingway blames on Zelda. Poor crazy Zelda, who, he says, was jealous of Scott, and liked to see him drunk, knowing he wouldn't be able to work. And what may be just as fantastic is Hemingway's explanation of why he began to shy away from Scott. He saw that Scott liked walking in on him to interrupt him, and saw that it was all a plan to make it impossible for him to work. This leaves us with

Fitzgerald doing to Hemingway what Zelda was doing to Fitzgerald. It gets mixed up and very complicated. But you must remember they were two men who dramatised everything, simply everything, including each other.

As the book draws to an end there is a curious revelation which is almost shocking in its candour. The idyllic love between Hemingway and his wife had continued up to the writing of 'The Sun Also Rises.' When they are ski-ing happily in the Alps, some rich people seek them out. A rich girl moves in with them, and in no time Hemingway has two women, and then finally he has only one and it isn't Hadley any more. 'Then you have the rich and nothing is ever as it was again,' he says, and his life took another turn, and with sourness he blames the rich for moving in on him and taking away his happiness. Was he so weak and helpless in the presence of the rich? It is such a surprising revelation one can't at first quite believe it, and then comes the thought, it must be true, for it is the first time Hemingway has ever deliberately put himself in a bad light.

Note

1 Ford did a blurb for 'In Our Time,' praised 'The Sun Also Rises' in 'Vanity Fair' and wrote an Introduction to 'A Farewell to Arms,' but he did not write a front-page review in the 'Herald Tribune.' Callaghan may be confusing Ford's work with Virginia Woolf's front-page review of 'Men Without Women.'

100. NELSON ALGREN, 'NATION'

198 (1 June 1964), 560-1

Nelson Algren (1909-1981) was an American novelist. He wrote 'The Man with the Golden Arm' (1949) and 'A Walk on the Wild Side' (1955).

The vital difference between this youthful American in love with his wife, his writing, food, wine and race-horses, was that the others had arrived at the Moveable

Feast directly from a picnic in Kansas City or St. Paul, but he had come to his place by way of death.

Paris to the Fitzgeralds was only a farther place on a meadow of endless sun. But Hemingway had so narrowly missed having no place at all - 'I'd felt my life flutter like a handkerchief in the wind' - that he knew how swiftly all good days are taken away. Hemingway was a young man learning how to sleep again.

But his hold on life having once been loosened, it now became all the more tenacious for that. The tension that began to pervade his writing derived from this tenaciousness, and lent him a perspective larger than that indicated by a phrase like 'lost generation.' When Gertrude Stein tried to pin it on him he rejected the label.

A French garage owner, impatient with a young mechanic who was goofing on Miss Stein's car, reproached him: 'You are all a lost generation.' Whereupon Miss Stein turned her irritation onto the nearest American - 'All you young people who served in the war are a lost generation, you drink yourselves to death' - who happened to be Hemingway.

'Don't argue with me, Hemingway,' she added firmly. 'It does no good at all. You're all a lost generation exactly as the garage keeper said.'

She wasn't prophesying the destiny of a generation; she was merely expressing the irritation of a car owner who finds the car isn't ready.

And Hemingway, having disputed her reluctantly and still feeling salty, walking home alone and catching a view of a heroic statue of Marshal Ney, turned his own irritation on the Marshal. 'What a fiasco you made of Waterloo!' Who was calling who lost? 'All generations were lost by something and always had been and always would be - the hell with her lost generation and all the dirty, easy labels.'

Hemingway wasn't lost. He would have been an expatriate even if he had never left Oak Park. His exile, like Villon's, was not from a land, but from the living. His need was not for a country, but for the company of men. Spiritually, therefore, he was closer to Villon than to Scott Fitzgerald. And, for a fact, Villon understood Hemingway better than have any of the critics:

In my own country I am in a far-off land
I am strong but have no force nor power
Well-received, rebuffed by all
I win all yet remain a loser
At break of day I say goodnight
When I lie down I have a great fear of falling. (1)

If we consider that Hemingway, like Villon, was forging a style not out of literature, but out of his need, we see not only what style is, but what Hemingway was.

The man and the style were one: the style was the instrument by which his need was realized; and the need was for light and simplicity. Thus, in achieving this for himself, he touched multitudes enduring a murky complexity.

A critic who can discover that Hemingway was nothing more than an innovator is scratching in the wrong barnyard. Dependence upon the catch phrase 'lost generation,' in lieu of insight into a writer's work, is of no use at all. One must distinguish between a man who represents his time, like John Dos Passos, and one who, like Hemingway, made his time represent him.

Multitudes saw the Spanish Civil War by Hemingway's light, because the light was true. When we consider how many novels have been turned out in imitation of him as a writer, we can only surmise how many Americans have tried to *be* Hemingway, because the image felt true. This was the image of the man or woman who felt that to become aware of life's precariousness was to become more alive. He caused the complacent man, standing content in his own well-lit door, suddenly to sense the precipitous edge where life drops off into utter dark. The woman counting her hours slowly dragging down, was troubled by the death of Catherine Barkley: lest no tragic hour ever strike for her.

Hemingway's own tragedy was that the light didn't hold. The present reminiscence is pleasant, humorous - and evasive. 'For reasons sufficient to the writer,' he advises the reader, 'many places, people, observations and impressions have been left out of this book ... there is always the chance that such a book of fiction may throw some light on what has been written as fact.'

The light he throws here is upon others. It is the harsh light of exposure: he reserves a soft, blurring glow for himself. Reporting a dialogue between two raving dikes, overheard accidentally thirty-five years before, is a bit the book could have done without. He might have let the poor brutes be. But the spotlight is useful when he recalls Fitzgerald's relationship to Zelda, because it reveals the fashion in which Fitzgerald was cut down. It does not have that justification with Gertrude Stein.

Fitzgerald appears to have been a sorry stiff, too disturbed about his wife's threat that 'you can never make any woman happy.' The washroom incident in which Hemingway assures Fitzgerald that he (Fitzgerald) could make any woman happy, by taking his measurement, is both comical and ominous. That a woman, failing to find her own femininity, may conceal that failure by attributing it to lack of manliness in her husband, is a trick we've all caught onto by watching TV. But Fitzgerald, with nothing to tune in but a radio, turned to drink.

Hemingway was a tolerant opponent and a mean competitor, both. Henry Strater, the artist whose portrait of Hemingway illustrates the back cover of 'A Moveable Feast,' and who was close to Hemingway in Paris because he could knock Hemingway down as often as Hemingway could knock him down, remembers that their friendship ended on a fishing trip in a quarrel over a marlin. 'I hated his guts for twenty years over that,' Strater now recalls their feud, 'I never hated any man so much in my life.' Then he added: 'But of all the friends I've had, now dead, the one I most wish were alive today is Hemingway.' (2)

Notes

1 François Villon, Ballade-VI (c. 1460), 'The Complete Works of François Villon,' trans. Anthony Bonner (New York, 1960), 143.
2 Henry Strater, Hemingway, 'Art in America,' 49 (1961), 84-5.

101. FRANK KERMODE, 'NEW YORK REVIEW OF BOOKS'

2 (11 June 1964), 4-6

Frank Kermode (b. 1919), Professor of English at Cambridge, is the author of 'The Romantic Image' (1957), 'Wallace Stevens' (1960) and 'The Sense of an Ending' (1967).

This is about how Paris was in the early days when Mr. Hemingway was very poor and very happy and handling himself very carefully because he knew there were going to be some rough contests, not only with Mr. Turgenev and Mr. Stendhal but also with life, 'the greatest left-hooker so far, although many say it was Charley White of Chicago.' The sadness of the book comes at the end because it explains that something got lost and the author was no longer making love with whom he loved, an activity to which he attached much importance. But it also speaks very happily about Paris, which is the best place in the world to write in. It explains writing carefully: the great thing is not to describe but to make, not to invent but to omit. And to be a good writer, as Hemingway has formerly explained, you need a built-in shit-detector. With one of those, working well, you can purge not only your prose but your acquaintance; so this book tells how Hemingway detected Ford Madox Ford and Wyndham Lewis and even Gertrude Stein, though it also tells how and why he put up with Scott Fitzgerald. It also tells about skiing, horse-racing, and fire-swallowing; about fishing in the Seine and the troubles of waiters, and how the Kansas City whores drank semen as a specific against tuberculosis. If I make it sound a little as if the figure of Lillian Ross's Papa must be casting a shadow over the book I do it no wrong. But I do it wrong beyond question if I seem to suggest that it could have been written by any but a great writer. This is, in some ways, Hemingway's best book since the 1920s and that makes it altogether exceptional.

At the beginning we have him sitting in a café on the Place St. Michel writing Up in Michigan; he names the streets he walked by to keep out of the wind, as elsewhere his route is determined by the need to avoid food-shops. A girl waiting in the café provides a kind of emblem of what he is feeling, and gets into the act; he sees her when he breaks off to sharpen a pencil, and she belongs to him as he to his craft. Finishing the story he feels 'empty and happy, as though I had made love.' This passage, which is about writing, is written not only with the skills but in the manner acquired during the period in which it is set, and so is the book as a whole. Some of the older attitudinising Hemingway has got into it, certainly - a sort of sentimental understanding of his own gifts and problems. But the book has that sharpness and suggestiveness which Hemingway means to achieve when he pursues his famous policy of omitting the known, the familiar links with other experience. And the power of it comes from its being a return - though by a man still sentimentally engaged in the struggle for style - to the time when he first made that hero's effort. The old writes about the young Hemingway, but in the prose of the latter.

The coexistence in this writer of technical and personal ambitions which seem at odds with each other has attracted much comment. Technically he intends to purge his prose in the interest of accurately representing the structure of experience and the texture of the world. It is the getting rid of *littérature*. The young Hemingway was dedicated to this effort. He had been a fluent journalist, and had had to learn that the good thing is the thing done with difficulty. So he went hungry when he need not have done, and 'learned how to make a landscape from Mr Paul Cézanne' - the hardest kind, demanding strict technical application, like boxing and shooting. And he listened to Stein and Pound, 'Isn't writing a hard job, though? It used to be easy before I met you,' he wrote to Stein. 'I certainly was bad, gosh, I'm awfully bad now but it's a different kind of bad.' (1) He learned how to leave things out and get right the things he did not. To all this he returns at length in the new book, telling how he took up Cézanne in Paris where he had left him in Chicago, 'learning something from the paintings ... that made writing simple true declarative sentences far from enough to make the stories have the dimensions that I was trying to put into them.' And when the light went in the Luxembourg he called on Gertrude Stein and watched her 'alive, immigrant hair' as she told him 'many truths about rhythms and the use of words in repetition.' It was taking him a morning to write a paragraph, but he was in training, like a fighter.

This book is in the manner then acquired. But it is far from bloodlessly insistent on purely technical feats. It is explicit that a living man, a natural heavyweight, was involved in these cerebral experiments, and they are accompanied by beer, whisky and oysters. The technique involved a technician, human material which felt itself involved in the demands of harsh difficult skills. And the behaviour of this material under stress came to interest him more and more. Perhaps we remember best of all the stories in his first book Big Two-Hearted River, with its concentration on a sporting technique and a sportsman's life. But Hemingway moved on, as he had to, from paragraph to story, story to novel; and he moved also into larger attitudes - the hero and not his skill became the focus. This is probably why Gertrude Stein could say that in her view he wrote nothing so good after 1925, the date at which this book ends. It is certainly why he began to lay the foundations of the heroic Hemingway myth.

This myth has often been characterised as self-indulgence, as something very different from the genuine dedication with which he went about making a style. In life it produced the insecure toughness ridiculed by Stein and rendered more sympathetically, a quarter-century later, by Lillian Ross. In prose it produced a writer who, in Lionel Trilling's words, 'put away the significant reticences of the artist' and 'opened his heart like "a man".' (2) The ethics of Jordan, the aesthetics of Cantwell, the cult of honour in defeat, too rigidly expressed, loosen and trivialise the writing, which invites harsh comparisons with the rigorous truth-telling and uncompromised structures of the earlier work.

This is a not unfamiliar line of argument. And yet this book strongly indicates something that was always there to be seen; only this hero, for all his self-indulgence, could have developed the manner of 'In Our Time.' It is the same man throughout. The difference between the pre- and post-Stein Hemingways, as he himself represents it, was the difference between a man who could do a lot easily and a man who could do a little only fairly well, and with great irritation and pain. He was learning a difficult craft and learning to do it with one hand. He thought it heroic, and perhaps it was; anyway the man who did it became the suffering hero of the novels. It is worth noticing that Barnes's wound in 'The Sun Also Rises' is a very literary wound, and is obliquely compared with the mysterious accident of Henry James. (3) After that the wounded writer is replaced by all those other sportsmen-technicians who have to hold the line of maximum purity in the utmost exposure: (4) the bullfighter who, incapacitated by an accident, has to kill his bull with one good hand; Morgan's last fight, one-handed against an evil world; Cantwell's wounded hand, which the perfect contessa loves; and finally the Old Man and his bad hand. Once he had beaten a powerful Negro in an all-night hand-game at Casablanca; but now his hand betrays him. 'If he cramps again, let the line cut him off.' When he sleeps after returning with his skeleton fish, the boy sees his hands and weeps.

So the years in Paris were not only a time in which Hemingway was learning how to do it, but how to be heroic in doing it, one-handed. And there is an intelligible relation between the self-denial of the writing and the self-indulgence of the attitudes, between finding out how to do it 'so it will make it without you knowing it,' and being the big game man, the *aficionado*, (5) the marksman, the fisherman, the DiMaggio of the novel. The style is a painful stripping away of all that is not declarative. What goes in must have the same kind of authority as a manual of instruction in some manly technique. Now the man who makes such prose is affected by it, and develops an increasingly simplistic theory of manliness. Hence the attention paid to the life of honour ('this honour thing is not some fantasy I am trying to inflict on you. I swear it is true') or the life of pure timeless and mindless love, even the life of the mystic. But above all, as we see when the lines of the literary diagram grow sharper, it is the life of the heroic and gifted peasant.

Hence the cultivated fellow-feeling for proletarian heroes - bakers, bullfighters, fishermen, all possessing techniques to be maintained in purity by imperfect human equipment. The theme is most diagrammatically proposed in 'The Old Man and the Sea.' There the hero speaks as Hemingway's Spaniards spoke, an invented language, common and pure, evading the transience of refinement or of slang. It is not spoken English any more than the language of the characters in the Civil War book is Spanish. It is the language of Wordsworth's Michael, resettled, after all, in the tropics. (6) It is very understandable that 'The Old Man' was at first taken to be an allegory of some personal disappointment, perhaps over the reception of 'Across the River and into the Trees.' It is simply the fullest representation of a pastoral myth, the myth of the author reduced to the simplicity of a one-handed struggle against the world, saying everything by saying a little accurately.

In the meantime, what happens to the reticent, heroic prose? The truth, it seems, can be known only by simple men who cannot speak English. One consequence is a sort of bombast, for Great Ideas can be mooted and discounted at the same time, as when the Old Man argues that you are entitled to kill a fish if you love it, but at once reproaches himself with thinking too much. This is certainly a difficult line to hold without falling into self-indulgence, and the later Hemingway is marred by a great deal of this disingenuous *simplesse*. Only one sees how it is related to his virtues, and developed from them.

So, if we consider this posthumous book *ad hominem*, (7) it will strike us as very moving. It was written by a man who thought he had, over the years, disciplined his technique to the point where he could deal with what he called the fourth and fifth dimensions; (8) who had, year in and out, fought his handgame with language till blood came from under his nails; who knew that he could do it any length, yet published nothing in the last decade of his life except a *novella* of the crystalline variety, very different from the arduous prose of the first heroic period. And a few years later he began to write this book about the heroic apprenticeship. It opens with a passage which equals in subtlety and power anything in the great stories. 'Then there was the bad weather' is the first sentence - what was omitted before he arrived at this declaration? - and before the end of the first page we are in the midst of a painter's description of sewer wagons in the moonlight on the rue Cardinal Lemoine. Then he tells about the girl who got into Up in Michigan, and goes right on to a description of one of Stein's lessons. He wants it to be clear that this book is about writing, about the heroic apprenticeship.

Much of what he says of Paris is generally familiar from other books. But no other book is of this authority and distinction, and no other so strongly conveys (largely by omission, of course) the sense of time regained. This, however, is to be understood as a side-effect of the principal effort, which is to celebrate the hero and his struggles. What happened in Paris was important in so far as it helped or hindered him. Being in love, knowing Pound and Sylvia Beach, going hungry, watching the fishermen, helped. Racing, though absorbing, didn't, so it had to be given up. Many things were positive hindrances: people who interrupted him as he wrote in cafés, and were foully insulted; people who upset him by being homosexual; people who in one way or another were out to con you. Some of these were well-known people, and the most obviously interesting thing about the book is that it says disagreeable things about such people.

There is a malice here, recollected in tranquillity;(9) as in the pages on Stein, and those on members of what she called the lost generation. (Incidentally Hemingway's explanation of the expression '*la génération perdue*' is that Miss Stein got it from a garage proprietor who was reproving the help for slowness or ineptitude in repairing her Model T. This is far less convincing than John Brinnin's version, (10) which is that she borrowed it from a hotel-keeper who argued that men got to be civilised between eighteen and twenty-five, or never, and that a generation had missed its chance of civility because of the war.) It was obviously fun to get back at Stein for the nastiness of the Toklas book, and Hemingway invents some beautiful dialogue - which he could always do, and which she, he claimed, could not - to say wicked things about her. The two chapters on Stein are written like very good stories, especially the second, called A Strange Enough Ending, which has in it why he could never make friends with her again; the reason given is not, most of us would think, a good one, but it sounds good. Wyndham Lewis is disposed of in a hideous little vignette; Hemingway goes home afterwards and tells his wife, 'I met the nastiest man I've ever seen today.' 'Tatie, don't tell me about him.' she said. 'Please don't tell me about him. We're just going to have dinner.'

Ernest Walsh, who was dying of consumption, flaunted

a 'marked-for-death look': 'and I thought, you con man, conning me with your con.' Of Ford Madox Ford: 'I took a drink to see if his coming had fouled it.' Scott Fitzgerald is a kind of critical case, absurd and offensive but a writer. So to him is devoted the most elaborately written section of the book, a carefully devised tragic farce about a trip to Lyon, with a scene in which Hemingway takes Fitzgerald's perfectly normal temperature with an immense bath thermometer. The food and the conversation are remembered or invented with total authenticity. From start to finish this is the work of a great writer.

This, as Hemingway himself suggests, is a work of fiction, and ought to be considered among his novels. It is an ingenious and deliberate way of revisiting the sources of a great writer's strength; and it displays that strength as very little else of his had done in thirty years.

Notes

1 Quoted in Baker, 'Ernest Hemingway', 168.
2 See No. 58.
3 During a fire in Newport, Rhode Island, in 1861 James suffered an 'obscure hurt' which seemed to impair his sexual capacity.
4 'The Sun Also Rises' (New York, 1954), 168.
5 Fan.
6 The subject of Wordsworth's poem Michael (1800) is a shepherd. Kermode also alludes to Aldous Huxley's Wordsworth in the Tropics, 'Collected Essays' (1968).
7 As applying to Hemingway himself.
8 See 'Green Hills of Africa' (New York, 1935), 27.
9 See Wordsworth's phrase 'emotion recollected in tranquillity' in the Preface to 'Lyrical Ballads' (1800).
10 John Malcolm Brinnin, 'The Third Rose: Gertrude Stein and Her World' (1959).

102. TONY TANNER, 'ENCOUNTER'

23 (July 1964), 71-3

Tony Tanner (b. 1935), an English critic and Fellow of King's College, Cambridge, wrote 'Reign of Wonder' (1965) and 'City of Words' (1971).

> 'I talk with the authority of failure - Ernest with the authority of success. We could never sit across the same table again.' (Scott Fitzgerald - 'Notebooks.')

Gertrude Stein, sceptical as to Hemingway's toughness and jealous of his success, once wrote: 'What a book would be the real story of Hemingway, not those he writes but the confessions of the real Ernest Hemingway.' Well, now we have the nearest thing to that story we are ever likely to get. Of course it is not 'the real story.' It is a deliberately and rather felicitously constructed version of the twenties as a doomed idyll. He portrays a time of pure beginnings, when nothing was spoilt, when talent burgeoned with love, and when rich vivid impressions were eagerly hoarded up by the unclouded wondering eye. (He seems to have had total recall of all the meals he had during this time.) There are paragraphs of exquisitely accurate notation which evoke that time with undulled intensity. But he sees this time from the perspective of age, so that the dawn brightness is occasionally darkened by sombre intimations of twilight. The recaptured sense of the young time when everything was possible is sobered by the recurrent realisation that nothing lasts.

This is of course an exercise in nostalgia, but it is a controlled exercise: a few well-placed shadows prevent the vivid recollections from spilling over into deliquescent idealisation. The book starts with rain, cold wind, and stripped trees - 'Then there was the bad weather' - and in Hemingway's work such weather always carries overtones of menace, transience, and loss. It ends with Hemingway having been unfaithful to his wife and already suffering some of the corruption of success. Looking back at Eden Hemingway can see some of the trampled flowers, and while the stress is on innocent happiness there are muted portents of the fall and banishment to come. Hints - '"We're always lucky," I said, and like a fool I did not knock on wood' - and the final realisation - 'All things truly wicked start from an innocence. So you live day by day and enjoy what you have and do not worry. You lie and hate it and it destroys you and every day is more dangerous, but you live day to day as in a war.' But for most of the book the scene is as follows: Hemingway sitting safely in a familiar café (A Clean, Well-lighted Place?). He writes, eats, and drinks. Then he makes his way quickly, even cautiously, across Paris until he is home (as all Hemingway heroes long to find a true 'home'). There he makes love and relishes the sense of sanctuary. Occasionally there are marvellous trips or walks with his wife or some particular friend who shares his own quiet reverence for ordinary things.

But there are interruptions, intruders in paradise who stop him from working or soil the sacred intimacy of his home. Real toads in the ideal garden. Like Ford Madox Ford ('heavy, wheezing, ignoble presence'), Wyndham Lewis ('I do not think I have ever seen a nastier-looking man'), and the unnamed visitor who dares to enter Hemingway's 'home café' to be greeted - 'You rotten son of a bitch, what are you doing in here off your filthy beat?' There are some angels - Ezra Pound with his endless generosity and help, Sylvia Beach for lending books and money, the euphoric Pascin - but throughout the book one senses an almost neurotic resentment at the uninvited proximity of other people, a pugnacious fear of their contagion. This impression is strengthened by his amazing statement to Gertrude Stein when he is explaining his prejudice against homosexuals. 'I tried to tell Miss Stein that when you were a boy and moved in the company of men, you had to be prepared to kill a man, know how to do it, and really know that you would do it in order not to be interfered with.' Remember Malcolm Cowley describing how Hemingway always moved around like a boxer? (1) - and the incredible importance he attached to his sparring? One character in the the book says that Hemingway looks like 'a man alone in the jungle.' but he sounds more like an animal at bay in the jungle, snarling to scare off a threat which is sensed, feared, but not yet seen.

Even the humour in the book (and parts are very funny) is rather cutting - a weapon rather than a joy. Hemingway certainly reveals himself more nakedly than he can have intended. What he intends to look tough starts to appear neurotic. The book is written with a good deal of arrogance: every episode is turned to leave Hemingway looking tougher, more talented, more honest, more dignified than anyone else. When he touches on his faults - and 'touches' is the word - they turn out to be those of the sportsman (gambling) or of the dedicated artist (bad temper). When he does upbraid himself it is embarrassingly theatrical. 'You God-damn complainer. You dirty phony saint and martyr, I said to myself.' This pseudo self-criticism in Hemingway-ese is merely a matter of posturing - the reverse of self-knowledge. And behind all the aggressive implications that Hemingway alone has the secret of the good life, one detects the over-assertiveness of a man troubled by anxiety and fear, a man whose tight tough confidence seems strained by wariness and suspicion, a man mythologising himself to avoid confronting himself. A 'fragile' man, as someone once commented.

This makes one look again at the style. It is a prose marvellously attuned to registering distinct, unhurried impressions; (2) it is a prose of veracity, paying meticulous respect to the real. But it is also a defence strategy. Hemingway's prose seems to expect trouble. When it is not celebrating some safe idyllic moment of sensory delight, it is clarifying potential opposition. His words sometimes seem to have a sort of sentry quality - cautious to expect attack and disciplined to deal with it. He has interesting things to say about his style in this book. The rule that 'All you have to do is write one true sentence' to get started; the resolve to write 'one story about each thing that I knew about' (*i.e.*, separation is preferred to synthesis); the influence of Cézanne (just as Stein said she wrote 'Three Lives' looking at a still-life by Cézanne); the use of rhythms and repetitions which he learned from Stein (an important factor in Hemingway's creation of the stylised vernacular as a style); the theory of omitting things to achieve greater power; and perhaps most interestingly the description of Ezra Pound as 'the man who had taught me to distrust adjectives as I would later learn to distrust certain people in certain situations.' *Distrust*. That is what - in this book - one senses in the man and the style. When life isn't idyllic it is likely to be a fight (the importance Hemingway attaches to mutilation as evidence of genuine warriorship crops up again) - so, never relax your guard. The clean, controlled stoicism of Hemingway's earlier work still seems to me a major achievement - but when distrust becomes a style all is not well within. (In this connection it is perhaps interesting to note Hemingway's intense interest in routes. It is there in an early story like In Another Country and much in evidence in his later work. Here it occurs with varying accounts of traversing Paris. Of course it is part of Hemingway's scrupulous regard for topography, his interest in terrain; but remembering that on the last car ride before his suicide he was pathologically anxious about the route and kept on consulting the map, perhaps we can suggest that it is a symptom of some unusually deep anxiety. Does some of the intense step-picking care of his prose come from a general fear of losing the way?)

The most interesting and moving part of the book describes

his relations with Fitzgerald in France. Some of the glimpses afforded us are arrestingly authentic. Scott passing out 'at the table with his head on his hands. It was natural and there was no theatre about it, and it even looked as though he were careful not to spill nor break things': Scott's face suddenly paling into a 'death mask' while they are standing at a bar, his 'long-lipped' Irish mouth which 'worried you until you knew him and then it worried you more.' There is a shrewd analysis of the logic of the Fitzgeralds' drinking, and some chilling insights into Zelda's terrible destructive jealousy. Her smile, for instance, as yet another party got under way. 'I learned to know that smile very well. It meant she knew Scott would not be able to write.' There is an amusing account of a disastrous visit to Lyon and a comic chapter called A Matter of Measurements which is about exactly what you might think. Typically, it shows Hemingway in the role of confessor and adviser, a sort of calm superman counselling the fallen and weak. Clearly the careful Hemingway had to be wary of the Fitzgeralds and the chaos they brought in their wake: but what is irritating is the way he manages to patronise Fitzgerald, subtly cutting him down and belittling him. He admits in passing that Scott was a loyal friend, rather as a lord might accept fealty owing to him, but it is Hemingway who graciously stoops to offer a hand: 'I knew that no matter what Scott did, nor how he behaved, I must know it was like a sickness and be of any help I could to him and try to be a good friend.' This is a wretched distortion. In fact it was the successful Fitzgerald who pushed and helped the unknown Hemingway, and when Fitzgerald was really down and out, Hemingway, by way of friendship, included a cruelly contemptuous reference to him in his story The Snows of Kilimanjaro. Such distortion - one feels it runs through the book - suggests that the work was written not with the authority, but with the *anxiety* of success.

To turn to Fitzgerald is to enter a different world, or rather the world registered and approached in an entirely different spirit. Where Hemingway's work feels closed, constricted, aggressive, andd suspicious in its fierce accuracy, Fitzgerald's seems open, expansive, loving, always moving towards moments of lyric suggestiveness. Where Hemingway seems to be holding back, putting up defences, husbanding his resources, Fitzgerald strikes us as precipitously involved and exposed, giving himself to the moment, squandering himself until his life seems like an allegory of his times - his twenties the Boom, his thirties the Depression. There is no distrust in his tone: he prefers to celebrate life, to be generous to its fleeting nuances, and where he has to record failure, dissolution, and degradation, he does so with understanding, balance, and a compassionate poise such as is attained only by those who are uncompromisingly self-aware, unfaltering in honesty to the very heart of darkness and loss.

This means, for a start, that Fitzgerald is far more perceptive about Hemingway than Hemingway is about him. He respected and admired Hemingway all his life (he was even planning to make him the hero of a series of medieval stories!), (3) he praised the quality of his style ('a stick hardened in the fire'), and always spoke glowingly about the order and purity of his work. But he could also read the man plain. An early note reads ' it is undeniable that the dark was peopled for him,' and when Hemingway made the cruel reference in Snows Fitzgerald wrote to a friend: 'He is quite as nervously broken down as I am but it manifests itself in different ways. His inclination is toward megalomania and mine toward melancholy.'(4) But still - 'Somehow I love that man, no matter what he says or does.' To a friend he explained that it was all part of Hemingway's 'sadistic maladjustment' which made him go round knocking people down. The mixture of love and clear-sighted judgment is typical. Hemingway thought life ought to be lived in a certain way and he strove to shut out anything he did not understand or didn't approve. But Fitzgerald followed life wherever it led him, even when it led him to the bottom of the abyss. For this reason he can understand loss, waste, and the general mortality of human things much better than Hemingway, who tends merely to register them with dumb resentment. Fitzgerald was a romantic whose work includes a definite critique of romanticism: as in 'Gatsby' he understood both 'the dream' and the 'foul dust' that floats in its wake. His insight into complexities of character was far subtler than Hemingway's (compare the analysis of Gloria in 'The Beautiful and Damned' with the sentimental wish-fulfilment figure of Catherine in 'A Farewell to Arms'), and where Hemingway's early stoicism became a somewhat shrill and desperate tough-guyism, Fitzgerald's young abandoned revelry gradually gave way to true wisdom.

Notes

1 Malcolm Cowley, 'Exile's Return' (1934).
2 Tanner discusses this point more fully in 'Reign of Wonder' (1965).

3 'Philippe, Count of Darkness' was meant to be a historical novel.
4 'Letters of Fitzgerald,' ed. Turnbull, 243.

103. JULIAN MACLAREN-ROSS, 'LONDON MAGAZINE'

4 (August 1964), 88-95

Julian Maclaren-Ross (1912-64), an English novelist, wrote 'The Nine Men of Soho' (1946) and his autobiography 'Memoirs of the Forties' (1965).

In his posthumously-published book of memoirs, Hemingway takes us back to the Paris of his - and the century's - early twenties. Here we have again the two-roomed apartment in the rue du Cardinal Lemoine where Harry, the drunken failure dying of gangrene in The Snows of Kilimanjaro, having traded-in his talent for security and comfort, also lived; the green autobus and the Café des Amateurs (packed with poverty-stricken, sour-smelling local drunks) in the Place Contrescarpe; and the 'cheap tall hotel where Paul Verlaine had died,' on the top floor of which both Hemingway and Harry wrote their early work: the room cost Harry, at any rate, sixty francs a month, though Hemingway - possibly because Harry was at work in it - seemed to prefer writing in a café on the Place St-Michel or, later (when he moved to the rue Notre Dame-des-Champs), at the Closerie des Lilas. He shares many memories with this There-but-for-the-Grace-of-God-type other self: for instance skiing at Christmas in Schruns in the Vorarlberg, Austria (where Hemingway was known to peasants as 'the Black Kirsch-drinking Christ'), and playing poker with Herr Lent of the Alpine Ski School as described in both the story and the last chapter of 'A Moveable Feast'; but one feels that Paris during this period (1921-26) would have been Hemingway's own chosen happy-hunting-ground rather than Kilimanjaro, as with Harry.

I too was in Paris then, living not far away in a flat formerly belonging to the Irish poet James Stephens and, like Hemingway's, over a sawmill: indeed I must often have seen him, without knowing it, walking hungrily about the Luxembourg Gardens while I was watching Guignol and

Grangalet (1) at the age of ten, a time of life when one's perceptions are particularly sharp where the sights, smells, and weather in a foreign city are concerned, so I can vouch for the truth of how he says it was in the winter and summer; though (from later experience) for only the partial truth of what he says about the value of being 'belly-empty, hollow-hungry'.

'Hunger,' we are told, 'is good discipline and you learn from it' (Yes, how to try and avoid getting into this unpleasant state again). A lot of nostalgic nonsense is often written about poverty and hunger by successful authors who no longer have to experience them, and Hemingway here is no exception ('I learned to understand Cézanne much better and to see how truly he made landscapes when I was hungry. I used to wonder if he were hungry too when he painted; but I thought possibly it was only that he had forgotten to eat'. etc., etc.). Incidentally, the book is so full of descriptions of eating that perhaps the best place to read it would be in a restaurant or after a heavy meal.

About Hemingway's actual methods of writing, and theories concerning his craft, which he was always unwilling to discuss, one learns little more than can be found, rather more fully expounded and on the whole better expressed, in the interview with him in 'Writers at Work' (Second Series, 1963), much as the Paris and Austrian backgrounds are re-created just as vividly, in microcosm, during the Kilimanjaro flashbacks: 'A writer can be compared to a well.... The important thing is to have good water in the well and it is better to take a regular amount out than to pump the well dry and wait for it to refill'. (The well fills of itself with 'juice' overnight, providing you stop writing at a point where you know what is going to happen next). There is also the simile of the iceberg ('seven-eighths of it underwater for every part that shows') first encountered in 'Death in the Afternoon' ('If a writer of prose knows enough about what he is writing about he may omit things that he knows and the reader, if the writer is writing truly enough, will have a feeling of those things as strongly as though the writer had stated them. The dignity of movement of an iceberg is due to only one-eighth of it being above water.'). In 'A Moveable Feast', we are given an example of the iceberg-principle when the author casually informs us that one of his most effective early stories, Out of Season, really ended with the old Tyroler Peduzzi hanging himself (suicides have always been a prominent feature of Hemingway's work): the imaginary Old Lady who acted as conversational sparring-partner in 'Death in the Afternoon' would complain that the 'wow' or pay-off had once more been left out, but this non-stated climax, quite unsuspected by the reader until now, may be seen to account for the oppressive atmosphere of guilty malaise informing what on the face of it seems a semi-comic character-study.

A few more glimpses of the young writer at work are vouchsafed us: bringing The Three-Day Blow into being because of the wind outside the café where he wrote; deciding to start a long story about coming back from the war without mentioning the war itself (this seems to be Big Two-Hearted River, though certainly no one could guess the true subject from internal evidence); and once when interrupted by a homosexual bore ('Take your dirty camping mouth out of here') whom he attempts unsuccessfully to turn into a critic. The relationship with his first wife (who at one stage lost by accident all his MSS: an almost insurmountable setback) never seems entirely credible because presented too idyllically in his later manner - rather like the Colonel's relations with Renata in 'Across the River and into the Trees' - and Mrs Hemingway is portrayed as far too admiring and acquiescent for a flesh-and-blood woman, however much in love: a fault which first began to show during the conversations with a different 'Mem' (2) in 'Green Hills of Africa'. Only in the closing pages does the marriage, under the shadow of imminent dissolution, spring suddenly to life; and perhaps the finest passages are those in which Hemingway, with an abrupt return to his best form, draws up a terrible indictment of 'the good, the attractive, the charming, the soon-beloved, the generous, the understanding rich' who were in some way, during 'a nightmare winter disguised as the greatest fun of all', responsible for the break-up.

The real interest of the book lies, however, in his portraits of the famous contemporaries with whom he came in contact, and the self-revelation contained in the personal reactions which he now claims they aroused in him: for example, the force of loathing conjured up by his first sight of Wyndham Lewis (compared among other things to toe-jam and an unsuccessful rapist) seems out of all proportion until we remember the Dumb Ox essay in 'Men Without Art' (1934). Certainly Lewis seemed unaware of any antagonism: they evidently shared a distaste for the 'Dark Laughter' racial theories of Sherwood Anderson (according to Gertrude Stein, one of Hemingway's formative influences, whom he afterwards publicly repudiated in the parody 'Torrents of Spring'); and in his autobiography 'Rude Assignment' Lewis quotes a letter from Hemingway dated October 1927 in which the latter congratulates him on publication of 'Paleface' (also an attack on Anderson), adding: 'I have always had a great respect for Hemingway ... he is the greatest writer in America.' The subject of Lewis ('the nastiest man I've ever seen') appears by the way to be the only one on which Hemingway's and Gertrude Stein's accounts agree; according to his, she said: 'I call him "the Measuring Worm". He comes over from London and he sees a good picture and takes a pencil out of his pocket and you watch him measuring it on the pencil with his thumb. Sighting on it and measuring it and seeing exactly how it is done', while 'The Autobiography of Alice B. Toklas' states: 'He used to come and sit and measure pictures. I cannot say that he actually measured with a measuring-rod but he gave all the effect of being in the act of taking very careful measurement of the canvas, the lines within the canvas and everything that might be of use.' (3)

About Miss Stein herself, Hemingway is considerably more guarded (though quoting as new an anecdote about the death of Apollinaire already told in 'Alice B. Toklas', as well as his own interpretation of Ezra Pound and the injured armchair, and the origin of the celebrated 'lost generation' label, which he seems to think inapplicable yet adopted as an epigraph). He admits grudgingly that she gave him good advice about writing (the story Up in Michigan, dismissed by her as *inaccrochable*, (4) is evidence of this); she also attempted without much success to make him take a more tolerant view of genuine homosexuality, and recommended for after-work reading the novels of Mrs Belloc Lowndes (5) (which he seems, astonishingly, to have enjoyed). From their respective styles it is still hard to tell who influenced whom: whether Hemingway learned to simplify his prose from proof-reading 'The Making of Americans' or Miss Stein learned to write dialogue from 'The Sun Also Rises', and probably both claims are justified. He states that their friendship folded because he inadvertently overheard her quarrelling with a Lesbian friend: her version is that the breach occurred when she told him that 'remarks are not literature' ('Alice B. Toklas' actually gives two separate reasons for this observation: (1) that Hemingway had written that Miss Stein 'always knew what was good in a Cézanne'; (2) that, having previously accused E.E. Cummings of 'having copied everything', he had then praised 'The Enormous Room' as 'the greatest book he had ever read'). But the truth will never be known now, since as Hemingway himself says in another connexion: 'All those people are dead.'

He was obviously a good hater, and one who never forgot a fancied slight: Aldous Huxley's essay Foreheads

Villainous Low is remembered after all this time, even though the last destructive word is delivered obliquely, through the mouth of Miss Stein in a reported conversation. Joyce, Pound and Pascin come off scot-free (he is nevertheless extremely funny about Pound's well-meaning efforts to rescue 'Major' T.S. Eliot from the bank in which he was then employed); the full blast of his malice is reserved for a phoney poet and literary con-man named Ernest Walsh, now dead (of T.B.), forgotten and seemingly scarcely worth the trouble, and Ford Madox Ford.

In a very amusing chapter, where the 'wow' is certainly not omitted, Ford is shown obtusely explaining the location of a Bal Musette above which Hemingway had lived for two years (and where he enjoyed with the taxi-driving proprietor the same drink recalled by Harry in Kilimanjaro). It is doubtful, however, that Ford would in reality have mistaken Aleister Crowley for Hilaire Belloc (6) (see the section on Starting a Review in his 'Selected Memories'), or that he would have gloried in 'cutting' Belloc as a 'cad'; what seems more likely is that he got their names mixed up, an inherited failing admitted in his Table Talk. It is also possible that Ford, in pontificating upon the definition of a 'gentleman' (Hemingway did not qualify), believed that an American would be genuinely interested in an analysis of this quaint form of English snobbery, or that he was simply sending himself up; an example of Ford's poker-faced fun is given in Harold Loeb's recent reminiscence printed in the 'London Magazine': (7) a young woman was startled on being informed with apparent seriousness that she could now tell her grandchildren she had danced with Ford Madox Ford, whereas he was plainly paraphrasing Liszt's remark to himself as a child; moreover, he would be unlikely to have 'severely' corrected a waiter for a mistake which he had not made, after dilating upon the existence of waiters as human beings in another Selected Memory entitled A Shameful Episode.

Hemingway's insistence on the 'heavy, wheezing, ignoble' presence of a man who had helped him as an editor (he even tastes his brandy cautiously to see if Ford's coming had fouled it) remains puzzling, although the reason for it may be found in 'Alice B.Toklas', where Ford is also reputed to have said of Hemingway: 'He comes and sits at my feet and praises me. It makes me nervous.' (8) But if he is unfair to Ford, one cannot complain of the picture presented of Scott Fitzgerald, the golden boy of American literature, who arrived slightly tarnished upon Hemingway's scene wearing a Guards tie, and proceeded to turn straightaway into a living death-mask under the influence of alcohol. Fitzgerald emerges as a tiresome hypochondriacal nuisance when drunk ('You can sit there and read that dirty rag of a French paper and it doesn't mean a thing to you that I am dying'), yet nonetheless endearing and a victim of his wife's literally insane jealousy of his talent: showing with impersonal pride when sober a ledger listing all sales, royalties, and other sums received for his stories, or giving 'a sort of oral Ph.D. thesis on Michael Arlen', whose books Hemingway found unreadable, although there is an odd occasional echo of the Armenian's mannered facetiousness in some of his dialogues with the Old Lady in 'Death in the Afternoon':

> *Old Lady:* That's a very nice line about lust.
> *Author:* I know it. It came from Andrew Marvell. I learned how to do that by reading T.S. Eliot.

Fitzgerald, however, outlived his meteoric fame as chronicler of the Jazz Age, and died too early to become a legend in his own lifetime, which does a writer more harm than too much whisky; Hemingway, on the other hand, did: and came to put almost as much work into perpetuating his personal myth as he had previously put into perfecting his style. 'Death in the Afternoon', containing much of his purest writing and most exact observation, equal in precision to the skill of the bullfighters which it celebrates, forms a bridge across the river and into the trees growing - figuratively - on the 'Green Hills of Africa'.

In this latter book the self-made legend may be seen to start, with Hemingway in a newly-created 'Personal Appearance Artist' (9) rôle as a gruff, laconic hunter on safari, complete with Little Woman (or, as he actually called her, 'Mem-Sahib') as feed. The opinions on literature so clearly expressed in 'Death in the Afternoon' have become dogmatic pronouncements (though in his 'Writers at Work' interview he attributed this to the character of his interlocutor, the Austrian Kandisky); rancour towards confrères - Gertrude Stein and Thomas Wolfe among them - first shows itself, and the ability to laugh at himself (conspicuous in the account of his bullfighting misadventures) has largely atrophied. 'To Have and Have Not', the most underrated of his novels, was a partial recovery, comprising some interesting technical experiments and the last two women (Helen Gordon and Marie Morgan) whom he was able to imbue with life (compare Maria, the 'Little Rabbit' of 'For Whom the Bell Tolls' with Brett Ashley and Catherine Barkley, or Maria's love affair with Robert Jordan to that between Catherine and Frederic Henry in 'Farewell to Arms'); the minor characters - Mr. Sing, Eddy the rummy, Bee-Lips the lawyer, the drunken Vets, the mad Spellman, even the murderous Cuban, to say nothing of the occupants of the yacht basin so harshly arraigned in the last sequence - constitute a gallery of portraits very different in calibre from the Hollywood stereotypes of the Spanish War novel; while in 'Across the River and into the Trees' there are no minor characters, except the egregious Grand Master and other admiring flunkies whose function it is to further glorify the already inflated ego of Colonel Cantwell, plus a pock-marked grotesque (10) embodying Hemingway's inexplicable grudge against a distinguished (though, in his day, overrated) fellow-writer.

This novel represents a penultimate phase in Hemingway's development which few readers of 'Farewell to Arms' could possibly have envisaged: not even the author's appearance in the play 'The Fifth Column', thinly disguised as a pseudo-drunken newspaperman who turns out to be a kind of Scarlet Pimpernel, like the dual-rôle protagonist of a Doug Fairbanks silent, could have prepared us for his complete self-identification with the Colonel, a professional soldier as romantically conceived and lovingly treated as any woman's magazine hero, whose stiff upper lip approximates closely to that of the British officer-type which he derides and despises, and whose sexual prowess with his titled Italian 'thoroughbred' day-dream-girl is so embarrassingly plugged:

> 'This is good for you, Daughter. It is good for all the ills that all of us have and for all sadness and indecision.'
>
> 'I have none of those,' she said ... 'I am just a woman, or a girl, or whatever that is, doing whatever it is she should not do. Let's do it again, please, now I am in the lee.'

One would have imagined from passages such as this, which read as if written by one of his less-talented imitators, that Hemingway was forever sunk, but he possessed a built-in buoy which allowed him to rise again to the surface (he also, by implication, claimed possession of a 'built-in, shock-proof, shit detector', but this must have been out of order during the writing of 'Across the River and into the Trees'). His physical metamorphoses in private life may be traced, in Leo Lania's 'Pictorial Biography', (11) from the photograph (captioned 'The Successful Author') resembling a handsome Hollywood actor in the rôle of the young Al Capone, to the rugged, bearded incarnation of Nobel prize-winning 'Papa': a character-part to be played, obviously, by Edward G. Robinson; yet, hidden somewhere behind these strangely-chosen masks, the fastidious, dedicated inventor of the iceberg-technique lived and worked on: here is 'A Moveable Feast', in which he reverts briefly to his real, former self, to prove it.

The acceptance of My Old Man for the 'Best Short Stories' anthology, (12) and the dedication of the volume to him by Edward J. O'Brien ('a gentle shy man, pale, with pale-blue eyes, and straight lanky hair he cut himself, who lived then as a boarder in a monastery up above Rapallo') was a turning-point in those far-off days when he had to be tough indeed to survive the lost MSS. and the rejection-slips; for, unlike Scott Fitzgerald, he never compromised by altering his endings to suit editorial requirements.

He knew, however, that he must soon write a novel: '... it seemed an impossible thing to do when I had been trying with great difficulty to write paragraphs that would be the distillation of what made a novel.... When I had written a novel before, the one that had been lost in the bag stolen at the Gare de Lyon, I still had the lyric facility of boyhood that was as perishable and as deceptive as youth was.' (Gertrude Stein had found this first effort wanting: 'There is a great deal of description in this, she said, and not particularly good description. Begin over again and concentrate.') So Hemingway went into training by writing 'longer stories as you would train for a longer race', and the result was 'The Sun Also Rises': first draft 'written in one sprint of six weeks', and rewritten during the winter of 1925-26.

It is quite customary nowadays for critics to state that Hemingway was not really a novelist at all, on the grounds that 'To Have and Have Not' and 'Across the River and into the Trees' were started as short stories (while 'Farewell to Arms' can of course be read in a potted form - with an even more downbeat ending - as A Very Short Story). Possibly no definitive verdict on this point can be reached until his huge novel of the Second World War is published at last. Nevertheless 'The Sun Also Rises' stands up extraordinarily well to a re-reading. One of the author's ambitions was to convey 'experience to the reader so that after he or she has read something it will become a part of his or her experience and seem actually to have happened': not only does he succeed in this, but whole passages of dialogue have sunk deep into one's memory, so that it comes as a shock to realize, on finding them here, that they were not overheard in real life at some time in the past. As a summing-up or sort of testament, no satisfactory equivalent exists for the activities of subsequent generations, and only one attempt to do for the fifties what Hemingway did for the twenties comes to mind: Chandler Brossard's 'Who Walk in Darkness', (13) one of the first American hipster or 'Underground'-type novels, couched in the Hemingway idiom and starting with a sketch of an unsympathetic character's background in much the same way as 'The Sun Also Rises' begins with an outline of Robert Cohn's. One's opinion of the latter opening, which seemed at first reading a marvellous technical device, leading to the devastating and apparently delicate throwaway by which we are only told of the narrator's terrible disability in Chapter IV, is naturally qualified now in view of the knowledge that the first two chapters were suppressed, presumably because they dealt outspokenly with the operation performed on Jake (an amputation, incidentally - like that self-inflicted by the boy on Christmas Day in God Rest You Merry, Gentlemen - Hemingway has explained, rebutting a critic's assertion that 'Jake was emasculated like a steer'). But the original impact is in no wise weakened, and the choice of Jake's predicament (apart from the dimension of tragedy lent thereby to the novel) remains an inspired one, by which he is both onlooker and participant up to a point: thus avoiding the snag present in many first-person narratives where the protagonist as detached observer often seems too remote from the people and events he describes to be entirely human.

Hemingway's career began and ended with suicide: Indian Camp, the first story printed in the volume 'In Our Time', featured a prospective father who cut his throat rather than endure the sight of his wife's sufferings in labour, and the ensuing dialogue between the boy who witnessed this and his own father, the doctor, assumes an added poignancy now. 'In Our Time' and 'The Sun Also Rises' are seminal works and their early influence (as Hemingway said of Joyce) 'was what changed everything, and made it possible for us to break away from the restrictions': all writers of his own and future generations have cause to be grateful to him. Had he never written the magnificent volumes of stories which followed, he would be assured of another kind of immortality than that which poor Nick Adams, as a boy, believed to be his on that morning up in Michigan: 'on the lake sitting in the stern of the boat with his father rowing, he felt quite sure that he would never die.'

Notes

1 French version of Punch and Judy puppets.

2 Memsahib, a lady.
3 Stein, 'Autobiography' (London, 1933), 134.
4 Not publishable, on the analogy of a painting too indecent to be hung.
5 Mrs. Belloc Lowndes (1868-1947), popular English Catholic novelist, and sister of Hilaire Belloc.
6 Aleister Crowley (1875-1947) was a self-styled magician and mystic. Hilaire Belloc (1870-1953) was an English historian, poet, essayist and Catholic apologist.
7 Harold Loeb, Ford Madox Ford's 'The Good Soldier': A Critical Reminiscence, 'London Magazine,' 3 (December 1963), 65-75.
8 Stein, 'Autobiography,' 236.
9 Wyndham Lewis, 'Men Without Art' (London, 1934), 115.
10 Sinclair Lewis.
11 Published in 1961.
12 'The Best Short Stories of 1923' (Boston 1924).
13 Published in 1952.

104. PHILIP YOUNG, 'KENYON REVIEW'

26 (Autumn 1964), 697-707

Philip Young (b. 1918), American critic and Professor of English at Pennsylvania State University, is author of the influential 'Ernest Hemingway' (1952, rev. ed. 1966) and editor of several books on Hemingway.

Most of us can remember without much trouble the discovery Hawthorne imagined having made in the storeroom of 'The Custom-House.' Among 'aged cobwebs,' 'bundles of official documents,' 'musty papers' and 'similar rubbish' he came upon a 'small package ... done up in ... ancient yellow parchment' and tied with 'faded red tape.' The package contained 'the record of other doings and sufferings,' 'the groundwork of a tale' that became, after the author had allowed himself 'much license' with the record, 'The Scarlet Letter.' (He thought eventually to deposit the package with the Essex Historical Society.) (1)

Now, as related by Mary Hemingway, we have a sort of counterpart to that happy event. This is in the discovery of some notebooks, packed away in two old trunks recovered from the storage basement of the Paris Ritz, where they had rested for some thirty years. The 'trunks' were 'two small, fabric-covered, rectangular boxes, both opening at the seams,' wherein were found, amidst 'ancient newspaper cuttings ... a few cracked and faded books, some musty sweatshirts and withered sandals,' several 'blue-and-yellow covered penciled notebooks.' After Hemingway had transformed them into what he says 'may be regarded as fiction,' these notebooks became 'A Moveable Feast'. (One hopes they are destined for final disposition in the Kennedy Library (2) with the rest of his papers.)

There is a little more to this. Just as Hawthorne notes in his sketch that he was happier in the composition of this work than at any time since he left the Old Manse (where of course he spent the early years of his marriage), so may Hemingway have found some happiness in writing sketches about places and events in the early years of *his* married lives. Lastly, with Hemingway's first posthumous work before us, it is a little awesome to hear Hawthorne, referring to a political 'decapitation' that lost him his job in customs, conclude the passage: 'the sketch which I am now bringing to a close, if too autobiographical for a modest person to publish in his lifetime, will readily be excused in a gentleman who writes from beyond the grave.'

And so now Hemingway's book appears, in the year and very month of the centenary of Hawthorne's actual demise. It is probably gratuitous to mention a 'movable festival' (May Day) in the 'Blithedale Romance,' but an additional afterthought is harder to resist - that this is not the first time these two unlikelies have been hitched together. I once noted (in the Minnesota American Writers pamphlet on Hemingway) (3) that the chief point of his 'Across the River and into the Trees,' 1950 (the notion of a person's sense of identification with a place most painful to him), had its classic American expression in this same introductory 'Custom-House' in 1850. Time and literature are playing tricks on us.

Though his words, themselves astonishingly alive, surely come to us from beyond the grave, how readily will Hemingway be excused? (Hawthorne caught hell for his little sketch.) In life Hemingway maintained where he could a pretty steady vigilance against the slightest injury to his reputation. And though he often let down the bars himself he was quick to take offense at any uninvited invasion of his privacy. Whatever principles lurked in these attitudes seem to have applied only to the living, and to have existed chiefly for the benefit of of himself alive. But reputations do not end with the death of writers, as he was ever well aware, and several are going to suffer from the holes fired into them here. So descendants of the dead live on, and a few people at least are going to be hurt. What Fitzgerald confided to Hemingway after lunch at Michaud's, the dialogue with Ford Madox Ford in the Closerie des Lilas, what Hemingway overheard in Miss Stein's apartment one spring morning - these bullets are likely to keep on hitting home as long as the targets are up. In each of these cases Hemingway has already been taken severely to task for telling tales out of school.

All the jokes in 'A Moveable Feast' are on other people; Hemingway comes out - steadily, effortlessly - smelling like a *vin rosé*. Underneath his well-known openness and generosity there was a mean, wary streak. He couldn't have been all that good nor they, perhaps, all that vulnerable. It is possible to make exactly the same objection to this book that many people, including Hemingway, made to Lillian Ross's once-notorious profile of him (which, incidentally, some of his chapters rather resemble). This objection would be that the sketches do not give much sense that the writers attacked were, much of the time anyway, serious and hard-working people. If his cruelty is to be excused, and it will be as Miss Ross has been, it will have to be with reference to the fierceness of competitive spirit without which he, at least, could not have been champion at all or ever, and to the *éclat* (4) with which these people are shot down. This was the fighter he said he was and, considering the infirmities of the late years, this is perhaps his most remarkable comeback, following as it does on the abortive Dangerous Summer, which he himself did not think well enough of to publish in full. We will eventually forget the belligerence and arrogance, along with a lot of other things, by summoning up the same 'strange excuse' with which Auden let off Yeats: 'Time ... Worships language and forgives/Everyone by whom it lives.' (5)

Hemingway shared in this devotion, and his success is with language. It is the shock of immediacy, the sense of our own presence on the streets he walks or in the cafés where he writes, talks, or drinks, that makes the book. When he is hungry so are we. And when, for instance, a small check enables him to break the fast at Lipp's, thought then as now to have the best beer in Paris, and he orders a great one, a *distingué*, and *pommes à l'huile* (6) and a large sausage, this reader, who was only reading (it's not all *that* immediate), was driven ravenous. Or take the first little sketch in the book. It is too cold to write in his room so he goes to a café, sees a pretty girl there, works on a story, drinks a *café au lait* and decides to go where there will be snow instead of rain. Nothing has happened, the girl is wholly anonymous, the story is not named. But the scene is etched in the reader as if a diamond had scratched glass.

There are flaws in the diamond. Some of the dialogue with Hadley is unreal and a little embarrassing; sometimes the borders of sentimentality are skirted if not transgressed. But for the most part the prose glitters, warms, and delights. Hemingway is not remembering but re-experiencing; not describing, making. In several cases the results are comparable to his fiction. So much have things changed that he could have invented names for the characters and called the sketches stories, reversing the process whereby editors once rejected the stories as sketches. Then the book would seem like a book of stories, but a little like a novel, too, as does 'Winesburg,' which he once called his first pattern, or 'In Our Time.' And the novel would pick up a little more than the unity of place from the sense of irretrievable loss that haunts it - loss of the spirit of youth, innocence and springtime, soon to pass.

This sense of melancholy is present from the start. The keynote sounds faintly on page six: 'all Paris belongs to me and I belong to this notebook and this pencil.... I felt ... both sad and happy, as though I had made love....' But it is amplified in reminiscence and by hindsight. 'We're always lucky,' he said to Hadley, 'and like a fool I did not knock on wood.' Later we are told that for luck he carried in his pocket a chestnut and a nearly worn-out rabbit's foot, so precarious was his happiness.

> Life had seemed so simple that morning when I had wakened and found the false spring and heard the pipes of the man with his herd of goats and gone out and bought the racing paper.
>
> But [Cold Pastoral!] (7) Paris was a very old city and we were young and nothing was simple there, not even poverty, nor sudden money, nor the moonlight, nor right and wrong nor the breathing of someone who lay beside you in the moonlight.

This is by no means the best of it, but the style that had years ago begun to seem self-conscious and *faux-simple* (8) came back to life toward the end, and must itself have helped sustain him for a while. A few excursions into self-imitation aside, most of 'A Moveable Feast' is either witty (this was always his most underrated virtue) or hardhitting, or moving and evocative.

Just as the book is well written it is good on the subject of writing - Hemingway's writing, that is. When once Mrs. Hemingway commented that the manuscript was not much about him he objected that it was - 'by *remate*,' a term in jai-alai which she translates 'by reflection.' And this is true; even when the focus, as so often, is on someone else there is an unflagging sense of his presence, of himself. But the largest part of the book's biographical value lies in what he has to say about the writing. The deep well-spring was there, and he explains how he tapped it and kept it flowing. He speaks much more directly than before about the 'dimensions' he was trying to put in his stories, though at the time 'it was a secret.' He explains specifically how he did not put a 'real life' suicide into the story called Out of Season 'on my new theory that you could omit anything if you knew that you omitted and the omitted part would strengthen the story and make people feel something more than they understood.' This passage goes on very nicely:

> Well, I thought, now I have them so they do not understand them. There cannot be much doubt about that. There is most certainly no demand for them.... And as long as they do not understand it you are ahead of them. Oh sure, I thought. I'm so far ahead of them now that I can't afford to eat regularly. It would not be bad if they caught up a little.

The theory worked eventually; people did catch up, more or less. It only took time and it only needed confidence, as he said.

Thoughts: There is a pretty good game here for burgeoning scholars. Try to find out exactly what was left out of other stories written according to this theory. (We have the answer to Out of Season; we have long been in a position to know that another suicide - the father's - was left out of Fathers and Sons; further it might be argued that when he leaves himself pretty much out of some of the tales in this book his felt presence adds an enhancing dimension.) But there would be few winners, unless maybe Carlos Baker. It took twenty-five years for someone to see and say in print what was missing, and not understood but felt, in Big Two-Hearted River - namely that the protagonist on his fishing trip was back and in bad shape from the War. (9) But unfortunately this example, cleared up over a decade ago, is the only other one Hemingway, perhaps cannily, gives away here; it is just after thinking over his new theory that he finishes the beer, leaves Lipp's, goes elsewhere for coffee and begins to write that same story, which is easily identified by the presence of the trout, the river, and the statement: 'The story was about coming back from the war but there was no mention of the war in it.'

The book contains many pleasant shocks of recognition (10) for *aficionados*, particularly in those parts of it which serve as a partial gloss on the flashbacks in the familiar Snows of Kilimanjaro. In the story the protagonist, Harry, about to die, thinks back to the opening scene of 'A Moveable Feast' - the Place Contrescarpe, the Café des Amateurs and the drunkards, the hotel where Verlaine died, the Boucherie Chevaline and the Bal Musette - regretting that 'he had never written a line about Paris. Not the Paris that he cared about.' But now his maker has, and later Hemingway tells an uncomprehending Ford about his connection with the proprietor of the Bal, which is the same connection Harry remembered. In another flashback Harry thinks back to the Vorarlberg, Schruns and the skiing; the Madlener-Haus and the card games with Herr Lent when they were snowbound; 'he had never written a line of that.' But now he does, extensively and with the same names and settings. He also writes it now with the same fierce resentment of the 'rich bitch' and rich people generally that helped animate the story; in addition he gives an account of his first marriage, and how his connection with the rich was the beginning of the end of it - things only touched on in the story. In short Hemingway lived to write in 'A Moveable Feast' at least part of the book Harry did not live to write in The Snows of Kilimanjaro.

It is also possible for the knowing to identify such things as the story Hemingway was writing in the opening sketch of the book (though in reviews both Frank Kermode and Alfred Kazin have independently misidentified it as Up in Michigan); (11) it is clearly an early Nick Adams item called The Three-Day Blow. The same people can play guessing games about various 'so and so's' who are insulted along the way (Cocteau? Harold Loeb? Wyndham Lewis?). And sometimes they will not need to guess. For instance when Fitzgerald speaks of 'those absolutely bloody British' in a café - especially of 'that girl with the phoney title who was so rude and that silly drunk with her. They said they were friends of yours.' 'They are' - it seems likely that the drunk is Mike Campbell, *né* Pat Swazey. And it seems much more than likely that the woman is our old friend and his fiancée, Lady Brett Ashley, in life Lady Duff Twysden (though it does not hurt to know that Fitzgerald's 'Letters' confirm his dislike of her).

Queries: Has anyone noticed how Fitzgerald seems to have countered Hemingway's portrait of the lady with his own toward the end of 'Tender is the Night'? Here Brett appears to reappear as Lady Caroline Sibley-Biers, who has been arrested for disguising herself as a sailor and picking up a girl. And thinking of such an aberrant escapade, doesn't a touch of Zelda's Paris behavior - making Scott 'jealous with other women' - put one in mind of both Lady Caroline's little lark and a neglected Hemingway story called The Sea Change? How about an episode involving Zelda's husband and a centigrade thermometer? Isn't this the germ of another story called A Day's Wait?

But enough of that. The book was not written for specialists so much as for the many who have paid the price of it. They may have been overcharged for so small a volume, but they have not been cheated by privacy, for the best things in it are completely public. As in the novels, for instance, anyone can divide the good guys from the bad. The good, beside the wife, Hadley, are Pascin, Joyce, Sylvia Beach, Ezra Pound and Evan Shipman. The bad are Ford, an aspiring critic and arrived homosexual named Hal, Zelda Fitzgerald, Wyndham Lewis and Ernest Walsh. However the two persons who get most space, Gertrude Stein and Scott Fitzgerald, are not so easily classified. Miss Stein evolves from good to bad; Fitzgerald dangles somewhere in between.

The sketch of Ford, called by Lewis Galantière in the 'New York Times Book Review' a 'thin and stupid anecdote,' (12) is a malicious little masterpiece, deft, controlled and an absolute joy. Hemingway just got his subject to talk, which was easy, and then put it down with a lancet. At the end poor huffy-puffy Ford no longer needs piercing. The section on Ezra Pound and his Bel Esprit, a society he helped to found 'to provide a fund to get Mr. Eliot out of the bank so he would have money to write poetry,' is very fine. ('This seemed like a good idea to me and after we had got Mr. Eliot out of the bank Ezra figured we would go right along and fix up everybody.') Another nice little piece concerns an obscure poet and opium eater, Ralph Cheever Dunning. In Pound's absence he was briefly in Hemingway's charge, and one Sunday morning Pound's concierge shouted up at Hemingway's window a sentence that gave happiness to Evan Shipman and to this reviewer: *'Monsieur Dunning est monté sur le toit et refuse catégoriquement de descendre.'* (13)

But Stein and the Fitzgeralds get three sketches apiece,

and these sections - by turns funny, sad and horrible - probably overshadow anything in the book but the *remate* presence of the author of it. The portrait of Miss Stein is not a painting, but an evolving story which starts in friendship, moves to a qualified affection, and explodes at the end in a scene as shocking as any in Hemingway, once famous as a shocker. The pictures of the Fitzgeralds, especially a wildly funny account of a trip from Lyon to Paris in a car from which Zelda has had the top cut off, are also merciless and sobering. This story of the trip reaches its peak in a scene where Fitzgerald is dying, without symptoms, of congestion of the lungs in a hotel, and insists that Hemingway take his temperature, which he does, employing *faute-de-mieux* (14) an absolutely unaffected bath thermometer 'with a wooden back and enough metal to sink it in the bath.' ('I shook the thermometer down professionally and said, "You're lucky it's not a rectal thermometer."') The second installment, which argues that out of jealousy Zelda set about to destroy her husband, is not at all funny, but rings true. The last sketch of Fitzgerald may indeed, however, 'be regarded as fiction.' In this one Hemingway tries to relieve Scott of worry, inspired by Zelda, about the size of his personal equipment. The conversation is plausible, even convincing, but two trips, first to *le water* to check the proportions, then another to the Louvre for the purpose of comparing them with the statues, have the look of invention. Despite doubt, however, the episode is funny, awful and sad all at once, and the ending of this recital is sad and a little cruel in a different way. Many years later Georges, the bar chief of the Ritz, where Fitzgerald in his fame is supposed to have been a center of attraction, asks Papa 'who was this Monsieur Fitzgerald that everyone asks me about?... You write about him as you remember him and then if he came here I will remember him.'

In part the appeal of this little, almost trivial book lies in the fact of Hemingway's active and communicated presence in the great years of Americans in Paris, an ideal expatriation that thousands of literary people, born too late, have dreamed of ever since. There was never for us anything like it; never such a sense that the arts were being born anew, or such exhilaration at having escaped this country. The wine was nearly free, the food was excellent and cheap, it was a good place to work, or not work; a couple could live well in this then-finest of cities on $25.00 a week. Many have tried to re-establish it all in Paris, or Rome, or elsewhere, but the arts are not being born anew, things have come to cost as much in many places as they do at home, and now we are teaching them how to drink.

But if it were simply a matter of time, place and nostalgia other writers would have been able to turn the trick, which they have notably failed to do. The difference is that this little collection of anecdotes and reminiscences is a minor work of art. The principles and particulars of poverty, the pleasures of food and drink disciplined by the shortage of cash, always how the weather was - these things and others are the texture of the book functioning almost thematically under the word-by-word spell of the style. This gentle effort toward unity is climaxed in the last scene, There is Never Any End to Paris, which is set mainly in Austria and has mostly to do with the skiing there: the magician has moved the activity so far to the side that you are not watching what else he is up to, and you do not see how he does it when suddenly there is the book, wrapped up and ending on the same sad loving note with which it began.

Then the tones of malice and superiority ring fainter, and one remembers the terrible need for reassurance that caught Hemingway up during the months of acute depression in his last two years, when he felt that after all he had been knocked out and nothing he had ever written was worth a damn. As George Plimpton guessed in an early review, one function of this book was probably therapeutic. It was as if by 'touching down' at these places and times, and even specific bottles and meals, the author could bring back the serenity and order that were failing him so badly. We know he had done this sort of thing before, as in Big Two-Hearted River. And now he must touch down once more, with the same fanatical precision. We know, again via Mary Hemingway, how she and her husband walked over and over the routes he walks in this book, partly to check their accuracy. Everything must be absolutely and exactly right. Many months later she got a friend to re-check the itinerary. Finally she herself 'flew over and retraced all the steps Ernest wrote he took, first by myself and then with my friend....' It turned out that Hemingway had misspelled the names of two streets. Nothing else was amiss. But it was a loyal, worthy thing for her to do. She honored the therapy even though the patient was deceased.

Notes

1 In Salem, Mass.
2 In Cambridge, Mass.
3 Philip Young, 'Ernest Hemingway' (Minneapolis, 1959).

4 Dazzling way.
5 In Memory of W.B. Yeats (1939).
6 Half-pint of beer; potatoes in oil.
7 John Keats, Ode on a Grecian Urn (1819).
8 Falsely simple.
9 Philip Young, 'Ernest Hemingway' (London, 1952), 19.
10 The title of Edmund Wilson's anthology of American writing (1943).
11 Alfred Kazin, Hemingway as His Own Fable, 'Atlantic', 213 (June 1964), 54-7, and Kermode, No. 101.
12 Lewis Galantière, 'New York Times Book Review,' 10 May 1964, 26.
13 'Mr. Dunning has climbed on the roof and absolutely refuses to come down.'
14 For want of something better.

105. MARVIN MUDRICK, 'HUDSON REVIEW'

17 (1964-5), 572-9

Marvin Mudrick (b. 1921) is an American critic, and Professor of English at the University of California, Santa Barbara. He is the author of 'Jane Austen' (1952) and 'The Man in the Machine' (1977).

A revised version of this article was reprinted in Marvin Mudrick, Hemingway, 'On Culture and Literature' (New York, 1970), pp. 117-27, and the author has asked that it be used here.

'A Moveable Feast' is the legacy we could hardly have dared hoped for. Yet in the Preface, at the very outset, the dead author speaks with the voice to which, during the last three decades of his life, he coercively accustomed us:

> For reasons sufficient to the writer, many places, people, observations and impressions have been left out of this book. Some were secrets and some were known by everyone and everyone has written about them and will doubtless write more.

That stiff metronomic swagger, and the pretense of large,

efficiently withheld implications, together make up Hemingway's public manner, the prose style and life style that dominate his last thirty years, the unsubtle virus of his literary influence, the old impostor's parody of the young writer whose Paris apprenticeship this book belatedly celebrates, and whose voice it so sadly recollects.

The distinction between the young man in Paris and Papa on safari must be made against some resistance, since even the most sensible of Hemingway's critics assume a qualitative continuity in his work. They will grant an occasional failure - 'Across the River and into the Trees' seems to have appalled everybody except Carlos Baker (1) - but they anticipate, and are rewarded by, triumphant recoveries. So 'The Old Man and the Sea,' that reduction to mushy parable of the Hemingway fish-and-game know-how, is discussed by Philip Young as if it were one of Beethoven's last quartets; and Young is almost equally impressed by numerous other exercises in the musclebound public manner. Young's book is nevertheless the best on Hemingway, because its reading of the Nick Adams stories - of the first and vintage Hemingway - makes sense of the stories, and nonsense of the dumb-ox label affixed to their hero by critics from Wyndham Lewis to D.S. Savage: 'His typical central character, his "I,"' writes the latter, 'may be described generally as a bare consciousness stripped to the human minimum, impassively recording the objective data of experience'; Hemingway's fiction constitutes 'a special form of that which might be termed the *proletarianization* of literature: the adaptation of the technical artistic conscience to the subaverage human consciousness.' (2)

The thesis of Young's book proposes, on the other hand, that critics like Savage are describing, if anybody at all in Hemingway's fiction, not Nick Adams, 'the Hemingway hero' (the author's own persona and very nearly his autobiographical self), but a possible standard for Nick to aim at, 'the code hero,' the bullfighter or prizefighter or big-game hunter, who teaches Nick (or Hemingway) 'to try and live by a code,' though 'the lessons' are not always 'of the sort the hero can immediately master.' Nick himself, neither a dumb ox nor a deadpan reporter, nor a man so skilled in his vocation as to perform it with the unreflective ease that Nick envies and would like to emulate, is

> ...sensitive, masculine, impressionable, humorless, honest, and out-of-doors - a boy then a man who had come up against violence and evil and been wounded by

> them. The manhood he had attained was thus complicated and insecure, but he was learning a code with which he might maneuver, though crippled, and he was practicing the rites which for him might exorcise the terrors born of the events that crippled him.

The stories about him must be read not separately but collectively, as a sort of mosaic-novel, an unexplained segment here and another very much elsewhere in time and place though always about the same life, scattered pieces only ultimately converging into the full picture; and their common subject is the traumatic event (or events) that Nick passes through, relives in sickness and nightmare, tries to forget or put out of mind, never quite escapes from or grows beyond: the stories are, in Young's phrase, 'bound tight about a core of shock.'

The old writer of 'A Moveable Feast' might agree, as he recalls an afternoon that the young writer spent with Gertrude Stein. The redoubtable lady, having just made a practical objection to the '*inaccrochable*' - as of a painting too indecent to be hung - language of a story of his (she herself wished and expected to be published in the 'Atlantic Monthly'), proceeded to a somewhat qualified defense of homosexuality:

> Miss Stein thought that I was too uneducated about sex and I must admit that I had certain prejudices against homosexuality since I knew its more primitive aspects. I knew it was why you carried a knife and would use it when you were in the company of tramps when you were a boy in the days when wolves was not a slang term for men obsessed by the pursuit of women. I knew many *inaccrochable* terms and phrases from Kansas City days and the mores of different parts of that city, Chicago and the lake boats. Under questioning I tried to tell Miss Stein that when you were a boy and moved in the company of men, you had to be prepared to kill a man, know how to do it and really know that you would do it in order not to be interfered with. That term was *accrochable*. If you knew you would kill, other people sensed it very quickly and you were let alone; but there were certain situations you could not allow yourself to be forced into or trapped into. I could have expressed myself more vividly by using an *inaccrochable* phrase that wolves used on the lake boats, 'Oh gash may be fine but one eye for mine.' But I was always careful of my language with Miss Stein even when true phrases might have clarified or better expressed a prejudice.

The old writer is at last trying to come at the truth of his experience directly, not, as the young one did, obliquely and implicitly, not evading it by bluster and tricks as Life Magazine's champion bull-thrower learned to do. For the pathos of Hemingway's reputation is that he got it years after his best work has been done, and that he felt obliged to sustain it by accepting and coarsening the public rôle of the true-born American writer: tough, terse, athletic, unliterary (this omnivorous man of letters who read every book he could lay his hands on), 'a bare consciousness stripped to the human minimum, impassively recording the objective data of experience.'

The reputation had its lethal effect on criticism, which either attacked the public image as if it were all there was of Hemingway, or praised virtually all of Hemingway as if the public image were quite unrelated to the work. Even Young's book, good as it is on the Nick stories, founders on the public image, since Young's thesis doesn't help him to distinguish between the early master and the old impostor. The real thing (Big Two-Hearted River, for instance, Young's examination of which is a model of intelligent analysis in support of a critical position) gets confused with so brassy a counterfeit as The Short Happy Life of Francis Macomber. It is bad enough that Macomber exhibits Hemingway's crudest sketches of his code hero and his bitch-heroine; but worse that the code has been simplified into imbecile bravado: if a man runs away from a charging lion he is a coward, and if he stands to face it he has confirmed his manhood. Nick Adams - the boy in The Doctor and the Doctor's Wife, the youth in The Battler, the man in Big Two-Hearted River - inhabits a world in which the problem of choice, unlike Macomber's, is unresolvable by any single action, and more difficult than lions.

The style of the Nick stories - however it may have launched itself with tips from newspaper reporting, Sherwood Anderson, Miss Stein - is as original and personal an invention as anything in literature; but it is also one of the narrowest in range, and among the least usefully imitable. Just as Lawrence speaks of 'shedding one's sicknesses in books,' (3) so Hemingway speaks of writing as the writer's own therapy: 'If he wrote it he could get rid of it. He had gotten rid of many things by writing them.' Still, Lawrence's 'sicknesses' have a breadth of curiosity, an impetus into the outer world, an intimate and hereditary connection with literary tradition, that ventilate and generalize the great resourceful style that bears them. The sickness that Hemingway tries to get rid of has no such outward impulse, it seeks only to withdraw from any further contact and damage; and the style it generates is an opaque thin membrane against which it obscurely presses and reluctantly defines itself without quite breaking through into a void of hysteria (except now and then, as in A Way You'll Never Be and, perhaps, Homage to Switzerland). Some of the most remarkable effects of this barely managed control occur in extended passages of dialogue:

> 'Come on back in the shade,' he said. 'You mustn't feel that way.'
>
> 'I don't feel any way,' the first girl said. 'I just know things.'
>
> 'I don't want you to do anything that you don't want to do -'
>
> 'Nor that isn't good for me,' she said. 'I know. Could we have another beer?'
>
> 'All right. But you've got to realize -'
>
> 'I realize,' the girl said. 'Can't we maybe stop talking?'
>
> They sat down at the table and the girl looked across at the hills on the dry side of the valley and the man looked at her and at the table.
>
> 'You've got to realize,' he said, 'that I don't want you to do it if you don't want to. I'm perfectly willing to go through with it if it means anything to you.'
>
> 'Doesn't it mean anything to you? We could get along.'
>
> 'Of course it does. But I don't want anybody but you. I don't want any one else. And I know it's perfectly simple.'
>
> 'Yes, you know it's perfectly simple.'
>
> 'It's all right for you to say that, but I do know it.'
>
> 'Would you do something for me now?'
>
> 'I'd do anything for you.'
>
> 'Would you please please please please please please please stop talking?'
>
> He did not say anything but looked at the bags against the wall of the station. There were labels on them from all the hotels where they had spent nights.
>
> 'But I don't want you to,' he said, 'I don't care anything about it.'
>
> 'I'll scream,' the girl said.
>
> The woman came out through the curtains with two glasses of beer and put them down on the damp felt pads. 'The train comes in five minutes,' she said.
>
> 'What did she say?' asked the girl.

'That the train is coming in five minutes.'
The girl smiled brightly at the woman, to thank her.

Later writers, including Hemingway, radically mistook the vibrations of such dialogue (from Hills Like White Elephants) and fabricated a whole subliterature of stylized detectives, criminals, deep-sea fishermen and smugglers, virtuous and easy-virtue ladies, all of whom lavishly and complacently protected the reader from polysyllables and complex sentences. But the Nick stories, and such related ones as Hills Like White Elephants (the unnamed young man is really Nick, and has Nick's troubles), are in fact waking nightmares: the early Hemingway style is the indispensable discipline that keeps them from erupting into psychosis; it could scarcely be more inappropriate, except as parody, to the expression of an assured and knowledgeable reticence.

Hemingway did not, at any rate, maintain the early style and its preoccupation. Soon he had less to say about Nick and more about the code hero, in such stories as Fifty Grand and The Undefeated, more about the code itself in all the novels: if the Nick stories are classifiable as the nightmare stories, the second group might be designated the know-how stories. In even the best of these the style appears more mannered and sententious, less continuous with its material. The preoccupation with merely keeping sane gives way to a shallower and less convincing preoccupation with physical competences, especially when there is the flavor of death in them: expertness in a dangerous athletic vocation signifies moral delicacy or at least intense moral awareness, as if to court death in a ceremony of skill (like the bullfighter, or the big-game hunter) is finally to live well. In even the better novels - 'The Sun Also Rises' and 'For Whom the Bell Tolls' - the effort to refract the external world through the style which had so successfully subjectivized and rejected it produces the sense of strain and affectation that is, in the public mind, the Hemingway style, 'impassively recording the objective data of experience.' The irreducible sickness is still there, but the novels, when they consider it at all, grotesquely simplify it (as with Jake Barnes) or pretend that it will yield to vocational or political or erotic affirmations. Hemingway's novel-heroines are particularly offensive because they sound like the girl in Hills Like White Elephants compelled to read affectionate lines she doesn't believe to a man pretending he isn't Nick: the dialogue between the lovers in 'A Farewell to Arms' is deprivation itself, displayed in the frozen attitudes of a period coyness; this novel in which Nick is to be saved by passion precipitates him into the most puerile of daydreams. The last step, which Hemingway takes in stories like Macomber and The Snows of Kilimanjaro as well as in the late novels (except 'For Whom the Bell Tolls'), is self-parody: the old impostor betrays the youthful master by attaching his name to parodies of the code, parodies of the style, emetic effusions of self-pity (as in Kilimanjaro), parodies of masculinity and pride.

'A Moveable Feast' makes another beginning. Hemingway's unexorcised sense of hurt and injury continues to cramp and trouble the all too recognizable style but 'A Moveable Feast' is an unexpected book by a not yet secure old master, it shoots for the moon and accomplishes moments of pride, amusement, melancholy, and - most unexpectedly - love. It has fine wry vignettes: the encounters with Miss Stein, and their terrible climax in the overheard conversation between her and her 'friend'; the comic and catty description of Pound's efforts to raise money from penniless writers (like young Hemingway) so that Eliot could leave his job at the bank and devote all his time to writing; the evening with the painter Pascin and his girls:

> 'Chez Viking,' the dark girl said.
> 'Me too,' her sister urged.
> 'All right,' Pascin agreed, 'Good night, *jeune homme*. Sleep well.'
> 'You too.'
> 'They keep me awake,' he said. 'I never sleep.'
> 'Sleep tonight.'
> 'After Chez Les Vikings?' He grinned with his hat on the back of his head. He looked more like a Broadway character of the Nineties than the lovely painter that he was, and afterwards, when he had hanged himself, I liked to remember him as he was that night at the Dôme. They say the seeds of what we will do are in all of us, but it always seemed to me that in those who make jokes in life the seeds are covered with better soil and with a higher grade of manure.

The best episode is Hemingway's account of Scott Fitzgerald. Gleaming with malice no doubt as well with moment-by-moment revelations of its subject (the memorable scenes in literary history will certainly include the one in which Hemingway reassures Fitzgerald about the adequacy of his sexual equipment), it is much closer to an absolute statement of the case than what Fitzgerald himself tried to write in 'Tender is the Night,' the minor tragedy of the weak, gifted man destroyed by a ferociously competitive wife:

> Zelda had hawk's eyes and a thin mouth and deep-south manners and accent. Watching her face you could see her mind leave the table and go to the night's party and return with her eyes blank as a cat's and then pleased, and the pleasure would show along the thin line of her lips and then be gone. Scott was being the good cheerful host and Zelda looked at him and she smiled happily with her eyes and her mouth too as he drank the wine. I learned to know that smile very well. It meant she knew Scott would not be able to write.

- a wife whose irreversible victory over her husband is to go mad:

> That night there was a party to welcome us at the Casino, just a small party, the MacLeishes, the Murphys, the Fitzgeralds and we who were living at the villa. No one drank anything stronger than champagne and it was very gay and obviously a splendid place to write. There was going to be everything that a man needed to write except to be alone.
>
> Zelda was very beautiful and was tanned a lovely gold color and her hair was a beautiful dark gold and she was very friendly. Her hawk's eyes were clear and calm. I knew everything was all right and was going to turn out well in the end when she leaned forward and said to me, telling me her great secret, 'Ernest, don't you think Al Jolson is greater than Jesus?'
>
> Nobody thought anything of it at the time. It was only Zelda's secret that she shared with me, as a hawk might share something with a man. But hawks do not share. Scott did not write anything any more that was good until after he knew that she was insane.

Much has been said about the cruelty of Hemingway's portrait of Ford Madox Ford. But Hemingway had perfected his hatreds too (his treatment of Wyndham Lewis makes his attitude toward Ford appear almost kindly); and the dialogue he records - though it may well have been that Ford was putting him on with a poker-faced travesty of the English gentleman - is a very funny epiphany of transatlantic relations:

> 'Was Henry James a gentleman?'

> 'Very nearly.'
> 'Are you a gentleman?'
> 'Naturally, I have held His Majesty's commission.'
> 'It's very complicated,' I said. 'Am I a gentlman?'
> 'Absolutely not,' Ford said.
> 'Then why are you drinking with me?'
> 'I'm drinking with you as a promising young writer. As a fellow writer in fact.'
> 'Good of you,' I said.
> 'You might be considered a gentleman in Italy,' Ford said magnanimously.

That concluding adverb, which none of the previous Hemingways would have indulged, is a sign of the fresh start, in which adverbs and metaphors are allowed to amplify and relax the texture of the prose:

> 'I think it would be wonderful, Tatie,' my wife said. She had a gently modeled face and her eyes and her smile lighted up at decisions as though they were rich presents.

For Hemingway at the very end took the risk of attempting his authentic love story. We will never know just what Nick or Hemingway was suffering from, or whether it was many things, or whether all these sufficient things screen off the genuine unfaceable article: his puritanical home, his ambitious and disappointed mother, his war wounds, his father's suicide.

'A Moveable Feast' suggests something besides: a broken heart. The heroine - Hemingway's only live and persuasive heroine - of 'A Moveable Feast' is the first Mrs. Hemingway. The book is in praise of her and of what he lost when he let her go, since losing her he gave up not only her love and his but his youth and his friends and Paris, everything that encouraged him to write the early stories and that he suppressed in order to emerge as the formidable and nerveless public figure:

> When you have two people who love each other, are happy and gay and really good work is being done by one or both of them, people are drawn to them as surely as migrating birds are drawn at night to a powerful beacon. If the two people were as solidly constructed as the beacon there would be little damage except to the birds. Those who attract people by their happiness and their performance are usually inexperienced. They do not know how not to be overrun and how to go away. They do not always learn about the good, the attractive, the

> charming, the soon-beloved, the generous, the understanding rich who have no bad qualities and who give each day the quality of a festival and who, when they have passed and taken the nourishment they needed, leave everything deader than the roots of any grass Attila's horses' hooves have ever scoured.

The vision of youth in an unspoiled spring is the vision that the old writer would give most, and heartbreakingly tries hardest, to evoke:

> When I saw my wife again standing by the tracks as the train came in by the piled logs at the station, I wished I had died before I loved anyone but her. She was smiling, the sun on her lovely face tanned by the snow and sun, beautifully built, her hair red gold in the sun, grown out all winter awkwardly and beautifully, and Mr. Bumby standing with her, blond and chunky and with winter cheeks looking like a good Vorarlberg boy.
>
> 'Oh Tatie,' she said, when I was holding her in my arms, 'you're back and you made such a fine successful trip. I love you and we've missed you so.'
>
> I loved her and I loved no one else and we had a lovely magic time while we were alone. I worked well and we made great trips, and I thought we were invulnerable again, and it wasn't until we were out of the mountains in late spring, and back in Paris that the other thing started again.

There are no charging lions or leaping marlin in 'A Moveable Feast,' or wars or rumors of wars. That Hemingway could have resolved to risk such a candor of private regret and longing against the grain of his so carefully cultivated reputation, less than a year before his death, is the proof of the strength he could still muster, and the most touching reminder of the splendid young writer he was trying to recall. The book is new, and stands with the best of his early stories.

Notes

1 At least three other critics liked the novel: Charles Poore, 'New York Times,' 7 September 1950, 29; John O'Hara, 'New York Times Book Review,' 10 September 1950, 1, 30-1; and Elliot Paul, 'Providence Sunday Journal,' 10 September 1950, sec. VI, 8.

2 D.S. Savage, Ernest Hemingway, 'The Withered Branch' (London, 1950), 24, 31.

3 D.H. Lawrence, 'Collected Letters,' ed. Harry Moore (London, 1962), I, 234.

106. ANDREW LYTLE, 'SEWANEE REVIEW'

73 (Spring 1965), 339-43

Andrew Lytle (b. 1902), an American professor, novelist and critic, is the author of 'The Velvet Horn' (1957).

A great hazard to an artist is his reputation. Except to that small body of readers who look to the word for meaning, the reputation is almost sure to be false to the work, composed as it is of the accidents of personality, at best the embodiment of the quality of artist as man. This implies the artist as man capable of making a lot of money. In a secular world, which sets profit instead of utility as the reward of work, money is the final judgment of any act, including the creative act. The matter is simple: if you make a lot of money from a story (especially from secondary sources such as the movies, etc.) you have to spend it or invest it. In either case think a lot about it. This takes time and the work suffers. Only a great devotion to a craft can resist the Lilliputian entanglements. (1) The critics of the Higher Illiteracy are the whipping boys of such reputations. It saves them the strain of reading. Apparently most of these fellows who have treated publicly of Hemingway's 'A Moveable Feast' have let the reputation bemuse them beyond the grave. Death is a time for summing up, of judgment. Perhaps they believe no more in death than in life.

Hemingway was not just a reputation; he was also an artist, but an artist who faltered and assumed the various masks of his public personality. Acting is a secondary art, depending upon the work of others: in this instance the illusion of a whole work which actually was only partially delivered. Or so it may seem. But this is a half truth. After first reading 'A Moveable Feast' I thought his publishers had done him a disservice. I now feel the book is extremely revealing: the public personality was there from the start; even in his apprenticeship it was there, the struggle between the ego and its transformation in the artefact. Most craftsmen suffer this conflict, and either end up as artists or personalities. Apparently Hemingway never made the choice, even if he was aware that a choice existed. It is always hazardous to read the inward decisions in the outward action, but there is a curious evasion in the introduction to this book. The reader is given the choice by Hemingway of reading 'A Moveable Feast' either as a memoir or as fiction. Obviously this is a false choice. Was he trying to get himself off the hook, or had he come to think that he might over-ride all forms in the self-regard of that carnal omniscience of his?

There are too many hooks to get free of; so it must be the devouring omniscience which defines the pathos of the action here. These early days in Paris were wonderful days. So we are told, and we are prepared to believe them so, until we begin to wonder at the wonders. There is not an associate of his, who conceivably might be his rival, or to whom he owed anything, that receives anything but denigration of character or profession. Not once does he show any human sympathy or charity towards his fellow man. The method is very workable. The professional competence of each is betrayed through the deficiencies and follies of a personal private nature. Towards Ford Madox Ford there is malice and hatred, so obvious that his craftsmanship fails him, and one wonders if Ford did not help him most of all. But then there is Gertrude Stein. He sat at her feet, was her errand boy, and drank her wine; yet in an obscene kind of false prudery he pretends to flee the sounds of her love cries coming from the room nearby. He remained long enough to hear them distinctly: or is this fiction? At one point at Pound's request Hemingway helps raise funds to get Eliot out of the bank so that he can be more free to write. This turns out to be unnecessary; so Hemingway gambles away the money he raised at the races and accuses Eliot of leading him into immorality. But he didn't really mean it - it was a kind of jest - for obviously he was the writer, the only one and hence the money should have gone to him. And how can you take what is properly yours?

At first Pound seems an exception. His praise for Pound is extravagant, but a closer reading leads to doubt. Pound is excessively loyal to his friends in praise of their work, but this loyalty is disastrous to his judgment. Except for Hemingway, Pound's choice of friends seems no better than his literary judgment. For example, Wyndham Lewis is 'nasty.' He quotes Miss Stein as saying Lewis is a measuring worm. This makes him a nasty measuring worm. Certainly his quality of evil lacks the 'dignity of a hard chancre,' and that's really some lack of dignity, as anybody will agree. But in Lewis's presence (Pound and Hemingway were sparring) Hemingway '- tried to make him (Pound) look as good as possible.' He found this hard to do; so we must add that to Pound's bad literary judgment, in sport (virility) he is no better. His wife, however, was built well. Physically and mentally Pound seems to be undone by his virtues.

Hemingway is very amusing about Scott Fitzgerald. There are many pages exposing Fitzgerald's foibles about his health, showing the infantile fears in the grown man and artist, until the reader soon wonders how this child-man had maturity enough to write at all. And wonders further when Fitzgerald consults Hemingway about 'measurements' which Zelda, his wife, presents to her husband as grounds for complaint. At the friend's invitation they retire to the W.C. for an examination, and there the husband learns the heraldic difference between at rest and rampant. Still not quite reassured the husband is taken to the Louvre to see the naked statues. But neither art nor heraldry nor professional, though friendly advice, seems quite to do, because finally Zelda, the wife, is jealous of the Muse. She keeps her husband on a round of parties, so that he won't be able to do his work. This may be a true observation, but it is not the only one. Years later at the Ritz bar in Paris a former chasseur (2) asks papa who this man Fitzgerald is. People keep asking him but he doesn't remember. Maybe if papa writes about him, then he will remember who he was. To have a rival alive only in your imagination and at the mercy of your craft must be wonderful triumph, if this is the end of art; and if you forget that out in the world, as an objective fact, 'The Great Gatsby' and other of his works still are and are read.

Now why is it that Hemingway wants to be the only one, the only artist and the only man? Why does he want Paris without people? Nor is he content to be the patron of the living and his elders in the crafts, but the past too he wants to envelop in so far as he recognizes what he considers his kind of virility there. But how can anybody, without the severest delusion, speak of Marshall Ney, as Mike Ney, as if he and Ney were old buddies and messmates? It has puzzled me a long time, Hemingway's hatred, at least contempt for tourists. It has seemed so inordinate and actually so irrelevant to the actions of his fictions, for example, 'The Old Man and the Sea.' After reading 'A Moveable Feast' I think I know. The tourist can go home. Hemingway couldn't. He lived in exile and the kind hardest to bear, self-exile. His residence at Key West was barely in the country; then Cuba, just outside. Later the far isolated West, where the home-tourists matched the International set he wrote about. Why this is so is nobody's business. He had doomed himself to the life of the perpetual tourist, forever in foreign parts, wandering to and through the wonders advertized. No scene, no mountain, not any city, even Paris, could be home. It is pathetic, his self-identity with Paris, with the restaurants, the streets and parks, as if they were laid out for his pleasure and sole appreciation. He in this book named the streets, the two ways to a given destination, to show his knowledge and control, against all those tourists intruding upon his exile. He only showed by this his isolation. Who when at home consciously says or thinks - Now I'm going two blocks up Main then turn off on Vine a block, right on College and into Mr. Maney's Avenue? Instinctively following the known ways and the known patterns of behavior - this is being at home. Here one gardens without being conscious of the strangers in town. Or fishes without saying it is serious, as opposed to those who play at it because it is the thing to do. One fishes. One makes love. You don't have to insist that it is good or that a good meal is fine to eat. His ignorance of this is the pathos of Hemingway's curiosity about the private lives of his acquaintances. The insensitive reporting of what is private shows the need for intimacy and knowledge of a neighborhood that is one's own. But Hemingway has none; only the International set. Paris cannot be his or any foreigner's. The conventions there could not restrain him or instruct him in the difference between the public and private thing, because they were not his conventions nor could ever be his mores. He has bitter things to say about the family, but Paris would not be without families. The intimacy he feels in his 'café' is the very domesticity of café life and its communal feeling. The one thing, the crucial thing, he never saw about Paris was that it was the capital of the French, the true head of a people. Parisians were Parisians, but when the distinguished provincial from Provence or Normandy came to Paris, he did not lose his local identity. He came to Paris, the head, as the representative of his province to give and receive, but no Provençal ever let himself be confused with a man from Normandy. The International set never got involved with the reality of this life, for this life stood for the order in the state and its meaning. Try to imagine the International set at a Guermantes salon. (3) By its nature this set thrown up after the first world war is in exile, with only its appetites to depend upon. Hence the continual reference to good food and drink and the love-making; but finally this must have seemed meaningless, for it did not prevent Hemingway's first marriage from breaking up. He could blame it on the rich, but more than appetite sustains this ancient institution. There is a name for it, well understood. Adultery. It was his, perhaps, but how could he blame himself? He was in another country, and besides the wench was dead. (4)

Notes

1 After being shipwrecked in Lilliput, Gulliver awakes to find himself tied up by the tiny inhabitants.
2 Porter.
3 The aristocratic characters in Proust's 'Remembrance of Things Past.'
4 Christopher Marlowe, 'The Jew of Malta,' IV.i (c. 1589).

'By-Line: Ernest Hemingway' (1967)

107. PHILIP YOUNG, 'CHICAGO TRIBUNE BOOK WEEK'

28 May 1967, 6

It was a dirty trick on a fellow, this digging up his journalism. Or so in effect Hemingway wrote his first bibliographer, Louis H. Cohn, even though all the poor man wanted was to enter the titles on a list. Nobody had any business resurrecting that stuff, Hemingway went on, to put it in competition with what he had written for keeps.

Thirty-six years have passed since that little outburst, and behold. Most of what Hemingway wanted buried as he left it has conspicuously been exhumed by the very publishers whose prize author he was. And already a blurb writer has blundered into the boobytrap of Hemingway's prophetic invention. The pieces that make up 'By-Line: Ernest Hemingway,' we are confidently informed, 'hold up better than some of the early novels.' They also make a 'more important book than "A Moveable Feast" and a more worthy posthumous volume.'

For quite a few reasons that is nonsense. But the publishers, having brought out a book that is not going to do a thing to devalue anything else Hemingway ever wrote, are making perfectly good sense. Not that they are quite the first with such a collection. Following close on the writer's death there was a fastback (short here for fast-buck paperback). Stunningly mistitled 'The Wild Years,' (1) it reprinted materials from the Toronto papers that were first to run the Hemingway by-line. But happily this shoddy compilation did not have wide circulation. Now the whole range of Hemingway's mostly-foreign correspondence, selected by a reputable professor of Journalism (2) and built to last, is going to get around a lot. All that's needed is that those who read it should read it for what it is: writing that was at first the meal ticket, before long the moonlighting, of a man who really had a different job.

Hemingway was frequently uncomfortable in journalistic disguise. At times he appears to have taken the role as a way of getting in on the action. In the heat of fighting the Germans an American soldier asked a question for everyone: 'What are you doing here if you don't have to be here?' The response, 'Lots of Money,' is not the answer nor was meant to be. But even in war, where for this writer the action so often was, he admitted that 'sometimes it doesn't seem the right man in the right place'; he thought occasionally of 'leaving the whole thing and going back to writing books....' A Situation Report out of Havana in 1956 is final. First quoting Cyril Connolly on the folly of 'all excursions into journalism' (since there 'we condemn good ideas, as well as bad, to oblivion'), Hemingway promises himself that 'you will never again interrupt the work you were born and trained to do until you die.' The Cuban report is truly a swan song, the last piece in the book.

Nevertheless, he was now and again a marvelous correspondent. After the sorcerer's apprenticeship during which, short of his 21st birthday, he began to turn out feature stories that are even now not particularly embarrassing, he became overnight quite as good as professional. Almost in spite of himself, then, and without the enormous pains he took with his fiction, he turned out good copy. If it was no less minor than he thought, it was certainly less ephemeral. That is what this book clearly establishes.

The evidence is in five parts, beginning with the Toronto newspaper stories, 1920-1924, which skip lightly from this continent to Paris, thence all about Europe clear to Constantinople. Some political reporting is extraordinary for the precocious shrewdness of a writer who is supposed to have no politics. But our man abroad was just as concerned with cultivating hotels, fishing, bullfights, etc. And some of these preparatory pieces, shortly to mature in 'The Sun Also Rises,' are already perfectly ripe in their own way. By Part Two, 1933-1939, practically everything has changed. An obscure cub has taken off into the trees. All of a sudden a famous man of letters is writing letters to 'Esquire' - making, as it were, his first appearance in person. And at the apogee of his career. At least that's what we used to be told. Some serious folk were offended by all that big-game hunting and deep-sea fishing, during a depression, with a war on the way.

The truth of the matter is that Hemingway wrote some satisfactory things for 'Esquire.' And they are here; often carrying pleasant shocks of recognition. For instance, there is the nugget out of which 'The Old Man and the Sea' was much later fashioned. More important, 'By-Line' offers a good opportunity to reconsider that bothersome business of the hairy chest. Not every reader is going to care so passionately as Hemingway if sailfish 'tap a bait' or not. (Definitely not!) And surely he misfired in his Notes on Dangerous Game, which is one of a few items that should probably have been excluded from the book. But a good deal of the fishing and hunting is so fresh and warm that even if one does not practice these sports it is not hard to find vicarious gratification in them. As for the rest, we may note that although it is not in 'By-Line' Hemingway did write a savage Depression Piece for the 'New Masses.' (3) And note as well that an unfrivolous 11th edition of John Bartlett's 'Familiar Quotations,' which allowed him 5 entries, took 3 of them from a single 'Esquire' letter called Notes on the Next War. Let it be pointed out last that an earlier letter to the same magazine, called simply Old Newsman Writes, is now more familiar to most: 'All good books ... are truer than if they had really happened' (this is the heart of it) 'and afterwards it all belongs to you ... the people and the places and how the weather was.' That selection is now headed for the anthologies, which for journalism is some sort of immortality.

Dispatches for NANA, 1937-1938, on the war in Spain make up most of the third section. None of them measures up to Old Man at the Bridge, which so far is the latest of Hemingway's stories to be elevated to the canon of his 'Collected Short Stories.' But like the story several of these reports were cabled out of the battle for the Ebro Delta, and it is a tribute to them that they remind one of the story without suffering from the comparison. Part Four is war once more: analyses of the big picture in China (1941) for the late 'PM,' close-ups in the European Theater for 'Collier's' (1944). The Chinese dispatches display a hitherto unexploited talent for the clarification of large problems. Those from Europe begin with the long, tense, fouled-up day 'we took Fox Green beach,' continue through the liberation of Paris and beyond, and reveal that quick sharp eye for immediate problems for which Hemingway had long been famous.

Abruptly the last section begins (and ends) with life and Miss Mary in Cuba, but consists substantially of The

Christmas Gift, which some will recall reading years ago in 'Look.' This long, rambling, really awful, but awfully funny, account of his two plane crashes in Africa has many curious features, among them a striking piece of self-analysis occasioned by the reading of his own obituaries. In 'almost all, it was emphasized that I had sought death all my life. Can one imagine that if a man sought death all of his life he could not have found her before the age of 54?' He can see the 'facile theory' as a 'quick solution to a complicated problem,' however. So much for his interpreters. (4)

But the sense that a personality is writing is nearly always present in his fiction, and even more so in his non-fiction, where little stands between reader and that distinctive self who has been so intensely interesting for better than four decades. In that sense 'By-Line' makes interpreters of us all, and few will come away with preconceptions intact. Better late than never, one reader (this one, who seldom fishes and has never hunted) was startled to see, at rare moments, description of these activities become evocation and then suddenly revelation. Somehow one fails to respond properly to the bulls, but it is all at once clear on reading 'By-Line' that taking the lives of fish and animals was for Hemingway an essentially aesthetic experience that brought emotions entirely comparable to those aroused by the experience of great painting or music. The 'whirr of wings that moves you ... more than any love of country,' the beauty of a great marlin, whose every jump was a sight to stop the heart, and at whose boating one is 'purified,' and welcome in the brotherhood of the 'very elder gods,' these things are not faked. The long, broad gap between Hemingway the sportsman and Hemingway the writer has closed for at least one of his students. This book doesn't often get outside the perimeters of its genre, and every bit of it is prose. But in many passages artist and man-outdoors are indivisible.

Notes

1 'Hemingway: The Wild Years,' ed. Gene Hanrahan (1962).
2 William White.
3 Ernest Hemingway, Who Murdered the Vets? 'New Masses,' 16 (17 September 1935), 9-10.
4 Young himself is the leading proponent of the 'obsession with death' theory.

108. STANLEY KAUFFMANN, 'NEW REPUBLIC'

156 (10 June 1967), 18, 35

This collection of Ernest Hemingway's journalism will comfort anyone with strong feelings about him, pro or con. Those who like him will be able to trace here the development of his eye and ear; they will recognize the sources of much in his fiction and they can admire its transmutation. Those who dislike him will be able to substantiate that he was, from youth, a perennial youth; that he spent much of his life flopping on the beach like a struggling whale stranded between the seas of war, pretending that tiny pools like bullfighting and big-game hunting gave him equivalent opportunities.

At the risk of seeming impartial, which I am not, I think there is substance in both views of Hemingway. I think he was a genius, and I cannot see why his career - or that of any artist - should be averaged out, like a sociological table. What finally matters is his best work. Hemingway's comprises a large number of stories and his two first extraordinary (though flawed) novels. This work was epoch-making and is, apparently, imperishable; more, it exemplifies a view of experience and art, a ruthless modernism, toward which much of literature had been moving, consciously and unconsciously, for a century. That is why he had such an overwhelming influence so quickly.

On the other hand, relatively early in his career he became a public fool, a conscious 'character,' an undernourished scavenger on his former self. Both views of him find some support in this new collection.

Which was not supposed to exist - at least as constituted here. The editor, William White, begins with a frank quotation of Hemingway's statement that he did not want his early newspaper articles republished. These articles, written through 1923, make up more than a quarter of this collection; the rest is 'post-fame' magazine and newspaper work. White's justification for disregarding the author's wishes is that Hemingway used much of the material in his fiction anyway. Tenuous though this logic is, I am glad that it satisfied White. Charles A. Fenton's 'The Apprenticeship of Ernest Hemingway' (1954), which referred to and quoted from those early articles, had whetted my appetite for this book. Now it is interesting to read some of them. That, I suppose, is the real test of the value of publishing marginalia: not whether it provides more grub for pedantic ferrets but whether it repays reading readers.

White has been highly selective. He includes only 29 out of the 154 pieces that Hemingway wrote for the 'Toronto Star' between 1920 and 1923 (doubtless many of the exclusions are justified, but I would like to have read the omitted Lloyd George interviews); 17 of his 31 'Esquire' articles; nine of his 28 dispatches on the Spanish civil war; all seven of his articles on China for 'PM' in 1941; his six World War II dispatches for 'Collier's'; some of his postwar sports stuff for various magazines; his 'Look' articles on his African plane crash, and some other odds and ends. I was glad not to see The Dangerous Summer, the long bullfight chronicle he wrote for 'Life' in 1960.

When one reads the early work of a man who later became an eminent artist, one tends to see in it too many presages of his later qualities. But, so far as hindsight permits, I think some of the later Hemingway can be seen in the 'Star' dispatches. I discount such touches as this paragraph from a Spanish article in 1922:

> Vigo is a pasteboard looking village, cobble streeted, white and orange plastered, set up on one side of a big, almost landlocked harbor that is large enough to hold the entire British navy. Sun-baked brown mountains slump down to the sea like tired old dinosaurs, and the color of the water is as blue as a chromo of the bay at Naples.

This sort of writing is the splashy stuff of 'ace' journalism. But the emerging Hemingway can be seen in such a line as this, from another Spanish dispatch in 1923: 'It was very exciting, sitting out in front of a café your first day in Spain with a ticket in your pocket that meant that rain (1) or shine you were going to see a bullfight in an hour and a half.' In 1923, *before* Hemingway was Hemingway, before he had altered the stylistic taste of his time, it took great calm nerve to write 'It was very exciting' - just like that, with no further fuss; and to plunk down the succeeding elements in that sentence one after another, almost coldly but with increasingly heating effect. Oh, yes, it seems common enough now.

These early articles have some historical value, too. His account of a commercial airline flight from Paris to Strasbourg in 1922 has the quality of a contemporary newsreel. His descriptions of the personalities at the Genoa economic conference in 1922 are cut cleanly and quickly. His report on Mussolini, whom he met in a group interview in 1923, is exceptionally prescient. Much of his later reporting, too, is incisive. In particular, his Chinese articles are the work of a man who knew warfare, knew something of Chinese problems, and had an eye for character. (White says in his introduction that these Chinese articles 'were all written from notes made abroad after his return to New York.' Nevertheless they are all datelined abroad, and in one of them Hemingway speaks of 'the Burmese sun outside the hotel window as I write this.' As this was, probably, written in the old Ritz on Madison Avenue, I think it must have amused Hemingway. It certainly amused me.)

Some of those early articles are historical in another sense. They contain comments about foreign places that are supposed to be eye-opening and awesome to the folks at home - the roots of Hemingway's notorious travel snobbism. Forty years have outdated the intrepid explorer of byways in Spain and Turkey - more in tone than in facts. The only kind of travel writing that is possible today is travel *hints*, what your readers can do next summer when they are where you are.

For me, this collection divides sharply in two: the material written before he became famous and the material written later. The former not only displays his sources but it also certifies the courage of the break he made in his life. With a wife and a small child to support (it would have been courageous enough without them), he turned his back on an increasingly successful newspaper career to forge himself into a serious writer. This action, especially in view of the radical change in style that he was advancing (not originating), is for me much more heroic than all the subsequent lion-plugging and marlin-tugging, which is easier.

The post-1933 journalism is, for the most part, sad, both in its lack of weight and its weightier revelation. Most of the Cuban and Key West writings, in which he unattractively builds the unattractive Papa character, are the empty motions of a writer who wants to keep busy to keep his eyes off the vacancies inside him. (I suppose he also needed the money.) The Spanish war - to put it bluntly - rescued him temporarily, but soon again he sank into sports writing and that most facile species of Beautiful Prose: nature writing. All one needs for this work are adjectives of color and a basic conviction that man is especially corrupt when compared with trout and elk.

As many have noted, Hemingway thrived on wars; but the Second World War arrived too late. The novel that came out of it, 'Across the River and into the Trees', is, even to partisans, his least defensible work. His journalism of that war is his nadir as correspondent:

> You love a lot of things if you live around them, but there isn't any woman and there isn't any horse that is as lovely as a great airplane, and men who love them are faithful to them even though they leave them for others. A man has only one virginity to lose in fighters, and if it is a lovely plane he loses it to, there his heart will ever be. And a P-51 can do something to a man's heart.

Wartime can do something to a man's head, but even so, it is hard to reconcile such writing with the author of The Three-Day Blow.

Let us draw a veil - a transparent one, to be sure - over his latter-day affection for such American ornaments as Leonard Lyons and Walter Winchell. (2)

The prime effect of this collection - both parts, before and after the Papa figure - is to confirm for me the value of his posthumous book 'A Moveable Feast.' Some have attacked this book as the work of a mean-spirited man. It is certainly the work of a man with meanness in his spirit. To me, who have just reread much of it (I wrote about it in this journal May 9, 1964), it now seems more moving than before. The journalism of the early 20's, with its combined feelings of power and insouciance, underscores the daring of the plunge he took from that platform of security; and the later journalism, most of it, emphasizes the gap between the young man and the old - and it is the consciousness of that gap that generates the pathos of 'A Moveable Feast.' His last book shows us that he knew what had happened; much of this collection shows it happening. Read in conjunction, these two books illuminate an artistic tragedy.

Notes

1 Not true. If it rains, bullfights are cancelled.
2 Popular newspaper columnists.

109. MALCOLM BRADBURY, 'NEW STATESMAN'

75 (22 March 1968), 386-7

Malcolm Bradbury (b. 1932) is an English novelist and critic, Professor of English at the University of East Anglia, and the author of 'Eating People is Wrong' (1960) and 'Stepping Westward' (1965).

Hemingway's curious power - which becomes in the end his curious weakness - is that he built up his authority as a man of letters by not being, in the familiar sense, a man of letters at all. This authority derived from relating a craft of verbal procedures and literary methods to a personal style, one that was to become even for himself a mythology (his wound was the most famous since Philoctetes, (1) his sleepless nights the best known since Lady Macbeth's). Most of the exemplary literary lives of the modern period are conducted in two worlds, set off against each other, jointly providing virtue and conviction for the work: Wilde the writer as aristocrat, Eliot the poet as bank-clerk, Faulkner the novelist as farmer. The alternative is Bohemia; but that gives technique but not material, art but not human value.

Hemingway tried it in Paris in the 1920s and it did not do. 'The Rotunders', he says in one of the pieces of journalism that make up 'By-line':

> are nearly all loafers expending the energy that an artist puts into his creative work in talking about what they are going to do and condemning the work of all artists who have gained any degree of recognition.

His 'The Sun Also Rises' is the classic work on the American expatriate-bohemians, centred in Paris and around the Rotonde, but it is a book *about* not an exemplary product *of*. So Hemingway made himself the writer as *guru* by drawing on three other life-styles - those of the journalist, the sportsman, the soldier of fortune. What they have in common is skill, expertise and the sense of having been there when it was happening - the sense of salvation through control and utter knowingness.

That is why the journalism concerns us, even though Hemingway himself insistently cut it off from the other work:

> If you have made your living as a newspaperman, learning your trade, writing against deadlines, writing to make the stuff timely rather than permanent, no one has the right to dig this stuff up and use it against the stuff you have written to write the best you can.

True; but we can use it *with* the best stuff to see how it got that way. For journalism led through into the other work; more, it provided not only its materials but its sense of virtue, stylistic and moral. It became part of Hemingway's method of self-presentation and his way of exploring and capturing the world. Most of the pieces in 'By-line' are not, after all, hard news but personal journalism - stories behind the news and insights on his own life. Hemingway began as an ordinary reporter on the Kansas City 'Star'; but after the war when he moved to the Toronto 'Star Weekly' he was engaged on special assignments, which took him to Europe and into serious writing. The later journalism comes out of even more specialist assignments - the dispatches from the Spanish Civil War for the North American Newspaper Alliance; the 'Collier's' journalism from World War II, which enabled Hemingway to liberate the Paris Ritz; and so on.

The role of war correspondent cohered many things for him, and he performs, of course, superbly well. But this is because it enables him to chart the universe he wants to know. The early pieces on Europe for the 'Star Weekly' are, for instance, the exploration of a distinctive European geography: a Europe of the falling mark, the rise of Mussolini, the retreat from Constantinople, bullfights in Pamplona, fishing the Rhône - that is the geography behind the Hemingway hero. Passages from these pieces transfer directly into the short stories and the novels. In addition, there is beside the creation of the distinctive Hemingway universe the steady development of a language and a personality. The volume gradually shifts in rhetoric and tense-usage, and above all in the use of the first-person - the first-person who finally coheres the world around himself and finalises it. By the end of the volume Hemingway is reporting a world possessed by himself. Virtue by now is pure Hemingway virtue - so this, about his wife:

> She can also sing well with an accurate and true voice, knows more generals, admirals, air marshals, politicians and important persons than I know dead company commanders, former battalion commanders, rummies, coyotes, prairie dogs, jack rabbits, leaders of café society, saloon keepers, aeroplane drivers, horse players, good and bad writers and goats.

'The Fifth Column' - the play Hemingway wrote under the Madrid shelling, first published along with 49 stories in 1939 - probably really counts along with the journalism too; indeed Philip Young, who provides the commentaries in 'By-line,' suggests the reports he wrote at the same time are better. It's set in a Madrid under siege from the Loyalist troops, and it's about an Anglo-American named Philip who operates, behind a playboy façade, with the counter-espionage branch of the International Brigade. Forced, for reasons never made entirely apparent, to choose between the war and a 'bored Vassar bitch' in attendance at the Madrid hotel where most of the action takes place, he chooses the war.

The trouble with the play is that the texture of the relationships never really gets thick enough; for instance, the girl, though she spends most of her time in Philip's room, never discovers his political involvement, despite the presence of soldiers, special agents and a corpse on the other side of the partition. The play also uneasily covers up for the murder of Loyalist supporters by the revolutionary forces - a kind of terror the existence of which, incidentally, Hemingway denied in some of his dispatches.

But the biggest problem is that the superb gift for controlled dialogue that runs through the novels slackens under the extra duties that dialogue in drama must bear. The play depends, therefore, very much on the specific claims on us that the journalism makes - I was there; this is how it worked; this knowledge makes a man a man. It's not, of course, all there is to Hemingway, and we will never regard either the dispatches and longer pieces collected in 'By-line,' or 'The Fifth Column,' as essential work. What both books do is to illuminate a man whose life was so crucially a part of his art - illuminate the steady search for the right life-style, and the paradox that goes along with it: that when it comes, when the style is achieved, when Hemingway is his own hero, the work falls off. In 'The Fifth Column' the lapses are already as much moral as structural, and by the later work the hard-shell hero has become too complete, too lacking in openness, to give us the world any more. That sad voyage runs through the journalism, and this is its primary interest.

Note

1 In Greek mythology, an archer abandoned by his people because of his stinking wound, but recalled when the oracle declared he was essential for the capture of Troy. Edmund Wilson used him in 'The Wound and the Bow' (1941) to symbolize the artist's relation to society.

110. TONY TANNER, 'LONDON MAGAZINE'

8 (May 1968), 90-5

It was always clear that there was a close connection between Hemingway's journalism and the distinctive prose he evolved in his fiction. This rich collection of his despatches and articles brings that connection into clearer focus. One example: at the head of each story in 'In Our Time' there is an impersonal piece of prose apparently unrelated to the narrative which follows. All of these pieces are about some moment of war, violence, or death, and many of them are derived from Hemingway's experiences as a reporter. Here is an extract from a report in the 'Toronto Star' in 1922 sent from Adrianople describing refugees. 'Twenty miles of carts drawn by cows, bullocks and muddy-flanked water buffalo, with exhausted, staggering men, women and children, blankets over their heads, walking blindly along in the rain beside their worldly goods.... It is a silent process. Nobody even grunts. It is all they can do to keep moving. Their brilliant peasant costumes are soaked and draggled.... A husband spreads a blanket over a woman in labour in one of the carts to keep off the driving rain. She is the only person making a sound. Her little daughter looks at her in horror and begins to cry. And the procession keeps moving.'

And here is an extract from the piece in 'In Our Time' which is based on this experience. 'Water buffalo and cattle were hauling carts through the mud. No end and no beginning. Just carts loaded with everything they owned. The old men and women, soaked through, walked along keeping the cattle moving. The Maritza (1) was running yellow almost up to the bridge.... Women and kids were in the carts couched with mattresses, mirrors, sewing machines, bundles. There was a woman having a kid with a young girl holding a blanket over her and crying. Scared sick looking at it. It rained all through the evacuation.' The changes are slight but they reveal something of Hemingway's art. The selection, juxtaposition, and placing of the naked visual impressions is more subtle and economic. The colourful costumes have gone so that nothing will distract from the yellow river and the dark mud, the overall muted drabness. The silent movement of river, animals, and people is linked. The rain - always ominous in Hemingway's extremely weather-conscious prose - is stressed at the end. And the sentences are whittled down in an attempt to give the illusion of an absence of syntax, because syntax is the human mind arranging its thoughts and perceptions and Hemingway preferred to give the impression that the facts arranged themselves. One impression now stands isolated between two full stops though it is not a sentence - 'Scared sick looking at it.' - and anyone who is familiar with 'In Our Time' will recognise the deliberateness with which Hemingway has singled this out for special focus. For the narrative part of the book is mainly about Nick Adams and in the previous story (Indian Camp) he too has watched a painful child-birth and in addition the horribly cut throat of the father who could not stand it - and he too was 'scared sick looking at it'. And we begin to realise how subtly Hemingway has organised that book. The prose passages are cameos of the violent world into which Nick Adams is being initiated: the stories themselves deal with this initiation. And half way through Nick Adams appears in one of the prose passages, wounded and surrounded by corpses and rubble. This is the moment when Nick literally encounters the shattering violence of war; and this is the moment when he makes a 'separate peace'.

From the start Nick has found that the world can scare you sick just by looking at it, and his need and aspiration is to achieve a stance, a personal style, which can control that fear, keep down the rising horror, extrude the dread and nausea that continually threaten to undermine him. Philip Young has shown how intimately this is related to Hemingway's own experience of being wounded, and clearly Hemingway's prose is continually doing what Nick Adams has to learn to do. Those famous sharp, rinsed perceptions are not the product of a great mindless eyeball as some critics have thought. On the contrary, Hemingway's mind was excessively vulnerable, and his prose with its meticulous attachments to the external world was a perpetual ritual to ward off the undermining nightmare of uncontrolled thought. The limit that this deliberate extrusion of thought put on his development as a writer is clear; in the life it became tragic. But it is the presence of an unstated and controlled fear or horror which gives his best prose the tension and imperilled clarity which make it so much more than a collection of itemised sensations. This may seem a long way from a review of Hemingway's journalism but there is a continuity between the prose of the reporter and that of the writer. It controls the same fears; it formulates the same strategies for survival; it holds onto the world in the same way. And like the fiction, the journalism is really about two things - war, and peace.

In one piece called Old Newsman Writes Hemingway says of himself 'it has been interesting to watch his progress from an herbivorous (outdoors, the spring, baseball, an occasional half-read book) columnist to a carnivorous (riots, violence, disaster, and revolution) columnist', and this perfectly expresses the dual nature of the experiences in which he was so often engaged and in which the herbivorous and the carnivorous were strangely mixed. Thus, in one of a superb series of news letters from the Spanish Civil War he describes the preparations in a village expecting an assault. He puts before us the clatter of guns, the slant of bayonets, the settling smoke, and then 'you picked an armful of spring onions from a field beside the trail that led to the main Tortosa road. They were the first onions of this spring and, peeling, one found they were plump and white and not too strong. The Ebro delta has a fine rich land, and, where the onions grow, tomorrow there will be a battle.' More comment than that he does not permit himself, and it is comment enough. It brings home to us the 'herbivorous-carnivorous' nature of the moment. In the midst of war, nature is apparently at peace. On the other hand, when Hemingway got away from men into nature (he liked the Gulf Stream and 'the other great ocean currents' because they were 'the last wild country there is left'), so far from abandoning himself to pastoral passivity he was either shooting, or hunting, or fishing - that is, he himself was introducing moments of death into nature's quietnesses. Some of the pieces in which he describes these various activities are marvellously vivid - for he can describe the flight of a bird, the leap of a fish, the movement of a wild animal, in a way which can cause an access of wonder and vitality in the most sedentary non-sportsman - and of course this was more than just pastime for Hemingway. For not only was he haunted by the fact of death, he was obsessed by it and his way of avoiding the fear of it was by continually approaching and confronting the fact of it. Two quotations from the Spanish reports may be juxtaposed here. 'The day was so lovely that it seemed ridiculous that anyone should ever die'; and 'we lifted him, still limp and warm, to the side of the road and left him with his serious waxen face where tanks would not bother him now or anything else and went on into town'. Death comes in the afternoon of the loveliest days.

In the remarkable piece about his two air crashes in Africa called The Christmas Gift Hemingway makes an important distinction concerning his preoccupation with death.

'In all my obituaries, or almost all, it was emphasised that I had sought death all my life. Can one imagine that if a man sought death all of his life he could not have found her before the age of 54? It is one thing to be in the proximity of death, to know more or less what she is, and it is quite another to seek her. She is the most easy thing to find that I know of.... If you have spent your life avoiding death as cagily as possible but, on the other hand, taking no backchat from her and studying her as you would a beautiful harlot who could put you soundly to sleep for ever with no problems and no necessity to work, you could be said to have studied her but you have not sought her.' Hemingway was indeed a student of death who spent a good deal of time in proximity to its innumerable manifestations. If this made his imagination seem somewhat carnivorous this was because he lived through a particularly carnivorous age. Perhaps half these pieces are about various wars and one begins to get some sense of the many images of violent death which must have imprinted themselves on Hemingway's vulnerable retina. And sometimes the control cracks: 'In modern war there is nothing sweet nor fitting in your dying. You will die like a dog for no good reason. Hit in the head you will die quickly and cleanly even sweetly and fittingly except for the white blinding flash that never stops, unless perhaps it is only the frontal bone or your optic nerve that is smashed, or your jaw carried away, or your nose and cheek bones gone so you can still think but you have no face to talk with. But if you are not hit in the head you will be hit in the chest, and choke in it, or in the lower belly, and feel it all slip and slide loosely as you open, to spill out when you try to get up, it's not supposed to be so painful but they always scream with it, it's the idea I suppose, or have the flash, the slamming clang of high explosive on a hard road and find your legs are gone above the knee....' He cannot stop - his head is full of death. And he never stopped studying it. If there was a war, there he was to be found. ('If you want to know how it was in a LCV(P) on D-day when we took Fox Green beach and Easy Red beach on the sixth of June, 1944, then this is as near as I can come to it.' He was the man, he suffered, he was there.) (2) Between the wars if he is not himself struggling with some animal, he is as often as not at the bull-fights. Included here are his first accounts of bull-fighting, which he discovered exactly mid-way between the two World Wars. (3) Of one matador's performance in killing five bulls he says 'each one was a separate problem to be worked out with death' and one can immediately see what the bull-fight meant to Hemingway, and how it relates to his own prose. If death is your preoccupation then valour is your need, and that too he could study in the bull-ring just as his own life and writing formed a continuous demonstration of bravery, that grace under pressure which became for him an ethic. In one short piece he describes going round second-hand shops seeing what war medals were worth, what was 'the market price of valour'. Nobody was interested. 'You could dispose of a second-hand mouth-organ. But there was no market for a D.C.M.... So the market price of valour remained undetermined.' This is a bitter irony directed at an indifferent society, but it also suggests that valour is a private thing, mattering little to society but greatly to the self.

It is easy to point to the limitations of Hemingway's prose, and some of the later pieces reveal the grace stiffening into a stilted posture. But there is enough in this book to remind us once again that he was one of the important writers of our time. Some of the pieces commenting on political situations make interesting reading, even though they are more impressionistic than analytic; and many of his comments on literature - including a moving and deeply felt tribute to Conrad - show how carefully he worked out his own aesthetic. His tendency to discuss historical and literary figures as though they were boxers or jockeys and rank them accordingly is obviously somewhat reductive; but it is all part of his compulsion to see all life in terms of competition just as he filled his own life with a series of deliberately undertaken tests and planned struggles. In any case there are plenty of good historians and literary critics but only one Hemingway. One final comment on this welcome collection: it reveals more of the humour in Hemingway than his books do. There are a number of passages which read like Mark Twain, who developed clowning into a deliberate strategy in 'Innocents Abroad'. (4) Hemingway plays the clown too, on many occasions, and for similar reasons. It was a way of surviving in unfamiliar and possibly threatening territories; it is also a way of coping with fear. And this surviving and this coping Hemingway made his own particular business. It is this underlying seriousness and tension which redeems most of his journalism from the ephemerality and contingency usually inherent in this activity.

Notes

1 Turkish river, east of Alexandropoulos.
2 Walt Whitman, 'Song of Myself' (1855), section 33: 'I am the man, I suffer'd, I was there.'
3 Hemingway actually wrote his first article on bull-fighting in the 'Toronto Star Weekly,' 20 October 1923.
4 Comic travel narrative published in 1869.

'The Fifth Column and Four Stories of the Spanish Civil War' (1969)

111. CARLOS BAKER, 'SATURDAY REVIEW'

52 (20 September 1969), 36-7

Hemingway's contribution to the literature of the Spanish Civil War included a spate of news dispatches for the North American Newspaper Alliance; the script for a Loyalist propaganda film, 'The Spanish Earth'; a three-act play, 'The Fifth Column'; a series of angry essays for the short-lived American periodical 'Ken'; four semi-autobiographical short stories relating to besieged Madrid in the spring and fall of 1937, and finally 'For Whom the Bell Tolls,' which, whatever its faults, is still the best novel in any language about the Spanish conflict of thirty years ago.

The bulk of this material has already appeared in book form. The chief exception, apart from some of the more ephemeral journalism and propaganda, consists of the four short stories, first published in 'Esquire' and 'Cosmopolitan' as the terrible decade of the 1930s drew to a close, and now brought together, with a reprint of 'The Fifth Column,' to provide a small but welcome addendum to the Hemingway fiction shelf.

The reappearance of the play reminds us once again that Hemingway's forte was fiction rather than drama. The setting is the Hotel Florida on the Plaza de Callao just off the Gran Via of Madrid. This was the place where Hemingway lived while serving as a war correspondent in the fall of 1937, when the play was written. His companion at that time was Martha Gellhorn, later to become his third wife. The hero of the play, Philip Rawlings, is a self-portrait of Hemingway as he might have been if he had actually engaged in counter-espionage while ostensibly writing for the newspapers. With a singular lack of gallantry Hemingway gives his heroine, Dorothy Bridges, certain superficial characteristics of Miss Gellhorn, and sets up a dawning love affair as background for the cloak-and-sword activities of his hero. At the end, predicting that the world is in for fifty years of undeclared wars, Philip chooses continuing participation in the fight against fascism rather than retirement into domesticity with Dorothy. But the dramatic conflict between these two goals is far too easily resolved, mainly because Hemingway himself never succeeded in making family life and the production of babies a sufficiently alluring counterforce to the joys of pseudo-political involvement in deeds of derring-do.

Except for fulfilling Hemingway's prediction about wars, the years have not been kind to 'The Fifth Column.' Its level of credibility now approximates that of 'The Mark of Zorro' (1) - to which, oddly enough, it bears some other resemblances.

With the stories, however, we enter another realm. Hemingway garnered the materials for them while he was working on 'The Spanish Earth' with Joris Ivens and John Ferno in and around Madrid in the spring of 1937. Between bouts of assisting the film-makers he continued to report the progress of the war for NANA. At the same time, as was his invariable custom, he concentrated on keeping his eyes, his ears, and his literary sensibilities alert for people and situations that were in his judgment too good to waste on newspaper dispatches, that might indeed provide the material for genuine works of art.

The four stories from this period that he considered worthy of survival are Night Before Battle, Under the Ridge, The Denunciation, and The Butterfly and the Tank. Read as a series they provide an interesting test case for one of Hemingway's favorite public statements about the art of fiction: that if a writer merely reported on an incident he had personally experienced, his work would be flat; only 'invented' stories could achieve the requisite roundness and depth. But 'invention' for Hemingway never meant abnegation of the actual; he would have agreed with Wallace Stevens's dictum that 'the real is only the base, but it is the base.' (2) With Hemingway invention was largely an architectonic process - the reconstituting of the original elements to form a new superstructure reared on the foundations of the actual.

The least 'inventive' story in this group, Night Before Battle, is also the longest. The events it depicts belong to the second week of April 1937, and the locales are

Chicote's Bar on the Gran Via, the basement restaurant of the Gran Via Hotel, a ruined apartment house overlooking the Casa de Campo, and Hemingway's own room at the Hotel Florida, which often served as a rest and recreation billet for war correspondents, members of the International Brigade, and Loyalist aviators. The story turns upon Edwin Henry's attempts to cheer up Al Wagner, an American Communist tank officer who must renew the attack against Rebel positions next day. It is a good story, incorporating an astonishing amount of information about the life of foreigners in wartime Madrid while achieving unity by keeping Wagner and his problems in central focus.

What especially distinguishes Under the Ridge and The Denunciation is Hemingway's skill at synecdoche, the art of suggesting the universal by means of the particular. Under the Ridge, based on one of his photographic expeditions with Ivens and Ferno into the hilly Jarama sector, concerns the fierce resentment of a Loyalist soldier from Badajoz against the cold-eyed 'discipline' of a pair of Russian battle police, who execute a deserter with no more compunction than they would have about shooting a rabbit. The ridge of the title becomes in effect a line of demarcation between the native Spaniards and the 'foreigners,' and the story subtly dramatizes the essential conflict between these two groups in the Loyalist ranks.

In The Denunciation a waiter at Chicote's denounces to Seguridad headquarters a devil-may-care customer whom he recognizes as a Fascist spy. A frequent visitor in Spain, Hemingway had many friends on both sides, and was constantly struck by the ironies of civil war, particularly that one which turned people he had admired into enemies. In a fit of tough tenderness at the end of the story the narrator claims responsibility for the denunciation because, he explains, the spy Delgado 'was an old client of Chicote's and I did not wish him to be disillusioned or bitter about the waiters there before he died.'

Hemingway's powers of invention were memorably engaged by an incident he knew only from hearsay. A light-hearted civilian named Pedro who was squirting waiters at Chicote's with eau de cologne from a flit gun was first beaten and then murdered by three humorless, trigger-happy soldiers. The story struck Hemingway so forcibly that he told it twice - rather lamely in the first act of 'The Fifth Column,' and at length in The Butterfly and the Tank, which John Steinbeck told Hemingway was one of the best short stories of all time: merely to have *seen* it as a story was an act of triumph, to have written so superbly was 'almost too much.' Hemingway's skill in developing metaphors from the circumstances of his narrative was one of the hallmarks of his genius. Here, as Steinbeck undoubtedly recognized, the basic metaphor is evolved unerringly from a matrix of invented or observed particulars, raising the story well above the level of mere reportage, even if not to the height at which Steinbeck rated it.

The appearance in book form of these four stories ought to add appreciably to our sense of Hemingway's stature as a writer of short fiction. It is our misfortune that he never made good on his original plan to write 'The Fifth Column' as a short novel rather than as a play. As fiction, it might have succeeded; as drama, it unhappily does not.

Notes

1 A popular novel by Johnston McCulley (1924).
2 Wallace Stevens, 'Opus Posthumous,' ed. Samuel Morse (London, 1957), 160.

112. PHILIP YOUNG, 'NEW YORK TIMES BOOK REVIEW'

21 September 1969, 6

There was a time when the author of this book had misgivings about everything in it. He wished he had turned the material of his only full-length play, 'The Fifth Column' - 'The Four Ninety-Five Column Marked Down From Five,' he once called it - into a novel. (A better idea was the shorter piece of fiction he originally intended.) And for a while, he complained, these 'Four Stories of the Spanish Civil War' 'wouldn't come.' It was not long, however, before they did. Three appeared in 'Esquire' and one in 'Cosmopolitan.' Then the play was published, and produced, with its proper title. Now, roughly three decades later, it is surprisingly good to have back these tales of the Last Great Cause, for the first time, under one book cover.

They grew, of course, out of Hemingway's considerable experience of the Spanish war as a correspondent for the North American Newspaper Alliance and as a participant in filming 'The Spanish Earth.' More specifically, they grew from adventures in and around besieged Madrid -

particularly in the Hotel Florida and in a bar called Chicote's. The book is unified, then, in time, place, and action. It is unified even more by the dominating presence of the author, who is to be found alive on every page. That presence slants the focus, but also gives the book its sharp distinction. This is immediate, unmistakable Hemingway.

He nowhere appears entirely without disguise, but the leading character in all these pieces is clearly the writer of them. He is Philip Rawlings, protagonist of the play, and he is narrator of the stories, most often called Edwin Henry (E.H.). The adventures in counterespionage as Philip were wishful invention; the experience behind the stories was pretty much actual. Indeed, in the latter case, there is a question as to how autobiographical fiction differs from autobiographical journalism - the best, that is, of the dispatches the correspondent filed from Spain, which were reprinted a couple of years ago in 'By-Line: Ernest Hemingway.' The answer is that the difference lies more in quality than kind. As good as some of that correspondence was, all four of these stories are better than any of it. (A fifth, Nobody Ever Dies, was wisely not reprinted; a sixth, Landscape With Figures, remains unpublished.)

In theory the writer distinguished sharply between journalism and what he put down 'for keeps.' But in practice the line sometimes faded out of sight - except that as a rule the fiction was written with more care. (The reviewer has seen a typescript of one of these stories, 'Night Before Battle'; it is heavily and significantly revised.) Hemingway seems also to have saved the best stories for fiction. As a result, the stories beat the dispatches. They are more memorable and more moving.

The Denunciation starts as if it were to be a feature story on Chicote's, where 'the good guys went,' but it becomes a genuine story when an incident of espionage picks it up and carries the load. The Butterfly and the Tank, which John Steinbeck thought among the 'very few finest stories' ever written (1) is more of a problem. Is it completely *written*? During the action the manager of the bar tells the narrator, 'You must write a story about this' - something the narrator has already told us he intended to do. The manager also insists on, and explains, the title. The question, then, is if Hemingway found a different and effective way here to tell a tale, or if instead he has presented the material for one? To a lesser extent both Night Before Battle - grim but also lively and at times funny - and Under the Ridge - even grimmer and not funny at all - raise the same question.

But it would be a bad mistake to bog down in the problem of genre - for, however their true nature is to be described, all four stories are deft, absorbing, and they stay with you. The play may be something else. Its author himself called it 'probably the most unsatisfactory thing I ever wrote.' Not explaining why he did not recollect his emotion in tranquillity (rework his drama back in this country) he blamed his avowed failure on the 'honestly impossible writing conditions' in his room at the Florida, which was frequently shelled during his stay there - a room which is most literally described as the principal set in the play. It is as if the author were living on stage, an impossible place to write indeed.

And so 'The Fifth Column' is autobiographical drama. Philip Rawlings, its leading man and a Loyalist agent, justified his apparently dissolute existence as a 'third-rate newspaperman' on the ground that he is really a 'second-rate cop.' So Hemingway justified what Rawlings's mistress calls 'this absolutely *utter* playboy business' on the ground that he was turning it to literature. (Except for her unbelievable stupidity, Dorothy the mistress, is an accurate portrait of fellow journalist Martha Gellhorn.) As elsewhere, the author gets good comic mileage out of the speech of those for whom English is not the native tongue. The hotel manager is hilarious. Actually all of the horseplay is amusing. But the utterly serious business depends for its impact on our believing in the hero's romantic political convictions - when, as Under the Ridge makes clear, the author himself was uncertain of them. In the play, Philip nobly renounces Dorothy for the cause; in life Hemingway married her.

At one point, Philip mentions to his mistress people who have 'done such things that it would break your damn heart if I tried to tell you about it.' Precisely Hemingway's purpose in the book: to tell us about such things. Despite his fascination with warfare and his cheerful wit, he is also trying to tell us that war is hell. (All the good themes are old stuff.) And if he fails to break our hearts, exactly, his stories reach deep enough to touch them.

Note

1 Quoted in Baker, 'Ernest Hemingway,' 403.

113. STEPHEN SPENDER, 'NEW YORK REVIEW OF BOOKS'

13 (25 September 1969), 5

Stephen Spender (b. 1909), an English poet and critic, wrote 'The Destructive Element' (1934) and an autobiography, 'World Within World' (1951). This excerpt is from a long review of books about the Spanish Civil War.

The Spanish Civil War crystallized this feeling that the final reality - of Fascism, capitalism, and, finally, of Stalinism - was an incommunicable terror. The writers who fought in Spain had submitted to its testing, even if they were destroyed by it.

Ernest Hemingway's position was close to this, though exceptional and *sui generis*. He went to Spain with the declared intention of writing about it. But no one was so foolish as to think that he had to submit to the test of the ultimate reality of the conflict in order to do so. He was the notorious exceptional case of a kind of War Horror Expert whose qualifications were already public knowledge. He was expected to write about war because war was his obsession. To him it was a pure condition of being, transcending even his loyalty to the Republican side.

Having him in Spain was like letting Edgar Allan Poe into a small cellar containing one mad cat. (1) He had passed all the tests already, faced the horrors, died the deaths. The only test Spain did offer was to ask Whether He Was Still Up To It, a question probably of greater interest to himself than to anyone else. He passed easily. When he read at Carnegie Hall, to the Second American Writers' Congress, (2) a text about war, he left no doubt that he was speaking about the ultimate reality - Captain Ahab personally addressing the real white whale - an experience by comparison with which the Cause had shrunk into being mere occasion. Mr. Weintraub quotes from this speech:

> ...It is very dangerous to write the truth in war and the truth is also very dangerous to come by. I do not know which American writers have gone out to seek it ... and when a man goes to seek the truth in war he may find death instead. But if twelve go and two come back, the truth will be the truth and not the garbled hearsay

> that we pass as history. Whether the truth is worth some risk to come by, the writers must decide themselves. Certainly it is not [? *sic*] more comfortable to spend their time disputing learnedly on points of doctrine. And there will always be new schisms and new fallings off and marvellous exotic doctrines and romantic lost leaders, for those who do not want to work at what they profess to believe in, but only to discuss and maintain positions, skillfully chosen positions with no risk involved in holding them. Positions to be held by the typewriter and consolidated with the fountain pen. But there is now, and there will be from now on for a long time, war for any writer to go to who wants to study it. (3)

The reality of the Cause which is fought for here seems to have disappeared into the war itself, which becomes the ultimate reality.

War's ultimate reality was also of course a test of qualities of human behavior which Hemingway took to be those of the real person. There goes along with this a view that people who go to wars should not complain about what they find there: hence Hemingway's quarrel in Spain with Dos Passos for being discomfited because one of his friends was shot as a spy. (4) In the collection of four stories and a play called 'The Fifth Column' recently published, there is a curious story called The Denunciation in which Hemingway as the thinly disguised narrator - who is also a well-known writer - seems to accept responsibility - perhaps as an object lesson to Dos Passos - for getting someone shot.

The scene is a Madrid café called Chicote much favored by its clients, to which the writer goes one afternoon. An old waiter comes over to him and, pointing out a guest at another table, says he is a Fascist spy. The writer at once recognizes the man as a certain Delgado whom he knew before the war, and with whom he had been on very friendly terms. He takes it for granted that Delgado is a Fascist spy, for he had met him among friends who held extremely reactionary views, and he had once, after a hunting party, won in a bet a sum of money which he knew Delgado could ill afford, but which he cheerfully paid up.

The waiter wants advice: Should he denounce Delgado? The writer at first hesitates and experiences some contemptible scruples of the literary man, but then encourages the waiter to do so. The waiter telephones the police, and the writer, feeling a bit squeamish about the prospect of seeing his old friend arrested in front of his eyes, goes back to his hotel from where, later on, he calls Pepé, a friend who is in the *Seguridad*, (5) to ask whether they have picked up Delgado. Pepé says yes, it all went off smoothly and Delgado will be shot tomorrow. The writer asks Pepé a favor: to tell Delgado that it was he and not the waiter who denounced him to the police. The story ends with the writer reflecting that doubtless Delgado had gone to Chicote's because all the clients at that café had a kind of special feeling about the place. 'So I was glad I had called my friend Pepé at *Seguridad* headquarters because Luis Delgado was an old client of Chicote's and I did not wish him to be disillusioned or bitter about the waiters before he died.'

The moral of this seems to be that in a war one should yield up one's friends to the secret police with a good grace and without fussily demanding that before being shot they should be tried. The ending has a conceited smugness which to my mind makes even a famous First World War story of Rudyard Kipling yield place to it in any competition for the most morally repugnant story ever written. Rudyard Kipling's story is about a dear old English spinster in the employ of a family whose son has been killed on the western front, who goes out into the garden and shoots dead a wounded German pilot whose machine has crashed nearby.(6) The spinster lady at least has the excuse that the pilot, given the opportunity, would have killed *her*. But in Hemingway's story there is not even any evidence beyond the waiter's and the writer's opinion to prove that Delgado was a spy. On such evidence as Hemingway provides, Delgado might equally have denounced the writer, for having hunted and taken bets and frequented aristocratic company before the war.

The Denunciation is obviously a story with a moral, horrid as it is. Yet in another story, Under the Ridge, where Hemingway is using his experience and his imagination and not preaching toughness, there is a truth which undermines any moralizing. Under the Ridge is an extremely vivid account of a battle in the midst of which the narrator visits a part of the front where there are various kinds of troops, some of them anarchists. He has a conversation with an Extremaduran who is extremely hostile and surly, and mistakes him for a Russian. Soon after this he notices a Frenchman get up with a very serious expression on his face and simply walk away from the front, behind the lines. A few minutes later the Frenchman is followed by two leather-jacketed military policemen. The soldiers notice this and tell the narrator how a boy called Paco who deserted this front was brought back by the Russian police and as an example shot at the very spot from which he had deserted. The writer suddenly thinks that the Frenchman 'could walk out of battle not from cowardice, but simply from seeing too clearly: knowing suddenly that he had to leave it: knowing that there was no other thing to do.' Comparing these two stories I can only conclude that when Hemingway was justifying war and toughness, he could be maudlin with a hideous inverted sentimentality, but that when he was simply observing and experiencing, war did move him to truthful observation and deep imaginative insight.

Notes

1 Poe's The Black Cat (1843).
2 In 1937.
3 Quoted in Stanley Weintraub, 'The Last Great Cause' (London, 1968), 198, which was also reviewed by Spender.
4 José Robles Pazos, Dos Passos' Spanish translator, was executed in 1937.
5 Police.
6 Mary Postgate (1915).

'Islands in the Stream' (1970)

114. CHRISTOPHER RICKS, 'NEW YORK REVIEW OF BOOKS'

15 (8 October 1970), 17-19

Christopher Ricks (b. 1933), Professor of English at Cambridge, is the author of 'Milton's Grand Style' (1963) and 'Tennyson' (1972).

'You're going to write straight and simple and good now. That's the start.' The faded adjuration in 'Islands in the Stream' is from one half of Hemingway to his other half - from the lonely uncorrupted painter Thomas Hudson to the companionable corrupted novelist Roger Davis. 'That's the start': and 'Islands in the Stream,' which is the end, is not straight or simple or good. Written mostly in 1951, ten years before he shot himself, it is Hemingway's last novel; it comes hard on the callous heels of 'Across the River and into the Trees,' and it opens up the Parisian reminiscences (it has its own such) which petrified as 'A Moveable Feast.' It had grown into a four-part enterprise, but Hemingway salvaged 'The Old Man and the Sea,' and what now remains is Part I Bimini, Part II Cuba, and Part III At Sea.

Bimini is Thomas Hudson in the 1930s entertaining the three sons of his two wrecked marriages; they fish; their love leaves him open to his loneliness, and then the death of two of them leaves him nothing but lonely. Cuba is Thomas Hudson clandestinely war-efforting in about 1942; his other son (the eldest) has been killed as a pilot; Thomas Hudson drinks; he meets his first wife who is all he ever wanted. At Sea is Thomas Hudson commanding the pursuit of some German U-boat survivors; the Germans die, and it may be that the wounded Thomas Hudson is about to too.

The three Parts part. According to Carlos Baker: 'he hoped to make each section an independent unit. Later he would accomplish the welding job that would unify the whole.' But nothing could ever have welded these together - they desperately don't fit, which is both why Hemingway had to write the book and why he didn't publish it. The fissures can't even be leaped, let alone welded. Part III is At Sea and so is the book. 'There aren't any answers. You should know that by now. There aren't any answers at all.' But when Thomas Hudson says answers, Ernest Hemingway means questions.

Devious and secretive, 'Islands in the Stream' is an elaborate refusal to say what is the matter with Thomas Hudson. It calls him Thomas Hudson throughout, which makes the reader's relationship with him at once utterly stable and aloofly unadvancing. The book makes it impossible for us to know what is the matter with him (and so at the same time to know what was the matter with Hemingway) by an ingenious circumvention: it proliferates good reasons for him to be in a bad way. What - it asks incredulously - is the matter with him? Haven't his marriages broken up? Doesn't he still despairingly love his first wife? Aren't all his sons killed? Isn't his work as a painter threatened by drink and indiscipline? Isn't he enduring the joyless dangers of furtive seamanship in a war which seems merely six of one and half a dozen of the other? What more do you want? Well, yes: but apart from the 'work' one (which doesn't ring true but does ring revealingly false), all of these stand rather as *ex post facto* (1) constructions than as living pains. The great swordfish here escapes; the mighty fish which Hemingway here most adroitly lands are indeed prize-winning specimens but are red herrings.

That Thomas Hudson feels the worthlessness of it all, this comes through. But his creator, with that kindliest of protectings which is usually a self-protecting, decides against any painful exploration of what is the matter: instead he scatters matters. The gap then yawns - sometimes like a crevasse, sometimes like a yawn. The 'sinister acumen' which W. H. Mellers half-praised in Hemingway thirty years ago ('Scrutiny,' 1939) (2) is here bent to not giving anything away - or rather to giving away haystacks with the odd poisoned needle in them. As in the Father Brown story where there are too disconcertingly many murder weapons, (3) so here there are altogether too many things which could have killed Thomas Hudson's spirit. 'He did not know what made him feel as he did.' Nor did his creator - or if he did, he wasn't telling. The enterprise is intricately self-defeating, at once locally steered and drivingly uncontrollable ('It was as though he were hooked to a moving anchor'). It resembles 'Hamlet' as it seemed to T.S. Eliot. Eliot sought an objective correlative, 'a set of objects, a situation, a chain of events which shall be the formula of that *particular* emotion'; what he found was pathology and failure:

> Hamlet (the man) is dominated by an emotion which is inexpressible, because it is in *excess* of the facts as they appear. And the supposed identity of Hamlet with his author is genuine to this point: that Hamlet's bafflement at the absence of objective equivalent to his feelings is a prolongation of the bafflement of his creator in the face of his artistic problem. Hamlet is up against the difficulty that his disgust is occasioned by his mother, but that his mother is not an adequate equivalent for it; his disgust envelops and exceeds her. It is thus a feeling which he cannot understand; he cannot objectify it, and it therefore remains to poison life and obstruct action. (4)

Thomas Hudson's three sons are slaughtered for the cruellest of markets: not commercialized sentimentality, but authorial escape. They are thrown off the sled so that Thomas Hudson - alias Ernest Hemingway - may get away. And why the frantic flight? What do you mean, those may not be wolves at all - didn't you see me throw the children to them? It was Fitzjames Stephen who was wittily perturbed about infant mortality in Dickens: in Dickens 'an interesting child runs as much risk ... as any of the troops who stormed the Redan.' (5) In Hemingway - a trooper who stormed Redans for all he was worth - the children ought to ask danger-money. Two sons abruptly die in a car, and one in a Spitfire; such things happen, (6) but the book should not make out that this precipitates Thomas Hudson's bitter hopelessness. He does not really want to live whether they live or not.

'But why did I ever leave Tom's mother in the first place? You'd better not think about that, he told himself.' Thomas Hudson's favorite form of communication with himself is telling himself. Yet we should apply a remark of Thomas Hudson's about that other kind of telling, the sharing of confidences. 'Telling never did me any good. Telling is worse for me than not telling.'

That is Thomas Hudson manfully not expatiating to others on his grief, but it goes for the plight of the whole book. Instead of telling, telling himself. 'Work, he told himself.' 'You'd better not think about that': was there ever a book so obsessively about not thinking about things? And yet the more often the phrase rings out, the more strangely it rings. Must there not be some quite other thing about which Thomas Hudson cannot bear to think, some deepest vacancy which these self-injunctions are to ward off? Or is it that when Thomas Hudson says he'd better not think about something, he means he'd better not think?

> ...and Thomas Hudson thought he had never seen a lovelier face nor a finer body. Except one, he thought. Except the one finest and loveliest. Don't think about it, he told himself.
>
> Let's not think about the sea nor what is on it or under it, or anything connected with it. Let's not even make a list of what we will not think about it. Let's not think of it at all. Let's just have the sea in being and leave it at that. And the other things, he thought. We won't think about them either.
>
> All right now. Don't think about that either. If you don't think about it, it doesn't exist. The hell it doesn't. But that's the system I'm going on, he thought.
>
> He knew they [the discovered German bullets] were the rest of his life. But he did not wish to think about them now....
>
> 'You truly think we will have a fight?' 'I know it. Do not think about that. Think about details.'
>
> Well, it keeps your mind off things. What things? There aren't any things any more. Oh yes, there are.
>
> He knew there was no use thinking of the girl who had been Tom's mother nor all the things they had done and the places they had been nor how they had broken up. There was no use thinking about Tom. He had stopped that as soon as he had heard.
>
> There was no use thinking about the others. He had lost them, too, and there was no use thinking about them. He had traded in remorse for another horse that he was riding now.

> Go ahead and drink the rest of your drink and think about something good. Tom's dead and it's all right to think about him. You'll never get over it. But you are solid on it now.

The instances are desolate and desolating - and not the less so for the utter unsolidity of this last sentiment (twenty pages from the end). It is not just Thomas Hudson who so unremittingly fingers his concealed wound as never to reach for his bow. Hemingway had become all wound and no bow. (7)

And the other horse that Thomas Hudson was riding now? A bankrupt duty, that of pursuing those Germans. Gone is Hemingway's old vengeful zest of which Edmund Wilson wrote so piercingly ('indulgence in that headiest of sports: the bagging of human beings') (8) - and a good thing it is gone. But what is left is not the disinterested but the uninterested. 'Get it straight. Your boy you lose. Love you lose. Honor has been gone for a long time. Duty you do.' But so truncated and impoverished a notion of duty does not do its duty: it - and in both ways - does for duty.

> Well, I know what I have to do, so it is simple. Duty is a wonderful thing. I do not know what I would have done without duty since young Tom died. You could have painted, he told himself. Or you could have done something useful. Maybe, he thought. Duty is simpler.

But too much simpler, so much so as to be no stay (even when lacquered with hard-wearing irony) against emptiness and terror. Hence the fierce flashes of the old Hemingway - the boy's blistered struggle with the swordfish, or a bloody gloating fight at the dock. Thomas Hudson's friend Roger - with an excuse but no real reason - smashes up a meanly abusive man. But it turns sour, and not just for Roger. Roger is the stronger and more skilled fighter. As so often in Hemingway, we are offered a 'hideous moral spoonerism: Giant the Jack Killer.' That is C. S. Lewis's dismayed evocation of 'Tamburlaine,' (9) and Hemingway has things in common with Marlowe. There is the single stylistic feat which is indeed a 'mighty line' (10) and yet in both senses of the phrase. There is the reducing of life to the sensation and the sensational. And there is the problem of how much in the end someone can know about men who know so little about women. It was a disaster for Hemingway that he had no daughters; it might have been a disaster for them if he had.

But Marlowe didn't live till he was sixty, didn't have to find out that his simple (though simply equivocal) code wasn't only inadequate to the complexities of love and of steadfastness but was inadequate even to most of the simlicities of life. It is impossible to read 'Islands in the Stream' without thinking of Hemingway's suicide. So much of the book is about suicide, and often the anecdotes are so little to the point as to make it likely that the point is not where Hemingway is pretending. There is the pig which swam out to sea.

> '*¡Qué puerco más suicido!*' Thomas Hudson said.... 'I'm sorry your pig committed such suicide.' 'Thank you,' said Thomas Hudson. 'We all have our small problems.'

There is the detailed irrelevance of 'The suicide gentleman':

> We all called him Suicides by then so I said to him, 'Suicides, you better lay off or you'll never live to reach oblivion.'

Is it a laugh that (successful) Suicides is good for? And there is the discussion of committing suicide by eating phosphorus, and by drinking dye, and by setting yourself on fire. And there is Roger's mistress, who killed herself.

> 'You wouldn't ever do that.' 'I don't know,' Roger said. 'I've seen it look very logical.' 'One reason you wouldn't do it is because it would be a hell of an example for the boys. How would Dave feel?' 'He'd probably understand. Anyway when you get into that business that far you don't think much about examples.'

But Hemingway did think about the hell of an example which his father had set. John Berryman has set it down:

> Tears Henry shed for poor old
>   Hemingway
> Hemingway in despair, Hemingway
>   at the end,
> the end of Hemingway,
> tears in a diningroom in Indiana
> and that was years ago, before his
>   marriage say,
> God to him no worse luck send.
>
> Save us from shotguns & fathers'
>   suicides.

It all depends on who you're the
father of
if you want to kill yourself -
a bad example, murder of oneself,
the final death, in a paroxysm, of
love
for which good mercy hides?

A girl at the door: 'A few coppers
pray'
But to return, to return to Hemingway
that cruel & gifted man.
Mercy! my father; do not pull the
trigger
or all my life I'll suffer from your
anger
killing what you began. (11)

Notes

1 Done afterward, but having a retroactive effect.
2 See No. 57.
3 G.K. Chesterton, The Secret Garden, 'The Innocence of Father Brown' (1911).
4 T.S. Eliot, 'Selected Prose' (London, 1975), 48.
5 Fitzjames Stephen, The Relation of Novels to Life,' 'Cambridge Essays' (London, 1855), 174n. The Grand Redan in Sebastopol was besieged in 1855.
6 André Malraux's twin sons actually were killed in a car crash in 1961 and his wife had died after falling under a train in 1944. Hemingway may have known about this.
7 An allusion to Edmund Wilson's book.
8 See No. 62
9 C.S. Lewis, 'English Literature in the Sixteenth Century, Excluding Drama' (Oxford, 1954), 52.
10 Ben Jonson, 'To the Memory of Shakespeare' (1623).
11 John Berryman, 'His Toy, His Dream, His Rest' (London, 1969), 164.

115. JOHN ALDRIDGE, 'SATURDAY REVIEW'

53 (10 October 1970), 23-6, 39

John Aldridge (b. 1922) is an American critic and Professor of English at the University of Michigan, and the author of 'After the Lost Generation' (1951) and 'In Search of Heresy' (1956).

At the time of his death in 1961 Hemingway is known to have at least four book-length manuscripts in various stages of preparation. There were the two nonfiction books: 'A Moveable Feast,' his collection of Paris sketches published posthumously in 1964, and 'The Dangerous Summer,' of which three portions dealing with the Ordoñez-Dominguin bullfights of 1959 had appeared serially in 'Life' in 1960. In addition, he had been working on a very long but presumably unfinished novel called 'The Garden of Eden' and a book often referred to as the Land, Sea, and Air Novel based on Hemingway's experiences during World War II.

In spite of the quantities of gossip that have accumulated around the Hemingway tragedy over the last nine years, very little has been said about his still unpublished works. According to Carlos Baker, his official biographer, the complete text of 'The Dangerous Summer' is now 'locked away' at Charles Scribner's Sons and seems a generally mediocre piece of writing. Judging by the quality of the 'Life' instalments, one would suppose that as a book it would be best kept locked away. Since 1961 it has been impossible to obtain reliable information on either the status or the whereabouts of the two fiction manuscripts, 'The Garden of Eden' and the Land, Sea, and Air Novel, (1) and reports circulated during Hemingway's lifetime were contradictory in the extreme. There is some evidence that he may have worked sporadically on both right up to his final illness and breakdown. But one does not know how far he had progressed or what disposition was later made of them. It may be that they were among the unfinished materials found on his work table after his suicide. It may also be that they were finished and placed in deposit - as his widow and others have said was sometimes his custom - in bank vaults, at his publishers, or with certain trusted bartenders.

In any case, information has been so meager that

undoubtedly few people outside Hemingway's immediate circle of family and friends were even aware that such a work as 'The Garden of Eden' existed until Baker referred to it in his biography. The description he gives there is far from complete, and it would appear that he saw only a draft of the work in progress. But if the book is as preposterously bad as he makes it seem, one can only hope that the novel's publication will be delayed until such time as it can safely be offered as a literary curiosity too ancient to be any longer embarrassing. Baker characterizes it as 'an experimental compound of past and present, filled with astonishing ineptitudes ... a long and emptily hedonistic novel of young lovers in the old days of Grau-du-Roi and the Costa Brava: page after page of their talk was filled with inconsequential commentary on the color and condition of their hair, the food and drink they were always consuming, and the current state of their sun-tanned skins.' (2)

This is all we have heard about 'The Garden of Eden,' and it would seem to be more than enough. About the original manuscript of the Land, Sea, and Air Novel, on the other hand, we have heard a great deal for years, but what we have heard has told us little. In fact, ever since 1949 when Malcolm Cowley writing in 'Life' confirmed the many rumors that Hemingway was engaged on a big new book about the war, the Land, Sea, and Air Novel has been the most widely publicized literary mystery of the past two decades. Scarcely any of the information released during Hemingway's lifetime contained more than an oblique reference to the book's theme or subject matter. One learned only that the action was supposed to be divided into three parts corresponding roughly to the different phases of Hemingway's experience of the war, first as captain of his cruiser, the 'Pilar,' during its service as an improvised submarine-chaser in the waters around Cuba, then as a correspondent with the RAF over France and Germany and finally with the Fourth Infantry Division during the Allied drive across Europe. Most of the publicity took the form of reports concerning his rate of progress with the book, and these were so contradictory that they served only to deepen the air of mystery surrounding the whole enterprise. They even caused one to wonder whether the book actually existed.

Cowley said that Hemingway began writing it before Pearl Harbor and by 1949 had completed more than a thousand pages. But as early as 1946 Hemingway had announced that he had completed 1,200 pages - a report which, if true, would indicate that in the following three years he made no progress at all. The columnist Leonard Lyons has been quoted as saying in 1954 that 'the long novel is finished and is in a safe-deposit box in a Havana bank.' But Hemingway apparently had not heard the news, for in July of 1955 he was still apprising the public of his progress. In fact, he seemed actually to have lost ground. The number of pages he said he had completed had dropped mysteriously to 900. Then a year later in a 'Look' article (3) he wrote that he had reached the 850th manuscript page, evidently having lost another fifty pages in the interval. Finally, more than two years later, his rate of loss having sharply accelerated, he is reported to have told Earl Wilson (4) that he had 'finished page six-sixty-seven today.'

These contradictions may or may not be important in themselves. They may indicate only that Hemingway was speaking on one occasion of rough-draft pages and on another of finished pages. But they may also indicate that there was some real ambiguity about his progress on the book and perhaps about his imaginative relation to his materials. Surely, there is some ground for suspicion on both counts. If, as Cowley claims, Hemingway actually began the book before Pearl Harbor, he appears to have been sufficiently cavalier in his attitude toward it to be able to interrupt the writing again and again to do other things and even to take on other and, one would think, much less important literary projects. Between Pearl Harbor and 1949, in addition to his Q-boat operations with the 'Pilar,' he had been extremely active as a war correspondent, had produced a large quantity of journalism about his experiences, written several introductions to books, and edited the 'Men at War' anthology, and in 1949 had suspended all other operations to write 'Across the River and into the Trees.' By 1952 the only material remotely related to the Land, Sea, and Air Novel which he apparently had ready to publish was 'The Old Man and the Sea,' and that book had nothing to do with the war at sea.

Hemingway's desultory progress on his big novel might not by itself have seemed especially disconcerting when one considered his temperamental restlessness and the wide range of his interests. But there were certain facts that made it deeply disconcerting. For one thing, it was not at all like him to suspend work on his important books for long intervals. In the past he had followed a carefully disciplined routine and rarely allowed himself to be distracted from the writing of a book until it was finished. Yet now he appeared to be almost frantically seeking distraction and taking advantage of any excuse, however trivial, to avoid full commitment to the big novel.

Second, contrary to the statements made by his intimates, it had also not been Hemingway's habit in the past to put finished manuscripts in the bank for extended periods before publishing them. (He evidently did not follow this practice in the case of any of his earlier books.) One does not know whether the big novel, as originally conceived, was ever finished. But if it was and Hemingway thought it successful, there is little likelihood that he would have postponed its publication, particularly at a time when he is known to have been acutely conscious of the need to bolster his reputation with an important new work. Hence, it may be that either he was unable to finish the book as he had planned it, or he did finish it and was dissatisfied with the result.

Hemingway might well have had his doubts, for there was good reason to suppose that he could no longer rely on the absolute rightness of his instincts or work with anything resembling his old energy and endurance. He had apparently been in failing health for quite some time, perhaps even as far back as the war. But the injuries he suffered in the two African plane crashes of 1954 apparently brought him in the next few years to a condition of virtually complete physical and mental breakdown. It seemed obvious also from the internal evidence of the work published in the Fifties that his physical deterioration had been accompanied by a decline in creative vitality. In 1950 he published 'Across the River and into the Trees,' surely the poorest of his novels, and even though 'The Old Man and the Sea' represented for many people a triumphant recovery, it could also be seen to have a quality of specious attractiveness and efficiency that in fiction so often results from the avoidance of more problems than are confronted and overcome. It was, in short, a safe book in the sense that it was made up of the best of Hemingway's old market-tested materials, stylistic and dramatic effects which at one time had been arrived at with some real originality and risk through a vital engagement of life, but which were now merely postures and autographs of famous but dead emotions. The problem was not only that Hemingway was sounding like himself in a manner that seemed synthetic. It was also that the self he sounded like was not the self he any longer was. Writing for him had apparently ceased to be an act of self-discovery and had become an act of self-resuscitation.

At any rate, as various commentators have indicated, Hemingway originally planned 'The Old Man and the Sea' as a coda or perhaps a fourth part to the sea section of the Land, Sea, and Air Novel. But, significantly, he chose instead to publish it as a separate short novel. While continuing to work on the big book, he may slowly have revised his original plan to the extent of limiting the action to those experiences relating to the sea only. It may also be, as Carlos Baker suggests, that certain of the materials concerning the war in Europe were incorporated into 'Across the River and into the Trees' and presumably were either used up in that way or never completed as a separate section of the projected long work. In any case, Hemingway may have decided - or his widow may have decided after his death - that a publishable novel could be made out of the sea materials alone, and it is this section, or surviving version, of the big book and not the big book itself (the remainder of which if it was ever written, is still not accounted for) that has now been published, with some emendations by Mrs. Hemingway, under the title 'Islands in the Stream.'

In it Hemingway tells the story of a painter named Thomas Hudson - whose circumstances and experiences in some ways closely resemble his own - during three phases of his life: in the mid-Thirties on the island of Bimini, where Hudson is living alone after a divorce and is visited by his three sons; a number of years later in Cuba during the war, when Hudson is involved in secret antisubmarine activities using his cruiser as a Q-boat; and a short time afterward when Hudson and his crew set out in search of survivors from a destroyed German submarine, this episode culminating in a gun battle and Hudson's wounding.

Knowing that this may well be the last new Hemingway novel we will ever see, one approaches it with a mixture of wariness, awe, and considerable anxiety, hoping that through some charity of the gods it will turn out to be very good, but knowing also the chances against the novel's being other than very bad. It would be nice homage to be able to pronounce it a masterpiece. There is diminishment for each of us in the possibility that the book might prove a disaster. But the worst diminishment of all: if honesty forces it upon us to be equivocal, finicky, and faint, to say, as unfortunately one must, that the book is neither very good nor very bad, but that it is both, in some places downright wonderful, in others as sad and embarrassingly self-indulgent as the work of any sophomore.

In this respect it resembles 'For Whom the Bell Tolls' perhaps more closely than it does any of the earlier novels. There are other obvious similarities between the two books, but they are most strikingly similar in the way each brings together in a single narrative - at times within the space of a single page - some of the best and worst features of Hemingway's writing. The interesting thing, furthermore, is that these features relate in both books to the same kinds of material. Those sections that are devoted mainly to the description of physical action are almost invariably excellent. Those in which the physical action is interrupted to give Robert Jordan and Thomas Hudson an opportunity to *think*, to analyze their feelings or to find intellectual justification for doing what they are about to do, are as vapid and pretentious as such passages nearly always are in Hemingway. Luckily, the two kinds of material are not present in equal amounts in either book: the passages describing physical action far outnumber the passages of intellectual analysis in both. But the element that finally saves 'For Whom the Bell Tolls' is missing from 'Islands in the Stream.'

In the latter there is no coherently formed or sufficiently compressed narrative structure in which the action can take on the intensity or the meaning it would seem potentially capable of developing. There is also no thematic design strong enough to support the weight of Hudson's sagging cerebral muscles or to give his thoughts the kind of relevance to the action that Jordan's can finally be seen to have. Where 'For Whom the Bell Tolls' is held together by the rigid economy of the form and the tightly interlocking relationship of events occurring over a period of a few days, the new novel is composed of episodes much more widely spaced in time and only vaguely connected by an evolving plot. The result is that such dramatic tension as may be generated in any one of the episodes tends to be dissipated in the lapse of time separating it from the next. The problem is not simply that the book is divided into three parts but that, as a novel, it *disintegrates* into three parts or long short stories, and these are related only by the fact that Hudson is the central if somewhat opaque character in all of them.

Yet taken separately, as, given the looseness of structure, they must be taken, many of the episodes contain the most exciting and effective writing Hemingway has ever done. There is a marvelous ocean-fishing sequence in Part I, the account of a protracted and agonizing struggle by one of Hudson's young sons to bring in a giant fish. The pathos of the boy's almost superhuman effort - which of course ends in last-minute failure - is brilliantly evoked, and one realizes that here is a dimension of Hemingway one has seen before but perhaps not often enough, that side of his nature which was capable of responding not merely to bluster and bravado but with admiration for bravery in the weak and with tenderness toward weakness in the brave. There are also some nicely comic scenes in a Havana bar that are reminiscent of the better moments of 'To Have and Have Not,' and the best sustained piece of writing in the book, the long story of the search for the German submariners ending in the gun battle. This is one of the most impressive descriptions of physical action to be found in Hemingway, comparable to the finest of them all, the account of El Sordo's last stand on the hilltop in 'For Whom the Bell Tolls.'

Yet in spite of the high quality of individual episodes, one still senses a deficiency in the whole, which another comparison with 'For Whom the Bell Tolls' may help to clarify. When he wrote that book, Hemingway was still close enough to the values and emotional responses of his early career to be able to use them to give a plausible edge of tragedy to Robert Jordan's story. Jordan was the climactic Hemingway hero and the last of the heroes able to embody convincingly the old attitudes about life, love, courage, and death. Even so, one saw that the old attitudes were being stretched extremely thin in Jordan. Already the Hemingway style, which had once been not merely a certain choice and arrangement of words but the verbalization of a distinct metaphysical view of experience, showed signs of hardening into a stance. The conviction was beginning to drain out of it, and it was obvious that Jordan, in those rather maudlin moments of introspection, was struggling hard to keep his old attitudes intact.

But one also saw that this very feature of the novel, this element of ideological strain, helped to provide it with its considerable dramatic tension. There was the conflict, never finally resolved, between Jordan's World War I negativism, the rather effete *Weltschmerz* (5) of Jake Barnes and Frederic Henry, and the requirement imposed by his situation that he be positive and idealistic in his beliefs. Jordan had continually to persuade himself that he believed in the Loyalist cause, just as he had to persuade himself that he believed in the war and, with less success, in 'Life, Liberty, and the Pursuit of Happiness.' (6)

Then there were the other sources of dramatic tension: the conflict between the desires of love and the demands of duty; the difficulties Jordan encountered in trying to persuade the guerrillas that they should help him perform a mission in which he himself could not entirely believe; the poignancy of all emotions in the face of danger and the threat of death. There was all that Jordan stood to lose by the action of blowing the bridge. There were Maria and his possible future with her. There were all the experiences of life he had always enjoyed and wished to be able to enjoy again. These elements helped to convert what was in some ways a too heavily melodramatic novel into a work that had some real artistic complexity and truth.

But the situation of Thomas Hudson is very different, and the difference helps to account for what is most wrong with the new novel. Hudson is primarily the product of his past losses, sorrows, and mistakes. He has already lived a long life, and he has been much damaged in the process. No longer positively committed to the early Hemingway values, he yet retains the early skepticism which in him is fast souring into hopelessness. The simple fact is that, unlike his predecessors, he no longer believes in life and no longer enjoys life. By the time he is faced with his own certain death, he is carrying nothing but grief over the death of his three sons, the failure of his marriages, and all the emotions he is no longer able to feel. Nothing motivates him to take action except a vague stubborn sense of duty. He does not believe in this war or in any wars, and the idea of Life, Liberty, and the Pursuit of Happiness has become for him a sad joke indeed. Consequently, Hudson confronts his death like an automaton. He has gone through the motions and put on a good show, but he has had nothing to lose from the start. Hence, his actions have had no meaning. When he dies, he will be ready to die, not for the cause, not in order to save the girl he loves, but because he is tired to death of life. There is sadness in this but no real tragedy, because there is no sense of missed possibility, no conceivable alternative to dying.

It is evident that as he grew older Hemingway came to identify himself more and more explicitly with his fictional heroes and to draw increasingly on his own emotions and experiences in the creation of his heroes. Jake Barnes and Frederic Henry were essentially fantasy projections of what in some secret part of himself Hemingway wished he might be like. But Thomas Hudson and Colonel Cantwell of 'Across the River and into the Trees' are realistic projections of the tired, ailing, and disillusioned man he had by then actually become. And as the distance narrowed between himself and his heroes, his writing lost a crucial dimension. He began to try to *live out* his fantasies instead of projecting them in his fiction. His fiction became devitalized because the real force of his creativity was being expended in living the experience he imagined. It is even conceivable that in the end Hemingway succumbed to the limitations of the philosophy he had for years been developing in his work and endeavoring more and more to practice in his life. But that philosophy was tenable only for a young and healthy man who could afford to be cynical since his hold on life was vigorous, and he could never really believe in the possibility of his own death. Thus, when because of age and failing health, Hemingway could no longer do the things that made you feel good afterwards, when the eyesight began to go and the legs went bad, and the condition of the liver would not allow you to drink, and it was no longer fun to hunt or fish or make love, then the limitations of that philosophy became intolerable. By then, however, there was no turning back. There was no way of building another more durable or complex set of values. Hemingway had succeeded in becoming his heroes, and finally he was beginning to die with them.

But art, when everything else failed, was always there. In the past there had always been art, the one dependable source of new hope and self-renewal. The world could collapse and it would not matter so long as you wrote carefully and well and tried always to write an absolutely true book. When he went down into the basement of his house that summer morning and selected the weapon that would end his life, Hemingway evidently forgot about art. It is a pity, because if art had saved him in the past, there was still a chance it might save him once again. There was, in fact, an excellent chance. For, in spite of its defects, the best parts of 'Islands in the Stream' make clear that he had in his last years enough talent left to serve art successfully. If he had been able to recognize this and believe in it, he might have put the shotgun away and gone back upstairs to bed. But all he could believe in was the black emptiness and the pain. Besides, in that moment Hemingway had arrived at the kind of despair he had spent his whole life in flight from, the kind he could no longer evade through the killing of big game in Africa or by writing about the death of his heroes in his books. All the heroes were dead now. There was only himself.

Notes

1 See Philip Young and Charles Mann, 'The Hemingway Manuscripts' (1969). Many of these manuscripts are now in the John F. Kennedy Library.

2 Baker,'Ernest Hemingway,' 538. Grau-du-roi is on the Mediterranean coast, southeast of Montpellier.

3 Ernest Hemingway, A Visit with Hemingway: A Situation Report, 'Look,' 20 (4 September 1956), 4-5.

4 A gossip columnist.

5 World-weariness.
6 Thomas Jefferson, Declaration of Independence (1776).

116. JOSEPH EPSTEIN, 'WASHINGTON POST BOOK WORLD'

11 October 1970, 1, 3

Joseph Epstein (b. 1937), American critic and editor of the 'American Scholar,' is the author of 'Divorced in America' (1974) and 'Familiar Territory' (1979).

Ernest Hemingway was the first of the American writers we came to know too well. In twentieth-century America he practically invented the role of the novelist as celebrity, and in this regard he was most truly Papa, the daddy of a great many novelists to come. During the last twenty or so years of his life Hemingway's celebrity most closely approximated that of a movie star, with consequences that were mixed at best. One lingering result is that today, more than nine years after his death, the experience of reading him is akin to watching a favorite actor - Humphrey Bogart, say, or Gary Cooper - on the late show. As with Bogart and Cooper, two highly stylized actors, so with Hemingway, a highly stylized writer, one doesn't really expect any surprises but instead looks for the old solid performance, anticipates the same marvelous moves that first captivated us so many years ago.

In 'Islands in the Stream' one finds very few surprises but most of the old Hemingway moves intact. Although this ample, somewhat rambling, posthumously published novel offers no radical departures from the body of Hemingway's work, its appearance, nonetheless, is salutary for his reputation. Since his death by suicide, the critical line on Ernest Hemingway has been drawn extremely taut: so taut, indeed, as to constitute a noose, leaving his literary repute dangling from the gallows of contemporary criticism. Briefly, the current critical line on Hemingway has reduced him to being the author of one good novel ('The Sun Also Rises'), a handful of excellent stories, and the originator of a once elegantly simple prose style that over the years dried up and flaked off in self-parody. Such are the sweeping swings of critical opinion that in less than a decade Hemingway's reputation appears to have gone from that of a major (if not *the* major) American novelist to that of a writer of little consequence: from - to use a boxing analogy of the sort he was so fond of - the heavyweight champ to just another bum.

The swing from champ to bum can partly be explained by the manner of Hemingway's death and the curious twists his literary fate has taken since that sad event. The first of Hemingway's posthumously published books was 'A Moveable Feast,' his memoir of Paris and the expatriate community of the 1920s. Very much a mixed bag of a book, it has some beautifully lyrical moments but many more low viciously mean ones, as Hemingway used his memoir to strike out against old friends, chief among them F. Scott Fitzgerald and Ford Madox Ford. Whatever else one might care to say about it, it is a book that left a bad taste in the mouth. Next came Carlos Baker's full-blown biography, 'Ernest Hemingway: A Life Story,' a friendly enough work but a badly misguided one. Disdaining treatment of any connection between Hemingway's life and his work while at the same time offering insight into the life itself, Baker retreated into factuality and produced a book that made his subject seem a tedious if not hollow figure.

But more damaging than anything in print was the way Hemingway died. It is not difficult to understand why his family at first attempted to hide the fact that he had committed suicide. In tripping the triggers of that double-barreled Boss shotgun on the morning of August 1, 1961, (2) Hemingway accomplished an act that succeeded not only in demolishing himself but one that threatened to demolish his work as well. Other writers - Hart Crane, for example - have taken their own lives, and the act seems only to have authenticated their pain and enhanced the stature of their work. Not Hemingway. If anything, taking his own life seemed to throw into doubt, if not utterly to disqualify, almost every word he had ever written. It made it appear that Hemingway, one of whose favorite mottoes was *il faut (d'abord) durer* - 'first of all, endure' - a writer who in so many novels and stories had stressed physical courage as the crowning virtue above all others, could not, when it came to the crunch, himself take punishment. As the shotgun went off it was as if all those bullfighters, big-game hunters, fishermen, ambulance drivers, and soldiers were blown to smithereens. Not merely Ernest Hemingway but the Hemingway hero seemed to die that morning in Ketchum, Idaho.

More than any other modern American writer, Hemingway illustrates the hazards of personality in literature - the hazards, that is, of the writer interposing himself between his books and their audience. While he lived, he was his own best press agent: since his death, this same press agentry has been the principal obstacle in the way of his books getting a fair reading. Theoretically, nothing about a writer's personal life ought to affect the way one reads his work: in point of fact, almost everything one knows about a writer affects one's reading of him. It was Hemingway himself who sedulously encouraged the close identification between his own life and that of his fictional characters. A writer can probably do his work no greater disservice. While fashions in writers' personalities change - Hemingway's emphasis on his own excessive virility today seems merely embarrassing - good writing remains good writing. Thus Hemingway's personality, which once added an extra luster to his writing, has in recent years threatened to obliterate it.

But once Hemingway's personality is set aside, what becomes clear is that he was neither so great a writer as he pretended nor so inconsequential a writer as the current critical revaluation of his work would have him. This fact emerges from 'Islands in the Stream,' the first of Hemingway's fiction to be published since his death. What is so useful about the novel's appearance is that it allows us to gauge afresh his achievement and his faults - and in a way that rereading his earlier books, which have all been filmed, discussed, and 'explicated' half to death, no longer allows. In all fairness, it should be pointed out that 'Islands in the Stream' is not an altogether 'completed' novel: it was originally worked at during the late 1940s and early 1950s, and had Hemingway lived long enough he may well have taken it out of his bank vault, where he used to place all his manuscripts to age and mellow before returning to polish or otherwise rework them for publication. Yet as it stands the novel contains all of Hemingway's strengths and weaknesses - his worst, which can be terrible, and his very best, which can be no less than wonderful.

'Islands in the Stream' is a novel of three parts - the first magnificently executed, the second merely interesting, and the third quite trashy. (According to Baker, a fourth was initially planned, but it evolved independently of the others and was published separately as 'The Old Man and the Sea.') Its hero is one Thomas Hudson, a painter who, in the novel's first section, is living on the island of Bimini. Although he is successful in his work, Hudson's life has otherwise been a fairly complete disaster. He has, we learn early on, run through two marriages which produced three sons. His best days were the days of his first marriage when he was a happily struggling painter in the Paris of the 1920s, and these are already well behind him. 'What he cared about was painting and his children and he was still in love with the first woman he had been in love with.' On Bimini Hudson lives a carefully ordered life, but it is an order made possible only by the strongest self-discipline:

> He had trained himself not to quarrel with women anymore and he had learned how not to get married. These two things had been nearly as difficult to learn as how to paint in a steady and well ordered way. But he had learned them and he hoped he had learned them permanently.

This is a novel about human loss, one in which a man's armor against the world is stripped away leaving him alone and exposed. The middle-aged Hudson has already suffered loss before the action of the novel begins: apart from his work and his three sons, who do not live with him, he lives in the main off the dry bread of nostalgia, which, like his liquor, he takes in very careful rations. It is said of Hudson by other characters in the novel that he has 'inner resources,' but Hudson himself seems to know how fragile these resources are, and how, should they ever be shattered, the chaos would rush in to flood his life.

Bimini, the first section of 'Islands in the Stream,' has to do with the visit of Hudson's three sons to the island for their summer vacation with their father. Detached from the remainder of the novel, Bimini would be one of the best longish short stories Hemingway wrote, standing alongside The Short Happy Life of Francis Macomber and The Snows of Kilimanjaro. It has, to be sure, some of the traditional Hemingway faults: the rather too easy division of the world into good guys and bastards, the rampant use of the word 'fine' in lieu of description for any thing or person the author approves of, occasionally stilted dialogue, etc. But so clean and clear and powerful is the rest that these minor points come to matter very little. The quality of insight, which is used sparingly to begin with, is high and the description of land and seascape can be dazzling - the natural world is most truly Hemingway's real element, and his is perhaps the only significant modern body of modern fiction that does not depend upon an urban setting. On a sheerly technical level, he has never been better than he is in long stretches of Bimini. There is a scene in which Hudson's second son puts up a six-and-a-half-hour battle with a giant fish that, in perhaps one-twentieth of the space, shows up 'The Old Man and the Sea' for the pseudo-Biblical second-rate goods that that novel is.

But the lyrical beauty of 'Bimini' is shattered, and Hudson's controlled life with it, when at the end of this section of the novel he learns that his two younger sons, as well as their mother, have been killed in a motor accident in Europe. On the boat that Hudson takes across the Atlantic to attend their funeral there is a scene of a few brief pages depicting Hudson's sorrow that is unsurpassed for a description of this flat almost literally unspeakable emotional state. Hemingway, moreover, captures it at the level of detail - '(Hudson) sat in the deep comfortable chair and drank his drink and learned that you cannot read "The New Yorker" when people that you love have just died' - which is perhaps the only true level on which it can be approached. In other of his novels Hemingway has created heroes who are courageous, admirable, even tragic, but Thomas Hudson, at least in the Bimini section, is the first Hemingway hero who is likable.

Somewhere early in the Bimini section one of Hudson's sons remarks, as he is retelling the story of his early life in Paris, 'Make something happen, then, pappa,' and one wants to say the same to Hemingway throughout the last two parts of the novel, which are so very inferior to the first part. The second part takes place in Cuba some years after the first; its time is during World War II and Hudson has just been informed that his last remaining son, his oldest boy Tom, has been killed in the line of duty as a fighter pilot. There are some brilliant flashes every now and again, especially the accounts of Hudson's cats, but the whole is rather skeletal and appears not to have been worked over with the same care as the first part of 'Islands in the Stream.'

The third part of the novel, At Sea, is a simple disaster - a prolonged mistake. In it Hemingway has Hudson, in writing reminiscent of the shoddiest prose from 'To Have and Have Not,' chasing the crew of a wrecked German submarine around the Caribbean. It is characteristic of Hemingway at his most limited that he could conceive of no other way to end this beautifully begun novel than to put the by-now totally bereft Hudson through the paces of a somewhat empty exercise in physical courage.

As long as a writer is alive, it makes sense to judge him by his worst work, holding it up to him as an example of his cheating on the promise of his talent. When a writer is dead, however, it is his best work that ought to be remembered. And parts of 'Islands in the Stream' offer a solid reminder of how good Hemingway could be when he was working well. That he did not always work well he himself seemed to know better than anyone, despite the bravura pose he must have felt it necessary to put on. In his biography, Carlos Baker tells how once, during a blocked period near the end of his life, the tears streamed down Hemingway's face because he could not write and believed he would never be able to again. (2) He was a pro - and if not a great writer of the caliber of Stendhal, Turgenev, or Flaubert, an important and a damn good writer nevertheless.

Notes

1 Hemingway actually died on 2 July 1961.
2 Baker, 'Ernest Hemingway', 657.

117. JOHN UPDIKE, 'NEW STATESMAN'

80 (16 October 1970), 489

John Updike (b. 1932) is an American novelist. He has written 'Rabbit Run' (1960), 'The Centaur' (1963) and 'The Coup' (1978).

This book consists of material that the author during his lifetime did not see fit to publish; therefore it should not be held against him. That parts of it are good is entirely to his credit; that other parts are puerile and, in a pained way, aimless testifies to the odds against which Hemingway, in the last two decades of his life, brought anything to completion. It is, I think, to the discredit of his publishers that no introduction (the American edition does carry a very terse, uninformative note by Mary Hemingway) offers to describe from what stage of Hemingway's tormented later career 'Island in the Stream' was salvaged, or to estimate what its completed design might have been, or to confess what editorial choices were exercised in the preparation of this manuscript. Rather, a gallant wreck of a novel is paraded as the real thing, as if the public are such fools as to imagine a great writer's ghost is handing down books intact from Heaven.

So we are left to perform the elementary scholarly decencies ourselves. Carlos Baker's biography speaks of a trilogy about the sea that Hemingway, amid the distractions of Cuba, the cockfights and double daiquiris and proliferating hangers-on, carried forward with enthusiasm in late 1950 and early 1951. The third item of the trilogy, The Sea in Being, was separately, and triumphantly, published as 'The Old Man and the Sea'. The first part, The Sea when Young, seems to have been an abridgment of an earlier, disastrously long and bad novel called 'Garden of Eden'. The middle section, The Sea when Absent, has for its hero an American painter named Thomas Hudson and, in the form that Hemingway announced as 'finished' by Christmas of 1950, answers the description of the section entitled Cuba in the book Collins has published. The Island and the Stream (*sic*) had become, by mid-1951, the working title of the first section, presumably the revamped Garden of Eden. Baker says: 'It contains "wonderful parts" that he hated to cut out, but he was now clear that it must be reshaped to the style and tempo of the other three sections.' (1) Of the 'other three', one is the story of Santiago that would soon be a separate novel, one is the Cuba mentioned above, and the third is 'the sea-chase story', which, in Hemingway's opinion, was 'impregnable to criticism' and was almost published, in 'Cosmopolitan', in two instalments. In the book just published, this sea-chase is the third section, At Sea, and the first section, whose adjusted title does for the whole, is entitled Bimini.

What we have, then, is a trio of large fragments, crudely unified by a Caribbean setting and the nominal presence of Thomas Hudson. Bimini is a collection of episodes that show only a groping acquaintance with one another; Cuba is a lively but meandering excursion in local colour that, when the painter's first wife materialises, weirdly veers into a dark and private region; and At Sea is an adventure story of almost slick intensity. Hudson, if taken sequentially, does not grow but dwindles, from an affectionate and baffled father and artist into a rather too expertly raffish waterfront character into a bleak manhunter, a comic-book superhuman holding unlooked-for bubbles of stoic meditation and personal sorrow. Some conscious attempt is made to interlock the characterisations - the manhunter remembers that he is a painter, and gives us some hard-edged seascapes to prove it; the bar clown intermittently recalls that he is drowning his grief at the death of a son - but the real congruence of these masks is involuntary: all fit the face of Ernest Hemingway.

Whereas an achieved novel, however autobiographical, dissolves the author and directs our attention beyond him, 'Islands in the Stream', even where most effective, inspires us with a worried concern for the celebrity who wrote it. His famous drinking, his methodical artistic devotion, his dawn awakenings, his women, his cats, even his mail (what painter gets anything like a writer's burdensome, fascinating mail?) are all there, mixed with less easily publicised strains, dark currents that welled into headlines with his last madness and shocking suicide. The need to prove himself drives Thomas Hudson implacably toward violence and death. His enemy, pain, becomes an object of infatuation. Even in the first, most lyric passages, when he is visited on Bimini by his three sons, what lives for the father-narrator are scenes of savagery - the machine-gunning of a shark, a boy's day-long wrestle with a monstrous swordfish, the child, bent double, bleeding in hands and feet, held fast to the fighting chair by the surrounding men, his guardians, so he can experience 'love':

> 'Well,' David said with his eyes tight shut. 'In the worst parts, when I was the tiredest I couldn't tell which was him and which was me.'
>
> 'I understand,' Roger said.
>
> 'Then I began to love him more than anything on earth.'

As if to insulate his fatherhood from his frightful passion for violence, Hemingway creates in this section (never to reappear) another alter ego, a brawling, brooding writer named Roger Davis, and thrusts upon him a gratuitously brutal fistfight, as well as a number of reckless and self-destructive traits that the placid morning painter Thomas Hudson has supposedly outgrown. But in 'Cuba', Hyde has been reunited with Jekyll, and Hudson - always a fond describer of guns, and a lover of blood sports - seems right at home among drinking companions who cheerfully remark, of prostitutes who gave imperfect service, 'We ought to have poured gasoline on them and set them on fire.' Later, Hudson himself, asked by his wife if their only son is dead, answers with the amazing monosyllable, 'Sure.' The final episode, At Sea, sees Hudson's fulfilment as a killer, and Hemingway's as a master of the casually cruel touch. A large 'obscenely white' crab offends Hudson: 'the man shot him between his eyes and the crab disintegrated.' Removing a bullet from a sun-dried corpse is 'like cutting into a pie'. A grenade eliminates a wounded German: 'How is the Kraut in the bow?' 'He's a mess.' Truly Hudson tells himself, 'The horrors were what you won in the big crap game that they run.' Well, the author is helping run this crap game, and it takes a little disintegration to keep him happy; unable to decide which of the hero's three boys to kill, he kills them all, two in one section and the third, with comic rigidity, in the next.

Hemingway of course did not invent the world, nor pain, mutilation, and death. In his earlier work his harsh obsessions seem honorable and necessary; an entire generation of American men learned to speak in the accents of Hemingway's stoicism. But here, the tension of art has been snapped and the line between sensitive vision and psychopathy has been crossed. The 'sea-chase story' is in many ways brilliant, but it has the falsity of the episode in Hemingway's real life upon which it was based. In the early days of World War II, he persuaded his friends in the Havana Embassy to let him equip his private fishing launch the 'Pilar' as a Q-boat, with bazookas, grenades, bombs, and machine guns. His dream was to lure a Nazi submarine close enough to toss a bomb down the hatch. He staffed the 'Pilar' with cronies and, fruitlessly, but displaying much real courage and stamina, cruised the Cuban coast. Everything in At Sea is true, except the encounter with Germans and the imperatives of the mission, which was not demanded from above but invented and propelled from within. Such bravery is not grace under pressure but pressure forced in the hope of inducing Grace.

And even love becomes a species of cruelty, which divides women into whores and bitches on the one hand and on the other a single icy-perfect adored. Some American reviewers have complained that the first wife is unreal; to me she has that hard reality of a movie star (which in the book she is), a star on the screen, with 'the magic rolling line of the hair that was the same silvery ripe-wheat colour as always'. But it is an easy transition from the image of this loved and lost woman, this enforcer of proud loneliness, to the cool grey pistols Hudson sleeps with:

> 'How long have you been my girl?' he said to the pistol. 'Don't answer,' he said to the pistol. 'Lie there good and I will see you kill something better than land crabs when the time comes.'

Love and death: fused complements in Hemingway's universe. Yet he never formulated the laws that bind them, never achieved the step of irony away from himself. He tried; this book opens in a mood of tonic breadth and humour, and closes with a sharp beatific vision of himself, Hudson, dying and beloved:

> 'I think I understand, Willie,' he said.
> 'Oh shit,' Willie said. 'You never understand anybody that loves you.'

The new generations, my impression is, want to abolish both war and love, not love as a physical act but love as a religion, a creed to help us suffer better. The sacred necessity of suffering no longer seems sacred or necessary, and Hemingway speaks across the Sixties as strangely as a medieval saint; I suspect few readers younger than myself could believe, from this sad broken testament, how we *did* love Hemingway and, after pity feels merely impudent, love him still.

Note

1 Baker, 'Ernest Hemingway', 583.

118. IRVING HOWE, 'HARPER'S'

241 (October 1970), 120-5

The first four paragraphs of this long review, which discuss Fellini's portrayal in his film '8½' of a director suffering a crisis of work, have been omitted.

I

It is a similar difficulty [a creative crisis] that afflicts Ernest Hemingway's posthumous novel, 'Islands in the Stream,' a very strange book full of both pleasing and disastrous things. Its very title suggests an awareness on Hemingway's part that he could manage, by now, only ill-connected portions of a narrative - at most, separate panels of representation - and that he must therefore fall back on the plea that the chaos of existence provides a rationale for his inability to achieve a unified work of art.

'Islands in the Stream' was apparently composed during the 1950s, toward the end of Hemingway's life and soon after the critical failure of his extremely poor novel, 'Across the River and into the Trees.' Always thin-skinned, Hemingway had been badly hurt by the rather brutal attacks that book had called out. His troubles, however, went much deeper. At the very peak of his reputation, when he was steadily feeding the public legend of Hemingway the Wise and Aging Swashbuckler ('Papa' to all those publicity-keen sons and daughters), he experienced a loss of confidence, fearing that his powers as a writer and perhaps as a man were waning. Nor could he comfort himself with the praise of cronies, journalists, and women whom he needed about him but did not finally respect. The fear that seems to have consumed him was of a rapid creative disintegration, that 'crack-up' his old friend Scott Fitzgerald had experienced. It was as if all the terrors he had struggled with in his youthful work and so brilliantly objectified through the discipline of art, had now come back to torment his later years. Late middle age seems peculiarly destined for the re-enactment of adolescent emotions, both those of self-love and those of self-contempt.

Hemingway, according to his biographer Carlos Baker, worked during these years in fits and starts, beginning and then putting aside several manuscripts, apparently dissatisfied with all of them. We can now see why. One of these manuscripts has been carved into a book by his last wife, Mary, and though it contains some beautiful things - we are, after all, talking about a master - 'Islands in the Stream' isn't going to add much to Hemingway's reputation.

The book centers on a middle-aged painter, Thomas Hudson, who lives wifeless in a beautiful house in Bimini. He has, of course, had many wives but none has remained with him, and now he looks forward to a visit from his young sons. Extremely famous, he yet has trouble sleeping at night, for he is haunted by memories of bad marriages and fears that he is losing his grip as an artist. In short, our old friend and hero, Ernest Hemingway in all-too-transparent disguise.

Almost everything wrong with the book follows from this emotional overlap between author and protagonist. Perhaps because artists are more prone to self-scrutiny than Army officers, Hudson doesn't quite come off as the bumptious loudmouth that Colonel Cantwell does in 'Across the River'; but he is still hard to take, at least with the narcissistic fondness that Hemingway proposes. Hudson does, it is true, respect the life of complex consciousness, even if he knows little about it, and in his middle-aged shakiness he seems closer to Hemingway himself than does anyone in his other novels. But simply as a character, he is a grossly self-indulgent and pompous fellow. His crippling limitation is that he deeply reflects his creator yet isn't a deeply created figure. One looks through him, toward the Hemingway psyche, but not into him, as a man interesting in his own right. His bouts of pettishness and generosity; his fumbling realization that something is missing in his life, perhaps what the race calls wisdom; his spasms of self-pity followed by a climactic test of courage - all this leads one not to a self-contained imaginary world but to a series of illicit speculations. First, to an uneasy curiosity about Hemingway's own life; then, to troubling echoes of his earlier books; and finally, to wondering once again about the boyishness of aging American men. For the cult of manliness which dominates this book, though with much less self-assurance than in his earlier books, is finally a boy's idea. You need only compare Hudson-Hemingway with the middle-aged characters of the European masters in order to be convinced that both as an individual figure, insofar as he is one, and as a national type he is callow, inexperienced, and unripe. Callow, inexperienced, and unripe despite his plethora of wives, perhaps because of them. That now and again Hemingway recognizes as much is extremely touching, a sign that he wants to break past those limitations of mind and feeling that marked even his most brilliant work and became disastrous later on.

The book moves - it doesn't move very much - on two planes: the external action, often interesting for pages at a time, and the inner life of Hudson, mostly tiresome. Hemingway's evident desire to probe his own loss of nerve and thereby get away from his encrusted *persona* arouses sympathy and respect; but most of the time his vanity is too overpowering for his desire to be realized and we are brought back to the kid-stuff bravado, the tight-lipped posturing, the endless narcissism of his later books. A small yet telling example: in his years of fame Hudson develops a sort of feudal mentality as all too innocently he keeps telling us about the endless loyalty of his retainers. How they all love him, how they all care for him, this great warrior-artist of many loves! There is even a long section about a cat alleged to be so devoted to Hudson that the poor creature, in violation of all known laws of cathood, trembles with nervous anxiety at the prospect of seeing master leave the house. The effect of all this is very sad and a little ugly, somewhat like that of an aging woman who keeps telling you how 'devoted' her old lovers still are.

II

In Bimini, the first part of 'Islands in the Stream,' we see Hudson in his house, a troubled man who 'had exorcised guilt with work insofar as he could' and who now recognizes he has been 'undisciplined, selfish, and ruthless.' He gets mixed up in a local brawl in which his friend Roger Davis, a failing popular writer who can be taken as a double of Hemingway's inferior side, beats up some rich visitors. What strikes one, in reading these flaccid and rather ugly pages, is how painful it is that the great master of narrative pacing, the Hemingway who could make tightness of phrase into a moral virtue, should now write so slackly, as if he must hang on to an incident for pages of chatter simply because he doesn't quite know what to do next. There follows, nevertheless, a quite charming section in which Hudson's three sons come to visit, and here the talk is bright, the feeling pure, and the action vibrant. But then comes a spoiling visit by a lovely named Audrey Bruce - for that's what women do, they *spoil* the good times of men - and after that, the terrible news that that two of Hudson's sons have been killed in an accident in Europe. Shaken but fighting for control, Hudson goes off to Europe. The writing as a whole reminds one of a phrase Hudson uses in regard to his friend Davis: 'Some sort of a sureness that he's lost.'

Part II, a complete disaster, is set in Cuba during the early years of World War II, with a cloak-and-dagger mystification that could thrill five-year-olds, for Hudson is now commander of a small boat chasing German submarines (based on Hemingway's own work in the Caribbean at this very time). There is a long, dragging bar conversation between Hudson and some cronies which centers on a lady with large hips and heart of gold named Honest Lil. Suddenly an unexpected appearance is made by Hudson's first wife, a still glamorous actress on a mission to entertain the troops. Though Hudson has learned about the death of his oldest son in the European war, he grants himself a few hours of precious love with the boy's mother who, we are steadily reminded, is his own true love. At the end Hudson tells himself, 'Get it straight. Your boy you lose. Love you lose. Honour has been gone for a long time. Duty you do.' The sad thing about Hemingway in his years of decline is that precisely when he wants to strike a note of introspection he starts most to swagger.

Part III, At Sea, constitutes a notable recovery. It is a tense and exciting story in which Hudson, firm beyond grief, commands his boat of American irregulars searching for some stranded U-boat sailors. Hudson is now off liquor, pretty much; free from self-concern, mostly; and devoted to the job at hand, which is to hunt down the Germans without glorifying - one is grateful for this touch - the ugliness of killing. These pages I found myself reading with a happy surrender to primitive suspense, as well as with pleasure at seeing Hemingway once again in command of his material. Yet, gripping as this part is in its steady accumulation of narrative tension, it isn't the kind of writing a great writer can ever content himself with. Certainly it isn't what a Kipling or a Conrad would have contented himself with, though a Stevenson might have. And to his everlasting credit Hemingway knows this. The chase of the German sailors ends in a gun battle; Hudson's crew wins out, though he himself, now a stoical but recovered warrior, is fatally wounded. The more obvious openings to heroics Hemingway resists here, and the grubby little shoot-out at the end of the book yields no unambiguous tribute to any virtue, not even 'duty.' Because he knows that he must deepen his adventure through an infusion of consciousness, because he sees that no story of battle can ever achieve in its own right the kind of significance a truly ambitious writer aims for, Hemingway keeps returning to the inner life of Hudson. Alas; it is like moving from shiny pebbles to thick mud.

The book does not move, there is no commanding idea - and not the kind of billboard-idea that Fellini's intellectual wants but the kind of emotionally resonant and personal idea that Fellini's director looks for. Nor is the problem of a kind certain academic or formalistic critics might stress: that from Part to Part new sets of characters are introduced and the old ones left to flounder, or that no effort is made dramatically to link the materials of each Part. The problem goes deeper and has to do with perceptions less easy to pin down - with the kind of firm and disciplined vision of life which, for example, pervades every chapter of 'The Sun Also Rises' or 'The Great Gatsby.' This is what Hemingway lost, this is what he struggled to recover, and this is what he did not find.

III

In his early writing Hemingway had very quickly come to

his one abiding subject: panic at the thought of psychic disintegration and then those kinds of inner struggle by which men can find momentary places of survival. He was not so foolish as to suppose that fear can finally be overcome; all his best work is concerned with improvising a truce in our hopeless encounter with fear. But he touched upon something that went beyond this, something that emerged in his fiction as the most personal kind of experience yet also showed the imprint of twentieth-century history. His great subject was the panic that follows upon the dissolution of nihilism into the bloodstream of modern consciousness, the panic that finds unbearable the thought of the next minute and its succession by the minute after that. We all know this experience even if, unlike Jake Barnes in 'The Sun Also Rises,' we do find it possible to sleep at night; we know it because it is part of modern life and because Hemingway drove it into our awareness once and for all.

He touched upon the quick of our anxieties, and for the moment of his excellence stood ready to face whatever he saw. The compulsive stylization of his prose was both barrier and principle of contrast to that shapelessness which is panic by definition. Against the terror of the external, the only protection Hemingway could establish through his work, and his characters in their lives, was the principle of stylization. Stylization implies a self-consciousness and then a stiffening of style, its transformation into a code or ritual of mannerism - which means, I think, to forgo the greatest of all styles, the style of transparency. Still, in extreme situations this stylization could be a delicate impediment to chaos, a papery shield between the self and everything beyond it. Stylization became the pomp of the vulnerable, infinitely touching in 'The Sun Also Rises,' supremely tragic in A Clean, Well-Lighted Place.

It is a defense that, by its very nature, cannot be long maintained, and that is perhaps one reason Hemingway worked best in short forms. His stories, and even his one great novel, bear more than a casual resemblance to lyric poems. Conceivably he might have persisted in using such forms and have kept turning out fine if increasingly predictable short fictions. But despite Faulkner's notorious and unjustified slur, Hemingway did take risks. (1) He took the risk of moving beyond the relative safety of his stylization and of trying not merely for the large novel as a form but also for what the large novel implies: a commanding idea or vision about man's place in society.

In 'Islands in the Stream' you can see Hemingway struggling desperately with both his need for some concluding wisdom - what, at the end of our journey, do we take the human enterprise to be? - and his habitual tough-guy swagger in all its sodden mindlessness. I say Hemingway struggled desperately, yet on the face of it this book shows few signs of struggle: the writing is usually smooth and there is little of the *gaucherie* (2) of 'Across the River.' Here, for example, is the opening paragraph of At Sea:

> There was a long white beach with coconut palms behind it. The reef lay across the entrance to the harbor and the heavy east wind made the sea break on it so that the entrance was easy to see once you had opened it up. There was no one on the beach and the sand was so white that it hurt his eyes to look at it.

This is accomplished prose, and its syntax and rhythm are calculated to remind us of Hemingway at his best. That, I fear, is just the point. One has the impression in reading such passages of a writer caressing the phrases in his hand, the way a gambler who has had a run of bad luck will caress the dice: yes, if I go through the old motions, carefully and slowly, I will recover those insinuating rhythms, those phrases of captivation I used to command. Once the virtuoso of rapidity, Hemingway now writes in a kind of slow motion, especially in the first two Parts, hoping to recapture, through the recollection of old ways, the old assurance of tone.

It is not enough, and he knows it. Some element is wanting, call it idea or vision or coherence, some word that could make the world of his imagining come whole again. Hemingway keeps struggling, Hudson hiding his bewilderment. Hemingway summons the old motions, Hudson slides into age. The conclusion seems to me a terrible one: an artist's, a man's, search for moral growth can disable his performance, crippling him with the knowledge of what he doesn't know.

Notes

1 See Harvey Breit, William Faulkner, 'The Writer Observed' (London, 1957), 282: 'I rated Hemingway last [of the five best contemporary American writers] because he stayed within what he knew. He did it fine, but he didn't try for the impossible.'
2 Awkwardness.

119. EDMUND WILSON, 'NEW YORKER'

46 (2 January 1971), 59-62

It is almost impossible to describe the new posthumous Hemingway book, 'Islands in the Stream,' from the point of view of what happens in it without making it seem preposterous. It gives us Hemingway as a concoctor of self-inflating fantasies at his most exhibitionistic. You have him in his Cuban residence, very thinly disguised as a painter, one Thomas Hudson, showing his sons how things ought to be done and how to behave like men (his younger brother Leicester has explained how Ernest like to instruct him); you have him in his favorite bars, where he can bully his hangers-on, subjecting them to his sarcasm and otherwise putting them down, and as captain of his own boat, maintaining a good-natured but effective discipline among a gallant crew that adores him. All this time, he is being brought drinks by his servants, by the waiters, or by the members of his crew. One of the last, who drinks too much, is wisely and firmly checked, and in a moment of equally firm self-discipline Hudson makes the dramatic gesture of throwing 'high over the side' and letting 'the wind take it astern' a glass of 'gin and coconut water with Angostura and lime.' In his relations with other people he is always on top, always the acknowledged 'champion' that Hemingway aspired to be in his writing when he boasted that he was 'trying to knock Mr. Shakespeare on his ——.' (I am sorry, in the interests of decorum, to be obliged to leave blanks in my quotations from Hemingway.) The most outrageous departure from plausibility, which is also the weakest of the episodes, occurs when Hudson's first wife, long divorced and now a singer entertaining the troops, makes a point of looking Hudson up and eagerly goes to bed with him. This woman is not in any way recognizable as Hemingway's first wife but all too recognizable as a well-known friend of Hemingway's. (1) But why, one asks, if these two characters in the novel can enjoy such passionate love, did they ever separate? They are agreed not to talk about the past; they acknowledge that they were both to blame. But why can they not be reunited? Nothing is ever explained.

It has always surprised me that the more or less imaginary Hemingway, the myth about himself that he managed to create by the self-dramatization of his extensive publicity and, in his fiction, by the exploits of some of his heroes, should have imposed on the public to the extent it did. The grumbling or bristling reaction on the part of certain reviewers to Mr. Carlos Baker's biography, which took account of the petty and cruel and ridiculous aspects of his subject, makes it plain that the ideal Hemingway was a living reality to many of his admirers. It is true that he was capable of courage, that he was capable of doing certain things very well. But actually, from the beginning, it was not merely the exploits of his heroes, athletic or sporting or military, that made his best stories compelling; it was the strain they conveyed of men on the edge of going to pieces, who are just hanging on by their teeth and just managing to maintain their sanity, or of men who know they are doomed to inexorable defeat or death. The real heroism of these characters is their fortitude against such ordeals or the honor they manage to salvage from ignominy, humiliation. It is this kind of theme in Hemingway that makes his stories exciting and stimulating. Will the hero last? How long will he last?

Now, with all its preposterous elements, this imperfect work, 'Islands in the Stream,' makes one feel the intensity of a crucial game played against invincible odds as one has not quite been able to do in connection with any of his last three finished novels - 'For Whom the Bell Tolls,' 'Across the River and into the Trees,' 'The Old Man and the Sea.' It has never been pulled tight or polished, as Hemingway would undoubtedly have done, for his sense of form was exacting. Everything goes on too long, even the most effective episodes: the boy's struggle with the monstrous swordfish - which he loses; the hunt for the Germans among the reefs at the time of the Second War - which results in Hudson's being shot by them. The barroom conversations are allowed to run on to a length that has no real point and in the course of which our interest slackens. These would all - if Hemingway had taken time to treat them with his characteristic technique - have surely been condensed to far fewer pages. That he knew well how much work there was still to be done is made clear by Mr. Baker's quotations from his letters to Charles Scribner. 'The Old Man and the Sea' and 'For Whom the Bell Tolls' are more satisfactory from the point of view of form, yet they seem to me a good deal less interesting than 'Islands in the Stream.'

They are less interesting because only here is Hemingway making an effort to deal candidly with the discords of his own personality - his fears, which he has tried to suppress, his mistakes, which he has tried to justify, the pangs of bad conscience, which he has brazened out. This effort is not entirely successful; hence, I imagine, his putting the manuscript away. You are never allowed to know exactly what has happened in Thomas Hudson's past. He is always admonishing himself that he must not allow himself to think about it, so in order to avoid this he orders a drink. The reader clearly sees the drink but not the memory that is being stifled. One is made to feel acutely, however, an ever-present moral malaise. The painful gnawing, amid jolly scenes of drinking, in affluence and beautiful weather, is perhaps more insistently here made to ache than in any of Hemingway's other books since 'The Sun Also Rises.' There is something more than needlings of conscience; there is that certainty of the imminent death that has threatened in so much of his writing. And the book is given special force and dignity by one's knowledge of the writer's suicide. He invents for his own family, as they figure in the story, deaths that did not actually occur. Two of Hudson's sons are killed in a motor accident, and a third is killed in the war, whereas in reality, though Hemingway's boys were involved in a motor accident, they were not fatally injured, and one who had served in the war and disappeared for a time turned out to have been only taken prisoner. Hemingway himself was not shot by a German, like his hero in 'Islands in the Stream.' He did not even come to grips with the enemy- though he had formerly suffered injuries so frequent that they seem almost to have been self-inflicted - in his one-man campaign against submarines. He died in retirement, by his own hand. It was the dread, the pressure, the need for death, the looming shadow, no doubt, of the memory of his father's suicide, that drove him so determinedly to meet it.

This book contains some of the best of Hemingway's descriptions of nature: the waves breaking white and green on the reef off the coast of Cuba; the beauty of the morning on the deep water; the hermit crabs and land crabs and ghost crabs; a big barracuda stalking mullet; a heron flying with his white wings over the green water; the ibis and flamingoes and spoonbills, the last of these beautiful with the sharp rose of their color; the mosquitoes in clouds from the marshes; the water that curled and blew under the lash of the wind; the sculpture that the wind and sand had made of a piece of driftwood, gray and sanded and embedded in white, floury sand. But to bunch in this way together these phrases of the section called At Sea is to deprive them of the atmosphere of large space and free air and light, of the sun and rain on the water, in which the writer makes us see them, and to see them always in relation to the techniques of fishing and navigation.

Though the whole thing centers on Hudson and though Hudson is kept always in the foreground, there is a certain amount of characterization of his family and friends and retinue - especially in the case of the boys, with whom Hemingway can come closest to identifying himself. The ability to characterize with any real insight has never been Hemingway's gift. Of the surface of personalities he has always been very observant, and of voices and ways of talking he is a most successful mimic. In his book of reminiscences of Paris, he reproduces for one who has known them the hoarse British gasps of Ford Madox Ford, the exasperating nonsense of Scott Fitzgerald so faithfully that one can hear them speaking, and one can also hear the tones and turns of speech of persons one has never known. But one is made aware, particularly in 'A Moveable Feast,' whose characters are real people, how little their friend - or companion - could actually have known about them: what was going on in their minds, what they were aiming at, what they were up to. And his judgments were almost always disparaging. He wanted to make everyone else look ridiculous or morally reprehensible. It was only Ezra Pound who escaped - rather surprisingly, since Pound had once been useful to Hemingway, and it was usually to the people who had helped him or to whom he owed something in a literary way that he was afterward to make a point of being insulting. But in 'Islands in the Stream' he allows himself little scope for malignity. He is able to be fond of most of his characters, since they all respect and obey Thomas Hudson, are glad to be molded or guided by him. '"Tommy,"' says his second in command, when Hudson is dying, '"I love you, you son of a bitch, and don't you die." Thomas Hudson looked at him without moving his head. "Try and understand if it isn't too hard." ... "I think I understand, Willie," he said. "Oh —— " Willie said. "You never understand anybody that loves you."' This is sentimental and 'self-serving,' but it does show, perhaps, on Hemingway's part an attempt to take account of his non-comprehension of other people.

The mimicry of himself by Hemingway has also been mainly on the surface; the malaise itself has been kept there - sometimes, as in A Clean, Well-Lighted Place, without any indication of what it is that is troubling the character. We are not even, as in Big Two-Hearted River, told explicitly that there is any cause for disquiet, yet this idyll, which is simply an account of a solitary fishing expedition, is related to something in the background that is never even referred to, which makes the fisherman concentrate with special attention on every baiting of the hook, every catch, every cooking of the fish in the open air. That something, as Hemingway was later to explain, was the young man's experience of the war. Now, in 'Islands in the Stream,' the experiences that have been pushed down out of sight are continually rising into consciousness; but not even here, as I have already said, are we told exactly what they are. In order to keep them out of his consciousness, Thomas Hudson takes another drink or plunges on into his program of action. Yet in spite of this the mythical figure of Hemingway is constantly breaking down, becoming demoralized by the memory of past betrayals of women who have trusted and loved him, betrayals of his heroic idea of himself. The situation is made truly tragic by the fact that the mythical Hemingway did have a certain basis in reality. After all, he did not always fail or make a fool of himself, though he needed, I think, an audience, if of only one, to appreciate and applaud him. His triumphs were partly actual and were of a kind that, for his larger audience, seemed to satisfy two typical American ambitions: that of becoming an accomplished outdoorsman and that of making a great deal of money. What had been lost was a part of an ideal self that had partly been realized.

I do not agree with those who have thought it a disservice to Hemingway's memory to publish this uncompleted book. Nor do I agree with those who, possessed by the academic mania of exactly reproducing texts, declare that Mrs. Hemingway and the publisher should have printed the manuscript as Hemingway left it, without making the cuts she explains. The author is not to be charged with the defects of manuscripts which he did not choose to publish and for which he can now take no responsibility, nor his editors with making those works more coherent if the editing has been done with good judgment. I imagine that this book, in the long run, will appear to be more important than seems to be the case at present, and I believe that Mrs. Hemingway is to be encouraged to go on to publish further manuscripts.

Note

1 Probably Marlene Dietrich.

120. PAUL THEROUX, 'ENCOUNTER'

36 (February 1971), 62-6

Paul Theroux (b. 1941) is an American novelist and travel writer, and the author of 'Saint Jack' (1973), 'Picture Palace' (1978) and 'The Great Railway Bazaar' (1975).

Ernest Hemingway imagined himself, as all his admirers now do, a heavyweight, a literary hard puncher and even physically a formidable opponent. He valued the attributes that the American male (and the Karamojong warrior) (1) value. His biographer shares the attitude and the metaphor: 'He ... dealt, almost singlehanded, a permanent blow against the affected, the namby-pamby....' He took enormous pleasure in flooring a muscular Negro with his bare fists, and delivering a manuscript he could say, 'I'll defend the title again against all the good young new ones.' He spoke of the discipline needed for writing as similar to that for successful boxing; he was proud of his good health, doing exercises, running, swimming and rising early while he was engaged on a book; and he saw his writing career in terms of the ring: 'I started out very quiet and I beat Mr.Turgenev. Then I trained hard and I beat Mr. de Maupassant. I've fought two draws with Mr. Stendhal.' He had the humility to add, 'But nobody's going to get me in the ring with Mr. Tolstoy....' His line was that he could lick practically any man in the house.

He was a destroyer and so are many of his characters: even the gentle Santiago recalls a triumphant arm-wrestling match (with a muscular Negro); others of his characters are fighters, inclined towards pugilism. One sees the glamour: his destroyers come in pairs and all eyes are on them; it is one big man against another and implies competition, ultimately a winner and a loser. We are to admire the winner (Hemingway, not Turgenev; Santiago, not the Negro). But the very reverent biographer concedes bullying: 'Throughout the month of May, Ernest's behaviour was often that of a bully.' Professor Carlos Baker is referring to Hemingway ruining his friend's catch of a large marlin by firing a tommy-gun at some circling sharks which, maddened by the taste of their own spilt blood, devour most of the marlin. Later in that same month Hemingway beats up Joseph Knapp, a New York publisher. Both of these incidents, tidied up to make the gunner heroic and the fight with the rich intruder a justly-deserved victory, are retold in 'Islands in the Stream', with the *envoi*, (2) black calypso singers immortalising the fist-fight with a song as, in 1935, they 'celebrated Ernest's victory with an extemporaneous song about the "big slob" from Key West'.

The boxer recalls his famous matches, the novelist his novels; a boxer is bigger than any of his fights and though writing is hardly a competitive art, much less a sport, the novelist postured deliberately to be bigger than any of his novels. The question of 'style', a favourite boxing word, is fundamental to a discussion of Hemingway's work; not style as a literary value but style as a posture, emphasising the face, the voice, the stance. Hemingway blamed the bad reviews of 'Across the River and into the Trees' on his photograph that appeared on the dust jacket ('Makes me look like a cat-eating Zombie'); the voice is familiar ('You got very hungry when you did not eat enough in Paris...'); and the stance? Always the boxer's: 'Am trying to knock Mr. Shakespeare on his ass.'

The reputation is all, and counts for more than the writing. Asked who is the most popular American writer in the Soviet Union, the Russian journalist says, 'Papa.' The note of friendly intimacy is common; it is the man that matters. The American writer produces a good book and acquires a reputation. The reputation displaces the idea of literary quality: the idea of the author is much more important than the ideas in the work. Interesting, the number of academics who care so deeply about the man's adventures and leave the work unread, or see blasphemy in a low evaluation of it. Hemingway claimed to dislike academics, but those that flattered him were welcomed at his haunts and in his house; he yarned them, feeding them lines, took them on his boat, and wrote them candid letters. In the letter refusing Carlos Baker permission to write a biography, Hemingway mentions ('with almost bewildering frankness') how he practised *coitus interruptus* with his second wife. (The fact appears in Professor Baker's recent biography, 'Ernest Hemingway - A Life Story'.)

Since the aggressive narcissism of commerce and the vanity of money are the driving forces of reputation-making, the progress of the reputation is best described in the language of the stock-exchange. A writer appears on the market; he has considerable long-term upside potential; he gets a divorce and hits a slump, his plane crashes in jungle and this is a technical rally; he tumbles and bottoms out, he meets resistance at the buyer level, then rallies again and inflates and firms up and meets a negative critical flow, and so forth. This does not have much to do with writing, but Hemingway's reputation grew without much reference to his work, and in the years since his death, aided by the urgent whisperings of fact-finders and anecdotalists, it has rallied and consolidated sideways. Now a 'new' novel has been found; it was written twenty years ago and apparently abandoned by the author. It is technically his last novel and its publication is a triumph for those obsessed with the man.

The novel has no literary importance, but its personal candour is essential. This is of course the basest motive for reading; contemptuous of the art of fiction, the reader is interested in the book only in so far as it gives access to the author: 'This is just a story but Ernest Hemingway is writing it....' The satisfactions are finding out how Hemingway drank and handled a boat, and spoke, and made love, and treated his friends. These revelations are considered important, for once the reputation is made and the novel is a study rather than a pleasure (or a bore), the hero of the novel is its author. Fortunately for Hemingway his life began to be studied before he failed as a novelist, so it was never acceptable to say, 'This novel is bad.' The novels were aspects of the man, and the man's heroism was never questioned.

'Islands in the Stream' is divided into three parts. In 1951 Hemingway said that parts 2 and 3 were 'in shape to publish', but he did not publish them. The novel (to use the publisher's term; it is really nothing of the kind) is set in the Caribbean and seems originally to have been intended as a study of the sea. Previous titles of the sections were The Sea When Young, The Sea when Absent, and The Sea in Being, retitled in the present edition as Bimini, Cuba and At Sea. The sections are loosely linked by the common subject of the sea and by the main character, Thomas Hudson, who is 'in appearance, manner, and personal history ... clearly based on Ernest himself' (according to Professor Baker). There was a fourth section, and Thomas Hudson was not the hero of it. This was the story of an old man, Santiago, who caught a marlin and battled to save it; it was published (Hemingway had some reservations about its length) as 'The Old Man and the Sea'. Professor Baker reports that Hemingway was very enthusiastic about the unpublished parts of the book he was calling 'The Island and the Stream', but rather than publish it he turned from it and wrote 'A Moveable Feast', his last book, parts of which are prefigured in the reminiscences of Thomas Hudson. Hudson, in his youth, also lived with his wife and small child over a sawmill in Paris in the 1920s, and had a cat named F. Puss and liked the bicycle races and drank in cafés with James Joyce and Ezra Pound.

Here, perhaps, is the reason Hemingway never published 'Islands in the Stream'. It was autobiography - this is clear from the duplicated recollections in 'A Moveable Feast' - but he wanted it to read as fiction. He wrote it at an age when most novelists turn to autobiography, but rather than reveal the novel as that, he published the story of Santiago and spent the last three years of his life writing a straightforward reminiscence, to which he added ambiguously in the Preface, 'If the reader prefers, this book may be regarded as fiction....' It is hard to say whether he would have published the present novel, had he allowed himself to live a few years longer. This is crucial because a writer can only be held responsible for what he publishes himself and stands by; he can't be blamed for writing a bad book that he chose to leave in a bottom drawer.

Thomas Hudson is a painter. He has been divorced and he lives in different places in the Caribbean. He seems to have a separate personality for each place. In the first section of the book, on the island of Bimini, he is a reticent friend, a quiet drunk and a devoted father; he fishes with his three boys and does a little painting of the Winslow Homer (3) variety. The second section is set largely in a bar in Havana; here Hudson is a bar-fly, drinking and betting, and talking at some length to an elderly prostitute; he does no painting. A sea chase occupies the whole of the third section; Hudson is a bullying, Bogartesque ship's captain pursuing Germans along the coast of Cuba. Three episodes, hardly stories, and except for Hudson, who alters but does not grow, the episodes bear no relation to one another. The three boys, Hudson's children, are all dead by the time the second section opens, possibly to give Hudson nothing to live for, though more likely because Hemingway couldn't think of any way of working them into the conversation with the elderly prostitute or the pursuit of the Germans. The artless novelist has his reasons for disposing of characters, usually no more complicated than the eldest boy's in 'Jude the Obscure', when he hanged himself and his siblings: 'Done because we are too menny.'

Hudson gets little satisfaction (but evidently lots of cash) from his painting. He is, for most of the book, an aggressive self-absorbed man for whom killing a big fish and disembowelling a German are ways of proving one's manhood. It is the philosophy of combat - perversely based on killing one's friend, for the noblest combat is destroying something beautiful, something one values. 'In the worst parts, when I was tiredest, I couldn't tell which was him and which was me,' says Dave, one of the sons, after the fish has been caught and killed. Incapable of creation, these characters see beauty in destruction; considering themselves men, in the proverbial sense of the word, their ambition must be to win: to kill the lion, to floor the Negro, to catch the fish, to have always the winning hand. Achievement is irrelevant here (Hudson's painting is all but dismissed as daubing) because achievement implies solitary creation. Winning is another matter: one wins by beating one's opponent. Thus, most strangely: 'Am trying to knock Mr. Shakespeare on his ass.'

> 'All fights are bad.'
> 'I know it. But what are you going to do about them?'
> 'You have to win them when they start.'

Failure is losing, because losing is humiliation, unbecoming to a man: 'Get it straight. Your boy you lose. Love you lose. Honour has been gone for a long time. Duty you do.' That is Hudson at his lowest point, a loser. He recovers, but others are not so lucky, for the last loser deserves it, as the winner deserves his success. The loser's mortality proves more than the winner's physical superiority - it implies the winner's immortality. So much for the fist-fight between Roger and the wealthy yachtsman, which Roger wins, saying, 'That guy was no good, Tom.' And Thomas Hudson agrees: 'You taught him something.' The implication is that the yachtsman has been taught that he will never win a fist-fight with a man Hemingway conceives to be morally superior. In this case the man should know better: Roger is a writer and the snivelling yachtsman he defeats is a publisher.

Hemingway insists on the rightness of the philosophy. Consequently there is an interminable repetition of the words fine and good and true and wonderful and brave and necessary, all applied to bullying and mean-spirited and unworthy acts, 'a wonderful chase,' 'a fine shot,' 'a beautiful kill.' A sententious utterance, implying if not employing one of these words, closes each incident. After Dave hooks the swordfish and yanks on him for six hours (and twenty-five pages of the book), the motto is, 'But there is a time boys have to do things if they are ever going to be men.' An odd thing for a painter to say; but Thomas Hudson is no creator.

There is a great deal of killing in the book, practically all of it gratuitous, as when the swordfish is killed or Thomas Hudson shoots a land crab that appears on his path ('...the crab disintegrated.... Poor old crab, he thought....') or the Germans are shelled. Murder is necessary and it is a shame it makes one feel bad:

> Then why don't you care about anything? he asked himself. Why don't you think of them as murderers and have the righteous feelings that you should have.... Because we are all murderers, he told himself. We all are on both sides, if we are any good, and no good will come of any of it.
>
> But you have to do it. Sure, he said.

We all are on both sides: 'I couldn't tell which was him and which was me,' says Dave when the fish is dead; and 'He was a pretty good guy,' Willie says of the German he's blown to bits. The philosophy demands the sentimentality of pity. And grief is self-pity. Here is Hudson revealing the death of his son to the mother of the boy, his ex-wife:

> 'That isn't it,' she said. 'Tell me, is he dead?'
>
> 'Sure.'
>
> 'Please hold me tight. I am ill now.' He felt her shaking and he knelt by the chair and held her and felt her tremble. Then she said: 'And poor you. Poor, poor you.'
>
> After a time she said: 'I'm sorry for everything I ever did or said.'
>
> 'Me, too.'
>
> 'Poor you and poor me.'
>
> 'Poor everybody,' he said, and he did not add, 'Poor Tom.'

A very large number of suicides, by various means, are mentioned in the novel as well, remarked upon with a kind of queer joy. Obeying the perverse logic of destruction, the destroyer as hero, it is consistent that after subduing or killing every powerful thing on earth, the man, to maintain the image of his invincibility, kills himself. The warrior runs upon his own sword. Self-slaughter is the only acceptable end for the destroying hero; any other death is humiliating defeat. Hudson does not commit suicide. At the end of the book, wounded by Germans for whom he has developed an eager affection, he is full of self-love and self-loathing which, combined, turn to pride and a satisfied self-pity. Motto: 'You never understand anybody that loves you.'

The Hemingway stamp, that cauliflower earmark that characterises his worst fiction, is everywhere apparent. Hudson reflects on catnip: 'There still should be some catnip in the shelf of drawers of the cat room if it hasn't gotten too dry and lost its force. It lost its force very quickly in the tropics and the catnip that you raised in the garden had no force at all.' Hudson has a drink: '...strong with the real Gordon's gin that made it alive to his tongue and rewarding to swallow.... It tastes as good as a drawing sail feels, he thought. It is a hell of a good drink.' The descriptions of food and wine are given lovingly, while love-making is reduced to utter vagueness: 'He did something.... She did something else....'

The novel is offered as something of a departure for Hemingway, with 'a rich and relaxed sense of humour.' But nearly all the humour depends on seeing bullying or ridicule as comic: attempting to set a dock on fire, humiliating the yachtsman or taking the mickey out of a tourist or 'a fine old whore,' or teasing a sleepy-headed servant. In each case there is a victim who is weak or passive; he is made a figure of fun and one is meant to find him contemptible and so laughable. The humour has Thomas Hudson and his friends in stitches, and in many places Hudson says how much he is enjoying himself, but he is an embittered, heartless, unquestioning and deluded man. Physical superiority is what Hudson cares about, but he is old and life is unbearable for him.

The disappointment and the sour regret give the novel the tone of a suicide note. It is sad to think that Hemingway wrote it, and understandable that he left it in a bottom drawer.

Notes

1 A primitive tribe in Uganda.
2 Postscript.
3 American landscape and marine painter (1836-1910).

'The Nick Adams Stories' (1972)

121. LOUIS RUBIN, 'WASHINGTON STAR'

23 April 1972, C-6

Louis Rubin (b. 1923), Professor of English at the University of North Carolina, is the author of 'Thomas Wolfe' (1955) and a study of Southern writers (1963).

Publication of the Nick Adams stories of Ernest Hemingway as a group, with previously unpublished and uncompleted material originally involved in the fragmented saga of Hemingway's first and most autobiographical of fictional protagonists, constitutes a fascinating and valuable bit of creative editing.

What Philip Young has done is to go through the unpublished Hemingway material, recognize and identify the scraps, episodes and unfinished fiction that belong to the Nick Adams stories, and present the thing as a whole - a chronological fictional unit beginning with young boyhood and carrying the protagonist through the first world war and into adult life as an author in Europe. Fittingly, the last story is Hemingway's Fathers and Sons, which was written later than most of the other Nick Adams material and describes an older Nick, driving westwards with his son, and thinking about his own father, now dead.

Young has distinguished between the Nick Adams stories that Hemingway actually completed and published and the manuscript material by setting the latter in italic type. There is apparently no tampering with the text as Hemingway wrote it, and the reader can recognize at once what is unfinished work.

The value of this compilation is at least threefold. In the first place, it gives us insight into Hemingway's creative processes and his ideas of what fiction should be. His theory about fiction - that the more than can be 'left out' of a story, the stronger what is left will be as art - is dramatically visible for inspection here, and most notably in the case of Big Two-Hearted River, in which what is left out is why the protagonist is off fishing by himself, and what are the forces that lie behind his obvious state of extreme tension. It turns out that originally Big Two-Hearted River concluded with a long, semi-stream of consciousness monologue in which Nick Adams, who is clearly Hemingway here, thinks about his literary career, his war experience, and about friendship, marriage, and what he wants to do and be as a writer. The passage is anachronistic - it contains material and experience that chronologically belong long after the time of the fishing trip.

Another valuable result of publishing the material in this form is that it offers us all manner of insight into the sensibility of Ernest Hemingway. A long narrative entitled The Last Good Country, which was left unfinished, involves the young Nick Adams with his family, in particular his sister, in a way that none of the published Nick Adams stories do. The episode is apparently a greatly augmented development of an actual incident involving the youthful Hemingway's violation of the game laws when he shot and killed a blue heron, and his sister helped him get to his uncle's house before a game warden could apprehend him. Hemingway transforms this into a full-fledged flight into the deepest woods by Nick and his sister, with the crime that occasioned it made more serious and less distasteful. The story gets very close to barely sublimated incest; whether Hemingway recognized this, or whether he abandoned completing it for other reasons, is unknown.

The memorable story entitled Indian Camp in which Nick Adams witnesses his father performing a Caesarean operation on an Indian woman, only to have her husband commit suicide because he cannot stand the pain his wife is experiencing, turns out to have had an opening section in which the young Nick is left alone in the camp by his father, who has gone off hunting. Nick's fear of the woods, and of death, and his knowledge that his father has some contempt for his fearfulness, give a new emphasis both to the end of the published story, to Hemingway's insistence in later life on branding his father as a coward, and to the early origins of the famous Hemingway preoccupation with death and heroism.

Several stories and parts of stories set in the period after the first world war, when a still-youthful Nick is living a carefree life with companions male and female, fishing, swimming, and, in one instance, having an affair with one of the girls, give us a glimpse of Hemingway's own experience during a time little written about, but full of significance for the later fiction. I was surprised to find that editor Young places the stories entitled The End of Something and The Three-Day Blow chronologically in this period, rather than before the war. His reasons for doing so, upon reflection, are obvious, and yet the naivete and innocence of Nick Adams in these stories seem more appropriate to the Hemingway of the pre-Europe days. This in itself is interesting; for the persistence of these qualities in the 'mature' Hemingway of the post-war years gives us a different picture from the customary stereotype of the youthful Hemingway being changed overnight into the tough, cynical, winner take nothing adult by the horrors of war on the Italian front.

The third and perhaps the best result of the publication of the unfinished Nick Adams material along with the published stories, however, is that it makes available to us some excellent writing. In particular, I think of the story or novella The Last Good Country. This contains some of the best writing Hemingway ever did. It is a shame that, for whatever reason, he did not see his way to finishing it. Another good specimen is the story, apparently close to finished form, entitled Summer People. To be sure, it is not the absolutely best Hemingway - but then, neither is a great deal of his short fiction of the 1920s the best Hemingway. Why Hemingway did not publish it is hard to say; perhaps (most oddly, considering his usual practice) it was too close to real life, and might therefore have given pain to real persons. In any event, it's excellent Nick Adams, and good to have available.

This is a fascinating collection. The fragmentary nature of the new pieces does not really interfere seriously with one's enjoyment. What we have is a more complete view of Hemingway as Nick Adams - and by this I mean the aesthetic experience of taking part in the writer's creation of himself in this guise. So much of reading Hemingway comes down to just that. No 20th century writer ever projected himself more into his work, not merely with autobiographical material but in the sense of dramatizing, through style and attitude, the persona of the creator.

The famous Hemingway style does not exist in a vacuum;

it involves the reader's being able to apprehend the achievement of simplicity out of complexity, grace under pressure. When it is working right, no writer is more compelling. In the Nick Adams stories, written in the 1920s, the style is usually working right, and this not only in the completed, published stories but in much of the new material in this collection. 'The Nick Adams Stories' represents an addition to the Hemingway canon of more worth than the unpublished novel 'Islands in the Stream,' and of at least equal importance as 'A Moveable Feast.' Which is no more than to say that it offers a great deal of vintage Hemingway, and that is all one can ask.

122. WILLIAM ABRAHAMS, 'ATLANTIC'

229 (June 1972), 98, 100-1

William Abrahams (b. 1919), an American biographer and editor, is co-author of 'Journey to the Frontier' (1966) and 'The Unknown Orwell' (1972).

Of course, the most important aspect of the posthumous life of a writer is that his work should live: that it should survive and endure, as Hemingway's at its best has done and will continue to do. But this, though it is the most important, is only one aspect of living posthumously.

There is also the life of the legend that thrives after a writer's death, especially if he has already been 'a legend in his own lifetime' - like Hemingway, a more glamorous figure than merely a writer. Posthumously, the legend is kept alive by a flow of gossip and the production of memoirs (whether adulatory or derogatory hardly matters) from friends, relatives, rivals, and hangers-on, until in time the legend comes to loom as large as, if not larger than, the work itself. (It is my own conviction that the single most powerful factor operating against a true appreciation of Hemingway the artist is the quasi-mythic, all too public and publicized figure of 'Papa Hemingway,' self-created by Dr. Hemingstein and brought to its apogee, or nadir, by A.E. Hotchner.)

Finally there are the posthumous publications, the

most immediate evidence of a continuing life - those gatherings of a previously published but uncollected work (in Hemingway's case his journalism and his stories of the Spanish Civil War) or manuscripts the writer left behind, finished and awaiting publication, or in a fragmentary state, or finished and put aside with dissatisfaction. So it is that now, some ten years after his death, we have yet another 'new' book with the name Ernest Hemingway on the title page, which brings together some of his classic achievements in the short story, along with a story (one of his earliest) and parts of stories and episodic fragments of a novel - all being published for the first time. Even if one has faults to find with the enterprise, as I do, for anyone who is an admirer of Hemingway, as I am, it must count as an event, though a considerably lesser one than either 'A Moveable Feast' or 'Islands in the Stream.'

'A Moveable Feast,' his memoir of Paris in the 1920s, and an important addition to the Hemingway canon, was the first of the posthumous publications (1964). It posed no editorial problems or uncertainties for the reader. This was a manuscript that the author had completed and prepared for publication, even including a preface, and Mrs. Hemingway supplied an admirable, brief, informative Note that told all one needed to know about the composition of the book. It might have served her as a model for any further posthumous works over which she has presided: 'Ernest started writing this book in Cuba in the autumn of 1957, worked on it in Ketchum, Idaho, in the winter of 1958-59, took it with him to Spain when we went there in April, 1959, and brought it back with him to Cuba and then to Ketchum late that fall. He finished the book in the spring of 1960 in Cuba, after having put it aside to write another book, "The Dangerous Summer," about the violent rivalry between Antonio Ordoñez and Luis Miguel Dominguin in the bull rings of Spain in 1959. He made some revisions of this book in the fall in 1960 in Ketchum. It concerns the years 1921 to 1926 in Paris.' For 'Islands in the Stream,' the novel published in 1970, Mrs. Hemingway's Note was a good deal less satisfactory: 'Charles Scribner, Jr., and I worked together preparing this book for publication from Ernest's original manuscript. Beyond the routine chores of correcting spelling and punctuation, we made some cuts in the manuscript, I feeling that Ernest would surely have made them himself. The book is all Ernest's. We have added nothing to it.' But even if one grants that Mrs. Hemingway's and her husband's critical judgment precisely coincided, it would have been illuminating to know what the 'cuts in the manuscript' were and where they occurred. In one sense, then, the book is truly 'all Ernest's'; in another, it is not. (Ultimately, I suppose, we may expect an annotated, complete 'Islands in the Stream,' much as we have had the final version of 'Lady Chatterley's Lover,' then the first version, and now, coming out this summer, the *second* version.)

For 'The Nick Adams Stories' Mrs. Hemingway offers no Note at all; instead there is a modest preface by Philip Young, helpful in its biographic details, but unpersuasive in its argument. The book is a collection of all the stories in which the character Nick Adams (conventionally, but too simply taken as the author's *alter ego*) plays a role, however slight. (Indeed, in at least one of the stories, told in the first person, he is not even named, so that it might well be someone else's history.) The stories are arranged chronologically, not as they were written, but as the events they describe occur. To Mr. Young these 'events of Nick's life make up a meaningful narrative in which a memorable character grows from child to adolescent to soldier, veteran, writer, and parent - a sequence closely paralleling the events of Hemingway's own life.' In short, some of the most masterly short stories written by an American in this century are made to serve as chapters in a shadow fictional autobiography or autobiographical novel, just as the same material was made the basis for a dreadful movie of the early 1960s called 'Hemingway's Adventures of a Young Man.'

There is, I feel, a serious misconception at work here: to believe that a short story and a chapter in a novel are essentially the same, that a succession of stories about a character make him more 'meaningful,' more 'memorable,' more 'understandable.' But a novel is not a story: the method of the novelist is very different from that of the short-story writer. A story, to the degree that it succeeds as a work of art, contains within itself all that we need to know aesthetically, though I will grant that this may not be the case if one chooses to read it as a document in the author's biography.

Mr. Young asks us to consider 'the trouble with Big Two-Hearted River. Placed where it was - at the end of "In Our Time," the first collection - it puzzled a good many readers. Placed where it goes chronologically, following the stories of World War I, its submerged tensions - the impression that Nick is exorcising some nameless anxiety - become perfectly understandable.' But surely, it is the sense of some 'nameless anxiety' that haunts the story and gives it its extraordinary depth and poetry. Literalism may be crucial to the journalist; it can suffocate the artist; and Hemingway, perhaps it needs to be said again, was one of the most conscious of artists. He knew what he was about in writing his stories; he was a master of omission and suggestion, of cadence and epithet. The secret of his art, or one of its secrets, is its appearance of giving more in fact than it does. And indeed, one wants no more from the self-contained story: we leave it with a sense of its absolute rightness. Would we alter by so much as a centimeter our admiration for Joyce's The Dead, for example, if it were preceded by a succession of episodes from the early life of Gabriel Conroy?

As I have suggested, the assumptions upon which the collection is based strike me as altogether wrong-headed. But this is not to deny the pleasure one is afforded by reacquainting oneself with one marvel after another. That matchless opening of In Another Country:

> In the fall the war was always there, but we did not go to it any more. It was cold in the fall in Milan and the dark came very early. Then the electric lights came on, and it was pleasant along the streets looking in the windows. There was much game hanging outside the shops, and the snow powdered in the fur of the foxes and the wind blew their tails. The deer hung stiff and heavy and empty and small birds blew in the wind and the wind turned their feathers. It was a cold fall and the wind came down from the mountains.

I have no idea how many more posthumous Hemingway books we can look forward to. (The new stories in the present collection, set in italics to distinguish them from the ones already published, are recognizably lesser or apprentice work. It is quite obvious that the author knew this himself and put them aside, which is not to say that it was ill advised to bring them to light.) One volume that is sorely needed, and that would testify perfectly to the enduring life of Hemingway's art, is a complete Collected Stories, carefully edited, that would bring together all the published stories, arranged chronologically as written, and in a separate group, perhaps as an appendix, the stories that he chose not to publish in his lifetime. No doubt the arguments concerning Hemingway's 'place' will continue for years to come; but the existence of such a volume as I have proposed would reaffirm, whatever the dispute over degree, a true master.

Select Bibliography

BIBLIOGRAPHY

HANNEMAN, AUDRE, 'Ernest Hemingway: A Comprehensive Bibliography,' Princeton, 1967. 'Supplement,' Princeton, 1975. An excellent, exhaustive work, which also lists library holdings of the manuscripts and a thorough bibliography of criticism.

BIOGRAPHY

ROSS, LILLIAN, 'Portrait of Hemingway,' New York, 1961. A bitchy 'New Yorker' profile (1950) of Hemingway as Dumb Ox.

BAKER, CARLOS, 'Ernest Hemingway: A Life Story,' New York, 1969. A factual, objective, respectful life, with almost no analysis or interpretation of his character.

MEYERS, JEFFREY, Ernest Hemingway's Four Wives, 'Married to Genius,' London, 1977, 174-89. Considers the relationship between Hemingway's marriages and novels, between his emotional and artistic commitment.

DONALDSON, SCOTT, 'By Force of Will: The Life and Art of Ernest Hemingway,' New York, 1977. Records what Hemingway thought on important subjects (fame, politics, war, love, art, death) and constructs a model of his mind and personality.

CRITICISM

BAKER, CARLOS, 'Hemingway: The Writer as Artist,' Princeton, 1952; 4th revised ed., 1972. The standard work on Hemingway's art; a close reading of his fiction with emphasis on style, technique and craftsmanship.

YOUNG, PHILIP, 'Ernest Hemingway,' New York, 1952; revised ed., University Park, Pa., 1966. The most stimulating interpretation of Hemingway. Young places him in the American literary tradition and stresses his traumatic wound, obsession with death and exorcism of terror through art.

YOUNG, PHILIP, Our Hemingway Man, 'Kenyon Review,' 26 (1964), 676-97. An amusing account of the rather abysmal books on Hemingway that appeared in the early 1960s.

ASSELINEAU, ROGER, ed., 'The Literary Reputation of Hemingway in Europe,' New York, 1965. A useful study of the reception of Hemingway's work in England, France, Germany, Italy, Scandinavia and Russia.

REYNOLDS, MICHAEL, 'Hemingway's First War: The Making of "A Farewell to Arms,"' Princeton, 1976. A study of the background, sources and genesis of the novel.

MEYERS, JEFFREY, Hemingway's First War, 'Criticism,' 19 (1977), 269-73. Review-essay of Reynolds' book.

COLLECTIONS OF REPRINTED ESSAYS

McCAFFERY, JOHN K.M., ed., 'Ernest Hemingway: The Man and His Work,' Cleveland, Ohio, 1950. The first and most comprehensive critical survey, including essays by Gertrude Stein, Malcolm Cowley, Max Eastman, Delmore Schwartz, Alfred Kazin, James Farrell and Edmund Wilson.

BAKER, CARLOS, ed., 'Hemingway and His Critics: An International Anthology,' New York, 1961. Published just after Hemingway's death, with essays by a cosmopolitan range of critics, including George Plimpton, André Maurois, Lionel Trilling, Harry Levin, Mario Praz and Arturo Barea.

WEEKS, ROBERT, ed., 'Hemingway: A Collection of Critical Essays,' Englewood Cliffs, N.J., 1962. A volume in the Twentieth Century Views series, including Lillian Ross, Leslie Fiedler, D.H. Lawrence, Philip Young, Sean O'Faolain and Leon Edel.

BAKER, CARLOS, ed., 'Ernest Hemingway: Critiques of Four Major Novels,' New York, 1962. Essays on 'The Sun Also Rises,' 'A Farewell to Arms,' 'For Whom the Bell Tolls' and 'The Old Man and the Sea' by James Farrell, Philip Young, Mark Spilka, Lionel Trilling, Mark Schorer and Carlos Baker.

WALDHORN, ARTHUR, ed., 'Ernest Hemingway: A Collection of Criticism,' New York, 1973. A less substantial collection of eight essays in the McGraw-Hill Contemporary Studies in Literature series.

WAGNER, LINDA, ed., 'Ernest Hemingway: Five Decades of Criticism,' East Lansing, Mich., 1974. Reprints twenty-two essays on Hemingway's development, work method and individual novels, including studies by Edmund Wilson, Robert Penn Warren, Carlos Baker, Paul Goodman and Richard Bridgman.

Index

The index is divided into two parts: I Ernest Hemingway; II General Index.

I ERNEST HEMINGWAY

II GENERAL INDEX